Hyam Plutzik and the Mosaic of Time

Essays and Selected Poems

Immigrant Worlds & Texts

Series Editor
Maxim D. Shrayer (Boston College)

Editorial Board
Rosana Kohl Bines (Pontifical Catholic University of Rio de Janeiro, Brazil)
Anna Lushenkova Foscolo (Jean Moulin Lyon 3 University, France)
Luis Krausz (University of São Paulo, Brazil)
Boris Lanin (Adam Mickiewicz University, Poland)
Holli Levitsky (Loyola Marymount University, USA)
Hilla Peled-Shapira (Bar-Ilan University, Israel)
Valentina Parisi (University of Macerata, Italy)
Fedor Poljakov (University of Vienna, Austria)
Marco Sabbatini (University of Pisa, Italy)
Mitsunori Sagae (Soka University, Japan)
Franck Salameh (Boston College, USA)
Hana Wirth-Nesher (Tel Aviv University)

Hyam Plutzik
and the Mosaic of Time

Essays and Selected Poems

Edited by
Victoria Aarons,
Holli Levitsky,
and Hilene Flanzbaum

ACADEMIC STUDIES PRESS
BOSTON
2025

Library of Congress Cataloging-in-Publication Data

Names: Aarons, Victoria, editor. | Levitsky, Holli, editor. | Flanzbaum, Hilene, editor.
Title: Hyam Plutzik and the mosaic of time : essays and selected poems / edited by Victoria Aarons, Holli Levitsky, Hilene Flanzbaum.
Description: Boston : Academic Studies Press, 2025. | Series: Immigrant worlds and texts | Includes bibliographical references and index.
Identifiers: LCCN 2024055643 (print) | LCCN 2024055644 (ebook) | ISBN 9798887197357 (hardback) | ISBN 9798897830077 (paperback) | ISBN 9798887197364 (adobe pdf) | ISBN 9798887197371 (epub)
Subjects: LCSH: Plutzik, Hyam, 1911-1962--Criticism and interpretation. | American poetry--Jewish authors--History and criticism.
Classification: LCC PS3531.L86 Z68 2025 (print) | LCC PS3531.L86 (ebook) | DDC 811/.52--dc23/eng/20250131 LC record available at https://lccn.loc.gov/2024055643 LC ebook record available at https://lccn.loc.gov/2024055644

Copyright © Academic Studies Press, 2025, collection

ISBN 9798887197357 (hardback)
ISBN 9798897830077 (paperback)
ISBN 9798887197364 (adobe pdf)
ISBN 9798887197371 (epub)

Book design by PHi Business Solutions
Cover design by Ivan Grave

Published by Academic Studies Press
1007 Chestnut Street
Newton, MA 02464, USA
press@academicstudiespress.com
www.academicstudiespress.com

For Tanya Roth Plutzik

Contents

Acknowledgments — ix

Introduction: "Memory knows no walls": Hyam Plutzik and the Mosaic of Time — 1
Victoria Aarons, Holli Levitsky, Hilene Flanzbaum, and Sandor Goodhart

1. Hyam Plutzik's War — 15
   Eric J. Sundquist

2. The Universe Is No Consolation: Hyam Plutzik, Jewish History, and the Nature of Post-Holocaust Poetics — 34
   Cary Nelson

3. Hyam Plutzik and Gabriel Preil: Trajectories of Jewish American Poetry — 71
   Naomi Sokoloff

4. "So!" Reading "The Importance of Poetry, or, The Coming Forth from Eternity into Time" — 89
   Sandor Goodhart

5. Hyam Plutzik's *Horatio* as Cautionary Epic: Writing the Cold War Everyman — 117
   Edward Brunner

6. Elegy for a Mythic Warland: Hyam Plutzik's Wartime Poems and Letters from England — 140
   Phyllis Lassner

7. When We Begin with Loss: Revisiting the Early Poems of Hyam Plutzik — 155
   Monica Osborne

8. Judaic Time and Eternity in Hyam Plutzik's Poetry — 168
   Timothy Parrish

9. "The Great Betrayals are Impersonal": The Abstract Demons
   of Hyam Plutzik's *Apples from Shinar*   192
   Kristin Boudreau

10. Hyam Plutzik and the Lowercase Jew   208
    Rodger Kamenetz

11. Hyam Plutzik: "Value the Intermediate Splendor"   215
    Jacqueline Osherow

12. "Scorn Will Not Save": Plutzik's Negative Capability   222
    Betsy Winakur Tontiplaphol

13. "But something can be said": Ethics, Memory, and Midrash
    in the Work of Hyam Plutzik   235
    Stella Setka

14. The Saturated Forgetfulness of Liturgical Memory   252
    Sara R. Horowitz

15. Hyam Plutzik's Rod and Creel: Fishing, Jewish Identity,
    and the Legacy of American Antisemitism   279
    Maxim D. Shrayer

16. The Outcasts of Rochester, or, The Fantastic Poetics of Hyam Plutzik   312
    Noah Simon Jampol

17. This Is My Letter to the World: On Hyam Plutzik's Big Epistle   325
    Jenny Browne

Selected Poems   337

Contributors   437

Index   443

Acknowledgments

We would like to thank our contributors whose enthusiasm for this project from the very start has been remarkable. The range of approaches and enlivened readings in these chapters speaks to the enduring legacy of Hyam Plutzik, a poet of striking breadth and fluidity, whose arresting voice captures the tenor of a transformative historical, cultural, and literary era. The essays that emerge in this volume reflect the widening scope of Plutzik's oeuvre, a poet whose premature death cut short what might have been an even more productive and expansive literary career. The depth and deep engagement with which the contributors take on Plutzik's poetry suggests the continuing influence of this poet and the significance of his work.

The book's collection of selected poetry by Plutzik includes poems written over two decades. We would like to acknowledge The University of Rochester Plutzik Archives, which provided a valuable resource for accessing documents, including letters, handwritten poems, photographs, and other related materials. Independent scholar Ed Moran has also been an abundant resource. We would like to direct our readers to the Hyam Plutzik website, to learn more about Hyam Plutzik's poetry.

We wish to thank Trinity University and Loyola Marymount University for their support during the creation of this book, and our administrative and student assistants for their help in the final stages of completion.

We would like to acknowledge the editors of the *Journal of Jewish Identities* for kind permission to reprint "Hyam Plutzik's War," Chapter 1, by Eric Sundquist.

Introduction: "Memory knows no walls": Hyam Plutzik and the Mosaic of Time

Victoria Aarons, Holli Levitsky, Hilene Flanzbaum, and Sandor Goodhart

This collection of essays explores the life and work of Hyam Plutzik (1911–62), a poet, as one of our contributors notes, "teetering on the precipice of a historical moment," both culturally and artistically. Plutzik's work surfaced at a time of cultural change set against the historical rupture of the Holocaust and World War II. He was writing at a pivotal historical and cultural moment that gave rise to a changing Jewish presence in American letters. His poetry found its place among the emerging Jewish American literary voices of his time. Through close readings of his poems and analyses of his developing poetic voice, thematic and structural patterns, and recurring tropes, the essays in this collection approach Plutzik's contribution to American poetry as it intersects with and is informed by Jewish identity. That is, the essays examine Plutzik as a Jewish American writer, one for whom the tensions and dualities of identity for Jewish writers at his time and place surface throughout his body of work.

The son of Russian Jewish immigrants who arrived in the United States during the third great wave of Jewish immigration, Plutzik was versed in Yiddish, Russian, and Hebrew, as well as English. His poetry is inflected with the richly figured linguistic mosaic of his cultural inheritance, "a memory that knows no walls."[1] The essays in this collection thus explore Plutzik's preoccupation with themes of Jewish ancestry, Jewish history—both past and proximate, the passage and paradoxes of time, memory—collective and personal—as a fragile and

---

1 Hyam Plutzik, "Divisibility," in *32 Poems* (Miami, FL: Suburbano Ediciones, 2021), 7.

impermanent record, and Jewish liturgy and midrash, all a leitmotif set against the strains of Jewishness and the hybridity of Jewish American identity.

Hyam Plutzik and the Road to Literary Canonization

In the 1987 introduction to Hyam Plutzik's *Collected Poems*, Anthony Hecht, writing about the former's first collection, *Aspects of Proteus*, pays the poet a rough tribute by stating, "he is speaking in more than his own voice; he was deliberately and slyly appropriating the modes and tones of others."[2] Hecht does not specify what is sly about Plutzik invoking Proteus, the mythical shape-shifter, but those familiar with Jewish American literary history might suspect that Hecht compares Plutzik to canonical Anglo-Saxon darlings Shakespeare, Dickinson, Stevens, and last but not at all least Auden (no less than seven times!). Hecht does not say as much, but Plutzik's mutable voices and consciousnesses suggest one way to understand this poet. Does Plutzik employ various voices and forms to display a tour de force of poetic craftsmanship—is he deliberately "showing-off"? Or are these variations evidence of his trying to find himself as a poet?

In any case, Hecht's Introduction, juxtaposed with the collected essays in this volume, presents a complicated story about the politics and contingencies of canonization, one that contemporary champions of Plutzik's work must understand if they are to make the poet's case. Although it is tempting to blame the brevity of Plutzik's career for his obscurity—it is not only about how long he lived (Keats died at twenty-six)—but *when* he lived: the years between 1945 and 1960 presented extraordinary obstacles for Jewish American poets.

There is simply no way to talk about American poetry at midcentury without considering the gigantic presence of T. S. Eliot—the Anglophile poet, critic, and "dictator" of "literary tastes" (as Delmore Schwartz names him)[3]—and the pressures that Jewish American poets felt to join the tradition of letters upon which they had been formed. More than any poem that Eliot wrote, including "The Waste Land," Eliot's criticism mattered. An essay like "Tradition and the Individual Talent," which called for poets to see themselves as part of a cultural chain that evoked past great writers, or in his equally influential essay

---

2 Hyam Plutzik, *The Collected Poems* (Brockport, NY: BOA Editions, 1987), xvi. Henceforth, all references to *The Collected Poems* (CP) will be placed in parentheses.
3 Delmore Schwartz, "T. S. Eliot as Literary Dictator," in *The Collected Essays of Delmore Schwartz*, ed. David H. Zucker (Chicago, IL: University of Chicago Press, 1970), 312–313.

"The Metaphysical Poets," where he called for "the extinction of personality" as well as density, irony, and ambiguity became required form. That Eliot was—in both his poetry and his personal life—a genteel antisemite complicated issues to the point of crisis for many Jewish American writers. Yet few had the courage, or foolhardiness, to protest this element of Eliot's public face. Literary biography, however, reveals that amongst themselves—privately—Jewish American poets had a lot to say. Plutzik's poem—in which he tries to gently poke Eliot about his views—while not nearly as instructive as it might have been, illustrates just how much the older poet was on his mind.

Hecht barely mentions Eliot in his introduction; instead, he casts W. H. Auden as Plutzik's poetic brother. One might suspect that he is driven not so much by their poetic affinities as he is by Auden's biography. Although critics positioned Auden (and Auden positioned himself) as Pound and Eliot's literary inheritor, he quite crucially split with them when it came to their reactionary politics—including their feelings about Jews. Openly political, a socialist, a gay man whose longtime companion was Jewish, Auden becomes the anti-Eliot (as a public persona) even though he does not split with his poetics until the late 1950s. From the vantage point of 2024, Hecht's approach to Plutzik feels like an historical relic, and his glancing treatment of ethnicity seems incredible. Certainly, by today's measures, a child of Russian Jewish immigrants who does not learn to speak English until he is ten years old and ends his career by translating scripture—must be viewed under that lens—and seems to automatically signal his estrangement from American mainstream and literary culture.

We should note, of course, that Hecht was no rebel; a social conservative and poetic formalist, even in 1987, he shies away from talking about Jewish identity, in an era when the footprint of identity politics has already been outlined. But Hecht has ground to stand on: only a few of these poems name—or even allude to—Jewish subject matter. But why would they, given that Plutzik rightly perceived the critical distaste for such enterprises? Such an observation about the constraints on Jewish American poets calls to mind the material limitations on African American writers. Phillis Wheatley, for instance, who could not have written anything but poems praising her white masters if she wished the poems to be published—but whose poetry was later read while keeping these material conditions in mind—was found to have a level of irony, or "double consciousness"[4] that rendered the poems more palatable to readers in the twentieth and twenty-first centuries. One thinks also of a poet like Paul Laurence

---

4   Double consciousness is a familiar term in African American culture, first named by W. E. B. DuBois in the early twentieth century and then later applied to literature by

Dunbar, who wrote sophisticated and revelatory poems like "We Wear the Mask," but in order to sell books wrote reams of ballads full of dialect and easy rhymes. At the turn of the twentieth century, no artistic or cultural movement was more profitable than minstrelsy.

The material and market constraints on the creation of poetry are not often considered by American literary critics, hypnotized as we have been by the romantic beliefs that one holds about the genre. Since in most cases, poetry has little commercial viability, it has seemed irrelevant to talk about profit. True enough, but what about other pressures—critical praise, awards, academic recognition, and employment? For a poet as clearly ambitious as Plutzik, the fifties—when he published both of his major collections—were dominated by forces that were bound to confuse and contradict. Eliot and his acolytes, insisting on "an extinction of personality"[5] and yielding not to American tradition (much to the chagrin of William Carlos Williams who viewed "The Waste Land" as "A catastrophe for American letters")[6] but to the rules that Eliot had laid out: the ancient and classical traditions as well as the best that Europe had to offer. In 1949, Eliot's phrase "the best Europe has to offer" must have felt deeply ironic, that is, when Jews from all over the globe had come face-to-face with the worst. That the nation that had given us Goethe and Beethoven could also deliver such expansive murder was enough for Americans, Jews, writers, and others, to reinvest in the United States, and turn away from European models.

In the fifties, especially for second-generation Jewish immigrants, to be viewed as American was the biggest prize. Neither Plutzik, nor any other Jewish American poet published anything about what had happened to Europe's Jews until several decades later—although we do know that Plutzik, when he died, was working on a long Holocaust poem. Had he survived long enough to complete it, it is interesting to speculate on whether he could have published it. What publisher would have dared to break the silence that surrounded the slaughter of the European Jews?

Both Eliot's grip on poetic fortunes, and the silence surrounding the Holocaust, would begin to collapse. The publication of Ginsberg's "Howl" in 1956 was

---

Henry Louis Gates in *The Signifying Monkey: A Theory of African American Literary Criticism* (Oxford: Oxford University Press, 2014).

5   T. S. Eliot, "Tradition and the Individual Talent," in *Selected Essays*, ed. Frank Kermode (New York: Harvest/Farrar, Straus and Giroux, 1975).

6   Williams's famous utterance about *The Waste Land* has been reprinted in many places. See Jahan Ramazani, Richard Ellmann, and Robert O'Clair, eds., *The Norton Anthology of Modern and Contemporary Poetry*, vol.1, *Modern Poetry* (New York: W. W. Norton & Company), 53.

greeted with critical opprobrium and an obscenity trial, but also a larger audience than any other twentieth-century poem had gathered. When Robert Lowell, the most critically praised American poet and a white pedigreed Protestant, published *Life Studies* in 1959, he delivered a severe blow to the poetry of reserve and impersonality. Add to this the four-month trial of Adolf Eichmann which initiated a change in public awareness of the Holocaust. In those early days of the 1960s, Sylvia Plath published "Daddy" and "Cut" with their infamous analogization of the Nazis to American patriarchy. As off-putting and inappropriate as many found her comparison, Plath had clearly accomplished one thing: she had breached the surface of silence that had whitewashed ethnic difference and injustice.

The Jewish American poets who survived Plutzik would have time to discard the values they had inherited from the early part of the century and reinvent themselves according to more liberal values. One thinks prominently of Adrienne Rich who began her career as a disciple of Auden, who chose her work for the Yale Younger Poets Award in 1950. Rich will survive to renounce those early poems—saying she wishes she had never written them—and move on to a more political, personal and ethnic poetry. Or one might be rediscovered. When the politics of canonization changes to valorize both feminism and leftist politics, Jewish American poets, Muriel Rukeyser and Louis Zukovksy would get their due attention. Plutzik does not get this second act.

Where does this history leave us when we erect the structure by which Plutzik might enter the American poetry anthologies? Shall we remember him as Hecht has—inheritor of the Anglo-Protestant tradition carried forward by Emily Dickinson? Or by his affinities to Auden, the philosemitic inheritor of high modernism? And among a collection of over five hundred pages of poetry, must readers be compelled by his Jewish poems more than his others? Or should we read the poems with a double consciousness? To state the problem more practically, were Plutzik's work to be anthologized, what works would best represent him and locate future readers?

To present our vision of Plutzik, we are very carefully curating, as all anthologists do. It is prudent to remember that poets are not remembered by the totality of their oeuvre. Even those who revel in *all* the poetry of Emily Dickinson, for example, met her through a selection that an editor curated. And indeed, one wanting to introduce Robert Lowell to a new generation of readers would do better to present them with the confessional and political "Memories of West Street and Lepke" and not "The Quaker Graveyard in Nantucket," which is so densely wrought, allusive and historical that today's readers would have great difficulty connecting with it. Even more pertinent to Plutzik, one making a case for Auden today would anthologize "Refugee Blues," a poem that anticipates as early as 1939 the world's indifference to the plight of European Jews—a poem that had been virtually ignored for sixty years—in favor of more difficult and allusive poems about World War II, such as "In Memory of Sigmund Freud" or "September 1, 1939," to name just two.

In Plutzik's case, however, there are no installed favorites to dethrone. We amend this omission by offering our own selections of his "best" work, which cannot be definitive, but will, we hope, help future readers discover Plutzik for the first time, or anew. The poems we have chosen share certain elements: they are free of classical allusion; they are not in a borrowed voice of another poet or famous literary character. While they are not confessional (in that they give few details about the poet's life), they reflect the poet's deepest thoughts on human nature and its intersection with what we know about philosophy, history, and science.

The first poem of the collected edition, "To the Predynastic Egyptian Who Rests within the Entrance of the Metropolitan Museum," pairs ancient culture with contemporary vision. This is high culture indeed (Eliot would approve)—museums and knowledge of ancient civilizations—but it is also Plutzik's natural habitat. We believe that the poet has been there and has had these profound musings: this poem asks if those reading him now are any less guilty of the atrocities we believe of other ancient cultures. The limits of history and science to shed light on our current predicament is surely Plutzik's "flood" subject. In many of these poems, history is revealed to be full of viciousness and tyrants; science, rife with limitations, and philosophy, only a temporary comfort. It is through a philosophical lens that Plutzik examines a flawed human world. The very best of these poems, "Abner Bellow," describes a parallel universe and an awareness of quantum physics (when knowledge in this area was restricted to scientists): "What wanders under the meadow— / An inverse horrible shadow?" (CP 24). In another place, an underground entity, a specter, an evil antithesis mirrors the speaker, and calls him "to a strange dance." Plutzik's acute perception that human beings—and human civilizations—fall to evil surfaces in another early poem, "Identity" (CP 26), in which Plutzik describes how virtue disintegrates through the natural forces of entropy: "We need no deeper philosophy than subtraction," he writes, to understand how humanity is ground down by life on the planet.

Other poems that deserve special attention include "Divisibility" which, meditating on the "limitary nature" of walls, contains lines that readers will long remember for their epigrammatic quality: "But space flies through (a wall) like a mad commuter," or "Only a fool would cut the sea with a knife." In "If Causality Is Impossible, Genesis Is Recurrent," Plutzik argues with philosophers in order to find the miraculous in the quotidian, again in precise but deeply evocative phrasing.

Completing our selection would be "Because the Red Osier Dogwood," "To My Daughter," and "On Hearing That My Poems Were Being Studied in a Distant Place." In these poems, which may be read through a Jewish lens, the reader will find Plutzik to be a poet of accessibility, insight and wisdom. The essayists we have included here make their own case for which poems deserve attention. It will be up to future editors to examine the scholarship—gathered here and elsewhere—to evaluate which Plutzik poems will attract a new generation of readers.

Organization of Chapters

Most of the essays in this collection are newly conceived, the result of a studied list of accomplished scholars of poetics—many accomplished poets themselves—put together by the editors. Each scholar was asked to propose an essay topic that examined Plutzik's Jewish poetics, experiences, sensibilities, influences, or heritage. Several essays are revisions: Jacqueline Osherow presented an earlier talk on the same topic at the 2008 Jewish American and Holocaust Literature Symposium; an earlier version of Ed Brunner's essay was published on hyamplutzik.com (as was Osherow's); and Eric Sundquist's essay was originally published in the special issue "Post-Holocaust Culture and Jewish Identity" of the *Journal of Jewish Identities* (vol. 16, no. 1–2 [January/July 2023]).

As more readers, students and scholars of twentieth century poetry discover or re-discover Plutzik, the digital archive has grown into a multimedia space that opens up his personal and professional lives to further critical investigation (and enjoyment). The material archive of personal letters, photos, unpublished poems, and other miscellany housed at the University of Rochester, where Plutzik was on the English faculty for sixteen years, continues to grow as well, with additional correspondence and other materials discovered by friends and family members, adding to a treasured collection visited by many of the writers in this collection. In 2018, a formal partnership was drawn between the Plutzik family and the organizers of the annual Jewish American and Holocaust Literature Symposium in order to create the Hyam Plutzik Fellowship, an award given to a prominent literary scholar to deliver a keynote address on Plutzik's work as a Jewish poet. The Hyam Plutzik Fellowship has been awarded four times thus far: Cary Nelson (2018), Eric Sundquist (2019), Naomi Sokoloff (2022), and Sandor Goodhart (2023).

The chapters in this collection begin with essays by these four Plutzik Fellows. In "Hyam Plutzik's War," Eric J. Sundquist argues that in the unpublished poem "An Agadah of Hyam ben Samuel," Plutzik offers us in midrashic form "the story of the Jews," the story of "a match" whose "function" it is to "flare to fire, and to become ashes." In Sundquist's view, Plutzik here echoes an account of the Holocaust and perhaps a part of the "post-Holocaust poem" he was said to be constructing, one in which he would argue that "the Shoah, as well as the world war of which it was a part, could only be understood within the full sweep of Jewish history and culture." Plutzik was the son of an Orthodox rabbi, and his work was "included in anthologies edited by Ted Hughes and Sylvia Plath alongside poets such as Richard Wilbur, Howard Nemerov, and Anne Sexton." Plutzik was also "a three-time finalist for the Pulitzer Prize." Thus, Sundquist accounts for Plutzik's relative anonymity because of his poetic subject matter.

For example, Sundquist notes that Plutzik wrote "The House of Gorya" shortly after the war and meant it to take "the leading role" in a book entitled *House of Gorya and Other Poems*. Submitted to *Scribners* ("unsuccessfully," Sundquist points out), the poem remained unpublished during Plutzik's lifetime, although the remaining poems in the manuscript subsequently appeared as *Aspects of Proteus*. "If 'The House of Gorya' contains elements of Plutzik's unwritten Holocaust poem," Sundquist surmises, in this concentric scene, "we may imagine him anchoring an exploration of modern anti-Judaism in biblical events and traditional midrash in order to extrapolate from the particulars of Jewish tragedy to the universals of human conflict." "In its characterization of mid-century nationalist barbarism," Sundquist concludes, "'The House of Gorya' foreshadows Plutzik's intention, in his planned long poem, to address 'the victims of the various terrorisms and tyrannies of our time . . . victims of injustice in states not ordinarily tyrannical,' so that all people will be on guard against 'their extraordinary capabilities for evil.'"

In "The Universe Is No Consolation: Hyam Plutzik, Jewish History, and the Nature of Post-Holocaust Poetics," Cary Nelson begins with Plutzik's account of the testimony of a Holocaust survivor (described in 1960 as part of a plan for a "Holocaust poem") and a passage from "The House of Gorya" (submitted for publication in 1945 or 1946) detailing what Plutzik names "the chosen one." Reflecting upon the "impossible" task of writing about six million deaths, in an application for a fellowship to the Guggenheim Foundation in 1960, Plutzik speaks of the Holocaust as "the most immense subject for a poem in our time: the massacre of six million Jews by Hitler" and adds that "it is hard enough to write a requiem for one man, but six million! Is there such a number? Grief ends beyond one or two or three; beyond that there are only statistics." As Nelson observes, "It is time for a reevaluation of Plutzik's poetry focused in part on a generally unrecognized but defining feature of his work—how he established his identity as a Jewish poet in the immediate post-Holocaust decade when many writers, except those on the radical left, avoided direct and aggressive political commentary." Nelson's groundbreaking essay further opens the door to this unfinished project, one perhaps somewhat "darker" than critics have surmised. Scrolling through letters, published and unpublished poems, and an unpublished novel (written in his twenties), Nelson documents Plutzik's complicated journey through a Jewish history and tradition within the West that was only beginning to assume available public form at the moment of his demise.

In "Hyam Plutzik and Gabriel Preil: Trajectories of Jewish American Poetry," Naomi Sokoloff argues that one way to better understand Plutzik's work is to compare it with that of the poet Gabriel Preil. Like Plutzik, Preil was raised in a household in which Yiddish, Hebrew, and Russian were spoken. And like Plutzik, Preil made use of his Jewish past. Sokoloff examines Preil's "Chapters of Time, His and Mine" and Plutzik's "After Looking into a Book Belonging to My Great-grandfather, Eli Eliakim Plutzik." Sokoloff finds, however, that their approach to the subject matter differs. Preil writes more accessibly, comparing the fullness of the older bygone world with the "thin ice" of his own. In contrast, the narrator of Plutzik's poem finds only emptiness in worlds past: "blank fields" and "speechless graves." His darkness continues: "Here lie no one and no one, your fathers and mothers." Viewing the writers "in tandem," Sokoloff concludes, allows us to see the variousness of worldviews within the Ashkenazi Jewish community, which is often constructed as a singular voice.

Finally, in "So!" Reading "The Importance of Poetry, or The Coming Forth from Eternity into Time," Sandor Goodhart argues that Plutzik's poetry works through its performativity through both its concrete temporal physical availability on the page and its auditory recital. Giving voice to the victims of the Holocaust, Plutzik writes "that time has run out." Through close reading, Goodhart shows that the poem enacts both its subject matter and its commentary upon that subject matter by dividing itself into two parts: the first stanza offering us a spare image of a willow that "no man knows," located in a place where "no man goes / Nor bird flies," where the "willow fronts an empty road," and where a lone man "is marching down a road" (the same or another) "upon an abyss"; and a second in which the "rays of the sun" (and its "fire") engage "the poppies life and death." Goodhart places this poem amidst a series of deadly "equations" and other identifications that Plutzik makes—in literature, in rival poetic practices, in military life, in nature, in history, and in religious traditions.

Hyam Plutzik in Response to His Time

As all the essays in this collection make apparent, Plutzik was deeply engaged with the tenor of his times, both in terms of the patterns and preoccupations of other writers and poets, but also with the ethos of postwar politics and the lingering and deeply felt effects of World War II, the Holocaust, Hiroshima, and the Cold War.

Plutzik wrote much of his best work in the mid-1950s as the events of the Holocaust were beginning to lay claim to an American intellectual consciousness. Plutzik's own poem on the memory of the Holocaust remained, at the time of his death, however, incomplete. As scholars such as Cary Nelson, Eric Sundquist, Monica Osborne, Edward Brunner, and others make clear, Plutzik's poetry engages both implicitly and explicitly with the Holocaust. Indeed, a number of his published poems were dramatized in Robert S. Cohen's "Of Eternity Considered as a Closed System," first performed at "Partners of Hope," a 2007 Carnegie Hall concert held shortly after International Holocaust Remembrance Day in honor of the acts of courage that helped spare much of Bulgaria's Jewish population from the death camps.

The chapters that follow the four essays by the Hyam Plutzik Fellows are loosely linked conceptually and thematically, although as is apparent, there are overlaps and connections among all of the essays. Our hope for this volume is not only to introduce readers to the range, the patterns, and preoccupations inherent in Plutzik's oeuvre, but to begin a conversation among scholarly and creative approaches to his work.

In "Hyam Plutzik's *Horatio* as Cautionary Epic: Writing the Cold War Everyman," Edward Brunner argues that this complex work demonstrates Plutzik's refusal to situate himself as a "fifties poet" who is caught up in the logistics of formalist verse. In a detailed and sensitive reading of this long poem, Brunner shows its many complex and interrelated layers, situating it against the backdrop of World War II, the Holocaust, and Hiroshima. *Horatio*, as Brunner argues, "subtly involves its readership in examining the politics of the opening years of the Cold War." Horatio's role as a survivor, Brunner contends, echoes Plutzik's understanding of his own complicated position after World War II. Brunner proposes, then, that "Plutzik's own experiences in wartime ... both personal and general, dark as they might be, might find a catering within the framework of a literary work that exercised his own calling as a poet."

Phyllis Lassner's "Elegy for a Mythic Warland: Hyam Plutzik's Wartime Poems and Letters from England" examines Hyam Plutzik's wartime poems and letters to his wife Tanya from Norfolk, East Anglia, where he served at Shipdham airfield as information office in support of the D-Day invasion. Plutzik was impressed by the landscape, villages, and countryside. They suggested a mythic England, redolent with literary and wartime history: "Read in tandem, Plutzik's letters and the poetry Norfolk inspired resound with a mythic poetic nexus of relations that integrate the English landscape and its poets." Lassner shows Plutzik's letters and poems to reflect an elegiac relationship to the land, its people, and its real and mythic history. Juxtaposing the natural and human made worlds in poems such as "The Airman Who Flew over Shakespeare's England" and "On the Airfield at Shipdham," Plutzik reflects on American history and how the war against fascism reveals his own nation's identity and destiny. As Lassner concludes, "Bearing witness, the Jewish poet personifies the natural and manufactured worlds—man, beast, war machines, and the land, to delineate the costs of this necessary war as well as the collective responsibility we bear to save the future, as uncertain as it is."

Monica Osborne argues in her essay "When We Begin with Loss: Revisiting the Early Poems of Hyam Plutzik" that Plutzik's "entire body of work, both pre- and post-Holocaust [fits] into the genre of Holocaust writing." She suggests that "the events of the Holocaust and the plight of Jews under the rise to fascism that preceded it are fully present" in Plutzik's early work—in particular, the poems "The Three," "My Sister," and "Death at the Purple Rim." She writes: "bleakness, loss, hopelessness, and death are the tell-tale themes of all these works." Osborne continues that while his work usually only addresses the murder of millions of his people obliquely, Plutzik's vision of the Holocaust is a "darkness always both just behind and just ahead of [all Jews]." She advances the idea that for Plutzik the Jewish poet, poetry is "an expression of the beginning of thinking."

If poetic expression is the "beginning of thinking" for Plutzik, Timothy Parrish's "Judaic Time and Eternity in Hyam Plutzik's Poetry" considers how his poetic expression became the beginning of thinking as a *Jewish* poet. Parrish explores the dichotomy between the "tastemakers of twentieth century American poetry" and Plutzik's own very Jewish education. On the one hand, American literary critics have connected his work to poets like Emily Dickinson, Robert Graves, and Wallace Stevens. On the other, this very Jewish poet has not, until now, been seen and understood as a Jewish poet. Parrish writes that the part a "Judaic understanding of life has played in his poetry is so profound as to have been almost invisible to his peers."

Set against a haunting line from Plutzik's poem "To My Daughter," Kristin Boudreau, in "'The Great Betrayals are Impersonal': The Abstract Demons of Hyam Plutzik's *Apples from Shinar*," explores the way in which the theme of betrayal haunts Plutzik's poetry. Boudreau argues that while incorporating fragments of earlier writers, particularly Eliot, into his poem "For T. S. E. Only," Plutzik renounced the "dispassionate impersonality that Eliot advocated." Plutzik's turn toward the personal, exemplified by "For T. S. E. Only," shows the evolution of the poet's thought from his earliest work. The *insight* that directs, in particular, Plutzik's later work might be expressed thus:

> Without the poet's own personality—including, essentially, his consciousness and conscience—morality is only a set of laws. Plutzik arrived at this insight, dramatized so eloquently in "For T. S. E. Only," not simply by reordering the impressions and experiences of earlier writers, but from his own lived experience, particularly as a Jew in mid-century America.

In his personal, coming-of-age essay "Hyam Plutzik and the Lowercase Jew," Rodger Kamenetz traces his own development as a young poet to Eliot's "Love Song of J. Alfred Prufrock." As Kamenetz acknowledges, in recognizing Eliot's antisemitism, he wrote a satire of Eliot in the form of burlesque in which he places Eliot in the hands of "a tribunal of rabbis" for "judgement and punishment." During the composition of this essay, however, he happened upon Plutzik's poem "For T. S. E. Only," which moved him deeply. Plutzik's more expansive position toward Eliot shaped Kamenetz's perspective. Eliot's Jew-hatred notwithstanding, Kamenetz writes that "Plutzik helped me realize a more common humanity—and the common failings—that unite us as poets, even including our brother Thomas Eliot." Kamenetz reflects on "what it must have been like to have been an American poet with the unabashedly Jewish name Hyam Plutzik writing in the 1950s and '60s at a time when the cult of Eliot reigned supreme in English Departments all over the US." Kamenetz acknowledges his "debt" to Plutzik as well as their "shared faith in the live-giving power of the poetic imagination."

In their essays, both Jacqueline Osherow and Betsy Tontiplaphol seek to characterize Plutzik as a poet whose words and images and allusions burn with paradox: an imperative of the writer as poet and Jew, inhabiting natural and ancestral spaces, the poems announce mysteries of time, space, language, existence. In "Hyam Plutzik: 'Value the Intermediate Splendor,'" Osherow identifies in Plutzik the twin engines of poetry: the necessary and the elusive. She writes, "poetry must always perform this balancing act between idealization and reality, between the self and the world, between 'the many dreams' and 'the world being as it is.'" Though God's hand in the world is of an "unnecessary roughness," the poet finds value in the "intermediate splendor" of the world between life and death—indeed, he "burns" within it.

Keats's notion of negative capability functions in a specific way for Tontiplaphol in "Scorn Will Not Save: Plutzik's Negative Capability." Addressing the elder poet directly in "For T. S. E. Only," Plutzik wonders whether it is possible for a

Jewish artist to suppress his identity enough to find value in an antisemitic line or poem, or to empathize with a culturally prominent poet (and "genteel" antisemite like Eliot) who deploys such images (even within the iconic poems for which Eliot is best known). Tontiplaphol writes: "After all, to be a Jew, Plutzik suggests in the poem 'Portrait,' is to bear the *weight* of identity; as the term 'portrait' intimates, the Jew is ever a bundle of distinctive particulars." Indeed, as Plutzik writes, "to be a Jew casually," is an impossible enterprise, one that would entail ignoring "A few thousand years of history." How, Tontiplaphol asks, and where, does a Jewish poet of his time find his literary home?

Similarly, in "'But something can be said': Ethics, Memory, and Midrashic Reading in the Work of Hyam Plutzik," Stella Setka identifies ways in which Plutzik's poetry has, at its center, an "elusive nightmarish history" that was difficult if not impossible for contemporary readers and critics to contend with. To read Plutzik as a fully Jewish poet, he must be understood "within the broader context of the history of antisemitism and its brutal climax." Reading through such an historical context reveals a poet determined to commemorate Jewish victimhood, despite the many American Jewish writers at the time who elided their Jewishness and remained largely silent about the Holocaust. Setka argues that Plutzik is fundamentally a post-Holocaust poet. For Setka, midrash offers a way to extend "the tools and tenets of the tradition to call attention to a history of loss and persecution while also celebrating the resilience and strength of the Jewish people." Midrashic reading of Plutzik's poetry creates difficult paradoxes for readers and, as a result, purposely and properly "denies the satisfaction of a mastered meaning."

In "The Saturated Forgetfulness of Liturgical Memory," Sara R. Horowitz investigates Plutzik's engagement with Jewish liturgical texts through a study of his partnership with the Rabbinical Assembly. She notes, "Although references to Jewish texts, tradition, history, and ethics weave through the poetic oeuvre of Hyam Plutzik, only in the last decade of his life did the poet engage with formal liturgy." Plutzik's engagement with Jewish religious texts, "weaving strands of liturgical allusions into the fabric of his poetry, [while] probing the ethics of Jewish memory and Jewish forgetting," created an ideal candidate to create a more literary prayer book. Horowitz details Plutzik's work with the Rabbinical Assembly and its complicated reception.

In his essay "Hyam Plutzik's Rod and Creel: Fishing, Jewish Identity, and the Legacy of American Antisemitism," Maxim Shrayer adopts fishing as a leitmotif in Plutzik's life and art, finding it useful as a lens through which to uncover the Jewish poet's challenges to assimilation. Shrayer envisions the art and craft of fishing for Plutzik as "a complex allegory of a Jewish poet's path into the Anglo-American literary mainstream," a career simultaneously contending with Jewish anxieties and

Christian antisemitism. As in the earlier essays, Shrayer hears in Plutzik's poetry an engagement with "towering English-language poets of high modernism," as well as other Jewish poets of the time, such as Paul Celan, who were struggling for ways to express themselves in a post-Shoah world. Shrayer argues that "Plutzik's best poetry showcases a richly gifted Jewish American poet at the crossroads of archaism and innovation," a man writing from a state of deep loneliness.

In "The Outcasts of Rochester, or, the Fantastic Poetics of Hyam Plutzik," Noah Simon Jampol reflects on Plutzik's lesser-known science fiction writing, demonstrating the ways in which he turns toward the genre of the fantastic to express the trauma that separates him from his poetic contemporaries: the reality of twentieth-century Jewish American identity following the Holocaust. Jampol considers Plutzik's 1952 science fiction story "The Outcasts of Venus," written under the pen name Anaximander Powell. Revealing it as a characteristic piece of twentieth-century American pulp fiction, it is nonetheless singularly remarkable for its "Holocaust-inflected" imagery.

The volume concludes with the poet Jennifer Browne's epistolary poetic response to Plutzik's *Letter from a Young Poet*. In "This Is My Letter to the World: On Hyam Plutzik's Big Epistle," Browne places Plutzik's "novella of a letter" to his college mentor in conversation with his own poems, as well as with the epistolary gestures and poetic styles of Rilke, Joyce, Dickinson, Bishop, and others. Browne writes the reply Plutzik never received, as well as a poetic meditation on the challenges and possibilities of mentoring young poets.

Bibliography

Eliot, T. S. *The Waste Land*. New York: Harcourt, Brace and Company, 1922.

Eliot, T. S. "Tradition and the Individual Talent." In *Selected Essays*, edited by Frank Kermode, 37–44. New York: Harvest/Farrar, Straus and Giroux, 1975.

Dunbar, Paul Laurence. *Lyrics of Lowly Life*. New York: Dodd, Mead and Company, 1896.

Gates, Henry Louis. *The Signifying Monkey: A Theory of African American Literary Criticism*. Oxford: Oxford University Press, 2014.

Ginsberg, Allen. *Howl and Other Poems*. San Francisco, CA: City Lights Books, 1956.

Plutzik, Hyam. *The Collected Poems*. Foreword by Anthony Hecht. Brockport, NY: BOA Editions, 1987.

Plutzik, Hyam. *32 Poems/32 Poemas*. Bilingual (English-Spanish) edition with a Foreword by Richard Blanco. Miami, FL: Suburbano Ediciones, 2021.

Schwartz, Delmore. "T. S. Eliot as Literary Dictator." In *The Collected Essays of Delmore Schwartz*, edited by David H. Zucker. Chicago, IL: University of Chicago Press, 1970.

Ramazani, Jahan, Richard Ellmann, and Robert O'Clair, eds. *The Norton Anthology of Modern and Contemporary Poetry*. Vol.1, *Modern Poetry*. New York: W. W. Norton & Company, 2003.

CHAPTER 1

Hyam Plutzik's War*

Eric J. Sundquist

At the time of his early death in 1962, Hyam Plutzik left among his unpublished poems "An Agadah of Hyam ben Samuel," whose title names him, according to tradition, the son of his father, Samuel.[1] The poem explicates its opening text: "It is the function of a match to be scraped against roughness, / To flare to fire, and to become ashes." In mythic time when matches could speak, one complained

---

Copyright © 2025 by Eric J. Sundquist

* Rpt. from Eric Sundquist, "Hyam Plutzik's War," *Journal of Jewish Identities* 16, no. 1 (2023): 165–80.

1 This essay derives in part from my "Blessed Mythmaker: The Poetry of Hyam Plutzik," which may be found on the Hyam Plutzik web site maintained by the University of Rochester: http://www.hyamplutzikpoetry.com/. https://drive.google.com/file/d/18y4aXAS0KLXStIN8wD3vcpbFi1qtEEbF/view. The earlier essay takes up a greater variety of Plutzik's poetry and includes more extensive annotations, which are here kept to a minimum. All quotations of poetry come from *The Collected Poems* (Brockport, NY: BOA Editions, 1987), page numbers cited in the text. Unpublished journal entries, lectures, and draft materials by Plutzik quoted below are from the Hyam Plutzik Papers held at the University of Rochester, abbreviated HPP in the text. I am grateful to Edward Moran and Melissa Mead for making these materials available to me. Thanks also to Saul Rosenberg, David Roskies, and Anthony Wexler for the comments and suggestions on earlier drafts. All quotations from the Bible are from *The Holy Scriptures, According to the Masoretic Text: A New Translation* (Philadelphia, PA: Jewish Publication Society of America edition, 1917; repr. 1942), which would have been the principle English version, other than the King James Bible, consulted by Plutzik, though he no doubt relied at times on a Hebrew text. Plutzik seems to have quoted Talmud from various English sources, again probably including his own translations. My citations are from the Soncino edition of the Babylonian Talmud, ed. I. Epstein (London: Soncino Press, 1935–52), online at https://www.halakhah.com/ (identified by the common abbreviation B. plus the name and folio of the tractate). Citations of Midrash Rabbah are from the Soncino print edition, ed. H. Freedman and Maurice Simon, 10 vols. (London: Soncino Press, 1983). General information about early Jewish history is drawn from the *Jewish Study Bible*, ed. Adele Berlin and Marc Zvi Brettler, 2nd ed. (New York: Oxford University Press, 2014); the Jewish Encyclopedia (http://www.jewishencyclopedia.com); and the YIVO Institute for Jewish Research (https://www.yivo.org/).

about such rough justice, wondering why the tribe of matches could not live safely "in comfort and amity." Like the Lord speaking to Job out of a whirlwind, a gigantic voice looming over the workshop replies: "Both the beauty and utility of a match / Are in their burning" (296). We might style this a parable or a legend, but in choosing aggadah, a mutable form of interpretive "telling" differentiated from halacha, the immutable "Law," Plutzik called upon the Talmudic texts and midrash, as well as noncanonical pseudepigrapha, produced in the centuries following the twin catastrophes of the Jewish War of 68–70 CE and not many decades later the failed Bar Kokhba Revolt, which effectively ended Jewish national history in ancient times. With the Temple and its rituals gone, sacrifice and religious practices centered on Jerusalem gave way to prayer, study, and textual interpretation marked by multiple, often highly inventive, readings, as well as fluid timeframes, such that patriarchs, prophets, and rabbis sometimes appear to inhabit the same worlds. Through collective acts of "exegetical imagination," to cite Michael Fishbane,[2] the sages and other commentators created a mythopoetic web of writing that laid a foundation for diasporic religious life.

We know from quotations in "Exhortation to the Artists" and "Commentary" that Plutzik consulted contemporary texts such as Jacob Ibn Chabib's *En Jacob: Agada of the Babylonian Talmud*, a five-volume medieval work translated by S. H. Glick in 1916, and it is likely that he was familiar with the monumental Hebrew anthology *Sefer Ha-Aggadah*, edited in 1908–11 by Hyam Nahman Bialik and Yehoshua Hana Ravnitsky. Whether or not Plutzik meant to establish a dialogue with such works, his citations and allusions portrayed the modern Jewish poet as an heir to rabbinical tradition—not least because the catastrophic watershed events that drove the Jewish people into a nearly two-thousand-year exile had in his day come full circle, so to say, with the Holocaust and Israeli statehood.

The parable of the match in "An Agadah of Hyam ben Samuel" invites several interpretations. It could refer simply to the brevity of life; or to a desire for sudden illumination; or to a poet's burning into brilliance and then being forgotten. But these options are secondary to the poem's historical trajectory. Here we have in miniature the story of the Jews, reaching from the match of Creation struck by God, variously figured in scripture and commentary as "light," "fire," "flame," "radiance," and "sparks," to the twentieth-century genocide of European Jews. Along the course of that story Jews had many occasions to experience God's rough justice and His seeming refusal to let them live in comfort and amity

---

2   Michael Fishbane, *The Exegetical Imagination: On Jewish Thought and Theology* (Cambridge, MA: Harvard University Press, 1998).

among other nations, while at the same time they believed the "utility" and "beauty" of lives in His care were sacred.

We do not need a particular point of reference to determine that "An Agadah of Hyam ben Samuel" is a post-Holocaust poem. Putting the question this way, however, alerts us to the important fact that Plutzik's poetry was written before the word "Holocaust" had come into common use and, after an initial postwar outburst of witness, analysis, and commentary, during years when attention to the Nazi genocide subsided before rapidly accelerating in subsequent decades.[3] In the 1960 "Plan for Work" he provided when applying for a fellowship to support an intended long poem on the subject, Plutzik, like many others in his day, used the prevailing formulation "the massacre of six million Jews by Hitler" (HHP: Box 4, Folder 8). He did, however, write in an era in which the question of Jewish resistance was much debated. These debates are not Plutzik's principal concern in the poem, but it is likely that he was inspired by "Blessed Is the Match," the last poem written by Hannah Szenes, a Mandate Palestine paratrooper dropped by the British into Yugoslavia to rescue Hungarian Jews before she was captured, tortured, and executed for her crimes against the Third Reich. The line that opens and closes Szenes's short poem, which provided the title of Marie Syrkin's 1947 biography, subtitled *The Story of Jewish Resistance*, reads: "Blessed is the match consumed in kindling flame."[4]

With Szenes's poem in mind, we might place "An Agadah of Hyam ben Samuel" in the centuries-long tradition of Jewish poems and songs addressing *Kiddush Hashem* (the martyr's "Sanctification of the Name"), from the book of Lamentations through medieval piyyutim and on to Shoah-era works such as Yitzhak Katzenelson's "Song of the Murdered Jewish People." At the same time, however, the poem's comic dimension allies it with the Yiddish humor of someone like Sholem Aleichem, just as its lesson that only when it is struck does the match produce "beauty" makes it one of Plutzik's many studies in the classical tradition of ars poetica. Far from parochial, Plutzik at mid-century was an accomplished poet unique in his interests and his demonstration that postwar Jewish identity might embrace poetry and ideas reaching from biblical antiquity to contemporary cosmology. Although there has been little scholarship to date on Plutzik, some of the most incisive has focused on his response, as a Jewish

---

3   For a collection of perspectives on this question, see David Cesarani and Eric J. Sundquist, eds., *After the Holocaust: Challenging the Myth of Silence* (New York: Routledge, 2012).
4   Hannah Senesh [Szenes], *Hannah Senesh: Her Life and Diary* (New York: Schocken Books, 1971), 256; Marie Syrkin, *Blessed Is the Match: The Story of Jewish Resistance* (New York: Jewish Publication Society, 1947).

poet, to both Nazism and the continued Cold War threat of totalitarianism.[5] Yet his range of reference tells us that he felt the Shoah, as well as the world war of which it was a part, could only be understood within the full sweep of Jewish history and culture.

* * * *

Born in 1911 to Russian Jewish immigrants and raised in a rural Connecticut home where the main languages were Yiddish, Russian, and Hebrew, Hyam Plutzik was first instructed by his father, an Orthodox rabbi, and later educated at Trinity College and Yale University, where he twice won the Yale Poetry Prize. Following military service in World War II and until his death, he was a faculty member at the University of Rochester. He was included in anthologies edited by Ted Hughes and Sylvia Plath alongside poets such as Richard Wilbur, Howard Nemerov, and Anne Sexton, and he was a three-time finalist for the Pulitzer Prize. That Plutzik is less well known today is owed in part to the exceptional variety of his work, which can only be hinted at in any given essay. Equally at home in lyric and narrative poetry, he was both a formalist and an experimentalist who fluently integrated science, mathematics, and philosophy into his work while drawing simultaneously on two distinct traditions: the classic works of the Western canon, including its mythological resources, mainly Greek but including Egyptian, Babylonian, Norse, and others, and the classic works of the Jewish canon that begins with the Hebrew Bible, whose stories, he said, in a lecture entitled "Poetry and Myth," "are the greatest and most powerful myths" (HPP: Box 34, Folder 11). At times, his Jewishness is inseparable from his craft, as in his translation of the Sabbath song "L'Cho Dodi" (or *Lekhah Dodi*, "Come My Beloved"). At other times, it is less direct, as in "Next Time I Shall Not Burn the Beehive," in which first the gassing and then the immolation of a hive of bees evoke the Shoah. We can see Plutzik's inspiration by dual traditions in small details, such as his attention to the linguistic bifurcation in the Canaanite root *Adon* that gives us, on the one hand, the Greek god Adonis, a key figure of death and renewal in his poetry, as in his Whitmanesque poem

---

5   See in particular Edward Brunner, *Cold War Poetry* (Urbana, IL: University of Illinois Press, 2001); Edward Moran and Steven Sher, "Hyam Plutzik's Horatio as Post-Holocaust Poem," accessed September 30, 2024, https://static1.squarespace.com/static/5682cb822399a3aa8df162ec/t/5b9866134d7a9cbbeaaf55bf/1536714260234/sher-and-moran-horatio-post-holocaust.pdf; and Cary Nelson, "The Universe Is No Consolation: Hyam Plutzik, Jewish Identity, and the Ethics of Post-Holocaust Reading," *Journal of Jewish Identities* 15, no. 1 (2022): 5–31.

"Sprig of Lilac," and, on the other, "El Adon Al Kol," a traditional hymn Plutzik also rendered in verse, and Adonai, the majestic plural signifying "Lord" that takes the place of the Tetragrammaton (YHWH) when the Ineffable Name cannot be uttered.

The duality appears on a larger scale in the rather elliptical titles of his first published volumes, *Aspects of Proteus* and *Apples from Shinar*. The former derives from the shape-shifting god of *The Odyssey* who reappears throughout Western literature and, for Plutzik, represents "modern consciousness," as he argued in a lecture entitled "The Protean Universe" (HPP: Box 34, Folder 13). Alluding to Joseph Campbell's influential *The Hero with a Thousand Faces*, in which Proteus is characterized as a "wily god" who stands for mythology itself, Plutzik might have been speaking of his own multivalent poetic practice when he added that "the world is the man with a thousand faces."[6] About *Apples from Shinar*, Plutzik said simply that "the plain of Shinar was where the garden of Eden was located, and the apple eaten." His assessment was based not on the Hebrew Bible, where Shinar is repeatedly associated with Babylonia and not identified as the location of Eden, but apparently on Christian iconography and vernacular wisdom about the kind of fruit growing on the fateful Tree of Knowledge. Plutzik borrowed apple motifs from Greek mythology in several poems, but *Apples from Shinar* insists that we acknowledge this alternative mythic dimension.

Shinar appears eight times in the Hebrew Bible, among them as the home of King Nebuchadnezzar, who destroys the First Temple and carries Israel "into the land of Shinar to the house of his god" (Dan. 1:2). Most famously, of course, it is the setting for the story in Genesis 11 when the whole earth's people, speaking the same language, migrate to the land of Shinar, where they build a city featuring a tower "with its top in heaven" to make a name for themselves lest they be "scattered abroad upon the face of the whole earth"—precisely the punishment the Lord inflicts upon them for their hubris in building the tower of Babel. After the dispersion of the people and the fracturing of Hebrew into alien tongues, the enumeration of the tribes of Noah resumes, concluding in Genesis 12 with the great drama of *Lekh Lekha*, the Lord saying to the man who will become the patriarch Abraham: "Get thee out . . . from thy father's house, unto the land that I will show thee. And I will make of thee a great nation." *Apples from Shinar* thus brings to the fore the dialectic of Jewish suffering and renewal that would be repeated many times in the Bible and later history.

---

6   Joseph Campbell, *The Hero with a Thousand Faces* (Princeton: Princeton University Press, 1972), 381.

In an early poem on the writer's craft, entitled "He Inspects His Armory," the gods of mythology appear to be dead, yet they are everywhere present throughout Plutzik's work, whether as mythic actors or as the names of constellations in poems such as "A Letter to Someone at Mt. Palomar" and "God and My Father." Nor was the Hebrew God dead. Unobservant though he may have been, Plutzik wrote of Jews as exponents of their own rich mythology, in which God, however inscrutable, was hardly less alive than He was for the prophets and sages. Plutzik wrote almost always in conscious reflection on his double heritage, but striking the right balance between the two was not without danger. In a remarkable letter about the poet's vocation, sent to his former Trinity College teacher, Odell Shepard, later published as *Letter from a Young Poet*, Plutzik confessed that he found it "an awesome thing to be a Jew and to know that one is hated by so many of one's fellowmen."[7] We see this exemplified in "Portrait," a painful poem about the costs of Jewish assimilation. Wearing an "ill-fitting garment," the "Greek shirt" that the poem reveals as the poisoned shirt of Nessus,[8] the young poet tries, without success, "To ignore the monster, the mountain— / A few thousand years of history" (112). We may surmise that Plutzik purposely alluded here to the "intolerable shirt of flame / Which human power cannot remove" in *Four Quartets*,[9] implicitly rebuking Eliot's antisemitism, as he did more forthrightly in "For T. S. E. Only," where he responded to Eliot's ugly Jewish stereotypes while at the same time addressing him as a poetic "brother" and inviting him to "weep together for our exile" (109–10). If ancient mythology and English literature gave Plutzik a vocabulary, it was in Jewish history and theology that he found the wellsprings of lived experience—and, more specifically, a complex and often disturbing lens through which to interpret twentieth-century Jewish life and the Shoah.

There is no evidence that Plutzik read deeply in Kabbalah, but in such poems as "An Equation" and "The Zero That Is All" he did think deeply about the nature of Creation embedded in the conundrum that God, at once infinite and without

---

[7] Hyam Plutzik, *Letter from a Young Poet* (Hartford, CT: Watkins Library at Trinity College, 2015), 68.

[8] In Ovid's *Metamorphoses*, among other sources, Heracles (Hercules) escapes the tormenting Shirt of Nessus, stained with the blood of the centaur Heracles killed to save his wife from rape, by throwing himself into a funeral pyre.

[9] T. S. Eliot, "Little Gidding," from *Four Quartets*, in T. S. Eliot, *The Poems of T. S. Eliot*, ed. Christopher Ricks and Jim McCue, vol. 1 (Baltimore, MD: Johns Hopkins University Press, 2015), 207.

beginning, "dwells in the depths of nothingness," as Gershom Scholem put it.[10] We find this darker view dramatized, for example, in "Of Objects Considered as Fortresses in Baleful Space," which erases the difference between the speaking "I" and his "brothers," an oak tree and a stone, all such things existing as islands "Upon a plain of nothing" (a refrain twice repeated), "Emergent out of nothing," and "Await[ing] the will of nothing" (116). The poem may count in the annals of mid-twentieth-century existentialism, but it likewise elucidates Plutzik's belief, outlined in "The Protean Universe," that by virtue of Einsteinian physics "matter has become nothingness," even as it echoes Job 26:7, where God, peering down into "naked" Sheol, the underworld of the dead, "hangeth the earth over nothingness." Plutzik, however, was less interested in God as a hidden cause than as a tragic actor, as we may see in "Commentary," where the Hebrew God appears without anthropomorphic form as an abstraction called the "Enthroned Will." Once, the poem tells us, this God had rivals in the Egyptian deity Ammon and the Greek Zeus, but now he sits alone in his great palace engaged in a single, eternal task: "to shape and reshape forever the crumbling substance ... the figurines / Wasting in air ... the dust, the dust" (20–21).

The "Enthroned Will" of "Commentary" seems to have little to do with God's will as it is figured, for instance, in the Kaddish ("Glorified and sanctified be God's great name throughout the world which He has created according to His will"). Rather, it has more in common with the pseudo-Freudian death drive in "The Geese," where "the screaming that comes from nowhere" portends "the will toward destiny, which is death" (98), or the force animating the ominous figure in "The Milkman." His biblical promise of milk and honey transmuted into opaque menace, this God stalks a wintry landscape "translating will to energy," empowered, like the Golems of folklore, by one of the secret names of God: "You are the thief of the secret flame, / The forbidden bread, the terrible Name" (121). Enemies of God's Will, not separate from but integral to it, like fallen angels, appear for Plutzik in many forms of negation. At times they appear as the ravages of time, decay, and death, and at others as the dark forces discovered by modern physics, psychology, and anthropology, all of which, he contended in "The Protean Universe," take part in the "trip to the underworld" afforded by discovery of an unconscious, where identity is "uncertain and shifting," even "demonic."[11]

---

10 Gershom G. Scholem, *On Kabbalah and Its Symbolism*, trans. Bernard McGinn (New York: Schocken Books, 1996), 102.

11 The word "demonic" is added in a handwritten emendation. Poems devoted to the "underworld" in mythic, psychological, and cosmological terms include "Those Who Write after Freud," "The Zero That Is All," "My Sister," "Abner Bellow," and "Dante in Our Time."

In poems such as "The Devil with the Minus Sign in His Right Hand," moreover, God's enemies are personified as Satan himself: "But what black thing wings from the lower quadrant? / See where he nears, breaking the timeless bliss!" (252).[12]

Plutzik's parables of Creation and its negation by demonic forces may have derived from the esoteric texts lying behind the Orthodox Judaism of his childhood, as well as from modern physics, but he also wrote as someone who had witnessed the catastrophe that engulfed the Jews of Europe. In his letter to Shepard, written in the wake of Pearl Harbor, Plutzik depicted the Axis powers as the camorra, the legendary Italian crime syndicate that later appears in the poem named for it as fallen angels who "plotted this before Adam was born, / To track us like hounds till we falter at last and fall." "The barbarian arises in every age" and must be met with "cold steel," Plutzik goes on to say in the letter, but in late 1941 he imagined only that the Jewish people might be made slaves under Hitler, unassimilable to Nazism but "left inviolate and unconquered as [they had] been throughout other periods of persecution."[13] By the time of a journal entry written on the eve of D-Day in England, where he served with the United States Army Air Corps, Plutzik succinctly identified Hitler as "the evil one."[14] Both immediately before the war and decidedly after it, in short, he wrote with a sense of evil rooted in Hebrew and Western tradition but now manifest in a contemporary world of totalitarian rule, radical antisemitism, and genocide.

* * * *

Before looking more closely at Plutzik's war poetry, we should therefore consider his conception of Creation from another point of view. "The Begetting of Cain" opens with what seems a conventional account of the Fall:

---

12 As in "An Equation," "The Zero That Is All," and other poems that call on a mathematical substrate, the figure of the "lower quadrant" signifies not only an underworld but also a Cartesian coordinate plane, which has zero at its center.

13 *Letter from a Young Poet*, 63, 75–76. The war was started, Plutzik writes, "by one of the lesser members of the camorra of the possessed," a formulation that connects the fallen angels of the Bible, the pseudepigrapha (the books of Enoch, in particular), and Western art and literature, most notably the novel by Dostoevsky variously translated as *The Possessed*, *Demons*, or *The Devils*.

14 Plutzik, journal entry of June 5, 1944: "The invasion of France began after all the years of preparation and all the wrongs suffered at the hand of the evil one." Quoted in Edward Moran, "The Life and Poetry of Hyam Plutzik," Hyam Plutzik, Poet, accessed November 16, 2022, http://www.hyamplutzikpoetry.com.

> Longing at twilight the lovesick Adam saw
> The belly of Eve upon the golden straw
> Of Paradise, under the limb of the Tree.
> He thought that none was near, but there were three ... (11)

Yet the third party in the poem is not the serpent of Edenic lore but rather a "creature of pointed ear, / Of the cleft hoof and the tight-mouthed sneer," who, in Plutzik's depiction, ensnares Adam and paradise itself in a net of evil:

> All were engulfed ...
> ... by the quenchless mind
> Roaming insatiate on the lowland, blind
> In its lonely hunger, lusting to make all things
> One with itself. (11)

The poem makes no mention of forbidden fruit or a serpent, nor does it place blame for the Fall on Eve. Because Satan in the Hebrew Bible appears not simply as the incarnation of evil but rather as an "adversary" or "accuser," and because the identification of the serpent with Satan as the devil incarnate belongs not to Genesis but to the New Testament, foremost in Revelation, Plutzik's Satan stands outside the Hebrew Bible's account. The "flutter of wings" that accompanies his "mastery," though it alludes to Yeats's "Leda and the Swan," identifies him as a fallen angel—specifically as Samael, who in rabbinical tradition refuses to bow down to God, or, out of jealousy of God, determines to avenge himself by seducing—or to be more exact, by raping—Eve. According to this mythology, which takes various forms, Samael comes to Eve riding on the serpent, and whereas Adam is the father of Abel (and later of Seth), it is Samael who is the father of Cain, made in his image, not God's or Adam's.[15]

"From Cain arose and were descended all the generations of the wicked, who rebel and sin," writes Rabbi Eliezer.[16] This tradition of the seed of Cain descending through Israel's enemies—Amalek, Esau, Edom, Rome, and so on—leads at length to Nazism, as in the German émigré artist George Grosz's 1944 painting

---

15 The rabbis argued that Samael, sometimes in the form of a serpent, "conceived a passion" for Eve (Genesis Rabbah 18:6) or said, "I will kill Adam and marry Eve" (B. Sotah 9b). In a variety of Talmudic readings, as well as pseudepigrapha, such as the 2 Enoch and the book of Adam and Eve, Samael is the prince of the demons, or sometimes the Angel of Death, who "injected a lust into" Eve (B. Shabbath 145b–146a), thereby creating evil passions.

16 *Pirke de Rabbi Eliezer*, trans. M. Friedlander (Skokie, IL: Varda Books, 2004), 183.

Cain, or Hitler in Hell, where a giant ogre-like Cain sits amid a heap of skeletons. Cain's lineage also appears in somewhat disguised form in other Plutzik poems; in "Elaboration on a Phrase of Rabelais," for instance, where he follows Rabelais in depicting his birthplace, Chinon, as the oldest city in the world, founded by Cain;[17] or in "The Mythos of the Man from Enoch," which refers not to the Enoch descended from Seth, whose line, continuing through the generations of Noah, is associated with worship of the true God, but instead with Enoch the son of Cain, whose progeny are associated in post-biblical literature with evil, violence, and corruption.

Cain and his descendants, that is to say, are not ancillary to Jewish history but essential to it, from Creation down to modern times. In his depiction of the Allies' war against Hitler, Plutzik seems always to have the seed of Cain in mind, yet he does not identify the propensity for malign actions with Nazism alone. In *Horatio,* a long narrative poem in the form of a legend-based sequel to *Hamlet* published in 1961, Plutzik addresses the crimes of totalitarian rule in a Cold War context but pays no explicit attention to the Shoah. Although we will never know what his unwritten long poem on the subject might have included, it was intended, he wrote in his proposal, "not to be primarily about Jews," let alone "a cry for vengeance": it will be an "exploration of the areas of evil in the human heart ... so that men, all men, may always be aware of, and on guard against, their extraordinary capacities for evil." Indeed, in Plutzik's view, war casts its own net of evil from which no nation or individual combatant, however just their cause, is immune. Thus, "Hiroshima" questions the moral comfort of those distant from the dropping of the bombs but nonetheless implicated in it, and "Bomber Base" asks about the responsibility of those, like Plutzik himself, who armed the machines of destruction:

> Hoist up the bombs carefully into the belly
> Of this great monster and do not look too closely
> At the work of your hands as you thread the fuse ... (37–38)

A different kind of qualification in his postwar judgment may be inferred in other poems, written just a few years after the war, that adopt a more distant, more contemplative stance. From the perspective of "The Airman Who Flew over Shakespeare's England," inspired by Plutzik's own postwar flight over defeated Germany, the English landscape is now a pastoral composition

---

17 François Rabelais, *Gargantua and Pantagruel,* trans. J. M. Cohen (New York: Penguin, 1955), 684–85.

of hayricks, woodlands, and steeples among "thrones of thatch ruling a yellow kingdom / Of barley" (101). "The Old War," a mellow short poem with a lilting rhythm, likewise circles around a few simple images summarized in the opening and closing stanzas:

> No one cared for the iron sparrow
> That fell from the sky that quiet day
> With no bird's voice, a mad beast's bellow...
>
> Home again to the barley-mother—
> Ten good sons, pilot and gunner,
> Radioman and bombardier. (94)

The apparent oblivion of those on the ground may owe something to Plutzik's further observation in his journal entry on the eve of D-Day where, after he described the work of loading bombs, he noticed in the background "a farmer harrowing an adjacent field behind a plodding horse," an image that circumspectly recalls, in Auden's "Musée des Beaux Arts," the farmer who "May / Have heard the splash of" Icarus plunging into the sea, though "for him it was not an important failure."[18] In any case, the deaths of the ten-man crew of a B-24 bomber brought to earth somewhere in the theater of war now belong, not many years later, to a fading event—"the old war."

The poem's elegiac mood is deepened in the image of the "barley-mother," which can be traced back to the Homeric *Hymn to Demeter*, the goddess of agricultural fertility. More immediately, however, it comes from a work that many poets writing in the wake of Eliot took to heart, namely, James Frazer's *The Golden Bough*, where the barley-mother is represented symbolically as the last sheaf harvested, thus placing the fate of the bomber crew within a ritual cycle of death and renewal.[19] Since for Plutzik such folklore was often rivaled by Hebrew traditions, he also alluded to the biblical fertility ritual of counting the *omer* ("measure"), the sheafs of barley harvested for the Feast of Unleavened Bread, during the fifty days between Passover and Shavuot, as described in Leviticus 23. We can find support for this reading in "After Looking into a Book Belonging to

---

18 W. H. Auden, "Musée des Beaux Arts," in *Collected Poems*, ed. Edward Mendelson (New York: Modern Library, 1991), 179.

19 James George Frazer, *The Golden Bough* (New York: Collier Books, 1963), 463–66. Plutzik cites *The Golden Bough* as an important influence in both "The Protean Universe" and "Poetry of Myth."

My Great-Grandfather, Eli Eliakim Plutzik," a poem devoted to the travails of Plutzik's Jewish ancestors in nineteenth-century Russia, nearly anonymous and unmemorialized in "speechless graves" (97), and inspired by the family's *Tikkun Leil Shavuot*, a compendium of passages from the Bible, the Mishnah, and other rabbinic commentary read by the observant in all-night study on Shavuot.[20] In rabbinical tradition, Shavuot came over time to commemorate the giving of the Law on Mount Sinai, but it was customarily a time for mourning past anti-Jewish violence and martyrdom. It is also notable that although few, if any, of the ten-man bomber crew were likely to have been Jewish, their number makes the *minyan* required to say Kaddish, and in this way, too, Plutzik's elegy suggests that mourning the dead is ameliorated by the prospect of new life to come.

As "The Old War" suggests, Hyam Plutzik's view of World War II, including the Shoah—truly an "old war" if we see it as just the latest in the long history of wars against Jews—cannot be appreciated without reference to a biblical and liturgical framework he took for granted. We see a further illustration in "The Miracle," an elegiac meditation spoken in the voice of a soldier bathing in the "mild waters of Betterton" at the "firing of the sunset gun," the time when the flag is lowered. Betterton is a resort town on the Chesapeake Bay where Plutzik camped during training exercises while stationed at the Aberdeen Proving Ground prior to shipping overseas.[21] Now, however, the war has ended. Although a return to the normal rhythms of life is not yet complete, the soldier, hearing a gull across the bay, speaks of himself past and present:

> The soldier heard and hears that cry
> To the running moment: *Stay! Stay!*
> *Over the valley of Ajalon!* ...
> O and the one who cried was I.
>
> War is done and that time is done,
> But nothing changes at Betterton.
> Much is lost but a strange thing won. (31)

---

20   The book is among those in Plutzik's library donated to the University of Rochester after his death. Its provenance is identified in a Yiddish inscription by Plutzik's father that reads, "My grandfather's Tikun Leyl Shavuot / Tikn leyl Shavues." Thanks to Kenneth Moss for the translation.

21   In a letter to his wife dated July 1, 1942, Plutzik described Betterton in rather pastoral terms: "We're on the bay itself here, our encampment being on a cliff over the shore. We have a swimming period daily. The water is very mild; the vista wonderful" (HPP: Box 5, Letters to and from Hyam Plutzik, 1926–March 1955).

The miracle announced in the poem's title takes off from the italicized lines, "*Stay! Stay! / Over the valley of Ajalon!*," which paraphrase God's intervention when Joshua does battle with a coalition of Amorite kings (Josh. 10:11–14). First, God rains "huge stones on them from the sky," and then, by making the sun stand still, He lengthens the daylight hours "until the nation had avenged themselves of their enemies" and the conquest of Gibeon is secured. Having hearkened to Joshua's voice, the passage concludes with "the Lord fought for Israel."

By this account, the miracle surpasses even the parting of the Sea of Reeds, when Moses likewise assures the people that "the Lord will fight for you" (Exod. 14:14).[22] Joshua is given to us as a skilled military commander, perhaps the greatest in the Bible, and yet victory at nearly every turn in his campaign requires divine intervention: Joshua commands the sun to stand still, but in doing so he speaks not to the sun but to the Lord. For a Jewish poet and war veteran writing in the wake of World War II, the potential role of God in the Allied military victory was sure to be of special interest. But before considering the strange final lines of "The Miracle," let us look at "The King of Ai," another postwar poem featuring Joshua.

In Exodus (17:8–14, 16) Joshua is counseled to do battle with Amalek, the shadowy archetypal enemy who first rises up against the Israelites during the journey out of Egypt and is subsequently named some half dozen times, perhaps most prominently in the book of Esther in the person of the villain Haman who plots to exterminate the Jews but instead is hanged for his crimes, a victory celebrated on Purim. In Plutzik's day, of course, it was Hitler, frequently compared by Jews to Amalek and Haman, who once again brought to the fore the admonition in Deuteronomy (25:17–19): "Remember what Amalek did unto thee ... thou shalt not forget," which reiterates the Lord's paradoxical instruction to Moses when the Amalekites are defeated in Exodus (17:8–15): "Write this for a memorial in the book and rehearse it in the ears of Joshua: for I will utterly blot out the remembrance of Amalek from under heaven."

The devastation of Ai follows fast on that of Jericho, in which we find the first instance of God's intervention on behalf of Israel, when the blasting of horns and shouting are enough to bring down the walls and expose the city to the destruction that ensues (Josh. 6:21). A comparable slaughter befalls the inhabitants of

---

22 The rabbis determined that the sun standing still for Joshua was one of the miracles experienced by Moses, Jonah, Elijah, Daniel, and others that God had commanded proleptically at the time of Creation ("I commanded the sun and the moon to stand still before Joshua"). See Genesis Rabbah 5:5.

Ai (in Hebrew, ha-'Ay*ha-'Ay*, "the ruin"), likewise put to the sword before the city is razed and its twelve thousand inhabitants wiped out (Josh. 8:26–9): "So Joshua burnt Ai, and made it a heap forever, even a desolation, unto this day. And the king of Ai he hanged on a tree until the eventide."

While turning the mellifluous word "eventide" into a repeated refrain circling around the hanging of the king and the havoc wreaked upon the city, Plutzik does not touch on Joshua's initial defeat by the soldiers of Ai, a punishment inflicted by God because one of the Israelites had violated Joshua's injunction against looting Jericho. History tells us, moreover, that the king and other dignitaries would not simply have been hanged but also impaled on stakes for public display. It may be details such as these that lie behind Plutzik's darker account of the "ravished city":

> God, God, for the evil done at eventide,
> For the bloody knife and the torch in the doomed city,
>
> And the girls who screamed on the sand by the gates of the city,
> And the strange seed within them at eventide—

And, indeed, it is not a partisan but a more evenhanded God whom Plutzik addresses:

> O God be merciful at eventide:
> Remember him you condemned by the flaming city,
>
> Where he lies under his cairn at the gates of the city,
> And the vultures circle the sky at eventide. (6)

Whereas the conquest of Ai in the Book of Joshua ends with Joshua building an altar, making burnt offerings, and reading to the assembled throng from "the book of the law of Moses"—that is, the Decalogue transported in the Ark (8:35)—here, in a shocking inversion, it is not the seed of Amalek but the seed of the Israelites that is planted in raped women, and here Amalek is not to be blotted out but remembered by God.

What, then, are we to make of the final line of "The Miracle"—"Much is lost but a strange thing won"? Was the strange thing the very survival of "the remnant," the *Sh'erit ha-Pletah*, much discussed in the wake of the Shoah? Or the birth of the nation of Israel? Or the Allied victory and, as it happened, the comparatively rapid assimilation of Jews among those nations, especially the United

States? Whereas some ultra-Orthodox Jews contended both during and after the war that the Shoah was God's judgment upon the Diaspora, might one not suggest to the contrary that God, as He did in Joshua's war with the Canaanites, intervened on behalf of Israel? Such a view might comport better with the idea that much was lost but a strange thing won; yet here, as elsewhere in Plutzik, the poem's power lies in painful, unresolvable ambiguities.

* * * *

After his destruction of Jericho, Joshua decreed that the city never be rebuilt, and yet, by the era portrayed in "The House of Gorya" (or Gurya, among other Talmudic variants), the city has not only been rebuilt but is renowned for its agricultural fertility and the home of a priestly population large enough to rival Jerusalem. Although "The House of Gorya" remained unpublished at the time of Plutzik's death, it had the leading role in a manuscript entitled "House of Gorya and Other Poems" that he submitted to *Scribners*, unsuccessfully, in 1945 or 1946 (later published as *Aspects of Proteus*, with the title poem removed). The title refers to a *bet midrash*, a "house of study," located in Jericho, which now suffers under the punishing rule of the Roman Emperor Hadrian:

> In the house of Gorya, in risen Jericho,
> Six dark men sat in heathen Hadrian's hour.
> The servant who brought them the black loaf of bread
> And the wine as meagre as Rabbi Hanania's face
> Startled their talk of the slavish Empire
> That stretched from Judea out to the great ocean.

Further depredations and idolatries taking place under "Caesar the fat-faced god," while "the ruined temple greyed on the holy hill," are catalogued before the scene turns back to the house of study and the sudden appearance of a mysterious, source-less voice:

> "There is but one—" As Rabbi Hanania poised,
> Bending so that his black beard was thrust
> Like an omen over them, they heard a voice speak forth:
> "There is but one in this generation of man
> Bearing such worth that the spirit of God touches him.
> But this age is unworthy of him." All turned as one
> To where Hillel sat, as quiet as a boy
> That listens to the memories of old men. (248)

The source of this aggadah about the great sage Hillel the Elder, a short version of which Plutzik typed in manuscript notes for the poem but seems never to have adopted as an epigraph, is B. Sanhedrin 11a:

> Once when the Rabbis were met in the upper chamber of Gurya's house at Jericho, a Bath-kol was heard from Heaven, saying: "There is one amongst you who is worthy that the *Shechinah* should rest on him as it did on Moses, but his generation does not merit it." The Sages present set their eyes on Hillel the Elder.

With the patriarchs long gone, the prophets dead, and the Temple in ruins, what the rabbis hear is not the voice of God but a *bat kol*, an "echo" of prophecy (literally, a "daughter of the voice") that in rabbinical literature typically praises particular biblical figures or sages.[23] As noted earlier, aggadah flourished following the watershed events of the Jewish War, concluded in 70 CE, and the calamitous Bar Kokhba Revolt in 132 CE, after which, as Stephen Mintz writes, it became the task of the rabbis to "shore up the battered paradigm of the covenant" and, as though assembling debris from a shipwreck, to "recall to mind a splendor that has been forever dismantled."[24]

The time of the poem would therefore seem to be important, but Plutzik leaves it uncertain. On the one hand, the mystical event seems to occur during the late life of Hillel, who is said to have lived from about 110 BCE to 10 CE. On the other hand, Plutzik's mention of "the ruined temple" locates the action in the interregnum between the destruction of the Temple and the failed revolt. A more specific reason to locate the poem between these events is the reference to Rabbi Hanania, presumably Rabbi Joshua ben Hanania, a leading sage who died in 131 CE on the eve of the revolt. His face is "meagre," as we might expect of one known for his conciliatory intercessions with the Roman authorities and his dialogues with Emperor Hadrian, who ruled from 117 to 138 CE. By most accounts, Hadrian was initially sympathetic to the Jews, to the point,

---

23 The *bat kol* is a successor to the Divine Voice heard, for example, by Moses: "When Moses went into the tent of meeting [. . .] he heard the Voice speaking unto him from above the ark-cover that was upon the ark of the testimony" (Num. 7:89). In two typescript drafts of the poem, Plutzik capitalizes "Voice," but he never writes "Daughter of the Voice" (as in his unused Talmudic manuscript note) or "bat kol."

24 Alan Mintz, *Hurban: Responses to Catastrophe in Hebrew Literature* (Syracuse, NY: Syracuse University Press, 1996), 57, 65.

it was said, that he intended to rebuild the Temple, but ultimately turned against them.[25] At the same time, because "The House of Gorya" goes on to speculate about postwar Jewish life, the catastrophe of the revolt is an essential part of the poem's context, nor can we ignore the admonition implicit in Joshua ben Hanania's reputed conciliation of a tyrant who proves to be no friend of Jews. Bar Kohkba's resistance to Hadrian's increasingly harsh anti-Jewish decrees, such as his interdictions against Torah study, circumcision, and holy festivals, and ultimately his erection of the temple of Jupiter on the site of the ruined Temple, ended according to tradition with some 580,000 Jews killed, many survivors sold into slavery, and most of the remnant scattered in a exile lasting almost two millennia.

As in much Talmud and midrash, however, temporal precision in the poem's setting matters less than the lesson conveyed. We see this clearly enough in the works of mourning that emerged in the aftermath, whether in Lamentations, the Tractate "Mourning," or the medieval *Midrash Eleh Ezkerah*, known in English as the "Ten Martyrs" prayer, or by its opening words, "These I Will Remember" (from Ps. 42:5), which memorializes sages murdered by the Romans around, but not confined to, the time of the revolt. For Plutzik, such temporal fluidity codified his transport of Gorya's message into the post-Shoah world. In the poem's second stanza, two millennia have passed. Hadrian's horses are now "Shadows, pressing silent hooves to the ground," his road "sunken beneath the imperial grass," and the name Hillel "beats thin / In the veins of history as a sleeper's pulse." The new era, which awaits "the chosen one, its saint," is an "epoch of great crimes and sanctimony" ruled by "the learned bigot, the well-groomed barbarian," a time when "willing slaves" and "hungry children" abase themselves before wealthy "whoremasters" (249).

In its characterization of mid-century nationalist barbarism, "The House of Gorya" foreshadows Plutzik's intention, in his planned long poem, to address "the victims of the various terrorisms and tyrannies of our time . . . victims of injustice in states not ordinarily tyrannical," so that all people will be on guard against "their extraordinary capabilities for evil." The universalization of "great crimes" in "The House of Gorya" may blunt the poem's force, but Plutzik is focused less on mass murder, let alone the event not yet known as the Holocaust, than on the evident potential for states to devolve into fascism and, just as important, on the less certain potential for redemption from world-scale catastrophe. In this "time of unworthiness [the chosen one] will be hidden," he writes, drawing on the idea

---

25 Genesis Rabbah, 64:10.

of the *Tzadikim Nistarim*, the "hidden righteous ones," one of whom may be the Messiah, who remains hidden because the age is not worthy of him.[26] In the poem's final stanza, moreover, the poet himself, perhaps the one now destined to hear the *bat kol*, emerges as the first-person speaker in search of the saint: "I seek that house in all the streets of the world" (249).

Plutzik was concerned about Jewish deracination, as we know from his self-incriminating depiction in "Portrait" or "On the Photograph of a Man I Never Saw," in which his Russian grandfather, whose beard, like Rabbi Hanania's, seems "blacker than God's / Just after the tablets / Were broken in half," foresees "the days / Of the fallen Law / In a strange place" (55). When Plutzik looked back some two thousand years in the wake of the Shoah, the challenge of restoring the covenant and the Jewish people was all the more acute. The lessons twentieth-century Jews might draw from the age of Hadrian and Hillel are not fully worked out in "The House of Gorya," but the poem is equally concerned with the fate of a larger world that has just survived a cataclysm in which some eighty million people died, in which millions more were exiled to alien lands, and from which colonized nations in Asia and Africa would soon emerge as sites of resistance and revolution. If "The House of Gorya" contains elements of Plutzik's unwritten Holocaust poem, we may imagine him anchoring an exploration of modern anti-Judaism in biblical events and traditional midrash in order to extrapolate from the particulars of Jewish tragedy to the universals of human conflict. The contemporary poet seeks not the Messiah but only a single person as worthy as Hillel, recognizable for "his dignity, his knowledge and his suffering"—a figure who might emerge in the Third World and might even be, like the Isaac who served bread and wine in the house of Gorya, a "lame servant waiting in the corner." Such a saint may or may not be Jewish, Plutzik appears to argue, but in any case his voice will not be addressed to Jews alone and must be heard by all. In the great remaking of the global order that Hyam Plutzik's generation was living through, mourning was not at an end, nor was the task of repairing the world.

---

26 More commonly known as the *Lamed Vav Tzadikim*, there are "thirty-six righteous ones" on whom depend the salvation, even the continued existence, of the world (B. Sanhedrin 97b, B. Sukkah 45b). The Messiah remains hidden, said Gershom Scholem, "only because the age is not worthy of him." See *On Kabbalah and Its Symbolism*, 6.

Bibliography

Auden, W. H. *Collected Poems*. Edited by Edward Mendelson. New York: Modern Library, 1991.
Babylonian Talmud. Edited by I. Epstein. London: Soncino Press, 1935–52. https://www.halakhah.com/.
Brunner, Edward. *Cold War Poetry*. Urbana, IL: University of Illinois Press, 2001.
Campbell, Joseph. *The Hero with a Thousand Faces*. Princeton, NJ: Princeton University Press, 1972 [1949].
Cesarani, David, and Eric J. Sundquist, eds. *After the Holocaust: Challenging the Myth of Silence*. New York: Routledge, 2012.
Eliot, T. S. *The Poems of T. S. Eliot*. Edited by Christopher Ricks and Jim McCue. Baltimore, MD: Johns Hopkins University Press, 2015.
Fishbane, Michael. *The Exegetical Imagination: On Jewish Thought and Theology*. Cambridge, MA: Harvard University Press, 1998.
Frazer, James George. *The Golden Bough*. New York: Collier Books, 1963 [1922].
Midrash Rabbah. Edited by H. Freedman and Maurice Simon. 10 vols. London: Soncino Press, 1983.
Mintz, Alan. *Hurban: Responses to Catastrophe in Hebrew Literature*. Syracuse, NY: Syracuse University Press, 1996.
Edward Moran and Steven Sher. "Hyam Plutzik's Horatio as Post-Holocaust Poem." Accessed September 30, 2024. https://static1.squarespace.com/static/5682cb822399a3aa8df162ec/t/5b9866134d7a9cbbeaaf55bf/1536714260234/sher-and-moran-horatio-post-holocaust.pdf; Accessed July 24, 2023.
Moran, Edward. "The Life and Poetry of Hyam Plutzik." Accessed July 24, 2024. http://www.hyamplutzikpoetry.com.
Nelson, Cary. "The Universe Is No Consolation: Hyam Plutzik, Jewish Identity, and the Ethics of Post-Holocaust Reading." *Journal of Jewish Identities* 15, no. 1 (2022): 5–31.
Pirke de Rabbi Eliezer. Translated by M. Friedlander. Skokie, IL: Varda Books, 2004.
Plutzik, Hyam. *Letter from a Young Poet*. Hartford, CT: Watkins Library at Trinity College, 2015.
———. *Hyam Plutzik Papers*, University of Rochester.
———. *The Collected Poems*. Brockport, NY: BOA Editions, 1987.
Rabelais, François. *Gargantua and Pantagruel*. Translated by J. M. Cohen. New York: Penguin, 1955.
Scholem, Gershom G. *On Kabbalah and Its Symbolism*. Translated by Bernard McGinn. New York: Schocken Books, 1996 [1961].
Senesh [Szenes], Hannah. *Hannah Senesh: Her Life and Diary*. New York: Schocken Books, 1971.
Sundquist, Eric J. "Blessed Mythmaker: The Poetry of Hyam Plutzik." Accessed September 30, 2024. http://www.hyamplutzikpoetry.com/. https://drive.google.com/file/d/18y4aXA50KLXStIN8wD3vcpbFi1qtEEbF/view
Syrkin, Marie. *Blessed Is the Match: The Story of Jewish Resistance*. New York: Jewish Publication Society, 1947.
The Holy Scriptures, According to the Masoretic Text: A New Translation. Philadelphia: The Jewish Publication Society of America, 1917. Repr. 1942.

CHAPTER 2

The Universe Is No Consolation: Hyam Plutzik, Jewish History, and the Nature of Post-Holocaust Poetics

Cary Nelson

> The victims speak, telling of their crime and punishment. Their crime is all too often that of merely being alive; the punishment is usually the fire, or sometimes the self-dug grave. I imagine passages: "I was so and so, I was so and so, I did such and such; for this I went into the fire."
> —Hyman Plutzik,
> from a 1960 description of a planned Holocaust poem

There will arise, in the repletion of time,
In every age the chosen one, its saint,
Whom the later days will corrupt when the great minds,
The sharp imaginations that discovered him,
Perish, and the little spirits play with history.
In the epoch of great crimes and sanctimony;
The hour of the learned bigot, the well-groomed barbarian;
Of immense knowledge and the conscience dead;
The murderer who loves humanity; and the king

Copyright © 2025 by Cary Nelson

> With a newer title, lording it in his halls;
> The willing slaves, multifarious in their abasement;
> The hungry children, the rich, worthy whoremasters—
> In the time of unworthiness he will be hidden.
>
> —Plutzik, "The House of Gorya"[1]

In a life that was prematurely cut short in 1962 at age fifty, Hyam Plutzik published three books of poetry: *Aspects of Proteus* (1949), *Apples from Shinar* (1959), and *Horatio* (1961). Despite the brevity of his mature writing life—just over twenty years—his posthumous *Collected Poems*, issued in 1987, adds uncollected and unpublished poems, some of which Plutzik hoped to include in another book, to comprise a substantial volume of three hundred pages.[2] While a planned long poem on the Shoah was never completed, as Edward Moran has importantly informed us, Plutzik described its themes and its major sections in detail in an October 14, 1960, fellowship application to the Guggenheim Foundation that is part of the Plutzik archive at the University of Rochester.[3] Plutzik's application describes it as a poem "on the most immense subject for a poem in our time: the massacre of six million Jews by Hitler," and adds, "it is hard enough to write a requiem for one man, but six million! Is there such a number? Grief ends beyond one or two or three; beyond that there are only statistics." To answer that impossible challenge by giving it an uncanny reality, the poem was to open with a scene "in which the six million ghosts appear at midday on Main Street." The poem was also to feature "a section dealing with Anne Frank"; "I expect," he writes in the plan for the poem, that she "will become an important figure in the poem. The idea of using her came to me soon after reading her diary some years ago." "I don't know whether I have the ability to do justice to this subject,"

---

1   Hyam Plutzik, *The Collected Poems* (Brockport, NY: Boa Editions, 1987), 249. Subsequent references will be in the text and identified as CP.
2   In addition to the *Collected Poems*, the most important resources for anyone interested in Plutzik's poetry are the extensive website at http://www.hyamplutzikpoetry.com and the large, well-organized Plutzik archive at the University of Rochester's Rush Rhees Library. The website includes a biographical essay, a film about his life, a bibliography, a series of scholarly essays, and many other resources. My thanks to Edward Moran for our conversations while I was working on this project and to Melissa Mead, archivist and collections librarian at Rochester. My thanks also to Holli Levitsky for inviting me to present a version of this paper at the 2018 annual Jewish American and Holocaust Literature conference. A revised and expanded version of this paper was published in the *Journal of Jewish Identities* in 2022. This version is further revised and expanded. Plutzik's poetry is reproduced and quoted here with the permission of The Estate of Hyam Plutzik.
3   A detailed register for the Hyam Plutzik Papers (forty boxes) at the University of Rochester library is available online at https://rbscp.lib.rochester.edu/finding-aids/D113.

he advises, "but I shall try."[4] Plutzik was determined, moreover, to capture the Shoah's meaning as a general human catastrophe as well.

Doing full justice to the overall topic of the Shoah, later to be more commonly known as the Holocaust, let alone all its victims, as Plutzik apparently realized, is fundamentally impossible. Of the six million individual victim's stories to tell, many are beyond any comprehension. What inner life is left to us of those selected for death at Auschwitz immediately on arrival? What of the experience of murdered children can be authentically recreated? The limits of the imagination may be implicit in Plutzik's decision to represent only six million *ghosts*, for whom our lamentation may stand in for or mediate representation. When Theodor Adorno qualified his famous assertion from "Cultural Criticism and Society" that "to write a poem after Auschwitz is barbaric," he allowed that "perennial suffering has a much right to expression as a tortured man has to scream."[5] That may have been the option left to Plutzik's ghosts. Giving Anne Frank a plausible presence in a narrative poem—up to the point when her diary ends—is an imaginable task. But the six million would flood a poem and incapacitate it.

Prosopopoeia, the rhetorical trope that gives a voice to the dead—Susan Gubar calls it, "impersonation of an absent speaker or a personification"[6]—could be effective for Anne Frank to the point where her diary ends and the special silence of the Holocaust takes over; after that, speech is impossible. We would then be in the zone of Dan Pagis's poem "Written in Pencil in the Sealed Railway Car," the text of which is abruptly aborted. Gubar argues that prosopopoeia "has remained the most noted phenomenon in English verse about the Holocaust, perhaps because the most notorious and decried ... poems composed in the cadences of the dead and dying emanate an unnerving invented proximity." Yet it also "holds out the promise of an unsettling empathic identification that connects without conflating the living 'now' and 'here' to the dead 'there' and 'then.'"[7]

Despite these challenges, it is fair to conclude that the projected Holocaust poem would, at least in part, lead Plutzik away from his characteristic strategy of indirection in social and political topics toward more intricately referential historical testimony. It is true, to be sure, that lyric poetry's often radical compression and frequent use of synecdoche amount to forms of indirection.

---

4   Hyam Plutzik Guggenheim Application, Box 4, Folder 9, Hymam Plutzik Papers, University of Rochester Library, Rochester, New York.
5   Theodor W. Adorno, *Prisms* (Cambridge, MA: MIT Press, 1981), 34; Adorno, *Negative Dialectics* (NY: Seabury, 1973), 326.
6   Susan Gubar, *Poetry After Auschwitz: Remembering What One Never Knew* (Bloomington: Indiana University Press, 2003), 178.
7   Gubar, *Poetry After Auschwitz*, 179–80, 189.

Those characteristics are behind Slavoj Žižek's claim that "poetry is always, by definition, 'about' something that cannot be addressed directly, only alluded to." That leads him to "correct" Adorno: "it is not poetry that is impossible after Auschwitz," Žižek writes, "but rather prose. Realistic prose fails, where the poetic evocation of the unbearable atmosphere of a camp succeeds."[8] Žižek's provocation is interesting, but it is empirically unsound. David Miller points that there are frequent poetic passages throughout modernism that make a strict poetry/prose distinction impossible. Antony Rowland argues that prose testimony also "often goes beyond positivistic details, adding an aesthetic 'layer' of mediation" and identifies such examples in prose by Primo Levi. Charlotte Delbo, he adds, "enmeshes poetic epiphanies in the main body of her non-fiction."[9] I would add that Jacques Derrida's entire career from *Of Grammatology* on makes it clear that plural and contradictory connotation is inevitable in all writing. Indirection and misdirection are everywhere. Self-reflexive metacommentary, foregrounding both authorial self-reflection and generic critique, are common to both poetry and prose. Yet, on a spectrum of generic strengths, lyric poetry's distinctive capacity for compression, as Rowland points out, gives special opportunities for "multiple—and co-existing meanings."[10] Moreover, the range of Holocaust poems is substantial, from the densely fact-based style of Charles Reznikoff's *Holocaust* to Paul Celan's cryptic late poems, from *Breathturn* to *Timestead*.

In 1941, writing a letter to a former teacher in what would be published decades later as *Letter from a Young Poet* in 2015 (the editors, not Plutzik, chose the title, with its allusion to *Letters to a Young Poet*),[11] Plutzik observes that "It is an awesome thing to be a Jew and to know that one is hated by so many of one's fellowmen."[12] The sentence trails off in ellipses, its implications perpetually undergoing new realization. Plutzik himself was still in the process of shaping his identity as a Jewish American poet. Born in 1911 in Brooklyn, the child of parents who

---

8   Slavoj Žižek, *Violence* (London: Profile Books, 2008), 5, 4–5.
9   Antony Rowland, "Poetry as testimony: Primo Levi's Collected Poems," Textual Practice 22, no. 3 (2008), 487–88, 489.
10 Rowland, "Poetry as Testimony," 494.
11 Whether Plutzik would have welcomed the Rilkean title is impossible to say, though he would not have wanted to promote the illusion that German culture provides a reliable antidote to barbarism. As Auschwitz survivor and Holocaust theorist Jean Améry writes, "No bridge led from death in Auschwitz to *Death in Venice*. Hesse's 'Dear Brother Death' or that of Rilke who sang 'Oh Lord, give each his own death'" (*At the Mind's Limits: Contemplations by a Survivor on Auschwitz and Its Realities* [Bloomington: Indiana University Press], 16).
12 Hyam Plutzik, Letter from a Young Poet (Hartford, CT: Watkinson Library at Trinity College, 2015), 68.

had emigrated rom what later became Belarus, Plutzik had spoken only Yiddish, Hebrew, and Russian at home. The family moved to a farm in Connecticut when he was a year old. Plutzik would learn English at age seven when he began attending a one-room Connecticut schoolhouse accommodating eight grades. He would later attend Trinity College as an undergraduate and graduate school at Yale. He was appointed an instructor in English at the University of Rochester in 1945, becoming the institution's first Jewish faculty member.[13]

I believe it is time for a reevaluation of Plutzik's poetry focused in part on a generally unrecognized but defining feature of his work—how he established his identity as a Jewish poet in the immediate post-Holocaust decade when many writers, except those on the radical left, avoided direct and aggressive political commentary. This effort to advance the recognition and documentation of Plutzik's Jewishness as a poet is shared with the online publication of Eric J. Sundquist's "Blessed Mythmaker." Part of what Sundquist demonstrates is that the Judaic grounding of a number of Plutzik's poems will only be apparent to readers with a substantial knowledge of Jewish history and culture. Moreover, Plutzik weaves Jewish and classical references together in ways that complicate and intertwine their meaning.

In the 2006 film about him, his widow Tanya describes him as a "neglected poet."[14] That characterization remains valid more than a decade and a half later. Part of what "doomed his verse to obscurity," Margot Lurie argues in a notable book review, was "an affinity for Jewish concerns."[15] Exactly what role unconscious antisemitism may have played in Plutzik's erasure—perhaps by way of an assumption that Jewish topics were simply marginal or less literary—is impossible to say. The chief task now is to correct the neglect.

By way of a fully representative range of poems, I argue here not only that Plutzik's story is fundamentally a Jewish one, and that the overall coherence and rhetorical sophistication of the 1987 *Collected Poems* is both remarkable and distinctive, but also that it presents a consistently darker vision than other critics have suggested. Although it includes both comic and occasional poems, its controlling vision is postapocalyptic, explicitly imbued with the themes and philosophical outlook that emerged from the rise of fascism in the 1930s and culminated in the defining events of World War Two.[16] Those events are two:

---

13   For more detailed biographical information, see Edward Moran's "The Life and Poetry of Hyam Plutzik."
14   The film *Hyam Plutzik: American Poet* includes biographical and critical commentaries, along with interviews by many of Plutzik's contemporaries.
15   Margot Lurie, "Golden Apples: *Apples from Shinar* by Hyam Plutzik," *Jewish Review of Books* 4, no. 1 (Spring 2013): 30.
16   Plutzik can use end rhymes to comic effect, as in "George Hobbs" (CP 29):
     I saw their arms together—

the Holocaust and Hiroshima. Plutzik did not, during his lifetime, write topical poems overtly about the Holocaust, but World War II remained an explicit subject, whether in "Bomber Base" from *Aspects of Proteus*, "The Old War" and "The Airman Who Flew Over Shakespeare's England" from *Apples from Shinar*, or the uncollected 1959 poem "On the Airfield at Shipdham," the latter commemorating the B-24 bomber base in Norfolk, East Anglia, where Plutzik was stationed as an ordinance officer in the Army Air Corps from 1944–45.[17] "Bomber Base," one of the more memorable poems anyone wrote about the war, records some of the work of preparing the B-24s for their bombing runs:

> Hoist up the bombs into the belly
> Of this great monster and do not look too closely
> At the work of your hands as you thread the fuse, performing
> The set procedure, till the thing is ripe for killing. (CP 38)

The lines document his own work at the base and the necessity of setting aside wartime reflection on the deadly mission built into the mechanical task of arming a plane. But he also thereby reads the organic reality back into the task by turning the bomber into a "great monster" with a bomb bay imaged as its belly. The Plutzik web site includes this passage from a June 5, 1944, letter to his wife, quoted from the Plutzik papers:

> The invasion of France began this morning, after all the years of preparation and all the wrongs suffered at the hands of the evil ones. It has been a cold and bitter day and now in the evening the sky is overcast and a drizzle is falling. The planes are out on a mission. Another officer and I stood under the wing of a grounded plane and saw them take off, one after the other, roaring in the long takeoff and then rising laboriously in the air. For hours later a roar could be heard above the clouds.

The conspiratorial tree.
Last night when on my knees

or

The issue of their plotting
One of them saw me come.
Suddenly they were mum.

17 He began his wartime service as a private in 1942 and ended with the rank of first lieutenant.

> How cold it must be in the sky now, and on the coasts of France!
>
> I went around with the men as they loaded three of the planes. The hoisting contrivance for the 500-lb'ers is ingenious. They worked as though fiends were pursuing them. Then when the bombs were up in the plane's belly, we fuzed them and threaded the arming wire. It was such a routine task, yet to think that this was a load of death for the enemy. The men are almost nonchalant in their work, except for their haste, yet even still they have a detestation for the fragmentate [sic] bombs
>
> On a bomber base in England, with a farmer harrowing an adjacent field behind a plodding horse, I pass the D-day of this war.

In its eight detailed stanzas, "Bomber Base" registers multiple forces in Britain and abroad that converge fatefully on a plane's mission, among them the "many messages coursing the earth / In this wartime night: of command, terror, despair; / In guttural syllables, in soft." As often with Plutzik, there is temporal convergence, as past, present, and imminent future intersect. He deftly manages tense changes that complicate those intersections. "Somewhere in the blackness" are the unseen guards "longing for home, / And a woman's arms," while in this ancient landscape "the stone weapons of dead men / Lie awaiting the outcome." The stone weapons invoke Britain's pre-history of ancient warfare and suggest that everything, all history, hinges on the outcome. "Already," he warns us, relating what the crews themselves know, "the enemy / Touches them with his instruments" as the planes lift into the air and register on German radar (CP 37). As the poem concludes, he recalls the bomber crews that pass through the base, their names and faces inevitably changing as new crews replace those whose planes went down, with their crews lost over Germany and the occupied countries; his lines infuse the poem's present time with elegiac undertones:

> *You remember that the faces changed often at the table,*
> *That you talked to them, that they had many dreams,*
> *That they were you yourself with a different number.*
> (Italics in original—C. N.)

The dining tables at the base host crew after crew, the faces changing as some die in the raids that follow. With high loss rates, it is a last supper for far too many, and such tables from more than one age are layered into the image. The numbers double as military designations and as fate's selection mechanism ("when your number is up"), but for Jews at least that last line has a special meaning: it reverberates with Holocaust implications. How many of us have thought about which direction we would have been sent on entering Auschwitz? It is part of our identity. A tattooed number on the arm still resonates for many alive today.

"The Old War" opens with a concise portrait of the miniaturized bomber, seen from a distance, that plummets to the earth as though it were a mechanical bird:

> No one cared for the iron sparrow
> That fell from the sky that quiet day
> With no bird's voice, a mad beast's bellow. (CP 94)

The shift from the half-naturalized "iron sparrow" to the "mad beast" that bellows carries the shock of every time a war violates norms by hurling categories together. The men's families are nowhere nearby to witness their deaths. The bomber crews return only to the indifferent "mother-barley" below, a reference evoking an impersonal fertility goddess whose embrace implicates timelessness, not family. "Sparrow, how many men did you bear?" the poem asks, and the answer makes it clear this is not a fighter plane but one of the bombers with larger crews that Plutzik serviced: "Ten good sons, pilot and gunner, / Radioman and bombardier." Sundquist adds that the ten-man crew evokes the minyan required for recitation of the Kaddish, giving the poem a Judaic edge for any Jewish reader.

In *Letter from a Young Poet*, Plutzik comments, after the Japanese attacked in the Pacific and "our men were dying at Pearl Harbor and Manila," that "the die is cast—by one of the lesser members of the camorra of the possessed,"[18] the Camorra being a mafia-style Italian criminal organization that may have existed for centuries. "The Camorra" is also the title of a chilling poem from *Aspects of Proteus* in which he tries to capture the persistence of an ancient, evil conspiracy whose targets may be Jews and whose members deceive the rest of us with false prayers seeking divine intervention:

> O they plotted this before Adam was born,
> To track us like hounds till we falter at last and fall
> Though we laugh behind doors and wear clever disguises.

---

18 Plutzik, *Letter from a Young Poet*, 63.

> For they were not all thrown in the burning gulf.
> There are those who remained behind and at convocations
> Fawn at the Lord and mumble the words of Hosannas. (CP 39)

The image of those "thrown into the gulf" alludes to Revelation 19:20 in which the beast and the false prophets or deceivers are "thrown alive into the lake of fire." But some avatars of the beast survived. As Plutzik was very much aware, Jews faced centuries in which pogroms and forced exile were carried out by those who believed they had god on their side. They were pursued relentlessly by men who might well have been hounds. His second book, *Apples from Shinar*, gathers poems that are not only post-Holocaust but also composed after the 1948 founding of the Jewish state. One of its substantial poems, the seventy-line "The Priest Ekranath" (CP 102-3), is a first-person narrative spoken by an invented Philistine priest, the Ekranath of the title.[19] Few readers then or since could have imagined that the task of defining one's identity as a Jewish American poet would have entailed writing an elaborate poem in the voice of an invented Philistine priest. In the opening stanza, the priest mentions Askelon (also Ashkelon) and Gath, two of the five Philistine city-states. Gath is the city where David took refuge as a fugitive from Saul, and it is also the birthplace of Goliath, the giant warrior whom David famously killed with his slingshot in the process of defeating the Philistines.

The poem amounts to prosopopoeia on behalf of an opponent who never existed and who voices his hostility toward the Jews before the concept of antisemitism was named. Ekranath's narrative is staged as a warning about the Hebrew peoples, who are constructed, in a manner wholly appropriate to the speaker, as unqualifiedly other—"these barbarians from the mountains, / From the anarchic hills come to destroy us." Elaborating on a wonderful conceit, the

---

19   Ekranath is likely an invented name, though it may be a portmanteau of Ekron, another of the five Philistine cities, and Anath, the goddess whom the poem probably references. It amounts to a linguistic puzzle to be decoded. It is not a name found in any ancient source (e.g., Bible, pseudepigrapha, Josephus, Philo, rabbinic text, etc.). Samson is taken to a Philistine priest, but the priest is unnamed. There is also a story in 1 Sam. 5 regarding the ark of Yahweh being taken to Dagon's temple in Ashdod, where the priests of Dagon are mentioned. The ark is then taken to Ekron, to the dismay of Ekronites. His drafts of the poem at Rochester [Plutzik papers, Box 11, folder 28] show he experimented with other titles—"The Priest Almater," "The Priest Hahanath"—before settling on the final title. The notes also show that he experimented with different arrangements of the names of the tribes at the poem's conclusion, no doubt seeking metrical enhancement of the incantatory effect, but never added the missing names. My thanks to several members on Brandeis University's Shusterman Fellows listserv for their assistance with this note.

priest complains "they have but a lone god" so stern and judgmental "he is their enemy." He invokes Anath, or Anat, the Canaanite goddess of violent passions—love, war, and sacrifice—and registers his offended protest that the Hebrew tribes "do not worship her nor any mother-goddess." She is known to enrich the fields with blood; without this "white Lady of splendid thighs and bosom" there will be no seedsman to "assure the fruit of field and man and animal."[20] Adonis is the god whom the priests represent as her lover, and in whose stead Ekranath testifies "I who am sanctified— / Having lain with the holy harlots at Askelon." Maintaining the priest's voice, the poem goes on to have him say

> ... Listen, you nations:
> They will lure you from your spontaneous ecstasies
> And positive possessions, and with themselves,
> Carry you forth on arduous pilgrimages
> Whose only triumph can be a bitter knowledge
> Out of the suffering they make our worth.

One such arduous pilgrimage was the journey through the Sinai after fleeing from Egypt. We are not only in the domain here of pagan complaints about the arrival of a monotheistic people that finds

> Our sunwashed cities despicable and meaningless,
> Our splendid artistic productions abominable,
> Our majestic pantheon foul as a kennel

but also in the territory of the pagan culture of the Nazis who overran much of Europe. All of Ekranath's complaints about the Hebrew tribes reverberate in the Nazi propaganda that so recently demonized the Jews. From Ekranath's perspective, the Hebrew tribes are an invading barbarian other, not only politically, culturally, and religiously, but also sexually.

Although the poem does not name him, the priest reports that he "met a certain one: / Sly as a jackal yet arrogant as a lion, / Rough-bearded, out of the desert," and that is clearly David. The poem is not only about the Philistine rage at the founding of the ancient Jewish kingdom, but also about antisemitic rage at the founding of the modern Jewish state. In the poem's final lines Ekranath testifies that through "the sacred harlot's embraces" he has learned

---

20 Anat is not named in the poem, though she is likely the goddess implied.

"the syllables / (Ah, they are powerful and barbarous!) / Of the secret incantation that gives them strength." But if we expect the poem therefore to close with the Shema it does not. Instead, it lists the names of eleven of the tribes of Israel:

> Hear how they thunder! Listen: *Issachar*
> *Levi simon reuben judah dan*
> *Zebulun asher naphtali menassah ephraim.*[21]

Recited without capitalization or punctuation, they form an incantation renewed for the present. The syllables of the names reverberate in a crescendo of pure sound that echoes through the centuries. As Margot Lurie writes in a review of a reprinted edition of *Apples from Shinar*,

> The roll call of Israelite tribes is unsettling not only because of its lofty authoritative tone, but because of its form. The tribes are not presented here in birth order, nor are they divided according to their mothers or territorial divisions. Only eleven names are listed, with Gad and Benjamin omitted. But while the names are presented irregularly, their appearance in the poem's final two lines marks a shift from the previously irregular meter into a thumping pentameter.[22]

That gives their recitation the character of a triumphal pronouncement.

If the legacy of the Holocaust echoes throughout the *Collected Poems*, however, explicit references to what was then the earth's newly nuclear present and future are mostly absent. Yet there are possible allusions to the use of atomic weapons in some of his works, as in the lines "In this mid-century / Screaming is easier . . . 'A poison bolus / Out of the sky has blasted your wife and child'" (CP 247). Consider as well the remarkable short poem "Two Hearts and an Arrow" from 1950 (CP 217):

> Deserted railroad sidings on Sunday
> Adumbrate the rust of our future,
> When the antiquarian will comment,
> "No, they were not wholly detestable.

---

21 Plutzik's list of eleven tribes omits the tribe of Benjamin. I do not have a convincing explanation as to why, though I imagine his reasoning combined both ancient and modern history.
22 Lurie, "Golden Apples," 31.

"Though the barbarians burned the libraries,
And the rocks are still radiant from their warring,
See, I have found in their more casual inscriptions
Hints of tenderness or only moderate hate."

This is a poem that anticipates how we will be viewed in a future time, something we can foresee now in the vacant silence of an abandoned, decaying railway spur, perhaps one of the abandoned lines to Auschwitz and other camps that were used to transport Jews to their deaths years earlier. The poem suggests that what we were and how we will be understood will be at once faintly recognizable and partly concealed (both meanings carried by "adumbrate") by the rust accumulated on disused rail tracks. With his typical wry humor, Plutzik imagines that by then we will be merely an antiquarian interest. In a debate among his fellows, the antiquarian sardonically pleads our case as enthusiastically as possible: we weren't *wholly* detestable. Our defining hatred was only "moderate," assuming hatred is amenable to moderation.

After alluding to Nazi book burnings in the opening line of the second stanza, a reference reinforced by his warning in *Letter from a Young Poet* that "a thousand books may go up in smoke on the Alexanderplatz,"[23] the speaker from the future tells us "the rocks are still radiant from their warring." Rocks heated and shattered from bombings do not long radiate their heat, but nuclear radiation can persist. Of course, Plutzik may only be metaphorically representing the intensity of our conflicts, but it seems a reference to atomic war is likely. Only then does Plutzik cash in his otherwise inscrutable title. "Two Hearts and an Arrow," as Edward Brunner proposed to me in an email, suggests a tree trunk carving by a lovestruck couple. Among the other "casual inscriptions" from our time that survive haphazardly, it displays limited "hints of tenderness." Other faint cultural survivals suggest we merely indulged ourselves in "only moderate hate," but those radiant wartime mementoes document the opposite. The poem not only reflects on the recent past but also predicts an imminent future, and in that future, as in the past, our relative investments in tenderness and hate may not reflect well on us. For a poem that shifts between past, present, and future and thus displays a certain temporal mobility, it is strikingly claustrophobic, unsurprisingly a characteristic of many Holocaust poems; they invoke a world, frequently Auschwitz or other camps, in which anything outside that imprisoned space ceases to exist for those confined there. Here it is a poem that arguably

---

23 Plutzik, *Letter from a Young Poet*, 77.

combines allusions to both the Holocaust and atomic war, references that empty our cultural legacy of any other meaning. As Brunner further suggested to me, poems like this "resound with a fierce restraint below which anger simmers."

Plutzik wrote but one, short, more explicit poem about nuclear war. Titled "Hiroshima," it was unpublished during his lifetime:

> The man who gave the signal sleeps well—
>   So he says,
> But the man who pulled the toggle sleeps badly—
>   So we read.
> And we behind the man who gave the signal—
>   How do we sleep? (CP 297)

The poem does not answer its question or offer an explicit moral judgment about the use of nuclear weapons. Instead, it registers the guilt and unease that must follow no matter what a military analysis might lead us to conclude. That guilt intensifies as the poem advances through its lines toward the public that granted its implicit consent. What signal did we give? How was it communicated? There are no easy answers. Unlike his Jewishness, however, there is only indirect evidence in the poetry that atomic war was a continuing preoccupation, but the vision of human affairs that pervades his work at mid-century is nonetheless imbued with a sense of tragedy marked by recent history. A bleak, postapocalyptic tone pervades his work.

That pattern began when Plutzik worked on an unpublished satirical novel about dictatorship in the 1930s, inspired by the rise of European fascism. Benito Mussolini had come to power in Italy in 1922 and immediately directed the police to begin eliminating the opposition. Laws were introduced giving him increasing dictatorial powers; within three years he established a dictatorship and by 1927 a full-fledged police state was in place. Hitler came to power in 1933. The novel written in 1934–35 was an experiment in more explicit, if mediated, political commentary, as opposed to what would become his more characteristic mode of indirection, until perhaps the planned but unwritten poem about the Holocaust.

His major 1935 poem, later submitted for the Yale Poetry Award in 1940, was his as yet still unpublished "The Seventh Avenue Express," a twelve-part 476-line poem ostensibly about the well-known New York City subway line. It is prefaced by a four-hundred-word "argument" reminding us that "always our comrade death is implicit, hinting his betrayal. Ever to each he turns some facet of his betrayal." Because the subway runs underground, Plutzik could use it to embody the largely hidden but emerging consequences of authoritarian governance. Opening with images of the train itself—"its windows throwing pale/ And fretful cubes of light on tunnel walls"—the poem quickly moves to characterize the subway riders:

> For here in the Earth, here in the home of worms,
> Voices are prisoned, speak with urgency
> From mouths that sag in weariness.

The riders' hands clench subway straps, "Not in salute to dictator or king, / Uneasily and million figures sway," here to be known by "clenched hand raised aloft and not in prayer / Or execration of God," or in revolutionary symbolism but in clinging to daily routine. Fascism was penetrating daily life. Evoking what will become a characteristic cluster of postapocalyptic tropes, he imagines this underground life will persist until it destroys us, "Until this city is the haunt of wolves" and "frogs croak out their loving song where once / The suave, tophatted gentlemen made love." The only trace of us would eventually be "the buildings tumuli / Of rust beneath the newborn, blazing stars." The dissolution of human civilization, succumbing to wild nature before an indifferent universe, is a signature displacement. It is also, to be sure, a familiar science fiction trope.

Until that moment comes to pass, "The Jew with his hunted eyes," and "Slav, / Saxon and Roman hold their place," but "Among them are those things that mimic men. / .. monsters from stele and monolith / Stand in our midst." Plutzik was very young, only twenty-four when he began writing "The Seventh Avenue Express," and it is partly a youthful fancy, but he nonetheless sensed the gathering malice: "The shells scream in the sky. The Very lights / Delineate a darkened land / ... The day is waning in an unknown West."

Although a few of Plutzik's published poems predate the outbreak of WWII in 1939—"My Sister" dates from 1938 and is the earliest poem included in *Aspects of Proteus*—none of them predate Hitler's ascension to power in 1933 or the advent of the viciously antisemitic Nuremberg Laws of 1935. The next phase of Germany's relentless assault on its Jews had its defining moment in 1938's Kristallnacht. These events and others were widely publicized in the US, and Plutzik was certainly well aware of them. The legacy of the Holocaust would continue to haunt him through 1959's *Apples from Shinar*. It obviously informs "Portrait," whose subject, perhaps Plutzik himself, "with what careful nonchalance ... tries to be a Jew casually" and thereby "to ignore the monster, the mountain— /A few thousand years of history" (CP 112). The passage is self-reflexive, as Plutzik, a nonobservant Jew, nonetheless feels his identity is historically, politically, and religiously shaped by his Jewish identity. As became clear when Europeans mounted their antisemitic assaults on equality in the late nineteenth century, Jewish assimilation is never complete; it is contingent and reversible.

Responding in part to the postwar frenzy of consumer capitalism, the poem effectively condemns those forms of assimilation that seek to replace historical memory, the personal investment in historical truth, including both long-term and recent Jewish experience, with consumerism. We are the equals of everyone else because we can all buy things. For one then wears but "the borrowed shirt . . . a shirt by Nessus." The same historical pattern would be among the forces motivating Adorno's critique of commodification and "the forces of commerce." The last stanza opens with a key characterization of its subject: "Notice how even when at ease he is somehow anxious, / Like a horse who wiffs smoke somewhere nearby faintly." That smoke, one could perhaps too easily deny, is from the ovens at Auschwitz. The unpublished prayer poem "Kaddish" also reads as a post-Holocaust text: "May he who establishes his peace on the heights bring peace and comforting also to us and to all Israel" (CP 270). But the eleven-month tradition of mourning for a family death does not suffice for the dead of the Shoah or for the people of Israel in its wake; that Kaddish prayer will now reverberate to the end of time.

"After Looking into a Book Belonging to My Great-Grandfather, Eli Eliakim Plutzik" (CP 97) is only readable as a Holocaust poem, even if its references once again are somewhat indirect. It opens with the first-person line "I am troubled by the blank fields, the speechless graves" (CP 97), which invokes not only the dead of the Shoah who have no living relatives to speak for them but also the vanished villages that have no remaining presence. They include obliterated Jewish cemeteries whose wooden tombstones have disintegrated. If we have words for the genocide itself—Holocaust, Shoah—we have "no word / For the thousand years that shaped this scribbling fist" that "carved upon wood." The killing fields and camps we can recall and name, but the "veldt dragging to Poland" trails a still longer history behind it. In the end, in the face of this palimpsest of absences there is necessary recourse to a placeless, rootless, diasporic form of mourning to which Jewish identity must testify: "Only *Here lies someone,* / Here lie no one and no one, your fathers and mothers." Plutzik is offering both a historical and theoretical intervention about diaspora post-Holocaust.

One of the most terrible of all Plutzik's poems readable as post-Holocaust commentary may be "The Geese" (CP 98), in which the passage of a squadron of migrating birds is first announced in sound, by "a miscellaneous screaming that comes from nowhere" that draws the observer's eye upward "at last to the moonward-flying" birds "arcing the spatial cold," skating the edge of the most unforgiving frigid temperature nature offers. The poem depicts fate, "the will toward destiny, which is death." But for a time, as the flock of birds hurls unwittingly "toward the secret marshes / Where the appointed gunmen mark the crossing," the sweep of their miraculous flight does not seem death-driven despite its "monomaniac passion." Indeed, in the poem's final line, which stands alone, we are told we must value the remnant, the flight before the flock meets its fate: "Value the intermediate splendor of birds." The poem is also about the intermediate civilization of the doomed Holocaust generation—before it meets its fate and vanishes. The anguish that now pervades the spectacle of their crossing is history's gift to us. Although Plutzik does not say so, perhaps he has in mind the fact that geese migrate in a V-shaped formation, symbolizing for us the fleeting character of our victory over death.

The Holocaust is also surely behind the need to address T. S. Eliot's antisemitism in "For T. S. E. Only" (CP 109–10), first published in 1955:

> You called me a name on such and such a day—
> Do you remember?—you were speaking of Bleistein our brother,
> The barbarian with the black cigar, and the pockets
> Ringing with cash, and the eyes seeking Jerusalem,
> Knowing they have been tricked. Come, brother Thomas,
> We three must weep together for our exile.

Eliot's rather modest exile is from his American birthplace to his chosen country, England, whereas the Jewish people's exile is from the Holy Land to the realms of the diaspora and from there, through the centuries, to further exiles from European countries. There would have been scant faint hope that Eliot could have found commonality with Bleistein and Plutzik and the Jews on the grounds of shared exile. The poem is a bitter appeal to an Eliot of potential sympathy, an Eliot who does not exist.

Eliot's "Burbank with a Baedeker: Bleistein with a Cigar" was published in his 1920 *Poems*. Among its uncompromising lines are these: "The rats are underneath the piles. The Jew is underneath the lot," lines that could well have been deployed by the Third Reich. But the issue is not only Eliot's antisemitism, which he confirmed repeatedly in poetry and prose over a number of years, but also the way it corrodes everything else he stood for as a major voice of modern poetry. For our purposes, the pressing issue is why Plutzik returned to highlight a 1920 poem thirty-five years after it was published. The continuing pressure of the twentieth century's defining genocide and the growing assault on Europe's Jews that lead up to it would seem the logical answer.

That may help contextualize the most telling challenge Plutzik issues to Eliot: "And now in the time of weeping you cannot weep" (CP 110). Now overshadowing the destruction of the Second Temple, the Holocaust is the supreme "time of weeping" in all of Jewish history, despite the pogroms, exiles, and categorical political, cultural, and religious acts of othering that preceded it. Because of his exalted literary status, Eliot stands at the forefront of the modern vocation Plutzik has chosen for himself. And so Plutzik asks Eliot, even now, in the wake of the apex of my people's suffering, will you not disavow your hatred? But of course Eliot never did. I am thus not inclined to impose on this poem a consoling sense of human fraternity as some readers have. It seems instead to offer forlorn witness to the brotherhood that antisemitism disavows, an awareness of which haunts Jewish identity. Like many post-Holocaust writers, Plutzik is not a poet of consolation.

In the final sections of his blank-verse epic *Horatio*, Plutzik reinforces the theme at the core of the four portraits that open the poem sequence. "Once I thought truth had a single face," the speaker reports, "And now? And now?" (CP 194). He can say so no longer. The book-length poem sequence narrates Horatio's lifelong journey to test people's memory of the concluding events in Hamlet's life and correct the misconceptions and transformations of the story that have multiplied. The task proves impossible. Myth, ignorance, and opportunism prevail; it seems no truth will hold. Every person he meets has a different and notably distorted account of the tragedy. That sense of loss and irresolution especially troubles those who need universal confirmation of modernity's most terrible truths. Horatio's resignation in the face of the mutability of truth and the erosion of its foundations comes after he has recounted the changes rung on the story of Hamlet over time and in different contexts.

The most explicit statement of the problem is in "Carlus," the dialogue with the slippery, manipulative, and somewhat threatening Danish prime minister, whom Anthony Hecht describes as "a cynical practitioner of *realpolitik* in the most Stalinist or Hitlerian style, to whom nothing is real or true, or anything can be made to be by brute assertion" (xviii). It was apparently written in the mid-1950s, most likely after McCarthy's 1954 censure by the Senate:

> "But," he blurted, "you persist in talking of 'truth.'
> Your devotion's for truth's sake. What, pray, is truth?
> What is this truth you would exhume from the grave?

> I am a practical fellow. Truth to me
> (Except, of course, for the doctrines of our religion)
> Is what I can see—a fact, no more or less." (CP 151)

The protagonist's frustrations with the erosion of political and historical awareness occur, for us and for the poet, in the face of the two absolute, implacable, incontrovertible truths of our age—that a genocide both intimate and industrialized was carried out with the active participation or passive consent of the nations of the world and that entire cities and their populations were intentionally obliterated in the blink of an eye. "What is this truth you would exhume from the grave?" seems readable in no other way. As Victoria Aarons recognizes, one of the poem's later questions—"If Moses is dead, how will Aaron speak?" (CP 159)—amounts to Holocaust lamentation. With Moses gone, there is no one to transmit God's messages to his priest Aaron. And we know the result: the multitudes turn toward the golden calf.

Like so many before him, Plutzik sees the worship of the golden calf beneath Mount Sinai as a parable applicable to his own generation. "On the Photograph of a Man I Never Saw" (CP 55) grounds the story in an autobiographical narrative that is immediately destabilized to acquire multiple referents. Each stanza operates with a conceptual and temporal hinge between the second and third lines, as the stanza flips between personal and mythic time:

> My grandfather's beard
> Was blacker than God's
> Just after the tablets
> Were broken in half.
>
> My grandfather's eyes
> Were sterner than Moses'
> Just after the worship
> Of the calf.
>
> O ghost! Ghost!
> You foresaw the days
> Of the fallen Law
> In the strange place.
>
> Where ten together
> Lament David,

> Is the glance softened?
> Bowed the face?

The poem offers no internal evidence to help us decide whether it refers to the speaker's or Plutzik's real grandfather. Instead, it testifies to a stern historical judgement that straddles Biblical and contemporary moments. For in our time the tablets with the ten commandments have been broken anew, with the worship of the golden calf being at least as damning as it is in the Exodus story. Only in the third stanza's pure lamentation can we comprehend the modern fact of the fallen law. And we too, as with the lost tribes, lament the loss of David's kingdom with its capital Jerusalem.

This double historical structure operates in *Horatio* as well. Composed from 1951–1955, *Horatio* is also effectively a fable about McCarthyism. It is no accident that the dialogue with a politician brings the issue to a head. As Edward Brunner writes in a masterful reading of the poem in *Cold War Poetry*, "It is never the case that this long poem alludes directly or even indirectly to particular events in the postwar years. Nevertheless, it is a work in which reputations are besmirched, often for reasons that are unscrupulous or that verge on personal vendettas" and "ends by glaring darkly at despicable circumstances which have compromised public discourse."[24] In the victory of political relativism and opportunism over the truth, the possibility of genuine historical witness is swept aside.

It was common for 1950s poets to address McCarthyism by implication rather than by direct critique, in part because there really was no venue in which to publish a poem explicitly attacking either the congressional committees or McCarthy himself. Editors understood that their rights to mail journals at discounted rates would be withdrawn if they published poems attacking the inquisition. As I have shown in *Revolutionary Memory*, however, some poets did write such poems, and they survive in their papers.[25] No one wrote a more searing set of such anti-McCarthy poems than another Jewish-American poet, Edwin Rolfe (1909–54), and he tried to publish a few, but even decidedly left-wing journals could not take the risk of publishing them. I published them for the first time in Rolfe's 1989 *Collected Poems*.

So Plutzik again opted for indirection, although no reader of *Horatio* with any political sophistication could miss the contemporary implications. The same

---

24 Edward Brunner, *Cold War Poetry* (Urbana: University of Illinois Press, 2001), 154.
25 See my *Revolutionary Memory: Recovering the Poetry of the American Left* and Edwin Rolfe's *Collected Poems* for examples of anti-McCarthy poems.

pattern of indirect and displaced contemporary implication informs his uncollected 1960 poem "On the Last Survivor of Our War, 1861–1865," where he tells us "The dead that Matthew Brady saw by the wall / Call too loud now to be denied" (CP 231). Plutzik had been stationed at several locations in the South during his World War II service, including Mississippi, so he was aware that the legacy of the American Civil War was still strong there. In the end, his broad national claim that the dead of a hundred years earlier call loudly to all of those alive is not universally true, though it was true for those culturally or psychologically still fighting the civil war. It is our dead, the dead of both World War II and, at least for Jews, the dead of the Holocaust who called loudly to us in that moment. The one-hundred-year anniversary of the start of the civil war provided the poem's occasion but did not define its contemporary relevance. When he concludes the poem by remarking "My God, how the storm of the generation passes, / How each wave is lost at last in the sand" he registers with others the concern that those more recent dead might pass from living memory. The same concern of course led the Israelis to capture Adolf Eichmann in Argentina that year and put him on trial in 1961 in Jerusalem, the event that made individual testimony such a strong feature of Holocaust memory. And in that moment the dead did "Call too loud now to be denied."

His long-unpublished poem "To Abraham Lincoln, That He Walk By Day" (CP 272-74) draws on empathy with African Americans grounded in that shared historical sense of suffering, discrimination, and injustice that drew many Jews to the civil rights movement:

> O Father Abraham, you know how wrongs grow fat
> On victim and doer, swallowing them both:
> One is destroyed, the other corrupted and tainted.
> The weary ages of injustice and brutality
> Do not fade out like a flying spark in the smithy:
> They burn deep and smolder till the full time
> When all, guilty and innocent, are consumed.
> For each man who is strung up, shot or castrated,
> Do you not think we shall have to pay a debt?

Plutzik hardly needs to remind us that another Father Abraham was father to the Jews in order to highlight the parallels, but he also insists on the distinctive features of black suffering. That includes the sexual violence enacted in lynchings. He insists that the necessity to remember must be paired with consequences. The American determination either to forget or misremember its history is implicitly paired here with the world's willingness to resist fully confronting the Shoah. Notable here is not just the sorrow he registers in a number of poems but also the very real anger he musters.

The most compelling act of witness incumbent on us is the need to bear witness to the presence of such evil. And evil is embodied in facts we cannot afford to see eroded. The "Salon on the Rue Galantiere" section of *Horatio* is set "In the Hyrcanian forest of aurochs and wolf / That we call Europe, that crouches out there barbarously" (CP 141). In *Hamlet*, Shakespeare invokes "th' Hyrcanian beast" as a symbol of barbaric malice. In the ancient world, in Hyrcania, now part of Iran, wild tigers were common. In Europe it was large horned wild cattle (aurochs), now extinct, and wolf packs, among other creatures, that roamed freely. For us it is altogether human beasts who threaten civilization. And they invade the present yet again. In the concluding section of his *Letter from A Young Poet*, written just after Pearl Harbor, he writes, "What I say is this: That the barbarian arises in every age. Sometimes he can be destroyed by laughter, sometimes by ridicule, sometimes by indifference, sometimes by legislation. Those are lucky generations when such measures can be used. And sometimes he can be destroyed only by the cold steel" (CP 76).

It is equally important that Horatio's second dialogue is with Faustus,

> ... the fierce-bearded Doctor I once had loved,
> Who now—I shall not name him here—has taken
> The old blasted path into damnation,
> And with his blood, abjuring gentle Christ,
> Matched his indenture with the Prince of Demons— (CP 135)

Plutzik will have been aware of those who made Faustian bargains with European fascism from Mussolini to Hitler to Francisco Franco. His brief unpublished poem "To Pablo Picasso, on His *Guernica*" (CP 253) testifies to his knowledge of the 1936–39 Spanish Civil War as the prelude to and testing ground for World War II and its mass slaughter of civilians. More dramatic still, however, is his 1950 preface to *Apples from Shinar*, unfortunately omitted from the *Collected Poems*, which functions effectively as a dedication to Spain's premier poet, Federico García Lorca, "murdered," as Plutzik emphasizes, "by Franco's bullies during the Spanish Civil War."[26] Plutzik pointedly asks "are there not many cities

---

26 Hyam Plutzik, "Peface," *Apples from Shrinar* (Midletown, CT: Wesleyan University Press, 2011), ix.

and many places that kill their poets? Places nearer home than Granada and the Albacín?" Here, he answers,

> the deaths are less brutal, more subtle, more civilized. Against us, luckily, there are no squads on the lookout. There is no conspiracy against us, unless it is a conspiracy of indifference. But there are more powerful things in the modern world (and people who are the slaves of things and people who are things) that move against poetry like an intractable enemy, all the more horrible because unconscious. They would kill the poet—that is, make him stop writing poetry.

This preface politicizes the whole book in multiple ways. It makes a statement about the cultural politics of the period, links the book to the great leftist cause of the 1930s, and reverberates through poems like "Portrait" with its condemnation of consumerist assimilation. Although *Apples* was published in 1959, Plutzik dates the preface October 1950, when it was produced for the Rochester Poetry Society. The effect is to indict the whole decade of the 1950s, not just its concluding years. García Lorca's death, however, is usually paired with Grenada, not with the Albacín, which is one of Grenada's districts. But the Albacín contains the Jewish quarter that thrived during Spain's long Muslim period. Once again, Plutzik embeds a cultural, historical, and distinctly Jewish allusion in a way that will not hail most readers. That may be part of why David Scott Kastan, in an otherwise sensitive afterword to the 2011 "special edition" reprint of *Apples*, says Plutzik "was not a Jewish poet, but a gifted poet who happened to be born Jewish."[27] Obviously, I disagree. The Albacín reference is as indirect as the inclusion of the name "Shinar" in the book's title. Shinar alludes broadly to Babylonia, site of the Tower of Babel and a place of exile for the Jews. In a November 1958 letter to Donald Hall, Plutzik writes "The plain of Shinar was where the garden of Eden was located, and the apple eaten."[28]

The preface is not alone in enriching our sensitivity to Plutzik's engagement with the events of his time. In a compelling letter Plutzik wrote to his wife Tanya on May 14, 1945, two days after his B-24 flight over a recently defeated Germany—quoted here from a copy of the single-spaced typed letter supplied to me by Edward Moran—Plutzik comments that "It gave one a strange sensation to fly thus over the land of the enemy, to think that, in the houses below, the

---

27 David Scott Kasten, "Afterword," *Apples from Shrinar*, 63.
28 The November 24, 1968, letter to Hall is from the Plutzik archive [Box 6, folder 10].

stunned embittered people lives in their defeat. The landscape was so beautiful that I could not help wondering how, from such beauty, could have been distilled the vicious brew of Hitlerism. From this very soil the most evil and ugly of things had come" (2). Yet as he flies over a landscape that alternates between ruined cities and green fields he also recognizes "the cities had paid the debt for Fascism" (3):

> The Hamburg waterfront was an indescribable chaos. Along both sides of the river lay the ruined factories and houses. There too the streets had often been obliterated; the jagged walls stuck up out of the devastation; a few lonely people passed. Outside the city land-battles had apparently taken place. On blackened hills whose vegetation had been burnt and blasted the tracks of armor could be seen twisted and crossing. (3)

Plutzik well realizes that German fascism did not arise from field and city; it arose from the German people. The beautiful landscape stands in for German and Western culture that offered no barrier to barbarism.

In the same section of *Letter from a Young Poet* Plutzik observes that "It is no wonder that the Jews have always been Hitler's main enemy. We are the people of the book; we are a symbol of the continuity he would break; we (with all our admitted faults) represent that element of conscience that he must eradicate entirely from mankind before he can implant his odious philosophy of brutality and selfishness in humanity."[29] And in a poignant moment, writing before the scope of Hitler's plans were known, Plutzik argues that the Jew cannot be drawn into a Faustian bargain with Nazism: "the Jew, compared to other people, would be comparatively fortunate in a Hitlerian world. . . . [H]is soul would be his own, for by the very basis of Hitlerism he is outside the pale; he cannot be accepted into the new philosophy even if he wishes to. Therefore will his spirit be left inviolate and unconquered as it has been through other periods of persecution." The Wannsee Conference, which inaugurated the Final Solution, would not take place until the following month, on January 20, 1942, but the systematic murder of the Jews of Ukraine had already begun with the June 1941 invasion of the Soviet Union in Operation Barbarossa. But it was not yet public knowledge, so I don't see Plutzik's observation as naive; it speaks instead to the fragile, tragic limits of our awareness in that moment of the reach of human evil, even as it

---

29 Plutzik, *Letter from a Young Poet*, 76.

acknowledges that the Jewish people will be victims, not perpetrators, when the legacy of the war is recognized.

But Plutzik also realizes Nazism and antisemitism meanwhile will spread: "Other people will be given the privilege of corrupting themselves; they will be given material bribes (ultimately more apparent than real) in order to make them accomplices to it all. And since the flesh is weak, many will yield, to their own final doom and that of their children."[30] Because he is a Jew, Plutzik understands how comprehensive is the evil the Nazis promote: "All that mankind has hoped for, they would negate."[31] The historical fact of the full realization of that comprehensive negation overshadows post-Holocaust life and the definitions we can offer of human identity. Awareness of our unlimited capacity for evil is part of what defines a specifically postmodern identity.

It is with the problem of evil, notably, that Plutzik chose to open his first book, devoting several beautifully crafted poems to the history of evil and its variations. As always with Plutzik, history speaks to and is layered into the present. We make contemporary choices in concert with those of the past whether we recognize it or not. But Plutzik knows the history of the twentieth century demonstrates repeatedly that we mostly deny such connections. The book's opening poem, "To The Predynastic Egyptian Who Rests within the Entrance of the Metropolitan Museum," points out that New York has given this ancient Egyptian a new tomb, "a mausoleum of granite / Which even the King would have longed for" (CP 3), then sardonically assures him

> ... The place of evil
> Where you met the jackals and were thrown into the pit
> Is not here, where civilized people pass and whisper
> On the long, clean streets.
> Your score is paid and the demons long since mollified.
> O do not think there is darkness in our days.
> Look upon us. We are not guilty, guilty.

Whether Plutzik really thought of a book of poems as a kind of mausoleum is difficult to say, but the poem about the entrance to the Met is placed at the entrance to his book, and the challenge it extends to the reader's illusions about modern civilization and inherited responsibility can hardly be mistaken.

---

30   Plutzik, *Letter from a Young Poet*, 76–7.
31   Plutzik, *Letter from a Young Poet*, 75–6.

Thus "Entropy" from the same book can be taken as a poem about the laws of physics, but its opening line—"I have seen the wound that matter makes in space"—more profoundly introduces a judgment about the doomed character of human life. The book's third poem, "An Equation," can be misrepresented as primarily reflecting Plutzik's interest in science, but the equation here is one between mythic time and the present, as a universal, eternal, and invincible will to evil coils itself around us:

> Coil upon coil, the grave serpent holds
> Its implacable strict pose, under a light
> Like marble. The artist's damnation, the rat of time,
> Cannot gnaw this form, nor event touch it with age.
> Before it was, it existed, creating the mind
> Which created it, out of itself. It will dissolve
> Into itself, though in another language.
> Its changes are not in change, nor its times in time. (CP 5)

Beyond birth and death, its mutations are without change; it does not age in time or even mark time's passage. Plutzik has imaged the serpent as a foil to and counter-power at once to human invention and the divine absolute. "It will not acknowledge the incense on your altars," the poem concludes, "Nor hear at night in your room the weeping."

A few poems further on we encounter "The Begetting of Cain" (CP 11), where Adam, besotted with Eve, does not see nearby the "Creature of pointed ear, / Of the cleft hoof and the tight-mouthed sneer":

> All were engulfed—these two, the birds of the air,
> The burrowers of the earth, by the quenchless mind
> Roaming insatiate on the lowland, blind
> In its lonely hunger, lusting to make all things
> One with itself. Brief as the flutter of wings
> Was his mastery, though ranging through world and void
> To the dusk-star shining. But all, all were destroyed:
> The two on the odorous earth in the garden there;
> The beasts, the birds in the nest, the fireflies in the air.

Once again, the allusion to modern history's recurring embodiment of absolute evil is clear. The poem's portrait of a remorseless, satanic will to dominate all creation—with its deeply unsettling lust "to make all things / One with itself"—seems unwarranted by events in the Garden of Eden alone. It requires the subsequent history we have inherited. Plutzik's metrical control, the punctuation of the message with rhymed couplets, all this underlines and strengthens the message, binds it formally and gives it no exit. There is no reason to write this poem and publish it in 1949 save the conviction that this is the world we have inherited and in which we live.

Given the widespread and continuing debates about the human capacity for evil prompted in part by Hannah Arendt's work, it is worth noting that Plutzik's poetic depictions are in harmony with Arendt's arguments in *The Origins of Totalitarianism* (1951), rather than with her "banality of evil" thesis in *Eichmann in Jerusalem* (1963). As Thomas White points out, in the earlier book "she argued that the evil of the Nazis was absolute and inhuman, not shallow and incomprehensible, the metaphorical embodiment of hell itself."[32] Plutzik insisted that the human capacity for evil is an ancient and infinite force of will that reached its exceptional zenith in the Third Reich.

"The Begetting of Cain" is in every sense a postwar poem burdened with the twin legacies of the Holocaust and Hiroshima, legacies that for Plutzik embody an eternal evil. This historical recognition cannot, however, be decisively settled by trying to determine the poet's intent. There are, to be sure, poets who have been explicitly focused on the Holocaust throughout their careers—from Paul Celan in France to Lily Brett and William Heyen in the US to Dan Pagis and Abraham Sutzkever in Israel—for whom one can set aside the question of whether or not a given poem addresses the Holocaust. Instead, one asks in what ways a particular poem inevitably does so and looks to intertextual echoes and connections to place the poem in the career-wide network of Holocaust commentary, consequence, and implication. There are other poets, conversely—from Randall Jarrell in "Protocols" and "A Camp in the Prussian Forest" to Sylvia Plath in "Daddy" and "Lady Lazarus" to Anthony Hecht in "The Book of Yolek" and "'More Light! More Light!'" to Jorie Graham in "History" and "From the New World"—who have each written several very powerful Holocaust poems that can be considered separately from their other work.

---

32 Thomas White, "What Did Hannah Arendt Really Mean by the Banality of Evil?" *AEON*, April 23, 2018, https://aeon.co/ideas/what-did-hannah-arendt-really-mean-by-the-banality-of-evil. Subsequent research, one may add, including Bettina Stangneth's *Eichmann Before Jerusalem*, shows that Arendt failed to recognize that Eichmann was not only an ideologically committed Nazi but also a major contributor to the horrors of the Holocaust. Claude Lanzmann's 2013 film *The Last of the Unjust* also makes a convincing case that Eichmann was an endlessly inventive master of torture and murder.

But that does not exhaust the impact that the Holocaust has had on post-war literature, culture, and human consciousness. It does not exhaust the ways the Holocaust and Hiroshima have redefined our individual and collective understanding of human potential and the human capacity for evil. It does not exhaust the way the century's defining genocidal project has changed our view of nation state responsibilities. Whether every contemporary poem merits an explicitly post-Holocaust reading is an appropriate subject for debate. David Miller suggests the Holocaust casts an omnipresent shadow over both poetic literariness and commentary: "the whole of post-medieval European literary culture, of which poetry was always the central emblem, has been irrevocably exposed as part of a 'tortured' existence."[33] In any case, poems taking on such major topics as these certainly do merit readings contextualized within the legacy of the Holocaust. While I believe it is useful and important to reflect on a writer's possible intent, as Derrida demonstrates, that does not exhaust the work language can do. Contemporary poems that address fundamental questions about human existence are now implicitly post-Holocaust poems. That can include poems about such apparently unrelated subjects as the potential for global warming to extinguish life on the planet.

Edward Brunner has an eloquent analysis of Plutzik's 1951 poem "And in the 51st Year of That Century, While My Brother Cried in the Trench, While My Enemy Glared from the Cave" (CP 114) which reflects the fear that the Korean War will escalate to the use of atomic weapons, but it is only the title, almost incongruously, that allows us to make that connection. As Brunner suggests, the poem's six lines conclude after obliquely invoking a threat to mother and child, "then longing to counteract it with a sheltering gesture":

> This star is only an augury of the morning,
> Gift bearer of another day.
>
> A wind has brought the musk of thirty fields,
> Each like a coin of silver under that sky.
>
> Precious, the soundless breathing of wife and children
> In a house on a field lit by the morning star.

---

[33] David Miller, "After Epic: Adorno's Scream and the Shadows of Lyric." In *The Bloomsbury Companion to Holocaust Literature*, ed. Jenni Adams (London: Bloomsbury Academic, 2014), 69.

This star, we may read with emphasis, is not the first light of a bomb bursting above, although one may worry that everything is at risk of being bought and sold with "a coin of silver," the thirty fields, as Brunner points out, alluding to the pieces of silver paid to Judas. The wish to protect the sleeping wife and children, Brunner concludes, "exists as little more than a helpless murmur, insufficient to counteract the nameless and unmentionable threat that stands at the horizon."[34]

Explicit Holocaust or Hiroshima poems, as we see, do not exhaust the burden that the twentieth century's pivotal and defining events place on post-Holocaust readers. The ethical burden of post-Holocaust reading necessitates receiving whatever we read in the historical context in which we live, and we live in the wake of those terrible events that changed everything. Analyzing a poem involves contextualizing its historical interrelationships whether or not the poet was consciously aware of them. No postwar interrogation of the destructive capacity of nation states can be mounted outside the shadow of the massive death toll in World War II and the apotheosis of those deaths in the death camps and in the ruins of two Japanese cities. But it is the Shoah that places the most deeply troubling and corrosive burden on subsequent generations. That is where questions about individual agency, identity, and complicity were forever transformed. And it is the place where genocidal malice combines collective planning and execution with infinite personal variations on how to belittle, dehumanize, and kill. It eviscerates every previous utopian dream and leaves us wary of every possible human future, for it forever changes our conceptions of what people are and what evil of which they are capable, undermining every humanist model of human nature and the fundamental character of human civilization.

Both writing and reading Holocaust poetry fall within the work of mourning, but it is mourning without end. All that Holocaust poems can offer contemporary readers is a kind of world-weary melancholy in the face of a thoroughly compromised civilization. For post-Holocaust generations the direct experience of survivor guilt has gradually been replaced by the more universal burden of a life lived without rationale for or confidence in sustaining values.

Plutzik accepts that burden in such poems as "As the Great Horse Rots on the Hill" (CP 91). Here is the fifth stanza:

> I observe the ordained explosions on the paper as I write,
> The pinpoints of flame in the wood on the table, and on the wall
> (Like a battlefield at night, or a field where fireflies flicker).

---

34 Brunner, *Cold War Poetry*, 229.

My hand, too, scintillates like a strange fish;
Fires punctuate the faces on the road;
A pox, a fever, burns in the tissues of the hills.
Thus you prepare the future for me and my loved ones.

That final line is repeated five times in the poem; it is the concluding line in all but one stanza, the only exception being the third stanza of one line only. It is not a poem anchored in a single event, but rather one that resonates with our inheritance of total war and suggests its "threads run / from time's instants to all the atoms of the universe." The poem's titular great horse rots on a hilltop, and as the poem directs us to look up we can see "the stars wink through his ribs." Perhaps what we see through his ribs is itself the Great Horse Constellation in the northern sky, the winged horse Pegasus of Greek mythology. The winged horse later became a popular emblem of inspiration, but neither that nor the stars in the night sky offer any consolation. Given that Plutzik was stationed in Britain, he may well have been aware that a silhouette of Pegasus ridden by Bellerophon, the Greek hero who captured him, was adopted by the United Kingdom's newly raised parachute troops in 1941 as their upper-sleeve insignia. Seen from the vantage point of World War II's darker legacy, we cannot expect that myth or any other set of beliefs will save us from history. Pegasus "rots on the hill."

As David Scott Kastan writes, "characteristically for Plutzik, eternity offers no comfort."[35] Throughout his poetry, Plutzik invokes nature or the wide character of the universe and then discounts the possibility it can offer either consolation or a perspective that changes the meaning of human history: "a swell of shadows / Destroys all sanctions of formal separateness." "What inner or outer flames may shine are random," he writes in "I Imagined a Painter Painting Such a World," "In the one, shadowed sea where all things melt" (CP 104). In "Elegy" (CP 51), written at some point from 1943–45 during his wartime service, the poem's subject walks "a plain vast and shadowy" until "the pale flame of the spirit sank / And flickered out in the last wilderness." Those who have "run their course" come to where "the minions of God regard them coolly and see / As in a fog the starved fires sinking." In the poem's last line, everything succumbs to "the poised darkness, the blows of the answerless Ocean." What alone distinguishes his subject is his dignity, his forbearance and restraint as he refuses to "swagger and shout." But that only means spurning "the poised darkness, the blows of the answerless Ocean." There is no route to any broader redemption.

---

35 Kasten, "Afterword," 70.

In "The Premonition" the speaker sets out "trying to imagine a poem of the future" and declares "'I am the poet of the damned'" (CP 95). In an uncollected poem from 1960, "The Marriage," he writes of "the silent nations, / the ghosts of the unborn," perhaps imagining those who would never be born because their parents were among the wartime dead. They lie "Under the canopy of galactic eyes," then rise to enter "a dark ship": "They saw the snow falling on the plains and the mountains / And the ice clasping all in its arms" (CP 232). "The Mythos of Samuel Huntsman," while witty and even sardonic about how we deceive ourselves about the solidity of our individual worlds—the poem's speaker opens by proposing that if he turns "the corner quickly" he'd "catch them preparing the scene, / Painting a tree or hanging the moon"—it is the revelation of the illusion that dominates:

> The surface is thin as a gilding of oil
> Upon an enormous lake
> Deep as infinity, vivid as a gas,
> On which they plant the lying rose
> To delude the sniffing child or the fool. (CP 99)

Even the heroism potentially available in a necessary war lends our fatal enterprises no grandeur. "The Old War" (CP 94) commemorates a bomber crashing to the ground, perhaps to the English countryside, but the return to the mothering earth is at best ironic. Even when nature is beautiful it embodies a stark human perspective. "Winter, Never Mind Where" (CP 107) opens with painterly portrait:

> The illusion is one of flatness: the sky
> Has no depth, is a sheet of tin
> Upon which the blackened branches and twigs
> Are corroded, burnt in
> By a strong acid

And again, here in "Two Voices and a Woodwind" (CP 119), the recourse to the universe brings no warmth:

> There are no bears, swans or heroes among the constellations—
> Only, throughout all space, branches budded with fire,
> From which, in an ether where never a wind shivers,
> Sift and sink the burning flower-flakes of time

What somewhat moderates this vision is the rhetorical skill with which it is given witness in the poetry. As Plutzik points out in the final lines of "Requiem for Edward Carrigh," the lines carved on his headstone are "Nothing can be done but something can be said at least" (CP 113). Carrigh is a pseudonym for John Wagenblass, a University of Rochester English Department colleague who had served in the US Navy in the South Pacific and participated in several major battles. He died of polio in 1949 at age thirty-seven:

> You suddenly left your house, your city, and your country,
> Traveling in the night, few knowing,
> To fight with a dark archangel in a desert.

He was lost to "the dull stones and the sterile earth / After the bitter climbing of forty-four years," but there is a more pitiless form of witness covering all: "The tireless eyes stare out of the sky, answering nothing, / And the silence is august and terrible."

There is also a kind of affectionate cynicism in Plutzik, most apparent in the four conversation portraits that open *Horatio*. While the portraits they paint are of men ill-informed or sinister, without nobility, the tone permits some tolerance toward their frailty. It is a more mature perspective than that embodied in the youthful "Seventh Avenue Express." There is as well a wry self-regarding humor in the two narrative poems that frame his career, "Death at the Purple Rim" and *Horatio*. Anthony Hecht in his introduction to the *Collected Poems* finds the first of these to be mock-heroic, but I am not sure I agree. Certainly, Plutzik is on one level lampooning himself as a young man who over dramatizes his decision to shoot a woodchuck that seems poised to raid a newly planted garden on a Connecticut farm. But the poem is composed on the eve of World War II, which lends a more serious meaning to lines like "As this beast dies here / So men have died and so will they die tomorrow." And observations like this— "where death and his foe had played at their cold, old game / With the loaded dice and the sneering eternal winner" (CP 82)—just do not admit unqualified assignment to mock-heroic comedy.

The poem that may most inscrutably embody the black humor component of Plutzik's work, however, may be "The Milkman" (CP 121), with its metronome rhymes, sing-song rhythms, and forbidding mixture of the prosaic and the threatening. It consists of six stanzas, but the key stanzas are the third, fourth and fifth:

> One night they will knock on the milkman's door,
> Their boots crunch hard on the front-porch floor,
> One-two, open the door.

> You are the thief of the secret flame,
> The forbidden bread, the terrible Name.
> Return what is let; go back where you came.
>
> One, two, the slam of a door.
> A woman crying: Who is there?
> And voices mumbling beyond the stair.

The first two stanzas allow us to imagine that the milkman, in familiar horror movie mode, is himself secretly a harbinger of evil. After all, he crunches through snow while "bad angels mutter" in apparent warning. We may ask ourselves whether he carries the "*Schwarze Milch*," the black milk of Paul Celan's "Todesfuge," to our doorstep. But the military-style and Nazi-like nighttime raid that follows, with its theological accusations—echoing the theft of the secret name of God and the violation of the eucharist—arguably reverse our expectations and lend the narrative an antisemitic edge. Daily life at its most ordinary is suddenly being upended; that is the horror, amplified by its absurd incongruity. As so often in history, those who demonize the Jews turn themselves into demons in the process.

Although there has been some fine work done on Plutzik—Edward Brunner has written compellingly about him in *Cold War Poetry* and the very valuable Hyman Plutzik Poetry web site includes several conference papers about his work, including Sundquist's expanded essay—Plutzik is not really very visibly part of the disciplinary conversation about modern poetry. Part of what I have tried to show here is that his formal skill, his rhetorical inventiveness, and the intellectual coherence of his work all suggest we should be reading and writing about him more widely. The thematic coherence of his work begins with "My Sister," the earliest poem he included in *Aspects of Proteus*. Plutzik's sister Molly died when he was nine. The poem contemplates what has happened in the seventeen years since, and it is stunningly macabre, focusing in part on "the slow rot of the bones in the Northern damp / Even the bones of that tiny foot that brought her doom" (CP 27). "Imagine the little skeleton lying there," he tells us

> Amid the monsters with lipless teeth who lie there in wait—
> The saurian multitudes who rest in that land—
> And the men without eyes who forever glare at the sky.

He is thinking both of a country beyond death and of a child's nightmares about what lurks in the dark. But he reminds us at the end that what lurks in the dark also walks the earth:

> The Man of War sits in the gleaming chair.
> Struts through the halls. The Dispenser of Vengeance laughs
> Crying victory! Victory! Victory!
>
> Victory.

The corrupting potential of the desire for vengeance continued to haunt decades of reflections on modern history. In laying out his plans for a Holocaust poem, he writes "I picture the poem not as a cry for vengeance but as an exploration of the areas of evil in the human heart." His goal is to craft an act of witness. As he writes,

> The massacre of the six million Jews must be remembered, not that a particular nation may be saddled with the crime but so that men, all men, may always be aware of, and on guard against, their extraordinary capacities for evil. For the vastness of the crime makes it almost incredible, and that which is incredible is forgotten or ignored, once the generation of those who grieved personally is past. The job is to make the event credible, to show that it really happened. And for this, one needs not history, but a poem.

Part of the challenge, as he saw it, was to combine the monstrous particularity of the crime against the Jews with a broad witness to the Holocaust as the defining event of the century's many crimes. Of the five sections he describes, the third will catalogue by name "with some narrative and expository material, names of the victims of the various terrorisms and tyrannies of our time: Communist, Fascist, and other; victims of the tyrants who had no ideologies but were for themselves only; victims of injustice in states not ordinarily tyrannical; victims of the bestialities of war; victims of the isolated malicious impulse that none the less reflects the maniacal stain of our time."

In his 1958 letter to Donald Hall, Plutzik worries unrealistically that *Apples from Shinar* might be too politicized a title. The plan for his long Holocaust poem demonstrates he realized he would have to cross that line and was prepared to do so. No more was he to embody a Jewish identity indirectly. The fifth and final section of the poem indeed was to fuse the personal, the historical, and the political—in its widest and most telling sense—in a searing act of testimony:

A section on the little town in Russia from which my parents came to this country, and in which my ancestors lived for perhaps a thousand years. Its name is Lapich (which, I gather, means something like "Old Shoe" or "Peasants' Clog"). It is in what was once the old Czarist province of Minsk. It is near Bobroisk (famous as a strongpoint in World War II). Nearby, at the river Beresina, the armies of Napoleon foundered in their flight. In my childhood I heard many stories about the town from my father and mother, so it is quite vivid to me: a place inhabited by peddlers and scholars. And before his death, my father sent me at my request a long description of the town, as well as translations of letters from our few surviving relatives, recounting the fate of the family and their own harrowing experiences. From other sources he heard the following story (which I must check up on somehow): When the Nazis arrived, those Jewish inhabitants who had not managed to flee were herded to a spot on the outskirts, forced to dig a big pit, shot, and buried there. And all that remains of the community is a big mound of earth.

With this fifth section of his Holocaust poem, the testimony becomes personal. Plutzik apparently lost relatives in the town, which makes him a member of that Holocaust generation. Thinking about the five very different sections—from the six million dead to Anne Frank to the multitude of other period victims to his personal family history—it seems fair to conclude that this poem would not be rhetorically and stylistically uniform throughout. Bringing my argument full circle, the poem would more likely be one of the mixed forms that David Miller and Antony Rowland describe. It could include lyrics and narrative. It would likely include positivistic and metaphoric passages. Both direction and indirection would be entirely possible. We will never know.

This was perhaps to be the transformative poem of Plutzik's career. And yet of course he did not live to write it. But think about and plan it he did. In a way his whole career was leading up to this moment. We have warrant to rethink his body of work in the light of this plan for a Holocaust poem, a plan we are lucky enough to have. Yet we may also be haunted by the special significance of a substantial but unrealized Holocaust poem. We can easily enough at least partially imagine the ghosts of those six million victims appearing on a city street. That was to be the opening section of the poem. But that is a visual image; the words that would in their way flesh out those ghostly figures and give them voices will never be heard. And so, like so many of their fellow murdered Jews, they remain voiceless, unrepresented. An unwritten Holocaust poem is unlike an unwritten poem on any other topic; it is uniquely burdened by the traumatic conditions and possibilities for collective Holocaust memory and representation. It creates at once a defining absence and an additional layer of meaning in this poet's legacy.

Even without this ambitious plan, however, Plutzik is in a deep sense a post-Holocaust poet. One of the compelling consequences is Plutzik's ability to embed a post-Holocaust message in every natural image he crafts. If Gerard Manley Hopkins found God's imprint in everything, Plutzik find's death's defining absence equally omnipresent. Indeed, that simultaneously enabling and disabling condition extends beyond his subject matter and his perspective on the human condition to encompass his view of what possibilities are left to poetry itself after Auschwitz. As many of the quotations from Plutzik's work offered above suggest, one cannot find confidence here in poetry's capacity for transcendence. It is no longer guaranteed a privileged place in culture. As David Miller concludes, "We can conceive of poetry after Auschwitz, then, as a purgatorial zone of literary meaning, neither the outright inferno of absolute poetic meaninglessness nor the paradise of lyric felicity" (77). "Like the shadows or outlines of people on the walls of Hiroshima in the aftermath of the dropping of the A-bomb," he adds, "it may well be that what remains for poetic language after the deeper hell of the death camps are only the shades of lyric. There are no lyrics after Auschwitz, only the shadows of lyrics" (78). Coming to terms with his Jewish identity for Plutzik meant carving a literary mission out of that narrowed territory; it amounts to a poetry of witness, not a guide to help us triumph over the history we have inherited. It would be difficult to read the prophecy from "The House of Gorya" that opens this essay in a more affirmative and empowering way, difficult as well to believe we have escaped what he describes there as "the time of unworthiness."

Bibliography

Aarons, Victoria. "A Genre of Rupture: The Literary Language of the Holocaust." In *The Bloomsbury Companion to Holocaust Literature*, edited by Jenni Adams, 27–45. London: Bloomsbury Academic, 2014.

Adorno, Theodor W. *Negative Dialectics*. Translated by E. B. Ashton. New York: Seabury, 1973.

———. *Prisms*. Translated by S. Weber and S. Weber Nicholson. Cambridge, MA: MIT Press, 1981.

Améry, Jean. *At the Mind's Limits: Contemplations by a Survivor on Auschwitz and Its Realities.* Translated by Sidney Rosenfeld and Stella P. Rosenfeld. Bloomington: Indiana University Press, 1980.

Brunner, Edward. *Cold War Poetry.* Urbana: University of Illinois Press, 2001.

———. "Hyam Plutzik's *Horatio* as a Postwar Text: Dream-Work, Verse Drama, Underground Myth." Hyamplutzikpoetry.com. Accessed August 7, 2024. https://www.hyamplutzikpoetry.com/commentary-brunner.

Gubar, Susan. *Poetry After Auschwitz: Remembering What One Never Knew.* Bloomington: Indiana University Press, 2003.

Choy Christine, and Ku-Ling Siegel, dirs. *Hyam Plutzik: American Poet.* 2006, 55:00. Accessed August 7, 2024. http://www.hyamplutzikpoetry.com/videos/.

Johnson, Kimberly. "Beyond the Thule of Possibility: The Task of Hyam Plutzik's *Horatio*." Hyman Plutzik Poetry. Accessed August 7, 2024. https://static1.squarespace.com/static/5682cb822399a3aa8df162ec/t/5682f45369a91ad70f63a39a/1451422803063/johnson-thule-of-possibility.pdf.

Lurie, Margot. "Golden Apples: *Apples from Shinar* by Hyam Plutzik." *Jewish Review of Books* 4, no. 1 (Spring 2013): 30–31.

Miller, David. "After Epic: Adorno's Scream and the Shadows of Lyric." In *The Bloomsbury Companion to Holocaust Literature*, edited by Jenni Adams, 65–80. London: Bloomsbury Academic, 2014.

Moran, Edward. "The Life and Poetry of Hyam Plutzik." Hyamplutzikpoetry.com. Accessed August 7, 2024. http://www.hyamplutzikpoetry.com/life-and-poetry.

———. "T. S. Eliot and Hyam Plutzik: 'Hypocrite Lecteur, mon Semblable, mon Frere.'" Paper presented at T. S. Eliot Conference, Washington University, St. Louis, MI, September 2009.

Moran, Edward, and Steven Sher. "Hyam Plutzik's *Horatio* as Post-Holocaust Poem." Hyman Plutzik Poetry. Accessed August 7, 2024. https://static1.squarespace.com/static/5682cb822 399a3aa8df162ec/t/5b9866134d7a9cbbeaaf55bf/1536714260234/sher-and-moran-horatio-post-holocaust.pdf.

Nelson, Cary. *Revolutionary Memory: Recovering the Poetry of the American Left.* New York: Routledge, 2001.

Osherow, Jacqueline. "Value the Intermediate Splendor." Hyman Plutzik Poetry. Accessed August 7, 2024. https://static1.squarespace.com/static/5682cb822399a3aa8df162ec/t/5682f5bedf4 0f38ac4378b60/1451423166682/osherow-intermediate-splendor.pdf.

Plutzik, Hyam. *The Collected Poems.* Foreword by Anthony Hecht. Brockport, NY: BOA Editions, 1987.

———. *Apples from Shinar.* Afterword by David Scott Kastan. Special ed. Middletown, CT: Wesleyan University Press, 2011.

———. *Letter from a Young Poet.* Hartford, CT: Watkinson Library at Trinity College, 2016.

"Polio Strikes Down Faculty Member, Two Undergraduates in Single Month." *Rochester Alumni-Alumnae Review*, October–November, 1949, 10. https://www.lib.rochester.edu/IN/RBSCP/Databases/Attachments/Reviews/1949/11-1/1949_October.pdf.

Rolfe, Edwin. *Collected Poems.* Edited by Cary Nelson and Jefferson Hendricks. Urbana: University of Illinois Press, 1993.

Rowland, Antony. "Poetry as testimony: Primo Levi's *Collected Poems*." *Textual Practice* 22, no. 3 (2008): 487–505.

Shapiro, Sidney. "Hyam Plutzik, American Poet: The Making of a Remarkable Course." Hyman Plutzik Poetry. Accessed August 7, 2024. https://static1.squarespace.com/static/5682cb822399a3aa8df162ec/t/5682f7b49cadb697dd8ac74a/1451423668358/shapiro-osher-2.pdf.

Sundquist, Eric J. "Blessed Mythmaker: The Poetry of Hyam Plutzik." Hyamplutzikpoetry.com. Accessed August 7, 2024. https://drive.google.com/file/d/18y4aXA50KLXStIN8wD3vcpbFi1qtEEbF/view?pli=1

Stangneth, Bettina. *Eichmann Before Jerusalem: The Unexamined Life of a Mass Murderer*. Translated by Ruth Martin. New York: Vintage, 2014.

White, Thomas. "What Did Hannah Arendt Really Mean by the Banality of Evil?" *AEON* (April 23, 2018). https://aeon.co/ideas/what-did-hannah-arendt-really-mean-by-the-banality-of-evil.

Witte, Phillip A. "Fiction or Imaginative Truth: Poetic and Dramatic Modes in Hyam Plutzik's *Horatio*." Hyman Plutzik Poetry. Accessed August 7, 2024. https://static1.squarespace.com/static/5682cb822399a3aa8df162ec/t/5cad4767e5e5f0b52f40502a/1554859879462/witte-fiction-or-imaginative-truth.pdf

Žižek, Slavoj. *Violence*. London: Profile Books, 2008.

CHAPTER 3

Hyam Plutzik and Gabriel Preil: Trajectories of Jewish American Poetry

Naomi Sokoloff

Two Jewish American Poets

Hyam Plutzik was born in 1911 in New York. The language of daily life in his family was Yiddish, and he was exposed at home also to Hebrew and Russian. He first spoke English at age seven in elementary school. Over time he acquired a masterful command of the English language and made a distinguished career in poetry. Among other honors, he was named a finalist for the Pulitzer Prize in 1961.[1]

Gabriel Preil, too, was born in 1911, though in Estonia. He arrived in the US in 1922, settling in New York. His was a Yiddish-speaking family that valued both traditional Jewish learning and Modern Hebrew literature, and Preil himself went on to a career as a celebrated poet composing first in Yiddish and then, most famously, in Hebrew. Among the honors he received was Israel's 1992 Bialik Prize for literature.[2]

Looking at poems by Plutzik and Preil side by side can provide occasion to think about Jewish American writing as a multilingual phenomenon and as

---

Copyright © 2025 by Naomi Sokoloff

1 For biographical background on Plutzik and an overview of his development as a poet, see Anthony Hecht's foreword to *Hyam Plutzik: The Collected Poems* (Brockport, NY: Boa Editions, Ltd., 1987), xi–xix. Other information is available from the American Academy of Poets, accessed August 8, 2024, https://poets.org/poet/hyam-plutzik.

2 For biographical background on Preil and a detailed account of his development as a poet who published in both Yiddish and Hebrew, see Yael Feldman's influential study *Modernism and Cultural Transfer: Gabriel Preil and the Tradition of Jewish Literary Bilingualism* (Cincinnati, OH: Hebrew Union College Press, 1986).

a site for cross-cultural expression. Both poets made their mark as American modernists, and both infused reference to Jewish topics into their poetry. However, coming from different sets of conventions and linguistic points of departure, the two men took different paths in their development as poets. Notably, their writing careers follow different trajectories in relation to the Jewish components of their work.

Consider, first, Hyam Plutzik. He moved from the Yiddish of his childhood into English, but proudly claimed Jewish identity in an era when it was not fashionable for poets to do so. According to Howard Schwartz and Anthony Rudolf in their survey of modern Jewish poetry, from the beginning of the twentieth century until at least 1960

> the primary ambition of most American Jewish poets was to make a contribution to the rich English language literary tradition. With a few exceptions of poets such as Charles Reznikoff, Karl Shapiro and Alter Brody, most poets of the older and middle generations saw Jewish life and tradition at the periphery of their lives, and in some cases there was even a shrinking away from it.[3]

In contrast, significant examples of Plutzik's poetry in the 1940s and '50s made overt mention of Jews and allusions to Jewish tradition.[4] Eric Sundquist has documented and elucidated some of those references. They include an early poem "On the Photograph of a Man I Never Saw," in which Plutzik muses respectfully on a Russian grandfather whose eyes were "sterner than Moses,'"[5] and another piece "The Miracle," which alludes to the biblical story of Joshua. The poem "Portrait," from a 1959 collection[6] comments on deracinated, Diaspora Jewry trying to assimilate and unsuccessfully attempting to conceal Jewishness. An unpublished piece called "House of Gorya" refers to Rabbi Hillel and other Talmudic figures, and in "An Agadah of Hyam ben Samuel," the poet inserts himself directly into Jewish literary lore by displaying his own Hebrew name along

---

3 Howard Schwartz and Anthony Rudolf, eds., *Voices within the Ark: The Modern Jewish Poets* (New York: Avon Books, 1980), 378. Schwartz and Rudolf include three poems by Plutzik in their landmark anthology: "The King of Ai," "The Begetting of Cain," and "On the Photograph of a Man I Never Saw." See pages 588–590.
4 Eric Sundquist, "Blessed Mythmaker: The Poetry of Hyam Plutzik," Hyam Plutzik, Poet, accessed August 21, 2024, https://drive.google.com/file/d/18y4aXA50KLXStIN8wD3vcpbFi1qtEEbF/view.
5 From Plutzik's *Aspects of Proteus* (New York: Harper and Brothers, 1949).
6 From Plutzik's collection *Apples from Shinar* (Middletown, OH: Wesleyan University Press, 1959).

with the Hebrew term for "legend" (agadah). In addition, Plutzik demonstrated knowledge of Hebrew and Aramaic by translating several texts from Jewish liturgy into English.[7] Moreover, in a speech he drafted celebrating the art of Sholem Aleichem, Plutzik wrote fondly about the linguistic richness of Yiddish—especially the versatility of Yiddish insults.[8] Toward the end of his life his concern with Jewish materials seems to have been increasing; he was planning a long poem about the Holocaust, featuring six million ghosts on Main Street.[9]

In her assessment of Plutzik's achievements, Margot Lurie notes that the poet's affinity for Jewish content may have helped doom his verse to neglect.[10] In Plutzik's era, Jewishness was not popular. And yet, from today's vantage point, readers may conclude that he was ahead of his time. It makes sense to count him as a forerunner to later trends in Jewish American poetry. Plutzik's death in 1962 cut short his career and it is not possible to know where the future might have led him, but it is clear it preceded a surge of creativity by others in decades to come. Many poets eventually turned to Jewish topics while writing in English. From the 1970s on, to mention just a few, think of Jerome Rothenberg, Cynthia Ozick, and Myra Sklarew; from the 1980s: Marge Piercy, Adrienne Rich, and Irena Klepfisz. Since the 1990s many poets have been unapologetically incorporating their knowledge of Judaism and Jewish sources into their poetry. Names that come to mind include Allen Grossman, Marcia Falk, Chana Bloch, Linda Zisquit, Peter Cole, Yehoshua November, and Richard Chess.[11]

Gabriel Preil followed a path different from Plutzik's. He worked in distinctively Jewish languages and he was deeply grounded in Jewish culture.[12] Yet, in his writing Preil moved away from incorporating allusion to Jewish texts.

---

7   These include "L'cho Dodi" and "Kaddish," in *The Collected Poems*, 266 and 270.
8   From the Hyam Plutzik archives at the University of Rochester. My thanks to Edward Moran and Melissa Mead for providing me access to these materials.
9   Cary Nelson, "The Universe Is No Consolation: Hyam Plutzik, Jewish Identity, and the Ethics of Post-Holocaust Reading," *Journal of Jewish Identities* 15 (2022):5–31.
10 Margot Lurie, "Golden Apples," *Jewish Review of Books* (Spring 2013), https://jewish-reviewofbooks.com/articles/115/golden-apples/.
11 Many other prominent poets—such as Muriel Rukeyser, Philip Levine, and Allen Ginsburg—bring Jewish identity into their work in less direct or more ambivalent ways. For an informative overview of Jewish American poets and how they relate to Judaism and religion, see Maeera Y. Shreiber, "Secularity, Sacredness, and Jewish American Poets: 1950–2000" in *The Cambridge History of Jewish American Literature*, ed. Hana Wirth-Nesher (New York: Cambridge University Press, 2016), 182–201.
12 Allison Schachter, *Diasporic Modernisms: Hebrew and Yiddish Literature in the Twentieth Century* (New York: Oxford University Press, 2012), 152–184. Important commentary on the poet can be found in Dan Miron, "*Bein haner lakokhavim*" [Between the candle and the stars], in *Collector of Autumns: Collected Poems 1972–1992*, ed. D. Miron (Jerusalem: Bialik, 1993).

He is known for shedding the kind of references to classic Jewish sources that had been so prominent in the work of previous American Hebraists. Literary forebears such as Benjamin Nahum Silkiner, Israel Efros, Ephraim E. Lisitzky, Hillel Bavli, Eisig Siberschlag, Simon Halkin, and Abraham Regelson, who had shaped Hebrew writing in early twentieth-century America, favored highly elevated language laden with allusions, pathos, and rhetorical flourishes. Preil pulled away from that style. He embraced lower diction, understatement, and irony. Indeed, his poetry was known for its closeness to conversational Hebrew—which is remarkable, given that his first visit to Israel was not till 1968, long after he had published a number of books of poems. Precisely because Preil's work distanced itself from the allusive burdens and figurative language of Hebrew romanticism, he was welcomed by Israeli poets who sought similar qualities in their own art.

Part of the reason Preil was able to introduce innovation into Hebrew verse was that he had knowledge of modernist trends in English and Yiddish poetry. His own work responded to and was indebted to the imagism of Amy Lowell, HD, and Ezra Pound, along with the work of Inzikh poets such as Yankev Glatstein. Preil was also familiar with the writing of many other poets from the Anglo-American canon, including Walt Whitman, Robert Frost, and Wallace Stevens. Literary historian Alan Mintz observes that, although other American Hebraists took an interest in British and American literature, "only in Preil's case does the poetry itself maintain an active dialogue with developments in modern English verse."[13] At the same time, Preil received little attention on the mainstream American literary scene. He was acknowledged among Hebraists and Yiddishists as a major poet, but the readership for those languages in America was always small and dwindled considerably during Preil's lifetime. He remained, and still remains, insufficiently recognized as an *American* poet, contributing to American poetry.

From this brief outline of Plutzik's and Preil's accomplishments, a number of parallels suggest themselves. Of the same generation, of Eastern European background, and from overlapping geographies, the two poets shared a double heritage rooted in Anglo-American poetic tradition and Jewish textual tradition. Both men were recognized and honored during their lifetimes, but both remained outliers in the historiography of American literature. Some intriguing details round out this picture: both Preil and Plutzik wrote introspective poetry,

---

13   Alan L. Mintz, *Sanctuary in the Wilderness: A Critical Introduction to American Hebrew Poetry* (Stanford, CA: Stanford University Press, 2011), 324. Chapter 14 (pages 323–354) focuses on Preil's poetry.

both were enchanted with New England, and both wrote landscape poems. Both felt an affinity for Whitman (Plutzik wrote MA work on Whitman; Preil translated Whitman into Hebrew), and both publicly condemned T. S. Eliot for his antisemitism.[14] Yet the two apparently never met, they moved in different circles, and scholarship has not directed attention to comparison of their work. Considering the two in tandem has value because it can demonstrate how two Jewish American writers negotiated dual cultural attachments, one moving from more to less focus on Jewish material and the other moving from less to more. Reading these poets together points to the mobility and changeability of Jewish culture within American settings of the twentieth century, illustrating cultural identities that are dynamic, not static. In the process, comparison can encourage models of Jewish American literature that take into account multiple languages and that also acknowledge poets' shifts in their Jewish identity or relationship to Jewish literary materials over time.

One place of striking intersection in writing by Preil and Plutzik is in two poems that focus on the past and on family heritage: Preil's "Chapters of Time, His and Mine" and Plutzik's "After Looking into a Book Belonging to My Great-Grandfather, Eli Eliakim Plutzik." As these titles indicate, both poems deal with intergenerational bonds. Paramount in each is a longing for connection with Eastern European Jewish life. A comparison of these texts is especially compelling because each poem, in its own way, laments a vanished world and at the same time asserts the poet's ties to a literary past. Those connections sustain him and his own writing. Consequently, a concomitant loss and renewal of Jewishness propels each poet to new creativity. Furthermore, when comparing these elegiac poems, it is important to keep in mind each poet's awareness of the Holocaust. Neither text directly incorporates reference to catastrophe, but scholars have noted that immense collective loss stands in the background of each poet's output. Cary Nelson finds in Plutzik's oeuvre a pervasive sense of the Holocaust as the defining event of the twentieth century; Natasha Gordinsky identifies a similar awareness as an overarching element of Preil's work.[15] She considers nostalgia a key to his poetry and posits that it is especially keen because the past for

---

14   The two men did not meet, but their paths crossed in tangential ways in shared milieus. For instance, during WWII Preil wrote scripts for the Office of War Information; Plutzik's future wife, Tanya, worked at the OWI in New York when she met Hyam in 1942. Ed Moran, personal correspondence, February 2, 2020.

15   On how Preil strove to come to terms with the Holocaust and his uses of nostalgic discourse, see Natasha Gordinsky, "Nostalgia as a Literary Device: Gabriel Preil's Diasporic Condition," *Hebrew Studies* 58, no. 1 (2017): 401–424.

Preil was inaccessible: he was an immigrant to the US whose early life was in a far-away place, and in that place the Holocaust destroyed what once had been.

A Poem by Gabriel Preil

Preil's "Chapters of Time, His and Mine" is the more straightforward and accessible of the two poems; moreover, it has been discussed more extensively in critical commentary. Therefore, remarks on this piece can serve as a useful point of departure for comparison with Plutzik. The two poems share similar themes, and highlighting elements of Preil's work that are clear and easy to understand can help bring to the fore aspects of Plutzik's poem that resist initial reading. In other words, comparison between the two poems can alert us to elements that are sotto voce in one but more openly acknowledged in the other.

> Chapters of Time, His and Mine
>
> Take a look at Grandpa, young in his Lithuanian town.
> Early in the morning he would rise,
> And after prayer jot down his new comments on the Law,
> Then prepare an essay for *Hamelitz*,
> And discover qualities of manna
> In stale bread and hot water.
> He was a great man.
>
> Take a look at *me*, a young man on American soil.
> Not exactly an anomalous creature
> writing poems in Hebrew. A man
> whose prayer is mute, sipping at noon
> a tepid morning-cup and convincing himself
> he'd found in it a taste of something rare, dreamt.
>
> To each man his manna in his own time.
> This is an autobiographical pill
> approved for consumption only until the budding [dawning]
> of the quarter of this century.
> From now on—days are clowns
> dubiously skating on very thin ice.

> It's hard to imagine what Grandpa would have said about them—
> I, however, would have liked to have lived in *his* time.
> (1976)
> Translation by Yael Feldman

Preil opens this poem with an imperative: "Take a look at Grandpa." The poet observes, and bids his reader observe, the ancestral world. There, a young man rises assiduously every morning to pray, to write commentary on religious texts, and to prepare articles for *Hamelitz*, the influential Hebrew newspaper that operated from 1860 till 1904. By noting family ties to this figure, the speaker establishes a literary heritage. He is heir to someone who had knowledge of the classic sources and who also played a significant role in the extraordinary revitalization of Hebrew as a modern language. The tone of admiration is evident. As Alan Mintz points out, the poet even describes the grandfather using the phrase "adam hamaalah"—words translated here as "a great man," but which appear in the Bible as a kingly epithet[16] So, Preil's poem clearly defines the grandfather as a man of distinction. In the next stanza a self-deprecating statement emerges through words that parallel those of stanza one: "Take a look at *me*." The poet defines himself as a bit of an oddity: a Hebrew writer in America. Moreover, he writes at a time when readership for Hebrew literature has decreased dramatically, and when the center of Hebrew as a spoken language has moved definitively to Israel. Only a tiny minority of Americans—and a small minority of American Jews—knew or could read Preil's poetry in the original in late twentieth century. Altogether, the speaker's efforts pale in comparison with those of the grandfather who worked in multiple impressive genres, and who combined publication in the Modern Hebrew press with time-honored engagement with religious texts. Further emphasizing contrast between the generations, the grandfather drinks boiling tea, while the American grandson makes do with a lukewarm cup. His daily fare does not possess the vitality, boldness, intensity, or religious fervor—the taste of manna—he imagines in the other man's life. The poem adds yet another unflattering comparison by noting that grandfather prays with commitment, whereas the grandson's prayer is muted.[17]

---

16 In 1 Chron. 17:17, David uses that phrase to acknowledge the honor of being chosen for royalty. See Mintz, *Sanctuary in the Wilderness*, 332.
17 See discussion of this poem in Feldman, *Modernism and Cultural Transfer*, 1986. In the Hebrew original of the poem, the phrase describing the grandson reads "*mitpalel mitokh elem*"—wording which suggests not so much quiet prayer as a person who struggles to pray.

Disappointment about this state of affairs registers in the speaker's conclusion, "To each man his manna in his own time." The turn of phrase here relies on sound play (man/manna) to link each individual to his own lot in life.[18] Keep in mind, though, that the dispiriting contrast is an imagined one, one that comes from a deliberate attempt to idealize the past. Preil never knew his grandfather, and so the presentation here is a "willed exercise" rather than an act of recollection.[19] In the final stanza, the poem underscores that idealization. In almost expository prose, these lines sum up the central premise of the poem: that the poet draws inspiration from the past. The speaker states, explicitly, that he prefers the earlier era to his own. One distinction between the Hebrew and the English translation is worth noting here, because it underscores the speaker's sense of displacement and of living in the wrong environment. The last line, in the English version, uses the word "however" ("I, however, would have liked to have lived in *his* time."). In Hebrew, the expression used is "mikol makom"—literally, "from any place." The mention of place, joining with the mention of time and separation ("zmano") reinforces the reader's awareness that Preil sees himself as a Diasporic figure, dislodged both spatially and temporally from a world that would have suited him better. The reader's knowledge that the Holocaust has destroyed that world makes the sense of loss even more poignant.

Although the observations of the opening and closing stanzas are conveyed in simple, direct, language and in a conversational framework, the third stanza offers a rather baffling image: a clown skating on thin ice. It helps to know that the Hebrew word translated here as clown, "muqiyon," appears in the Talmud, where it means "fool."[20] Preil is stating that to continue to write Hebrew in America, in the second half of the twentieth century, is a fool's errand. The poet looks back wistfully to a time when the revival of Hebrew was an exciting, forward-looking venture, and he contrasts that era with his own: a dangerous one in which the reality of a Hebrew poet is not quite a reality and so resembles "keraḥ-lo-keraḥ" (literally, ice-not-ice). Indeterminacy of the surface on which the skater skates indicates that there will be no certain future, if any, for the Hebrew poet in America.

---

18   The translation felicitously echoes the Hebrew. Sound play in the original text differs lexically, but works to much the same effect: "kol ish lemano bizmano."
19   Mintz, *Sanctuary in the Wilderness*, 331.
20   Ibid., 333.

A Poem by Hyam Plutzik

Turning now to Plutzik's poem, we find a shorter text. Laconic and compact, it compresses significance into few words. Meaning waits to be unpacked from an elliptically lyrical style.

> After Looking into a Book Belonging to My Great-Grandfather,
> Eli Eliakim Plutzik
>
> I am troubled by the blank fields, the speechless graves.
> Since the names were carved upon wood, there is no word
> For the thousand years that shaped this scribbling fist
> And the eyes staring at strange places and times
> Beyond the veldt dragging to Poland.
> Lovers of words make simple peace with death,
> At last demanding, to close the door to the cold,
> Only *Here lies someone.*
> Here lie no one and no one, your fathers and mothers.
> —(1959)[21]

Like Preil, Plutzik from the start emphasizes the verb *look*. As the title tells us, perusing a book inspired the poem, and, as Plutzik's biographers tell us, the book in question was *Tikkun Leil Shavuot*.[22] This is a traditional religious text, compiled for all-night study sessions to celebrate the Feast of Weeks.[23] From that book the poet turns his gaze to a wide vista. As was also the case for Preil, gazing across space takes the poet back in time, and this poem, too, laments loss and severed connections to ancestors. Plutzik's poem, though, is more contemplative, more melancholy, and more keenly attuned to erasure of the past. For Preil, Hebrew provides a living link to earlier generations. Not only does he write in the same language his forefathers used, he attempts to enlist others, in the here-and-now, to share his vision and feel connection to the past. That is, he demands action in the present through the imperative "take a look." Doing so, moreover, he conjures a scene of industrious activity: the grandfather diligently at work. Plutzik, in contrast, musters less immediate connections. He writes in English, not in the

---

21 Plutzik, *Collected Poems*, 97.
22 Correspondence with Edward Moran.
23 Sundquist, "Blessed Mythmaker."

language of his ancestors, and he does not issue a command. Instead, he composes a reflection. Indeed, the title and the first line of the poem may be read as a continuous, single sentence—"After looking into a book [...] I am troubled"—and the rest of the poem reflects on how the glance into the book leads to a feeling of unease. Furthermore, again contrast to Preil's poem, the phrase "looking into" is less imperative than evocative; it implies research, distanced philosophical consideration rather than unmediated engagement. Finally, the findings of that research stress inactivity and silence. Rather than an image of industrious activity as in Preil's poem, the speaker in Plutzik's poem perceives "blank fields" and "speechless graves." Both poets write about cultural heritage and centuries of family ties, but Preil champions the Hebrew of the past while Plutzik suggests there is no adequate verbal expression to convey what is gone.

In particular, what has been lost is names. Carved upon wood, they have worn away. This scene stands in stark contrast to what Jewish tradition dictates. For Jews, names of the dead are to be honored and preserved. It is customary to engrave names on stone, a more durable material than wood. What's more, Jewish epitaphs tend to include personal information about the deceased, such as the descriptors "modest" or "important" for a woman or "perfect and upright" for a man. Those words are often accompanied as well by a title, depending on the age and position of the person. After that comes mention of paternal lineage, followed by the surname of the person who died.[24] Lines 1–3 of Plutzik's poem emphasize the absence of just such markers of personal worth and community status: here lie "no one and no one." This absence of names then puts into relief the prominent announcement of a particular name in the title of the poem. The specificity and length of the title signal that the poet is fighting back against forgetting, effacement, and anonymity. Moreover, the name in the title reverberates with multiple meanings that bestow honor on the dead man. "Eli" means high, that which is exalted. The name Eliakim, "he whom God will raise up," bears further connotations of eminence. In the Bible, several honorable and accomplished men are named Eliakim.[25] The title also explicitly designates Eli Eliakim Plutzik as "great-grandfather." While Preil refers to his grandfather as "adam hamaʻalah"—the "great man," Plutzik, too, in a more understated way, calls attention to great-ness. Finally, paying heed to names takes on further

---

24 For information on other elements of Jewish tombstones see for instance Heidi M. Szpek, "Jewish Epitaphs," accessed August 7, 2024, http://www.jewishepitaphs.org/epigraphs-2/.
25 Those biblical figures include the governor of the palace of King Hezekiah of Judah, as well as King Jehoiakim, whose original name was Eliakim and who assisted Nehemiah in rebuilding the walls of Jerusalem.

significance in view of pervasive concern with the Holocaust in Plutzik's work. The poet's insistence on mentioning his ancestor's full name calls to mind the efforts of Yad Vashem, the Israeli Holocaust memorial authority, which works to identify and honor individual Jewish victims of Nazi genocide. For each person whose death can be documented, Yad Vashem keeps a separate file in the Hall of Names in Jerusalem. That project bears the lyrical label "Lekhol ish yesh shem" ("Each One Has a Name"), borrowing words from a famous poem by Zelda [Schneerson Mishkovsky]. Plutzik's short, lyrical poem with its long title expresses a similar sentiment. It singles out the individual and acknowledges the value of individual lives.

How does the speaker in the poem express his troubled feelings? One way is through the deft use of simple words that quietly generate multiple meanings. Consider the line "since the names were carved on wood." The word "Since" can be understood two ways. In one, it serves as explanation; that is, because the grave markers were not stone, the names haven't lasted. This reading emphasizes feelings of loss. But the same word can also serve as an indication of temporality. "Since" may refer to the time span during which family heritage has become erased, the "thousand years that shaped [the poet's] scribbling fist." Interpretation #2 emphasizes a sense of belatedness. The poet is a latecomer; his hand and his writing have been shaped by a long history, reaching back over many centuries. The choice to fold several implications into the word "since" gives the impression that the speaker feels a mix of emotions: loss, and also arriving too late to recover what was lost. He carries a disturbing burden that cannot easily be voiced, and while his vocabulary carries a surplus of meaning, it is subdued and constricts expression; the result is to convey a queasy tension— intensity of feeling and a sense that it is impossible to adequately give voice to that feeling.

The reference to "this fist" and "the eyes" adds to the impression of unease. On first reading, those phrases disorient. The reader is left wondering, whose fist? Which eyes? On second reading the logical conclusion is that the hand and the eyes are the poet's own. Impersonal phrasing here, suppressing first person pronouns, cloaks the speaker in anonymity. The "My" and "I" of the title and first line have disappeared. Individuality is deemphasized. The result is to incorporate the speaker into the same extended chain of nameless ancestors that he memorializes in the poem. Subsequently, lines 4 and 5 indicate that connection to the past is neither simple nor automatic. Here, heritage is a matter of "strange places and times" and the poem introduces the word "veldt," an incongruous lexical item, to dramatize strangeness. Signifying open, uncultivated country or grassland in southern Africa, the term seems out of place in a poem that contemplates family history in Eastern Europe. The poet opts for a word that makes the past foreign and that amplifies his sense of displacement.

Through the double meaning of "since," the muffled, oblique reference to self, the de-familiarizing effect of the word "veldt," and the long, somewhat convoluted sentence that makes up lines 2–4, the poem wrestles with articulating unspeakable loss. Together with other word choices that heighten the register (for example, the quasi-rhyme "wood"/"word," and the parallelism of the phrases "blank fields" and "speechless graves"), these elements of the text render Plutzik's verse non-conversational. They afford it solemnity, and they contribute to a style that is at once stately, enigmatic, and, though unadorned, neither facile nor plain.

The poem itself, as it draws to a conclusion, calls attention to the topic of simple expression and so invites the reader to consider how simplicity contributes to Plutzik's art. See line 6, which pivots from personal reflection to generalization: the poet notes that "Lovers of words make simple peace with death." That is, those who cherish language come to terms with mortality by recording few words on gravestones: "Only *Here lies someone.*" This line (8), is the shortest one in the poem; its brevity reinforces the idea that mourners rely on brief words and thereby find closure (they "close the door to the cold").[26] Plutzik's own use of the same unadorned wording ("Here lies") merits comment, though, because it is not so plain in meaning. It calls to mind Jewish tradition and the custom of writing on a gravestone "poh nitman" (פ״נ)—"here is buried." Plutzik does not use that Hebrew phrase; this means that his words intimate familiarity with Jewish custom, yet Hebrew remains hidden. It, too, is buried—unmarked, like the nameless dead—lying beneath the surface of the poem.

In view of that move, consider the last line of the poem: "here lie no one and no one." The emphasis on anonymity, of course, contrasts with "*Here lies someone.*" The poet's sorrowful acknowledgment that names have been forgotten is perhaps the most accessible line in the poem. Readers, including those not familiar with Jewish epitaphs, will discern bitter irony in Plutzik's turn of phrase. Indeed, this poem—like Preil's—ends with a declarative summation of its central idea: graves, woefully, have been desecrated; forgetting is lamentable. However, readers with cultural knowledge of the phrase "poh nitman" may discover another dimension to the poem: they can appreciate that Preil's thinking is informed by Jewish tradition even while Hebrew itself is absent. In a poem about lost

---

26 The firm iambs of line 8 (*ONly HERE lies SOMEone*" contrast with the metrical irregularity elsewhere in the poem. The rhythm of line 8 works together with the brevity to reinforce the impression of simplicity.

connections with the past, traditional language itself is muted. The text itself both invokes and severs continuity with the past. The distinction from Preil is clear: Preil in his poem regrets discontinuity with the past, but writing in Hebrew reasserts a direct continuity with the figure of the grandfather who was a Torah scholar and also published in *Hamelitz*.

The final words of the poem do offer a small measure of repair, of restitution to previous generations who have been denied recognition. The speaker specifies that the ones buried are "your fathers and mothers." This closing asserts connection to the dead, honoring them as progenitors. Adding the phrase "fathers and mothers" gives them stature. At the same time, the word "your" insists on personal attachment, and this point raises the question: who is being addressed? Using a second person pronoun, the poet could be speaking to himself, or to his readers. Use of the plural (fathers/mothers) suggests reference either to multiple ancestors of his own and/or to ancestors of a wider public. Any of these possibilities would emphasize belonging and community. The text is inclusive of those who came before and those who are readers in the here and now. While Gabriel Preil ends his poem by looking to the future with trepidation, Hyam Plutzik ends on a note that is sad, but not without consolation.

Those final lines that turn to readers and include them also encourage them to reread the opening of the poem. Since readers are thinking in line 7 about closing the door "to the cold," perhaps it is necessary for them to go back to line 1 and reconsider the "blank fields" mentioned there. Are they blank because they are covered with snow? Does "cold" refer metaphorically to death, or is it a literal reference that demands reinterpretation as a winter landscape? The "cold" here is not like the image of "ice-not-ice" in Preil's poem. That phrase was entirely figurative, whereas Plutzik's poem presents more uncertainty about the status of words. Perhaps they are literal, perhaps figurative, perhaps both, or perhaps first one and then the other. The poet challenges us to see meaning unfolding, as readers cast a backward glance and read themselves and personal attachments into the opening scene. Note that line 7 mentions "last demanding" and the simple response that "lovers of words" supply. Line 9, though, stands in ironic contrast to what is simple. It makes demands on us—to reread, to fill in the blanks, as it were, to explicate what Plutzik leaves unsaid, to identify with the poet, and to involve ourselves in his sorrow. For Jews, the demand is also something more: to become part of a long cultural chain. That was true of Gabriel Preil's poem, as well, but "Chapters of Time" speaks directly to a collective "you" ("Look"—"re'u"). Hyam Plutzik is less straightforward. His poem opens possibilities for community and strengthened ties to the past, but in a more oblique and tenuous way.

Reframing Jewish American Literature

What, then, emerges most saliently from a comparison of these two poems, both of which offer thoughts on family, express reverence for forebears the poets never actually met, and convey a sense of personal loss amplified by collective losses of the Holocaust? For one thing, reading them in tandem enriches each of them, calling attention to details that readers might otherwise miss. The vestiges of Hebrew in Plutzik's poem become more legible in juxtaposition to Gabriel Preil's poem; the direct address, the imperatives, and appeal to Jewish community in Preil's poem gain emphasis in comparison with Plutzik's more oblique, understated approach. Significantly, such details help put into relief multiple layers of cultural attachments that give rise to this poetry. Each poet both seeks connection with the past and acknowledges disconnection from it, reaches out for community and contends with the slipperiness or elusiveness of contact, grapples with continuity and discontinuity. Their work contributes to a Jewish American literature that is constantly negotiating with its Jewish roots and American heritage.

Accordingly, reading these poems together also invites consideration of how the two writers fit into wider frameworks of literary history. Looking at the two poems can contribute to the "transnational turn" in American Studies. That line of thought, which has gained wide recognition in the past two decades, has reshaped the field to acknowledge diverse, pluralistic voices within the US. The trend has been to highlight the multiple identifications and allegiances of individuals and groups, while taking into account that American literature is not restricted to English-language texts alone. Recent scholarship has called for fully recognizing Jewish American literature as fundamental to such conversations.[27] Comparison of Preil and Plutzik can certainly add to those discussions. Keep in mind, as well, that although there has been growing attention to American Hebraism by scholars in the field of Jewish literature,[28] few studies have specifically discussed American Hebrew poetry in conjunction with other Jewish

---

27 Roberta Rosenberg and Rachel Rubinstein, "Introduction," in *Teaching Jewish American Literature*, ed. Roberta Rosenberg and Rachel Rubinstein (New York: Modern Language Association, 2020), 1–20.

28 Recent scholarship on American Hebrew literature includes Stephen Katz, *Red, Black, and Jew: New Frontiers in Hebrew Literature*. (Austin: University of Texas Press, 2009) and Michael Weingrad, *American Hebrew Literature: Writing Jewish National Identity in the United States* (Syracuse, NY: Syracuse University Press, 2011), in addition to Mintz, *Sanctuary in the Wilderness*, and Schachter, *Diasporic Modernisms*.

American writing. Juxtaposing Preil and Plutzik can help reframe understanding of Jewish American poetry and encourage us to see it in a more holistic way, one less compartmentalized by linguistic division. In this regard, it's worth noting that previous historiography has been criticized for its Ashke-normativity and its overemphasis on early twentieth-century writers of Eastern European background. Hyam Plutzik and Gabriel Preil, even though they both come from Ashkenazi background, exemplify difference within this demographic category.

Discussion of these two poets can also help us think about the diversity and diffuse audiences of modern Jewish literature broadly speaking, reaching beyond American shores. Literary historians have come to see attempts at defining what Jewish literature *is* as an exercise in futility. Rather than looking for unity in modern Jewish writing, they have been focusing on phenomena that are multinational and multilingual and that include writing aimed at both Jewish and non-Jewish readers.[29] Following the lead of Dan Miron (particularly, in response to his book *From Continuity to Contiguity: Toward a New Jewish Literary Thinking*), they have emphasized that Modern Jewish literature is characterized not by a unitary tradition but by

> dualities, parallelisms, occasional intersections, marginal overlapping, hybrids, similarities within dissimilarities, mobility, changeability, occasional emergence of patterns and their eventual disappearance, randomness, and, when approximating a semblance of significant order, by contiguities.[30]

Such a description applies aptly to the relationship between Preil and Plutzik. The two poets overlap, at times, in geography. Preil spent most of his life in

---

29 Dan Miron, *From Continuity to Contiguity: Toward a New Jewish Literary Thinking* (Redwood City, CA: Stanford University Press, 2010), based on work published earlier in Hebrew, is an indispensable contribution to critical debate over the nature of what constitutes modern Jewish literature. Another very informative volume about ideas on this topic is *Modern Jewish Literatures: Intersections and Boundaries*, ed. Sheila Jelen, Michael Kramer, and Scott Lerner (Philadelphia: University of Pennsylvania Press, 2011). Of particular interest is the introduction and, in connection with Preil, the chapter by Anita Norich, "Hebraism and Yiddishism: Paradigms of Modern Jewish Literary History" (327–42). For a survey reviewing scholarship on Hebrew modernism as a transnational phenomenon, see Rachel Harris, "Cosmopolitan, Diasporic and Transnational: The Flourishing of Hebrew Modernism, *Modernism/Modernity* 21, no. 1 (2014): 361–368.

30 From Shachar Pinsker's review essay that discusses Miron's approach: "What Is Jewish Literature?," *New Republic*, December 7, 2011, https://newrepublic.com/article/97062/jewish-literature-dan-miron-continuity-contiguity.

New York City; Plutzik was born there, grew up in Connecticut, and then resided for years in Rochester. The two poets' shared roots in Eastern European Jewish experience led to parallels and occasional shared thematic elements in their writing; those patterns happen to emerge in a pointed way in "After Looking into A Book Belonging to My Great-Grandfather, Eli Eliakim Plutzik" and "Chapters of Time, His and Mine." The dissimilarities between the poets, though, are also evident: each poet had knowledge of English, Yiddish, and Hebrew, but each used that knowledge in different measure for creative art. In short, theirs is not a single, inherited tradition or set of poetic conventions. The word "contiguity" is thus highly pertinent to our understanding of Plutzik and Preil. The definition of contiguity includes notions of proximity, adjacency, or kinship. It allows us to appreciate each poet's distinctive artistry while also exploring each poet's connections to Jewish culture.[31]

The question of predecessors raises yet another concept that can provide a framework for understanding Plutzik and Preil: authorial affiliation, the way writers align themselves with other writers or highlight their connections with colleagues and precursors so as to craft an artistic identity. As David Hadar has explored in his book *Affiliated Identities in Jewish American Literature*, one way that writers establish such associations is by forming literary movements or by penning manifestoes, but those are not the only options. An alternative is for writers to mention other literary figures within their own texts—for instance, to incorporate them as characters in works of fiction.[32] The poems we have looked at by Gabriel Preil and Hyam Plutzik both make this kind of affiliative effort. Each poet invokes an ancestor, a writer or bookish forefather, and thereby infuses Jewish cultural associations into his own work. Bear in mind that the autobiographical element here is less about reminiscence or about revealing

---

31 While his poetry presents culturally hybrid work that draws on Anglo-American literary background together with Judaic elements, we should not obscure the fact that many of Plutzik's poems are not Jewishly oriented—they cover many topics, including science, math, philosophical meditation, humor, war, and more—nor should we minimize the fact the Preil wrote extensively on Jewish topics even as he pulled away from the kind of hyper-allusive style that was characteristic of Hebrew romanticism. His oeuvre includes multiple poems that engage with Jerusalem, Jewish history, and poetic predecessors (Ibn Gabirol, Yacov Fichman, Uri Nissan Gnessin, David Fogel, and more).

32 David Hadar, *Affiliated Identities in Jewish American Literature* (London: Bloomsbury Academic, 2020). Gordinsky, *Nostalgia as a Literary Device* comments on how Preil establishes an artistic genealogy by mentioning a variety of writers and painters in his poems. The references include not only Jewish figures but also Poe, El Greco, Van Gogh, and others, as well. Via literature, these artists acquire a kind of belonging and intimacy they did not have in life.

personal life than about actively seeking out literary attachments, acknowledging progenitors, and constructing cultural networks. The two poets write about the past becoming illegible, occluded, or ignored, but they nonetheless value memory and they keep the past tethered to the present by linking themselves to a chain of Jewish books and writing. Reading Plutzik and Preil side by side therefore invites us to insert them, together, into a global network of Jewish writers.

In keeping with those considerations, the value of comparing Plutzik and Preil will not be to establish a new canon of Jewish American writing nor to try to redefine centers and margins in literary history—though, certainly, it is meaningful to call attention to two poets who deserve to be more widely known. More crucially, it is exciting to enlarge discussion of how American poets, in all their diversity, have grappled with the centrifugal forces of Modern Jewish literature and with tensions between continuity and discontinuity. Looking at these two poets can underscore how their modes of expression evolved over time, emerging out of multilingual circumstances. Furthermore, the ways that their poetic trajectories intersect can help highlight the dynamic aspects of Plutzik's and Preil's cultural identities and creativity. Theirs is not a single, inherited tradition; instead, they contribute to a lively, ever-shifting, transformative one.

Bibliography

American Academy of Poets. Accessed August 8, 2024. https://poets.org/poet/hyam-plutzik.
Feldman, Yael. *Modernism and Cultural Transfer: Gabriel Preil and the Tradition of Jewish Literary Bilingualism*. Cincinnati, OH: Hebrew Union College Press, 1986.
Gordinsky, Natasha. "Nostalgia as a Literary Device: Gabriel Preil's Diasporic Condition." *Hebrew Studies* 58, no. 1 (2017): 401–424.
Hadar, David. *Affiliated Identities in Jewish American Literature*. London: Bloomsbury Academic, 2020.
Harris, Rachel. "Cosmopolitan, Diasporic and Transnational: The Flourishing of Hebrew Modernism." *Modernism/Modernity* 21, no. 1 (2014): 361–368.
Hecht, Anthony. Foreword to *Hyam Plutzik: The Collected Poems*, xi-xix. Brockport, NY: Boa Editions, Ltd., 1987.
Jelen, Sheila, Michael Kramer, and Scott Lerner, eds. *Modern Jewish Literatures: Intersections and Boundaries*. Philadelphia: University of Pennsylvania Press, 2011.
Katz, Stephen. *Red, Black, and Jew: New Frontiers in Hebrew Literature*. Austin: University of Texas Press, 2009.
Lurie, Margot. "Golden Apples." *Jewish Review of Books* (Spring 2013). https://jewishreviewofbooks.com/articles/115/golden-apples/.
Mintz, Alan. *Sanctuary in the Wilderness: A Critical Introduction to American Hebrew Poetry*. Stanford, CA: Stanford University Press, 2011.

Miron, Dan. "Bein haner lakokhavim" [Between the candle and the stars]. In *Collector of Autumns: Collected Poems 1972–1992*, edited by Dan Miron. Jerusalem: Bialik, 1993.

———. *From Continuity to Contiguity: Toward a New Jewish Literary Thinking*. Redwood City, CA: Stanford University Press, 2010.

Nelson, Cary. "The Universe Is No Consolation: Hyam Plutzik, Jewish Identity, and the Ethics of Post-Holocaust Reading." *Journal of Jewish Identities* 15 (2022): 5–31.

Norich, Anita. "Hebraism and Yiddishism: Paradigms of Modern Jewish Literary History." In *Modern Jewish Literatures: Intersections and Boundaries*, edited by Sheila Jelen, Michael Kramer, and Scott Lerner, 327–42. Philadelphia: University of Pennsylvania Press, 2011.

Plutzik, Hyam. *Aspects of Proteus*. New York: Harper and Brothers, 1949.

———. *Apples from Shinar*. Middletown, OH: Wesleyan University Press, 1959.

———. *Hyam Plutzik: The Collected Poems*. Brockport, NY: Boa Editions, Ltd., 1987.

Preil, Gabriel. *Asfan stavim: shirim 1972–1992* [Collector of Autumns: Poems 1972–1992]. Edited by Dan Miron. Jerusalem: Mossad Bialik, 1993.

Rosenberg, Roberta, and Rachel Rubinstein. "Introduction." In *Teaching Jewish American Literature*, edited by Roberta Rosenberg and Rachel Rubinstein, 1–20. New York: Modern Language Association, 2020.

Schachter, Allison, *Diasporic Modernisms: Hebrew and Yiddish Literature in the Twentieth Century*. New York: Oxford University Press, 2012.

Schwartz, Howard, and Anthony Rudolf, eds. *Voices within the Ark: The Modern Jewish Poets*. New York: Avon Books, 1980.

Pinsker, Shachar. "What Is Jewish Literature?" *New Republic*, December 7, 2011. https://newrepublic.com/article/97062/jewish-literature-dan-miron-continuity-contiguity.

Shreiber, Maeera Y. "Secularity, Sacredness, and Jewish American Poets: 1950–2000." In *The Cambridge History of Jewish American Literature*, edited by Hana Wirth-Nesher, 182–201. New York: Cambridge University Press, 2016.

Sundquist, Eric. "Blessed Mythmaker: The Poetry of Hyam Plutzik," Hyam Plutzik, Poet. Accessed August 21, 2024, https://drive.google.com/file/d/18y4aXA50KLXStIN8wD3vcpbFi1qtEEbF/view

Szpek, Heidi M. "Jewish Epitaphs." Accessed August 7, 2024. http://www.jewishepitaphs.org/epigraphs-2/.

Weingrad, Michael, *American Hebrew Literature: Writing Jewish National Identity in the United States*. Syracuse, NY: Syracuse University Press, 2011.

CHAPTER 4

"So!" Reading "The Importance of Poetry, or, The Coming Forth from Eternity into Time"

Sandor Goodhart

And it's time, time, time
And it's time, time, time
And it's time, time, time, that you love,
And it's time, time, time.
—Tom Waits, from Rain Dogs (1985)

Structured time, the blessing of a foundation for measure and purposive action, is one of civilization's great gifts. But in extremity the forms of time dissolve, the rhythms of motion and change are lost. . . . The death of time destroys the sense of growth and purpose.
—Terence Des Pres, from The Survivor (1976)

The disaster ruins everything and leaves everything intact.
—Maurice Blanchot, The Writing of the Disaster (1980)

Time runs out.
—Hyam Plutzik, "The Last Fisherman" (2011)

Copyright © 2025 by Sandor Goodhart

The Writing of/from the Disaster

My thesis in what follows is that all of Hyam Plutzik's writing is effectively a "writing of the disaster," to use a term that I borrow from Maurice Blanchot's seminal 1980 volume *L'écriture du désastre*.[1] The French word *écriture* can of course mean "writing in general." But it can also mean "handwriting," "signature," or simply "hand," as we say in English, or even just "notes," "notebooks," or "jottings." And, of course, the French conjunctive *du* commonly translated as "of" or "of the" and meaning "about" or constituting a description of some kind, can also mean "from," as in "deriving from" the disaster or "a symptom of" the disaster. And the specific way in which Plutzik gets at this Jewish connection, I would like to suggest, is through the theme of time.

Time is clearly Plutzik's subject, as virtually every commentator has noted. It is a theme Plutzik inherits from Wordsworth and the romantic poets (among others) and that continues into writing of the current day. "Time equals death minus now" is the important formula that I would use for consideration of these writers. And the theme of almost every poem of Plutzik's reflects that "equation." Time is the brute fact of decay, of decomposition, complementary perhaps to the famous second law of thermodynamics described by physical cosmologists with the colloquialism that things run down, that entropy or randomness at large increases in the universe in rivalry perhaps with the potential for poetry, which is perceived as being linked, if only temporally and temporarily, to survival.

How so? "Coil upon coil," Plutzik writes in an early poem, "the grave serpent holds / Its implacable strict pose under a light / Like marble."[2] "The grave serpent" is the serious serpent, the serpent perhaps of biblical Edenic fame, but also the serpent of the grave. "There is no force stronger," Plutzik writes,

---

[1] The essay that follows is an expanded version of my presentation before the Jewish American and Holocaust Literature Symposium, South Beach, FL, November 13, 2023.

    Jewish themes are everywhere in Plutzik's poetry. But all of it looks forward to what Ed Moran identifies in the archived papers as "a poem on the Holocaust," one that Plutzik never lived to complete but on which he appears to have been working, if Sundquist and Nelson are right, since just after the war. Working in the context of these researchers and commentators, I regard this essay as a further expansion of the Jewish connection, in contradiction to David Scott Kastan's charged assertion that Plutzik "was not a Jewish poet, but a gifted poet who happened to be Jewish," a claim Kastan makes in his afterword to the 2011 republication of *Apples from Shinar* as a "special edition" that includes excerpts from Plutzik's *Horatio*.

[2] Hyam Plutzik, "An Equation," in *The Collected Poems*, forward by Anthony Hecht (Brockport, NY: BOA Editions, Ltd., 1987), 5. *The Collected Poems* will henceforth be cited as Plutzik 2017.

"(In the sweep of the monomaniac passion, time) / Than the will toward destiny, which is death":[3]

> ... The artist's damnation, the rat of time,
> Cannot gnaw this form, nor event touch it with age.
> Before it was, it existed, creating the mind
> Which created it, out of itself. It will dissolve
> Into itself, though in another language.
> Its changes are not in change, nor its times in time.[4]

"There is no change," Plutzik writes in another poem, "but only re-creation / One step ahead."[5] "If these lesser things are subsumed within the Good," he proposes in still another poem,

> These corrupt shapes: desk, mirror or tree—
> The falsely transliterated, strangely planed
> Creatures of eyesight and the sentient bones
> (Themselves in the web of the spider), then all times
> Are poses of the one actor, Time: he
> Who is ape of eternity, and the acorn neglected among leaves
> Encircles, now in this very heartbeat, a forest
> Of oaks that have no horizon;[6]

This "coiled serpent," Plutzik continues, "quivering under a light / Crueler than marble, unwinds slowly, altering / Deliberate the great convolutions."[7] This serpent, death, is "a dancer,"

> A mime on the brilliant stage. The sudden movement,
> Swifter than creases of lightning, renews a statue:
> There by its skin a snake rears beaten in copper.[8]

---

3   Hyam Plutzik, "The Geese," in *Apples from Shinar: A Book of Poems: Special Edition* (Middletown, CT: Wesleyan University Press, 2011), 15. *Apples from Shinar* will henceforth be cited as Plutzik 2011.
4   Plutzik 1987, "An Equation," 5.
5   Plutzik 2011, "If Causality Is Impossible, Genesis Is Recurrent," 9.
6   Plutzik 2011, "The Zero That Is All," 27.
7   Ibid., 5.
8   Ibid.

And, as such, this "coiled serpent" is not affected by ritual, nor by suffering: "It will not acknowledge the incense on your altars, / Nor hear at night in your room the weeping."[9]

Limitation itself, for Plutzik, differentiation, separateness, is in fact already an illusion. Things project shadows in which they are embedded, he tells us, and within the larger shadow—namely, suffering—all things "melt" and are bathed in a "subjective night," a reference perhaps to the night (*layla*) of Genesis 1, which is the name given to a darkness (*hoshech*) that is older than the opposite of light, a darkness which also occurs as part of the quotidian cycle of evening (*erev*) and morning (*boker*):

> Like successive layers of leaf that dwindle the sunlight
> Are the overlapping cumulative shadows
> Projected by things, which huddle in them darkly
> Within the greater shadow: suffering.
>
> Breaching the shores of matter a swell of shadows
> Destroys all sanctions of formal separateness;
> And objects, transposed of vesture, take doubtful values
> Like hulks vaguely discerned under the tides.
> What inner or outer flames may shine are random
> In the one, shadowed sea where all things melt,
> While through all, the superior dark, the subjective night
> Encloses and bathes the universe.[10]

For Plutzik, there is an intensely personal connection to this theme. Time, he was aware, after a point, was clearly running out for him. The unpublished poem "Cancer and Nova" reflects upon this imminent connection explicitly:[11]

> The star exploding in the body;
> The creeping thing, growing in the brain or the bone;
> The hectic cannibal, the obscene mouth.
>
> The mouths along the meridian sought him,
> Soft as moths, many a moon and sun,

---

9   Ibid.
10 Plutzik 2011, "I Imagined a Painter Painting Such a World," 23
11 Plutzik 1987, "Cancer and Nova," 246.

Until one
In a pale fleeing dream caught him.

Waking, he did not know himself undone,
Nor walking, smiling, reading that the news was good,
The star exploding in his blood.

The onset of mortal illness ("the creeping thing") comes to some extent as a surprise, framed as "he" was within the dimension's poetic rhyme. "The mouths . . . sought him . . . until one . . . caught him." "Waking" and "walking," "he did not know himself undone." "Reading that the news was good," all the while the star was "exploding in his blood," a noun that looks as if it might rhyme with the adjectival qualifier "good" but in fact fatally opposes the quality of the news he was reading.

But there is also another connection beyond even the personal, biological, and generally humanist tradition in which Plutzik is so clearly invested. If I turn to the work of Terrence Des Pres, and especially to his book *The Survivor*, it is to link this theme of time in historical terms, to recast it in terms of the Holocaust.[12] What the Jews lacked, among other things (both those who survived and those who did not), was time, Des Pres writes:[13] "The death of time destroys the sense of growth and purpose."[14] And for Plutzik, the sense of insufficiency, or decay, or decomposition, or rot he finds everywhere peeks through the rubble in a poem like "Portrait," in which he appears to take himself explicitly to task for it. "Notice with what careful nonchalance / He tries to be a Jew casually," Plutzik writes, "To ignore the monster, the mountain— / A few thousand years of history."[15] His references to the ancient biblical tradition—the Greek and the Germanic especially—concretize this same concern.

It may be that if we want to understand Plutzik's poetry, we need to understand his thoroughgoing obsession with time (and the onset of death that it signals) throughout his work as much a symptom as an observation. The poetic voice is, thus, a witness to the experience of the Jews in the Holocaust just a few years earlier, Jews with whom he had "no personal connection" and about

---

12 Terrence Des Pres, *The Survivor: An Anatomy of Life in the Death Camps* (New York: Oxford University Press, 1976), 11–12.
13 Cf.: "For most, their [the survivors'] own good luck, simple facts of time and place come to be 'almost a miracle' (ibid.). Terrence Des Pres, "Lessons of the Holocaust," *New York Times*, April 27, 1976.
14 Des Pres, *The Survivor*, 12.
15 Plutzik 2011, 31

which experiences he says "he personally remembers nothing." Yet these are experiences and stories he would like to tell rightly (and in fact feels deeply committed to telling) but at the same time feels barred from telling for a variety of reasons—perhaps not unlike Hamlet's friend Horatio feels regarding the story of Hamlet in Shakespeare's most famous play.

In order to pursue these themes—especially the lack of time, with particular reference to survival and Jewish history and the continuation of the effects of trauma with which he has no personal connection and about which he remembers nothing—I want to consider several poems. The first is "The Importance of Poetry, or the Coming Forth from Eternity into Time" which I will read in detail, explicating each line, and in some instances each word, in the way I might do so in a college classroom. The second poem is "Of Objects Considered as Fortresses in a Baleful Space" in which for a moment the poet steps "outside of time," so to speak, in order to talk as "never-guests."[16] A third, about which I will comment only briefly, is "Portrait," quoted in part above, in which the poet addresses Jews explicitly and Judaism implicitly.[17] Finally, I will address *Horatio*, the long poem he submitted to his publisher in the fall of 1961, shortly before his passing in January of 1962. This poem details the failure, in the protagonist's view, of generations of critical responses to the man Hamlet that Horatio knew (and implicitly in the author's view, the play *Hamlet*, and the man Shakespeare), and perhaps more as well.

"The Importance of Poetry"

Here is the text of Plutzik's poem. It is taken from the second edition *Apples from Shinar* (2011).

The Importance of Poetry, Or the Coming Forth from Eternity into Time

> Beyond the image of the willow
> There is a willow no man knows
> Or watches with corruptible eyes.
>
> Deep in a field where no man goes
> Nor bird flies
> The willow fronts an empty road.

---

16   Ibid., 35
17   Ibid., 31

> The bird hovers in other skies:
> World where only these wings exist.
>
> And elsewhere, alone, upon an abyss,
> The man is marching down a road
>
> As the rays of the sun are drawn together
> By a curved glass and rekindled to fire
> So, to the poppies life and death,
> So does desire
> Draw them and bend them and bind them so,
> So the noise of the wings can at last be heard
> And the willow-image do grace to a bird
> And the ghost on the roadway give them word
> Not for forever, only a day.[18]

The word "or" in the title of the poem clues us in right away to the richness of its meaning. Does this "or" mean "in other words," *c'est à dire* in French—the importance of poetry or, in other words, what is the same thing as "the coming forth from eternity into time"—whatever that phrase might mean? Does this "or," in the title, this titular "or," so to speak, denote choice? Do we choose "the importance of poetry" or do we choose "the coming forth from eternity into time"? It's the same problem in fact that we find in Shakespeare's *Hamlet*, for example, in the famous "To be or not to be" speech, where the protagonist asks the same question. Does the word "or" in the phrase "To be or not to be" designate an appositive ("to be" or, in other words, "not to be," as, for example, we might speak of a ghost or an apparition as both being and not being, as the presence of an absence). Or, does the word "or" in the phrase mean choosing (between being and not being, for example, between living and not living)? To be, or alternatively, not to be? In other words, suicide. For Hamlet, the "question" is: What if being turns out to be just another form of not being, of play-acting, of living with ghosts? Then, is taking steps toward really not being (i.e. bringing on death) so outlandish?

And what in fact does the phrase "the coming forth from eternity into time" mean? It sounds like something that might be found in the philosophic writings of Franz Rosenzweig—for example, in *The Star of Redemption*, where

---

18 Ibid., 25

Rosenzweig speaks of creation, revelation, and redemption.[19] Or perhaps it's akin to the philosophic work of Emmanuel Levinas, who speaks of "the infinite within the finite"—not the infinite *and* the finite, nor the finite *within* the infinite, but, precisely, the infinite *within* the finite, the "more within the less," "the container within the contained"—as our access to the eternal within the limited realm of time. It is an access or gateway in Levinas's view that he finds in the human face, or in certain written works that act like a human face (one of which, for Levinas, is Torah, another of which is the writing of Shakespeare), or in certain nonwritten cases (like the nape of the neck in a man in line after World War Two in one of the European DP camps). These are accesses or gateways for Levinas that always open us to our infinite responsibilities for other human beings, to the unlimited scope of our ethical obligations to the other individual.

In his title, then, is Plutzik opposing poetry to the coming forth of the infinite into the finite, which is also the project of Genesis in the Hebrew Bible, the problem of creation? Or is Plutzik saying they are one and the same? Is he opposing the literary to the religious, creation by the poet, the human maker, to creation by God, the divine Creator? Or is he saying that they are in fact the same thing, that the "importance of poetry" is its capacity to work as a version of the coming forth of the infinite into the finite—that poetry is perhaps the human cognate of Genesis in the Hebrew Bible?

There is a third possibility that I mention somewhat in passing. Has Plutzik made a hidden or secret pun on the letters of the English word? We know of course that Kabbalah relies on the esoteric or hidden tradition that derives not from the words of holy scripture as Talmudic and midrashic exegetical readings do (and as Eric Sundquist in his essay reminds us), but from the letters, from, in this case, the English letters. Has Plutzik made a pun on the Hebrew word *or*, which means "light," in the title of his poem? Has he asked in effect, "What is the importance of poetry?—*or*, light, the coming forth from the eternal into time? Does poetry do what God does in Genesis, namely, inaugurate creation, that bringing forth of light from the infinite into the finite? But before we get carried away by just the title of his poem, let us look more closely at the poem proper.

"Beyond the image of the willow / There is a willow no man knows / Or watches with corruptible eyes." The situation for the poet appears to be what we might term "Kantian." Kant introduced into a generally accepted tripartite

---

19   Franz Rosenzweig, *The Star of Redemption* (Notre Dame, IN: University of Notre Dame Press, 1985).

division of the universe the conception of a bipartite one. Before Kant, thinkers like Locke, Wolff, Berkeley, and Hume spoke commonly of three realms: (1) "world out there"; (2) sense or sensory impressions generated by encounters with the world "out there;" and (3) human understanding or interpretation that would result from transforming sense impressions of the world out there into practical usable content. Kant said, in effect, that there are in fact only two realms: (1) the world out there and (2) one that begins with sense impression (what Kant called the *Anshauung*, sometimes translated as "intuition," and which designates the way the world confronts us aesthetically, the way we perceive the *schau* or show through the sensory organs and thus the way the world "shows up" for us), and that leads to human understanding, which now becomes the way in which we translate that sensory impression into interpretation or narrative.

For Kant, then, there is still "a world out there," a brute reality, or what he calls the "noumena," by which he means that into which one can in fact bump one's feet or stub one's toe, a guardrail; but, he adds, there is no noumenal way of getting at that world. There are only phe-noumenal ways of getting at the world "as such," ways that proceed from sensory impression to human understanding, ways that came later to be called the "phe-nomenal" world, the world built of phenomena, when the study of that world and its logic became the branch of philosophy known as "phenomenology."

Moreover, Kant said—and here is where, in addition to the barrier of the noumena, what Kant said rendered his theory bipartite rather than tripartite—that the sensory or aesthetic impressions that we have of the world (for example, through the eyes), are inseparable from human understanding but are already fully traversed by interpretation or that same human understanding. When we are seeing, we are always already interpreting; there is no interpretation-free way of viewing things; what we call "sense impressions" are in fact that region of interpretation in which we think that interpretation is not operative. There are many books that explain at greater length this idea of the constructed nature of seeing.[20]

So, "Beyond the image of the willow," Plutzik writes, "There is a willow no man knows," or one that the human being "watches [although] with corruptible eyes," with eyes, that is to say, that are already fully immersed in and dominated by human interpretation. There is a willow. Plutzik is not a solipsist any more than Kant is. There is a willow out there. But there is no access to that

---

20 John Berger, *Ways of Seeing* (London: Penguin 1972).

willow through language or, more precisely, through the language of images, which are always visual and always proceed through the eyes. One can have no knowledge of the willow in that way, knowledge of the kind that one might expect to get through language. If we think we have access to it, it is because we are looking with "corruptible eyes," which is to say with eyes already fully contaminated by one interpretation or another, by a story about that willow, by a narrative.

What, then, is "out there" for Plutzik? "Deep in a field where no man goes / Nor bird flies," he writes, "The willow fronts an empty road." "An empty road!" The place where this willow resides that no man goes, and no bird flies, is not "place" at all, or even just a sort of floating shapeless nothingness, but a "road," a pathway, a "diachrony" we might say if we were to employ a technical term from philosophy, a "sequentiality," or seriality, something that leads us from one locus to another, from place A to place B, but that is itself neither A nor B. Moreover, the poet adds, this "road" is "empty." There are no individuals traveling on it.

The willow "fronts" this empty road. The word "front" used as a verb in the 1950s in the United States had a very particular meaning. We speak commonly today of a "front" as a noun in a military context, of the place where the real battle is really taking place, for example, where hand-to-hand combat might be happening. But in the 1950s, in America, it also referred to McCarthyism, to deception, as for example in the title of Woody Allen's *The Front*. Allen tells the story of individuals working in Hollywood who were discredited by McCarthy and often lost their livelihoods after appearing before the House Un-American Activities Committee where they were accused of communist sympathies. On occasion, others stood in for the accused or "fronted" for them before the committee. It is perhaps not entirely ironic that Senator McCarthy was finally defeated only when soldiers, on Eisenhower's command, showed up at these infamous hearings.

Moreover, it is not only human beings that are missing from this picture where the willow fronts an empty road. There are in fact no nonhuman creatures there either. Is not the natural universe also missing from this place (or nonplace)? Is the phrase "no birds" figurative language for no nature? Is it possible that the willow that "there is" is simply a front, a cover, for an emptiness? The poet doesn't tell us. We learn only that this willow "fronts," or lies about, or deceives us about, or substitutes for, a road on which no one—man or bird—is traveling.

Significantly, the bird "hovers in other skies: / World where only these wings exist." "Hover" is an especially interesting word in this context. Plutzik grew up in a household speaking Yiddish and Hebrew among other languages. So, he would have known very well when he came of age as a poet that "hover" translates a very important word in the opening verses of the Hebrew Bible, verses that occur even before the creation of light is described, words that describe divine action.

Here is the opening of the Hebrew Bible in Hebrew (transliterated) and then in English:

> Bereishyt bara elohiym, eit hashmayim v'eit ha'aretz,
> Ve ha'aretz hayta tohu ve vohu,
> Ve hoshech al penai t'hom
> Ve ruah elohiym merahephet al penai hamayim
> Vayomer elohiym l'or vayhi or

> When God set about to create the heavens and the earth,
> The earth [being] without form and empty,
> Darkness [being] upon the face of the deep,
> And a wind from God hovering over the face of the waters,
> Then God said, "Let there be light" and there was light. (Gen 1:1)[21]

"Hover" is what God does here—or what the "wind from God," the "breath" of God, the *ruah elohim* does—over the face (*panim*) of the waters (*hamayim*), just before God says, "Let there be light." "The bird," Plutzik writes, "hovers in other skies: / World where only these wings exist."

What is he saying? That the "bird" that is missing from the field in which there is a willow—but which no man knows and to which no man goes—hovers in other skies? That the bird in other words is not missing entirely, as if the reference were to some kind of illusion?

Rather, secondly, and perhaps even more importantly, that the bird is not just any bird, but a very specific bird, a bird, or bird-like creature, an avionic agency, we have fashioned from the earliest texts in Jewish tradition, as divine—specifically, that the bird is God-like and does what God (*elohiym*) is perceived to do?

> Beyond the image of the willow
> There is a willow no man knows

---

21 My transliteration and translation, following Rashi.

> Or watches with corruptible eyes.
> ....
> Deep in a field where no man goes
> Nor bird flies
> The willow fronts an empty road.
> ....
> The bird hovers in other skies:
> World where only these wings exist.

"The" bird hovers in "other skies." The hovering we might find in Genesis 1:1, for example, the hovering undertaken by the divine creator (a hovering, or *merahephet*, that the rabbis say, perhaps with a midrash in mind, reminds us of a mother hen tending to her nest) takes place "elsewhere," in other skies. This hovering reflects a nurturing relationship, then, the caring of one individual for another and takes place elsewhere than in the image we have of the willow which in fact fronts an empty road.

Where does it take place? In a "World," the poet says, a universe, a place or locus within which things can occur; but in this case, a place "where only 'these wings' exist." What wings? The wings of the bird no doubt. But also the wings we have been describing in describing the bird, namely, the wings that exist in the sounds of language and especially those of this poem. The willow fronts an empty road. And elsewhere there are birds whose being is constituted by exclusively figurative image-bound language.

The choice would seem to be between a willow that fronts an empty road and wings that exist in their fullness and embodiment only in the saying of them in words and stories told about them, language that exists only as a signal or trigger or protection for an emptiness leading from place to place, locale to locale, and language that echoes embodied construction, means of locomotion specifically—wings—but only in the literary or religious imagination. Language that performs and language that denotes or describes.

What about the "man," the one who neither knows nor goes? Does he exist somewhere between these two alternatives, between language that fronts an empty road and figurative language? "And elsewhere, alone, upon an abyss, / The man is marching down a road." So there is a "where" after all in which "man" or mankind or the human species resides, or at least is active. It is distinctly an "else-where," but a where nonetheless, a place or placeholder, a locus in which things may happen. Moreover, that "man" is doing something. He is engaging in some form of behavior.

But what precisely is that man doing? What characterizes that human behavior? He is "marching," doing what a soldier does—in a military or a political context, for example—following the orders of a commander or a cause. And the place in which he is marching is lodged over or "upon an abyss." Is it over a "deep" or *t'hom*, perhaps, invoking the biblical context Plutzik invoked earlier with the hovering bird? Moreover, the poet tells us, the man there is "alone," solitary. There is no one there with him.

Let us summarize what we have said so far. Thus, in the first half of this poem at least, there are three distinct situations: (1) an "image of the willow"; (2) a willow "beyond" the image of the willow (where there is an empty road that the willow is "fronting"); and (3) a man "marching down a road" sustained over an abyss. An image, a willow, and a man on a road. Is it the same road for which the willow is fronting? It is hard to say for sure. Probably not, since the latter road is described as "empty," while this one is attended by a man, although he is "alone" doing whatever he is doing. Beyond the image of a willow, there is a willow that no man knows, a field where no man goes (and that fronts an empty road), and a road down which a man is marching alone, suspended over an abyss. There are not a lot of characters or activity in the first part of this poem!

"The Importance of Poetry" II

Here again is the second part of the poem. I have numbered the lines for easier reference.

> 1 As the rays of the sun are drawn together
> 2 By a curved glass and rekindled to fire
> 3 So, to the poppies life and death,
> 4 So does desire
> 5 Draw them and bend them and bind them so,
> 6 So the noise of the wings can at last be heard
> 7 And the willow-image do grace to a bird
> 8 And the ghost on the roadway give them word
> 9 Not for forever, only a day.

Thematically, the second section appears to be quite similar to the first. Many of the same references recur. The "wings," images, the "willow," the "road," a "bird"—they are all there. But here in the second stanza, they are all treated now somewhat differently. It is not the existence of the wings that is at issue this time, but their "noise." It is not the willow—whether known or unknown by "man"—that is now at stake, but a hyphenated form—the "willow-image." It is not simply the empty road "fronted" by the willow, but "the roadway," a roadway now graced by a bird and a ghost.

And that difference of treatment reflects a different cosmological setting. For if we return to the sequence in Genesis 1, it is as if we have moved on from creation to a portion of its refinement. It is as if light (created on day one), and subsequently the sun (created on day four)—as a further refinement of that light rather than the introduction of a new element to light, waters, and earth—have been declared into existence; as if the human creature (*ha-adam*) has been created (on day six), subdivided in chapter two into female (*isha*) and male (*ish*), suffused with desire in chapter three, and the wings of the divine bird fluttered (to express frustration?) at the requisite expulsion from the Edenic state at the end of chapter three for their disobedience; and as if language—for example, the language of scripture—now serves as a means of communication (throughout the rest of scripture), and that this is not forever, that it is only temporary or time-limited, and that after creation, and revelation, redemption is sure to follow. These new thematic and cosmological dimensions or stories introduced in the second part of the poem are strategically heightened by what we might call a sudden unexpected but detailed "metricalization" of the language. The metrical differences concern mainly rhyme and rhythm. There is certainly rhyme in the first section of the poem, rhyme and near rhyme, even repetition at points. Thus, in Part One, "knows" and "goes," "eyes," "flies," and "skies." But also "exist" and "abyss," even "road" and "road."

But in the second part, rhyming is suddenly more focused. Fire and desire, or heard, bird, and word. There is repetition. The word "so" is used four times (lines 3, 4, 5, and 6 in the above numbering): So, / So / so, / So. Vowels echo each other as near rhymes (coupled with voiced and unvoiced fricatives): tog-*eth*-er and d-*eath*. Consonants repeat each other—witness the guttural g sounds of grace, ghost, give.

Regarding rhythm, there is similarly some rudimentary structure in the first part. We could read the first section as four beats and most of the lines as tetrameter. But we would have to bend or shape the language somewhat awkwardly to do so. The language in the first part remains closer to natural speech patterns. And we might alternatively read many of the lines equally as three beats or trimeter rather than tetrameter.

But in the second part that structure is considerably more grounded. Speech patterns match more naturally metrical patterns. Eight out of the nine lines are already strictly tetrameter. No alteration is necessary to get them to match. Perhaps more importantly, each line is different from all the other lines. The same configurations (or patterns of stressed and unstressed syllables) appear in nine different configurations. One set moves largely from anapests to iambs, the other from dactyls to trochees.

Here is a chart registering those lines and movements. S equals stressed; u equals unstressed.

[1]A   uuS/ uuS/ uS/ uSu/:   tetrameter: anapest, anapest, iamb, amphibrach
[2]A[1]   uuS/ (u)S/ uuS/ uuS/: tetrameter: anapest, iamb, anapest, anapest
[3]B   Suu/ Su/ Su/ S(u)/:   tetrameter: dactylic, trochee, trochee, trochee (soft)
[4]C   Suu/ S(u)/ -- / -- /:   dimeter: dactylic, trochee (soft)
[5]B[1]   Suu/ Suu/ Su/ S(u)/:   tetrameter: dactylic, dactylic, trochee, trochee (soft)
[6]A[2]   uuS/ uuS/ uuS/ uS: tetrameter: anapest, anapest, anapest. iamb
[7]A[3]   uuS/ uSu/ uS/ uuS: tetrameter: anapest, amphibrach, iamb, anapest
[8]A[4]   uuS/ uuS/ uS/ uS: tetrameter: anapest, anapest, iamb, iamb
[9]B[2]   Suu/ Su,/ Suu/ S(u):   tetrameter: dactylic, trochee, dactylic, trochee (soft)

Of the nine lines, eight are clearly tetrameter, with four syllabic beats per measure. Of the kinds of beats (stressed and unstressed syllables) in the poem, we find that twelve are anapests (uuS), eight are trochees (Su), six are iambs (uS), six are dactylics (Suu), and two are amphibrachs (uSu).

So what? What, we may ask, is the point of all this metrical intensification in the second part of the poem? What is the point of the distinct difference and similarity between the parts? How, if at all, does it change our view of things for us to know this metrical structure? What is the relation of Part Two to Part One?

One answer, I suggest, is sequence. The second part of the poem completes and enacts the subject matter about which Part One is speaking. The "noise of the wings can at last be heard"—for example, in the repetition of the word "so," a bit of which I have tried to echo in the writing of this essay. We watch poetic creation take place before us, on the page, before our "corruptible" eyes, in the very language of the poem, its very sounds as we would hear them. We experience, in a distinctly sensorial fashion, the fluttering of the "S's" in "these wings."

If Part One divides poetic language into poetic image, inaccessible reality, and an isolated traveler or observer, Part Two allows us to recognize that Part One was in fact already performative and not just constative or descriptive. The distinction between the two, between the constative and the performative, the descriptive and the illocutionary, turns out to be illusory. Poetic language is all finally performative. In other words, the constative or descriptive is precisely that region of the performative that thinks it is not performative but constative. This is a move that echoes the way that the *Anschauung* in Kantian thinking imagines it is connected sequentially to the world and to human understanding but in fact turns out to be exclusively a feature of human understanding, namely, the one part that thinks that way with no necessary external affirmatory connection attached to it.

Why is Plutzik writing in this fashion? Is he trying to enact a speech act theory of poetic language—the kind that might be encountered in J. L. Austin's *How to Do Things with Words* or the Yale English Department of the 1960s?[22] Or are there more humanist reasons behind his activity? Is Plutzik suggesting in this way that a full-figured natural image, an inaccessible willow fronting an empty road, a man marching alone down a roadway overpassing an abyss might be more convincing as a representation of reality, more humanly compelling, if enacted or performed before us in the poem itself as "these wings," offered even as a level of understanding comparable to and perhaps in rivalry with that underlying scriptural biblical writing? Is Plutzik enhancing in Part Two what he said in Part One, showing that his creation is like God's creation?

Or is it about something else entirely? Not about the value of poetic language at all over the "plain of nothing" in which it may be exerted or exhorted, or even about practical considerations (personal, biological, biographical, or other), but rather about what might be deemed the relevant historical circumstances, what might be called an "historical oversight" (in the poem "Portrait"), a "miscellaneous screaming that comes from nowhere" (as he says in "The Geese"), a screaming or oversight which leads the poet to conclude "There is no force stronger / (In the sweep of the monomaniac passion, time) / Than the will toward destiny, which is death." And that what we should do, as a consequence, in the interim, is "Value the intermediate splendor of birds"?

Could it be, in other words, that Plutzik's use of poetic language in Part Two as an enactment of the subject matter of Part One is not an adornment, or supplementary accompaniment, of any kind, but in fact a way of talking about what we might name (recalling Blanchot) the "writing of the disaster," writing, that is to say, that is both "about" the disaster (and outside of it, at a distance from it) but also at the same time "from" the disaster (from somewhere within it), and

---

22 J. L. Austin, *How to Do Things with Words*, 2nd ed. (Cambridge, MA: Harvard University Press, 1975).

constituting, thereby, a veritable witness to it or symptom of it? The word *du* in the French title of Blanchot's book from which this phrase comes, *l'écriture du désastre*, means both, as noted at the outset of this essay, the writing or signature or handwriting or notes about the disaster, but also the writing or signature or handwriting or notes from within the disaster, as its symptom or witness or testimony.

Is Plutzik's poetry his witness, his testimony, to the Holocaust? And if so, how so?

We seem to be left with two distinct interpretations. How do we choose between them? A "part one" and a "part two." A part one made up of a "beyond," where no man knows or goes, a place where a bird hovers (but only "these wings" exist), and a road where a solitary man marches over an abyss; and a part two where to the drugs, or "poppies," "life and death," desire draws, bends, and binds so that the wings can be heard, the image seen, and ghosts communicate, if only temporally and temporarily? That might be considered a less than ideal set of options!

One option would seem to render all as one gargantuan cinematic illusion—as the poet ponders in "If Causality Is Impossible Genesis Is Recurrent" (2011):[23]

> ... As in the cinema
> Upon the screen, all motion is illusory.
> So if your mind were keener and could clinch
> More than its flitting beachhead in the Permanent,
> You'd see a twinkling world flashing and dying
> Projected out of a tireless, winking Eye
> Opening and closing in immensity—
> Creating, with its look, beside all else
> Always Adamic passion and innocence,
> The bloodred apple or the yellow flower.[24]

In this context, in this "perfect nothing," even God would be a construction and must be "presupposed":

> The abrupt appearance of a yellow flower
> Out of the perfect nothing, is miraculous.
> The sum of Being, being discontinuous,

---

23 Plutzik 2011, 9.
24 Ibid.

> Must presuppose a God-out-of-the-box
> Who makes a primal garden of each garden.
> There is no change, but only re-creation
> One step ahead.

Take, for example, the phrase "The poppies life and death" in the poem. What if, what we consider to be so important, namely, "life and death," are, from the point of view of the poetry, or of God, no more than, say, "poppies," brief transient vegetation, so to speak, fragrant flowers, drugs, if you like, desire, that make us feel this way or that way, involuntarily, for a brief fleeting period of time. Emulating the natural world, the human world thus deals with flourishes in growth and transience:

> As the rays of the sun are drawn together
> By a curved glass and rekindled to fire
> So, to the poppies life and death,
> So does desire
> Draw them and bend them and bind them so,
> ....
> Not for forever, only a day.

And yet, at the same time, we feel there must be more, that there must be a better choice available, as the title suggests. Is it possible, for example, that poetry for Plutzik is simply a way of asking questions, as Maurice Blanchot suggests literature in general may be a way of asking questions, both as a form of independent observation perhaps and as extension of the subject matter it is registering? Poetry would not be in that case the first agency or phenomenon to pose questions in such a way. Biblical scripture has already been doing so, we may observe, throughout our history in the West, in response to other disasters, a "mountain" of them, in fact, over a "few thousand years of history" (as Plutzik says in "Portrait").

If we ask what Plutzik is finally saying to us in this poem—about poetry, about biblical scripture, or about the Holocaust—certain things are clear. Inherited from the English and European romantics, his subject matter is time—that there is not enough of it left, that it is running out. Time equals death minus now. He experienced it viscerally, within his own body. But more importantly (for him) in relation to the Holocaust, it is the Jews who had no time, for whom time had run out. As such, his discussion constitutes, in effect, I would suggest, a witness to that experience, a tribute to it, a testimony to it.

But we are left, then, with the following question. Where does that leave us in the post-Holocaust era? Is there simply "nothing," in the world around us or outside that world, for us, or for those who experienced the Holocaust in close-up? There is for Plutzik an elemental world to be sure, one that is "one-sided" as Levinas and Kant might say, a brute reality, so to speak, but with no brute way of getting at it; and in that context, God might well be imagined as an illusion of narrative language, the projection of the human realm outside of it. Or, is that conceptualization simply what the victims of the Holocaust felt like, whether Plutzik himself would share that view or not? Is Plutzik's existential approach to poetry, in other words, a tribute to the survivors, a witness to their unique and indelible perspective, or his own independent view? Or is it somehow both?

How precisely, in other words, is Plutzik's poem linked to the Holocaust? The connection is clearly through time. But how does the poem articulate the link to time? The key, I suggest, may be in the poem's final line. The word "time" itself appears, of course, in the poem's title—"the importance of poetry, or the coming forth from eternity into time." But the last line of the poem is also about time. And there, in those final moments, it seems almost arbitrary and interruptive. "As the rays of the sun are drawn together . . . So, to the poppies life and death . . . does desire / Draw them and bend them and bind them." And then, out of the blue, it seems, we get the qualifier: "Not for forever, only a day." Temporally. Temporarily.

How does the last line relate to the subject matter of the poem, namely, to the metricalization of the first part that we identified as characterizing the second part, the gap between figurative language—the willow—and the empty road, the fact that the observations of the first part turn out to be a construction rather than reality?

Could the poem be about what we have called elsewhere "the posthumous," about living "after death," living after the end of time? Is that what the sudden jolt of "not for forever, only a day" is about, the sudden repeated dactyl-trochee combination? The poem abruptly ends with the words "not for forever, only a day." Is that line too an enactment—as the rest of the second stanza is an enactment—of the limited temporality and so the connection we are looking for?

Is it, perhaps, for example, an instance of Kant's noumena, what Kant says we bump up against, death as impossibility? Not death as "the possibility of impossibility," as Martin Heidegger famously says, but as impossibility itself. As an interruption, a discontinuity. The Jews had no time. Does the poem enact that "no time" of the Jews, that stoppage, or radical cessation, that stopping short, so to speak, by in fact stopping short? To say the poem reflects an awareness of the posthumous would mean living with the awareness that it may all suddenly end, which would mean to act, in effect, as if that death, that impossibility, has already occurred, as if death is less a future possibility than a premise. As, for example, in the poem it does.

If we had only stanza one, in other words, the poem might well be regarded as utterly bleak. Then stanza two appears and for a moment, things seem more hopeful. Like the natural world, the human world is also driven. But what drives it is desire. Desire acts like rays of light. It draws, bends and binds in order that (a) the wings can be heard; that (b) the willow may assume the image of a bird: and that (c) the empty figure of a man—the ghost on the road—may enable communication to occur. So far, so good. Things would seem to be on the up and up. But then we learn (d) that all of this occurs only for a brief time, and then: poof! It's all gone. Like the Jews of the Holocaust. Whatever else this "man" in Plutzik's poem lacked, he lacked time.

Does that sudden radical cessation with which the poem concludes, then, give us the relation of stanza two to stanza one in a larger context? Does it explain for us the link of the poem to the traumatic memory of the Holocaust that seems to have been transmitted?

Stanza two may not be about the Bible after all, but about the relation of the human world in which figurative language does occur and which is entirely time-limited. Notice that the last word of the last line—"day"—does not rhyme with any of the earlier line endings. And the rhythm of the final line is equally disparate. The double dactylic structure of "Not for forever" matches the dactylic structure of "so does desire," but then the repeated dactyl "only a day" seems oddly repetitive, a strange add-on, and, as such, calls us back to reality.

So "where," then, we may ask, is stanza two vis-à-vis stanza one? If stanza one constitutes the bleak reality—the willow fronting an empty road, birds elsewhere (namely, in figurative language), a solitary human marching over an abyss—"where" are these "rays" or this "desire" doing whatever they are doing in stanza two? In what "place" does stanza two occur? One answer, of course, is in poetry! The "importance of poetry," the poet says, is its enabling of the "coming forth" from the eternal into the finite temporality of such images. Time occurs not just at the end of the poem, in its final line, but in the first words we read as well, in its title. But in that title—since titles, we commonly assume, tell us the essence or what is essential about what is to follow—these words perhaps give us a clue to what we might expect. "The Importance of Poetry, or the Coming Forth from Eternity into Time."

We thus return to the reading of the English word "or," about which we spoke at the beginning of this essay. Are we dealing with a question of choice versus one of apposition or synonymy, or with one of light itself, which we might understand as a performance of both of those options? Poetry, which is to say, the metricalization of language in rhythm and rhyme, as itself the site (among other sites) where the infinite obtains within the finite (poetry, or, in other words, the infinite within the finite)? Or poetry considered as metricalization itself, as an alternative to that creation from the eternal into the temporal, to that genesis, either in the natural universe or in the biblical scriptural texts (poetry on the one hand, the infinite within the finite on the other)? Or, if we take the word "or" as light, as a pun on the Hebrew word *or*, then perhaps the two previous alternatives are: (1) poetry as light, as doing what religious scripture does, what God does in the natural universe, poetry as creation, or in Plutzik's understanding, as re-creation or (2) poetry as an alternative to what God is said to be doing in the natural universe, or what is said to be happening in religious scripture, poetry as a salvific gesture, perhaps even a messianic one, documenting, bearing witness to a mountainous tradition, a monstrous tradition, of suffering?

In either case, in other words, a response to time: as (1) enactment of the coming forth of the eternal or as (2) alternative to the coming forth of the eternal. Poetry, in both cases, as a response to what the Jews lacked. The introduction of the problematic nature of time, in both the poem's title and final line, as Plutzik's response to the Holocaust. Temporality. Temporarily.

There is little time (or space) left in this essay to consider other poems with the same intensity. But let us gather more information on its questions that might be pursued in other contexts, as an extension of what we have begun to do here with Plutzik's poetry. Let us turn to another poem in which the poet speaks of hovering over an abyss on a "plain of nothing."

"Of Objects Considered as Fortresses in a Baleful Space"

Here is the text of another of Plutzik's poems from *Apples from Shinar*. If we thought the previous poem was bleak, consider the following:

> I and the other intruders,
> The oak and stone my brothers,
> Stare at one another
> Upon the plain of nothing.

> As if to ask what wonder
> By willing or by blunder
>
> Could lead to this encounter
>
> Upon the plain of nothing.
>
> (As if to ask what meeting
> Could overmatch the wonder
> Of opaque hostile Being
> Emergent out of nothing.)
>
> The nothing is a glitter
> Wicked, a frosty water,
> Upon which no words scatter,
> Not hallo, sob or laughter.
>
> Upon their petty islands
> The something and the something,
> Knowing or blank, in silence
> Await the will of nothing.
>
> One, one, and one,
> Mysteries of the moon,
> And the always never-guests,
> None, none.[25]

I have something in common with the natural universe and the elemental universe, the poet appears to say, with the oak and stone respectively: we are both "intruders" and neither of us belong. We stare blankly at each other, as if wondering what could have brought on this encounter, here, on this "plain of nothing." We stare as if to ask "was it some mistake or some miracle with which we had nothing to do, that brought us here, given that there is nothing we share?" We ask ourselves what could have overcome the natural state of "opaque hostile being" that one could have expected to be emergent from "out of nothing."

---

25 Ibid., 35.

The "nothing" is what glitters. It is made of shiny surfaces, shiny objects that simply reflect back at us the light shining on them. And that is in fact what constitutes its wickedness. It is like the surface of chilled water that words penetrate but from which they do not emerge—not unlike light shined on a black hole in space. There is no greeting. No emotional response of any kind—neither joy or unhappiness. Upon the islands of these failed interlocutors—something and something, knowledgeable or without awareness, in silence—we await no external intention. We give no response. We feel no responsibility. We sustain no relationship. I and the two others. One, one, and one. Gravity alone is at work. We are moved like the tide in the sway of the moon. And the "never-guests," those admitted in this interlude without time, those who find themselves briefly in this place (or nonplace) of "not-ever," we are not even "something," not even "one." We are simply none. None.

Where is God in this discussion, we might ask? Where is love? Where is responsibility or infinite obligation for the other individual? Where are the Jews? Where is Jewish history?

"Portrait"

Here is another poem of Plutzik's that addresses some of those questions, if obliquely. "Notice with what careful nonchalance / He tries to be a Jew casually," he writes, "To ignore the monster, the mountain— / A few thousand years of history."

> Of course he personally remembers nothing,
> And the world has forgotten the older objections—
> The new ones not being socially acceptable:
> Hangdogs, hiding in the privies and alleys of the mind.
>
> It is agreed
> That he of all men has gained the right to his soul.
> (Though like the others he no longer believes in one).
> He lives in his own house under his oak.
> He stands by his car, shod in decently-grained leather.
> He is smiling. His hair is peacefully in place.
> His suit is carefully pressed; his cravat harmonious.
>
> Whose father, it is whispered, stubbornly cried old clothes
>   and bric-a-brac,

> He of all men might yet be master of self, of
>   self-possession
> Were it not (how gauche and incredible!) for the one ill-
>   fitting garment—
> The historical oversight in antique wardrobe—
> The shirt, the borrowed shirt,
> The Greek shirt.
>
> Notice how even when at ease he is somehow anxious,
> Like a horse who whiffs smoke somewhere nearby faintly,
> Notice with what nonchalance,
> The magazine in his hand and the casual cigarette to his lips,
> He wears a shirt by Nessus.[26]

His suit is carefully, "carefully pressed" and the poet's account might well be one of self-mastery or "self-possession," except for one significant "historical oversight"—one whiff of smoke somewhere. Is the smoke a reference to the crematoria? For example, at Auschwitz? Is he, the poet, in his distinct modernism, his new-born postwar energy (he, whose father was a bric-a-brac salesman), in fact, wearing the poisoned gift of the Greeks? ("Beware of Greeks bearing gifts," goes the old adage). Is his "borrowed shirt," his "Greek shirt," the clothing of his ancestors' oppressors? "Are his words clothes or the putting off of clothes" he will ask in another poem in which a similar self-criticism is lodged ("On Hearing That My Poems Were Being Studied in a Distant Place").[27]

Horatio

Or consider, finally, *Horatio*.[28] What of the book-length poem that he completed just before the end of his life? The poem is ostensibly a continuation of Shakespeare's *Hamlet*. The stakes there are already very many. Is Plutzik's final book, *Horatio*, about Shakespeare the dramatist? About the discovery of theatricality—of ghosts, of "being nothing"—in Shakespeare's life, in the context of having written plays like *Richard II*, in which Richard speaks, just before his own

---

26 Ibid., 31.
27 Plutzik, 1987, 237.
28 Plutzik 1961.

death, of "nothing"?—"[W]hat'ere I be, / Nor I nor any man that but man is / With nothing shall be pleased, till he be eased / With being nothing."[29]

Or is Plutzik's book about the death of Shakespeare's son, Hamnet, an event that took place shortly before Shakespeare wrote *Hamlet*, at a distance away from London, in Stratford, during what may have been the plague (although some scholars dispute that account)?

Or is Plutzik's book about the "infinite variety" of critical readings of Shakespeare's play that Samuel Johnson announced in the eighteenth century, and which in the nineteenth century on the one hand, both go back to its historical sources in the medieval writer Saxo Grammaticus and develop fanciful new modern interpretations of the play and even of those sources, or, on the other hand, develop substitutive allegorical narrative accounts in contexts of which the plays are then to be read—failed revenge accounts, accounts of failed mourning rituals, accounts of unacknowledged unconscious desires and the like?

Or is Plutzik's book finally about its protagonist, Horatio himself, and his stated failure to fulfill his commitment to his friend, his promise to tell his friend's story?

But maybe we have gotten the setting of the book wrong entirely. Maybe it is not about Hamlet or Shakespeare or Shakespeare criticism or Horatio at all. Could it not also be about the Holocaust and the inability to tell that story, the fact that all the stories about it are wrong or misguided or at best partial? In the poem, Horatio alone remains a witness to the history he feels committed to retelling. Is the idea that the poem is about Horatio itself already the first fiction? Is the poem really, finally, for Plutzik, about the impossibility of talking plausibly about a different subject matter in his own life, namely, about the Holocaust? Or about its indelible effect? Its destructive capacity even upon our future ability to talk about it? And, as such, is this poem the first sketch, so to speak, for the poem that Plutzik says he has been writing his whole life (and for which he left us only the notes), about time and death and the lack of it for the Jews?

Commentary on the Holocaust

What, in other words, if Plutzik's obsession with time and its destructive potential is in fact an obsession with the Holocaust, with the Jews who ironically

---

29 William Shakespeare, *Richard II*, in *The Norton Shakespeare*, ed. Stephen Greenblatt (New York: Norton, 2009), 5.5.38–41.

didn't have enough if it, and whose stories he feels he is not able effectively to tell, a failure that is not so much the result of personal incapacity (and his own eventual succumbing to mortal illness) or even personal absence (since he was not there) but the result of the traumatic nature of the experience, an experience that foreclosed for its victims not only their lives and the experience they went through but the capacity for they themselves or for others to talk about it? To read Plutzik, we need to read not only Shakespeare and the poetic tradition and the natural universe and the critical writing within the scientific and humanistic disciplines—of literature and philosophy—that reflect upon Shakespeare, the poetic tradition, and the natural universe, but also the Holocaust.

What would it mean precisely to do that, to "read the Holocaust?" The Holocaust is not a text but a conglomeration of historical events. To "read" the Holocaust can only mean to read its effect upon its victims—upon those who died, first of all, also the effect upon its witnesses, both those close up and those at a distance, those who were there and those who were not. To read, in short, the language of the ghost (or of ghosts) which always only say, as the ghost of Hamlet's father says to the actor playing the character Hamlet: "remember me."

"Happiness," many writers have observed, is a "brief fleeting interlude in a long drama of pain." Famously attributed to Thomas Hardy and Henry James, among others in literary history, that sentiment certainly applies to the writing of Hyam Plutzik. An anecdote is told that on his deathbed, Henry James was asked a question by Gertrude Stein. "Henry, Henry," she is said to have asked, "what is the answer?" To which James is said to have responded, "Gertrude, Gertrude, what is the question?" And then he died. The constant reference in Plutzik's work to time or temporality and the sense that there is not enough of it indelibly recalls an earlier generation of Jews whose situation was considerably more dire, and yet from which in succeeding generations one continues to struggle unsuccessfully to free oneself, as if that struggle and its repetition of the traumatic events in small ways were itself somehow the point, as if that struggle and its failure were a dislocated way of paying tribute to and doing justice to that haunted and haunting legacy. The vaunted ideas of "survivor's guilt" and of "traumatic transmission" certainly open the door to a discussion about that gesture when it occurs in succeeding generations; but, I would suggest, they may also fail to get at the core of the problem, which entails being locked in a vortex in which all attempts to get out are also inevitably efforts that insure that one stays locked within, which is to say, locked in a black hole or black box from which no light can escape and to which, if we are to trust the cosmologists and cosmogonists who write about it, all matter in the universe will one day be reduced.

In an uncollected poem (1987) about his own poetry "On Hearing That My Poems Were Being Studied in a Distant Place," Plutzik writes the following words that may remind us of Hamlet's remarks to his mother, Gertrude, about his "inky cloak and customary... suits of woe" (1.2.77):

> "Here," they say, "he suffered; here was glad."
> Are words clothes or the putting off of clothes?[30]

The poet expounds his point:

> The scene is as follows: my book is open
> On thirty desks; the teacher expounds my life.
> Outside the window the Pacific roars like a lion.
>
> Beside which my small words rise and fall.
> "In this alliteration a tower crashed."
> Are words clothes or the putting off of clothes?
>
> "Here, in the fisherman casting on the water,
> He saw the end of the dreamer.
> And in that image, death, naked."

"Here, in the fisherman casting on the water," he writes, "He saw the end of the dreamer. / And in that image, death, naked." And in "The Last Fisherman," which was in fact the last poem in the first edition of *Apples from Shinar* in 1959 (since the sequence "The Shepherd" from *Horatio* was added to the 2011 revised edition), Plutzik writes:

> He will set his camp beside a cold lake
> And when the great fish leap to his lure, shout high
> To three crows battling a northern wind.[31]

---

30 Plutzik 1987, 237.
31 Plutzik 2011, 41.

And then he concludes the poem with a reference to time, water, waning, waiting, and wonder.

> Time runs out as the hook lashes the water
> Day after day, and as the days wane
> Wait still for the wonder.

Bibliography

Austin, J. L. *How to Do Things with Words*. 2nd ed. Cambridge, MA: Harvard University Press, 1975.

Berger, John. *Ways of Seeing*. London: Penguin 1972.

Blanchot, Maurice. *The Writing of the Disaster*. Translated by Ann Smock. Lincoln: University of Nebraska Press, 1995 [In French: *l'Écriture du désastre*. Paris: Gallimard, 1980].

Des Pres, Terrence. "Lessons of the Holocaust." *New York Times*, April 27, 1976.

———. *The Survivor: An Anatomy of Life in the Death Camps*. New York: Oxford University Press, 1976.

Hyam Plutzik, Poet. Accessed August 7, 2024. https://www.hyamplutzikpoetry.com/.

Kastan, David Scott. "Afterword" to *Apples from Shinar*, by Hyam Plutzik, 61–73. Middletown, CT: Wesleyan University Press, 2011.

Plutzik, Hyam. *Apples from Shinar: A Book of Poems: Special Edition*. Middletown, CT: Wesleyan University Press, 2011.

———. *Horatio*. New York: Athenium, 1961.

———. *Hyam Plutzik: The Collected Poems*. Forward by Anthony Hecht. Brockport, NY: BOA Editions, Ltd.,1987.

Rosenzweig, Franz. *The Star of Redemption*. Notre Dame, IN: University of Notre Dame Press,1985.

Shakespeare, William. *Hamlet*. In *The Norton Shakespeare*, edited by Stephen Greenblatt. New York: Norton, 2009.

———. *Richard II*. In *The Norton Shakespeare*, edited by Stephen Greenblatt. New York: Norton, 2009.

Waits, Tom. "Time." Track on *Rain Dogs*. RCA Studios, 1985.

CHAPTER 5

Hyam Plutzik's *Horatio* as Cautionary Epic: Writing the Cold War Everyman

Edward Brunner

Published at a moment when American poets generally resisted any invitation to include a role for politics in their work and as a result refused even attempts to produce poetry that might have an influence on political thinking, Hyam Plutzik's *Horatio* stands apart as a distinctly bold intervention, its acceptance in 1961 as one of the finalists for a major literary award a remarkable achievement. Appropriating material from Shakespeare's *Hamlet*, Plutzik shapes a long poem that initially presents itself as no more controversial than one more homage to a major text that has for decades invited adaptation. "*Hamlet*, famously, is a work existing across multiple editions, countless productions, and infinite appropriations," as Lisa Gitelman notes, adding that "[i]t doesn't exist in any one place as much as it exists anywhere and everywhere its interpretations do."[1] What Plutzik brings in his sequel, however, is more than a little distinct and quite unexpected: *Horatio* offers, as it proceeds, an increasingly clear demonstration of a poem that subtly involves its readership in examining the politics of the opening years of the Cold War.

In a virtuoso act of balancing, Plutzik imagines the activities that Horatio would have undertaken in his lifelong pursuit of the charge given to him by

---

Copyright © 2025 by Edward Brunner

1 Lisa Gitelman, *Paper Knowledge: Toward a Media History of Documents* (Durham, NC: Duke University Press, 2014), 6. Adaptations are serious business, especially when it comes to *Hamlet*. Adaption theorist Julie Sanders describes it as the play that has "canonical standing... in any study of Shakespearean reception and appropriation." She devotes an entire chapter to "Shakespearean Appropriations." See her *Adaptation and Appropriation* (New York: Routledge, 2006), 52.

a dying Hamlet to "report me and my cause aright" (*Hamlet*, 5.2.140) at the same time as he appreciates the pressures for such a task in a nation handling the aftermath of war. Plutzik's access to the situation of Horatio consists in his own experience as a war veteran, as well as his growing knowledge of the extent of the Holocaust; together, these called for a sensitivity to the conditions of trauma that would be faced by many. To confront the challenges of an aftermath of war that had evolved into a cold war—with ongoing skirmishes globally, but also repressive measures subtly placed within the nation—Plutzik believed it might be best if those very issues attained a visibility of sorts if they were mapped onto an imaginary Denmark (already mapped by Shakespeare onto Elizabethan times). Figures who could help define that project had been helpfully developed by Shakespeare who placed at the side of the play's heroic prince an everyman who could witness political events up close. Plutzik's own wartime experiences and his knowledge about the conflict more generally, dark as they were, could be fitted into the framework of a literary work that challenged his skill as a poet.

Adaptations are mechanisms for portability; they recontextualize their originals for use in other settings. *Horatio* exemplifies that mobility and hones it to a critical edge. While Horatio's struggles can seem like battles from a remote time, they provide us with observations that import analytic distance into our time. What we take away, moreover, is not a roadmap with a broad overview of a political terrain but rather a way to find parallels we might use. The failures of Horatio—to whom Plutzik generously extends his understanding—let us focus on the need for certain kinds of action to be taken.

Horatio as Appropriation

While *Horatio* is in many respects a pivotal text for Plutzik, at the same time it is a clear extension of the short lyrics that Plutzik had been collecting in his prior two volumes. These poems stand off to the side of the lyric tradition that views poetry as an opening to an interior sensibility. They favor observations that call for engagement in problems that are both philosophical (confronting inescapable dilemmas) and social and political (confronting issues that need solutions). Plutzik's poetics begins by acknowledging a world that is inherently challenging—and which remains in place—but that forms a backdrop for seeking perspectives that administer some relief.

Such relief often takes the form of an opening, an edge, that the poem insinuates and leaves the reader to fulfill. "Jim Desterland" (a work that originally appeared in 1955 in the mass-distributed softcover anthology *New World Writing*) is a strikingly clear example, especially as it is one of a handful of poems in which Plutzik is determined to portray a world anxiously threatened by nuclear catastrophe. For such poetry to proceed, it required a cloak of security. "Only in allusive and tentative ways," historian Paul Boyer writes, did the "Atomic Bomb begin to make its way into post-1945 American literature."[2] The anxiety that surrounds the bomb is inseparable from its reality.

Plutzik's poem opens with its eponymous figure at a mundane moment, fishing alone in a boat off Pondy Point, apparently safely enclosed and surrounded by silence. Suddenly, "The doors swung open, the little doors, / The door, the hatch within the brain." After erupting into a "thunder-noise" the poem shifts: "The doors swung shut" and "all was as it was before." This open door, closing door refrain occurs throughout the poem. "Jim Desterland" reaches back to one of the earliest iterations of what would evolve over centuries into poetry: the riddle. What is the event that opens doors and then closes them just as suddenly? The last stanza of the poem offers an ominous answer.

> There is a roaring in the skies,
> The great globes make, and there is the sound
> Of all the atoms whirling round
> That one can hear if one is wise—
> Wiser than most—if one has heard
> The doors, the little doors, swing wide.[3]

As in other poems of the 1950s, the reference to "atoms" provides both a clue as well as, in its allusiveness, a denial. This terrible threat endures because it is akin to the unmentionable, so that when one hears it despite its silencing, it is at once to become "wiser than most."

Poetry, in Plutzik's hands, offers a chance to be "wiser than most," where what is meant by wisdom is aligned with ethical considerations and thoughtful alternatives. These possibilities are woven throughout Shakespeare's play. Hamlet is,

---

2   Paul Boyer, *By the Bomb's Early Light: American Thought and Culture at the Dawn of the Atomic Age* (Chapel Hill: University of North Carolina, 1994), 247. Two other nuclear poems, "Two Hearts and an Arrow" (dated 1950) and "Hiroshima" (undated), are analyzed with thoughtful care in Cary Nelson, "The Universe Is No Consolation: Hyam Plutzik, Jewish Identity, and the Ethics of Post-Holocaust Reading," *Journal of Jewish Humanities* 15, no. 1 (January 2022): 5–31.

3   Hyam Plutzik, *The Collected Poems*, Foreword Anthony Hecht (Brockport, NY: Boa Editions, 1987), 96. Hereafter, parenthetical citations refer to this edition. "Jim Desterland" was selected by Richard Wilbur for inclusion in a paperback anthology among poems by E. E. Cummings, W. S. Merwin, Barbara Howes, Rolfe Humphries, and others in *New World Writing VIII* (New York: Mentor, 1955), 164–165.

to be sure, a character who can be and has been described in a variety of ways, but as an example who holds interest for Plutzik, he might appear to be a figure standing at an intersection where the warrior culture that is conventionally the bastion of admirable leadership might now be interrogated, possibly even displaced.[4] What interpreters have usually relegated to the background of *Hamlet* could well rivet the attention of Plutzik, magnified by his own experience as a veteran. His service in England with aircraft bombing crews flying in and out of Europe would have shown the violence of warfare as it affected both those in the military and the civilians who became targets, with delivery mechanisms whose efficiency had too many parallels in World War II.[5]

To one familiar with the military, but by no means absorbed in it, the sterling line "Something is rotten in the state of Denmark" (1.4.90) is no offhand remark. The play opens with the country existing in the aftermath of a major battle in which Hamlet's father defeated the king of Norway, both leaving behind a next generation of two sons. It is no accident that the king's ghost is seeking his son while garbed in full battle regalia, appearing in "warlike form / In which the majesty of buried Denmark / Did sometimes march" (1.1.47–49). Horatio witnesses a ghost whom he describes to Hamlet as "Armèd at point exactly, cap-a-pe" with his "beaver up"—technical talk for full armor encasement with an open visor (1.2.200, 230). Indeed, soldiers are standing night watch because preparations in defense of the country are well under way, with "a daily cast of brazen cannon / And foreign mart for instruments of war," as Marcellus says, prompting Horatio to relay a rumor that young Fortinbras of Norway has gathered an army "to recover of us by strong hand ... those foresaid lands / So by his father lost" (1.1.102–104). Soon after, ambassadors Voltemand and Cornelius return from Norway with an assurance that no threat is emergent while simultaneously entreating permission for an army led by Fortinbras to pass through Denmark, an outfit heavily armed for a campaign against Poland (2.2.60–79).

---

4 Some might find this very conflict between physical violence and sensitive communication at the dawn of literature in the opening pages of the *Iliad*. See Emily Katz Anhalt, *Enraged: Why Violent Times Need Ancient Greek Myths* (New Haven, CT: Yale University Press, 2017), esp. 13–29. Others might claim that Shakespeare's version of a revenge play offers an alternative to the round of murders that escalate in Kyd's *Spanish Tragedy* in which the vengeance pursued in the warrior culture leads always to more vengeance. Hamlet's hesitations, for which he is always seeking a justification, threaten to break the cycle of revenge. Hamlet's Wittenberg education complicates every action.

5 Plutzik's "Bomber Base," 37–38 and first collected in *Aspects of Proteus* (New York: Harper & Brothers, 1949). throws sharp light on these elements. See Nelson, "The Universe Is No Consolation," 8–10.

The new king Claudius seems prone to accept this arrangement, especially as it is accompanied by a payment of "three score thousand crowns" (2.2.73).

This militarization forms an emotional background for events in the play. Is the ghost maneuvering not only to replace Claudius with his son as rightful heir but also to lure his son away from his dilettantish preoccupations following his education in intellectually advanced Wittenberg University, an institution that privileges the study of humanism over more practical matters such as warfare? Hamlet's reluctance "to take arms against a sea of troubles" (3.1.59) is a mixed metaphor that pointedly notes how militarism is an unlikely solution to widespread problems—a trenchant insight that is lost in the entanglements of considerations at the highest level in the "To be or not to be" speech. In the same regard, an exchange between Hamlet and a captain in Fortinbras's army who complains they are gathered to "gain a little patch of ground / That hath no profit in it but the name" (4.4.19–20) goes unnoticed. A self-absorbed Hamlet turns this encounter into a lesson about how greatness lies in finding a "quarrel in a straw / When honor's at the stake" (4.4.54–55). But a veteran seasoned by years of warfare might be suspicious of such a large army assembled for so minor a task. What else might be afoot?[6]

Any one of these details, most of which are relayed in a passing phrase or a moment in the background (and many of which would be a candidate for editing-out in a production)[7] could function as triggers for Plutzik's appreciation

---

6   For one thing, there is the status of the ghost of Hamlet's father, never quite resolved, with Hamlet himself wondering if it is an "honest ghost" (1.5.238); he tests his suspicion by subjecting Claudius to *The Murder of Gonzago*. Catholics saw ghosts as spirits temporarily freed from Purgatory to return to seek justice in order to earn points that would mitigate their eternal suffering; Protestants, with no afterlife apparatus such as Purgatory distrusted ghosts as demons bent on disorder. Gillian Bennett discusses this aspect of the play in *Alas, Poor Ghost! Traditions of Belief in Story and Discourse* (Logan, UT: Utah State University Press, 1999), 139–145.

7   William Empson notes: "The insistence on the dangers of civil war, on the mob that Laertes does raise, and that Hamlet could raise but won't, and that Fortinbras at the end takes immediate steps to quiet, is rather heavy in the text though nowadays often cut." See "Hamlet," in *Essays on Shakespeare* (Cambridge: Cambridge University Press, 1986), 87. The essay is a revision of "*Hamlet* When New," *Sewanee Review* 61 (Winter– Spring 1953), which may well have fallen under Plutzik's eyes. F. O. Matthiessen also considers the exchange between Hamlet and the captain in act four to be important, regretting that nineteenth-century productions often omitted it. See "The Responsibilities of the Critic," the 1949 Hopwood Lecture in which Matthiessen sketches a critic who has just the proclivities that Plutzik's work merits ("I do not see how the responsible intellectual in our time can avoid being concerned with politics" [287]). The Hopwood Lecture, a major event at the time, was widely read. Its first publication is in *Michigan Quarterly Review* 55, no. 24 (Summer 1949): 283–292.

of the pressure exerted on Horatio to carry out the memorialization of his dear friend, fallen in the pursuit of a just cause, a situation that for many might be the dominant emotional problem of the early years of the Cold War. Under any circumstances it would be a challenge for the sole survivor of a massacre to take up the charge of Hamlet's dying words, especially when they claim the world will be worsened by his absence and that anyone who fails to see this has withdrawn into the self-satisfaction of "felicity": "absent thee from felicity awhile, / And in this harsh world draw thy breath in pain / To tell my story" [5.2.147–149]). The charge is a necessary one, but almost impossible to fulfill, as anyone knows who has lost companions and friends, brothers and sisters, to unexpected and violent conditions. That kind of storytelling only ends with one's own death. All in all, then, Plutzik's engagement with *Hamlet* sympathetically honors the many in his own generation who carry such a burden. His sequence places them within the lineage of a classic text, and in the process, insists that their grief is not wasted but is central to defining the unsettled and unnerving years that open onto the Cold War. It is just the kind of calling that Plutzik as a poet would recognize and embrace.

Plutzik's decision to proceed with a sequel also falls in line with recent theorizing about the kind of work that adaptations perform, especially when they take shape as a sequel. Marjorie Garber proposes that sequels are almost always never a simple return to a previous work and are likely to be something more: a compulsive revisitation driven by a desire to reconsider events—even to correct, adjust, and reshape them, which always turns out to be impossibly endless. The sequel, in Garber's estimation, can dramatize a need to get right or come to terms with that which would otherwise exist as a gap or an omission. She goes so far as to connect sequel writing with Freud's view in *The Interpretation of Dreams* of the dream as the product of the sleeper's compulsive return to a moment of trauma. The dynamic of the dream springs from its readiness to cope with that which remains unprocessed, left over as unfinished emotional work, to rearrange "the dream-thoughts into an intelligible and apparently consistent scenario that 'makes sense.'"[8]

Of course, there is no clear way to confront the events which begin and end World War II—the Holocaust and Hiroshima; and that lingering incompleteness is definitive. The territory of the dream, however, sanctions a range of maneuvers that Plutzik energizes, some of which Victoria Aarons has located in Holocaust literature, such as a tendency to "defamiliarization" in which an author explicitly

---

8   Marjorie Garber, "Sequels," in *Quotation Marks* (New York: Routledge, 2003), 75. Garber comments further in chapter 9, "McGuffin Shakespeare," 147–175.

repurposes familiar forms. Plutzik reworks fashionable trends in poetry in each of *Horatio*'s three major sections. When proceeding in a sociological frame, in Part One, he places verse drama as a popular form but one whose limitations he wants to expose. In the anthropological emphasis in Part Two he regards myth-making modes as expressions of frustrated longing. And the climactic discoveries in Part Three turn upon psychoanalytic self-consideration that becomes disabling and enabling. More important is the recurrence, at the end of each of the poem's three major parts, of the community voicing, though it is mitigated and blurred, that Aarons associates with an insistence on sustaining an emergent future.[9] Profound loss resists closure because the event is at once deeply personal and massively inconceivable; but it also sets in motion resourceful inventions, and is, though not itself a work that openly joins with Holocaust literature, clearly a text that is keenly aware of the Holocaust.

Horatio as Verse Drama

One of the earliest reviews of *Horatio* is by William Dickey, a poet from the generation after Plutzik's, in the prestigious *Kenyon Review* in 1961. Though only two paragraphs, it offers insightful guideposts designed to intrigue readers. Dickey proposes that "each of the parts of the poem has its own validity" so they can be read on their own though together they deliver a force that is "cumulative." The gathering force is most evident, Dickey writes, when Plutzik develops a relationship between the language of his own writing and "Horatio's task of defending his friend's memory." And here Dickey uses "symbol" as his shorthand for complex poetic language when he explains that "Plutzik's language deepens and becomes richer" as "the uses of symbol increase, and symbols themselves come to be understood in more and more serious ways."[10] Each of the three parts deserves understanding in the service each delivers to "defending [a] friend's

---

9   Victoria Aarons, "A Genre of Rupture: The Literary Language of the Holocaust," in *The Bloomsbury Companion to Holocaust Literature*, ed. Jenni Adams (London: Bloomsbury, 2014), esp. 33, 38.
10 William Dickey, "One Alexandrian, Some Greeks and Others" [review of poems by George Seferis, Edmund Keeley, Hyam Plutzik, Thomas Kinsella and William Goodreau], *Kenyon Review* 23, no. 4 (Autumn 1961): 708. It is a mystery why so supportive a review has gone unnoticed. It is by any standard a robust endorsement of the work as a successful "blend of fact and legend" in poetry that is "assured and independent." The review appears in the same issue as "Next Time I Shall Not Burn the Beehive" (610), a poem in which Plutzik witnesses a somewhat conventional event, the purposeful extinction of a beehive, as complexly

memory." When Plutzik aptly entitles Part One "What a Wounded Name," he softly invokes a memory associated with those fallen in battle.

In this opening segment, wounding is not going to be a remote event in *Horatio*, but one that is repeated almost obsessively. A kind of damage is already evident in the brief Prologue to the work, occurring on the parapet where Shakespeare began his play and where the ghost first appeared. Bernardo and Horatio are deep in a freewheeling dialogue in which Horatio, using Hamlet's words, defines him as a king "of infinite space." Their dialogue is broken when a clock striking midnight sounds a changing of the guard and, abruptly: "the rumble of armored footsteps on the flags / Left unsaid; what would not have been said" (126). This soon, then, the atmosphere in Elsinore has become supercharged with suspicion. A conversation is broken off in mid-sentence, silenced as men in armor advance toward them. Unlike the play *Hamlet* where the guardians called out "Who's there?" in the poem *Horatio* there is no hailing, no address, only a "rumble" that signifies many feet and military muscle. If "Who's there?" inaugurates the action of *Hamlet*—it is a play that questions identities—then a menacing rumble that stifles conversations between friends inaugurates *Horatio* as a poetic sequence that will show friendship under threat.

The four stereotypical figures distributed across the quartet of poems in Part One offer a portrait of facets of the Danish society that overlay and intersect with the moral panics that defined the Cold War in its opening years. The hostler's tabloid version of events recalls the era's anxieties about mass culture, in which authorities prosecuted publishers for disseminating cultural narratives that were crudely packaged for ignorant readers; a modern-day instance of the hostler as a gatekeeper to dwelling spaces away from home might have been a connoisseur of *Classics Illustrated* comics.[11] By casting *the* Doctor Faustus as an academic superstar, Plutzik demonstrates the fear that intellectuals will spawn systems that can be highjacked in the service of political movements (the poem's emphasis on "being" recalls Martin Heidegger's association with the fascism popular in his time).[12] The high-flying chatter of the wealthy into which Horatio is drawn as a diplomatic envoy to France resonates, as it sometimes does

---

seen through the lens of the Holocaust. The poem is erroneously included among the set of "Unpublished Poems" in *The Collected Poems* (250).

11 For a portrait of how the newly fledged comic book industry spread xenophobic narratives that undermined public confidence, see Paul S. Hirsch, *Pulp Empire: The Secret History of Comic Book Imperialism* (Chicago, IL: University of Chicago Press, 2022).

12 The extent to which Heidegger's work was compromised by Nazism has been examined most recently by Richard Wolin, *Heidegger in Ruins: Between Philosophy and Ideology* (New Haven, CT: Yale University Press, 2023).

in novels by Henry James, with a fear that America's self-conscious new role as a partner with Europe will find its innocence tarnished by the sophistication of nations with ancient roots.[13] And the most alarming threat is borne out by Carlus as a prime minister who closely resembles authoritarian spokespersons that derided "schoolmen's logic," while raising fears about a future when "you tempt the populace / With impossible, dangerous dreams" (153).[14]

These four dialogue-based poems present themselves as examples of verse drama, widely admired by writers of poetry in the late 1940s and 1950s as a vehicle for transforming poetry into a popular art. T. S. Eliot had plays in verse on Broadway in 1949 and again in 1954, and when Monroe Spears reviewed Christopher Fry's plays for *Poetry* in 1951, he opened with the blanket statement: "Verse drama seems now the one hope of regaining any large audience for poetry."[15] Archibald MacLeish hailed verse drama as offering the promise of a

> true theatre for poets; a theatre in which the imaginative ear, not the pedantic eye, would provide the audience; a theatre in which cadence would be heard and image would be confronted and the inwardness of human action might appear: a theatre also in which poetry could regain what it cannot long exist without—a public.[16]

In Plutzik's hands, however, the very idea of a type of poetry that delivered a simplified product to the public was useful for only one thing: it was available to expose a process in which a product was being simplified. Another look at these confrontations shows that Plutzik has staged one encounter after another

---

13 James's novels in an international setting, when read during the Cold War, wonder how America might be an equal to Europe without losing its openness (and even innocence) in the midst of networks of complicity. Those components, so inextricably entangled in the figure of Daisy Miller, for example, can be fatal in the wrong context. A more general concern for the relation between America and Europe in the Cold War years is examined in Brett Gary, *The Nervous Liberals: Propaganda Anxieties from World War I to the Cold War* (New York: Columbia University Press, 1999).

14 One likely contemporary model for Carlus is Joseph McCarthy, on display throughout Thomas Doherty, *Cold War, Cool Medium: Television, McCarthyism and American Culture* (New York: Columbia University Press, 2003).

15 Monroe K. Spears, "Christopher Fry and the Redemption of Joy," *Poetry* 78, no. 1 (April 1951), 28–32.

16 Archibald MacLeish, Foreword to *This Music Crept by Me Upon the Waters* (Cambridge, MA: Harvard University Press, 1953), n.p.

that back away from engagement. In each one, Plutzik summons a nemesis for Horatio who can be revealed as ignorant or self-satisfied or disengaged or menacing; they participate in faux conflicts. It is true that as Plutzik traces Horatio's "failures" to defend Hamlet's honor he ushers us on a tour that reaches across all levels in society. At the same time, we cannot help but wonder at the rigidity of Horatio, for as each effort to memorialize Hamlet "fails," the memory of Hamlet can only grow, in Horatio's view, more perfect, more unassailable, more supernal.

Plutzik understands that verse drama is effective but fatally limited: it resembles the political cartoon that was a feature of newspaper editorial pages, using caricature to spot an excess that exposes a policy mistake without investigating it. It strands Horatio in a situation that is essentially static. It is possible, though, that its ultimate end is at least to blunt the violence of the warrior culture by displacing it with even-handed verbal exchanges. This is a glimpse of a positive turn that occurs at the end of the fourth poem, in which Carlus as prime minister, after numerous warning threats to Horatio, insists he must break off their talk (actually, it is monologue in which he lectures Horatio), claiming an urgent appointment with the king. However, as Horatio exits the castle, the king spots him, calls him to his side, and the two walk together in conversation for an hour, after which they embrace. The moment is fleeting but positive: it underscores exchanges between powerful figures that may curtail Carlus's malign influence, and above all it supplants conflict with conversation. Plutzik recognizes persistence as a fragile value that is superior to its alternatives.

Horatio as Underground Myth

Although Dickey's review notes that the language in *Horatio* enlarges from each multi-poem section to the next, that observation is not shrill enough to prepare for the poems in "The Shepherd," Part Two, works that in multiple ways depart from the neatly curtailed exchanges in the caricatures of Part One. The three poems in Part Two set us before a seaside campfire in the wilderness where an aged Horatio in masquerade (accompanied by his bailiff) is astonished by a violently distorted version of the *Hamlet* story. It is a narrative that Norman Friedman has described as "full of folk-tale exaggerations . . . a horrible and distorted thing"[17]—an observation that underscores that all the exchanges in

---

17   Norman Friedman, "The Wesleyan Poets, IV: The In-Between Poets," *Chicago Review* 19, no. 3 (June 1967), 84. In his review, Friedman is commenting on "The Shepherds" as collected

Part one took place in cloistered settings. In the remote country, though, Hamlet has become "Ambleth," as Plutzik takes scraps from predecessor texts that Kyd and Shakespeare might well have drawn upon for their versions, appropriating the names of the players (such as "Feng" for Claudius) much as they appear in a probable source for Shakespeare, the fifth volume of Belleforest's *Histoires Tragiques* (1576), based on information in Saxo Grammaticus's twelfth-century manuscript *Historia Danica*.[18] Plutzik stirs these primitive forerunners into a stew of conspiracy theories and tales of corruption at the highest level delivered for uneducated laborers on the late shift to consume with delight to help pass the long, cold night. Horatio's horrified reaction to the devaluing of Hamlet's reputation thus confirms how completely the world can destroy the beloved, in a setting that renders it nearly impossible to restore any part of this apparently ever-evolving myth to pertinence. "The Shepherd," then, fails, as it were, to shepherd—fails to guard and pass along accurate information to another generation. Yet the poetry in these three poems that make up Part Two, to the extent that they afford a glimpse of something like a view that an underclass or a laboring class might endorse as reflecting a real-world situation, may well be counted among this work's most brilliant turn—though it too is sharply engaged with the issues of its time, including a new attentiveness to anthropological understandings of myth and religion.

In an era when the New Criticism was in its ascendancy, the only serious counterweight to the ahistorical linguistic practice of the New Critics was myth criticism. The case for myth as an omnipresent underpinning for creative endeavors of all kind—especially poetry—had been made with enormous élan by Robert Graves in *The White Goddess* (1948), whose subtitle is *A Historical Grammar of Poetic Myth*, a study which has been described as "an often impenetrable wilderness of cryptology, obscure learning, and apparently *non sequitur* reasoning brought to bear on a thesis that has its roots partly in historic fact, partly in generally accepted anthropological hypotheses, and partly in pure poetic intuition."[19] Plutzik indirectly acknowledges Graves in one of the poems

---

in *Apples from Shinar* as part of a five-part review of all the Wesleyan University Press poets since the series began under Richard Wilbur's guidance in 1959. Plutzik is called "a poet of genuine vision" who "encompasses subjects, ideas, and attitudes of the first importance" (79), and by placing him in a fourth tier (out of five), Friedman elevates him into a superior group.

18 Edward Hubler, "A Note on the Sources of 'Hamlet,'" in William Shakespeare, *The Tragedy of Hamlet, Prince of Denmark (1600–1601?)* (New York: Signet, 1963), 183.

19 Douglas Day, *Swifter Than Reason: The Poetry and Criticism of Robert Graves* (Chapel Hill: University of North Carolina Press, 1963), 157.

from *Apples from Shinar* "The Priest Ekranath," when the speaker notes that the mountain barbarians worship temple harlots whom they regard as extensions of "the White One or the White Lady" (102). Plutzik's own suspicion of the mythic dominates an undated, unpublished poem, "Strange Diners at the Café Parnassus" which compares "mythmakers / Eating their own marrow" to the cannibalistic Ugolino of Dante's *Inferno*, Canto 33. Rather than confronting what the poem calls "the war-brought sorrow," Plutzik proposes that the mythmakers instead are turning upon themselves: "The fever out of hunger / Has brought the private illusion, / The hallucination, / And the convulsion, / The sly aside / And the crude explosion" (257–58).

An allegiance to "the mythic" was not uncontroversial. For Philip Wheelwright, it became a crucial strategy for poets who hoped to tap into energies that the New Critical emphasis on the linguistic might dissipate. Indeed, the "aesthetic surface" of a work was important, Wheelwright writes, only as it offers a promising entrée to "mythic depths."[20] But others, like Leslie Fiedler, understood that identifying exactly what constituted "the mythic" was a problem that some poets regarded as compelling by itself. Writing in 1952, Fiedler identified some poets who "can ironically manipulate the shreds and patches of out-lived mythologies, fragments shored against our ruins." These figures (he cites Eliot's *The Waste Land* in his remark, but he also turns to Joyce, Pound, and Thomas Mann) were "writing finally not archetypal poetry, but poetry *about* archetypes, in which plot (anciently, *mythos* itself) founders under the burden of overt explication."[21] But even this sophisticated description of myth in poetry fails to capture Plutzik's procedure in this section of *Horatio* which takes its defamiliarization a further step. Far from foundering under a burden, Plutzik offers an explicatory framework in which the tales he proposes that disarm Horatio reveal the active and ingenious struggles of those who live far from the centers of power where much, if not everything, depends on skills of deception and animal cunning. As a result, the narratives they produce, as fragments shored against what the shepherds perceive as their ruins, are ultimately revealing: they sharply register moments in which, if only in a dreamy and fantastic way, the very powerful are subverted, thwarted, or even injured. Even as these tales fantastically garble the events of *Hamlet* as we know them, and certainly provide a sequel

---

20 Philip Wheelwright, "Aesthetic Surface and Mythic Depth," *Sewanee Review* 65, no. 2 (April–June 1957): 279–293.
21 Leslie Fiedler, "Archetype and Signature: A Study of the Relationship between Biography and Poetry," *Sewanee Review* 60, no. 2 (April–June 1962): 253–273.

to them that is nothing short of monstrous, these distortions are carefully, even lovingly, explored by Plutzik.

The riddle, for example, abounds in Graves's study, holding his attention right from his book's beginning. In the bardic tradition, riddles breed new viewpoints, shifts of focus; they alter perceptions when their solution crystallizes a set of seemingly unrelated terms. What is "The strong creature from before the Flood / Without flesh, without bone, / Without vein, without blood, / Without head, without feet...," and so on? All is resolved, Graves shows, in the answer "The Wind."[22] Graves elicits riddles that have survived over centuries, admiring them for the information they carry, and Chapter 5 in *The White Goddess*, "Gwion's Riddle," explores a lengthy riddling poem whose unconventional wordings sustain various kinds of knowledge. In a sharp and provocative contrast, in a poem from this section entitled "The Book of Metamorphoses," Plutzik shows how the riddle can be used not to rouse curiosity but to quell it, to provide an aura of assurance and stability, as he demonstrates with the shepherds parading a set of riddles in which every "solution" simply identifies the ur-Hamlet figure Ambleth (174–175). The give-and-take of the call and response of a riddle remains, but the delivery of new knowledge at the end is stymied.

Such stasis amidst a display of activity that is almost frantic is not so much a critique of the shepherds as ignorant it is a portrait that reflects the unforgiving environment of the poverty they struggle to endure. The shepherd's simplified and violent version of the Ambleth tale quickly shifts from palace intrigue, about which they know little, to the forest and the sea which is their bailiwick. In their telling, human figures, for example, metamorphose into various animals, with Ambleth becoming a peer of five creatures each of whom has access to a body part of the murdered king, all of which Ambleth must acquire and reassemble. The quest has now become degrading, with the human falling away and the animal emergent. In the final poem, "The Harrowing of the House of Eyes," Ambleth seeks a degree of comfort in a setting as remote as the constellations in the sky. This final variant on the tale of Ambleth suggests an imperfect understanding of the tenets of a Christianity whose symbols are still in the process of evolving. At the same time, the endless eyes that seem always to be watching may be an impression familiar to the poor—a dismissive gaze that serves to weigh judgment. Here are the rules of Christianity, still new at this point, that place an archangel on display who oversees the guards that eventually eject Ambleth, now condemned to wander forever with only animals for companions.

---

22 Day, *Swifter Than Reason*, 17.

These new rules, Plutzik suggests by depicting them in a series of distorted actions, are no better than whatever the shepherds once followed, at least when it comes to fulfilling their expectations. Under Plutzik's sharply historicizing angle of vision, the mythic becomes not just a fragmentary tracing of a lost beloved, or even a search for a value that is half-forgotten, but a record of a current struggle taking place within a precarious culture as ill-informed laborers invent tales to comprehend their place as survivors in a hostile and unsettling universe, where events larger than life threaten their own sense of existence.

Only in the closing lines of Part Two is Horatio openly brought into the poem, where he is entirely unmoored by his brush with these distorting tales. There, Plutzik reveals a Horatio ill-equipped to comprehend what humanity may exist in the lives of the poor. He is horrified by the round-the-fire conversation that generates laughter in response to his well-meaning attempt to explain that he is the original of the so-called "Honorio" who figured in the tales just told. This concluding scene can be read as a mockery of mob mentality, exposing the underclass as incapable of understanding the subtle concepts that the dominant class so easily follows. After all, the shepherds quickly turn to chattering among themselves about small details, falling into low humor and easy jokes. But Plutzik arranges even these final passages so that we can appreciate the skepticism with which the shepherds greet Horatio's insistence that he was part of their story. They respond not with menace or rage but with undisguised hilarity, as if the old man had simply failed to appreciate that they had all been simply listening to stories together, sharing in the pleasure of "answering" riddles by returning to the same solution each time. And like warriors on a bivouac or enlisted men in the field, they turn away from large explanations and joke among themselves, carrying inventiveness along on a smaller scale, in a daily frame.

Plutzik may be remembering his own days among the all-male society that wartime breeds, but he is also writing generously here, as he records just what it takes to get through a long night. If it is a small moment, it also becomes surprisingly large, and it shows a quantum leap in perspective: the outsiders, the working poor, the forgotten others have not been included in the overall poem up until this section. Horatio's pathways have never ventured far from the well-traveled road. For Plutzik, who may have been placed among those outsiders at more than one point in his life, whether as a reporter in New York or a military man in England, it is time to draw attention to exclusion, especially since oral epics in this form, with their enticing riddles, and their indulgence in fantasy, as well as their questioning of the judgments of the privileged, may need to maintain contact with poetry's own origins at a time when the poet is a threatened species. At the same time, the bonds that exist among those living in precarity darkly suggest that warrior culture has a deep foundation that guarantees its persistence.

Horatio as Workbook

To Horatio's credit, the "horrible and distorted thing" that he takes as a wreck, as a misunderstanding, as an undoing of his life's work has become, as it were, his own ghost. It haunts him so sufficiently that, two years after, he sequesters himself at the remote corner of his holdings in a retreat from where he can contemplate failure on such a cataclysmic scale. The title for Part Three "At the Castle of Forstness" might describe a retreat under siege, but the five monologues that emerge at this late point in Horatio's life (he is seventy-six) provide Plutzik with a chance to change his own poetic approach once again, this time within a contemporary format that is powerful enough to deliver a series of remarkable insights, including a distinctly somber conclusion that is, in its context, one of Plutzik's most lyrical performances. This is perhaps the most richly speculative writing of Plutzik's career, and it is a vehicle for Horatio to confront his shortcomings. That process expands this segment of the work: the sweep of Horatio's deliberation now embraces not just veterans but all who are reacting to the burden of massive loss, so that an inkling of the long poem on the Holocaust that Plutzik did not live to begin may have its origin in these ruminations. If there is an underlying lesson in Part Three it is that one should not immortalize those who have fallen but rather choose to live a life in their stead; to be open to what is to come, rather than gripped by what has happened. We are poised to consider now that it is not the details of Hamlet's story that Hamlet was charging Horatio to deliver "a-right"—the charge was to live his own life without forgetting Hamlet.

In the quiet and silence of Forstness, Horatio opens himself to a series of self-interrogations whose rigor takes its cue from the confessional verse pioneered by Robert Lowell's 1959 collection *Life Studies,* much of which had appeared in prestigious journals such as *Partisan Review* in the mid-1950s. Lowell's confessional verse had psychotherapeutic overtones as it revisited events from a personal past with a clarifying intent. For Lowell, this poetry celebrated the struggle to escape delusional memories, to proceed in a clear-headed direction even if it meant discarding cherished notions. Honing Lowell's precedent, Plutzik's confessional verse uses Horatio's voice as a channel for zigzagging in and around moments of the past.

A breakthrough comes early and unexpectedly when Horatio realizes that Hamlet's charge to him was not a self-serving request but a maneuver to block Horatio from following him in death. Now Horatio sees there was

> An expression
> On that dying face I could not understand,
> So hid away, but know now that it spoke
> No more of Hamlet but of Horatio:
> ....
> Hoping indeed the current of the world would seize me
> And give me its own strongest reasons for breath;
> Meaning "Live!" when saying "Live for me!";
> Meaning "Horatio live and be yourself!" (192)

This echoes the message that Henry James's Lambert Strether delivers in *The Ambassadors*, an injunction that also arrives belatedly.[23] Expanding the scope of Hamlet's words by deepening their significance bonds Horatio to Hamlet in a different way, not as an ideal to incorporate within but as a companion to bear within—not a guiding beacon but a memorable confidante: "I was his friend the way I could be a friend" (193). Plutzik presents a Horatio who gradually spins one speculation after another, and as he rehearses his considerations, he now begins to sift through an aftermath landscape where there is no certainty to seek. "Once I thought truth had a single face" (194), Horatio realizes in the first of these monologues. This acceptance that there is no single-faced truth concerns Horatio, who wonders if he is wandering close to what he calls "the pit of Carlus"; his belief is that the "question of belief is relevant" (197). But in a second monologue Horatio introduces a Hamlet who has multiple selves—"thing of earth, a lover of milkmaids," "the abstract man . . . the man beyond himself," "a damnable melodramatist / Who loved players, [and] would rather act than do." As these coalesce before him, he begins to move in conversation with them. When he considers that Hamlet as friend may have been more interested in acting out roles than accomplishing tasks, Horatio can speak back to him: "Pardon me, Hamlet!" The complex person who is emerging anew, then, is not simply

---

23 "Live all you can; it's a mistake not to. It doesn't so much matter what you do in particular, so long as you have your life. If you haven't had that what *have* you had? (Book Five, Chapter 2). F. O. Matthiessen elevates this sentiment into "the quintessential expression of a dominant theme that runs through James' work," in his *Henry James: The Major Phase* (New York: Oxford University Press, 1944), 25.

Hamlet but also Horatio, who has come now to spot the difference between a personality with multiple interests such as Hamlet has and a Carlus who is single-minded and evasive: "A silent fellow, truly, and most admirable / At striking little nooses in the grass" (197).

These forays are some of Horatio's earliest preparations for confronting the negative images spawned by the shepherds, and he begins to view them with distance: "A thing that flew / From the dark tongue the old man has changed me" (19). When he begins to acknowledge his own bad dreams ("Once in a nightmare I saw / The lark lying dead on the heavenly stairs" [198]), he can recall the nightmare of a "battle that flickers up over the world . . . / Which touches the farthest atom with its ripples" (200). (Plutzik cannot resist being proleptic here.) But Horatio now faces ruminations that could be deeply unnerving by summoning the tangible presence of a younger Hamlet—"You appear again, Hamlet"—and the lines of the poem launch into a garrulous idiom, in a voice we have not previously heard:

> Tell me, what do you think
> Of our mutual enemy, our friend Old Croaker?
> Does he not have the gift of tongues? Tomorrow
> Shall I not send him off to Wittenberg
> To occupy the chair of philosophy
> (Where since old Faustus sold his soul to Satan
> The faculty has been more or less
> Than a row of empty noddles)? Done! (200–201)

This is the way Horatio talked with Hamlet. This goofing-around voice endows Horatio with a youthful mobility so that when his next digression sends him wandering into dark corners that unfurl a "philosophy of dust . . . by which King Alexander / (So I have heard) might make an excellent bunghole" (201), the recurrence of Hamlet's voice has a saving effect. The reference is Hamlet's riff on Alexander and bungholes, for which Horatio served as a delighted straight man, with Hamlet "innocently" redeeming the anal references at the last minute (5.1.204–219 for the entire anecdote). The memory sends Horatio spiraling away from mortality to discern a quality in Hamlet that sustained playful speculation, and the memory allows Horatio to return and complete Hamlet's riff by evoking Alexander's teacher—that is, Aristotle: "There was in him / A principle spurning this wretched Was / For Could-Be, Might-Be, which Alexander's teacher / Throned in a neighboring bunghole, still holds higher" (201–202).

In the fourth monologue, Horatio is no longer haunted by the shepherds' narratives but has become one who is able to understand how a bleak and disorderly regime has now penetrated everyday life. In passages that recall Orwellian inversions in which opposites exchange places, in which humans perform as animals, and mirrors promulgate images that spill into the streets (204–206), the tirade stands as a barely disguised portrayal of a mass culture driven by advertising slogans that have invaded the political realm. The vividly surreal imagery embodies what Plutzik had stated as a conclusion to his 1961 afterword "Creativity and Poetry" in which "every day colossal forces make our language muddier and muddier":

> The air is full of the jargon of the mass-media and the gobbledygook of organizational life. Hucksters using the very techniques of poetry for their own ends, din our ears with carefully calculated praises of toothpaste, dandruff removers, headache pills and motor cars. Is it any wonder that many people, with a cautious realization at the back of their heads, have come to distrust all purveyors of the word—poets included—figuring them not as dedicated spirits, but as men who will say anything for gain. (304)

What Plutzik presents as analytic observations in an essay, Horatio experiences as visceral outrage. Horatio's ability to confront so deranged a world is possible because he understands that Hamlet had been, in effect, practicing a politics of the impolitic that was itself designed to confront such a world: an impolitics errantly driven by an inquisitory spirit that was fearless in its readiness to zigzag as called for—but never reaching down to Horatio's own politics of the politic, a temperamental distinction that allied Horatio with "the red-faced ostler, Carlus and the rest" (207).

If Horatio is driven, in his final monologue, to arrive at a highly self-critical image in which he accepts his failure to redeem Hamlet's memory, Plutzik also opens the doors in Horatio's memory that reveal what he did accomplish. He had twice mentioned earlier in these monologues that he has served ten kings, but at this moment, when he rehearses a list of the ten it is a startling taxonomy of the catastrophic. It begins with a not surprising takeover and the start of a legitimate succession (the two Fortinbras family members) only to wobble, tip, collapse, and explode: "The first and second Fortinbras, then John / Who died in Palestine; Petrus the Ruddy; / Jacob who ruled a year and the second Jacob / Who shocked our bishops by wishing his body buried / In a hogshead of red wine instead of a coffin / And Wulfstan who loved to run a race and fell / Running into the Swedish cannon" (209). The durability of a nation to survive this clownish parade of leaders is most likely the handiwork of Horatio, who even now is modest in acknowledging that Hamlet did receive mercy (burial in an official plot) "but awaits the trickier payment: / Justice from men" (210). He summarizes his own contribution as the work of "one who was rather venerable than worthy, / Not only to work good, but to speak and indite / With authority" (210). At the same time, he concludes that these accomplishments are undermined by "slow obliteration / Which time works," erasing more and more, "Leaving a beam as memorial, a mound / The hint of a little hill, then nothing, nothing, / And all is borne over by the cruel river" (210).

Plutzik has not so elaborately guided Horatio through a tangled set of memories, reviving powerful moments that had perhaps been willfully suppressed, to construct a portrait so clearly defining Horatio only to abandon him. Exhausted, and expecting nothing but a moment of relief, anticipating emptiness, Plutzik now walks Horatio into the next stage of his life in which time is anything but a "cruel river." Time, as it is manifest in the forthcoming coda is always performing a looping-back, capturing and rearranging moments to form unanticipated depths, as the final lines affirm.

A Coda, a Breakthrough, and Solace

A conversation arises at the close of all three parts of *Horatio*, and each part ends with an endorsement of communal discourse, and even though all three are by no means dramatic or extravagant, the emergence of continuity is a welcome alternative to physical combat. Plutzik is not given to ending with a dramatic finale. Part One concludes with Horatio chatting with the king in his garden; Part Two ends with shepherds dropping into a slapdash conversation; and so the last lines in Part Three, to the extent they restore a sense of community, do not proceed with demonstrative brio. Nonetheless, intricate overtones resonate through the moment when Horatio, his self-analysis over, makes his way to the parapet of his castle for some cool night air. Though Horatio may climb the stairs to the parapet having convinced himself, as Plutzik shows, that he is at the end of his days, that his time is limited and that time, in any case, is a "cruel river" that only moves in one direction as it steadily bears away all that is most valued, Horatio now finds himself showered with impressions and surrounded by discoveries, all of which elegantly if subtly demonstrate that time may always be available for looping back. The scenario begins with an impression that one moment resembles a particular earlier moment—and then another, and still another, with each one brought close by Horatio's use of deictic pointers such as "there," "that," and "here" which bring a scene directly before us:

> —Bernardo?
> You stand *there* while we wait a midnight bell—
> And *there* when we speak of the dreadful deeds of a day!
> And Hamlet, you are *that* shadow when your father's wraith
> Appears at the stairhead *there*, and you both withdraw
> *Here* to the sheer wall to consult in secret . . . [Emphasis mine, ellipses in original]

Folded together are three earlier moments, all in Elsinore: the midnight bell where Bernardo and Horatio enter in act one, scene one in *Hamlet*, the talk with Bernardo interrupted on the evening after Hamlet's death in the prologue to *Horatio* (125–126), and the meeting in act one, scene three in *Hamlet* as Hamlet follows his father's ghost. Notably, the last event that brings together one who is living and one who is not living occurs not "there," not over and away, but "here," right where Horatio now stands.

The two questions that emerge are each decidedly unanswerable—the very kind of questions most necessary to ask: "Who can explain / From what fugitive grace the heart will take its ease? / Or find the shy spring from which joy flows?" They effortlessly slip free of the adamant thinking that has heretofore gripped Horatio in his reflective retreat. And now, hearing the song of "the bird," that too becomes a moment of looping back.[24] By realizing the songbird's "first note carried a mid-note's richness" Horatio turns restorative, capturing the bird's addition to a darkness that was "already sweetened by your voice." With ears "at first closed to your mercy" he now pursues such notes by realizing what he had not heard earlier, a re-assemblage parallel to "a violet poised on the knowledge of its own ascension," associating knowledge with self-production. He now admires the bird's own self-production, which began by singing in the shadows of the

---

24 Plutzik is intent on gathering here as many echoes of earlier moments that he can. The anonymous bird singing out of schedule (it has just struck midnight) recalls the folk beliefs Marcellus lists in act 1, scene 1, lifting the moment back into time: when the "season comes / Wherein our savior's birth is celebrated, / The bird of dawning singeth all night long / And then, they say, no spirit dare stir abroad, / The nights are wholesome, then no planets strike, / No fairy tales, nor witch hath power to charm / So hallowed and so gracious is that time" (1.1.158–164).

stairs, then "fluttered over the stage / To a new perch in the dark" from where it sang as it lofted itself to the "moon's edge," flying higher as if in greeting to the stag who has slowly been occupying "the moonlight field," only to survey it "like a king" and withdraw. That stag, viewed militaristically as "broad-antlered," has become ancillary, banished to a shadow, in no way as playfully fulfilling as the song-bird who holds Horatio's attention completely in the last words of the poem that now loop back all the way even to the moment before Horatio began his climb to the parapet: "Bird, you brushed my sleeve as I came to the stair" (211). This address, a conversation of sorts, constructs an imaginary community that "depends on the persistence of memory," which is, Aarons powerfully reminds us, "a persistence fulfilled by testimony in the face of loss."[25]

The flurry of activity in the last lines of *Horatio* carries no slogan or motto as a takeaway—nothing could be further from Plutzik's poetics—but it underscores his consideration at work throughout. It is worth repeating what may be the probable lesson: not to immortalize the fallen but to live in their stead, not turning them into stone statues but breaking against time to recall them, to continue their conversations, to imagine their presence. *Horatio* itself is multilayered, revising one set of poems after another, and inviting other adjustments of all sorts, including alternate approaches to *Hamlet*. Even more important is that his consideration of Hamlet and his impolitic politics may have helped focus Plutzik on his last project, the exorbitant and extraordinary long poem on what he called "the most immense subject for a poem in our time" that begins not with just one ghost but six million, that would have led him, Hamlet-like, into unpredictable confrontations by following where his inquisitive spirit would take him. As Cary Nelson has shown, such inquiries can lead to finds that others might have turned away from crossing lines to embody a Jewish identity, and peering into corners that call out for clarity no matter what. Pondering how to launch an "impossible challenge" as he examines the opening of the poem at the beginning of his essay, Nelson locates the very scholars who would sustain such a work, and in the final pages he takes words from the proposal that conceives how the fifth section of the poem would end, describing it in such detail that "the transformative poem" of Plutzik's career comes before us as "uniquely burdened."[26] A politics of the impolitic leads, Emily Apter writes, into a "disentrenchment" that breaks "patterns of routine dealing, power-brokering, and lobbying that limit imagination

---

25 Aarons, "A Genre of Rupture," 38.
26 Nelson, "The Universe Is No Consolation," 5–7, 27–29.

and political experiment."[27] Plutzik's *Horatio* ultimately affirms a Hamlet-like impolitics that challenges entrenched positions by pursuing unexpected lines of thought that must lead where they may.

Bibliography

Aarons, Victoria. "A Genre of Rupture: The Literary Language of the Holocaust." In *The Bloomsbury Companion to Holocaust Literature*, edited by Jenni Adams, 27–46. London: Bloomsbury, 2014.

Anhalt, Emily Katz. *Enraged: Why Violent Times Need Ancient Greek Myths*. New Haven, CT: Yale University Press, 2017.

Apter, Emily. *Unexceptional Politics: On Obstruction, Impasse, and the Impolitic*. London: Verso, 2018.

Bennett, Gillian. *Alas, Poor Ghost! Traditions of Belief in Story and Discourse*. Logan, UT: Utah State University Press, 1999.

Boyer, Paul. *By the Bomb's Early Light: American Thought and Culture at the Dawn of the Atomic Age*. Chapel Hill: University of North Carolina Press, 1994.

Day, Douglas. *Swifter Than Reason: The Poetry and Criticism of Robert Graves*. Chapel Hill: University Press of North Carolina, 1963.

Dickey, William. "One Alexandrian, Some Greeks and Others." Review of *Horatio*, by Hyman Plutzik. *Kenyon Review* 23, no. 4 (1961): 702–709.

Doherty, Thomas. *Cold War, Cool Medium: Television, McCarthyism and American Culture*. New York: Columbia University Press, 2003.

Empson, William. "Hamlet." In *Essays on Shakespeare*. Cambridge: Cambridge University Press, 1986.

———. "*Hamlet* When New." *Sewanee Review* 61, no. 1 (1953): 15–42.

Fiedler, Leslie. "Archetype and Signature: A Study of the Relationship between Biography and Poetry." *Sewanee Review* 60, no. 2 (1962): 253–273.

Friedman, Norman. "The Wesleyan Poets, IV: The In-Between Poets." Review of *Apples from Shinar*, by Hyam Plutzik. *Chicago Review* 19, no. 3 (1967), 64–90.

Garber, Marjorie. *Quotation Marks*. New York: Routledge, 2003.

Gary, Brett. *The Nervous Liberals: Propaganda Anxieties from World War I to the Cold War*. New York: Columbia University Press, 1999,

Gitelman, Lisa. *Paper Knowledge: Toward a Media History of Documents*. Durham, NC: Duke University Press, 2014.

Hirsch, Paul S. *Pulp Empire: The Secret History of Comic Book Imperialism*. Chicago, IL: University of Chicago Press, 2022.

Hubler, Edward. "A Note on the Sources of 'Hamlet.'" In William Shakespeare, *The Tragedy of Hamlet*, edited by Edward Hubler. New York, Signet, 1963: 183–195.

Kyd, Thomas. *The Spanish Tragedy*. Edited by J. R. Mulryne. London: Ernest Benn Limited, 1970.

---

27 Emily Apter, *Unexceptional Politics: On Obstruction, Impasse and the Impolitic* (London: Verso, 2018), 97.

MacLeish, Archibald. Foreword to *This Music Crept by Me Upon the Waters*. Cambridge, MA: Harvard University Press, 1953.
Mathiessen, F. O. "The Responsibilities of the Critic." *Michigan Quarterly Review* 55, no. 24 (!949): 283–292.
———. Mathiessen, F. O. *Henry James: The Major Phase*. New York: Oxford University Press, 1944.
Nelson, Cary. "The Universe Is No Consolation: Hyam Plutzik, Jewish Identity, and the Ethics of Post-Holocaust Reading." *Journal of Jewish Humanities* 15, no. 1 (2022): 5–31.
Plutzik, Hyam. *The Collected Poems*. Foreword by Anthony Hecht. Brockport, NY: Boa Editions: 1987.
———. "Jim Desterland." In *New World Writing VIII*. New York: Mentor, 1955. 164–165.
Sanders, Julie. *Adaptation and Appropriation*. New York: Routledge, 2006.
Spears, Monroe K. "Christopher Fry and the Redemption of Joy." *Poetry* 78, no. 1 (1951), 28–32.
Wheelwright, Philip. "Aesthetic Surface and Mythic Depth." In *Sewanee Review* 65, no. 2 (1957): 279–293.
Wolin, Richard. *Heidegger in Ruins: Between Philosophy and Ideology*. New Haven, CT: Yale University Press, 2023.

CHAPTER 6

Elegy for a Mythic Warland: Hyam Plutzik's Wartime Poems and Letters from England

Phyllis Lassner

Hyam Plutzik enlisted in the Tenth United States Army in 1942, and in May 1944 was sent to Shipdham Air Base near the city of Norwich, the capital of Norfolk, a county in the region of East Anglia, on the northeastern coast of Britain.¹ He was among the 1,500,000 American military personnel in Britain who were preparing for the D-Day invasion of Europe on June 6, 1944. Plutzik served as ordnance officer in the Forty-Fourth Heavy Bomb Group for the Second Air Division, Eighth United States Army Air Force, the unit responsible for the maintenance and loading of one of the Allies' most vital weapons, the B-24 Liberator bombers. Although ordnance work suited his organizational and managerial skills, on July 25, 1944, Hyam wrote his wife Tanya that "all this leaves one dissatisfied and restless."² He would have preferred more intellectually and culturally stimulating work. The opportunity finally arose when he was

---

Copyright © 2025 by Phyllis Lassner

1   Plutzik's use of the word "England" in his letters and poems from Shipdham suggests a timeless, mythic landscape, but historically, England only became part of the United Kingdom in 1801. Ralph Charles Atkins, "United Kingdom," Britannica, accessed August 7, 2023, https://www.britannica.com/place/United-Kingdom.
2   Hyam Plutzik to Tanya Plutzik, July 25, 1944, accessed October 1, 2024, https://www.dropbox.com/sh/jah52kjyhcuoi1f/AAD3SfcSrOh5vTM8MPjHWeHza?dl=0.
    All letters from Hyam Plutzik to Tanya Plutzik derive from the above website. Dates will be cited in the text.

appointed Education and Information Officer, organizing lectures, teaching courses, and accepting "the constant incredible job of explaining to the fighters why they were fighting."[3] He also helped establish a library in Norwich and enjoyed offering informal lectures on American life and culture to local residents. This was an especially sensitive activity at a time when the local population could easily have found the large American presence overbearing. In fact, the US War Office produced a six-page cultural guide in the hope of minimizing tensions with the host population.[4] As his letters and activities in nearby towns convey, Plutzik was very aware of his delicate position as an American soldier in a foreign land that faced incessant threat of bombings and invasion.

Although Plutzik's responsibilities left little time or creative energy for writing poetry, his imaginative observations found their way into his letters from Shipdham to Tanya. All through 1944 and until he left England in 1945 these letters are filled with lyrical reflections on the Norfolk countryside and its villages and towns that he visited while roaming on a bicycle. Military restrictions on identifying specific places also encouraged Plutzik to generalize his impressions, as he wrote to Tanya on May 18, 1944:

> Never was there a greener land than England. The countryside is breathlessly beautiful, a little world of fresh fields surrounded by hedges; pools of clear water; and trim houses of stone or brick. The weather is cool, even chilly sometimes, but the grass is the deepest green, with buttercups, daisies, and dandelions scattered about.

It was only well after the war, when he had settled into his life's work of teaching and writing that Plutzik was able to translate and formalize his memories of Norfolk into poetic expression.

Plutzik's Norfolk poems align with his letters to Tanya to capture the mundane exigencies of life on the airbase, as well as his imaginative vision of an ancient land beset by war. Often written late in the evening, his letters express a longing for home as well as both frustrations and achievements of the day. Encounters

---

3   Edward Moran and Steven Sher, "Hyam Plutzik's Horatio as Post-Holocaust Poem," Hyam Plutzik, Poet, accessed October 10, 2023, http://www.hyamplutzikpoetry.com/commentaries/.
4   "American Armed Forces," D-Day Revisited, accessed October 1, 2024, https://d-dayrevisited.co.uk/d-day-history/planning-and-preparation/american-armed-forces/. Both British and American war departments organized programs to foster amicable relations. See American Battle Monuments Commission, accessed October 1, 2024, https://www.abmc.gov/news-events/news/americans-great-britain-world-war-ii-online-interactive-released.

with a surly roommate and constant bureaucratic logjams are intercut with his appreciation of the ground crews' meticulous work and the pleasures of his countryside jaunts. As he wrote to Tanya on June 8, 1944, two days after D-Day, "I'm still marveling at the speed, spirit, and agility with which my men do their work." The poems transform the quotidian of Shipdham into meditations that channel his memories into meanings he finds or creates about the impact of centuries of war on the places he found so inspiring. Expressed both compactly and expansively, in different metered, rhymed, and unrhymed forms, these poems create a metaphorical historical chronicle that extends from an ancient warland to an unprecedented global war.

This essay will demonstrate how Plutzitk's letters from Norfolk and poems express an emotional, historical, and critical intensity that delineates his responses to the war through the lens of his eighteen-month British experience. Living and working within the restricted parameters of preparing for a monumental battle, hidden behind a security curtain of total secrecy, and with only brief excursions beyond, Plutzik's poetic imagination forged lasting connections with Britain's embattled history, its enduring rural landscape, and compelling literature.

Read in tandem, Plutzik's letters and the poetry Norfolk inspired resound with a mythic poetic nexus of relations that integrate the English landscape and its poets, as he muses in a letter to Tanya about his visit to Stratford and Shakespeare's house on April 18, 1945: "everywhere one goes the relics of great age, mellow under the mantle of time. . . . [T]here was an ineffable solidity about it all; the buildings had become a veritable part of the landscape, a part of the earth surrounding it. And over all the city hung the odor of lilacs, now in bloom." As Edward Moran infers from Plutzik's epic poem *Horatio*, the war poems should be read as imagining the "rugged landscapes and seascapes in East Anglia" as a geological record of its ancient history, "one of the four main kingdoms of Anglo-Saxon England in the centuries before the Norman invasion of 1066."[5] Plutzik's poems of wartime Norfolk, anchored in the climactic moments of preparing for the D-Day invasion, form a temporal kaleidoscope, oscillating between the urgency of the present and "East Anglia the ancient," as his poem "Bomber Base" declaims.[6] On June 5, 1944, Plutzik's journal entry envisions the anxious present as coterminous with the region's sylvan rural past: "On a bomber base in England, with a farmer harrowing an adjacent field behind a plodding horse, I pass the D-day of this war."[7]

---

5   Moran, "Hyam of Norwich," Paper delivered at JAHLIT, November 2017.
6   Hyam Plutzik, "Bomber Base," in *Collected Poems* (Brockport, NY: BOA Editions, 1987), 37.
7   I thank Ed Moran for sharing Plutzik's journal entry.

Plutzik's letters from Shipdham express both the loneliness of an American soldier far from home and the wonders of exploring an ancient land, including the resonance of its iconic sites, battles, and literary traditions. The past of Norfolk is envisioned lyrically in his poem "Bomber Base" as the unfettered continuity of rural life: "the thatched farmhouse sleeps in the dark" while the poem "I Have Read in the Book of the Butcher Boy (In Time of War)" imagines Shakespeare's "thyme-sweet" Avon as a sanctuary, an idyll of domesticated, protected, and protective nature ("Bomber Base, 37").[8] With a catalyzing juxtaposition, "Bomber Base" simultaneously exposes the East Anglian landscape as an ancient and present warland: "Upon the fields the stone weapons of dead men" ("Bomber Base," 37). Plutzik's poetry creates a cultural and historical continuum of war as a lens through which he processes the multivalent significance of D-Day and establishes a bridge between British and American poets of World War II—poets who have only been studied as separate, literary canons.

From Poetic Legacies of World War I to Poetic Confrontations with World War II

Despite the unprecedented events of World War II, many American and British poets represented it as shadowed by poetic responses to the horrific battles, losses, and contested outcomes of World War I. The cacophonous cadences and anti-lyricism that marked modernist responses to the war's open wounds remained hauntingly influential. As Paul Fussell argues, as the scarred and broken veterans of the Somme and Passchendaele revealed, and as so much postwar literature confirms, "redemptive notions of patriotism, heroism, and even elegiac sentiment had been effectively exhausted by WWI."[9] Noting the impact of the First World War on the Second World War, Catherine Reilly posits that "the disillusionment engendered during the years 1914–18 and those that followed ensured that in 1939 there was no glorification of war or false patriotism,

---

8 Hyam Plutzik, "I Have Read in the Book of the Butcher Boy," in *Collected Poems*, 58.
9 Paul Fussell, *The Norton Book of Modern War* (New York: Norton, 1991), 311. Phillipa Lyon worries that "Apart from the sense of history repeating itself, there is a related concern that there is nothing 'original' to be expressed in war poetry," that "the war poet's work here seems at least as defined by the demands of social duty as by those of aesthetic expression," *Twentieth-Century War Poetry* (Basingstoke: Palgrave, 2005), 93, 94.

just a calm acceptance of what had to be done."[10] With few exceptions, poets on both sides of the Atlantic recognized that the threat against which World War II would be fought had already, throughout the 1930s, revealed itself as distinctively "evil," as Plutzik's June 5, 1944 letter to Tanya contends. Although many poets rejected the idea that warfare produced a unified sense of purpose or "had a salutary effect on anyone," they "did not turn against the war . . . as they realized that the alternative to fighting Nazi Germany and imperialist Japan would be even worse."[11]

The Imprint of World War II on British and American Poetry

Both British and American poetry reveal querulous and searching responses to World War II, registering the sense that although the events they experienced and witnessed "were too devastating to capture in words, . . . they nevertheless were compelled to write about them" (Oosdijk, 2). Adam Piette describes the restrictive conditions that both complicated and resolved this ambivalence. American poets and their British counterparts shared "the power of unexpressed feeling wartime generates, especially in a superheated propagandized and censored environment. It was also true that the brevity and concentration of poetry suited the intensities and fractured experiences of wartime during the long hours of waiting."[12] Such paradoxical resolve is voiced in a retrospective poem by American poet Howard Nemerov "D Day Plus 20 Years." In Diederik Oostdijk's interpretation, Nemerov shows the ironic need for "words to express [...] the Silence [that] seems to be the most appropriate reaction to D-day and World War II" (Oosdijk, 2). In response to "the only necessary war of modern history," both American and British writers created poetic forms that might echo the syntactical ruptures and discontinuous tempos of post-World War I poetry, but their often unsettling condensations and analogies register a sense of urgency to commit to this distinct war while enduring its emotional

---

10 Catherine Reilly, Introduction to *Chaos of the Night: Women's Poetry and Verse of the Second World War* (London: Virago, 1984), xxii.
11 Diederik Oosdijk, *Among the Nightmare Fighters* (Columbia: University of South Carolina Press, 2011), 5. Future references to this book will be cited parenthetically in the text.
12 Adam Piette, "War Poetry in Britain." in *The Cambridge Companion to the Literature of World War II*, ed. Marina Mackay (Cambridge: Cambridge University Press, 2009), 16.

and ethical costs.¹³ As British war poet Laurie Lee concludes, to achieve victory over Fascism, he would be forced "To camouflage compassion and ourselves / Against the wretched icicles of war."¹⁴ Brian Gardner notes "That 1945 heralded history's most cruel and bitter peace was not a cause for jubilation. The poets knew this, accepted it."¹⁵ The combination of recognizing the war's necessity along with its inconceivable human toll produced poetry that in Margo Norris's analysis, demonstrates "virtually every innovation produced in the immense range of Anglo-American modernism, from local specificity and realism to classical allusion and referential obliquity, from the primness of regular meter and rhyme to the idiom of slang and the vernacular of obscenity."¹⁶

Alan Ross, a poet who served in the Royal Navy, expressed his understanding of both the war's exceptionality and its wearisome cycles by creating a poetry of mournful reportage. Like a fraternal twin to Plutzik's poem "Bomber Base," in which "every wartime night" brings "command, terror, despair," Ross's "Naval Base" depicts the war on the seas as both deadly and "The same routine, continuing the war until it ends" ("Bomber Base, 37).¹⁷ Plutzik shared a similar sense of the war's onerous rhythms in his January 22, 1945 letter to Tanya: "To many, the daily work becomes no more than a circular routine; to others there is the danger of each mission. So that in the background of the memories of their comrades are the ghosts of the men who did not come back."

In "Bomber Base," the relentless cycle of each "day's struggle" expands to encompass the uncanny specters of ancient warriors who, like the airmen of World War II, "Lie awaiting the outcome":

> The bombs shatter the factory and many are blasted.
> The broken machine crashes into the hill.
> The young men die in manifold agonies. ("Bomber Base," 37)

---

13   Brian Gardner, Introduction to *The Terrible Rain: The War Poets 1939–45* (London: Methuen, 1966), xxii. Future citations from Gardner will be cited in the text.
14   Laurie Lee, "The Armoured Valley, in Gardner, *The Terrible Rain*, 133.
15   Gardner, Introduction, xxii.
16   Margot Norris, "War Poetry in the USA," in Mackay, *The Cambridge Companion to the Literature of World War II*, 44. Eric Sundquist identifies Plutzik as an "American modernist accomplished in the arts of lyric and narrative Poetry" whose sources included "classic" Western mythology and the Hebrew Bible, "but he also wrote as someone who had witnessed the catastrophe that engulfed the Jews of Europe." See Eric Sundquist, "Blessed Mythmaker: The Poetry of Hyam Plutzik," accessed November 1, 2023, https://drive.google.com/file/d/18y4aXA50KLXStIN8wD3vcpbFi1qtEEbF/view.
17   Alan Ross, "Naval Base," in Gardner, *The Terrible Rain*, 119.

Densely compacted with alliteration that echoes both the completed mission and its inherent destructiveness, like a stuttering fall, "bombs, blasted, broken" attest to the lacerating suffering of the airmen, as well as that of the nameless enemy below. With journalistic precision, these lines report an inevitable wartime tragedy as testimony and commemoration, eschewing mythology or analogy as rhetorically anodyne, as moral masquerades. For almost all American and British World War II poets, it can be said that "the issues of the war seemed clear beyond all ambiguity," allowing Ross and Plutzik to "concentrate on recording a kind of existence as accurately as possible."[18] That this project would remain a challenge is evident in Plutzik's letter to Tanya on June 16, 1944: "In these exciting and world-shattering days each man sees only what is before his eyes, and to try to estimate his part in the total struggle is an impossibility. And to try to get a comprehension of the total struggle from the small part he himself plays is even more impossible."

Among the ethical challenges characterizing much World War II poetry is how to represent a sense of urgency to defeat the Axis powers coupled with anxieties about the boundless reaches and continuum of war. Plutzik's "The Miracle," set at the "mild waters of Betterton," imagines the global war extending to American shores.[19] The poem recalls the poet's stay in the Maryland resort town, but transforms its bucolic landscape into a war zone, as though there is no such thing as a safe haven in this world war ("The Miracle," 31).[20] Instead, "a soldier bathing in the sun" becomes a casualty of "the firing of the sunset gun," attacked by the transfiguration of nature's nurturing beauty into a weapon of destruction.[21] Invoking *"the valley of Ajalon"* provides an interpretive gloss that connects a continuous stream of biblical battles with the breadth of World War II ("The Miracle," 31). The ancient

---

18   Waterman, Introduction to *Poets of the Second World War* (Northcote: Tavistock, 2016), 3.
19   Hyam Plutzik, "The Miracle," in *Collected Poems*, 31.
20   Plutzik's sense of the war as reaching home fronts as well as battlefields addresses the argument that only combatants who are direct witnesses can write war poems. William Logan asks, "Shouldn't the poet be any soldier or civilian who simply lived through the war, whether within sound of the fighting or a continent away, writing in the passion of the moment or the ruptured tranquility long after?" See William Logan, "World War II Poetry, Reloaded," *Southwest Review* 98, no. 4 (2013): 554.
21   Plutzik, "The Miracle." Plutzik wrote about this stay in a letter to his wife (July 1, 1942): "I write this sitting at the door of a tent under an apple tree [...]. The name of this place is Betterton, and it's across Chesapeake Bay from Aberdeen Proving Ground. We're on the bay itself here, our encampment being on a cliff over the shore. [...] The water is very mild; the vista wonderful. It's really a vacation for me, despite the inconveniences of living in a tent and being roused up in the middle of the night to take part in sham battles." Thanks to Edward Moran for referring me to this letter.

saga begins with the story of Joshua, who prayed for a miracle to prevent the sun from setting so that the Israelites could avenge themselves on the Amorites.[22] "The Miracle" resonates with Ajalon's battles as inconclusive and therefore haunting the hopefulness of the D-Day invasion.

Hyam Plutzik on an English "Plain Vast and Shadowy"[23]

There is no indication that Plutzik interacted personally with British poets or that their wartime writing was available to him, but the analogues and discontinuities Plutzik draws between past wars and the present firmly establish his artistic, historical, and experiential connection with British wartime poets. Many references in his letters to Tanya and in his later writing confirm his deeply felt connection to Britain's cultural heritage. Examples include his lyrical descriptions of Norfolk, references to Shakespeare, Keats's "Ode on a Grecian Urn," and Robert Graves.[24] His letter of August 28, 1944 identifies with other servicemen who might have read and shared the sentiments sculpted on the gravestone of the poet William Cowper (1731–1800): "like all men he suffered in this life; he saw many evils; and the fates buffeted him cruelly.... And now, after many years, other men read these words and felt their meaning, being all far from home in a strange land, in the great whirlpool of war."[25] That British literature influenced Plutzik's "thinking is apparent in his letter to Tanya of May 29, in which he recounts how he had "begun to read *The Mayor of Casterbridge* by [Thomas] Hardy, interrupting my perusal of [J. M.] Barrie's *Little Minister*." Only a week before D-Day, these were apt choices, melding the anxiety and optimism that characterized preparations for the monumental invasion and the visions of Hardy's humanistic, but dark determinism with Barrie's redemptive melodrama of human charity.

British and American war poets inscribed similar tensions, tedium, and anxieties as they attended to the technical minutiae of their training and prepared

---

22 The valley was a crucial approach to the roads leading to Jerusalem in both General Allenby's 1917 campaign and in the 1948 War of Independence. See *Encyclopedia Judaica*, s.v. "Aijalon," vol. 2, A–Ang (Jerusalem: Keter Publishing, n.d.).
23 Plutzik, "Elegy," 51.
24 On Graves, see Edward Brunner, "Hyam Plutzik's Horatio as Postwar Text: Dream-Work, Verse Drama, Underground Myth," Hyam Plutznik, Poet, accessed May 1, 2023, www.hyamplutzikpoetry.com/commentary-brunner.
25 Edward Moran shared this quote from Plutzik's letter.

the weapons, amphibian transports, and planes for the invasion of Europe.[26] Recording the homely details of armed service in "All Day It Has Rained," British poet Alun Lewis domesticates the war zone with language, rhymes, and diction that intertwine the mundane and the precarity that both civilians and combatants experienced: "Smoking a Woodbine, darning dirty socks / Reading the Sunday papers—I saw a fox."[27] The tedium of inaction is noted in D. Van Den Bogaerde's poem "Steel Cathedrals," where "It seems to me, I spend my life in stations / Going, coming, standing, waiting [. . .] A cigarette, a cup of tea, a bun, / and my train goes at ten."[28] In Plutzik's poem "Bomber Base," memories of domestic routine as integral to the war's terrors are embedded in the longings of fighting men "for home, / And a woman's arms, / a warm bed in a house" ("Bomber Base," 37).

Unlike the unequivocal lyricism of Plutzik's letters, his poems configure the landscape as deceptively pastoral, as camouflaging its actual history as an ancient and present battleground.[29] This duality shapes his poem "The Airman Who Flew over Shakespeare's England," which opens with a majestic image of reassuring continuity:

> A nation of hayricks spotting the green solace
>
> Of grass,
>
> And thrones of thatch ruling a yellow kingdom
>
> Of barley.[30]

---

26 "The combined operation in the European theater required both nations (and their respective militaries) to work hand in hand. In fact, the Supreme Allied Command was an integrated staff [. . .]. In addition, a joint school was created in London just for D-Day so the two nations could understand each other's doctrines and staff planning procedures." Email correspondence with Dr. John M Curatola Lt Col USMC (Ret), military historian, Institute for the Study of War and Democracy, The National World War II Museum, April 27, 2023.
27 Alun Lewis, "All Day It Has Rained," in Gardner, *The Terrible Rain*, 36–37.
28 D. Van Den Bogaerde, "Steel Cathedrals," in Gardner, *The Terrible Rain*, 90.
29 David Miller maintains that "There are no lyrics after Auschwitz, only the shadows of lyrics." See his "After Epic: Adorno's Scream and the Shadows of Lyric," in *The Bloomsbury Companion to Holocaust Literature*, ed. Jenni Adams (London: Bloomsbury, 2014), 78. Sean Singer observes that "Plutzik's finest work [. . .] balances wonder and terror with a clean, focussed intelligence" See his "Craft: Hyam Plutzik," accessed October 1, 2024, https://drive.google.com/file/d/1diJ7-ns8YvDUMlrYV7sJUIHbERRjw3dm/view.
30 Hyan Plutzik, "The Airman Who Flew over Shakespeare's England," in *Collected Poems*, 101.

As the poem ends, however, the image of a ruin, originally a fort built by William the Conqueror in 1068, undermines the rhapsody of perennial regeneration:[31]

> Over the castle of Warwick frightened birds
>
> Are fleeing,
>
> And on the bridge, faces upturned to a roaring
>
> Falcon. ("Airman," 101)

Although, as Eric Sundquist observes, the poem was inspired by Plutzik's "postwar flight over defeated Germany,"[32] its trajectory charts the airman's journey through time and space, across British history, from the bronze age "circle of stones" to "the road to Shottery," the childhood home of Anne Hathaway, Shakespeare's wife ("Airman," 101). But then, subverting the idea that the nation's complex culture and complicated history can be repurposed as a tourist playground, the poem's itinerary includes "monstrous constellations / Of cities" ("Airman," 101). This is only one image throughout Plutzik's war poems of the human potential for dehumanizing innovations. Bringing this potential to its climactic conclusion is the poem's tableau of war as an assault on the natural order. The "fleeing" birds are threatened by a predator, a "roaring Falcon," suggesting the metamorphosis of a creature of nature into a monstrous creation of war ("Airman," 101).

This poem and others construct Plutzik's memory of Norfolk as both a harmonious land and people and a theater of war, the combination of which tells a story of Britain having withstood, adapted to, and absorbed incursions by others into itself as a phantom memory. As he wrote to Tanya on July 2, 1944, "The print of great age, of thousands of years of history is stamped upon all. The multitudes of men—Roman, Norman, Saxon—who have walked upon this ground have left their character here—intangible but still existent, something at the very edge of the mind, like a half-remembered tune." Curiously, Plutzik did not cite the dark side of Britain's history, that of its violence against others from ancient times onwards. Etched into the character of Norwich is its history of Britain's first blood libel against the Jews in 1144, inciting pogroms that instead

---

31 Over the centuries, Warwick Castle has been reconfigured as a fortified castle, a country mansion, and finally as an amusement/theme park.
32 Sundquist, "Blessed Mythmaker."

of garnering sympathy, led to their expulsion in 1290.³³ Other civil and religious wars, and rebellions also revealed the nation's oppression of its others. Even the poem's seemingly peaceful reference to "the pilgrims along the holy roads / To Walsingham" recalls a politically motivated religious assault, Henry VIII's destruction of a Catholic shrine in 1538.³⁴

Plutzik's poems about England form a narrative about the alloyed but contradictory convergence of war's disfiguring operations and the essentiality of World War II. In turn, the structural analogues in "On the Airfield at Shipdham" reveal the war's transformative effects on poetic tropes by creating a fraught symbiotic relationship between human, nonhuman, and mechanical agents. Although "Airfield" was not collected as part of *Aspects of Proteus*, its figure of a lark evokes the mythical Proteus, representing human mutability. A tribute to Shakespeare as well, this figuration recalls both the song "Hark, Hark! The Lark at Heaven's Gate Sings" from Shakespeare's *Cymbeline* and Sonnet 29, in which the narrator experiences an emotional transformation from desolation to joy when he is inspired by the lark's happy song.³⁵ In Plutzik's poem, "The Lark at Heaven's Gate," Chapter 5 of his epic *Horatio*, war overtakes nature's ecosystem: "The war flickers forth like a sudden flame . . . / Over the earth the sky and the sea; subsiding; / Rising again a thousandfold."³⁶ The narrator admits that "the dreadful deeds of a day" have kept him from listening to a bird singing with "mercy" and sweetness; but then acknowledges its power as ascendant ("The Lark," 211). The narrator in "On the Airfield at Shipdham" is far less sanguine, observing the lark as engaged in a struggle to survive. Like other birds in Plutzik's war poems, the fate of the lark signifies that of the imperiled nation, and therefore lyrical reveries of the natural world no longer obtain. Instead, the narrator sees "The

---

33 Edward Moran interprets Plutzik's silence about this atrocity in his "Hyam of Norwich." Jews were falsely accused of the ritual murder of a boy, William of Norwich. In a speech at a 2023 interfaith Passover seder, the mayor of Norwich, Kevin Maguire, apologized to the Jewish community for these atrocities. See Gary Toberman, "Norwich Lord Mayor's 'Heartfelt Apology' to Jewish Community for First Blood Libel," *Jewish Chronicle*, April 18, 2023, Blood Libel." *Jewish Chronicle*, April 18, 2023, https://www.thejc.com/news/community/norwich-lord-mayors-heartfelt-apology-to-jewish-community-for- "first-blood-libel-696qu GLZlNoUh74Q8doxv6?utm_.

34 This was part of Henry's campaign to overrule the Vatican's power. See Gary Waller, *Walsingham and the English Imagination* (Ashgate: Aldershot, 2011).

35 Shakespeare, William, *Cymbeline*, in *Folger Shakespeare Library*, ed. Barbara Mowat, Paul Werstine, Michael Poston, and Rebecca Niles (New York: Simon & Shuster, 2020); "Sonnet 29," *Folger Shakespeare Library*, accessed March 7, 2023, https://folger.edu/explore/shakespeares-works/Sonnets.

36 Hyam Plutzik, "The Lark at Heaven's Gate," in *Horatio*, in *Collected Poems*, 209.

small lonely singer beating its wings / Against the pull of the old and evil earth," and therefore it is now "too late ... to praise its song ...," especially with "The beasts with guts of metal groaning on the line."[37] "On the Airfield at Shipdham" is a disconsolate elegy, mourning the natural order as wounded by the war that requires extreme, irrevocable measures.

With similar condensation and emotional impact, a war plane in the poem "The Old War" is figured as "the iron sparrow," transforming one of nature's more innocuous creatures into an instrument of war.[38] Choosing a sparrow rather than a bird of prey and endowing it with an assertive "I" anthropomorphizes the war plane as self-conscious of its role as both agent and victim: "Ten good men I bore in my belly ..." ("The Old War," 94). Externalizing the poet's ethical consciousness, the plane is inextricably entwined into nature's cycle of life and death in which the organic nature of war necessitates saving lives with destructive force. Bearing "'Ten good sons, pilot and gunner, Radioman and bombardier,'" the plane crashes into the land Plutzik lyricized in his letters but must now be viewed mordantly ("The Old War," 94). The "mother-barley," recalling the "yellow kingdom of barley" evoked in the poem "The Airman Who Flew over Shakespeare's England," endows the landscape with both the grandeur of its literary heritage and the recurring scars of war ("The Old War," 94).[39] Mother nature in this ecosystem bears life and accepts death as her due, reabsorbing the "Ten good men" who are consumed by another natural element transformed by war: *Fire swarming high and higher!*" (original italics).[40] Cary Nelson regards the poem's movement as a "shift from the half-naturalized 'iron sparrow' to the 'mad beast' that bellows and carries the shock of every time a war violates norms by hurling categories together."[41] Plutzik's English poems cohere as a narrative in which romantic tropes of nature's timelessness and regeneration must be sacrificed to absorb and express the poet's anxious response to the war's climactic moment.

Yet as Plutzik's May 14, 1945 letter to Tanya reveals, while flying over defeated Germany, he imagines nature as a living organism, as personifying a nation's moral character: "The landscape was so beautiful that I could not help wondering how, from such beauty, could have been distilled the vicious brew of Hitlerism.

37　Hyam Plutzik, "On the Airfield at Shipdham," in *Collected Poems*, 225.
38　Hyam Plutzik, "The Old War," in *Collected Poems*, 94.
39　Ibid.
40　Ibid.
41　Cary Nelson, "The Universe Is No Consolation: Hyam Plutzik, Jewish Identity, and the Ethics of Post-Holocaust Reading," *Journal of Jewish Identities* 15, no. 1 (January 2022): 9.

From this very soil the most evil and ugly of things had come."⁴² With parallel attention to the landscape, but in searing contrast, on his return flight "It was good to see England. Its fields did not have the precision and regularity of those in Germany. They were diverse, as though a more ingenious and imaginative mind had made them—a free mind."⁴³ Although their rhymes and rhythms vary, the conceptual structure of Plutzik's Shipdham poems harmonizes around the persistence of his historically inflected ethical consciousness. The Allies' victory did not produce roseate promises. Instead, Plutzik reflected on the unsettled peace that defined the cultural and political contexts of the 1950s, the decade during which he was writing his war poems. As Brunner proffers, Plutzik questions "the long-standing view that most postwar writers deliberately chose to disengage themselves from political and historical contexts."⁴⁴

Plutzik's historical consciousness is evident in *The Outcasts of Venus*, his 1952 science fiction adventure novel that links the terrors of the 1930s to political anxieties of the Cold War and McCarthy era. For Brunner, the opening chapter recalls the "rescue missions of the 1930s in which group after group of Europeans—Jews, but also left-wing intellectuals and other 'undesirables' like homosexuals—eagerly sought passage to America. Too few of those ships, as history reveals, ever found a safe port" (Brunner). Five years into the war, as the Holocaust escalated, Plutzik expressed both his anger at the Nazi perpetrators and relief at the rough justice they earned. On June 7, in anticipation of D-Day's success, he wrote to Tanya: "The filthy fascists are tasting the bitter brew now of their own making!" By August 14, his judgment had solidified: "listening to the epochal news out of France today I feel more than ever that this horrible war is now marching toward a conclusion. It was a long time waiting for this moment. When I think back at the time when the Nazi hordes were posturing and goosestepping over a continent, this time of retribution seems like a dream too good to be true almost."⁴⁵ As Cary Nelson comments, "Like many post-Holocaust writers, Plutzik is not a poet of consolation" ("The Universe," 15).

---

42 Qtd. in Edward Moran, "The 'Soldier Poetry' of Hyam Plutzik as Revealed through His War Letters, 1944–45," JAHLIT Conference, 2016.
43 Qtd in ibid.
44 Brunner, "Hyam Plutzik's Horatio as Postwar Text."
45 Sundquist, Nelson, and Moran interpret Plutzik's response to the Holocaust. Historians agree that attempting to save the Jews was never part of the goal to defeat the Axis powers. See the US Holocaust Memorial Museum exhibition "America and the Holocaust," accessed October 1, 2024, https://www.ushmm.org/collections/bibliography/the-united-states-and-the-holocaust.

Plutzik never doubted the necessity of World War II, but his poem "Elegy" is also a lamentation for its irrevocable losses. The poem portrays a dystopian Anthropocene in which "the pale flame of the spirit sank / And flickered out in the last wilderness."[46] Resembling human detritus, forecasting searing images of Holocaust survivors, spectral wraiths wander "on a plain vast and shadowy . . . / As in a fog the starved fires sinking" ("Elegy," 51). Towards the end of the poem, however, this despairing portrait is transformed by the narrator's defiant "metamorphosis" in which "a kindred spirit" is revived: "Together they spurned the immense coils of Being, / The poised darkness, the blows of the answerless Ocean"("Elegy," 51). "Elegy," as Moran and Sher observe, "was the only poem [Plutzik] finished there, where it was hard to write or 'think for oneself'—the poem came to him while walking under the wings of a B-24 bomber and watching men head for a mission."[47] "Elegy" both encapsulates and expands the poet's response to the war as an emotionally wrought ethical journey, from apprehension to resistance. Followed by the realization that "the test goes on," Plutzik considers the possibility of regeneration but in an uncharted, always precarious future ("Elegy," 51). Plutzik's postwar war poems condense his journey, as a Jewish poet confronting, as he wrote to Tanya: "all the wrongs suffered at the hands of the evil ones." Bearing witness, the Jewish poet personifies the natural and manufactured worlds—man, beast, war machines, and the land—to delineate the costs of this necessary war as well as the collective responsibility we bear to save the future, as uncertain as it is.

Bibliography

American Battle Monuments Commission. Accessed April 5, 2023. https://www.abmc.gov/news-events/news/americans-great-britain-world-war-ii-online-interactive-released.

Atkins, Ralph Charles. "United Kingdom." Britannica. Accessed August 7, 2023. https://www.britannica.com/place/United-Kingdom.

Brunner, Edward. "Hyam Plutzik's Horatio as Postwar Text: Dream-Work, Verse Drama, Underground Myth." Hyam Plutznik, Poet. Accessed May 1, 2023. www.hyamplutzikpoetry.com/commentary-brunner.

D-Day Revisited. Accessed May 1, 2023. https://d-dayrevisited.co.uk/d-day-history/planning-and-preparation/american-armed-forces/.

Encyclopedia Judaica. S.v. "Aijalon." Vol. 2, A–Ang. Jerusalem: Keter Publishing, n.d.

"Preparations for D-Day." Europe Remembers. Accessed May 1, 2023. https://europeremembers.com/story/preparations-for-d-day/.

---

46   Plutzik, "Elegy," 51.
47   Moran and Sher, "Hyam Plutzik's 'Horatio' as Post-Holocaust Poem."

Fussell, Paul, ed. *The Norton Book of Modern War*. New York: Norton, 1991.
Gardner, Brian, ed. Introduction to *The Terrible Rain: The War Poets 1939–1945*, xvii–xxv. London: Methuen, 1966.
Holocaust Encyclopedia. s.v. "America and the Holocaust." Accessed April 5, 2023. https://www.ushmm.org/collections/bibliography/the-united-states-and-the-holocaust.
Lee, Laurie. "The Armoured Valley." In *The Terrible Rain: The War Poets*, edited by Brian Gardner, 133–134. London: Methuen, 1966.
Lewis, Alun. "All Day It Has Rained." In *The Terrible Rain: The War Poets 1939*–1945, edited by Brian Gardner, 36–37. London: Methuen, 1966.
Logan, William. "World War II Poetry, Reloaded." *Southwest Review* 98, no. 4 (2013): 540–565.
Lyon, Philippa. *Twentieth-Century War Poetry*. Basingstoke: Palgrave, 2005.
Miller, David. "After Epic: Adorno's Scream and the Shadows of Lyric." In *The Bloomsbury Companion to Holocaust Literature*, edited by Jenni Adams. 65–80. London: Bloomsbury, 2014.
Moran, Edward. "The Soldier Poetry of Hyam Plutzik as Revealed through His War Letters." Paper Delivered at Jewish American and Holocaust Literature Conference, 2016.
———. "Hyam of Norwich," Paper delivered at JAHLIT, November 2017.
Moran, Edward, and Steven Sher. "Hyam Plutzik's Horatio as Post-Holocaust Poem." Hyam Plutzik, Poet. Accessed October 10, 2023. http://www.hyamplutzikpoetry.com/commentaries/.
Norris, Margot. "War Poetry in the USA." In *The Cambridge Companion to the Literature of World War II*, edited by Marina Mackay, 43–55. Cambridge: Cambridge University Press, 2009.
Nelson, Cary. "The Universe Is No Consolation: Hyam Plutzik, Jewish Identity, and the Ethics of Post-Holocaust Reading. *Journal of Jewish Identities* 15, no. 1 (January 2022): 9.
Oosdijk, Diederik. *Among the Nightmare Fighters*. Columbia: University of South Carolina Press, 2011.
Piette, Adam. "War Poetry in Britain." In *The Cambridge Companion to the Literature of World War II*, edited by Marina Mackay, 13–25. Cambridge: Cambridge University Press, 2009.
Plutzik, Hyam. *Collected Poems*. Brockport, NY: BOA Editions, 1987.
———. Letters to Tanya Plutzik. Accessed October 1, 2024. https://www.dropbox.com/sh/jah52kjyhcuoi1f/AAD3SfcSrOh5vTM8MPjHWeHza?dl=0.
Reilly, Catherine. Introduction to *Chaos of the Night: Women's Poetry and Verse of the Second World War*, edited by Catherine Reilly, xxi–xxvi. London: Virago, 1984.
Ross, Alan. "Naval Base." In *The Terrible Rain: The War Poets 1939*–1945, edited by Brian Gardner, 119. London: Methuen, 1966.
Shakespeare, William. *Cymbeline a Tragedy*. In *Folger Shakespeare Library*, edited by Barbara Mowat, Paul Werstine, Michael Poston, and Rebecca Niles. New York: Simon & Shuster, 2020.
———. "Sonnet 29." Folger Shakespeare Library. Accessed March 7, 2023. https://folger.edu/explore/shakespeares-works/Sonnets.
Sundquist, Eric. "Blessed Mythmaker: The Poetry of Hyam Plutzik." Accessed November 1, 2023. https://drive.google.com/file/d/18y4aXA50KLXStIN8wD3vcpbFi1qtEEbF/view.
Toberman, Gary. "Norwich Lord Mayor's 'Heartfelt Apology' to Jewish Community for First Blood Libel." *Jewish Chronicle*, April 18, 2023. https://www.thejc.com/news/community/norwich-lord-mayors-heartfelt-apology-to-jewish-community-for- "first-blood-libel-696quGLZlNoUh74Q8doxv6?utm_.
Van Den Bogaerde, D. "Steel Cathedrals" In *The Terrible Rain: The War Poets 1939*–1945, edited by Brian Gardner, 90–91. London: Methuen, 1966.
Waller, Gary. *Walsingham and the English Imagination*. Ashgate: Aldershot, 2011.
Waterman, Rory. Introduction to *Poets of the Second World War*, 1–18. Tavistock: Northcote, 2016.

CHAPTER 7

When We Begin with Loss: Revisiting the Early Poems of Hyam Plutzik

Monica Osborne

> We speak suggesting that something not being said is speaking: the loss of what we were to say; weeping when tears have long since gone dry; the surrender which the invisible passivity of dying announces but does not accomplish—human weakness.
>
> —Maurice Blanchot[1]

The images in Hyam Plutzik's poem "The Three"—published in 1933 and for which he won the Yale Poetry Award—are bleak. Tantalus, the very embodiment of eternal suffering, looks over "the gloomy dome of hell."[2] The mythological figures are fallen and emaciated, immobile and barren. The world of the gods is now one of souls stripped bare. They are images that end in futility rather than salvation, producing only repetitions of themselves. The first poem that Plutzik published and for which he received recognition is a postapocalyptic vision grounded in loss and tragedy and ending in the desolation of "repetition on repetition." It feels strangely like a post-Holocaust poem at some moments:

Copyright © 2025 by Monica Osborne

1   Maurice Blanchot, *The Writing of the Disaster*, trans. Ann Smock (Lincoln, NE: University of Nebraska Press, 1995), 21.
2   Hyam Plutzik, "The Three," Hyam Plutzik, Poet, accessed October 1, 2024, https://www.hyamplutzikpoetry.com/poem-the-three.

> Tantalus turned his wondering face to Ixion then.
> Ixion said: "Do you not know the gods are gone?
> All their vassal souls in Hell are liberated;
> We alone are left to toil forever. The gods fled,
>
> But we were forgotten. Our doom is irrevocable,
> Bound into the very laws that govern nature.

The gods, here, are gone. They have fled. They have forgotten those who worship them, those who recount stories about them. The doom of these people—which people, we wonder?—are "bound into the very laws that govern nature." It is difficult not to read these lines through the lens of Jewish history, the most thoroughly researched moment of which is, for better or worse, the Holocaust. It's not so unthinkable, then, to place Plutzik's entire body of work, both pre- and post-Holocaust, into the genre of Holocaust writing. I would suggest that the events of the Holocaust and the plight of Jews under the rise of fascism that preceded it are fully present in Plutzik's early work—"The Three," "My Sister," "Death at the Purple Rim," and even perhaps the newly published "The Seventh Avenue Express," written in 1934, though it is set in Depression-era New York City and seems to consciously avoid the death Plutzik fixates on in the others. Bleakness, loss, hopelessness, and death are the tell-tale themes of all these works.

Plutzik the Jewish Writer

"Evil is infinitely profound," writes Jewish French Lithuanian philosopher Emmanuel Levinas in "Poetry and the Impossible." "Its texture is thick and inextricable. Its impregnable fortresses survive at the heart of a refined civilization and deep in the souls conquered by grace."[3] Here Levinas describes the path of the French Catholic poet Paul Claudel from antisemitism to the point at which he "ultimately recognizes Judaism" in 1939, as the events of the Holocaust are beginning. Levinas notes that it is "incredible" that this evolution "lasted until the eve of Auschwitz, and that it took no less than" the appearance of such blatant atrocities against Jews for Claudel to "arrive at a definite reassessment" of the Jewish people. Claudel's reputation as a poet is grand, and it was poetry that functioned as "a means of attaining knowledge" for him. Indeed, writes Levinas,

---

3   Emmanuel Levinas, *Difficult Freedom: Essays on Judaism*, trans. Seán Hand (Baltimore: Johns Hopkins University Press, 1990), 128.

"this is probably the very definition of poetry—the thing that makes language possible." If poetry makes language possible, it also makes understanding possible. Poetry provides a means of both understanding and articulating the great tragedies of our time as well as the ones that both precede us and lie before us.

No doubt the beginnings of fascism in Europe—not to mention the Great Depression in the United States—in the year this poem was published informed its imagery. There is a prescience in the lines of "The Three," a haunting that comes not so much from the past but primarily and eerily from the future, a foreboding of all that was just around the corner. It is a poem that resides upon the cusp of an historical moment: we all stand teetering on the precipice of something catastrophic as we read it. The year 1933 began with the appointment of Adolf Hitler as chancellor of Germany in January. Less than two months later, the Reichstag was set on fire under suspicious circumstances; this fire would quickly be used as a pretext to seize complete power. A day later, numerous German civil liberties were revoked and hundreds were arrested as Germany rounded up its so-called political opponents. By the middle of March that same year the Nazi flag was flying and the Third Reich was declared. By the end of that month Dachau, the first Nazi concentration camp, was opened. It was clear that the year held no auspicious beginnings, and the terrifying historical events that marked the rest of the year were many: a train hurtling through time, moving so quickly that all was a blur when seen through the glass. Book burnings, the gestapo, a complete seizure of power by the Nazis: this was the landscape against which Plutzik's first published poem appeared.

It was certainly a strange year for any Jewish poet to begin the process of coming into his or her own, let alone for Plutzik, who was not one to distance himself from his Jewish identity. Cary Nelson has noted that, indeed, Plutzik's post-World War II task was in part to define himself precisely as a "Jewish poet in the immediate post-Holocaust decade when many writers, except those on the radical left, avoided direct and aggressive political commentary."[4] There are writers who happen to be Jewish, and who, at the very least, no doubt take great pains to keep this identity private or minimal in a world that prefers a less complex and fraught identity. They are the ones who, at worst, can always be counted on to wave a flag or carry a banner or become an apologist for the antisemitic ideologues that appear over and over throughout history at different times and in different places. These are the Jews on whom Plutzik would reflect years later in "Portrait":

---

4   Cary Nelson, "The Universe Is No Consolation: Hyam Plutzik, Jewish Identity, and the Ethics of Post-Holocaust Reading," *Journal of Jewish Identities* 15, no. 1 (January 2022): 7.

> Notice with what careful nonchalance
> He tries to be a Jew casually,
> To ignore the monster, the mountain—
> A few thousand years of history.

To be casually Jewish is to live in a constant state of deceiving one's self, to pretend that the past isn't simply past; it never existed at all. To live in this way is to "ignore the monster, the mountain" that is anti-Jewish hatred, a hatred as old as the beginning of time or, at the very least, "a few thousand years of history." "Portrait" was published in 1959 in *Apples from Shinar*. Although the famous trial of Nazi Adolph Eichmann, which made the ordinary man's role in the murder of millions of Jews crystal clear to the world, was still nearly two years away, by this time it was all but impossible for the world to deny what had happened to Jews during World War II. But lest readers think, mistakenly, that the postwar period is the only time period to which Plutzik refers here ("the monster, the mountain"), we are reminded that this is one of many dark moments in Jewish history, a "few thousand years of history." Plutzik's frustration with Jews who can be "casually" Jewish is palpable.

And so, there are writers who happen to be Jewish; and then there are Jewish writers. Plutzik, who was born in 1911 in Brooklyn, New York to Jewish émigrés from Russia (current-day Belarus) and who grew up speaking Yiddish, Hebrew, and Russian at home, was the latter: keenly aware of his position as a Jew in a world increasingly hostile to Jews, but unwilling to downplay those crucial elements of his identity. "It is an awesome thing to be a Jew and to know that one is hated by so many of one's fellowmen," he wrote in a 1941 letter to a former teacher.[5] Some have suggested that the overtly Jewish themes and concerns of some of his work were responsible for its ultimate obscurity, despite the fact that Plutzik won numerous prestigious awards during his lifetime and was a three-time finalist for the Pulitzer Prize.[6] That said, it is important to note that

---

5   Hyam Plutzik, *Letter from a Young Poet* (Hartford, CT: Watkinson Library at Trinity College, 2016), 68.

6   In her 2013 review of Plutzik's *Apples from Shinar* for the *Jewish Review of Books,* Margot Lurie quotes Eric Ormsby's assessment of Plutzik's early poetry, which Ormsby claims tries "to recreate a credible Shakespearean voice in American verse" and "doomed his verse to obscurity." Even Harold Bloom omitted Plutzik from his anthology of American religious poems, which both Ormsby and Lurie find suspect. But Lurie follows up Ormsby's assessment with another theory for why Plutzik's work was doomed to obscurity: "an affinity

while we may currently refer liberally to the "obscurity" of Plutzik's work, it is an assessment that is quickly becoming obsolete, not least with the publication of this book and the Plutzik Poetry Series at the University of Rochester, which has welcomed over three hundred leading literary figures to the university campus, including Nobel, Pulitzer, and National Book Award winners, and poets laureate from both the US and Britain.

In 1933 as a graduate student at Yale, Plutzik was just beginning what would be a three-decade career as a writer and had no idea that the very Jewishness that defined him would be the basis for what would ultimately be millions murdered across the ocean in another continent. Certainly he had no way of knowing just how brutal and bleak the scenes of the real world would become as they played out on Hitler's stage. And yet, when we read the dismal lines of "The Three," it is almost impossible not to see the landscapes of the death camps stretching out before us, each prisoner a Tantalus or Ixion or Sisyphus, forced to "endure their destined, long frustration." It is difficult not to read in these images the plight of the Jew in the modern world. But this was not 1938, when the horrors that had been planned for years were starting to materialize for all the world to see, and while such horrors were only just around the bend, they had not yet become truly visible, save to those with the keenest of insights and perceptions—those of course were the ones who fled Nazi Germany before 1938, the ones who saw all of the signs and read all of the writing on the crumbling walls. But as we now know, those were few and far between, with most German Jews having settled into a mindset of disbelief: we are Germans, too, after all. From where, then, did Plutzik draw these prescient images? One answer is perhaps found in the loss of his sister, twelve years before "The Three" was written—a loss he would write about four years after publishing "The Three," in 1937, in a poem called "My Sister," just as the most brutal terrors were about to commence in Nazi Germany.

Poetry as the Beginning of Thinking

Much of Plutzik's work is grounded in personal losses, traumas, and absences. He was an close observer of the world around him, but especially the world nearest to him in physical proximity, as his earliest poems demonstrate. But first, "How does one begin thinking?," Philippe Nemo once asked Levinas, to which

---

for Jewish concerns second only in English poetry to A. M. Klein's." See Margot Laurie, "Golden Apples," *Jewish Review of Books*, Spring 2023, https://jewishreviewofbooks.com/articles/115/golden-apples/.

Levinas responded: "It probably begins through traumatisms or gropings to which one does not even know how to give a verbal form: a separation, a violent scene, a sudden consciousness of the monotony of time."[7] Poetry, then, is an expression of the beginning of thinking.

In "Death at the Purple Rim," for instance, which first appeared in 1940, Plutzik describes a chilling confrontation between beast and man in the Connecticut countryside where he had spent time. The "Purple Rim" was the name given to the valley by a family Plutzik had known when he spent time laboring outdoors in the countryside, and the landscape is described at times in painstaking detail. We are meant to find ourselves in a specific place and time—Connecticut's northern hills, the gardens, the trails, the stone walls, the cattle grazing—while simultaneously reflecting on "the riddles the Sphinx / Propounded to Oedipus on a Grecian morning, / Or the song that the sirens sang." It is undeniably a poem about a moment in Connecticut. And yet it is 1940 and we cannot help but consider the collective, over-arching tragedies and traumas of the period in which Plutzik wrote. Indeed, "Death at the Purple Rim" was written at a time after nearly a decade of American newspaper reporting on Hitler and Nazi Germany. Other than an unfinished and unpublished poem about the Holocaust, Plutzik—for all his so-called obsessions with Jewish themes and imagery and topics—never really addressed it specifically. Of the unpublished project, Edward Moran and Steven Sher tell us that in 1954, applying for a Ford Foundation fellowship, Plutzik "mentioned plans for a long poem on 'man's inhumanity to man': 'the terrible atrocities which the 20th century has produced, with particular reference to the Nazis.'"[8] The poem was to be "a philosophical poem with narrative parts." Plutzik said he had "been collecting insights for the past four years"—while he was simultaneously drafting *Horatio*.

According to Moran and Sher, Plutzik called his planned work "the most immense subject for a poem in our times: the massacre of six million Jews by Hitler."[9] It was never to be finished, of course, but I would suggest that the assertion that Plutzik never really wrote about the Holocaust is not accurate, for we see the Holocaust in many of his poems, even those that precede its actual events more or less. It's a strange suggestion, to be sure. But whether or not we

---

7   Emmanuel Levinas, *Ethics and Infinity: Conversations with Philippe Nemo*, trans. Richard A. Cohen (Pittsburgh, PA: Duquesne University Press, 1985), 21.
8   Steven Sher and Edward Moran, "Hyam Plutzik's *Horatio* as Post-Holocaust Poem," paper presented at the ALA Jewish American and Holocaust Literature Symposium, Salt Lake City, UT, 2008.
9   Ibid.

read the Holocaust throughout Plutzik's body of work is contingent on what we understand when we hear the word "Holocaust." Certainly it is an historical event, generally said to have begun in the year 1938 with *Kristallnacht* and to have finished in 1945 with the liberation of the camps and the end of World War II. But as I have written with Sandor Goodhart: "Life after the Holocaust reveals to us . . . a darkness already there at the outset of the biblical tradition, one from which we might have learned about such destructive potentials had we wanted to learn, but to which we can now nonetheless turn as a guide in our ongoing exploration of narrative and its relation to the ethical."[10] The Holocaust, as it were, has always been with us. The events of 1938–1945 (and that is leaving out what began in 1933) were but a symptom of the darkness that both preceded and perpetuated it.

The Holocaust was an immense and inarticulable darkness, but it is also a darkness that harkens back to our origins, back to the beginning of the world, which we read about in Genesis:

> At the beginning of God's creating of the heavens and the earth,
> when the earth was wild and waste,
> darkness over the face of Ocean,
> rushing-spirit of God hovering over the face of the waters—[11]

A world that is "wild and waste," waters that are covered by a great darkness: our beginnings are entrenched deeply in chaos, a chaos that is a touchstone not of where we've been, but where we are going. The Holocaust is "less a new darkness than the same darkness, a darkness present all along and throughout our history in the West preserved for us in our scriptural texts, a darkness we may have forgotten but to which the Holocaust draws our attention as never before."[12] "The world is too much with us," William Wordsworth famously wrote.[13] He was hinting at our attachment to the material world, to things that are trivial and that prevent us from apprehending the natural world in all of its splendor. But the trivial things of the world, those things to which we attach ourselves fiercely and indefinitely, are symptomatic of our efforts to avoid a real encounter with and

---

10 Sandor Goodhart and Monica Osborne, "Introduction: Reading Darkness: The Key, the Letter, and the Beginning," *Modern Fiction Studies* 54, no. 1 (2008): 16.
11 Gen. 1:1–2. Quoted from Everett Fox's translation of the first five books of the Hebrew Bible: *The Five Books of Moses* (New York: Shocken, 1983). Gen. 1:1–2, quoted in ibid.
12 Goodhart and Osborne, "Introduction."
13 "The World Is Too Much with Us" was published in 1807.

understanding of the world and its dark origins. Indeed, the world is too much with us.

Plutzik understood this. But we know this only through a diachronic reading of both his work and life. It's not simply to read or understand something as it developed over time. It means understanding that at every point at which we pause to read a text, we are reading that same text from a different and new perspective, a perspective that is shaped and colored by everything that has come since, a perspective that contains more. So when we read Plutzik's earliest poetry through this post-Holocaust lens, we find that the darkness of the Holocaust—and the darkness of his post-1945 poems—is just a return to the darkness we never left.

The Traumatic Origins of "My Sister"

Trauma, whether experienced individually or collectively, is a common impetus for writing about death, loss, and absence. We tell or write stories, suggests Gabriele Schwab, "in order to defer death."[14] Such writing presents us with a paradox: the writing both acknowledges death and attempts to defer it, which, ultimately, is an impossibility. Writing is a form of resistance that doesn't move us farther away from death or trauma; rather, it brings us inside of it, as close as we can possibly be to understanding without ever understanding fully. "Stories are told to register a truth that cannot be found in the simple telling of facts," writes Sue Grand in *The Reproduction of Evil*.[15] The story that Plutzik tells in his 1937 poem "My Sister" shows us the traumatic core of his work. Mollie Plutzik was only two years old when she died. We know that she underwent a surgery on a Friday and then died on Sunday, March 2, 1919, and was buried in Waterbury.[16] That Plutzik returned to this loss so many years later but still so early in his literary career suggests that it was a profound loss from which he never fully recovered.

---

14 Gabriele Schwab, *Haunting Legacies: Violent Histories and Transgenerational Trauma* (New York: Columbia University Press, 2010), 41.
15 Qtd. in ibid., 41.
16 According to Deborah Briggs, Hyam Plutzik's daughter, this information was discovered in an excerpt of an obituary next to a note written in Samuel Plutzik's (Hyam's father) own hand in his Bible, which has since been sent to the Plutzik archive. "The little face that smiled so sweet our daughter Millie dies March 2 1919 age 2. Waterbury Conn. Hebrew Benefit ass'n Cemetery" (email from Deborah Briggs, October 7, 2023). It's unclear what the surgery was for, but Plutzik's poem suggests that perhaps it was a fall ("that tiny foot that brought her doom").

We sense viscerally, in this poem, the depth not only of Plutzik's pain at the loss of his young sister, but also the horror he experiences as he realizes that "the little skeleton lying there," underneath the ground, does so "in the crumbling shell of a world." This was 1937, and the world was only months away from that precipice of *Kristallnacht*. But this was a year that those with open eyes saw a great beast coming for all of us. It's not unthinkable that these moments of insight and presence awaken in us the traumas of the past, that we reach back into our traumatic core for guidance and insight, or even simply for familiarity. But what resides in the traumatic core? Story, one supposes, only story—which is to say, everything.

The poem opens with an image from the past:

> Now the swift rot of the flesh is over.
> Now only the slow rot of the bones in the Northern damp.
> Even the bones of that tiny foot that brought her doom.

Like the world reflected in Genesis 1, the *Beresheit*, Plutzik's body of work opens with absence and chaos. And while the language of "The Three" is certainly bleak and suspicious of any world that claims not to be, "My Sister," his second poem, moves from the universal and the collective to the personal and the individual. Plutzik brings us face to face with the image of his sister's corpse, a body long dead, but this is not an obituary; it's not a poem written as eulogy or memorial. There is little remembrance here. Rather, this is a return to something both foundational and fundamental for the poet. For, it is the "crumbling shell of a world" in 1937 that no doubt causes him to return to what may be his traumatic core. It is this world, devolving into the darkness that preceded it, in which Plutzik remembers his sister.

But is it really his sister whom he remembers here, or is she simply a touchstone to something larger and more enveloping? The world in which the poem places his sister is eerily familiar, reminiscent of the world of "The Three." For, her "little skeleton" lies "Amid the monsters with lipless teeth who lie there in wait— / The saurian multitudes who rest in that land— / And the men without eyes who forever glare at the sky." Likewise, in "The Three," Tantalus observes far-off Olympus from Tartarus, the deepest place in the underworld, and finds that the gods have gone missing, and that "under the clenched fists of ages palaces are crumbling." It's a world that is shifting into the darkness from which it originates. The irony is that the only thing that remains unchanged in "The Three" is that Tantalus, condemned to stand forever in a pool of water just under a fruit tree he can never reach, will be frustrated indefinitely, just as Sisyphus will continue, from the depths of Hades, to roll his boulder up a hill that has no peak. The gods may have departed, but they are not free to abandon their posts. "The accumulation of our pain will crush us," says Tantalus, "As the long march of infinity continues." Ixion, tied to his ever-spinning wheel of fire in Hades, has a different perspective:

> "... Insuperable powers
> Flay us; but the gods have in their humor
>
> Made us insuperable; ultimate defeat will never come.
> Instead of quick extinction we are tortured
> By mighty energies translated into pain.
> We are fagged runners. Continuing beyond endurance,
> Even fortitude is not for us, nor pride. We are ignored
> By the listless gods and the race of men existent."

The same could have been said of the Jews, both then and now: "Instead of quick distinction we are tortured ... We are ignored / By the listless gods and the race of men existent." Read diachronically, these words become darkly prescient of what would come. The poems last two lines—"Repetition on repetition ... Ixion fights with a rock ... The hungering of Tantalus arose again"—reveals the futility of imagining a world without death, without constantly pushing back against the threat of death.

Both poems are written from the perspective of those underground or in the underworld—no doubt Plutzik's way of grappling with how to understand what cannot be understand: that is, death. Putzik's sister looks up from beneath the ground and sees "ominous strangers ever entering," a "man who walks in the sky," who has come to cut the grass. It's a world, as in "The Three," in which time passes, revealing marked changes, and yet some things never change at all. For in the final lines of "My Sister," the "Man of War sits in the gleaming chair. / Struts through the halls. The Dispenser of Vengeance laughs, / Crying *victory! victory! victory! victory!*" It isn't just death that is inevitable, Plutzik seems to say; it is striving against it, the endless futility and frustrations felt more acutely by some groups of people than others.

In not writing directly about the six million and more, Plutzik articulates a larger and more chilling vision of the Holocaust as a darkness always both just behind and just ahead of us. We are always already both inside and outside of it. That is to say: we, at this moment and at every moment, are continuous with it. Recognizing this and re-orienting ourselves to a reading of literature and poetry in this way surprises us with the fact that it is not, after all, impenetrable or unbreachable. It is a rhetoric of separation throughout much of literary studies that orients us in this way, but the idea that there is a before and an after is but itself a fiction. We remember that in Cynthia Ozick's "Rosa," Stella supposes that there are three distinct versions of life: before, during, and after the Holocaust. But her aunt, Rosa Lublin the survivor, says: "'Before is a dream. After is a joke. Only during stays.'" In speaking the language of trauma, which locates the past ongoing in the present, Rosa collapses the separation between these periods. It's what Goodhart understands as the language of the Möbian, a figure that looks two-sided and "appears to have two distinct edges that cannot be crossed." It is a figure that appears to have a boundary, a crucial separation. But what "looks like it is on the 'other side' will turn out in fact to be the 'future' or the 'past' of where you are. What appears absolutely distant from you, separated by a nontraversable boundary, is really before you or behind you. You can reach that dislocated point without at any moment transgressing that boundary if you simply reorient yourself a quarter turn and follow the twisting path between your origin and your goal."[17] The twisting path that runs between Plutzik's early poetry and the Holocaust that it foreshadows is the one on which we reorient ourselves as we find the darkness that has always been with us.

When he was working on the Holocaust poem that never was finished, Plutzik wrote that it was hard enough to write a requiem for one man, so the question became how one can even begin to do justice when writing about six million. "Grief ends beyond one or two or three," he said, "beyond that there are only statistics." Some eighty-five years after the Holocaust began, we can read in Plutzik's early work the darkness, the devastation, the hopelessness of the Holocaust— the revelation and continuation of every violence against Jews since the beginning of time: "the monster, the mountain" that we drag behind us like Sisyphus pushing his boulder for eternity.

And so when Plutzik writes in "Death at the Purple Rim" (first appearing in 1940, during the war and before all of the horrors were known, but later published in 1949, after the war) about the "dream of each year" being smaller, we cannot help but read in retrospect. And when that "desperate final dream has tightened about you, / And encloses a space no bigger than you yourself, / It circles your neck and strangles you and you perish." Here is a reminder that the bleakness of his first two poems was an announcement of all that would come, a proclamation of the unavoidable bleakness of life in the modern world, perhaps

---

17 Sandor Goodhart, *Möbian Nights: Reading Literature and Darkness* (New York: Bloomsbury, 2017), 3.

especially for the Jew. Plutzik, here, is making good on his word. In the shared landscape of "Death at the Purple Rim" and "My Sister," even the beast is the same. In "Purple Rim" the beast that comes to "ravage the garden" he planted has eyes that are "piglike, his paws a hellish blackness." The speaker, presumably Plutzik himself, fears that the beast's "black paws" will "tear up the sprouts / And nibble them in the shade with his thieving mouth." It is a more dangerous version of the "black dog" in "My Sister" that "has come, but he does not play." The dog is a beast of the living world, haunting the decomposed body of Plutzik's sister, just beneath him, under the ground. But in "Purple Rim," the dog has become the beast; it not only haunts the speaker but actively torments him—and us.

In "A Memorial to Hyam Plutzik," Robert Hinman said:

> But, although the serenity that incorporates, even permits, gaiety and wit was certainly his, gaiety is not, in his poetry, his invariable, or even prevailing mood. The spirit of such a poet is the spirit of wholeness, of harmony, not vitiated, but rather ennobled by—as it ennobles—his basically tragic view of life. It is a spirit aware of joy rendered poignant by an undercurrent of sorrow, joy that can revel in the sweat of toil, "make a blessing of Adam's curse," without ignoring that it was and is a curse, without blinking at the desperate self-knowledge accompanying it, a self-knowledge he probed deeply even so early as his writing "Death at The Purple Rim."[18]

But I'm not certain that it was Plutzik's "view of life" that was "tragic." Plutzik was simply a careful observer of the darknesses, a poet who knew how to sidestep the separations in order to reorient himself—all so that he could read these darknesses. After all, are the images of his very first poem, "The Three," confined to the age of the era they signify or the moment in which the poem was written? Surely not. The devastated mythological figures, fallen and emaciated, immobile and barren but forced to toil indefinitely are not us; but they are also *not* us. Perhaps, as in the very first poem, what we call hell is now in this time more visible than ever, the deepest darkness become illuminated.

---

18 Robert Hinman, "A Memorial to Hyam Plutzik (July 13, 1911–January 8, 1962), accessed October 1, 2024, https://static1.squarespace.com/static/5682cb822399a3aa8df162ec/t/5682f3510ab377cb562c7a0e/1451422545918/hinman-memorial-to-hp.pdf.

Bibliography

Blanchot, Maurice. *The Writing of the Disaster*. Translated by Ann Smock. Lincoln, NE: University of Nebraska Press, 1995.

Fox, Everett. *The Five Books of Moses*. New York: Shocken, 1983.

Goodhart, Sandor. *Möbian Nights: Reading Literature and Darkness*. New York: Bloomsbury, 2017.

Goodhart, Sandor, and Monica Osborne. "Introduction: Reading Darkness: The Key, the Letter, and the Beginning." *Modern Fiction Studies* 54, no. 1 (2008).

Hinman, Robert. "A Memorial to Hyam Plutzik (July 13, 1911–January 8, 1962)." Accessed October 1, 2024. https://static1.squarespace.com/static/5682cb822399a3aa8df162ec/t/568 2f3510ab377cb562c7a0e/1451422545918/hinman-memorial-to-hp.pdf.

Levinas, Emmanuel. *Difficult Freedom: Essays on Judaism*. Translated by Seán Hand. Baltimore, MD: Johns Hopkins University Press, 1990.

———. *Ethics and Infinity: Conversations with Philippe Nemo*. Translated by Richard A. Cohen. Pittsburgh, PA: Duquesne University Press, 1985.

Nelson, Cary. "The Universe Is No Consolation: Hyam Plutzik, Jewish Identity, and the Ethics of Post-Holocaust Reading." *Journal of Jewish Identities* 15, no. 1 (January 2022).

Plutzik, Hyam. *Letter from a Young Poet* Hartford, CT: Watkinson Library at Trinity College, 2016.

———. "The Three." Hyam Plutzik, Poet. Accessed October 1, 2024. https://www.hyamplutzik-poetry.com/poem-the-three.

Schwab, Gabriele. *Haunting Legacies: Violent Histories and Transgenerational Trauma*. New York: Columbia University Press, 2010.

Sher, Steven, and Edward Moran. "Hyam Plutzik's *Horatio* as Post-Holocaust Poem." Paper presented at the ALA Jewish American and Holocaust Literature Symposium, Salt Lake City, UT, 2008.

CHAPTER 8

Judaic Time and Eternity in Hyam Plutzik's Poetry

Timothy Parrish

Who was Hyam Plutzik?

From 1933, when Steven Vincent Benet helped him win the Yale Poetry Award, to 2007 when Galway Kinnel, Hayden Carruth, and Donald Hall expressed their admiration in a PBS documentary, Hyam Plutzik's work has not been forgotten among those who care about modern poetry. The year after his death in 1962, Ted Hughes and Thom Gunn included his work in *Five Poets*. As Anthony Hecht shows in his foreword to *The Collected Poems* (1987), Plutzik's poetry demonstrates a clear familiarity with name brand-modernists such as Eliot, Frost, and Stevens. He also loved Shakespeare and rewrote *Hamlet* in his long, original poem, *Horatio*. Speaking of his relative obscurity, Eric Ormsby says he tried "to recreate a credible Shakespearean voice in American verse." More recently, David Scott Kastan, a Shakespeare scholar, echoes Hecht by placing Plutzik's work with that of Frost, Jeffers, Stevens, and MacLeish.[1] Were Plutzik trying to enter the canonical club of his era, his poems conveyed the proper mannerisms. But his poems were not like theirs. They came from beyond the pale, by which I refer to the Pale of Settlement established by the Tsars for the restricted residence of Jews. They go farther back than that—to the fall of the Second Temple and before that time as well. More than a poet's poet, Plutzik is a challenging poet steeped in Judaic tradition whose work remains to be rediscovered.

In his lavish appreciation of Plutzik, Hecht mentions Plutzik's familiarity with the Talmud and notes that "Holy Scripture" was "greatly important" to Plutzik

---

Copyright © 2025 by Timothy Parrish

[1] See Edward Moran and Phillip Witte, "A Great Stag Broad-Antlered: Rediscovering Hyam Plutzik," *Paris Review*, May 8, 2012.

and that he expected it to be important to his readers.² But among the tastemakers of twentieth-century American poetry there is little evidence that Plutzik's engagement with "Holy Scripture" influence their reading of him. Indeed, Hecht hardly makes the point before quickly moving on to connect his work with Robert Graves and Emily Dickinson, and then, almost breathlessly, noting how Donald Justice sees resemblances in Plutzik's poem titles to those of Stevens. Reading his peers' praises of his work, one almost wants to say that one finds so many different respectable and recondite poets of the Anglo-American tradition present in Plutzik's work that the reader may begin to wonder where Plutzik is amid this mélange of influences. Ideally, one should not have to point to his family history as the child of Russian Jewish immigrants to identify him as a Jewish poet. However, the crucial role that a Judaic understanding of life has played in his poetry is so profound as to have been almost invisible to his peers. This makes talking about Plutzik in the context of his career challenging, since one almost has had to present him as a different poet from the ones his peers knew and celebrated.

One may well ask, when is a poet formed? Is it when he first reads the most influential English poet of his life, T. S. Eliot, and thinks, yes, this manner of creating with words I want to master? Or does this process of becoming a poet happen experientially and occur before the future poet knows what a poem is? In the case of Plutzik, he knew Russian, Hebrew, and Yiddish before learning English upon reaching school age. To borrow from the title to one of his poems, he already knew himself as "Hyam ben Samuel," the son of Samuel, and was already absorbing the Judaic tradition from his family life where his father was a leader of the Jewish community and synagogue.

In a brief essay written the year before his death from cancer in 1962, Plutzik reflects on the status of the contemporary poet and the relevance of poetry to the modern world. He does not specify his complicated relationship with the English language or suggest in any way that he writes as a Jew. He speaks, simply, as a poet with no obvious affiliation other than the appreciation of poetry broadly conceived. Somewhat humorously, he divides the contemporary poet's limited audience into two groups: "those who neither respect him or understand him" and "those who respect him but still don't understand him" (303).³ It is easy to imagine that he was speaking of himself.

---

2 See Anthony Hecht, Foreword to *Hyam Plutzik: The Collected Poems*, ed. Anthony Hecht (BOA Editions Ltd. 1987), xiii.

3 *Hyam Plutzik: The Collected Poems*, ed. Anthony Hecht (Brockport, NY: Boa Editions Ltd, 1987), 303. Hereafter cited parenthetically as *Collected*.

"Creativity and Poetry" suggests an ambition beyond honorary membership in the rarefied poet's club. Noting that "the major themes of poetry are eternal," he nonetheless insists that poetry that strives to be "original" must "grapple" with "the experience of our time," which would include developments in science, philosophy, as well as contemporary questions regarding social mores and politics. His remarkable poem "To Abraham Lincoln, That He Walk By Day" speaks urgently to the issues of the civil rights protests and in so doing to an American national ideal no less than Whitman or Ginsberg did. Virtually no one read it while he was alive. One is unlikely to find it in writings about Lincoln or during courses on the civil rights movement. And, to be forthright, Plutzik is hardly a national poet. He almost never writes as an American. Poems like *Horatio*, among many others, delve into the thought of ancient Greece and Rome, and convey the range of his intellect. Like Eliot or Stevens, his poetry conveys a remarkable depth difficult to define—equal parts philosophical, historical, and aesthetic. But his poetry's depth reaches places their poetry does not touch—principally because it draws on Judaic understandings of history and time.

A poem such as "An Electromagnetic Phenomenon" uses contemporary science to describe the "veins of mind" that are "flung upward" to take in the sky. The "phenomenon" is but the poet's brain perceiving the natural world—including birds and butterflies, stars, and sun—as it becomes "a tangle in the mind" (*Collected* 236). In effect, the poem uses a phrase associated with science to describe the poet's interaction with the natural world. The tone is one of awe—it is religious, in other words. The poet exclaims, "there is a cobweb in my head!" This cobweb connects his perceptions to the natural world as "the current of music" made by the birds becomes entangled with the song in his head. But is this song merely an "electromagnetic phenomenon" or it something more, something derived from a recognition of being part of God's creation? In Plutzik, the terms of the question are not mutually exclusive. The poem does not play with the reader. It is a call to see as deeply as possible into the nature and history of things. It partakes of theologian Abraham Heschel's claim that "the will to meaning and the certainty of the legitimacy of our striving to ascertain it are as intrinsically human as the will to live and the certainty of being alive."[4] Heschel sees "this will to meaning" as an intrinsically Judaic concern and it imbues Plutzik's poetry at every turn.

Plutzik respects his peers, noting that "never in the history of English poetry has the general level of knowledge been so high and widespread among the

---

4   Abraham Heschel, *Who Is Man?* (Stanford, CA: Stanford University Press, 1963), 54. Hereafter cited parenthetically as *Who*.

general practitioners of the art" (*Collected* 302). On the other hand, he worries that their unprecedented will toward experimentation may cause them to remain unread except among themselves. In "Those Who Write after Freud," Plutzik sharply characterizes his peers. With what dexterity

> They run to obscurity
>
> Set up a maze
> As a hiding place,
>
> Become by choice
> A mysterious Voice. (52)

Yet, he wonders that despite their "difficulty," poets may get lumped with those who sell advertising—"men who will say anything for gain" (304). Plutzik may worry who his audience is for his poetry, but he does not write simply to have a reputation—or to be perceived as difficult or different.

In "Critique," Plutzik identifies T. S. Eliot as the mysterious voice these poets seek to emulate. For poets have developed a "horror of the obvious," "St. Thomas / (Stearns Eliot)" IS "sufficiently polyglot / Father and Nurse" to teach them that "to be devious is their safest course" (25). Eliot here is the god of Modernist Difficulty who presumably has provoked the high level of poetic practice among the modern poets who prize difficulty. "Genius is a rare bird," Plutzik observes in "Creativity and Poetry," that "will come to roost and roost where it will," before asserting that "we have no Shakespeare, and for ten years we have had no Dylan Thomas either" (302). The essay rather pointedly does not mention Eliot, just as it says nothing about his Jewish intellectual heritage. By then Plutzik had written and published "For T. S. E. Only," a poem directed specifically at Eliot, and it may be that his not mentioning the modernist was a form of rebuke and perhaps a recognition that his own work did not sit comfortably when read side by side with the elite genteel poets of his era.

In order to understand how Plutzik writes in a Judaic tradition going back to the scribes, it is worth thinking about Plutzik the uneasy Eliot reader and admirer. It may be that that the Plutzik who became the poet we know would not have existed had he not read Eliot. However, he would not have become the poet he is without being of a tradition that gave him a perspective to resist what I cannot avoid calling the shallowness of Eliot's individual tradition where mazes replace meaning. This is not to say that Eliot's poetry is merely a striving after difficulty so much as to say that for Plutzik difficulty is not the same thing as meaning. As we shall see, Plutzik's poetry resists modernist difficulty because it is always seeking a will to meaning beyond the poem itself.

Although only a child when Eliot published *The Waste Land* (1922), Plutzik became a poet when Eliot's work was defining what modern poetry could be. By the time he wrote "For T. S. E. Only," he was an established poet reflecting on his own relationship to the Anglo-American tradition. The poem is at once a plea, an accusation, and an expression of deep hurt. If we imagine Plutzik speaking directly to Eliot, we might almost think of it as a conversation between friends. As it happens, the offense is grave. The situation is so fraught that to bring it up is to put the friendship at risk. The poem's opening is remarkably direct. "You called me a name on such and such a day—" (109). This event happened in the past, but it rankles, it burns, in fact. He cannot let it go. The name referenced was not necessarily directed at the poem's speaker, but at "Bleistein our brother." Plutzik of course is referring to Eliot's antisemitic characterization of Bleistein,

> the barbarian with the black cigar, and the pockets
> Ringing with cash, and the eyes seeking Jerusalem,
> Knowing they have been tricked. (109)

This mocking description evokes Eliot's own language regarding Bleistein—it recontextualizes it so that Eliot's unselfconscious denigration of Jews is clear. Plutzik is like a surgeon removing Bleistein from Eliot's larger poetic practice, or body, in order to isolate and reveal the contamination of the representation. Decades before Eliot's antisemitism became part of mainstream academic discussion, he holds it up for the reader's inspection. And he is doing it as more than a gifted apprentice—as a gifted practitioner. He grasps the achievement of Eliot's poetry from the inside. One might say that Plutzik is part of this body since Eliot is one of the poets from whom he fashioned his own voice. To be inside of something, however, that also condemns you as foreign and dangerous is a very uncomfortable place to be. To change metaphors, how can one sit comfortably inside a house from which you know you have been excluded?

And then Plutzik makes a remarkable gesture. He calls Eliot "Brother Thomas." Is this a sarcastic reference to Eliot as the high priest of Anglo-American modernist poetry? Could he be mocking the avowedly Christian poet whose arrogance as a believer causes him to view the Jews as unfit for Jesus's teachings? The fourth stanza perhaps suggests such a reading.

> Or you may enwomb yourself in words or the Word
> (the Word is a good refuge for people too proud
> To swallow the milk of mild Jesus' teaching).

These lines tacitly remind Eliot that Jesus did not live his life (whatever his death may be said to mean) as a founder of a new religion that would conquer the distant continent that Plutzik and Eliot would share as countrymen; he was a rabbi enjoining Jews to live according to God's will. Eliot, however, having appropriated to himself the power of the "Word," has usurped this role and become lawgiver to modern poets. It's a role that strains Plutzik's Eliot.

> . . . the hunted look, the protestation,
> The desperate seeking, the reticence and the brashness
> Of the giver of laws to the worshippers of calves.

Eliot's confident tone and artistic distinction may even conceal some deeper poetic insecurity. Perhaps the poet's sense of his own refinement requires a scapegoat positioned as being oblivious to the elegant high culture surrounding him. Yet, the offending poet remains "brother Thomas," and is addressed as such throughout the poem. Rather than simply casting him off, Plutzik invites him to join their brother Bleistein and weep for their shared "exile." He must know it is an invitation unlikely to be accepted or even acknowledged.

It takes ten to make a minyan, and those ten must be practicing Jews, so the offer is not quite to pray together. One may think of this offer being like an invitation to a gentile to come for Shabbat. What is being offered is not a celebration, though, but an opportunity for commiseration and perhaps the healing of wounds. Exile suggests some sort of bond that precedes their knowing each other. After noting his friend's "hunted look" and "desperate seeking," he remarks that "at times you speak as if the words were walls." Here he refers again to Eliot as the poet-lawgiver, his tendency to define what and what does not count as poetic tradition and who may be said to claim this tradition. Among the walls he has built would be the one that divides Eliot from his brothers Bleistein and Plutzik. Plutzik would like to see this wall fallen and he topples it with a historical reference from a book they both share, the Bible.

> But your walls fell with mine to the torch of a Titus.
> Come, let us weep together for our exile.

With this single reference Plutzik reminds Eliot, the poet who provides learned footnotes to his most ambitious poem that their differences as Christian and Jew derive from an ancient historic moment in which the three of them still live.

In the New Testament, Titus was Paul's friend whose example made it so that new converts to the religious movement springing from Jesus' teaching need not be circumcised. It marked the moment where religious teaching from the

Judaic tradition to Gentiles did not require conversion. Judaic Law, in effect, was abrogated. These new converts who became disciples or apostles of Christ rather than adherents to a community based on laws derived from the Torah. After Titus, Jews who followed Christ would be lost among the growing legions of Christians. In some sense, to be a Jew meant one was not a Christian, despite a shared tradition, and to be a Christian was certainly not to be a Jew. In time, the Tanakh became the Old Testament to distinguish it from the New. Thus, after the tradition that separated Jesus's teaching from Torah evolved and created a new religion derived but separate from Judaism, Eliot the Christian poet arrogantly assumed for himself and his poetry the right to place Christianity above Judaism. Thus, despite his admiration for Eliot's poetic gifts, "at times," Plutzik notes, Eliot speaks "as if the words were walls," as if his words must form an uncrossable barrier between the poet and his Jewish reader. Eliot's poetry, his repudiation of Jews and their tradition, is, arguably, an extension of Titus's example. Such a perspective allows the self-declared Anglo-Catholic poet to dispense freely as they are decidedly not of his tribe. Worse, they might have been but chose not to be.

Each of the eight stanzas preceding the poem's concluding line ends with a version of the lament, "let us weep together in our exile" (109–10). These friends may have come from the same place, but history, wars, and prejudice divided them long ago. Still, Plutzik imagines they "could accommodate ourselves" (109). After all, they both admire Dante and dislike Chicago. To make possible this accommodation Eliot "must bow down / To our brother Bleistein here." Eliot must make amends. He must confess that they share more even than a poetic tradition. But Plutzik knows that Eliot cannot perform, what with Brother Bleistein smoking "an unaesthetic cigar" and therefore beyond the halls of rarefied aesthetic culture. Thus, in his disappointment that mimics bemusement, Plutzik proposes he "will stick a needle in your balloon, Thomas." That needle is this poem. Brother Thomas, in his role as poetic visionary, lacks what the poem calls "true compassion."

Plutzik writes as friend, brother, and fellow traveler in the high art and moral value of poetry. He suggests that Eliot "must bow" to Bleistein. If Eliot must "bow down" it is not only because he insulted Jews and the Judaic tradition, but also because he has violated the ideals of his most inspired poetry. Plutzik is calling out a self-mutilation at the heart of Eliot's work. To make this charge he calls on Dante—the Christian poet they both admire and whose work presumed to identify and categorize sins and their appropriate punishment. More a witness than a judge, the poet testifies,

> I see your words wrung out in pain but never the true compassion
> For creatures with you, that Dante
> Knew in his nine hells.

In *The Inferno*, Dante shows compassion for the suffering sinners—this quality is what makes the depictions of their punishment so affecting. Still, at one point he kicks the head of a sinner to prove his disdain for sin. Eliot has kicked the heads of Jews to prove what? That, in the words of "Burbank with a Baedeker: Bleistein With a Cigar," "the rats are underneath the piles" and "the Jew is underneath the lot?"[5]

In the diaspora, Jews have had to tolerate and constantly adjust to the fear their presence has provoked in others. When Eliot published "Burbank with a Baedeker" in *Poems* (1920), Adolf Hitler had not yet entered history and its antisemitism was casual and unthinking. When Plutzik published "For T. S. E. Only" in *The Apples from Shinar* (1959), it had been fourteen years since the Holocaust ended, and the word "Holocaust" had not come into use. There was yet no common word that marked that unthinkable crime against humanity. In this context, Eliot's antisemitism takes on a deeper meaning, just as Plutzik's invitation "to weep with us in our exile" offers Eliot the chance to join the Jews in the unbearable sense of loss of having one-third of their worldwide population destroyed in part because the sort of easygoing antisemitism Eliot glorified was a rampant cultural illness.

Whether Eliot read this poem, one has a hard time imagining him responding to it in the key in which it was written. Plutzik likely cannot either, so he speaks of how "now in the time of weeping you cannot weep" (109). This "time of weeping" presumably refers to the Holocaust. Reading Eliot after Hitler, Plutzik recognizes the Holocaust as another event in history that has come between them. By putting Eliot's writing into this broader history, he highlights both its vanity and its triviality. What moral authority is available to a poet of the first half of the twentieth century who mocks the Jews and does so from a place of willed ignorance? Eliot's depiction of Bleistein is a type of sickness. Recognizing that Eliot's offense is also an illness perhaps makes forgiveness easier. The poem's closing line combines accusation with forgiveness.

---

5   T. S. Eliot, *Poems* (Alfred A. Knopf, 1920), 18.

"You, hypocrite lecteur! Mon semblable! Mon frere!" (110)

My intent is not to stress that "For T. S. E. Only" is a Holocaust poem, but to highlight Plutzik's remarkable ability to recast contemporary poetry, and terms of traditional Judaic history, and theology. One can see a similar turn in a poem more obviously about the Holocaust, the self-referential "An Agadah for Hyam ben Samuel." It begins with an assertion: "the function of a match is to be scraped against roughness / To flare to fire, and to become ashes" (296). The poet imagines the matches speaking and one of them asks, "why should I be hurt?" Why, in other words, am I born to die. Given that the poem's title alludes to his father, Samuel, it may be read as a type of mourning. The light that is scraped that burns out with the match is the beauty and briefness of life itself. Or perhaps it's a reflection on the act of making poetry—a tribute to the vagrant nature of inspiration that may result suddenly in a poem that is only an approximation (ashes) of the spark that generated it. Hence, the poem ends with a voice answering, "Both the beauty and utility of a match / Are in their burning."

On this reading, the poem is concerned with the act of creation—a persistent theme in Plutzik's poetry—by which I mean the world made by God that God chose to make. In "Time and the Poem," Plutzik compares this "unexpected world" that appears "to an angel who slept / Through the seven crucial days" of creation to "a sudden poem." The comparison suggests an integral relation between poetry and creation that also shares a sense of the miraculous. For Plutzik, poetry aspires to silence—to reverberate as it were in God's eternal time. "Whatever is won is won forever," says the poet in "Of Eternity Considered a Closed System" (233). The same is true of "whatever it lost." A poem for Plutzik is something both won and lost forever,

> Out of my life I fashioned a fistful of words.
> When I opened my hand, they flew away. (237)

Or, as he writes in "Useful Prepared Speech for the Diffident Author of a Book of Poems Costing Three Dollars and Fifty Cents,"

> The beginning and ending
> Are the silence begun
> When the talking is done. (241)

Poems, like lives, are fragile, temporary. His poems are gifts he offers for having been created. Being created puts one into relationship with a divine presence that Plutzik's poems register nearly everywhere the poet casts his eye—in history or a tree. The fact of being created requires amazement, labor, and gratitude. Into that same silence from which God made the world, his poems will be returned.

In "Time and the Poem," the sleeping angel is the Adversary and his response to the poem that is the world is to defile it. To Plutzik, a poem, like a person, is "a coming forth from eternity into time" (106). His poems always assume that this life, no matter how it ends, is a gift—one has been created and thus been put into a mold not of one's making. If one is born into the Judaic tradition, one's birth is a blessing from God that is repaid by serving God which can take many forms, most clearly serving one's community and carrying on the spark of life by having children of one's own. A necessary part of one's life is also confronting its inevitable end while appreciating—as "An Aggadah" suggests—its utility and beauty.

So far, so good. But what if the poem concerns the Holocaust as "An Aggadah" surely does? As Eric Sundquist points out, Plutzik was likely inspired by Hanna Szenes's "Blessed Is the Match" (3).[6] She was a Mandate Palestine paratrooper who performed missions in Yugoslavia attempting to save Jews and was eventually caught and executed by the Nazis. "Blessed Is the Match" was her last poem. For many, the Holocaust meant a break with history and with God. For Szenes, it was something she fought against. Plutzik, too, fought against it as a soldier during the war. "An Aggadah," on the other hand, memorializes and reflects upon the Holocaust by attempting to balance the horror of its factuality against a continuum of Jewish history. In this sense, the title gives us the best clue to how we are to read the poem.

Aggadah is an ancient form of writing that engages the deepest questions of Judaism. Where Halacha refers to the absolute law of the Torah, Aggadah is closer to a folk tradition through which deeper meanings of the laws, often hidden, may be conveyed. The poem thus is telling a story, one that that necessarily involves specific Jews, Jewish history, and God. The first and last lines of Szenes's poem begin and end with the assertion, "Blessed is the Match consumed in kindling flame."[7] Plutzik's "Agadah for Hyam ben Samuel" speaks of the "function of a match" that is "to be scraped against roughness." This allusion, as Sundquist

---

6   Eric Sundquist, "Blessed Mythmaker: The Poetry of Hyam Plutzik," accessed October 1, 2024, https://drive.google.com/file/d/18y4aXA50KLXStIN8wD3vcpbFi1qtEEbF/view, p. 3.
7   Ibid.

suggests, pays tribute to Szenes as an exemplary poet and a fighter for justice.[8] By drawing on the ancient traditions, Plutzik commemorates the light that was the poet's life that resulted in this poem. Her death indicates that not only is each person born obligated to create their life through the choices they make, but what is won or what is lost is also won or lost forever.

If Plutzik's poem may be read as a tribute to her sacrifice for the Jewish resistance, the match being struck and burning itself out into an unfathomable darkness encloses her life within a sense of eternity. Her death, and by implication the Holocaust, is a continuation of history and obviously not a denial of God's presence. For this reason, the poem also concerns Plutzik's father, concealing Szenes and with her the Holocaust within this poem that names his father as the occasion of its writing. The poem places Plutzik's own biological life, given to him by his ancestors, as well as his densely allusive poetry into the event that took Szenes's life. He is acknowledging that the Holocaust concerns the Jews who survive it and the Jews who came before it. At the same time, the Holocaust is linked to traditions of Jewish history, storytelling, and rabbinic commentary going back to the beginning of the Diaspora and arguably to the moment depicted in "Time and the Poem," that is, the beginning of creation.

Does this eternity minimize the significance of the Holocaust? Of course not. Still, quietly, the poem gives the Holocaust a frame beyond itself. I borrow from the magnificent reading Sundquist gives the poem. "*Here*," he writes, "we have in miniature the history of the Jews, reaching from the match of Creation struck by God, variously figured in scripture and commentary as 'light,' 'fire,' 'flame,' 'radiance,' and 'sparks,' to the twentieth-century genocide of the European Jews" (2).[9] There is an arc to the history of the Jews and the Holocaust is not the end to Judaic history, in part because the ancient forms of Judaic writing may still address and frame it for future generations.

Within the light given by the match of creation, the poem enfolds the lives of Szenes, Samuel Plutzik, and Hyam Plutzik, and the Holocaust. If the Holocaust is sometimes seen as a break with history, Plutzik portrays it as being continuous with a Jewish history that is primarily concerned with a people's relationship to God. Plutzik often writes about history and historical figures who were not Jews, such as in "King of Ai," "The Airman Who Flew Over Shakespeare's England," "Predynastic Egyptian Who Rests within the Entrance of the Metropolitan Museum," and "To Abraham Lincoln, That He Walk by Day," among many others. It is important to note, though, that history and Jewish history may intersect but

---

8   Ibid.
9   Ibid., 2.

are not part of the same trajectory. As a practice, his poetry is consistent with historian Yosef Yerushalmi's observation that "Israel is under no obligation whatever to remember the past," only "God's acts of interventions in history, and man's responses to them" (11).[10] Even when writing about Eliot, his poem carries an aura of Judaic reflection, which isn't to say that God intervened in Judaic history through Eliot. The Holocaust may or may not have been such an intervention. In any case, its occurrence remains a medium for Plutzik to reflect on the presence of eternity, or God, in whatever act, great or small, happens in the world.

In his book about the Sabbath, Heschel argues that Judaism is a *religion of time* aiming at the *sanctification of time* (my emphasis—T. P.).[11] In Genesis, the seventh day is declared "holy." Heschel notes that in the Tanakh no object in space is declared holy. The Sabbath is not related to cycles of the moon or any of nature's events. It exists for the celebration of the eternal in time where the results of creation—of one's striving—gives way to dwelling in the "mystery of creation; from the world of creation to the creation of the world."[12] Temples may be destroyed, but not the Sabbath. Even apostasy, Heschel suggests, cannot do away with the Sabbath which always remains observed and celebrated. Consequently, "the primary awareness is one of our being *within* the Sabbath rather than of the Sabbath being within us" (21).[13] A world without the Sabbath, Heschel suggests, would be a world where an abyss separated humans from God. This is the world that Plutzik's Ixion foresees in "The Three" where technological prowess has replaced a belief in eternity.

In deciding which of Plutzik's poems would be included in *The Collected Poems*, Anthony Hecht omitted "The Three." His reasoning was that it is an apprentice poem and Plutzik had "judiciously" eliminated it from *Aspects of Proteus* (1937), his first book of poems.[14] I do not know why Plutzik sacrificed it. The poem is a remarkable mixture of Greek, Christian, and Judaic traditions where its Judaic component provides the framework for understanding the action depicted. It is important for understanding how Plutzik sympathetically engages other traditions from within a Judaic understanding of time, history, and being.

---

10   Yosef Hayam Yerushalmi, *Zakhor: Jeiwsh History and Jewish Memory* (Seattle: University of Washington Press, 1996), 11.
11   Abraham Heschel, *The Sabbath: Its Meaning for Modern Man* (New York: Farrar, Strauss and Giroux, 1979), 8.
12   Ibid., 10.
13   Ibid., 21.
14   Hecht, Foreword, 11.

When the poem begins, the Greek Gods have already been vanquished. The conqueror is the "Meek One," the "Galilean," presumably Jesus.[15] His followers are not portrayed sympathetically. They are "savage" and have "hewed down the shrines" leaving the gods to wander "like shades in erewhon" ("Three"). Plutzik tacitly associates the Greek Gods with Rome, since he uses their Roman names. And perhaps he is thinking of Rome as much as Greece which was transformed and partially overrun by Christianity. In any case, "the clan of the Olympians of Jupiter—was fallen," though in "a hole of hell" Ixion, Sisyphus, and Tantalus lived on ("Three"). The power of the great gods has become no more than dust on an urn, but the stories of these other figures abide as the legacy of this fallen world that the gods ruled but did not make. The distinction is important because the difference between believing in "God" the creator and "gods" who simply overran other deities to achieve power divides Israel from Greece and Rome.

The abrogation of power suffered by the gods curiously does not excuse Ixion, Sisyphus, and Tantalus from their punishments. Ixion remains tied to his wheel, Sisyphus still pushes his rock up the hill, and Tantalus is as thirsty as ever. They see the gods that ruled over them "prostrate" and vanquished and wonder why they are not free ("Three"). Vainly, they imagine their punishment has proven "the matrix of good rests in us." Surveying the gods' destruction, Ixion asks, "does the domain of Time extend forever?" He hopes that "duration" will give rest or perhaps for an "extra-Temporal Elysium." He wants to be excused from history, but this cannot happen. He longs for a cyclical time where he can once again live outside of his punishment. They imagine themselves forgotten by the future yet embedded within it. Out of their ceaseless repetition of their labors they foresee a future where humans are "webbed by chains of mechanism" and "their instruments control them." Their legacy will continue in "mortals" who "have spurned the gods" and "worship their own creations" in the form of technological achievement. Time for them is but the linear progression of their own repeating fates, albeit with the unquestioned convenience. Though they imagine time as eternal, they cannot conceive of it having a presence vaster than the ticking of clocks which is the basis of their punishment. They have lost the gods that sustained (and punished) them and are now trapped with no escape from the monotony of their existence. Indeed, insofar as their fates stand in for Humankind, not even death would free them from their pain. The "matrix of good" they claim is merely persistence in a task with no meaning beyond its ceaseless repetition. For them, the meaning of life is the loss of a meaningful life.

---

15 Hyam Plutzik, "The Three," *Hyam Plutzik, Poet*, accessed October 1, 2024, https://www.hyamplutzikpoetry.com/poem-the-three. Hereafter cited parenthetically as "Three."

Heschel suggests that humans experience life as something at stake that may be gambled away. At stake is no less than the meaning of life. In the poem, the followers of the Galilean chase away the gods—but only because the gods' order was already so fragile. It lacked permanence and gave no authentic meaning beyond power or comfort. "In all acts he performs," Heschel argues, "man raises a claim to meaning" (*Who* 54). That "The Three" details the dismal logic of surrendering this claim can be seen in the distinction Heschel draws between (Greek) ontology and (Judaic) theology. Where ontological thinking seeks to relate the human being to a transcendence called being as such (as in Heidegger, say) Judaic theology sees "the human being as more than being" and "seeks to relate man to divine living, to a transcendence called the living God" (69). "The self is in need of a meaning it cannot furnish itself" (56). Thus, the universe which Heschel calls "Being itself" can never "offer an answer to the question of the universe." That is the answer to Ixion's question whether Time extends forever. If "being" is only about "being as being," then life itself is but endurance of various tasks provided by the brute fact of existence. Heschel notes that "the Greeks formulated the search of meaning as man in search of a thought," where "the Hebrews formulated the search of meaning as God's thought (or concern) in search of man" (74). Thus, Heschel argues, "the tragedy of modern man is that he thinks alone." Trapped always in thoughts of his own affairs, "he has moved out of the realm of God's creation into the realm of man's manipulation" (76). In Plutzik's poem, Ixion, Sisyphus, and Tantalus embody this logic precisely. The cycle of punishment they forever endure is the result of thinking that "being" itself is the answer to existence.

For these mythological figures, there is no "time" beyond the time their suffering measures. Is there a worth beyond humans' inventions other than the ruins created for future humans to contemplate? Plutzik's poetry—whether it portrays the scattering of the Greek gods, a sprig of lilac, or a bomber being loaded—dramatizes the sanctification of time that permeates our passing through this world. This sanctification of time is also an acknowledgment of God as the creator. Poems such as "Magen Avot," "L'Cho Dodi," "El Anon Al Kalol," and "Kaddish" borrow from Jewish liturgy to praise God for having been created and being given the Sabbath. "Because he loves them, he brings now the holy tranquility / of the Sabbath to his people," he writes in "Magen Avot" (*Collected* 265). "Render greatness and holiness to the mighty name of God," "Kaddish" begins, and asks that "his kingdom flower in your time and in the whole of the house of Israel" (270). "Portrait" depicts the modern American Jew wearing "a borrowed Greek shirt" whose ancient beliefs no longer seem tenable in the modern world (112). The "borrowed Greek shirt" that signifies man's material success and social standing is also a remnant of Ixion's plight. That destiny has become available to the Jew who has, so to speak, lost the vestments of belief their fathers wore and kept despite many hardships.

If the "house of Israel" has perhaps lost its meaning to this Jew, it still exists in the Sabbath that he no longer observes. Plutzik's poems encounter the Sabbath in the most unlikely places. "Bomber Base," for instance, is a World War II poem set at an airbase that reflects upon the tiny acts leading to an act of massive destruction:

> The machines are quiet before the day' struggle.
> Geometric lines subtend the air at random.
> In the half-dark, propeller, wing and fin
> Loom out of space. (*Collected* 37)

They have been built from man's knowledge, which includes graphing space according to geometric lines that less map God's creation than demonstrate humanity's increasing mastery over it. Centuries of invention and experiment have formed the "propeller, wing and fin" of the airplane. Referring to its constituent parts, rather than the whole, gives the bomber plane a sense of doom. From the "half-dark" it "looms out of space," menacing, like the "great monster" of destruction it is. The poem details the messages going back and forth among humans concerning its mission and alludes to how "the enemy" is also doing the same. "Was there not a time when you turned aside to avoid crushing a beetle or marring a spider's web?" the poem asks. Humans may have learned to control nature by parsing it into atoms, but this control is as destructive as it is meaningless. Thus, "man grows wiser and older—and wickeder." "The work of your hands," the poem asserts, goes on until "the thing is ripe for killing." Ixion's wheel continues to spin.

As with "The Three," the poem resists this spinning by putting it into what Plutzik's poems frequently refer to as "Time" with a capital T. Quite simply, his poems exist to acknowledge time and are formed within it. Inflected by a sense of eternity, the poem's perspective conveys a context deeper than that of human action. Speaking of the various spotlights moving in the sky, the poem notes "There is always one whose beam rears motionless / Slashing up through the bowl of the Great Dipper" (37). The line suggests a continuity of existence between man and a beyond that cannot be measured. The acts committed on D-Day in the war are part of eternity and thus have a resonance beyond the daily contingencies that made them seem necessary. They exist in a moral universe where reflection is inevitable, which means God's presence. The poem ends with an italicized stanza written in the second person. Here Plutzik seems to be addressing himself and his own memories of serving in the war where "the faces changed often at the tables" and "that they were you yourself with a different number" (38). The poet's sense of identification with the soldiers lost or dead gives their acts a meaning other than having performed what was ordered—one deeper than having won or lost a battle. They live through the poem, obviously, but so does their enemy.

In "Bomber Base," World War II itself is not inconsequential. However, by placing its action within a sense of time that exposes the futility of understanding life merely as the dominion of space, or the exertion of power over the world, it provokes the reader to reflect upon the inadequacy of viewing time (or history) only as something by which we mark results or events. History does not exist for itself, or its own logic, but as acts within Time. The passing of the pantheon in "The Three" is meaningful not because something momentous seemed to have happened, but because its passing only calls attention to the vaster structure of which it is a part. In places, the voice of the poem seems to merge with this Time that is both present and absent. This beam in "Bomber Base" could refer to God but it also conveys the quiet stillness of the poet's voice—and its relation to the chaotic events it describes.

The last verse may be describing the entire history of the world, not just a battle from World War II. The event is linked to all human history under the observation of God. Neither is ordinary historical knowledge superfluous since Plutzik uses it to reflect on his own plight as a modern Jewish poet creating poetry that is something other than what advertisers and gifted maze-makers may make. As a Jewish poet, rooted in Judaic tradition, he understands his task to be one with the ancient biblical challenge of becoming a holy people. I do not think, however, that in "Portrait" he is calling on Jews to return to synagogue. Rather, his version of Israel, fragmented as it may sometimes seem, exists in a poetry which is touched by the sense of eternity—one might also say God's presence—that elevates the situations depicted in "Bomber Base" or "Portrait" into the most profound human meaning. Plutzik's poetry may be seen both to continue the rabbinic tradition and to engage modernists like Eliot. Their insistence on the sanctification of time, though, align them with Ahad HaAm's claim, "more than Israel has kept the Sabbath, the Sabbath has kept Israel."[16] Regarding Plutzik's future reputation, one wonders if the reader he deserves is not the reader of Eliot but one who recognizes his poems for the psalms that they are.

---

16   See Milton Steinberg, *Basic Judaism* (New York: Harvest, 1947), 130.

Bibliography

Eliot, T. S. *Poems*. New York: Alfred A. Knopf, 1920.
Heschel, Abraham. *The Sabbath: Its Meaning for Modern Man*. New York: Farrar, Strauss and Giroux, 1979 [1951].
———. *Who Is Man?* Stanford, CA: Stanford University Press, 1963.
Moran, Edward, and Phillip Witte. "A Great Stag Broad-Antlered: Rediscovering Hyam Plutzik." *Paris Review*, May 8, 2012. https://www.theparisreview.org/blog/2012/05/08/a-great-stag-broad-antlered-rediscovering-hyam-plutzig/.
Plutzik, Hyam. *Hyam Plutzik: The Collected Poems*. Edited by Anthony Hecht. Brockaport, New York: BOA Editions Ltd. 1987.
———. "The Three." Hyam Plutzik, Poet. Accessed October 1, 2024. https://www.hyamplutzikpoetry.com/poem-the-three.
Steinberg, Milton. *Basic Judaism*. New York: Harvest, 1975 [1947].
Sundquist, Eric. "Blessed Mythmaker: The Poetry of Hyam Plutzik." Hyam Plutzik, Poet. Accessed 27 Nov. 2023. https://www.hyamplutzikpoetry.com/commentaries.
Yerushalmi, Yosef Hayim. *Zakhor: Jewish History and Jewish Memory*. Seattle: University of Washington Press, 1996 [1982].

Figure 1. Plutzik in the Welles Brown Room, University of Rochester. While teaching he organized frequent readings for students and the community, creating a tradition which is continued to this day.

Figure 2. Plutzik, a lifelong nature lover and avid fisherman, is seen here engaged in contemplative reflection during the 1950s.

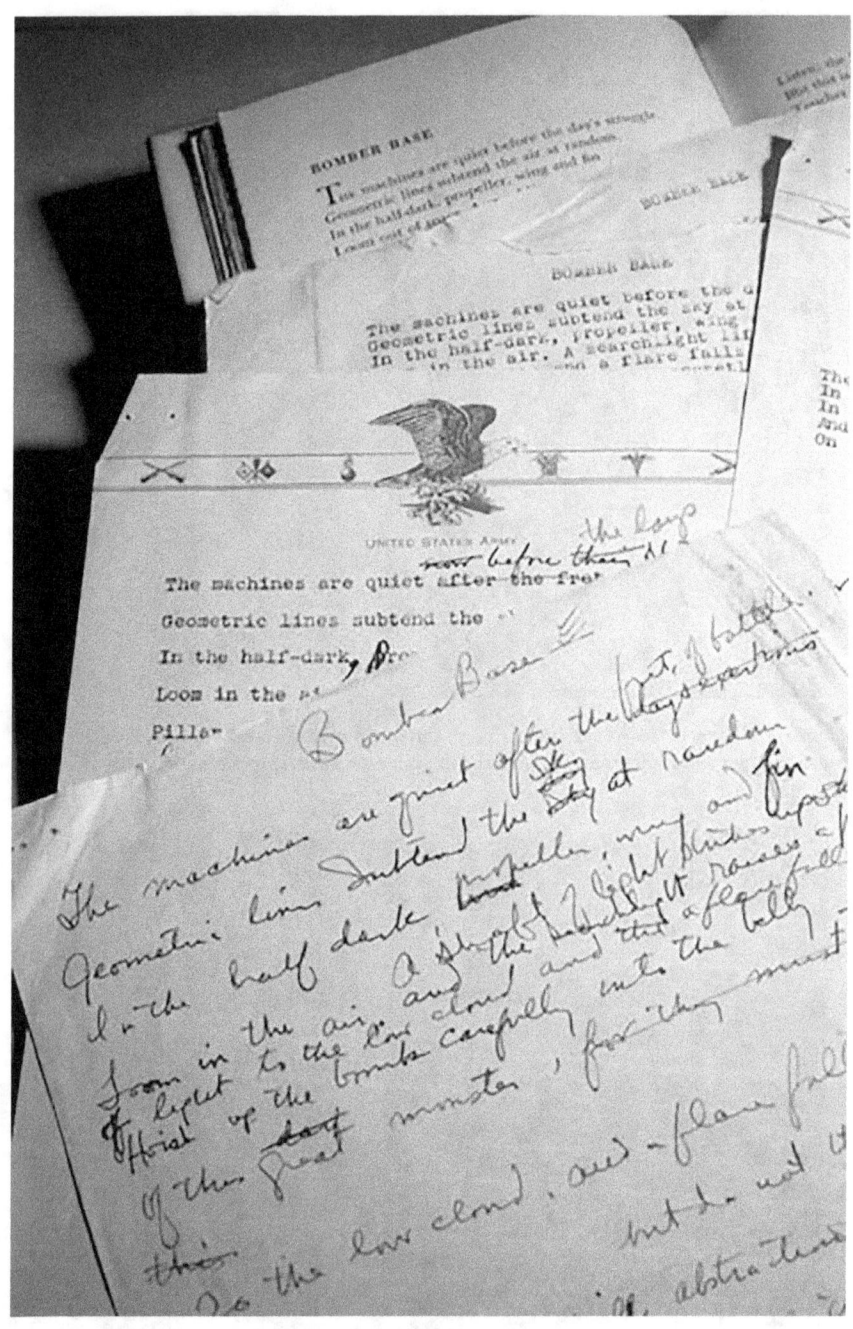

Figure 3. Manuscript for "Bomber Basse."

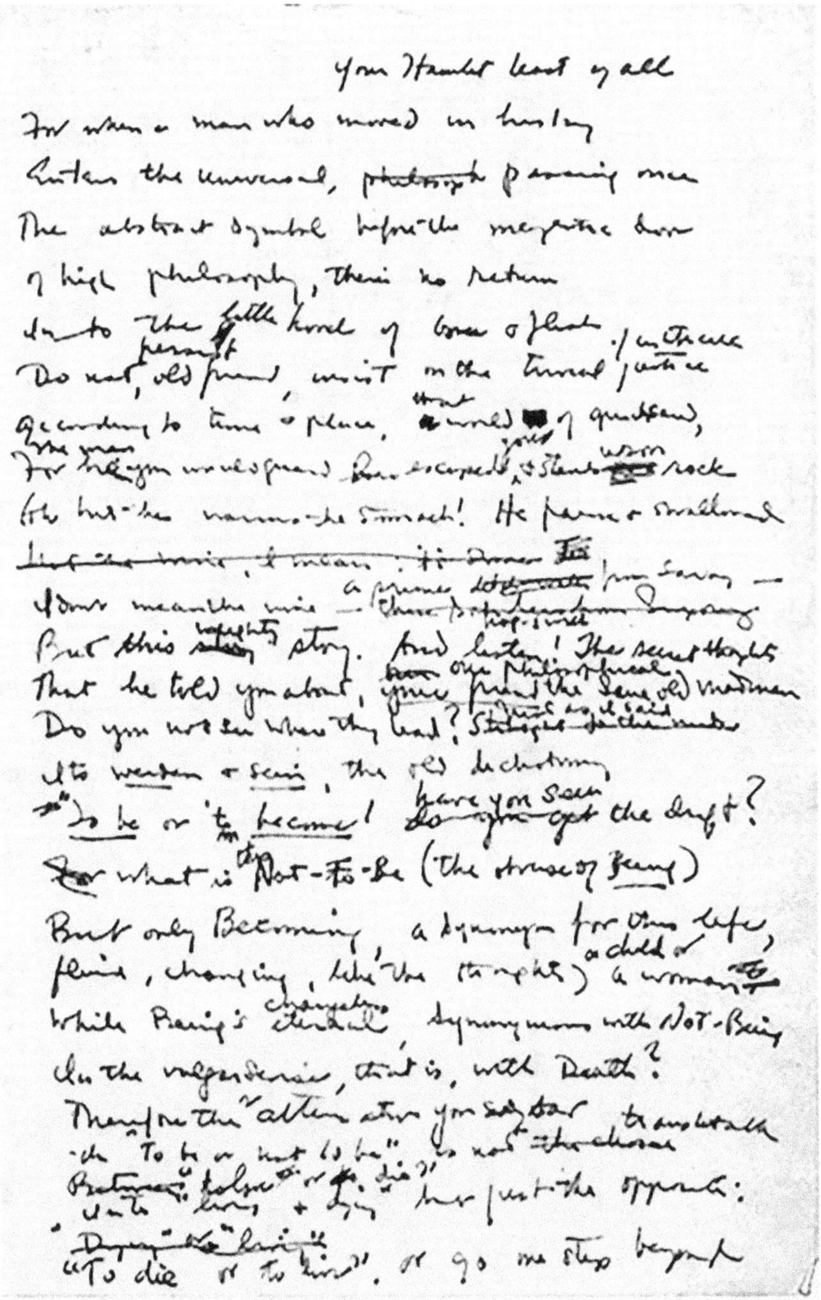

Figure 4. *Horatio* manuscript.

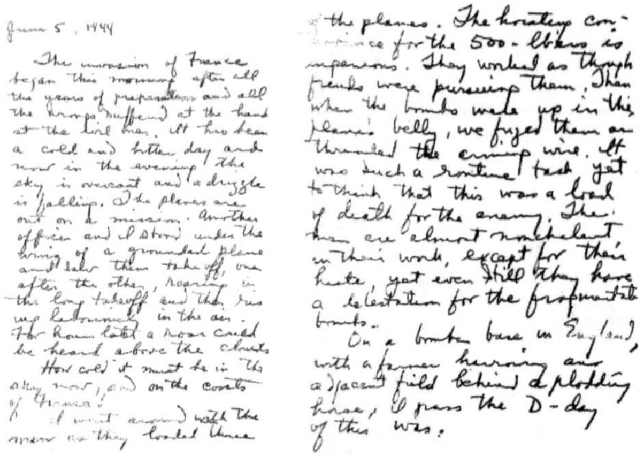

June 5, 1944

The invasion of France began this morning, after all the years of preparation and all the wrongs suffered at the hands of the evil ones. It has been a cold and bitter day and now in the evening the sky is overcast and a drizzle is falling. The planes are out on a mission. Another officer and I stood under the wing of a grounded plane and saw them take off, one after the other, roaring in the long takeoff and then rising laboriously in the air. For hours later a roar could be heard above the clouds.

How cold it must be in the sky now, and on the coasts of France!

I went around with the men as they loaded three of the planes. The hoisting contrivance for the 500-lb'ers is ingenious. They worked as though fiends were pursuing them. Then when the bombs were up in the plane's belly, we fused them and threaded the arming wire. It was such a routine task, yet to think that this was a load of death for the enemy. The men are almost nonchalant in their work, except for their haste, yet even still they have a detestation for the fragmentate bombs.

On a bomber base in England, with a farmer harrowing an adjacent field behind a plodding horse, I pass the D-day of this war

- Hyam Plutzik

Hyam Plutzik, WW II Soldier Poet, (1911-1962)
HyamPlutzikPoetry.com

Figure 5. Handwritten and typed D-Day letter by Plutzik.

Figure 6. Tanya Roth Plutzik and Hyam Plutzik were married in 1943 in Brooklyn, New York, moving to Rochester after the war where they remained until Hyam's death in 1962. Tanya (as of 2024) is 105 years old, living in the home she bought with Hyam.

Figure 7. Plutzik with his daughter, Roberta Ann (b. 1948), in a portrait taken for a magazine article featuring his poem "To My Daughter," taken in the 1950s in Rochester, NY.

Figure 8. Headshot of Hyam Plutzik.

Figure 9. Bible with signature of Samuel Plutzik.

Figure 10. Plutzik is buried in the large Jewish Cemetery at Old Montefiore in the Borough of Queens, New York City. In addition to his name (in English and Hebrew) and birth and death dates, a closed book is inscribed on his monument.

CHAPTER 9

"The Great Betrayals are Impersonal":[1] The Abstract Demons of Hyam Plutzik's *Apples from Shinar*

Kristin Boudreau

> To be, then, passionately impersonal
> Yet nourish the self, is the poetic dilemma.
> —Hyam Plutzik, "The Poetic Process"[2]

Hyam Plutzik's poem "To My Daughter" begins with an ominous image: "Seventy-seven betrayers will stand by the road." This poem, first published in 1951, appeared in Plutzik's 1959 collection *Apples from Shinar*. Like many of his poems, "To My Daughter" feels mythic, allegorical, its seventy-seven unnamed figures lining a road the daughter seems destined to travel. In its whispery syllables, its repeating phrases, and its open, meditative vowels, the poem suggests a lullaby, its speaker attempting to place comfort alongside difficult truth:

> Seventy-seven betrayers will stand by the road,
> And those who love you will be few but stronger.
> Seventy-seven betrayers, skilful and various,
> But do not fear them: they are unimportant.

Copyright © 2025 by Kristin Boudreau

1   Hyam Plutzik, "To My Daughter," in *Apples from Shinar* (Middletown, CT: Wesleyan University Press, 1959), 5.
2   Hyam Plutzik, "The Poetic Process," in *Aspects of Proteus* (New York: Harper and Brothers, 1949), 41.

With his weary, grieving lines, the speaker intimates that he has encountered figures like these before: he is as sure of their skill and variety as he is of their inevitable betrayals. How, then, can they be unimportant? What comfort does the speaker give his daughter when he urges her not to fear them?

> You must learn soon, soon, that despite Judas
> The great betrayals are impersonal
>
> (Though many would be Judas, having the will
> And the capacity, but few the courage).
>
> You must learn soon, soon, that even love
> Can be no shield against the abstract demons:
>
> Time, cold and fire, and the law of pain,
> The law of things falling, and the law of forgetting.
>
> The messengers, of faces and names known
> Or of forms familiar, are innocent.

As Cary Nelson notes, "Plutzik is not a poet of consolation" (16). Though it ends, shockingly, with the notion of innocence, this poem confronts us with many forms of betrayal. The small betrayals are unimportant only alongside the greater ones, those "abstract demons" that the speaker says have been prepared, like the grim future of another poem in this collection, "for me and my loved ones."[3] In the pages ahead we will briefly explore Plutzik's treatment of these abstract demons in this, his last collection published before his death in 1962. Before we do, we must consider Judas, who occupies a subordinate and parenthetical place in this poem not because he is unimportant but only because he is a rare case: many have the will and capacity for Judas's grievous personal betrayal, "but few the courage." The speaker's reference is tantalizing in all that it suggests and omits. In this poem about impersonality, Judas stands with "those who love" as the exceptions: the speaker mentions Judas's will, capacity, and courage—personal factors that might be compared to the strength of those who love the speaker's daughter. Despite his subordinate role in this poem, then, the figure of Judas—that most personal of betrayers, one of three whom Dante

---

3 "As the Great Horse Rots on the Hill," in Plutzik, *Apples from Shinar*, 7–8.

consigned to the last round of the last circle of hell—leaves an impression that will take on larger significance later in *Apples from Shinar.*

The speaker's list of more obscure threats, those "abstract demons," could be a table of contents for the poems in this collection: "Time, cold and fire, and the law of pain, / The law of things falling, and the law of forgetting." In 1951, as Plutzik was composing these poems, the demons had special significance for Jews. As early as 1941, writing to his former English professor not long before enlisting in World War II, the young poet had been thinking about his own people's particular susceptibility to the law of pain, even if he could see antisemitism in an impersonal light. "It is an awesome thing," he mused, "to be a Jew and to know that one is hated by so many of one's fellowmen."[4] Those ellipses are Plutzik's as he lays aside that unfinished thought and returns abruptly to an earlier reference in his letter. I like to think that Robert Pinsky resumed this thought thirty-four years later in "Poem about People," describing how the pain of impersonal hatred is almost unbearable:

> In the movies, when the sensitive
> Young Jewish soldier nearly drowns
> Trying to rescue the thrashing
> Anti-Semitic bully, swimming across
> The river raked by nazi fire,
> The awful part is the part truth:
> Hate my whole kind, but me,
> Love me for myself."[5]

It is difficult, these lines suggest, to take much comfort in the impersonality of racial hatred. Plutzik may have had two senses in mind for the line, "The great betrayals are impersonal." The first of course is the sense that these abstract demons—"Time, cold and fire, and the law of pain, / The law of things falling, and the law of forgetting"—are impartially meted out by a remote God or Universe. Or not: The poem "As the Great Horse Rots on the Hill," also in this collection, is partly a Job-like complaint against a universe that has carefully prepared physical decay for the speaker and his loved ones. Plutzik casts this poem in the rhythm of a Hebrew prayer drawn from Jeremiah 18: "As the pot in the hand of the potter, so are we in your hands. As the goblet in the hand of the

---

4   Hyam Plutzik, *Letter from a Young Poet* (Hartford, CT: Watkinson Library at Trinity College, 2015), 68.
5   Robert Pinsky, "Poem about People," in *Sadness and Happiness: Poems by Robert Pinsky* (Princeton, NJ: Princeton University Press, 1975), 4.

silversmith, so are we in your hands." While the original prayer affirms the smallness of human beings against the power of God, Plutzik's poem meditates on the meaning of aging, as he noted in an undated poetry reading.[6] Where the potter's clay is a communal "we" in the Hebrew prayer, Plutzik's subjects are much more individual, the image of their future more bleak:

> As the great horse rots on the hill till the stars wink through his ribs;
> As the genera of horses become silent, the thunder of the hooves receding in the silence;
> As the tree shrivels in the wind of time, as the wind Time dries the locust tree—
> Thus you prepare the future for me and my loved ones.

If the speaker feels the passage of time personally, he is more ambivalent about its source: Is it the impersonal demon of aging that torments impartially, "transform[ing] . . . a number of particles . . . in a certain moment in accordance with the laws of the universe," as he suggested at that same poetry reading, or have the rot, the silence, and the desiccation of time been carefully prepared for the speaker and his loved ones? Both the "law of things falling" and the "law of forgetting" appear in "The Old War," as "ten good sons, pilot and gunner, / Radioman and bombardier" fall from the sky. This poem was based on Plutzik's own wartime experience with the Heavy Bombardment Group stationed at RAF Shipdham in Norfolk, UK, where for nearly a year his B-24 outfit loaded bombs "for the mighty attack on Germany."[7] "The Old War" opens with an echo of the ploughman's indifference in Auden's "Musée des Beaux Arts": "No one cared for the iron sparrow / That fell from the sky that quiet day / With no bird's voice, a mad beast's bellow." Plutzik later recalled the origin of the one poem he'd written during the war. He composed "Elegy" in his head "one night while walking around under the wings of a B-24 bomber and watching the men head for a mission."[8] The poet's eyes on the departing bombardiers and the emerging elegy fill out the facts in this one spare sentence, suggesting the deeply

---

6   Reading from *Apples from Shinar*. Hyam Plutzik papers, D.113, Rare Books, Special Collections, and Preservation, River Campus Libraries, University of Rochester, Box 40. Hyam Plutzik Papers, D.113, Rare Books, Special Collections, and Preservation, River Campus Libraries, University of Rochester, Box 40.
7   Autobiographical Essay, 1949, Hyam Plutzik papers, D.113, Rare Books, Special Collections, and Preservation, River Campus Libraries, University of Rochester, Box 4, Folder 2, p. 4.
8   Hyam Plutzik, "Autobiography," Unpublished manuscript (1949), Hyam Plutzik papers, D.113, Rare Books, Special Collections, and Preservation, River Campus Libraries, University of Rochester, Box 4, Folder 2.

personal feelings Plutzik brought to the law of things falling—however abstract the law itself. As for the impersonal law of forgetting, it arouses strong feelings in the poem "After Looking into a Book Belonging to My Great-Grandfather, Eli Eliakim Plutzik," which opens with the speaker's dismay at history's blank tablets: "I am troubled by the blank fields, the speechless graves. / Since the names were carved upon wood, there is no word / For the thousand years that shaped this scribbling fist." While the speaker feels the genealogy that connects him to his ancestors, history itself is silent: "*Here lies someone.* / Here lie no one and no one, your fathers and mothers."

Impersonality, then, is no consolation and certainly no escape from emotion. Nor does the speaker intend consolation when he assures his daughter that "The great betrayals are impersonal." Plutzik may have had another meaning in mind with this line, a wry reference to T. S. Eliot, who had been to him both an influence and a tormentor. Eliot, of course, made the concept of "impersonality" nearly identical with himself as both a poet and critic, most notably in "Tradition and the Individual Talent," where he assures readers that "it is not in his personal emotions, the emotions provoked by particular events in his life, that the poet is in any way remarkable or interesting," but rather in the poet's distillation of emotions into an objective correlative. "The more perfect the artist, the more completely separate in him will be the man who suffers and the mind which creates." These lines, drawn from Eliot's most famous essay, appear in Plutzik's lecture notes on T. S. Eliot. Eliot ends his essay with a line that Plutzik did not quote but that, I will argue, informs many of the poems in *Apples from Shinar* and especially the poem Plutzik addressed directly to the senior poet. "The emotion of art," Eliot concluded, "is impersonal."

Eliot's influence on Plutzik's generation of poets and literary scholars was impersonal, professional, and altogether commanding. In *The Temple of Culture*, Jonathan Freedman describes "the absolute preeminence Eliot assumed in the booming literary academy of the 1940s and 1950s, especially in America."[9] Hyam Plutzik was part of this generation of American academics. He began teaching English at the University of Rochester in 1945 after the conclusion of his army service during World War II,[10] and he was among the first Jews to be admitted into mainstream institutions of higher education.[11] "To be a college

---

9   Jonathan Freedman, "Lessons Out of School: T.S. Eliot's Jewish Problem and the Making of Modernism," *Modernism/modernity* 10, no. 3 (2003): 420.

10 Plutzk, "Autobiography," 4.

11 As Freedman notes, these years constituted "the period in which an Anglo-American professoriate which had closed itself off to Jews, frequently on the not-un-Eliotic argument that

professor of English in this period," Freedman argues, "was, perforce, to come to terms with a model of literary history and cultural value that placed Eliot, the work Eliot esteemed (e.g. metaphysical poetry), and the religious vision that Eliot affirmed at the center of critical and pedagogical practice."[12] From the earliest years of Plutzik's academic career, he felt Eliot's critical and poetic dominance, and the intensity of his attention to Eliot is reflected in his papers at the University of Rochester archives. Plutzik's notes on Eliot overwhelm his collection of lecture notes for English 221: Modern Poetry, including twenty typed and handwritten pages on Eliot alone. In addition to their evidence of Plutzik's immersion in Eliot's poems and essays, these notes include quotations from some of Eliot's major critics. Represented here are Herbert J. C. Grierson's introduction to Eliot's *Metaphysical Lyrics and Poems of the Seventeenth Century* (1921), George Williamson's *The Talent of T. S. Eliot* (1929), I. A. Richards's *Practical Criticism* (1929), Edmund Wilson's *Axel's Castle* (1931), F. R. Leavis's *New Bearings in English Poetry* (1942), F. O. Matthiessen's *The Achievement of T. S. Eliot* (1958), and Eliot's own criticism, most expansively "Tradition and the Individual Talent" (1919). The margins of *The Waste Land* in Plutzik's personal copy of Eliot's *Poems: 1909–1925* are almost entirely covered with his handwritten notes, including sentences and phrases he copied from Cleanth Brooks's *Modern Poetry and the Tradition* (1939), Thomas MacGreevey's *T. S. Eliot: A Study* (1931), and other prominent critics from the first half of the twentieth century (see Figure 1). For a man who, in graduate school, had found the work of literary criticism "odious,"[13] Plutzik's diligence in understanding Eliot's poetic and critical principles attests to his recognition of Eliot as a literary giant with whom he would have to contend if he were to succeed as a professor of English.

Nor was Plutzik's deep study of Eliot motivated entirely by a sense of duty. The more established poet represented a modern approach to poetry that Plutzik wanted to emulate and that, as he put it, he was beginning to develop almost unconsciously. In his 1949 "Autobiography,"[14] written just five years into his teaching career at Rochester, Plutzik reflects on these changes to his poetic craft. Recalling that he had written almost no poetry during his service overseas,

---

one needed to have a thorough and deep –a feeling– knowledge of Christianity in order to understand a literary tradition suffused with that faith, began to open up to this previously excluded group" ("Lessons Out of School," 420).

12   Ibid.
13   Plutzik, "Letter," 21.
14   Plutzik, Autobiographical Essay.

nevertheless "some odd change or development seems to have taken place imperceptibly during this period, for I seem to express myself in utterly new ways. My very method [of] composition has changed. I write more deliberately now and am so much more at ease with subject and medium." Plutzik's evolving grasp of his art included a new independence from formal meter and a sharper editorial knife. Among his new ways of expression, he noted both his liberation "from the manacles of blank verse," which had been his nearly exclusive form before the war, and his more disciplined approach to diction: "I am much less romantic in my language, striving often for economy and precision rather than for vague music."[15]

Plutzik describes the evolution of his poetry as both the natural outcome of his maturing practice—part of that "odd" and "imperceptibl[e]" change taking place during the years when he wrote almost no poetry—and also the result of a conscious effort to find his voice. "So perhaps after a devious and fluctuating struggle," he concludes, "I have at last found my natural method of expression. I hope so. This search for an idiom is the modern poet's torment." That struggle included his study of T. S. Eliot, whose poetic principles dominate Plutzik's lecture notes and reflect the younger man's observations of his own work. A page of his undated notes on Eliot records this observation: "TS: tradition & enlargement of subject matter; greater economy of word & greater flexibility of rhythm."[16] Hyam Plutzik might have been describing his own developing "search for an idiom."

In a sentence that we might at first take as more evidence of Eliot's influence, Plutzik also mentions a turn toward the impersonal in his evolving poetic style: "I am . . . much less personal and introspective, much more prone to write about other people," he notes ("Autobiography," 5). However, in this context Plutzik's understanding of this word "personal" (meaning himself) is far different from Eliot's, who associates it with any individual's subjectivity, which he calls "personality." Eliot describes his ideal (that is, impersonal) poet not as a feeling consciousness but as a mechanism that reassembles the fragments of disembodied impressions and experiences. The poet, he writes, has

---

15 It was Mark Van Doren, Plutzik noted, who first pointed out his overreliance on blank verse. "It was directly as a result of his analysis and kind of criticism that I began to diversify my poetic form" ("Autobiography," 5).
16 Lecture Notes: T. S. Eliot, Undated, Hyam Plutzik papers, D.113, Rare Books, Special Collections, and Preservation, River Campus Libraries, University of Rochester, Box 31, Folder 17, p. 2.

not a "personality" to express, but a particular medium, which is only a medium and not a personality, in which impressions and experiences combine in peculiar and unexpected ways. Impressions and experiences which are important for the man may take no place in the poetry, and those which become important in the poetry may play quite a negligible part in the man, the personality. ("Tradition," 50–51)

This account of the poetic process uses the language of psychology in a mechanistic and distinctly unpsychological way, its agent not the poet but the "impressions and experiences" with which he works. Those impressions and experiences, in turn, are textual, mined from the literary and cultural works of previous ages. Although Eliot indicates that the impressions of earlier writers, put into words, create impressions in later readers that can be revived for yet other readers when they combine in new ways, his language distances the human, turning the poet into a medium or substance that enables the recombination of words. Plutzik's poetry, in contrast, remained attentive to the workings of consciousness that had lured him to the works of Plato, Emerson, and Whitman. Though he, like Eliot, admired John Donne, he was temperamentally drawn toward the Neoplatonic elements in Romantic writers. His early writings are full of meditations on consciousness. In his 1941 letter to Odell Shepard, he describes some of the dreams and questions that consumed him even as he was "prowling the streets [of New York] in search of employment."[17] "The old question of identity recurs to me often. What is the 'I' that my name represents? What is the self that I am, and who are the selves I talk to? Are we nodes of consciousness in a larger infinite nebula of consciousness?" (47). Many of his poems in *Apples from Shinar* play with the Platonic idea of an invisible, absolute world of which one might catch rare glimpses in the acts of ordinary life. "Jim Desterland" figures this glimpse as a door swinging open; in "If Causality is Impossible, Genesis is Recurrent" it is a "flitting beachhead in the Permanent." In a more skeptical mood, Plutzik wonders, with Emerson, if other humans are as real as he is. "Are they worlds, these other men, Thomas or Roger, / Like me, with their plague of conjurers / Or but lesser dolls in the scene of one / Who will deal alone with God?"[18] Emerson answers the question pragmatically: "Let us treat the men and women well: treat them as if they were real: perhaps they are."[19]

---

17 Plutzik, "Letter," 43–44.
18 Plutzik, "The Mythos of Samuel Huntsman," in *Apples from Shinar*, 16.
19 Ralph Waldo Emerson, "Experience," in *Essays and Lectures*, ed. Joel Porte (New York: Library of America, 1983), 479.

Plutzik's answer can be found in his poetry, and especially in one especially dramatic plunge into the personal. We don't know exactly when he first encountered Eliot's poem "Burbank with a Baedeker: Bleistein with a Cigar." The hand that had so tirelessly annotated *The Waste Land* had nothing to note in the margins of "Burbank," a poem that represents the modern age as devoid of love, meaning, dignity, and beauty. Through the travels of the Anglo-Saxon Burbank and the Jewish Bleistein, "Burbank" conjures the modern city of Venice from "time's ruins." Like many of Eliot's poems, the impressions here, both ancient and modern, constitute a pastiche of images from Western culture: the scraps of Venice come from Gautier's "On the Lagoons, "Andrea Mantegna's Venetian painting of St. Sebastian, Henry James' *Aspern Papers*, Robert Browning's "A Toccata of Galuppi," John Marston's masque, and Shakespeare's *The Merchant of Venice*. Other images and phrases are drawn from *Antony and Cleopatra* and *Othello*. The poem, which Eliot regarded as "intensely serious,"[20] reads like a tightly rhymed and metered rehearsal for *The Waste Land* and its images of physical and moral decay. A phrase in the epigraph puts these ruins in religious context: Eliot borrowed the passage *"Nihil nisi divinum stabile est. Caetera fumus"* from a streamer encircling an extinguished candle in Mantegna's 1490 *St. Sebastian*. Nothing is stable but divinity, it says; the rest is smoke. Like *The Waste Land*, where "withered stumps of time / Were told upon the walls," here "The smoky candle end of time / Declines." Plutzik's notes to *The Waste Land*— "Impotency of our time" (82)[21]—would be fitting commentary on "Burbank with a Baedeker: Bleistein with a Cigar." But in his copy of Eliot's poems, Hyam Plutzik left the margins of this poem blank (see Figure 2).

What did Plutzik make of the figure of Bleistein, the cigar-smoking "Chicago Semite Viennese" who makes his way through Eliot's Venice with "A saggy bending of the knees / And elbows, with the palms turned out"? Eliot's Venice is of course a historical Venice, written "not merely with his own generation in his bones, but with a feeling that the whole of the literature of Europe from Homer and within it the whole of the literature of his own country has a simultaneous existence and composes a simultaneous order."[22] Bleistein represents time's decline by joining the unnamed Shylock, indicated here by a reference to the

---

20   T. S. Eliot to Henry Eliot, February 15, 1920, in *The Letters of T. S. Eliot*, vol. 1, *1898–1922* (New Haven, CT: Yale University Press, 2011), 441.
21   Annotation, page 82 of Plutzik's copy of Eliot, *Poems*. Hyam Plutzik papers, D.113, Rare Books, Special Collections, and Preservation, River Campus Libraries, University of Rochester.
22   T. S. Eliot, "Tradition and the Individual Talent," in *The Sacred Wood: Essays on Poetry and Criticism* (New York: University Paperbacks, Barnes & Noble, 1966), 44.

Rialto, the commercial district where Shylock works as a moneylender. Whereas Shakespeare's Shylock endures abuse about his "moneys and [his] usances" (*The Merchant of Venice*, 1.3.435), Eliot's Bleistein signifies not only greed but also ruin and filth. "On the Rialto once, / The rats are underneath the piles. / The jew is underneath the lot." As James Longenbach notes, "this bit of parallel syntax, conjoining the fates of rats and Jews, is extremely provocative."[23] Eliot's words provoked Hyam Plutzik to put aside the ideal of impersonality and confront the poet directly in a poem he first titled "For Mr. Eliot Only" and later, "For T. S. E. Only."[24]

Written with not merely Plutzik's own generation in his bones, "For T. S. E. Only" starts with a direct address to "brother Thomas." Plutzik's speaker assumes the voice of the wounded and vengeful Shylock recalling the many insults and assaults he has endured from his Christian tormentors:

> You called me a name on such and such a day—
> Do you remember?—you were speaking of Bleistein our brother,
> The barbarian with the black cigar, and the pockets
> Ringing with cash, and the eyes seeking Jerusalem,
> Knowing they have been tricked. Come, brother Thomas,
> We three must weep together for our exile.

Plutzik's references to antisemitism recall Shylock's speech to Antonio upon being asked for a loan: "Shall I bend low . . . / . . . [and] Say this; / '"Fair sir, you spit on me on Wednesday last; / You spurned me such a day; another time / You called me dog–and for these courtesies / I'll lend you this much moneys?'"[25] In unearthing Shylock's wounded words, Plutzik restores the wound of antisemitism but not Shylock's vengeance. Instead, he calls to "brother Thomas" in a tone of reconciliation, as Edward Moran argues, addressing Eliot "as a fellow sufferer in exile" (5).[26]

---

23 James Longenbach, "A Response to Ronald Schuchard," *Modernism/Modernity* 10, no. 1 (2003): 49–50, 50.
24 "For T. S. E. Only" appeared in the *American Scholar* in 1925 and again in *Apples from Shinar* in 1959.
25 William Shakespeare, *The Merchant of Venice* (New York: Folger Shakespeare Library, 2009), 1.3.33–38.
26 Moran's essay perceptively demonstrates Plutzik's *caritas* in this address to Eliot, noting the poem's "deep sensitivity to the cultural markers and the language of Christian redemption, reproving Eliot only in the gentlest of tones for . . . his slurs on Jewish people."

Plutzik confessed in a recorded reading that he identified with some of Eliot's worst traits, which, he said, had "been associated historically with the Jews themselves." These include "a thundering of the law from the mountain, as it were, the sense of exile, the feeling that the temple is burnt, that the life of sanctity, of religion, is withered and must return if we are to be saved."[27] Having so earnestly labored to understand and apply Eliot's laws, as we have seen, Plutzik here looks behind the laws to the personality who issued them, as if discovering that Eliot's "impersonality" is a ruse, the show of objectivity masking an ugly psychological truth. The second stanza of "For T. S. E. Only" begins, "I see the hunted look, the protestation, / The desperate seeking, the reticence and the brashness / Of the giver of laws to the worshippers of calves."

Wallace Stevens disputed Eliot's famous claim of impersonality in 1922 after reading *The Waste Land* and confiding to his editor, "If it is the supreme cry of despair, it is Eliot's and not his generation's."[28] Plutzik's poem, while it does indeed approach Eliot with fellow-feeling, takes an equally oppositional stance to Eliot's poetic principles, scrutinizing them in the light of his poetic practice. Here, Plutzik accuses Eliot of using the words of the past, those essential elements of his poetry, as barriers to human compassion:

> Oh, you may enwomb yourself in words or the Word
> (The Word is a good refuge for people too proud
> To swallow the milk of the mild Jesus' teaching),
> Or a garden in Hampshire with a magic bird, or an old
> Quotation from the Reverend Andrewes, yet someone or something
> (Let us pause to weep together for our exile)
> Will stick a needle in your balloon, Thomas.

What has happened to Eliot's "historical sense," that perception of the past and its present that "compels a man" (as Eliot had written and of which Plutzik had taken dutiful note) to write with prior literary traditions "in his bones"?[29] In Plutzik's poem, that historical sense becomes a balloon, a distracting if fragile

---

27 Undated recording Ur_97_01. Reading from *Apples from Shinar*. Hyam Plutzik papers, D.113, Rare Books, Special Collections, and Preservation, River Campus Libraries, University of Rochester, Box 40.

28 Wallace Stevens, letter to Alice Henderson, November 17, 1922, in Alan Filreis, "Voicing the Desert of Silence: Stevens' Letters to Alice Corbin Henderson," *Wallace Stevens Journal* 12, no. 1 (1988): 17.

29 In his lecture notes, Plutzik draws two large asterisks and a small arrow pointing to the heading, "T. S. Eliot's Theory of Poetry: "First need of poet is historical sense, meaning tradition.

display that shields Eliot from empathy for his fellow humans. Plutzik had transcribed in his lecture notes a passage from Eliot's essay on the Metaphysical poets that argues for the necessary difficulty of modern poetry:

> It appears likely that poets in our civilization, as it exists at present, must be *difficult*. Our civilization comprehends great variety and complexity, and this variety and complexity, playing upon a refined sensibility, must produce various and complex results. The poet must become more and more comprehensive, more allusive, more indirect, in order to force, to dislocate if necessary, language into his meaning.[30]

Having refrained from commentary in those lecture notes, Plutzik speaks without restraint in this poem, revealing the cruelty of Eliot's refined sensibility and allusive dislocations, and making a mockery of impersonality with his direct address, his accusing tone, and the intimacy and exclusivity of the word "Only" in the title.

When Eliot first published "Burbank with a Baedeker: Bleistein with a Cigar" in his 1920 book *Poems*, he considered it "among the best [poems] I have ever done." Still, he understood that most readers would miss its high merits. "Even here I am considered by the ordinary Newspaper critic as a Wit or satirist," he complained, "and in America I suppose I shall be thought merely disgusting."[31] The speaker of Plutzik's poem admits to having been duped by Eliot's cleverness: "You drew us first by your scorn, first by your wit," he recalls, "[l]ater for your own eloquent suffering." Reflecting on the gulf between Eliot's "eloquent suffering" and his scornful depiction of the pain of others, the speaker suggests that Eliot's exile from humankind is the price of his wit: "We loved you first for the wicked things you wrote / Of those you acknowledged infinitely gentle. / Wit is the sin that you must expiate. / Bow down to them, and let us weep for our exile."

Forcing man to write w/ not only own generation in bones, but feeling of simultaneous existence of Eur lit & own land since Homer (T. S.)"
30 Lecture Notes: English 221. Undated, Hyam Plutzik papers, D.113, Rare Books, Special Collections, and Preservation, River Campus Libraries, University of Rochester. Box 25, Folder 11.
31 T. S. Eliot to Henry Eliot.

In introducing this poem at his poetry reading, Hyam Plutzik noted with dismay not only the antisemitism on display in this poem, but a larger problem with Eliot's brand of modernism. He described

> the modern artist too removed from his material, his world, human beings, . . . an artist-God who, like the God of Joyce's Stephen, retires from his creation to pare his fingernails. Are we too much like that? Yes, I find a coldness in Mr. Eliot, a coldness which, for instance, one does not find in Chaucer—who, like our contemporary friend, took a congregation of sinners on a journey and loved them, and enjoyed them, though no doubt he disapproved of their sundry wickednesses. . . . Well, Mr. Eliot doesn't love his unhappy ones–a typist and a cleric, Bleistein and the rest.

Chaucer displays his love and enjoyment of his sinning pilgrims, not only in their humor, their fellowship, their joy in earthly pleasures, and the charm of their stories, where their "sundry wickednesses" are revealed, but also in his character the Parson, the only moral church figure in *The Canterbury Tales*. The Parson's contribution to the pilgrimage is not a tale but rather a treatise on penitence, including the elements of contrition of the heart, confession of the mouth, and satisfaction through penance. Plutzik may have had Chaucer's Parson in mind when he commands "brother Thomas" to "bow down" to the "infinitely gentle" ones he has offended. He was clearly thinking, in contrast to Eliot's coldness, of the Parson's kind nature, his gentleness in reproving his fellow sinners:

> And though he hooly were and vertuous,
> He was to synful men nat despitous,
> Ne of his speche daungerous ne digne,
> But in his techyng discreet and benynge.[32]

Writing with earlier generations in his bones, Plutzik found in Chaucer an example of a moral sensibility that combined compassion with righteousness. He found another example in Dante, who appears in the final stanza of "To T. S. E. Only": "I see your words wrung out in pain, but never / The true compassion for creatures with you, that Dante / Knew in his nine hells." Even in the last ring

---

32 Geoffrey Chaucer, *The Canterbury Tales*, ed. Larry D. Benson (Boston: Houghton Mifflin, 1987), 31 ("General Prologue, ll. 514–518).

of the ninth and final circle of hell—the place named Judecca for Judas—Dante dwells not on the sin of Judas's betrayal but on his suffering. "That soul up there who suffers most of all," Virgil tells Dante, "is Judas Iscariot" (25:61–62).

Dante, like Plutzik, had spent long years studying his poetic elder. When he first encounters Virgil in Canto 1, Dante describes Virgil's importance: "O light and honor of the other poets, / may my long years of study, and that deep love / that made me search your verses, help me now!" (ll. 82-84). In contrast, Plutzik writes Judas into his account of T. S. Eliot, if only cryptically and namelessly: "you must bow down / To our brother Bleistein here, with the unaesthetic / Cigar and the somber look. Come, do so quickly, / For we must weep together for our exile." This command, "do so quickly," echoes Judas's betrayal of Jesus in John's gospel. After predicting his betrayal and identifying the man who will betray him, Jesus turns to Judas and tells him, "That thou doest, do quickly" (John 13:28).

This echo suggests faint confidence that brother Thomas will repent and bow down to the Jews he has insulted in his depiction of Bleistein. So too does the final line of the poem, an echo of *The Waste Land* that is itself an echo of Baudelaire's first poem, "To the Reader," in *Flowers of Evil*. "You, hypocrite lecteur! mon semblable! mon frère!," writes Plutzik, repeating Baudelaire's accusation that his reader falsely assumes the guise of purity and turning that charge against Eliot. Plutzik, who as we have seen saw something of himself in Eliot, found the coldness of Eliot's moral vision personally chilling. While incorporating the fragments of earlier writers, particularly Eliot, into "For T. S. E. Only," the poet renounced the dispassionate impersonality that Eliot advocated. Eliot's coldness, he seems to imply, was not a lapse from his theory but the necessary consequence of a theory that removed the individual from his works. Without the poet's own personality—including, essentially, his consciousness and conscience-morality is only a set of laws. Plutzik arrived at this insight, dramatized so eloquently in "For T. S. E. Only," not simply by reordering the impressions and experiences of earlier writers, but from his own lived experience, particularly as a Jew in mid-century America. Indeed, this was an insight that had been evident to Plutzik at least ten years earlier, when he published his first book of poetry, *Aspects of Proteus*. "To be, then, passionately impersonal," he wrote, "Yet nourish the self, is the poetic dilemma" ("The Poetic Process," *Aspects of Proteus*, 1949).[33]

---

33 Plutzik, "The Poetic Process."

Bibliography

Chaucer, Geoffrey. *The Canterbury Tales*. Edited by Larry D. Benson. Boston: Houghton Mifflin, 1987.

Dante, Alighieri. *Dante's Inferno*. Indiana Critical Edition. Translated and edited by Mark Musa. Bloomington: Indiana University Press, 1995.

Eliot, T. S. *Poems, 1909–1925*. New York: Harcourt, Brace and Company, 1936.

———. "Tradition and the Individual Talent." In *The Sacred Wood: Essays on Poetry and Criticism*. New York: University Paperbacks, Barnes & Noble, 1966 [1919].

Emerson, Ralph Waldo. "Experience." In *Essays and Lectures*, edited by Joel Porte. New York: Library of America, 1983 [1844].

Freedman, Jonathan. "Lessons Out of School: T. S. Eliot's Jewish Problem and the Making of Modernism." *Modernism/modernity* 10, no. 3 (2003): 419–429.

———. *The Temple of Culture: Assimilation and Anti-Semitism in Literary Anglo-America*. New York: Oxford University Press, 2000.

Moran, Edward. "T. S. Eliot and Hyam Plutzik: 'Hypocrite Lecteur, mon Semblable, mon Frere.'" Paper delivered at the T. S. Eliot Conference, St. Louis, MO, September 2009. https://static1.squarespace.com/static/5682cb822399a3aa8df162ec/t/5682f4f2d82d5ec8099bd075/1451422962573/moran-eliot-and-plutzik.pdf.

Nelson, Cary. "The Universe Is No Consolation: Hyam Plutzik, Jewish Identity, and the Ethics of Post-Holocaust Reading." *Journal of Jewish Identities* 15, no. 1 (January 2022): 5–31.

Pinsky, Robert. *The Sounds of Poetry: A Brief Guide*. New York: Farrar, Strauss, & Giroux, 1998.

Plutzik, Hyam. *Apples from Shinar: A Book of Poems*. Middletown, CT: Wesleyan University Press, 1959. Reprinted with preface by Hyam Plutzik, Wesleyan University Press, 2011.

———. *Aspects of Proteus*. New York: Harper and Brothers, 1949.

———. "Autobiography." 1949. Hyam Plutzik papers, D.113, Rare Books, Special Collections, and Preservation, River Campus Libraries, University of Rochester, Box 4, Folder 2.

———. *Letter from a Young Poet*. Foreword by Daniel Halpern. Hartford, CT: Watkinson Library at Trinity College, 2015.

Shapiro, Karl. *In Defense of Ignorance*. New York: Random House, 1960.

Stevens, Wallace. Letter to Alice Henderson, November 17, 1922. In Alan Filreis, "Voicing the Desert of Silence: Stevens' Letters to Alice Corbin Henderson." *Wallace Stevens Journal* 12, no. 1 (1988): 3–20.

"The Great Betrayals are Impersonal" | 207

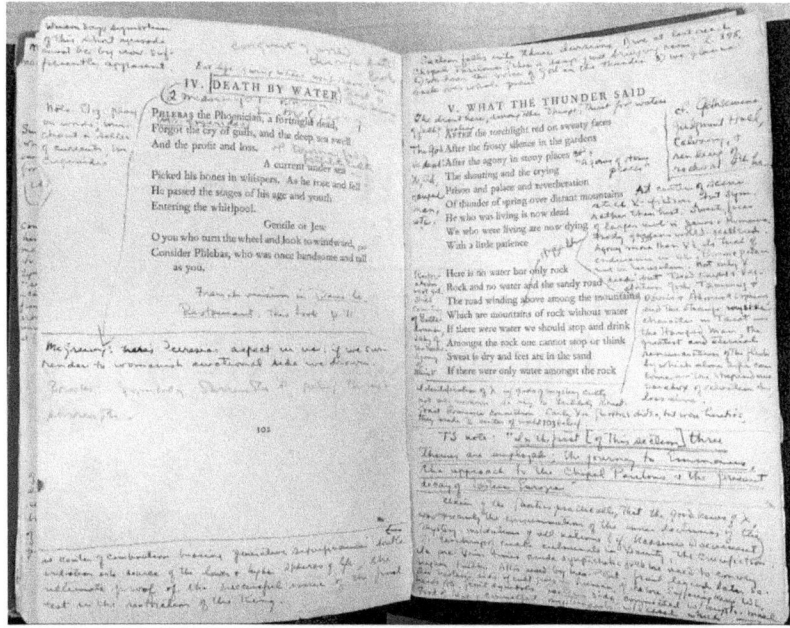

Figure 1. Hyam Plutzik's personal copy of T. S. Eliot, *Poems: 1909–1925* (New York: Harcourt, Brace and Company, 1936). Hyam Plutzik papers, D.113, Rare Books, Special Collections, and Preservation, River Campus Libraries, University of Rochester.

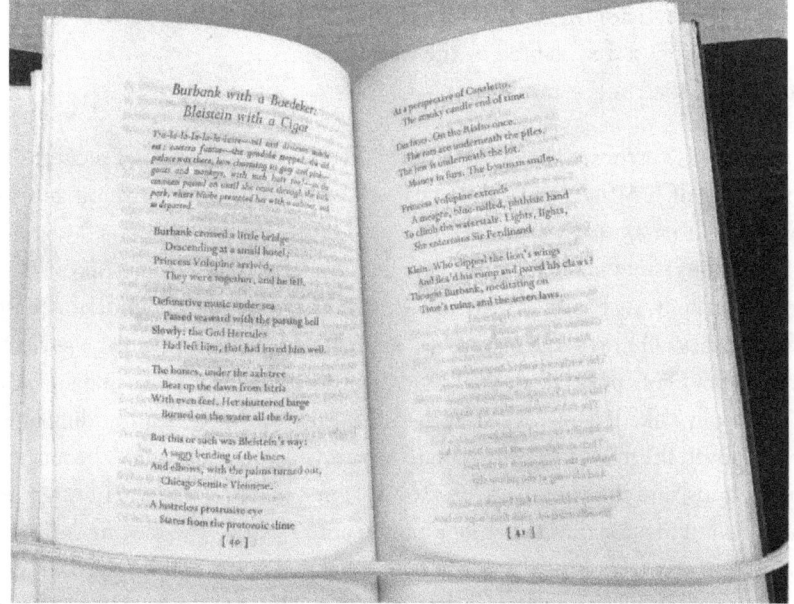

Figure 2. Hyam Plutzik's copy of T.S. Eliot, *Poems*. Hyam Plutzik papers, University of Rochester.

CHAPTER 10

Hyam Plutzik and the Lowercase Jew

Rodger Kamenetz

When I was fifteen, in the spring of 1965, I found myself marching on the old Baltimore Washington Highway with the Student Nonviolent Coordinating Committee. We were on our way to Washington, DC, to protest the murder of Reverend James Reeb in Selma. To keep up our spirits as a group we sang a hymn derived from Psalm 1:

> We shall not, we shall not be moved
> We shall not, we shall not be moved
> Just like a tree planted by the water
> We shall not be moved

But at other stretches, to keep myself occupied for the long miles, I recited "The Love Song of J. Alfred Prufrock" out loud, a poem I greatly admired and had committed to memory.

Now I don't know why at fifteen I found this love song so compelling. Maybe I took pleasure in knowing Prufrock was even wimpier than I was. I could mock his waspy tea party social life, his gentlemanly repression. It's odd considering that a Jew-hater wrote it, but Eliot's poem made me proud to be down-to-earth, frank, and Jewish.

That's why I liked "The Love Song"—but I also loved it with my budding poet's heart. I loved the music and the drama, the precision of the imagery, the magic of the rhythms, and the overall architectonics. I first discovered there how a poem could be not just a lyrical statement, but an entire world. The raw modernity of the diction was refreshing: "like a patient etherized upon a table" sounded new to me compared to the poems I'd read in school. I liked the mix of low and high

---

Copyright © 2025 by Rodger Kamenetz

culture: "sawdust restaurants with oyster shells" and "In the room the women come and go / talking of Michelangelo." But especially the ending as the meter returns to iambic bedrock and bursts into song:

> We have lingered by the chambers of the sea
> By sea-girls wreathed in seaweed red and brown
> Till human voices wake us, and we drown.

Eliot met me at the beginning of my lifelong love affair with poetry, and the mermaids (or were they sirens?) were inviting me from the flats of suburban life into the ocean of the archetypal.

So on that protest march in March 1965, I recited Prufrock's love song over and over while a tough Black ex-con in a denim jacket hollered at me, "Move it or I'm gonna put skirts on you." I have love for that naive kid who believed then that poetry and the Civil Rights movement and all that was good and just and beautiful could march together—me, the ex-con, and Eliot's mermaids on the road to freedom land. I was in that pleasurable state of mind Blake calls innocence and kabbalists call Eden. In that Edenic state I had no idea that T S. Eliot would have abhorred everything I was marching for, everyone I was marching with, and me too.

I fell in love with Eliot before learning he hated my kind. It broke my heart to discover I was that "rootless cosmopolitan" which, as he wrote in *After Strange Gods*, we could not do with too many . . . I, or my cousins and uncles were Bleisteins whom Eliot described as "Chicago Semite Viennese" and in the same poem ("Burbank with a Baedeker, Bleistein with a Cigar") as a tourist in Venice staring at a painting by Canaletto "with a lusterless protrusive eye," "from the protozoic slime"). In the same poem Eliot treated us to this little ditty: "The rats are underneath the pile / the jew is underneath the lot." (In a letter to his brother around the time of its publication in England Eliot singled out this poem and "Sweeney Among the Nightingales" as "intensely serious" and "among the best I have ever done.)"[1]

Eliot must have had a thing for the protrusive eyes of this Jew because in a manuscript of the *Waste Land* he imagined—in a parody of a Shakespeare song in the *Tempest*—Bleistein as a drowned man, his eyelids gnawed by crabs:

> Full fathom five your Bleistein lies
> Under the flatfish and the squids

---

[1] T. S. Eliot, *The Waste Land Facsimile and Transcript*, ed. Valerie Eliot (New York: Harcourt Brace, 1971), 18.

> Graves' Disease in a dead jew's eyes!
> When the crabs have eat the lids.
> Lower than the wharf rats dive.[2]

Apparently, he attributed the protrusion to Grave's disease—and you get a sense of the visceral hatred Eliot had for Jews in other proposed lines: "Those are pearls that were his eyes. See! / And the crab clambers through his stomach, the eel grows big..."[3]

Originally, Eliot thought of putting this poem at the very end of *The Waste Land*, but Ezra Pound talked him out of it :"I think your instinct had led you to put the remaining superfluities at the end. I think you had better leave 'em abolish 'em altogether or for the present."[4] But then Pound added, "If you MUST keep 'em, put 'em at the beginning before the 'April cruelest month.'"

One can only imagine how *The Waste Land* would read today if Eliot had picked up on this latter suggestion. Oh, what verbal acrobatics English professors would have to use to explain that one away. But I suspect they would have risen to the task because there is a well-established studious practice of averting eyes from Eliot's blatant hatred of Jews.

One has to wonder how in a relatively small corpus (fewer lines in total than Keats's *Endymion*) Eliot stuffed in so much Jew-hating. These are not accidental slips that can be easily overlooked, but bilge from a deep source of bile. Certain signature images and words rise up from every poet's unconscious, much as they appear in our dreams. In dreams we frequently see primordial images of fire, drowning, dogs, wolves, bears. A similar set of images and associations mark the work of every poet worth reading.

Eliot's poems associate Jews with animals commonly despised: rats, apes, raccoons. This material is visceral and, as Ed Hirsch remarked to me, the problem with Eliot's Jew-hating lines is not that they were his worst. Rather, Hirsch claimed, they were in some ways his "best" because his hatreds and aversions ran so deep. This may account for why his defenders seem to choose the strategy of simply reading around his disgusts, then glossing his work with a shiny polish of religiosity. That's not a luxury Jewish readers can afford.

Eliot also thought of beginning *The Waste Land* with "Gerontion," another Jew-baiting poem, which includes this gem:

---

2   Ibid., 121.
3   Ibid., 123.
4   Ezra Pound, *The Letters of Ezra Pound*, ed. D. D. Paige (New York: Harcourt, Brace and World, 1950), 233.

> My house is a decayed house,
> And the jew squats on the window sill, the owner,
> Spawned in some estaminet of Antwerp....

The lowercase "jew" in that line gave me the title of my poem and book—it is extraordinary how his hatred manifested itself in such intricacies as orthography. Having already memorized "Prufrock" but knowing little of his other work, I first discovered that poem after my girlfriend at the time gave me *The Complete Poems and Plays* for my fifteenth birthday. It was not a happy discovery. My grandfather and father were both landlords, and I can't read these lines now without thinking of them, barely human "Spawned" like frogs in a pond.

Eliot's hatred was written right into the poetry where it can't be avoided. Yet for generations teachers and professors have worked hard to teach us all that this bigot was "great," "important," "a representative of high culture," and most of all "Christian." I still feel some repugnance for people who praise Eliot as a Christian poet without holding him to account for his Jew-hating, for which, as the rabbis (in my poem "The Lowercase Jew") say,

> You never once apologized
> retracted, or removed those lines.
> You published them up to the end
> even after the war, you spoke of Jews
> whoring after strange gods—
> Eliot:
> But I won a Nobel Prize. Surely—
> Judge:
> —There are plenty of them in hell.

It took me years to sort out my anger—about forty, to be exact. My vehicle was a burlesque poem, "The Lowercase Jew." Thanks to a residency at the Vermont Studio Centers, I had the leisure to do what I call a "research poem." First I carefully listed every single Jew-hating line in Eliot. The poem imagines the poet has been brought up before a heavenly rabbinical court. His prosecutor, naturally, is that same "Chicago Semite Viennese," Bleistein, whom Eliot had visualized gnawed by crabs. His defense is Sir Ferdinand Klein. Both Bleistein and Klein appear as Jewish characters in "Burbank With Baedeker: Bleistein with a Cigar."[5]

---

5   T. S. Eliot, *The Complete Poems and Plays: 1909–1950*, ed. T. S. Eliot (New York: Harcourt Brace and World, 1962), 23–24.

That latter poem includes the world's first antisemitic line break. "She entertains Sir Ferdinand / Klein." Eliot resented Jews who worked their way into the British nobility viewing this as a nefarious sign of corruption of civilization.

In my poem, Bleistein and Klein each present their side of the case and in the end the rabbis need to decide the punishment. This is where I became stuck. I had to wrestle with my conscience and my resentment. My impulse was to send T. S. Eliot to hell, and I might have but for Hyam Plutzik.

When I came across Plutzik's elegant protest against Eliot's Jew-hating "For T. S. E. Only,"[6] it spoke to me directly. Though in tone and rhetorical approach his poem is admirably restrained, Plutzik is also addressing the same issue and, in his own way, the same anger:

> You called me a name on such and such a day—
> Do you remember?—you were speaking of Bleistein our brother,
> The barbarian with the black cigar, and the pockets
> Ringing with cash, and the eyes seeking Jerusalem,
> Knowing they have been tricked. Come, brother Thomas,
> We three must weep together for our exile.

My poem, with its courtroom set up, stands against Eliot in judgment, Hyam Plutzik had the confidence to address him directly as a brother—and to include Bleistein as a brother as well. The concluding word of each stanza, "exile," nicely tweaks Eliot by noting a commonality: Eliot, an American living in England, is like the Jews, an exile.

Plutzik builds emotion carefully. But in the last lines of his poem, he bares his teeth and expresses more fiercely the anger we both felt:

> Thomas, Thomas,
> Come, let us pray together for our exile.
> You, hypocrite lecteur! mon semblable! mon frère!

By quoting Baudelaire, Plutzik echoes Eliot's quoting Baudelaire at the end of the first section of *The Waste Land*—a gesture both erudite and a form of poetic justice. In my poem, which as a burlesque relies more on comic shtik, Eliot is forced to stumble over the Yiddish word for mercy, *rackhmones*.

---

6   Hyam Plutzik, "For T. S. E Only," in *Apples from Shinar* (Middletown, CT: Wesleyan University Press, 2011), 28–29.

I loved putting Yiddish in Eliot's mouth. Plutzik's erudition, his steady and gentle tone, his invitation to Eliot to weep with him over their common exile softened my anger and made me realize I had to take a gentler approach in my poem. In that sense Plutzik helped me realize a more common humanity— and the common failings—that unite us as poets, even including our brother Thomas Eliot. Plutzik's words of chastisement for Eliot could equally apply to me as I attempted to work through the hurt Eliot caused me when I was a young poet. And I took the lesson to heart:

> I see your words wrung out in pain, but never
> The true compassion for creatures with you, that Dante
> Knew in his nine hells. O eagle! master!
> The eagle's ways of pride and scorn will not save

Now, after reading Plutzik, hell seemed too harsh and so when it came to time to "sentence" Eliot, the rabbis on Bleisteins's suggestion send him to Jewish purgatory. But what is Jewish purgatory? The answer comes easily to Bleistein—and me:

> I propose you send him
> to Hyam Plutzik's grandson's bar mitzvah
> for the Jews it will seem an afternoon
> for him, a hundred years

I had often thought what it must have been like to have been an American poet with the unabashedly Jewish name Hyam Plutzik writing in the 1950s and '60s at a time when the cult of Eliot reigned supreme in English Departments all over the US. I think the name itself, along with his poem, above, made it seem just perfect for my burlesque. It was also an acknowledgment of my debt to Plutzik's example.

After the book, also titled *The Lowercase Jew*,[7] came out in 2003, I was happy that the Jewish Book Council sponsored a tour during Jewish Book Month. One of the stops was Rochester. I fully intended to read my Eliot poem because it almost always got a great response—but as I came into the JCC I was taken aback when I was introduced to a very formidable Tanya Plutzik, Hyam Plutzik's widow. The truth is I was shocked—a virtual reality had become flesh and blood. I realized I had no idea whether the Plutziks had a grandson who was bar

---

7   Rodger Kamenetz, *The Lowercase Jew* (Evanston, IL: Northwestern University Press, 2003).

mitzvaed. I asked Mrs. Plutzik and she said yes she did. I told her I was going to read a poem that mentioned her late husband and their grandson—as I didn't want to make her uncomfortable in any way. She was gracious and kind, and so with her permission I read it.

Many, many years later—in 2023—I was invited to read the poem at the annual JAHLIT conference. I met Hyam Plutzik's son Jonathan and his grandson Zach Hyam Plutzik and we shared a meal at the Betsy, the hotel which Jonathan owns and Zach manages. It was a special feeling. What had started as a line in a poem had sprung to life. It reaffirmed something else I have in common with Hyam Plutzik—a faith in the life-giving power of the poetic imagination.

Bibliography

The Bible. New International Version.

Eliot, T. S. *After Strange Gods: A Primer of Modern Heresy*. New York: Harcourt, Brace and Company, 1934.

———. "Burbank with a Baedeker: Bleistein with a Cigar." In *Poems, 1909–1925*, 5–6. New York: Harcourt, Brace and Company, 1925.

———. *The Love Song of J. Alfred Prufrock*. In *The Complete Poems and Plays: 1909–1950*, edited by T. S. Eliot, 3–9. New York: Harcourt, Brace and World, 1952.

———. "Sweeney Among the Nightingales." *The Little Review* 6, no. 4 (1919).

———. *The Waste Land Facsimile and Transcript*. Edited by Valerie Eliot. New York: Harcourt Brace, 1954.

Keats, John. *Endymion: A Poetic Romance*. London: Taylor and Hessey, 1818.

Phelps, Arthur N. *The Lowercase Jew*. New York: Greenleaf Publishing, 2003.

Pound, Ezra. *The Letters of Ezra Pound*. Edited by D. D. Paige. New York: Harcourt, Brace and World, 1950.

CHAPTER 11

Hyam Plutzik: "Value the Intermediate Splendor"

Jacqueline Osherow

What will become major concerns of Hyam Plutzik's lyric poetry are set out in the beautiful final stanza of his excellent and affecting World War II poem "Bomber Base":

> You remember that the faces changed often at the tables,
> That you talked to them, that they had many dreams,
> That they were you yourself with a different number.
> Probably, they would not have been very happy—
> The world being as it is—but they were young.[1]

These lines encapsulate a great deal of what is at the center of Plutzik's poetry, those fundamental paradoxes that establish poetry itself as both necessary and elusive. First of all, there is the seeming paradox of the singularity of any individual (the changing "faces," the "many dreams") alongside the fact that the poet cannot be differentiated from the rest of humanity ("they were yourself with a different number"). And then there is the paradox of life's extraordinary value ("but they were young") despite its inevitable disappointment and pain, ("Probably they would not have been very happy— / The world being as it is"). For Plutzik, poetry must always perform this balancing act between idealization and reality, between the self and the world, between "the many dreams" and "the world being as it is."

Even in his masterwork, the book-length poem *Horatio*, there is a significant poetic thrill of failure and disappointment alongside a kind of success. In devoting

---

Copyright © 2025 by Jacqueline Osherow

1   Hyam Plutzik, "Bomber Base," Hyam Plutzik, Poet, accessed September 3, 2024, https://www.hyamplutzikpoetry.com/bomber-base. All further references can be found at this website).

much of its energy to a clear demonstration of the post-Hamlet Horatio's inability to rise to the occasion of the hero, and submit to Hamlet's final request that he "tell my story," the poem explores the many instances of Horatio's failed telling (that is, his failure to make his hearers understand the story as he would have them understand it). It is only when the failed teller Horatio himself becomes a listener that he finally experiences a kind of success. Sitting with shepherds at a bonfire, Horatio hears a very elaborate telling of the amplified story of "Ambleth." However inaccurate, however mangled, however wildly elaborated, the story with which Horatio has been entrusted has been transformed into the stuff of myth, of call-and-response, of oft-repeated ritual. Horatio hears himself in the telling of Ambleth's story, though his name has been altered to "Honorio." And even though everyone laughs in Horatio's face as he says, "I myself was this Honorio," his claim is nonetheless made valid. He was indeed this Honorio. Through his efforts, the story with which he was entrusted has become legendary. The use of the nearly identical name "Honorio" in the poem makes clear that, even if Horatio has not succeeded in making the truth of the story known, his efforts have indeed been worthy of "honor." His emphatic claim to his position, "I myself," suggests his desire to acknowledge his role, and his pride in the position regardless of his failure to achieve the given request. The shepherd's telling is the result of Horatio's telling. He may not have succeeded as he hoped, but he hasn't failed.

Telling is, after all, a fraught enterprise in a world best understood through paradox. How one tells this story, and produces a poem under these circumstances is perhaps the major subject of Plutzik's work. From the very outset, in his early poem, "Divisibility," Plutzik's subject is the problem inherent in this paradox:

> The limitary nature of a wall
> Is partial only, to keep out dogs and insects,
> Contain the furniture, exclude the rain.
>
> But space flies through it like a mad commuter.
> Rooms are thus always strange, as if you entered
> Another by error in the same hotel,
>
> And saw incredulous no known landmarks,
> The bed moved, new luggage on the floor,
> And a window staring at you from the wrong corner.
>
> And desire goes through a wall as wild geese
> Pass and cry over reedy waters. Memory
> knows no walls. They are elementary limits.

> Only a fool would cut the sea with a knife,
> Or say to a wind: Exceed this line at your peril.

The only containable things are ordinary; indeed, even keeping out rain seems to be suspect. The only effect of walls is to alienate, to keep the speaker himself away from everyone else. What really matters, that is "desire" and "memory," can't be contained. These are, after all, rooms (the English translation of the Italian word stanzas), and Plutzik's rooms, his stanzas, are alien to him, unrecognizable; what matters won't inhere or stay. Indeed, what matters is by definition, what cannot be limited by the likes of him. The best he can do is "Pass and cry" like the wild geese, like desire. But then, there's a partial turnaround in the final couplet, which moves from lamenting the limitations of the poet's stanzas to celebrating limitlessness itself. It's as if the real poets are the sea and the wind. And since what's finally at stake is a "line"—an even smaller unit of a poem that a stanza or room—it's almost as if Plutzik, fool that he is, is challenging the wind to come up with a better line than "his"; the poem both declares its limitations and challenges them. After all: "Exceed this line at your peril" is the poem's last word; Plutzik, however foolishly, can be heard to challenge the wind to improve upon his poetic "line." And even if the implication is that Plutzik must surely lose, there is a lyric excitement in the challenge.

In Plutzik's poems, acknowledged limitation, such as "the world as it is," is still no reason to abandon one's "many dreams." Indeed, perhaps it's that limitation itself which is the catalyst for poetry. It doesn't really matter how the poet deals with the impossible, only that, one way or another, he takes it on. In "The Chinaman and the Florentine," he gives us two supremely celebrated poets:

> "This man for forty years studied a leaf;
> This man, the scattered leaves of the universe.
>
> This man lies in the earth at Ch'ang-hsi;
> This, in a crypt at the crossroads in Ravenna."

We have Dante, buried, in exile, at Ravenna, and, allowing for changes in the last half century of English spelling of Chinese place names, Tu Fu, who died in a place now called "Ch'ang sha." The opposition of their iconic enterprises—both involving leaves or pages—suggests that neither is exhaustive or absolute. In their opposite ways, each approached the unknowable, the inexhaustible. Each devoted a life to poetry and yet was buried; it's as if living and producing poetry were one and the same.

This same conflation of poetry and life itself seems to be made in the poem "To Those Who Look Out of the Window":

> To those who look out of the window at the night
> This passing moment, within the bounds of our city:
> We are not many, standing in the dark by the window,
> With the cool and starlit air brushing the face
> And our eyes hungry for the light-givers,
> The luminous ones, brightening the reaches of the sky.
> Of them our neighbors, the thousands and the thousands,
> Under all the rooftrees in the obscure streets and alleys,
> Let us not be reminiscent or piteous,
> If, in the coils of the serpent sleep long since,
> All unresisting they have become earthen.
> —But feel the brush of the wind on the face, the bath
> Of the light, the torment of beauty deep in the throat;
> And strive, in secret, this brotherhood so small,
> To climb the stairway out of the dust a moment
> Before the lying down to sleep and the surrender.

This poem's openness to a variety of meanings finally fuses those meanings. The speaker could be discussing the sleepless or the living; the "thousands and thousands" that "have become earthen" could be the dead or those who are satisfied with earth, whose "eyes" aren't "hungry for the light-givers." But whether "this passing moment" is life itself, or a restless moment in the dark by a window, that struggle to get beyond, to "strive . . . / To climb the stairway out of the dust a moment"—out of one's human limitations as well as one's mortality—becomes a kind of triumph in itself, simply in its opposition to "lying down to sleep and surrender." The very desire to struggle against mortality and to produce art, to produce a poem, is a kind of victory for "this small brotherhood," of the artistic. Striving to reach beyond dust and earth is in itself a thing of value, even if one must sleep and surrender at the last.

The stars here are profoundly inspiring, but in many poems, Plutzik establishes them as unattainable. Indeed, their very durability renders them suspect. In "Patterns of Earth," Plutzik is clearly skeptical of their power. Only what doesn't last is prized:

> Now the new grass is vivid with dandelions
> As last night the ancient sky was constellated.

And the Scorpion, the Dog, Perseus, and Hercules
Are less than the gold children of my field.

Whom I will name quickly, for their time is flying:
The Butcher, the Baker, and the Candlestickmaker.

They will be gone in a fortnight, fluff upon the wind,
And the bullies of the sky will resume their mastery.

Plutzik exults in his poetic powers even though he chooses no more significant names than those from a convenient nursery rhyme (and in the nursery rhyme he quotes, the line is followed by "turn them out or throw them out knaves all three"). Still, they are "the gold children of my field." It's their very temporariness, their future as "fluff on the wind" that makes them "vivid," as opposed to the "ancient sky," which is given the strange adjectival verb "constellated." The fleeting dandelions free up the artists, while the eternal stars block them, with their bullying "mastery." Similarly, in his poem "The Geese," Plutzik suggests that we "value . . . intermediate splendor." One wonders if the "miscellaneous screaming that comes from nowhere" and "Raises the eyes at last to the moonward flying / Squadron of wild-geese arcing the spatial cold" isn't on one level a comment, again, on his own poetry, which to him, perhaps, seems "miscellaneous," shrill, to "come from nowhere." But it does "raise the eyes" to a beautiful sight. And in a world where "There is no force stronger / (In the sweep of that monomaniac passion, time) / Than the will toward destiny, which is death," it does a service. As the poet urges at the poem's end, "value the intermediate splendor of birds." As he has now twice likened himself, as poet, to geese (before we had the geese who "pass and cry"), "the intermediate splendor of birds" could refer to his own poetry, for all its "shrillness."

If Plutzik is an imperfect artist, he's in good company. Plutzik suggests, in the closest form to a psalm that he produces, that God himself—genius though He is—could use a little editing:

Since, as we know,
Genius is superior to praise or blame,
He will not mind if I suggest:
"Fewer cold subjects please (they do not please!).
Really, your leafy stuff, Sir, is best."

But of course, those cold subjects prevail. And, in Plutzik's final, uncollected poems, the fleeting life, that is, death, becomes his own. There's a new urgency within the poems even before his own death is their subject. "The Belated Birds Having Taken Their Leave" begins once again with the poet settling for something small and fleeting in the place of stars. This time, it's not dandelions, but rather snowflakes. "The belated birds having taken their leave, suppose / This instant or two of barely falling flakes, / Each of a certain splendor the time of our stars." Once again, it's "intermediate splendor" that Plutzik is "valuing." "Our stars" are not *the* stars, but they too, possess "a certain splendor." There's always a qualifier to the splendor to which Plutzik claims access. And, once again, the great pleasure is also fleeting: "The glee on the upturned faces. Imagine / Arms raised on a hill to catch at Vega, / "That one I call Antares, and—" / "Why do you cry?" / "This snowflake died before I could give it a name."

Here the silliness of butcher, baker, and candlestickmaker is replaced by the wistful and understated acknowledgment of the fundamental impossibility of the poet's task; his subject is so fleeting, so short-lived that it can't be captured in poetry, can't be "named." Both the namer and the named diminish in the face of this failure. Whereas the named dandelions in the poem "Patterns" are, in short time, "fluff on the wind," the snowflake never gets its moment in poetry. And the stars, which here as in "Patterns" represent an unapproachable eternal, are not merely "bullies" but turn deadly when the fleetingness of human life is at issue. Here is "Cancer and Nova":

> The star exploding in the body;
> The creeping thing, growing in the brain or the bone;
> The hectic cannibal, the obscene mouth.
>
> The mouths along the meridian sought him,
> Soft as moths, many a moon and sun,
> Until one
> In a pale fleeing dream caught him.
>
> Waking, he did not know himself undone,
> Nor walking, smiling, reading that the news was good,
> The star exploding in his blood.

As in the other poems, there is a lack of awareness of the coming disaster, but here, of course, the stakes are higher, the loss incalculable.

Plutzik will, eventually, make his poetic peace, however sad, with even this loss, in his wonderful poem "An Agadah of Hyam Ben Samuel." An agadah is a brief tale, meant to explore or explain the inexplicable in the Torah or in life itself. Though he lived as a secular Jew, Plutzik was the son of a Rabbi, born Hyam Ben Samuel (Hyam, son of Samuel), and Hyam Ben Samuel is Plutzik's Hebrew name; it is the name with which he would have been called to the Torah for his bar mitzvah and named in any Jewish ceremony, marriage or indeed a funeral. Hyam Ben Samuel is the name engraved on his gravestone.

> Once there was a match in the days when matches could speak
> That complained: "Why should I be hurt?
> The surface of the match box is unnecessarily rough.
> I question the justice of the universe.
> Why cannot I and my friends
> Live in our match box in comfort and amity?
> Is fire necessary?"
>
> At which a gigantic voice cried out in the workshop:
> "Both the beauty and the utility of a match
> Are in their burning."

If we were to ignore the poem's title, we might see this as yet another poem praising what is fleeting. But the fact that the life in question is his own, and neither the dandelions, nor the snowflakes, gives the poem a unique pathos. If the poem, in its quiet way, rails against God and his "gigantic voice," against the unnecessary roughness of the universe, the poet himself does not, finally, disagree with God's harsh statement. He too has always found the greatest beauty (and, for the poet, "utility") in what will wind up as ash. There's a new intensity here: one doesn't simply "value the intermediate splendor" which has now become that brief moment between birth and death; one must "burn" with it, one must be that "intermediate splendor." Like the men whose faces disappeared from the table at the bomber base, "the world being as it is," the poet too, escaped, in dying, a certain amount of pain and disappointment. Like them, he too was "very young."

Bibliography

Hyam Plutzik, Poet. Accessed October 1, 2024. https://www.hyamplutzikpoetry.com.

CHAPTER 12

"Scorn Will Not Save": Plutzik's Negative Capability

Betsy Winakur Tontiplaphol

In the Afterword to the 2011 Wesleyan University Press edition of *Apples from Shinar*, David Scott Kastan writes that Hyam Plutzik's story "might" easily have been a "romantic" one, an archetypal "tale" of a "young poet with great promise who didn't live long enough fully to develop his gift." In reality, Kastan continues, Plutzik's "fate" was different." Although "he died too young," Kastan observes, Plutzik's "gift did develop," and through his "carefully measured poetry, precise but never precious," he became—and must be remembered as—"a significant American poet."[1]

I wouldn't challenge that assessment, but I'm keen to capitalize on—in fact, to *capitalize*, orthographically speaking—Kastan's oblique reference to English Romanticism, the nineteenth-century literary-aesthetic movement indisputably shaped by the early deaths of some of its youngest poet associates, among them George Gordon Byron, Percy Bysshe Shelley, and John Keats. Although there's no critical consensus as to whether those figures had sufficient time "fully to develop [their] gift[s]," their influence on nineteenth- and twentieth-century poetics was undeniably "significant," and it's impossible to imagine that Plutzik, both a poet and an English professor, was either unfamiliar with or indifferent to their work. Indeed, I would suggest that Plutzik, notwithstanding Kastan's eagerness to dissociate him from "romantic"/ Romantic types and "tale[s]," demonstrates in *Apples from Shinar* a concrete debt to Keats in particular. The youngest of the canonical Romantics and the first to die (at the age of twenty-five), Keats

---

Copyright © 2025 by Betsy Winakur Tontiplaphol

1   David Scott Kastan, Afterword to Hyam Plutzik, *Apples from Shinar* (Middletown, CT: Wesleyan University Press, 2011), 62.

matured rapidly over the course of his six-year writing career, which afforded readers both a body of "carefully measured" lyric poetry and a uniquely generative critical-philosophical position known, per the letter in which it originated, as negative capability. Keats's notion of negative capability functions, I argue, as an aspirational principle throughout *Apples from Shinar* but plays a special role in "For T. S. E. Only," the poem in which Plutzik addresses T. S. Eliot, who poached and distorted the description of the ideal artist that Keats had offered a century and change earlier.

Drafted in December, 1817, and addressed to his brothers George and Tom, Keats's negative capability letter opens (like much of the poet's correspondence) with an apology for not having written sooner and proceeds to offer a newsy account of recent entertainments, including evenings at the theater, dinners with friends, and a visit to a painting exhibition. In many ways, the letter is mundane—a Christmastime missive from an "affectionate Brother" who "has been out too much lately"[2]—but as it progresses, Keats's interspersed assessments of his social experiences and artistic encounters, offhand though they are, begin to cohere around a few crucial loci: the value of authenticity, the pleasure of intensity, and the necessity (from standpoints both moral and aesthetic) of emotional diversity. One recent outing, for example, "convince[d]" Keats "how superior humor is to wit in respect to enjoyment"—"These men," he complains, "say things which make one start, without making one feel, they are all alike"[3]— and in reflecting on Benjamin West's painting *Death on the Pale Horse*, he regrets that "there is nothing to be intense upon; no women one feels mad to kiss; no face swelling into reality." "[T]he excellence of every Art," he continues, "is its intensity, capable of making all disagreeables evaporate, from their being in close relationship with Beauty and Truth," and he identifies *King Lear* as a work in which "you will find this examplified [sic] throughout."[4] Waxing grateful for the Bard and ever more disgusted by the affectation of the "fashionables," whose corrupt perception generates objectionable "mannerism in their very eating & drinking, in their mere handling a Decanter,"[5] Keats approaches the letter's critical apotheosis. During a recent "disquisition" with his friend Charles Dilke, he recounts, "several things dovetailed in my mind, and & at once it struck me, what quality went to form a Man of Achievement especially in Literature & which Shakespeare possessed so enormously." "I mean," he continues,

---

2   John Keats, *Letters of John Keats* (Oxford: Oxford University Press, 1970), 42–43.
3   Ibid., 42.
4   Keats, *Letters of John Keats*, 42.
5   Ibid., 42–43.

> *Negative Capability*, that is when man is capable of being in uncertainties, Mysteries, doubts, without any irritable reaching after fact & reason—[Samuel Taylor] Coleridge, for instance, would let go by a fine isolated verisimilitude caught from the Penetralium of mystery, from being incapable of remaining content with half knowledge. This pursued through Volumes would perhaps take us no further than this, that with a great poet Beauty overcomes every other consideration, or rather obliterates all consideration.[6]

If the exposition in this famous passage vacillates somewhat frustratingly between the relatively straightforward (e.g., "remaining content with half knowledge") and the deeply abstruse (e.g., "caught from the Penetralium of mystery"), the term "negative capability" affords, in itself, a satisfying interpretive foothold. To be negatively capable, scholars agree, is to possess the ability to *negate*—that is, the capacity to turn off or otherwise suppress—the egoistic desire for clarity and permanence, for anything other than fleeting moments of intense "Beauty" or authentic expressions of "half knowledge." Whereas the egotist can't abide the discomfort of the incomplete or temporary, the artist embraces those experiences—and, in the process of doing so, cultivates egotism's opposite: empathy. To empathize is to experience (if only in fits and flashes) *others'* truths and perspectives, even the ostensibly "disagreeable" ones, and a few weeks after penning the negative capability letter, Keats would explicitly identify William Wordsworth, Coleridge's friend and collaborator, as "an Egotist."[7] "Every man has his speculations, but every man does not brood and peacock over them till he makes a false coinage and deceives himself,"[8] Keats complains of Wordsworth, celebrating instead a poetics of empathetic absorption, a literature (and creative practice) that prioritizes the feelings of its readers and the value of its subjects, *not* the voice of an all-knowing author. "We hate poetry that has a palpable design upon us—and if we do not agree, seems to put its hand in its breeches pocket," Keats declares in the February, 1818 "Egotist" epistle to John Hamilton Reynolds.[9] Instead, he asserts, "[p]oetry should be great & unobtrusive, a thing which enters into one's soul, and does not startle it or amaze it with itself but with its subject."[10] By October of 1818—not quite one year after he had coined the term

---

6   Ibid., 43.
7   Ibid., 60.
8   Ibid.
9   Ibid., 61.
10 Ibid.

"negative capability"—Keats would argue in yet another letter that the ideal poet is so adept at negation that he becomes selfless, identity-free. "As to the poetical Character itself," he writes to Richard Woodhouse,

> ... it is not itself—it has no self—it is everything and nothing— It has no character—it enjoys light and shade; it lives in gusto, be it foul or fair, high or low, rich or poor, mean or elevated—It has as much delight in conceiving an Iago as an Imogen. What shocks the virtuous philosop[h]er delights the camelion Poet. It does no harm from its relish of the dark side of things any more than from its taste for the bright one; because they both end in speculation. A Poet is the most unpoetical of any thing in existence; because he has no Identity—he is continually in for—and filling some other Body.[11]

As the foregoing description suggests, negative capability demands something akin to ego death—the successful poet, Keats implies, must pursue the annihilation of his own "Character." And although the Preface to *Apples from Shinar* begins with an anxious (Keats might call it "irritable" or Coleridgean) commentary on the literal and metaphorical forces that, in the twentieth century, "would kill the poet," Plutzik soon relaxes into a posture more negatively capable, more confident in the potency of fragmented or even *dying* poetic "product[s]" to "[triumph]" over such "conspirac[ies]."[12] There exist "powerful things in the modern world ... that move against poetry like an intractable enemy," Plutzik acknowledges, but those fearsome energies, he argues, cannot defeat poetic work in which "even one speck of the final distillate, the eternal stuff pure and radiant as a drop of uranium," appears.[13] Shades of Keats's "Beauty and Truth" abide in Plutzik's notion of "eternal stuff pure and radiant," and Plutzik's language of "speck[s]" and "drop[s]" echoes the rhetoric of partiality—"a fine isolated verisimilitude" and "half knowledge," in particular—that characterizes the negative capability letter. More broadly Keatsian, however, is Plutzik's titular commitment to dwelling in a world of "uncertainties, Mysteries, [and] doubts," of "disagreeables" that include even Iago-esque "enemies." Never directly addressed in the volume's Preface, the resonance(s) of the title *Apples from Shinar* must be

---

11 Ibid., 157.
12 Plutzik, *Apples from Shinar*, ix–x. I cite Plutzik's poetry (by line numbers) from this source throughout the essay.
13 Ibid., ix.

snatched piecemeal from "from the Penetralium of mystery," but it seems significant that Shinar is, from a biblical-mythological perspective, ground zero in arguments about linguistic confusion and expressive ambiguity. The site of the Tower of Babel,[14] Shinar witnessed humankind's misguided attempt to eliminate "uncertainties," "doubts," and partialities—to "build . . . a city and a tower with its top in the heavens," lest their community become "scattered abroad upon the face of the whole earth" (Gen. 11:4). Angered by the builders' hubristic insistence on something like divine completeness, God speaks—"'Come, let us go down and confuse their language there, so that they will not understand one another's speech'"—and then acts: "So the LORD scattered them abroad from there over the face of all the earth, and they left off building the city. Therefore it was called Babel, because there the LORD confused the language of all the earth, and from there the LORD scattered them abroad over the face of all the earth" (Gen. 11:7–9). But if the chaos of Babel and the attendant "Mysteries" of babble, or speech, are, per the story that Plutzik's title invokes, a form of divine punishment, they likewise generate opportunities for empathy, occasions to think *beyond* the self and its ego-straitened interests.

In addition to creating a discursive framework in which connection must be cultivated (rather than assumed), a post-Babelian reality consistently encourages a kind of Keatsian "speculation," a reveling in the diversity of the "scattered," be those components "foul or fair, high or low, rich or poor, mean or elevated." Such attitudes, Plutzik's title hints, have the potential to bear real fruit, to nourish like the overripe apples that "bend . . . the moss'd cottage-trees" in "To Autumn" (5),[15] the 1819 ode in which Keats, arguably at his most negatively capable, highlights the fleeting beauties that abide even in a season of impending death. Keats's autumn is a symphony of rot and endings—gnats that "mourn" in a "wailful choir" "[a]mong the river sallows," "full-grown lambs" that "loud bleat from hilly bourn," and southbound swallows that "twitter in the skies" (27–28, 30, 33)—and in "Beware, Saunterer, of this Desperado, a Mr. Bones, a Bad Actor," Plutzik seems explicitly to channel Keats's negatively capable description, warning a "[s]aunterer on this autumn track / That edges the garden" to "avoid the place where the dead rat lies," lest he be deprived the pleasure of sensing death's delicate and multifaceted *approach*: "Else how will you breathe

---

14 "Now the whole earth had one language and the same words. And as they migrated from the east, they came upon a plain in the land of Shinar and settled there" (Gen. 11:1–2).

15 John Keats, *John Keats: The Complete Poems* (Harmondsworth: Penguin, 1988). I cite Keats's poetry (by line numbers) from this source throughout the essay.

untainted the sweet / Rot of the indolent cucumber, / Apple smell, stubble-reek, pumpkin-vinegar?" (1–2, 4, 5–7).[16]

"Beware, Saunterer" appears midway through *Apples from Shinar*, but something more broadly negatively-capable informs the collection from the moment it opens with the winter-set "Because the Red Osier Dogwood." If autumn signals death's approach, winter signals its dominion, but in "the naked and forlorn season / When snow is winner," Plutzik writes, "the red osier dogwood / Is the winter lightning, / The retention of the prime fire (1–5)—an "isolated verisimilitude," as it were, whose striking "red branches" (14) represent, as Keats might put it, a "Beauty [that] overcomes every other consideration":

> For because the red osier dogwood
> Is the winter sentinel,
> I am certain of the return of the moth
> (Who was not destroyed when an August flame licked him),
> And the cabbage butterfly, and all the families
> Whom the sun fathers, in the cauldron of his mercy. (19–24)

If Plutzik's "certain" seems, at first blush, to counter Keats's epistolary injunction against resisting "uncertainties, Mysteries, [and] doubts," its shades of "irritable" Coleridgean "fact"-finding fade in the context of the poem's next lines, which treat "the moth" as merely an *emblem* of the scattered, a stand-in for the infinitely diverse "families" that roil about in nature's "cauldron." The grammatical singularity of "moth" notwithstanding, no individual or particular organism will "return," but *something* as yet unknown will rise, like a phoenix, from the "flame." Plutzik's "certain," then, conveys confidence not in facts but in inscrutabilities, not in logic but in the "speculation"—I borrow Keats's term—that the "the red osier dogwood" can be or cause anything beyond itself. And in the collection's subsequent poem, "The Dream about our Master, William Shakespeare," Plutzik doubles down on the notion that flashes of certainty derive from mystery and partiality. When a "midnight dream whisper[s] to" the speaker, it instructs him

---

16 Notably, Plutzik's list—cucumber, apple, pumpkin—recalls the catalogue of fruits and vegetables that consumes the first stanza of Keats's "To Autumn," which refers to "apples" (5), "gourd[s]" (7), and more. Additionally, Keats's second stanza describes a "cyder-press" (21)—a tool central to the processing of "vinegar," pumpkin or otherwise—while his final stanza employs the distinctive word "stubble": "barred clouds bloom the soft-dying day, / And touch the stubble-plains with rosy hue" (25–26). I highlight these similarities less to make a case about Plutzik's explicit borrowings from Keats—though I think that that case could be made—than to suggest that Keats was, acknowledged or not, a *presence* for Plutzik.

to "*take the lane / Into the green mystery / Beyond the farm and haystack at Stone*" (1–4; italics in original), in which space-cum-condition he will encounter the artist who, according to Keats, "possessed [negative capability] so enormously." Upon dream-entering "*the green mystery*," Plutzik writes, he "had one glimpse":

> . . . In a close of shadow
> There rose the form of a manor-house,
> And in a corner a curtained window,
> All was lost in a well of trees,
> Yet I knew for certain this was the place. (11–15)

Shrouded in darkness and "lost in a well of trees," Plutzik describes a space that evokes a literal "Penetralium of mystery," a "form[al]" sanctum of which his speaker gets but "one glimpse," barely a visual "half truth." The partiality of that vision nonetheless generates a fleeting "certain[ty]" of "place," a "fine isolated verisimilitude" with which Plutzik, unlike the Coleridge whom Keats denigrates, "remain[s] content." By the poem's close, in other words, its glancing certitude has re-dissolved into the broader substrate of not-knowing; constrained by "the hound of air, the ropes of shade / And the gate between that is no gate," Plutzik's speaker proves unable to meet Shakespeare "as he lived" (16–17, 20). As Plutzik suggests in subsequent poems, however, that loss really isn't one. "As the great horse rots on the hill," Plutzik observes in the piece that bears that title, it is "transmuted . . . / Till the stars wink through his skull" (1, 26–27), and throughout *Apples from Shinar*, ostensible losses and "rot[tings]" generate similar "wink[s]"—"glimpse[s]," flickers—of the authentic, of Keatsian "Beauty and Truth." Indeed, variants of the word "wink" appear throughout the collection, always signifying peeks into a cosmic "Penetralium." "If your mind were keener and could clinch / More than its flitting beachhead in the Permanent," Plutzik asserts in "If Causality is Impossible Genesis is Recurrent," "You'd see a twinkling world flashing and dying / Projected out of a tireless, winking Eye / Opening and closing in immensity" (9–13). Similar celestial imagery dominates "The Premonition," in which Plutzik, "[t]rying to imagine a poem of the future," envisions "a nameless jewel lying / Lurid on a table of black velvet"—"Light winked there like eyes half-lidded, / Raying the dark with signals, / Lunar, mineral, maddening" (1–6)—and he "winks" again in "The Mythos of Samuel Huntsman," whose speaker asserts that he "[has] seen through their plausible lies— / That of a uniform world" (7–8). Although it's tempting, the speaker of "Samuel Huntsman" intimates, to reach irritably for the facts—"But me they cannot expect // To wink forever, never to turn / And look at their empty stage /

Of space starless and planetless" (18–21)—the poem closes with "question[s]" still to be "wrestle[d]" and a "façade" that stands as yet un-"smash[ed]" (25–26).

But if "Samuel Huntsman" manifests, like "Red Osier Dogwood," "Dream About Our Master," and other pieces, a Keatsian appreciation for "isolated verisimilitude[s]" peeped with "eyes half-lidded," it also captures the annihilation of self that, according to Keats, allows the poet to sustain such a posture. The query with which "Samuel Huntsman" concludes speculates about the "worlds" of "others":

> Are they worlds, these other men, Thomas or Roger,
> Like me, with their plague of conjurors
> Or but lesser dolls in the scene of one
> Who will deal with God alone? (27–30)

The terms of the question are, in themselves, ego-diminishing: Plutzik's speaking persona is either one "world" among many or a divine plaything, a "doll" trapped "[i]n the desperate game which is God's" (6). And to obtain even a wink of an answer, Plutzik intimates elsewhere, is to let go of "self," "character," and "Identity"—Keats's terms—altogether. In "Jim Desterland," for example, a speaker "fishing off Pondy Point" abruptly encounters "the voice you never will hear / Filling the crannies of the air" (5–6) and, as a result, experiences a short-lived but radical boundlessness, a state of "camelion[ic]" no-self:

> The doors swung open, the little doors,
> The door, the hatch within the brain,
> And like the bellowing of ruin
> The surf upon the thousand shores
> Swept through me, and the thunder-noise
> Of all the waves of the seas.
>
> The doors swung shut, the little doors,
> The door, the hatch within the ear,
> And I was fishing off Pondy Pier,
> And all was as it was before. (7–16)

To fish, of course, is to *try* to catch, to "irritably [reach]" for a self-satisfying (even, perhaps, a self-nourishing) conclusion, but the speaking persona in "Jim Desterland" is caught himself, subsumed by "seas" that deluge "[t]he door, the hatch within the brain," in a manner that recalls Keats's definition of poetry:

"a thing which enters into one's soul." Though brief, the moment is profound, and in an effort to sustain it, Plutzik's fisherman, true to type, "mark[s] the place" and egoistically pursues that poetry like prey: "So day and night / I crouch upon the thwarts and wait" (21, 23–24). Plutzik himself, however, readopts in the poem's closing stanza a negatively capable passivity—the "wait[ing]" without the hunterly "mark[ing]" and "crouch[ing]." Devoid of a fishing "I," the last lines of "Jim Desterland" affirm that wisdom—"what one can hear if one is wise"—is, in fact, the product of self-dissolution, of "[t]he doors, the little doors, swing[ing] wide" (28, 30). And since, as Keats puts it, "[a] Poet is the most unpoetical of any thing in existence," the "wide[r]" those "doors" "swing," the better. To that end, Plutzik encourages dramatic self-annihilation in the collection's subsequent poem[17]—"Here lie no one and no one, your fathers and mothers," he writes (9)—and concludes "The Last Fisherman," the volume's final lyric,[18] with a prescription for achieving it: "Wait still for the wonder" (12).

I would suggest, however, that "For T. S. E. Only" as a limited case for negative capability, for the egoless "[w]ait[ing] still," that Plutzik cultivates throughout *Apples from Shinar*—and it represents, therefore, the volume's centerpiece. "What shocks the virtuous philosop[h]er delights the camelion Poet," Keats asserts, but "For T. S. E. Only" finds Plutzik exploring whether it's desirable or even possible for a Jewish artist to annihilate "Identity" enough to "delight" in (or even regard with poetical equanimity) a "disagreeable" as vicious as antisemitism—or to extend empathy to "an Iago" as threatening as a culturally prominent antisemite like T. S. Eliot. After all, to be a Jew, Plutzik suggests in "Portrait," is to bear the *weight* of identity; as the term "portrait" intimates, the Jew is ever a bundle of distinctive particulars, and to "[try] to be a Jew casually," Plutzik writes in that piece, is an impossible enterprise, one that would entail "ignor[ing] the monster, the mountain— / A few thousand years of history" (2–4). It's dangerous, too, since the Jew's attempts at "camelion[ic]" reinvention—at "filling some other Body," as Keats might put it—invite the kind of ridicule ("how gauche and incredible!" [18]) that, as "years of history" have demonstrated, always presages violence. His "father, it is whispered, stubbornly cried old clothes and bric-a-brac," so "even when at ease," Plutzik asserts, the Jew "is somehow anxious / Like a horse who whiffs smoke somewhere nearby faintly" (16, 22–23). Those "whisper[s]" of otherness, it would seem, are uniquely difficult to subsume within a mélange of "foul or fair, high or low,

---

17 "After Looking into a Book Belonging to my Great-Grandfather Eli Eliakim Plutzik"
18 I discount, as lyric, the excerpt from *Horatio*, which operates in a poetic tradition closer to epic.

rich or poor, mean or elevated"—and the existential "anxious"-ness that they induce, therefore, difficult to *re*duce to mere "irritab[ility]." Indeed, Plutzik suggests in "For T. S. E. Only," antisemitic rhetoric *always* feels personal—like an attack on his "Identity"—even when directed at another, and even when that other is an imaginary figure like "Bleistein," the caricatured Jew who appears in several of Eliot's poems[19] and to whom Plutzik refers explicitly as "For T. S. E. Only" begins. "You called me a name on such and such a day," he writes:

> Do you remember?—you were speaking of Bleistein our brother,
> The barbarian with the black cigar, and the pockets
> Ringing with cash, and the eyes seeking Jerusalem,
> Knowing they have been tricked. (1–5)

Antisemitic insults lobbed at other Jews, those lines indicate, trigger the *assertion* of self, not its negation, and Plutzik's "me"—"You called *me* a name," he says (my emphasis)—threatens to preclude even the most intuitive experience of empathy: empathy for the maligned individual "Bleistein" and the *many* people whom, for Eliot, he represents. Bleistein, as Eliot nastily portrays him, is a quintessential "reach[er]"—I invoke Keats's rejection of "irritable reaching"—whose full "pockets" and ever-"seeking" eyes are at odds with the partialities and glimpses that inspire the negatively capable poet, and Plutzik, too angry or frightened to "[fill] some other Body," risks succumbing, in that "me," to the art-forestalling egotism that Eliot projects onto the Jewish "barbarian."

Plutzik's "our," however, moves the poem in a different direction. The phrase "Bleistein our brother" initially conveys (or might be assumed to convey) a solidarity among Jews, and its plurality does indeed counter the egoistic "me" of the poem's first line. More radically self-negating, however, is the fact that that "our" soon stretches to include, in what becomes the lyric's loose refrain, Eliot himself: "Come, brother Thomas, / We three must weep together for our exile" (5–6). The *grounds* for that imagined brotherhood and shared "exile" are, in themselves, winks tenuous and unclear, but whether their anchor is political history ("your walls fell with mine to the torch of a Titus" [11]), American urbanity ("we both dislike Chicago" [14]), or modern poetry ("we loved you first for the wicked things you wrote" [39]), Plutzik identifies, in addressing Eliot "only," shades of solidarity sufficient to justify both a sense of common sorrow and the recitation of a common prayer—albeit not *the* Common Prayer

---

19 Bleistein most famously appears in "Burbank with a Baedeker: Bleistein with a Cigar," which appears to be Plutzik's primary focus.

of Eliot's adopted Anglicanism. In other words, in the poem's final refrain, the inarticulate weeping that has closed each of the first seven stanzas gives way to the articulacy of prayer—"Thomas, Thomas, / Come, let us pray together for our exile," Pluzik writes (47–48)—but since the Jew and the Anglican speak fundamentally different religious languages, it's a gesture that evokes both theological and Babelian multiplicity, that imagines a selfless and un-"irritable" openness to discursive diversity. Earlier in "For T. S. E. Only," Pluzik had warned Eliot against "enwomb[ing]" himself "in words or the Word," observing in particular that "the Word"—that is, the biblical message that Christian zealots, "incapable of remaining content with half knowledge," regard as indisputably singular and, as that definite article intimates, fixed—"is a good refuge for people too proud / To swallow the milk of the mild Jesus' teaching" (19–21). "[S]omeone or something," Plutzik continues, "[w]ill stick a needle in your balloon, Thomas" (23, 25), but Plutzik himself, having established his adversary's Word-made "balloon" as, in fact, a *womb*, refuses to abort, to eliminate his "brother." "The eagle's ways of pride and scorn," he concludes, "will not save" (46), and Plutzik opts instead to let "[t]he doors ... swing wide," to welcome Eliot to the "refuge" of mutual exile that he has, through inchoate flashes of empathic connection, imagined into existence. Indeed, whereas to "weep for" something is almost certainly to lament it, to "pray for" something is, perhaps, to *request* it as a holy boon, and the poem's last refrain, then, arguably reframes exile as a Keatsian "disagreeable," as an experience to "relish" with as much "gusto" as "bright[er] one[s]." Both the "dark" and the "bright," Keats asserts, "end in speculation," and "For T. S. E. Only" ends not only with that speculation-inducing refrain about "pray[ing]" for exile but also with an untranslated French quotation that gestures, in its very presence, to the generative losses cultivated on the plains of Shinar. It's the same Baudelairean exhortation that Eliot deploys in "The Waste Land"—"You, hypocrite lecteur! mon semblable! mon frère" (49)—but in Plutzik's hands, it functions less as a *critique* of those who would judge than as an invitation, even a summons. Hypocrisy, after all, is itself a state of "camelion[ic]" non-"Identity," and in inviting his *hypocrite lecteurs* to join his brotherhood with Eliot, Plutzik pushes against the limiting "only" of his own title and permits "the little doors" described in "Jim Desterland" to "swing" that much "wide[r]."

But if "pride and scorn will not save"—will not, that is, stave off life's "disagreeables"—neither will they sustain the poetic "quality ... which Shakespeare possessed so enormously." In other words, negative capability, as Keats describes it, is first and foremost an artistic virtue, and the close of "For T. S. E. Only" purposefully reconsiders Eliot's bigotry in the context of his poetic "Achievement." In addition to reengaging (and, as I suggested above, freshly applying) Baudelaire,

Plutzik compares Eliot's work to Dante's and finds it wanting with regard to that most Keatsian of features: empathy. "I see your words wrung out in pain," he writes, "but never / The true compassion for creatures with you, that Dante / Knew in his nine hells" (43–45), and that statement registers, to my mind, as a distinctly Keats-inspired challenge to the "[i]mpersonal theory of poetry" articulated in Eliot's 1920 essay "Tradition and the Individual Talent."[20] As the term "Impersonal" suggests, Eliot's foundational Modernist statement owes a substantial (if unacknowledged) debt to Keats's notion of negative capability and the poet who "has no character." "[T]he mind of the mature poet," Eliot argues, is merely a "finely perfected medium in which special, or very varied, feelings are at liberty to enter into new combinations,"[21] and when he famously specifies that he means to compare the poet to a chemical "catalyst" like platinum, he echoes Keats's oxymoronic claim that "[a] Poet is the most unpoetical of any thing in existence; because he has no Identity—he is continually in for—and filling some other Body":

> When the two gases previously mentioned are mixed in the presence of a filament of platinum, they form sulphurous acid. This combination takes place only if the platinum is present; nevertheless the newly formed acid contains no trace of platinum, and the platinum itself is apparently unaffected; has remained inert, neutral, and unchanged. The mind of the poet is the shred of platinum. It may partly or exclusively operate upon the experience of the man himself; but, the more perfect the artist, the more completely separate in him will be the man who suffers and the mind which creates; the more perfectly will the mind digest and transmute the passions which are its material.[22]

Whereas Keats, however, had who takes "*delight*" in both an Iago and an Imogen, Eliot envisions a poet "unaffected" by either—a poet, that is, who exchanges egocentric feeling for no feeling at all. Kastan claims that Plutzik "poetically [inhabits] a salutary midpoint between Eliot's passionless 'impersonality' and

---

20 T. S. Eliot, "Tradition and the Individual Talent," in *Criticism: Major Statements* (New York: Bedford/St.Martin's, 2000), 408.
21 Ibid.
22 Ibid.

the passionate self-absorption of many contemporary poets,"[23] but I would argue, rather, that Plutzik's theoretical position is, ultimately, equally at odds with *both* of those extremes. "Self-absorption" is undeniably non-Keatsian, but "passionless[ness]" is, too, and when Plutzik muses in "For T. S. E. Only," that "At times you speak as if the words were walls" (10), he intimates that an Eliot-esque *barrier* between "the man who suffers and the mind which creates" generates not poetry with its "doors swung shut," but rather poetry with no doors at all. Those airless Word-wombs, devoid of the "compassion" with which even Dante infused his "nine hells," threaten more than the morality of Eliot "the man." In fact, Plutzik insinuates, they threaten the visionary potency of Eliot "the mind"—and, of course, that of any writer who would aspire, the length of his career notwithstanding, to a place of literary-historical "significan[ce]."

Bibliography

Eliot, T. S. "Tradition and the Individual Talent." In *Criticism: Major Statements*, edited by Charles Kaplan and William Davis Anderson. 4th ed. Boston: Bedford/St. Martin's, 2000.

Kastan, David Scott. Afterword to *Apples from Shinar*, by Hyam Plutzik. Middletown, CT: Wesleyan University Press, 2011.

Keats, John. *Letters of John Keats*. Edited by Robert Gittings. Oxford: Oxford University Press, 1970.

———. *John Keats: The Complete Poems*. Edited by John Barnard. 3rd ed. London: Penguin, 1988.

Plutzik, Hyam. *Apples from Shinar*. Middletown, CT: Wesleyan University Press, 2011.

---

23 Kastan, Afterword, 66.

CHAPTER 13

"But something can be said": Ethics, Memory, and Midrash in the Work of Hyam Plutzik

Stella Setka

Despite having published five volumes of poetry in his lifetime and very nearly garnering a Pulitzer Prize for his work—shortlisted not just once, but several times—Hyam Plutzik has become "a neglected poet" in the years since his untimely death at the age of fifty.[1] His verse is not widely anthologized, and when it does appear in such volumes, one is likely to encounter only two or three of his poems. Part of Plutzik's exclusion from the American literary canon may be because his work, "Neither 'modern' nor Modernist," resists easy categorization.[2] Margot Lurie speculates that it was Plutzik's "affinity for Jewish concerns" that "doomed his verse to obscurity," and it is certainly reasonable to suggest that a latent antisemitism influenced mid-century responses to his work.[3] However, by closely evaluating critical assessments of Plutzik's poetry, we can identify an additional reason for the occlusion of his verse from American literary memory. In his Pulitzer juror's report of *Apples from Shinar* in 1960, Alfred Kreymborg argues, "We have another original in Hyam Plutzik. . . . While he is not a musical poet like most of his contemporaries, he more than compensates by the

---

Copyright © 2025 by Stella Setka

1 In one of her interviews, Tanya Plutzik comments, "All the big shots have him among the neglected poets." Christine Choy and Ku-Ling Siegel, dirs., *Hyam Plutzik, American Poet*, YouTube, 54′40, accessed August 4, 2024, https://www.youtube.com/watch?v=4zVK4XJYKp4.
2 Margot Lurie, "Golden Apples," *Jewish Review of Books* 4, no. 1 (Spring 2013): 30.
3 Ibid.

strength and depth of his writing and the power of his visions and personality."⁴ Louis Untermeyer's report echoes Kreymborg's: "Hyam Plutzik is a consciously thoughtful poet and his thoughts are never commonplace. He lacks music, but he substitutes tensity for tunefulness, and penetration for prettiness. His book ends with a gruesome and violent version (or perversion) of the Hamlet story. It is frightful but fascinating."⁵ While both reviewers seem attuned to qualities in Plutzik's verse that suggest "strength," "depth," and "tensity," they are overcome and perhaps repelled by its "frightful" aspects. These assessments of *Apples from Shinar* anticipate the Pulitzer committee's evaluation of *Horatio* in 1962: "It is primarily a tour de force—and forceful it unquestionably is. It is also ingenious in its kaleidoscopic shifts from melodrama to metaphysics, from straightforward narrative to involved nightmare.... This is not a book to be disposed of lightly."⁶ If these reports underscore the powerful impact of Plutzik's verse, they also emphasize the sense that many of his contemporaries found it inaccessible. The feeling that Plutzik's work was "beset with the past"⁷ confounded many contemporary reviewers, who lacked the language and theoretical paradigms necessary for contending with elusive, nightmarish history at its center. By reading Plutzik's poetry within in the broader context of the history of antisemitism and its brutal climax, we can clearly see in hindsight, as Cary Nelson argues, that "Plutzik is in a deep sense a post-Holocaust poet."⁸

Plutzik's plan to compose a long poem about the Holocaust, first documented in a 1954 Ford Fellowship Foundation application and referenced again in a 1960 Guggenheim Fellowship proposal,⁹ reveals a poet determined to commemorate the six million at a time when many American Jewish writers elected to elide their Jewishness and remain largely silent about the Holocaust.

---

4   Alfred Kreymborg, *Chronicle of the Pulitzer Prizes for Poetry: Discussions, Decisions, and Documents*, ed. Heinz-Dietrich Fischer (München: K. G. Saur, 2009), 208.
5   Stanley Kunitz Louis Untermeyer, *Chronicle of the Pulitzer Prizes for Poetry* (Berlin: Walter de Gruyter, 2009), 214.
6   Ibid., 243–244.
7   Hyam Plutzik to Mark Van Doren, November 20, 1946, Hyam Plutzik Papers, D.113, Box 5, Folder 4, Rare Books, Special Collections, and Preservation, River Campus Libraries, University of Rochester, Rochester, NY.
8   Cary Nelson, "The Universe Is No Consolation: Hyam Plutzik, Jewish Identity, and the Ethics of Post-Holocaust Reading," *Journal of Jewish Identities*, 15, no. 1 (2022): 28.
9   Hyam Plutzik, "Intellectual autobiography and proposed project" for Ford Foundation Fellowship, 1953 or 1954, Box 4, Folder 3, Hyam Plutzik Papers, Rare Books, Special Collections, and Preservation, River Campus Libraries, University of Rochester, Rochester, New York and "Guggenheim Fellowship Application Materials: Application forms, Correspondence, and Bibliographies, 1950–1960," Box 4, Folder 7, ibid.

In the former document, Plutzik establishes the rhetorical objective of his planned poem:

> The massacre of the six million Jews must be remembered . . . so that men, all men, may always be aware of, and on guard against, their extraordinary capacities for evil. For the vastness of the crime makes it almost incredible, and that which is incredible is forgotten or ignored, once the generation of those who grieved personally is past. The job is to make the event credible, to show that it really happened. And for this, one needs not history, but a poem. Many poems.[10]

Here, Plutzik seemingly revises Theodor Adorno's famous prohibition on Holocaust representation: after Auschwitz, it is the act of writing history, rather than poetry that becomes barbaric. Indeed, for Plutzik, the sheer enormity of the catastrophe produces a numbing effect: "it is hard enough to write a requiem for one man, but six million! Is there such a number? Grief ends beyond one or two or three; beyond that there are only statistics."[11] In these words, we see what Monica Osborne terms "a midrashic awareness," which "reminds us that such information, while critical to historical and cultural memory, is but a vast supply of representations of traumatic events."[12] Historical facts and figures, even documentary footage, are merely representations of the event that supply us with knowledge without a concomitant understanding. Plutzik's précis suggests a desire to move beyond the anesthetic effects of such information to establish, through the immediacy of verse, a greater sense of intimacy between the reader and the traumatic past, and indeed, in those of his works that remain to us, we recognize a poet who was already grappling with the weight of commemoration well before the popularization of the phrase, "Never forget."

In twenty-first-century reappraisals of Plutzik's work, scholars such as Eric J. Sundquist, Cary Nelson, and Edward Moran have laid the foundations for reading Plutzik as both a Jewish poet and a post-Holocaust poet. Moran, together with Steven Sher, has made a convincing case for reading *Horatio* as a work that is deeply concerned with the Holocaust. Nelson goes further to argue that "the

---

10   Ibid., Box 4, Folder 3.
11   Ibid., Box 4, Folder 7.
12   Monica Osborne, "The Midrashic Legacy," in *New Directions in Jewish American and Holocaust Literatures: Reading and Teaching*, ed. Victoria Aarons and Holli Levitsky (Albany: SUNY Press, 2019), 175–176.

legacy of the Holocaust echoes throughout the *Collected Poems*."[13] In this essay, I extend these assessments of Plutzik's body of work still further by examining how it adapts the Jewish exegetical tradition of midrash as a strategy for responding to historical trauma.

The son of an Orthodox rabbi, Plutzik received a traditional religious education, which is reflected in his repeated references to Talmudic texts in his poetry. Plutzik was not particularly observant in adulthood, preferring the "philosophical" aspects of Judaism and eschewing the Halakhic in favor of the Aggadic.[14] The latter's influence is evident in many of his poems, which evince a keen sense of midrashic awareness. As Sundquist's careful research has demonstrated, Plutzik consulted twentieth-century editions of Talmudic texts in both English and Hebrew, and in some cases, he cites directly from *En Jacob: Agada of the Babylonian Talmud*.[15] The impact of such texts on Plutzik's work cannot be understated; indeed, as Sundquist asserts, "through both explicit citation and embedded allusion he called attention to the role of the modern Jewish poet as an heir to this rabbinical tradition—not least because the catastrophic watershed events that drove the Jewish people into a nearly two thousand-year exile had, in his day, come full circle, so to say, with the Holocaust and Israeli statehood."[16] The fact that Plutzik openly references this tradition in his work is bold, but more radical still is the way that he uses the tools and tenets of the tradition to call attention to a history of loss and persecution while also celebrating the resilience and strength of the Jewish people.

Midrash began as a type of exegesis—the study and interpretation of Torah practiced by rabbis in the period of late antiquity. Although the term is still associated with the exegetical, midrash has assumed new meaning in literary studies as a theoretical process of engendering or evaluating texts. As a secular hermeneutic, midrash acts as "an imaginative narrative commentary composed after the initial narrative of experience" to offer a "reading" that articulates the significance of the event in the Jewish cultural imagination.[17] Thus, midrash is a form of representation that not only calls attention to itself as representation, but also

---

13 Nelson, "The Universe Is No Consolation," 11.
14 Hyam Plutzik, Poet, accessed October 1, 2024, https://www.hyamplutzikpoetry.com.
15 Eric J. Sundquist, "Blessed Mythmaker: The Poetry of Hyam Plutzik," paper presented at the Jewish American and Holocaust Literature Symposium, Miami, November 2019, Hyam Plutzik, Poet, accessed October 1, 2024, https://www.hyamplutzikpoetry.com/commentaries.
16 Ibid., 2.
17 Sara R. Horowitz, "Auto/biography and Fiction after Auschwitz: Probing the Boundaries of Second-Generation Aesthetics," in *Breaking Crystal: Writing and Memory after Auschwitz*, ed. Efraim Sicher (Champaign: University of Illinois Press, 1998), 290.

to the absence that necessitates the act of representation in the first place. It attempts to both read and highlight absence, interceding "to fill in cognitive and psychological absences in history and memory while also reproducing gaps ... that require of readers not distance but moral and emotional engagement."[18] If, in a biblical context, midrash "infers from ellipses or condensations a very human story and introduces dialogues that draw God deeper into the affairs of mankind,"[19] in the literature of the Holocaust, it "has the capacity to bring us closer to the experience of trauma about which we cannot speak."[20] However, as Rachel Salmon and Gerda Elata-Alster explain, even while midrash creates conditions that foster a sense of reader intimacy, it does not simplify the reading process. They suggest that midrash, by design, creates difficulties for readers and therefore "denies the satisfaction of a mastered meaning."[21] By transgressing boundaries between itself and the text(s) it is reading, midrash

> adopts a singular rhetorical stance which does not allow the reader to secure a "readerly" position *vis-à-vis* the text. That is to say, the reader is not provided with the sort of transitional directives which enable him (or her) to proceed with confidence in the footsteps of the writer. Presented with one view after another, it is the reader himself who must fill in the gaps in such a way as to construct narrative values. While thus not employing the usual rhetorical strategies of persuasion, the Midrash, by violating the narrative expectation it has itself provoked, "persuades" the reader to do much work himself.[22]

This "work" in which the reader must engage, then, is what produces the conditions within which an ethical engagement with the text arises. As Osborne cautions, "it is not enough to suggest simply that certain texts have been written with a midrashic awareness; rather to read a text midrashically is what allows

---

18   Ibid.
19   Geoffrey Hartman, "Midrash as Law and Literature," in *The Geoffrey Hartman Reader*, ed. Geoffrey Hartman and Daniel T. O'Hara (New York: Fordham University Press, 2004), 209.
20   Osborne, "The Midrashic Legacy," 173.
21   Rachel Salmon and Gerda Elata-Alster, "Retracing a Writerly Text: In the Footsteps of a Midrashic Sequence on the Creation of the Male and the Female," in *Hermeneutics, the Bible and Literary Criticism*, ed. Ann Loades and Michael McLain (New York: St. Martin's Press, 1992), 180.
22   Ibid.

its inherent midrashic components to materialize meaningfully."²³ In Plutzik's poems, the participatory qualities of midrash shift the act of reading from a passive experience to one of active engagement and ethical thinking.

Poetry lends itself quite well to midrashic thinking because of how it solicits the reader. In his anthology of American Holocaust poetry, Charles Adés Fishman observes that "Poetry, at its best, resists abstraction and permits us to feel again, to be wounded again."²⁴ Wounds abound in Plutzik's work, perhaps most glaringly in the poems that engage the painful aspects of Jewish history and the horrors of the twentieth century. Indeed, in poems such as "Entropy," Plutzik's poetry wounds in the way that it writes around the memory of collective trauma, centering absence without seeking its resolution. Because Plutzik foregrounds absence in this way, "we are drawn into the wound. The absence is made visible, finally, so that we can read it. Here we are as close to it as we can possibly be."²⁵ By situating the reader in such intimate proximity to the wounds of the past, Plutzik's verse also highlights that which precipitated those wounds: evil.²⁶ In the opening stanza of "Entropy," one immediately detects a midrashic awareness on the part of the author and a concomitant summons to the reader to proceed midrashically: "I have seen the wound that matter makes in space / The hole in the blank sheet of white paper."²⁷ This palimpsest of absences precedes references to the lives whose humanity—"tension of Being" sustains them "against the tightening spring / Of infinite number and the fires of nebular torment" until they are finally "crushed like a moth / In a child's hand." The "tightening spring" and "fires." Such lines, easily read as allusions to mass shootings and crematoria, are avatars of the evil enabled by antisemitism, which because it disavows the humanity of Jews also denies any sense of responsibility for their lives or their deaths. The "wound" and "hole" referenced in the poem's first two lines, then, emphasize not only collective trauma of the Holocaust, but also the history of antisemitism that provided the Nazis with its template.

The evils of Nazism were foremost in Plutzik's imagination even before the full extent of its crimes were widely known. In the mid-thirties, Plutzik began writing

---

23 Monica Osborne, *The Midrashic Impulse and the Contemporary Literary Response to Trauma* (Lanham, MD: Lexington Books, 2017), 6.
24 Charles Fishman, Preface to *Blood to Remember: American Poets on the Holocaust*, 2nd ed. (St. Louis, MI: Time Being Books, 2007).
25 Osborne, "The Midrashic Legacy," 175.
26 Similarly, Nelson argues that Plutzik's *Aspects of Proteus* (1949) devotes "several beautifully crafted poems to the history of evil and its variations." Nelson, "The Universe Is No Consolation," 20.
27 Hyam Plutzik, *Collected Poems* (Brockport, NY: BOA Editions Ltd., 1987), 16.

a seventy-two-page letter, something of an ars poetica, to his former professor and mentor, Odell Shepard, and did not complete it until late 1941. Although *Letter from a Young Poet* is distinctly American—reminiscent in some ways of Thoreau's *Walden* and Whitman's prose works—it also evinces an acute sense of the poet's Jewishness and what it means to be a Jew in a world of virulent antisemitism. Writing of his admiration for the Yankee, Plutzik observes regretfully,

> This dignity and independence of his are something which a Jew, for instance, can only regard with hopeless envy. The Jew is always trying to seek poise, to walk with unconscious dignity; but the very fact that he *tries* shows that he is conscious of his quest. His dignity, when he attains it, usually has a melancholy air, and there is uncertainty in his manner. He tries . . . but often he fails, and his trying becomes aggressiveness, or, on the other side, timidity. It is an awesome thing to be a Jew and to know that one is hated by so many of one's fellowmen . . .[28]

As Nelson observes, the final sentence "trails off in ellipses," which he interprets as a signifier of Plutzik's ongoing identity formation.[29] However, read in the broader context of Plutzik's work, with its emphasis on the dangers of antisemitism and the deep wound of the Holocaust, the placement of these ellipses functions as an invitation to the reader to proceed midrashically. Ellipses operate in language in the same way that suture operates in narrative, constructing meaning where there is an omission or gap.[30] Visually, ellipses resemble the puncture marks caused by stitches, prompting a recollection of the initial meaning of suture as the joining together of the edges of a wound. While we cannot see the wound itself, we understand the terrible signification of first the stitches and then the scar they leave behind.

If the text's elliptical ruptures signify the wound of history, they also stand in for what remains unknown. In this way, the ellipses function as an extension of the catastrophe itself, a visual signifier of midrashic opportunities for writing and reading. These actions carry with them an ethical significance, one that is best explained by way of the philosophy of Emmanuel Levinas, who maintains that we are charged with an infinite responsibility for the other, their responsibility,

---

28 Plutzik, *Letter from a Young Poet* (Hartford, CT: Watkinson Library at Trinity College, 2016), 69.
29 Nelson, "The Universe Is No Consolation," 8.
30 The strategic use of ellipses is a hallmark of works that narrativize historical trauma. See Stella Setka, *Empathy and the Phantasmic in American Ethnic Trauma Narratives* (New York: Lexington Books, 2020).

and their death.[31] Levinas regards "language, or discourse," as tied to ethical responsibility, and yet within this discourse this is a space for silence to be read as language."[32] In *Totality and Infinity*, he writes: "Words are said, be it only by the silence kept, whose weight acknowledges this evasion of the Other. . . . Speaking, rather than 'letting be,' solicits the Other. Speech cuts across vision . . . The formal structure of language thereby announces the ethical inviolability of the Other."[33] For Levinas, silence, like speech, is fundamental to discourse, and therefore, it functions as an ethical summons in the same manner. Plutzik's silence here—and the silences that his later poems highlight—summons us to read midrashically, both within specific poems as well across his oeuvre.

The function of the ellipses in *Letter from a Young Poet* is mirrored in Plutzik's use of dashes in several of his poems, most notably "Portrait." The function of the dash in poetry, like ellipses, is to signify silence or absence, to create a gap in the text that forces the reader's attention to the omission of language and to prompt midrashic interpretation. In "Portrait," Plutzik strategically situates the dash within lines that reference the past, and in so doing extends the wounds of the past into the present. For example, in the poem's opening stanza, its subject feigns "careful nonchalance" as "He tries to be a Jew casually," striving (and seemingly failing) "To ignore the monster, the mountain— / A few thousand years of history."[34] As Nelson notes, the passage is "self-reflexive, as Plutzik, a nonobservant Jew, nonetheless feels his identity is historically, politically, and religiously shaped by his Jewish identity."[35] The dash, which arrests the reader's pace and creates a gap within the poem's rhythm and opens a space of silence, also works extensionally to facilitate the emergence of the stories, lives, and losses encompassed in the "few thousand years of history" that haunt the poet's imagination, thereby connecting the reader to this fraught past in a way that gives rise to midrashic awareness and invites ethical engagement.

The sense that Plutzik is prompting a midrashic awareness in his reader becomes more apparent toward the end of his letter to Shepard, where he attests to the power and tenacity of the Jewish aggadic tradition in the face of persecution. Paradoxically, while Plutzik concludes that language cannot

---

31 For more on Levinas's philosophy of infinite responsibility, see Emmanuel Levinas, *Totality and Infinity*, trans. Alphonso Lingis (Pittsburgh, PA: Duquesne University Press 1969), sections 3 and 4.
32 Osborne, "The Midrashic Impulse," 22.
33 Levinas, *Totality and Infinity*, 195.
34 Plutzik, *Collected Poems*, 112.
35 Nelson, "The Universe Is No Consolation," 14.

defeat the Nazis, he believes that it is language and the Jewish discursive tradition that will ensure the survival of the Jewish people and convey the truth of their suffering. Plutzik laments warfare as "odious and diabolic," but he concedes that war "might be the only means by which a diabolic philosophy could be confronted and outfaced; in short, that it is a waste of time to use decent language in conversing with the Devil, since he mistakes decency for weakness."[36] And while Plutzik certainly followed his conviction that it was "better to adopt for the purposes of the struggle [the enemy's] own weapons" by enlisting in the US Air Force, it is to language that he turns both before, during, and after the war to highlight the "true suffering" that those—like his Jewish forebears in the Pale of Settlement and his contemporaries in Europe—suffered as the result of antisemitism:[37]

> It is no wonder that the Jews have always been Hitler's main enemy. We are the people of the book; we are a symbol of the continuity he would break.... A thousand books may go up in smoke on the Alexanderplatz, but there is one Book that is too heavy and too solid to become vapor. That and the infinite meanings that radiate from it and the associations with which it is tied will confront the destroyers when their fire turns upon themselves.[38]

Here, Plutzik operates metonymically, the "one Book" calling to mind the expression *Am HaSefer*, or the view of Jews as the "People of the Book," bound together across the diaspora by written and oral Torah, as well as the rabbinical texts that expound upon them. Indeed, it is this strong connection with sacred texts that has historically sustained and connected the Jewish people across time and space. Although he is writing nearly a year before the immense scale of Nazi atrocities had become public knowledge in the United States, Plutzik's discussion of burnings and "vapor" are nothing if not prescient, for Jewish bodies, like the sacred scrolls that perished in the destruction of synagogues on *Kristallnacht* and in similar prewar pogroms, were also disintegrating into smoke at death camps like Auschwitz and Buchenwald.[39] Prophetic, too, is his insistence in the

---

36 Plutzik, *Letter from a Young Poet* (Hartford, CT: Watkinson Library at Trinity College, 2016), 18–19.
37 Ibid., 19.
38 Ibid., 76–77.
39 "The United States and the Holocaust, 1942–1945," The United States Holocaust Memorial Museum, accessed August 12, 2024, https://encyclopedia.ushmm.org/content/en/article/

power of aggadic traditions, with their infinite meanings, to not only sustain the Jewish people, but also to "confront the destroyers." In Plutzik's verse, we observe a midrashic awareness that gives shape to loss while at the same time holding accountable the "barbarians" whose crimes engendered it. Here, as in subsequent poems, Plutzik establishes the modern Jewish poet as both "an heir to ... rabbinical tradition"[40] as well as a witness for whom commemoration is an ethical obligation.

If *Letter from a Young Poet* conditions us to read midrashically, it also primes us to consider themes that Plutzik explores in greater depth in his later works. A prime example of this is Plutzik's reference to a "camorra" in his letter to Shepard. Remarking on the recent bombing of Pearl Harbor, Plutzik writes, "the die is cast—by one of the lesser numbers of the camorra of the possessed."[41] The term "camorra," often associated with the Mafia, is more broadly defined as "a group of persons united for dishonest or dishonorable ends." The term and its suggestion of nefarious violence clearly resonated with Plutzik because it serves as the title of a poem in *Aspects of Proteus* (1949). The poem begins with the speaker's instinctive recognition of danger and oppression:

> They meet me at midday in implausible places;
> They strike at me with their daggers and when I cry out
> I am told there are no invisible highwaymen.
>
> I say that even at noon in the public streets
> Where crowds are chattering, fingers brush my throat
> And a whisper reveals the conspirators are here.

Significant here are the evocations of daylight, "midday" and "noon," which connote truth and clarity and, as a result, contrast sharply with the violence experienced by the speaker, violence that is dismissed by others who insist "there are no invisible highwaymen." The sense of gaslighting communicated in the first stanza is amplified in the second, where the "crowds chattering" fail (or refuse) to recognize the imminent danger posed to the speaker by the "conspirators." The indifference of the bystanders, who substitute insincere prayers for action on behalf of the persecuted Jews, leads to the catastrophe:

---

the-united-states-and-the-holocaust-1942-45.
40 Sundquist, "Blessed Mythmaker," 2.
41 Plutzik, *Letter from a Young Poet* (Hartford, CT: Watkinson Library at Trinity College, 2016), 63.

> O they plotted this before Adam was born,
> To track us like hounds till we falter at last and fall
> Though we laugh behind doors and wear clever disguises.
>
> For they were not all thrown in the burning gulf.
> There are those who remained behind and at convocations
> Fawn at the Lord and mumble the words of Hosannas.

By reading the "burning gulf" as a metonym for the recent war, we see Plutzik's concern that this camorra, though nominally defeated, persists in the form of the bystanders—casual antisemites—who refuse to assume responsibility for the horrors, both past and present, that have been and continue to be wrought by antisemitism. The threat, Plutzik's poem implies, has not abated, but simply transmuted. Reading midrashically, we can perceive a theme of ethical responsibility that is central to many of Plutzik's poems. In the context of "The Camorra," responsibility is framed as a need for vigilance and a warning to read the wounds of the past as cautionary. As he makes clear in "The Camorra" and elsewhere, Plutzik frames the work of the poet—bringing the reader face-to-face with the wounds of the past—as an ethical responsibility.

The weight of ethical responsibility, however, is tremendous, and the notion of infinite responsibility—the ethical demand placed on the subject—is endless. Levinas employs the metaphor of insomnia to illustrate the endless vigilance necessitated by the ethical encounter. As Levinas explains in an interview,

> The other haunts our ontological existence and keeps the psyche awake, in a state of vigilant insomnia. Even though we are ontologically free to refuse the other, we remain forever accused with a bad conscience. . . . I have described ethical responsibility as *insomnia* or *wakefulness* precisely because it is a perpetual duty of vigilance and effort that can never slumber.[42]

Plutzik's poems, haunted by ghosts, metonyms, and visual signifiers of a painful past, inspire a midrashic awareness that, in turn, "prohibits evasion."[43] We,

---

42 Emmanuel Levinas, "Dialogue with Emmanuel Levinas: Emmanuel Levinas and Richard Kearney," in *Face to Face with Levinas*, ed. Richard A. Cohen (Albany, NY: State University of New York Press, 1986), 28.

43 In his essay on the poetry of Paul Celan, Levinas identifies in the poet's work a quality of attention that he likens to ethical responsibility and conscience: "Attention—a mode of

like the poet, cannot look away because we are confronted by the "rectitude of responsibility."[44] However, although Plutzik's work demonstrates that he takes seriously the perpetual duty of responsibility, it also evinces a concomitant sense of weariness.

The weight of ethical responsibility is a key theme in "Exhortation to the Artists," which frames the subject of collective trauma within the context of the midrashic tradition. The poem begins by recounting to the Talmudic story regarding the mitzvah of *bikur cholim*, or visiting the sick:

> Rabbi Elazer once became sick. Rabbi Jochanan came to visit him.... Rabbi Elazer was weeping. "Why do you weep?" asked Rabbi Jochanan. ... "I weep," said Rabbi Elazer to him, "for the beauty which will decay in the earth." "For that indeed," Rabbi Jochanan said, "you ought to weep," and both wept."—The Talmud[45]

This Talmudic preface suggests that the mitzvah of *bikur cholim* is only complete when the experiences of the visitor and the patient are shared through a mutual empathy.[46] While, as Sundquist notes, "the passage in Tractate Berakhot (5b) from which Plutzik excerpts his epigraph deals more generally with suffering and chastisement, including the lesson that acceptance of suffering in this world may bring reward in the world to come,"[47] Plutzik's selective quotation of the passage from *En Jacob: Agada of the Babylonian Talmud* redirects our attention from the need to accept suffering to considering the broader implications of ethical responsibility. Although Elazer is ill, it is *he* who weeps first for *Jochanan's* mortality, an action that leads to mutual grieving. Feeling with the other means that one must open oneself up to suffering as well. Thus, Plutzik begins by exhorting

---

consciousness without distraction, i.e. without the power of escape through dark underground passages; full illumination, projected not in order to see ideas, but in order to prohibit evasion; the first meaning of that insomnia that is conscience—a rectitude of responsibility before any appearance of forms, images, or things. Emmanuel Levinas, "Paul Celan: From Being to the Other," in *Proper Names*, trans. Michael B. Smith (Stanford, CA: Stanford University Press, 1996), 43.

44 Ibid.
45 Plutzik, *Collected Poems*, 57.
46 Jacob Ibn Chabib, *En Jacob: Agada of the Babylonian Talmud*, vol. 1, trans. S. H. Glick (New York: 1916), accessed August 12, 2024, https://babel.hathitrust.org/cgi/pt?id=pst.000060816078&seq=5, p. 16.
47 Sundquist, "Blessed Mythmaker," 4.

us to ethical responsibility and with it, empathy, which unlike sympathy brings us into greater proximity with suffering.

The poem's first stanza extends the scene of Elazer and Jochanan's shared grief:

> Two weeping for beauty perished, husband
> And wife, lover and mistress, friend and friend,
>   Shall mark the world's end.

Reading "beauty" as a metaphor for "life," we see in this stanza echoes of the Talmudic discourse surrounding the primal story of Cain's fratricide: "Whoever takes a single life destroys thereby an entire world."[48] As John Llewelyn observes, murder is profound because "if the very expressing of [God's judgment] is expressed through the commandment, 'Thou shalt not kill,' that judgment owes some of its force to generations to come. For to kill the person facing me is to kill the *multiple* generations to which he or she might have given birth."[49] The "world's end" encompasses the exponential loss represented by the murders of the six million who appear, as ghosts, in the next stanza.

In the second stanza, one of startling self-reflexivity, Plutzik writes

> As I was spinning a fable for this page,
> There came ghosts weeping, two and two,
>   In pity, dolor, or in rage.

The ghosts here anticipate the ghosts Plutzik references in his plan for a Holocaust poem described in both his Ford Fellowship and Guggenheim proposals. Plutzik's plan was to craft a poem "in which six million ghosts appear at midday on Main Street," "giving it an uncanny reality." To Plutzik, it seems, the immensity of the Holocaust not only requires a poetics of ineffability, but also demands a poetics of empathy. Taken together with their Talmudic preface, these lines in "Exhortation to the Artists," summon readers and artists alike to bear witness to the "ghosts weeping." The range of emotions these ghosts carry signify a progression of emotional identification and intensity. Beginning with "pity," which signifies a sympathetic, albeit distanced feeling of sorrow and compassion caused by the sufferings and misfortunes of others,

---

48 *Mishna Sanhedrin* 4:5.
49 John Llewelyn, *Emmanuel Levinas: The Genealogy of Ethics* (London: Routledge, 1995), 119–20.

we progress to "dolor" and then "rage." In this transition from pity—something we typically feel for others—to sorrow and rage—feelings generally inspired by personal experience—we observe a marked shift in emotional investment. The ghosts signify the absent presence of those murdered in the Holocaust, and what remains is the infectious intensity of their emotional response. Emanating from formless, timeless voids, these mournful ghosts haunt ceaselessly, waiting, it seems, for the next reader to come along. The poem's speaker has no choice but to advance from sorrow to rage, and thence to action in the final stanzas. However, Plutzik also self-reflexively addresses the immense weight of this empathy and what it means, as an artist, to engage with historical trauma in this way. In the third stanza, which references Samson's destruction of the Philistine temple, Plutzik addresses the burden of this responsibility:

> Against the pillars of the heartless temple
> Throw, whom knowledge blinded, your brute skill
> Though it is yourself you kill.[50]

Here, it is the poet "whom knowledge blinded," and with his "brute skill"—art—he holds accountable the enemies of his people, those makers of the ghosts we encounter in the second stanza. Although it seems apparent that Plutzik views commemoration—as much an act of avengement as of lamentation—as an ethical obligation to those who died, the poet nonetheless communicates the profound cost of such art; it is, in many ways, an act of self-immolation.

In the poet's most profoundly commemorative poem "After Looking into a Book Belonging to My Great-Grandfather, Eli Eliakim Plutzik," originally published in *Apples from Shinar*, we observe repeated references to death, loss, and absence. The poem's title centers us in the space of textual encounter, explicitly linking the poet's relationship to the past and his own ancestry to language and texts. However, while the title seemingly prepares the reader for a meditation on a past that precedes the poet's birth, the poem's opening line undermines this expectation, connecting us instead to the speaker's meditations on a historical event much closer in time: "I am troubled by the blank fields, the speechless graves."[51] The first-person speaker directs our attention not to his forefather's book, nor to musings about the ancestor himself, but rather to his own pressing obligation to bear witness to the recent trauma of the Holocaust.

---

50 Plutzik, *Collected Poems*, 57.
51 Ibid., 97.

He is haunted by "blank fields" and "speechless graves," signifiers of the absence and silence that give shape to profound loss. Drawing our attention to these voids, Plutzik prompts us to proceed midrashically as we work to make sense of the relationship between the poem and its title. As Nelson observes, these lines "invoke not only the dead of the Shoah who have no living relatives to speak for them but the vanished European and Russian villages that have no remaining presence."[52] The Holocaust is a void in the poet's narrative, a disruption in the continuity of the story that he seeks to tell about himself and his family. It obscures his ability to imagine his ancestral past or the forbear whose name appears in the title and threatens to obliterate any sense of historical continuity. He explains, "there is no word / For the thousand years that shaped this scribbling fist / And the eyes staring at strange places and times."[53] The lack of language, "no word," echoes the namelessness of the victims—"no one and no one"—known only as "Lovers of words . . . your fathers and mothers" who in their silence exhort the poet to bear witness to their lives and deaths: "At last demanding, to close the door to the cold, / Only *Here lies someone*" (italics in original). Plutzik's engagement with his great-grandfather's book gives rise to a midrash that extends the past into the present; arrested by this unexpected encounter, we, too, are summoned to read midrashically, and thus through the poet's "eyes" we sit "staring at strange places and times / Beyond the veldt dragging into Poland." In this way, the poet extends the responsibility of commemoration to readers, implicating us in the ethical obligation to remember the loss of lives as well as the loss of memory. Although he cannot restore "the names carved upon wood," he makes their loss personal to us; they become our "fathers and mothers" as well.

In an unpublished poem, Plutzik muses on the function of poetry and the role of the poet, writing "a poem / Is merely the proem / To the author's intending— / That beginning and ending are the *silence* begun / When the talking is done."[54] In these verses, Plutzik provides a directive for how we should read, a key, as it were, that enables us to begin the process of interpreting the myriad gaps and silences that emerge from his work. We can ascertain the poet's intention, but, as Plutzik suggests, there are possibilities for meaning, for midrashic thinking, beyond the poet's words. The double emphasis on "*silence*," both italicized and underlined, emphasizes the importance of ascertaining the textual openings,

---

52 Nelson, "The Universe Is No Consolation," 14–15.
53 Plutzik, *Collected Poems*, 97.
54 Ibid., 241.

which, in turn, summon us to read midrashically. In this way, Plutzik's charge as a poet—the responsibility to remember, an ethical imperative—belongs to the reader as well.

Bibliography

Choy, Christine, and Ku-Ling Siegel, dirs. *Hyam Plutzik, American Poet*. Video, 54:40. Miami Jewish Film Festival, 2020. https://www.youtube.com/watch?v=4zVK4XJYKp4

Fischer, Heinz Dietrich, and Erika J. Fischer, eds. *Chronicle of The Pulitzer Prizes for Poetry: Discussions, Decisions and Documents*. München: K G Saur, 2009.

Fishman, Charles. Preface to *Blood to Remember: American Poets on the Holocaust*. 2nd ed. St. Louis, MI: Time Being Books, 2007.

Hartman, Geoffrey. "Midrash as Law and Literature." In *The Geoffrey Hartman Reader*, edited by Geoffrey Hartman and Daniel T. O'Hara, 205–222. New York: Fordham University press, 2004.

Horowitz, Sara R. "Auto/Biography and Fiction after Auschwitz: Probing the Boundaries of Second-Generation Aesthetics." In *Breaking Crystal: Writing and Memory after Auschwitz*, edited by Ephraim Sicher, 276–95. Champaign: University of Illinois Press, 1998.

Hyam Plutzik Papers. Rare Books, Special Collections, and Preservation, River Campus Libraries, University of Rochester, Rochester, New York.

Ibn Habib, Jacob. *En Jacob: Agada of the Babylonian Talmud*. Vol. 1. Translated by S. H. Glick. New York: n.p., 1916.

Levinas, Emmanuel. "Paul Celan: From Being to the Other." In *Proper Names*. Translated by Michael B. Smith, 40–46. Stanford, CA: Stanford University Press, 1996.

———. *Totality and Infinity*. Translated by Alphonso Lingis. Pittsburg, PA: Duquesne University Press, 1969.

Levinas, Emmanuel, and Richard Kearney. "Dialogue with Emmanuel Levinas: Emmanuel Levinas and Richard Kearney." In *Face to Face with Levinas*, edited by Richard A. Cohen, 13–34. Albany, NY: State University of New York Press, 1986.

Llewelyn, John. *Emmanuel Levinas: The Genealogy of Ethics*. London: Routledge, 1995.

Lurie, Margot. "Golden Apples: *Apples from Shinar* by Hyam Plutzik." *Jewish Review of Books* 4, no. 1 (2013), 30.

Mishnah Sanhedrin. Sefaria.org. Accessed July 14, 2023. https://www.sefaria.org/Mishnah_Sanhedrin?tab=contents.

Nelson, Cary. "The Universe Is No Consolation: Hyam Plutzik, Jewish Identity, and the Ethics of Post-Holocaust Reading." *Journal of Jewish Identities* 15, no. 1 (2022): 5–31. https://dx.doi.org/10.1353/jji.2022.0003.

Osborne, Monica. *The Midrashic Impulse and the Contemporary Literary Response to Trauma*. Lanham, MD: Lexington Books, 2017.

Osborne, Monica. "The Midrashic Legacy." In *New Directions in Jewish American and Holocaust Literatures: Reading and Teaching*, edited by Victoria Aarons and Holli Levitsky, 167–81. Albany: SUNY Press, 2019.

Plutzik, Hyam. *Hyam Plutzik: The Collected Poems*. Brockport, NY: Bookslinger, 1987.

———. *Letter from a Young Poet*. Hartford, CT.: Watkins Library at Trinity College, 2015.

Salmon, Rachel, and Gerda Elata-Alster. "Retracing a Writerly Text: In the Footsteps of a Midrashic Sequence on the Creation of the Male and the Female." In *Hermeneutics, the Bible and Literary Criticism*, edited by Ann Loades and Michael McLain, 177–97. New York: St. Martin's, 1992.

Setka, Stella. *Empathy and the Phantasmic in American Ethnic Trauma Narratives*. New York: Lexington Books, 2020.

Sundquist, Eric J. 2019. "Blessed Mythmaker: The Poetry of Hyam Plutzik." Paper presented at The Jewish American and Holocaust Literature Symposium, Miami, FL, November 11, 2019. Hyam Plutzik, Poet. Accessed October 1, 2024. https://www.hyamplutzikpoetry.com/commentaries.

United States Holocaust Memorial Museum. "The United States and the Holocaust, 1942–1945." Accessed August 12, 2023. https://encyclopedia.ushmm.org/content/en/article/the-united-states-and-the-holocaust-1942-45.

CHAPTER 14

The Saturated Forgetfulness of Liturgical Memory

Sara R. Horowitz

Although references to Jewish texts, tradition, history, and ethics weave through the poetic oeuvre of Hyam Plutzik, only in the last decade of his life did the poet engage with formal liturgy. Invited in the early 1950s to contribute to an ambitious project to modernize and re-energize the prayer service of the Conservative movement, Plutzik began to compose English language translations of traditional liturgical poems. Working with some of the key religious thinkers of the movement impelled Plutzik to lay out his thinking on the interrelation of prayer, language, aesthetics, and theology—and all of this in the context of the recent, shattering catastrophe of European Jews. His work on formal liturgy spills over onto other poems, weaving strands of liturgical allusions into the fabric of his poetry, probing the ethics of Jewish memory and Jewish forgetting.

Several sources mention Plutzik's consultancy with the Conservative movement. Preparing to explore the influence of American Jewish poets in contemporary liturgy, I looked for reference to Plutzik in any prayer book published by the Rabbinical Assembly or United Synagogue (respectively, the organization of Conservative rabbis and the federation of Conservative synagogues in the United States and Canada). Typically, these prayer books credit the English translation of the liturgy, and the prayer books are commonly referred to as such—for example, the Silverman *siddur*, or the Harlow *maḥzor* are twentieth-century prayer books edited and translated by Morris Silverman and Jules Harlow, respectively. In notes, the prayer books also credit non-Rabbinical Assembly contributors of English language versions of individual prayers—for example, the British writer Israel Zangwill and the

---

Copyright © 2025 by Sara R. Horowitz

American physician, and poet Solomon da Silva Solis-Cohen. But the only published trace of Plutzik's involvement with the prayer book are the translations of four Hebrew liturgical poems that appeared two and a half decades after the poet's death.

What was the extent of Plutzik's "consultancy" with the Conservative movement, and what did he produce for it? Why did he have no presence in their prayer books? Although one cannot step through a portal into the past, and one cannot eavesdrop on long-ago meetings and telephone conversations, unpublished documents and published records of meetings[1] allow us to reconstruct the scope and parameters of Plutzik's engagement with the prayer book, the ideas about the Jewish sacred that he brought to the table, and the influence of this work on the poems he composed during and after the period of consultancy. Secondary references to Plutzik's consultancy place it in the late 1950s.[2] But, in fact, his work on the prayer book began much earlier in the decade and lasted about two years. During this period, he was also working on poems that grappled with the Holocaust, Jewish history, antisemitism—issues central to Jewish identity.[3] Plutzik's intensive immersion in formal liturgy influenced the poems he would write, and his thinking about the issues that drive these poems shaped his commitment to revitalizing Jewish liturgy.

---

1   In reconstructing the details of Hyam Plutzik's consultancy with the Rabbinical Assembly of America Prayer Book Committee, I drew upon material in two archives: D113, Box 16, Hyam Plutzik papers, Rare Books Special Collections, and Preservation, River Campus Libraries, University of Rochester; in ARC.1000.007, Box 1, Jacob B. Agus Papers, Library of the Jewish Theological Seminary, New York, and other volumes at the Jewish Theological Seminary Library. I am grateful to Edward Moran for his assistance in locating the relevant holdings at the University of Rochester library. I thank Andrew Katz, public service librarian for special collections at the Jewish Theological Seminary Library for his help.

2   For example, Edward Moran understands the consultancy as emerging from Plutzik's friendship with Abraham Karp, who served as rabbi of Temple Beth El of Rochester in the mid- to late 1950s. See Edward Moran, "T. S. Eliot and Hyam Plutzik: 'Hypocrite Lecteur, mon Semblable, mon Frere,'" Hyam Plutzik, Poet, accessed October 1, 2024, http://www.hyamplutzikpoetry.com/commentaries, p. 3. In fact, it was Karp's predecessor who, in the early 1950s, brought Plutzik to the attention of the Prayer Book Committee. Similarly, Steven Sher and Edward Moran date Plutzik's key correspondence with the Prayer Book Committee as 1960, two short years before Plutzik's death. By then, however, the Prayer Book Committee that Plutzik worked with had been disbanded for over five years. See Steven Sher and Edward Moran, "Hyam Plutzik's *Horatio* as Post-Holocaust Poem," Hyam Plutzik, Poet, accessed October 1, 2024, http://www.hyamplutzikpoetry.com/commentaries, p. 14.

3   Sher and Moran note that in a 1954 application for a grant, Plutzik includes a plan to compose a book-length poem about Nazi atrocity and its implications.

The Poet and the Rabbi

Central to Plutzik's involvement in crafting Jewish liturgy in English is the working relationship forged with one of the leading advocates for modernization in the Conservative movement, Rabbi Jacob Agus. Agus's insistence that mid-century American Jews needed a new prayer book[4] galvanized the project that brought the two men together. Agus envisioned a prayer book designed primarily for home use, part of an ambitious plan to energize the Conservative movement in the years immediately following World War II. Serving as chair of the Prayer Book Committee of the Rabbinical Assembly, Agus realized that a large segment of the Jewish American community could not comprehend the Hebrew (and Aramaic) text of the traditional prayer book. For prayer to be moving and meaningful to contemporary American congregants, English translation was crucial. Even more, Agus understood that the English version of the traditional liturgy should be not merely competent, but inspiring. While he himself could produce a serviceable translation, he felt that a more literary eye was needed. Thus emerged the *shidduch*, or match, between the poet and the rabbi.

Agus's Prayer Book Committee included some of the luminaries of the Conservative movement.[5] From Agus's correspondence with committee members and others, and from discussions recorded in the proceedings of the 1954 and 1956 proceedings of the Rabbinical Assembly Convention, the dissatisfaction with previous translations was clear.[6] Reporting to his colleagues at the convention on in the committee's work to date, Agus explained the need to elevate the quality of the English translation. The ideal person for this, he explained, would "be able to do the entire job, namely, a person who would be acquainted with our theology, with our tradition, and who would also have literary facility, so that he could be entrusted with the preparation of a manuscript which the committee could then discuss"[7]—in other words, someone within the Rabbinical Assembly with literary talent and facility with classical Jewish texts. With no

---

4   In this essay, I use "prayer book" rather than the Hebrew *siddur* because that is the term used consistently by Agus, his committee, and the Rabbinical Assembly.
5   In addition to Agus, the members of the Prayer Book Committee included Rabbis Robert Gordis, Arthur Hertzberg, Hershel Matt, Arthur Neulander, and Stuart Rosenberg.
6   *Proceedings of the Rabbinical Assembly of America, Fifty-Fourth annual Convention, May 17–20, 1954* (Philidelphia, PA: Rabbinical Society of America, 1955), quotations from *Proceedings* are from this volume.
7   Ibid., 107.

obvious candidate, Agus himself prepared a preliminary draft manuscript of the new prayer book, and looked for literary talent outside the Rabbinical Assembly to help revise it. Conceptualizing this person's role as a "stylistic consultant," Agus sought someone who might be "theologically... trusted to be sensitive to ideas."[8] That person emerged through one of the members of the Prayer Book Committee.

A dynamic young rabbi still in his twenties, Stuart E. Rosenberg was the rabbi of Temple Beth El in Rochester, then considered among the leading congregations of the Conservative movement.[9] Rosenberg went on to forge a career as one of the most influential Conservative rabbis, publishing books of sermons and ideas about twentieth-century Judaism. In a 2007 documentary about Plutzik's life and work,[10] Plutzik's daughter recollects that although her parents had both been raised in Orthodox families, their own home was not religiously observant. But because of his religious background, Plutzik was invested in "asking life questions." While Plutzik did not attend synagogue services regularly, he would go there to "just talk about ideas and stuff. He was interested in sort of the philosophical issues." Plutzik's synagogue conversations must have impressed Rosenberg. Not only was Plutzik a gifted poet and writer, but he knew Hebrew, was familiar with classical Jewish texts, and he thought deeply and in a Jewish context. Rosenberg broached the prayer book project to Plutzik, and then connected him with Agus. In a letter to Agus dated October 7, 1953, Rosenberg wrote, "I had a long conversation with Professor Hyam Plutzik today. He is willing to take a half dozen or so of your translations and do stylistic revision. He will then be in a position to tell us if he can continue and also how long it will take, as well as the cost. We, too, will then be in a position to evaluate his work, to determine if we want him to continue."[11] Rosenberg gave Agus Plutzik's home address, urging him to send the poet his translations for review.

A month later, Plutzik sent Agus a sample of his work on the "batch of material," apologizing for the "lapse in time." Plutzik's work must have impressed Agus, because shortly after that, the two met for two days to discuss the prayer

---

8   Ibid.
9   Michael Brown, "Platform and Prophecy: The Rise and Fall of Rabbi Stuart E. Rosenberg as Foreshadowed in His Early Toronto Sermons on Leadership," *Jewish History* 23, no. 2 (2009): 195–217, https://doi.org/10.1007/s10835-009-9078-y.
10 Christine Choy and Ku-Ling Siegel, dirs., *Hyam Plutzik, American Poet* (2007), video, 54:41, accessed October 1, 2024, https://vimeo.com/165907660.https://vimeo.com/165907660.
11 Stuart E. Rosenberg to Jacob Ages 7 October 1953, Jacob B. Agus Papers, The Library of the Jewish Theological Seminary, New York, NY, ARC.1000.007, Box 12, Folder 2.

book project, the work required on Agus's manuscript, and the terms of Plutzik's consultancy. Plutzik returned from the meeting with the understanding that he would work up a revision to Agus's translation and compose some new translations, within about half a year's time.

To understand Plutzik's importance to the translation process, we need to consider the composition of the traditional Jewish prayer service. The bones of the service are a series of sections, each defined thematically by a particular blessing that opens with the Hebrew formula *barukh atah adonai*, the translation of which we will return to. Elaborating on the theme of each section are selections of biblical poetry and later liturgical poems called *piyyutim*.[12] The *piyyut* genre first emerged in the land of Israel in the third and fourth centuries CE, and developed further in the diaspora in the Middle Ages. Characterized as "complicated, allusive and linguistically novel verses,"[13] the *piyyut* draws on mystical sources, and features "sophisticated formal arrangements (rhyme, acrostics, sound devices)," as well as "enigmatic language (often incorporated with midrashic allusions) . . . and . . . Hebrew neologisms."[14] While contemporaneous audiences appreciated the "intellectual and aesthetic" sophistication of these liturgical poems, most congregants in mid-twentieth-century Conservative synagogues in America had neither the Hebrew language skills nor the knowledge of classical sources to appreciate them. Translating them in a way that would both carry their original import and aesthetics and at the same time make them accessible to this audience posed a formidable challenge—so much so that some members of the Rabbinical Assembly suggested including them only in the original Hebrew, without translation.[15] While Agus elsewhere explains that the prayer book would rely on existing translations of biblical passages (most likely from the Jewish Publication Society's 1917 edition), the

---

12 My discussion of the *piyyut* genre draws on Ezra Fleischer, *Shirat ha-kodesh ha-ivrit bi-yeme ha-benayim*. [Hebrew Liturgical Poetry in the Middle Ages] (Jerusalem: Keter, 1975; rpt. Jerusalem: Magnes, 2007); Ruth Langer, *To Worship God Properly: Tensions between Liturgical Custom and Halakhah in Judaism* (Cincinnati, OH: Hebrew Union College Press, 1998); Stefan C. Reif, *Judaism and Hebrew Prayer: New Perspectives on Jewish Liturgical History* (Cambridge: Cambridge University Press, 1993); and Tova Rosen and Eli Yassif, "The Study of Hebrew Literature of the Middle Ages: Major Trends and Goals," in *The Oxford Handbook of Jewish Studies*, ed. Martin Goodman, online ed. (Oxford Academic), accessed October 1, 2024, https://doi.org/10.1093/oxfordhb/9780199280322.013.0011, pp. 241-294.

13 Reif, *Judaism and Hebrew Prayer*, 158,

14 Rosen and Yassif, "The Study of Hebrew Literature of the Middle Ages."

15 *Proceedings*, 111-112.

piyyutim demanded new English versions. Agus understood that the work of a fine poet was imperative.

The minutes of the Prayer Book Committee's December, 1953 meeting[16] confirm that Plutzik had been brought on as a paid consultancy—or, as Plutzik refers to it in several documents, a "job"—not as a partnership with Agus or the Rabbinical Assembly. Plutzik's "duties," Agus explains, would be "to recast the poetic, interpretive and responsive reading sections of the manuscript and to formulate all other sections in the most effective way possible without departing from the literal meaning." In a different section of the minutes, Agus elaborated on the translation policy that would govern the prayer book: "interpretive versions shall be used when the literal translation is [crossed out: unacceptable] awkward on ideological grounds and sparingly also for other cases when literal translation is not ideologically objectionable." Agus's thinking about literal and interpretive translations is, of course, inherently problematic, because it does not acknowledge that all translation entails interpretation. This will emerge, as we shall see, as an issue between Agus and Plutzik, and between Agus and his committee as the project progresses. In any event, Agus and Plutzik agreed on a rate of six dollars per hour (roughly equivalent to seventy dollars in the mid-2020s). Moreover, Plutzik's work would be "subject to revision of this committee which has the responsibility for the text." By then, Plutzik had already put in one hundred hours on the project.

Translating a poem from one language into another must be seen as the creation of a new and original poem in the target language. In all his other compositions, Plutzik was the sole arbiter of his work, revising and rewriting to his own satisfaction. But the terms of this project demanded that he relinquish control entirely. That he did not own this work is evident from a typewritten comment on the unpublished "Prayer, from the Hebrew, to Him Who Lights the Earth," Plutzik's translation of a *piyyut* found in the *shaḥarit*, or morning prayer service: "NOTE: This translation was made when I was literary consultant to the Prayer Book Translation Committee of the Rabbinical Assembly of America. Permission to print this, I suppose, would have to be obtained from the Rabbinical Assembly."[17] But even more disquieting, the language, structure and imagery of his English renditions could be changed by a group of men

---

16 "Minutes of the Prayer Book Committee Breaker's Hotel, 12/28/53," Jacob B. Agus Papers, The Library of the Jewish Theological Seminary, New York, NY, ARC.1000.007, Box 12.

17 Hyam Plutzik, "Prayer, from the Hebrew, To Him Who Lights the Earth," n.d., Hyam Plutzik papers, D.113, Box 16, Rare Books, Special Collections, and Preservation, River Campus Libraries, University of Rochester.

who—however versed in Jewish texts and theology—were not poets. Plutzik might try to persuade the committee to accept his version, but he could not compel them to do so, nor prevent them should they choose to publish their emendation of his translation. At most, presumably, Plutzik could demand that his name be removed.[18] Such an arrangement could not have been easy for him.

What compelled Plutzik to agree to these terms? Certainly, economic factors must have played into his decision to take on this project. In the 2007 documentary about Plutzik, his daughter notes that Plutzik felt the economic pinch of raising four children on a professor's salary, and that he took on summer jobs. The consultancy would bring in much needed extra income. But there were likely other factors driving Plutzik to work on the prayer book: first, the interaction between him and Agus, with whom he worked intensively; second, their shared concern for Jewish renewal after the losses of the Holocaust; third, the possibility of a new and expanded audience for his work; fourth, an abiding commitment—evident in his oeuvre—to thinking through matters of theology, ethics, and the sublime.

At first glance, Agus[19] and Plutzik[20] appear very different—one an American pulpit rabbi deeply engaged in developing an American religious denomination, the other a poet and a professor of English literature at a secular American university. But elements of a common background and shared concerns made for a working relationship that—based on correspondence and other archival material—was productive and stimulating, if at times contentious. Agus and Plutzik were the same age, both born in 1911—the former in Poland, and the latter in Brooklyn to parents who had recently immigrated from Russia—although

---

18   In his report to the 1954 Rabbinical Assembly convention, Agus assures his colleagues that, following established practice, "Whenever we use a prayer composed by a person who is not a member of the Prayer Book Committee, he is properly compensated for his efforts." *Proceedings*, 111.

19   My discussion of Jacob Agus's biography and thinking draws on Steven T. Katz, ed., *The Essential Agus: The Writings of Jacob B. Agus* (New York: New York University Press, 1997), as well as on Agus's own writing, especially *Modern Philosophies of Judaism: A Study of Recent Jewish Philosophies of Religion* (New York: Behrman's Jewish Book House, 1941) and *Guideposts in Modern Judaism* (New York: Bloch Publishing Company, 1954).

20   My discussion of Hyam Plutzik's biography and his work as a poet draws on Steven Sher and Edward Moran, "Hyam Plutzik's Horatio as Post-Holocaust Poem," and Edward Moran, "The Life and Poetry of Hyam Plutzik." and Anthony Hecht, Foreword to *Hyam Plutzik: The Collected Poems* (Brockport, NY: Boa Editions, 1987), xi–xix.

both towns of origin are located in the present Belarus.[21] Both grew up with Yiddish and Hebrew as mother tongues, acquiring English only later. Each received a traditional Jewish education, which entailed fluency in biblical, rabbinic, and modern Hebrew, and familiarity with classical Jewish texts and liturgy. Plutzik's oeuvre is laced with allusions to Bible, midrash, and other Judaic sources. Moreover, his notes pertaining to the prayer book project, while written in English, are punctuated with words, phrases, even passages written in a handsome Hebrew hand. And while each man—albeit in different ways—remained profoundly tied to Jewish identity and Jewish issues, each also felt powerfully drawn to the broader world of secular thinking. Plutzik studied English literature at the undergraduate and graduate levels. I won't elaborate further on his cultural and philosophical reach, as it is evident from the scope of this volume. Agus studied in a Bialystok yeshiva where he was considered an *illui* (genius). When he was fourteen, his family left Poland for Mandatory Palestine, and two years later moved to Brooklyn, New York. He attended Yeshiva University High School where he learned both religious and secular subjects. Yeshiva University's educational philosophy—"the ideological presumption that all true human knowledge, the whole of creation, reflected God's wondrous ways"[22]—became Agus's lifelong attitude.

Ordained in the mid-1930s as an Orthodox rabbi, from early on Agus was something of a maverick, willing to contest widely held beliefs about Jewish practice. Eager to develop his intellectual reach beyond the Jewish world, he left the pulpit for graduate study in philosophy at Harvard University. There he first encountered criticisms of traditional Judaism. His graduate work entailed "explicating, disseminating, and defending the ethical and humanistic values embodied in the Jewish tradition."[23] Agus published his doctoral dissertation as *Modern Philosophies of Judaism*.[24] After completing his degree, Agus accepted a pulpit in a liberal Orthodox synagogue in Chicago. But he began to have doubts about Orthodox dogma and its resistance to modernization. He wanted

---

21   Agus was born in a shtetl called Sislevitch/Swislocz, then in the Grodno-Dobornik area of Poland (Katz, *The Essential Agus*, 1). Plutzik's parents came from "a little town in Russia" called Lapich, located near Bobroisk, in the province of Minsk, then Russia, as Plutzik notes in Hyam Plutzik, letter to Donald Hall, 24 November 1968, Hyam Plutzik papers, D.113, Box 6, Rare Books, Special Collections, and Preservation, River Campus Libraries, University of Rochester. Today both towns are in Belarus, roughly 250 miles apart.
22   Katz, *The Essential Agus*, 2.
23   Ibid., 3.
24   Jacob Agus, *Modern Philosophies of Judaism: A Study of Recent Jewish Philosophies of Religion* (New York: Behrman's Jewish Book House, 1941).

to invigorate and modernize American Judaism on a multi-denominational level but could not garner support from the Orthodox establishment. When the ultra-Orthodox Agudas ha-Rabbonim put him in *ḥerem* (excommunication) for some of his opinions in the late 1940s, he broke with Orthodoxy and joined the Conservative movement, which he felt had the potential to offer both American-born Jews and postwar immigrants an "intellectually and spiritually meaningful" Judaism. In addition to his work as a dynamic pulpit rabbi, he published prolifically. His 1954 *Guideposts in Modern Judaism*—which he wrote as he worked on the prayer book project—developed the concept of the American Jewish community as a "creative minority" that should emphasize "autonomy" and "creativeness", and "foster whatever cultural and spiritual values are generated by every individual interpretation, every aspiration, within the community."[25] One can easily see how Agus would be fascinated by the erudite and gifted Jewish American poet and professor who transmuted Jewish angst into a secular poetic idiom. And one can see how Plutzik would be intrigued by the rabbi with a streak of rebelliousness who wrote about philosophy, theology, and literature.

The Prayer Book Project

The prayer book project came at a fraught moment in Jewish history. The push for re-energizing the American Jewish community took on a particular urgency in the late 1940s and early 1950s. Still reeling from the brutal murder of the Jews of Europe and beyond, the center of Jewish life shifted to America. That the catastrophe weighed heavily on Plutzik is evident in his poems and other writing. Steven Sher and Edward Moran analyze in detail the ways in which Plutzik's long poem *Horatio* bears on the Holocaust.[26] Even in poems that do not directly address the Shoah, Eric J. Sundquist insists that Plutzik "wrote as someone who had witnessed the catastrophe that engulfed the Jews of Europe,"[27] and Cary Nelson demonstrates that "the legacy of the Holocaust echoes throughout"

---

25   Jacob Agus, *Guideposts in Modern Judaism* (New York: Bloch Publishing Company, 1954), 213.
26   Sher and Moran, "Hyam Plutzik's *Horatio* as Post-Holocaust Poem."
27   Eric J. Sundquist, "Blessed Mythmaker: The Poetry of Hyam Plutzik [final]," accessed October 1, 2024, https://static1.squarespace.com/static/5682cb822399a3aa8df162ec/t/5e3df6c7e14ad269a8b5badf/1581119183903/Blessed+Mythmaker+12-19+final.pdf, 16.

Plutzik's oeuvre.²⁸ Plutzik saw the Jewish genocide as both a contemporary catastrophe and part of the long arc of Jewish history and culture. He felt deeply connected to what happened—not only because he served in the United States military during World War II, but because it resonated deeply with how he understood Jewish identity and both Jewish and Western ethics. The murder of the Jews under National Socialism raises dark and difficult questions about God, secular humanism, and the future of Jews and Judaism. It propels the possibility—indeed, the imperative—for American Jews to take on the mantle of Jewish continuity. Agus, too, felt both the tragedy and the burden of the Holocaust, and the need to offer spiritual and ethical guidance to the American Jewish community. For many rabbis in the Conservative movement, the early 1950s was a time to consolidate its presence, to "crystallize," as Agus put it at one of the discussions of the Prayer Book Committee, what Conservative Judaism believed and stood for.²⁹ Thus, a shared sense of urgency drove both Agus and Plutzik in this project. The new prayer book would be both a means to and a concrete manifestation of the spiritual regeneration they hoped to achieve for the Jewish American community.

In addition to grappling with the shattering devastation of the Shoah, both Agus and Plutzik were intellectual giants, and their exchanges contended with other pressing questions, such as Jewish destiny in America, forging an ethics born of Jewish and secular thinking, developing a modern idiom for Judaism. While there are no recordings of their conversations, the existing correspondence between the two men and documents about their meetings offer traces of their discussions about sacred language and modernizing Jewish worship. In the vision that Agus put forth, the prayer book would help to revitalize American Jewish spiritual life in a way that did not slavishly imitate the recently destroyed centers of Jewish culture and spirituality in Europe. He envisioned a reimagined Jewish American synagogue that would engage its congregants and be fully of the modern world while drawing on organic links to an inherited tradition. He called for a liturgy that would make this tradition accessible to Americans without the language skills or the classical Jewish education necessary to read and understand the original. In addition to reshaping the flow of the Jewish prayer service, he saw as crucial a vivid and eloquent translation that would not diminish the power of the liturgy but transmit and amplify it. He wished to draw in the Jewish American community through the power of language and intellectual

---

28 Cary Nelson, "The Universe Is No Consolation: Hyam Plutzik, Jewish Identity, and the Ethics of Post-Holocaust Reading," *Journal of Jewish Identities* 15, no.1 (January 2022).
29 *Proceedings*, 109.

sophistication. The encounters between Plutzik and Agus, and Plutzik's wrangling with English translations of traditional Hebrew liturgical poems, presented opportunities for the poet to work through abstract ideas about Jews, the divine and sublime, and to find concrete form for them. Unlike poems composed out of the poet's sensibilities alone, these translations and the expanded conversations about them sought to engage a broad public who would read, chant, sing, and be moved by this language. This promised to bring Plutzik's work out of the more rarified circle of poetry lovers and into a more populist domain. How to move this potential audience played into the composition of the translations as much as how to express the poet's complex thoughts and feelings about the sacred.

Most often, Agus referred to Plutzik as a "stylist" or "stylistic consultant" to the prayer book project. However, the parameters of Plutzik's work—his mandate, if you will—remained under constant renegotiation. In part, this was because the nature of the work evolved. But also, in part, it was because Plutzik became increasingly invested in the work—because it mattered to him.

With the first sample of material that Plutzik sent Agus in November 1953, he explained in a one-page letter that it took some time for him to "get the 'feel'" of the project. Plutzik then articulated the principles that govern the work he has done. First, Plutzik explained, he aimed "to keep the English rendering vivid, elevated, readable, and (to the best of my ability) accurate." The parenthetical qualifier might be a modest disclaimer about Plutzik's knowledge of classical Hebrew, or it might be a nod toward the element of intervention that translation inevitably brings. He elaborated on that latter issue more explicitly later in the letter: "A literary retouching cannot, of course, dissociate itself from basic matters of interpretation of text, so doubtless I have stuck my neck out in a number of places." In this early work on the prayer book, Plutzik's letter lays out several different literary strategies that he employed, referencing specific examples. So, for example, Plutzik noted, for one *piyyut*, "my version has been essentially a line-by-line rephrasing of yours;" for another, he wrote a rhymed song; for yet another, he "cast [the English translation of a *piyyut*] into an irregular blank verse."[30]

In a later, undated document, which bears the heading "Memorandum to the Prayer-Book Committee,"[31] Plutzik outlined at length several issues for

---

30 Letter to Jacob Agus, November 8, 1953, Jacob B. Agus Papers, Library of the Jewish Theological Seminary, New York, NY, ARC.1000.007, Box 12, Folder 2.
31 Hyam Plutzik. "Memorandum to the Prayer-Book Committee," n.d., Hyam Plutzik Papers, D.113, Box 16, Rare Books, Special Collections, and Preservation, River Campus Libraries,

discussion with the Prayer Book Committee. He termed these "certain basic matters of style." But these are more than simply stylistic considerations. Underlying these issues of language, diction and register are ideas about worship, community, theology, ethics, and the relationship between the human and the divine. The care with which Plutzik elaborated his views to the committee indicates his desire to persuade them to see things as he does. It also indicates that these are matters he cared about, that the work was more than a "job." We might argue that it was vitally connected to his sense of Jewishness and perhaps even redemption and revitalization after the devastation of the Shoah.

After their initial correspondence and exchange of material, Agus asked Plutzik to address other English translations in the *siddur*—his own unpublished translations, and selections from the 1946 *Seder Tefilot Yisrael: Sabbath and Festival Prayer Book* published by the United Synagogue of America.[32] Plutzik did not simply tinker with these translations, making small "stylistic" improvements. He thought through what it means to engage in formal prayer and how language shapes that experience. In his first point to the Prayer Book Committee, he argued for a complete overhaul of the conventions of God-language, of how one addresses the divine. While the archaic and, to his mind, off-putting language of existing prayer book translation may well be "inevitable," having become "almost... a trademark" of the genre, he urged the committee to accept the revision of prayer language into "a fitting modern idiom."

The Language of Prayer

Plutzik pushed, for example, "with as much emphasis as I have at my command" against the use of "thee," "thou," and so on, along with "obsolete" verb forms endings (such as -est, -eth) and outmoded prepositions such as *unto* and *nigh* in favor of a contemporary diction with "immediate... impact."[33] Plutzik crafted his arguments in terms designed to move the members of the committee. "A prayer is of eternity," he reminds them, "but language is of a particular time and place." Acknowledging the attraction of retaining such conventional liturgical English locutions, Plutzik conceded that its "ceremonious" quality may well be "in

---

University of Rochester; and Jacob B. Agus Papers, The Library of the Jewish Theological Seminary, New York, NY, ARC.1000.007, Box 12.

32 *Seder Tefilot Yisrael: Sabbath and Festival Prayer Book*, ed. and trans. Morris Silverman (New York: Rabbinical Assembly and United Synagogue of America, 1946).

33 Plutzik, "Memorandum," 1.

keeping with the ceremony of religion itself," and that the "dignity," "formality", and "weight" attached to such language may seem fitting. He acknowledged that "a certain remoteness" conveyed by such language may suggest the divide between the divine and the human.[34]

Then, in an extended argument that goes on for five pages, Plutzik advocates in theological, aesthetic, psychological and ethical terms for modernizing the "diction" and "typology" of prayer. Drawing on his knowledge of classical and modern Hebrew, Plutzik notes that the liturgical second-person singular that addresses the divine is identical to the word used when addressing another person: *atah*. In other words, to be faithful to the original Hebrew, the translation of *atah* should not distinguish between the sacred and the mundane. *Atah*, Plutzik insists in an example chosen for its everydayness, "is exactly the same Hebrew term used in speaking to the grocer when ordering a bag of potatoes." And, he presses, that lack of distinction between God-language and human-language governs the conjugation of verbs, as well.[35]

For Plutzik, the implications go beyond mere "stylistic" preference. They signal the relationship between the Jew and the Jewish God. "Does not the Jewish worshiper, when he prayers [sic] in Hebrew, speak directly to God, familiarly, man to man as it were. *Atah* [handwritten in Hebrew letters] is not *thou*; it is *you*. It may have been *thou* some hundreds of years ago when the word was the accepted English second-person singular pronoun. And back in those days *thou* too was used in addressing the grocer as well as God."[36] Connected to Plutzik's advocacy of a less formal and more modern second-person singular form is what he calls the "typology" of God-language.[37] "God will forgive us," Plutzik insists, "if we neglect to capitalize personal pronouns in referring to him."[38] Especially because so much of liturgical text is spoken to God, the persistent capitalization of God's many names and invocations—second- and third-person pronouns, nouns such as "King," "Helper," "Redeemer" and "Shield" and so forth—visually impede the reader of the prayer book. "Any psychologist will tell us that capital letters retard reading."[39] So that the print of the prayer book not get in the way of the experience of those praying from its text, Plutzik advocates capitalizing only

---

34 Ibid.
35 Ibid., 2.
36 Ibid.
37 Ibid., 4.
38 Ibid.
39 Ibid., 4–5.

names, the word *God*, "and possibly the word *Lord* . . ."[40] Even if the concept of "God as king" commands "a certain formality,"[41] Plutzik repeatedly insists that there are "more *valid* way of giving dignity and formality"[42] to the language of prayer.

Moreover, Plutzik insists, the verb form endings attached to these obsolete forms work aesthetically against the experience of prayer. Plutzik understands aesthetics not as simply prettifying language, but as an important means for language to render its effect. Bearing in mind the intention to recite aloud parts of liturgy, Plutzik judges *-st* and *-est* endings "extremely uneuphonious," lending "a sibilance to a passage that is quite destructive to the music."[43] The aesthetic failings of this diction carry "practical disadvantages." To function effectively in synagogue worship—to create, in other words, sacred experiences for congregants in prayer—the English phrasing must "roll easily from twentieth-century lips."[44] To that end, Plutzik calls for replacing "stiff, inflated" vocabulary with words that feel simpler and more direct.[45]

In his view, the most important argument for employing modern, rather than obsolete, diction is "philosophical . . . I am even tempted to use the word 'ethical' . . ."[46] Using archaic diction and all that attaches to it renders the translation "artificial," and not "genuine." In this, Plutzik insists on going back to the original Hebrew as the determinant of the most appropriate diction choices in English, rather than being welded to an enchainment of translation choices past which might have once been "the best available" but are no longer so. To bring home this point, he cites two contemporary translations of Latin classics—Richard Lattimore's *Iliad* and C. Day-Lewis's *Aeneid*—and new Protestant translations of the Bible. These modern translations, he insists, come close to capturing how original audiences understood the texts.

These arguments about what constitutes appropriate liturgical diction in the second half of the twentieth century emerged from different aspects of Plutzik's life, education, and inner being. They drew on his youthful learning of Hebrew and Jewish practice and his familial legacy, along with his training as a poet and literary scholar, and his experience as a professor of literature. Rather than

---

40   Ibid., 5.
41   Ibid., 2.
42   Ibid., 3.
43   Ibid., 2.
44   Ibid., 4.
45   Ibid.
46   Ibid., 3.

seeming disparate, these elements shape his sensibility and the prism through which he understands this moment of Jewish crisis and possibility. His secular, or perhaps more correctly, his Western education, rather than pulling against his Jewish understanding, nourishes, and deepens it.

Plutzik's Memorandum suggests that, rather than simply regarding his consultancy as a "job" that taps his range of knowledge, the poet found his participation in the project deeply meaningful. In his laying out of the issues, Plutzik made clear that his engagement with the prayer book project and with Agus was intellectually, ethically, and spiritually significant. The passion and intelligence with which he mounted his arguments to the committee suggest that he sees an important place for the renewal of liturgy as part of the revitalization of Jewish spirituality in postwar America, after the devastation in Europe.

But in an undated typed letter from Agus to Plutzik,[47] Agus responded critically to a packet of translations that Plutzik had sent him. Rejecting some of them and calling for revision of others, Agus praises Plutzik's translation of the *piyyut Yishtabach*,[48] stating that he preferred it to the one published in the recent United Synagogue prayer book. He planned to include Plutzik's version in the new prayer book, but only with further revision. The closing blessing of a portion of the morning prayer service called *Pesukei dezimra* [Verses of praise], *Yishtabach* deploys a series of synonyms for praise. Since the liturgical section it closes consists largely of Psalms, *Yishtabach* links the act of praise with song. Because of its brevity, it is worth comparing here the version in the 1946 United Synagogue prayer book, translated by Morris Silverman, with Plutzik's version.

Silverman's translation:

> Praised be Thy name forever, O our King, Thou God and King, great and holy, in heaven and on earth. For unto Thee, O Lord our God and God of our fathers, it is fitting to render song and praises, hymn and psalm, ascribing unto Thee power and dominion, victory and glory, holiness and sovereignty. Unto Thee we offer Blessing and thanksgiving from this time forth and forevermore. Blessed art Thou, O Lord, exalted in praises, God of

---

47 Letter to Hyam Plutzik, n.d., Hyam Plutzik papers, D.113, Box 16, Rare Books, Special Collections, and Preservation, River Campus Libraries, University of Rochester. The first page of the letter is missing.
48 I use Agus's transliteration here.

thanksgiving, Lord of wonders, who takest delight in songs and psalms, Thou God and King, the life of the universe.[49]

Plutzik's translation:

> May your name be praised forever, our king and God,
> God of our fathers, majestic and holy monarch
> Of earth and sky, whom fittingly we render
> For the magnitude of your holiness and power
> Worship and laudation, hymn and psalm,
> Now and forever.
> Singing we bless you—
> You who delight in the loveliness of music—
> Lord of wonders, life-giver of the universe.

In translating *Yishtabach*, Plutzik put into practice the principles he articulated in his Memorandum to the Prayer Book Committee. As he noted to Agus in his letter of November 8, 1953, he has "cast [*Yishtabach*] into an irregular blank verse" so that it seems of a piece with the Psalms and passages of biblical verse that precede it. The translation eschews the archaic diction and typology that the earlier translation exemplifies. Plutzik capitalizes only the word "God," not the other references to God (and fudges the issue of "Lord" by placing it at the start of a line). One might view Plutzik's *Yishtabach* less as a translation, and more as an original poem created from the themes invoked in the original. Its language would, as Plutzik put it in the Memorandum, "roll easily from twentieth-century lips." Plutzik integrated the musicality of the Psalms that precede it in the prayer service, so much so that praise and prayer, and music merge—evoking the Levite services in the ancient Temple. Most daringly, in the seventh line Plutzik replaced the standard "Blessed art Thou, O Lord" with something entirely new. The phrase "Singing we bless you" connects the musicality of Temple worship with the music of poetry, and imagines a contemporary congregation singing this prayer-poem. While the poem marks a disparity between God and the worshipers—after all, it is we who praise God—it also suggests a similarity: both delight in music.

---

49 *Seder Tefilot Yisrael*, 86.

For Agus, Plutzik has taken a step too far. After praising the translation, Agus asked Plutzik to revise it, instructing him to make it "more literal." What Agus meant by "literal," in this instance, is not closer fidelity to the original Hebrew text. Indeed, Agus acknowledges that a translation need not be "exact" if "in a deeper sense, it grasps the truth that is involved in the naive words." Rather, Agus takes issue with the final three lines of Plutzik's translation. In fact, Plutzik's first rendition of the prayer had only six lines, ending at "Now and forever." At Agus's direction, he had added the closing three lines, constituting the blessing section of the prayer. But Plutzik's choice was too radical for Agus. The rabbi demanded that the translation retain the English formula "Blessed art Thou," the conventional translation of the Hebrew *barukh atah adonai*, which is the standard Hebrew beginning of Jewish blessings. Agus argued that Plutzik "cannot avoid the phrase, 'Blessed art Thou'" because of the phrase's "deep symbolic expression which cannot be eliminated." Agus made clear that Plutzik's radical departure from what had by then become the accepted English language formula cannot stand.[50]

In fact, Plutzik's choice opens on a set of questions that has vexed traditional scholars for centuries. Just what does it mean to say that God is *barukh*. We understand what it means for God to bless—whether the object of blessing be people, the sabbath, or anything else. People bless other people—prophets, a nation; parents, their children. But what does it mean to say that God is "blessed," as that formula has it? Who has the authority or power to bless God?

The fifteenth-century French Jewish philosopher Rabbi Joseph Albo understands the concept of *berakha*, commonly translated as "blessing," as an increase of *tov vashefa* [good and abundance]. In his *Sefer ha-'Ikkarim* [Book of Principles],[51] through an analysis of grammatical forms, Albo observes that the word *barukh* may refer both to the giver and the recipient of *hatov vehashefa* [the good and the abundance]. When applied to the recipient, *barukh* is a passive verb, indicating that the recipient is the one upon whom blessing has been conferred. When applied to God, *barukh* is an adjective, similar in form to other

---

50   Agus's dictum regarding translating the blessing reflects a broader decision about the use of pronouns pertaining to the divine. In his discussion of the prayer book at the 1954 Rabbinical Assembly convention, Agus asserted that after spending "a great deal of time" on that question, his committee has decided to use "thee" and "thou"—"because when it comes to prayer, it is more important to have the feeling of confrontation with the deity than it is to have a term that can be read as you run" (*Proceedings*, 107) and that such terms bring with it "reverence" (ibid., 108).

51   Yosef Albo, *Sefer ha-'Ikkarim* [the Book of Principles], accessed October 1, 2024, https://www.daat.ac.il/daat/mahshevt/ikarim/b7-2.htm.

divine adjectives, such as *raḥum* [merciful] and *ḥanun* [compassionate]. To utter the words *barukh atah*, then, is to recognize God as the source of goodness and abundance. As such, Albo observes (noting biblical prooftexts), *barukh* becomes a term that connotes a general praise and celebration [*hashehvah vehahilul bikhlal*] of the divine. With this in mind, Albo explains, the sages of the Talmud determined to use *barukh atah* to connote a recognition of *kol minei tovot* [all sorts of good] that humanity receives from God.

Agus's insistence on the English formula accords it the stature of the Hebrew original, in a sense; the English convention is venerable because old. But Plutzik's departure from the stiff English wording shakes up the prayer experience. Not only is his version, "Singing, we bless you," truer to the understanding of what *barukh* means when it pertains to the divine, but it also jolts those reciting the prayer out of a routine recitation whose meaning is lost. Moreover, the "we" links those participants in congregational prayer with the heavenly beings who sing God's praises in a subsequent portion of the liturgy. Elsewhere in his translations, Plutzik employs such substitutions for the formula as "we adore and bless you,"[52] or the simple "Blest is you." While Agus and his colleagues remained tied to the English convention, Plutzik's versions anticipate future changes in attitude. Decades later, for example, the American Jewish poet Marcia Falk would argue against the use of universal formulae, because "no convention of prayer ought to become completely routine, lest it lose its ability to inspire authentic feeling."[53] And in his 2002 Orthodox *Pathway to Prayer*, Mayer Birnbaum would employ the phrase: "You are the source of all blessing."[54]

Fundamental disagreements with Plutzik's choices led Agus to constrict "the function of a stylistic consultant." While Agus did "not rule out the possibility of an occasional, more creative approach," in general his critique of the work submitted indicates that what he now wanted from Plutzik was kind of tinkering—"stylistic adjustments"—with existing translations and Agus's own, new translations, both literal and interpretive. "And please," he instructed, "do not feel that you must suggest revisions, if, in your judgment, they are not needed" (undated letter, 3). At several points, Agus told Plutzik that his versions are *"theologically unacceptable"* (emphasis Agus's) (undated letter, 2), or that Plutzik has missed certain "theological nuances" (undated letter, 3) of the original Hebrew. While deferring a detailed response to Plutzik's Memorandum

---

52 From Plutzik's "Evening Prayer from the Hebrew."
53 Marcia Falk, Author's Preface to *The Book of Blessings: New Jewish Prayers for Daily Life, the Sabbath, and the New Moon Festival* (San Francisco, CA: Harper San Francisco, 1996), xviii.
54 Mayer Birnbaum, *Pathway to Prayer* (Nanuet, NY: Feldheim Publishers, 2002).

to a later date, Agus concluded, somewhat condescendingly, "Apparently, cooperation between theologians and poets is possible only in a more limited way" (undated letter, 4).

What caused Agus to temper his earlier enthusiasm for Plutzik's contributions, as a writer and a thinker? Agus was deeply invested in bringing the prayer book project to fruition. In an interim report of the Prayer Book Committee to the Rabbinical Assembly convention, Agus states, "I look at this project as a work of holiness. I have to do a great many things in the rabbinate, but I consider this project to be the holiest task assigned to me."[55] But the path was not a simple one. The members of the committee and the larger constituency of the Rabbinical Assembly held a broad range of opinions about what a prayer book should look like. Some wanted to retain the formal language that Plutzik pushed against; some argued against any kind of "interpretive" translation (as though it were possible to translate without interpreting); some objected to any translation that implied a theological position. While Agus believed that the prayer book could serve as an engine to "crystalize" the outlook of the Conservative movement, some of his colleagues argued against any kind of such crystallization. Hoping to salvage the project from the myriad of opinions about the manuscript-in-progress, Agus appealed to "the attitude of mutual toleration" that he asserted characterized the Conservative movement[56] and acknowledged that "our final result could only be a work of compromise" because "we have to reckon with the differences in viewpoint within our movement."[57]

While Plutzik understood that his work was subject to the approval of Agus and the Prayer Book Committee, his notes to himself reveal increasing frustration. "'Stylistic consultant': what is style," he writes in undated handwritten notes.[58] While he complied with Agus's demands for revision, he did not give up on the versions he really liked. "I'm correcting Agus [sic] version but including my own. His version OK but not inspiring."[59] Plutzik's vision of a modern prayer book that would revivify Jewish liturgy in America was more holistic than a sampling of translated *piyyutim*. He thought of the new prayer book as an oeuvre, with a unified and reconceptualized approach to diction and God

---

55 *Proceedings*, 110.
56 Ibid., 106.
57 Ibid., 104.
58 Hyam Plutzik papers, D.113, Box 16, Rare Books, Special Collections, and Preservation, River Campus Libraries, University of Rochester.
59 Undated handwritten notes, p. 2.

language, designed to reflect complicated concepts and to engage the reader / reciter of prayer. "Still, I get a feeling of *patching* (a bit of Klien [sic], a bit of Un Syn [sic], Hertz, etc. Ergo, a competent version, improvement by & large, yet lapses in high style, not a wk [sic] of [illegible]"[60] In his notes, Plutzik carries on an imagined and heated conversation with Agus. "What you are afraid of is not [illegible] but lack of adherence to formality." He continues, "You know the stuff you have is NG / What am I doing here. Neither I nor you know. Agus said dot 'I's' so why am I here." For Plutzik, undotted I's are hardly "the only thing wrong here."

Ultimately, much to Agus's disappointment, his prayer book project was scuttled.[61] It is beyond the scope of this essay to elaborate on the issues that defeated him, which included disagreements among his colleagues about the shape of the service and the parameters of the translations, along with complaints from disgruntled editors and translators of previous prayer books. Towards the end of the life of the project, colleagues reprimanded Agus for his "caustic reply" to criticism, for not being his "usual genial self."[62] Suffice it to say that none of Plutzik's translations were included nor was he credited in any subsequent prayer books issued by the Conservative movement. In 1961, the Rabbinical Assembly published a *Weekday Prayer Book*[63] shepherded by a new Prayer Book Committee headed by a newly appointed chair, Gershon Hadas, who prepared a new English translation. While this prayer book ignored most of Plutzik's recommendations about prayer diction and typology, it did follow his suggestion to forgo thee / thou language and archaic verb forms in favor of a more modern usage. According to introductory notes to the volume, "The adoption of the familiar second person in reference to the deity, revisions in the Hebrew text, and parallel changes in the translation were adopted in the effort to make our prayer book more readily accessible and more meaningful to the contemporary worshiper" (iii). Sidestepping issues of interpretation that so vexed Agus's project, the introductory notes assert that the original Hebrew "is faithfully reflected in the translation" except for only one prayer "which is an interpretation rather

---

60 Undated, unpaginated handwritten notes.
61 It is possible that Agus printed an abridged version of the prayer book in a limited run, for use in his Baltimore synagogue. Katz refers briefly to Agus producing a prayer book "for everyday use that allowed service to be of moderate length" by 1960 (8–9), although no such prayer book appears in Katz's exhaustive bibliography.
62 Albert I. Gordon, letter to Jacob Agus, March 5, 1954. Jacob B. Agus Papers, The Library of the Jewish Theological Seminary, New York, NY, ARC.1000.007, Box 12.
63 *Siddur Limot he-hol: Weekday Prayer Book* (New York: Rabbinical Assembly of America, 1961). Subsequent references to this edition will be in the text.

than a translation of the original" (iii). Plutzik's poetic renditions remained unpublished until several of them were included posthumously in the 1987 volume of *Collected Poems*.[64]

Memory and Forgetting

Notwithstanding the failure of the prayer book project to come to fruition, working on formal liturgy rippled into Plutzik's poems. Among his archived papers, in the same file box that contains his work for the Prayer Book Committee, are hand-written and typed versions of a poem whose title evolves from "Prayer to God for the Seasons of Death" to "Prayer in the Seasons of Death." The poem consists of four tercets and a couplet, with each line beginning with the word "Remember." Stanzas one and three begin with "Remember us"; stanzas two and four, with "Remember them"; and the final couplet, with "Remember them" and "Remember us." The poem opens in fall, with the first tercet evoking autumnal scenes, and each line progressing further into the season ("when the yellow leaves fall," "the leaves are on the ground," "the time of leafless trees"). The third tercet evokes winter—"the white flakes fall"—but also death of the natural world—"the time of the white death." But even in death, God is present: "the whiteness of Your kiss" may signal that God brings death, or that even death is encompassed by God's love. The even numbered tercets touch on the supernatural and on memory, evoking "ghosts who wander," who follow "wandering dreams," and become "blind wanderers in Your lands" in autumn, and then ghosts whose footsteps mar the snow. The poem asks that God "Remember" these "ghosts" and "the ghostly dreams they sorrow for," and "the seekers in Your ghostwhite lands." The concluding couplet ends in hope, evoking surety of the cycle of seasons when "the warm buds grow" and "the new sun greens the earth."

But in the present moment of the poem, this anticipated renewal has not yet arrived, and the poem asks that God "Remember them" and "Remember us" until then. "Them" references the antecedent "ghosts" of the second and fourth stanzas, who wander blindly, sorrowfully marring the pristine white snow. If we read this as a post-Holocaust poem, these are the murdered Jews of Europe. The "ghostwhite lands" evoke not only the wintery appellplatz of

---

64 Hyam Plutizk, *The Collected Poems* (Brockport, CT: BOA Editions, 1987). The published poems from the prayer book project include "Magen Avot" (265), "L'cho Dodi" (266–67), "El Anon [sic] Al Kol" (268), and "Kaddish" (270).

the concentrationary universe, but also the acres of fields covered in the ash of cremated victims. The ghosts do not so much haunt the bleak winterscape as hover over their own anonymous remains. The poem beseeches God to remember them—perhaps because for so many of the Shoah victims, no one remains alive to keep them in memory. In asking that God remember these unremembered Jews, the poet—and all of those who would recite this prayer-poem—perpetuate their memory, in essence, doing God's work. In other words, the prayer itself is both a call for and an act of memorialization.

But the poem is not only about memorializing the past. It reflects somberly on the present moment, and on the legacy of the Shoah. This becomes clear if we read "Prayer in the Seasons of Death" alongside another poem about the cycle of seasons and the promise of renewal, "Because the Red Osier Dogwood."[65] In the latter poem, the poet gazes upon the vividly red, bare branches of the dogwood shrub, seeing in them the promise of renewal during the season "When snow is winter." The flame-colored branches signal to the poet that, while all seems dead in winter, life forms—grasshoppers, snakes, frogs, crickets, and so forth—are merely suspended "over an abyss." The shrub intimates to the poet the "retention of the prime fires / In the naked and forlorn season," and "flames quietly" with the promise of the warmth of summer. If this poem, too, evokes the devastation of the Holocaust, the dogwood shrub keeps at bay thoughts of despair. The poet refuses to "believe the horror at the door, the snow-white worm / Gnawing at the edges of the mind . . ." but instead, remains "certain" of the return not only of nature, but "of the return of the moth / (Who was not destroyed when an August flame licked him)." The poem ends with an image of renewal, of a world set right, of the return of "all the families / Whom the sun fathers, in the cauldron of his mercy."

Although "Because the Red Osier Dogwood" ends with this strong affirmation, it does so with ambiguity. While the flame-colored branches of the osier dogwood invoke a fire that symbolizes creation and life, it is hard to dissociate it from the fires of the crematoria, synagogues, and other Jewish edifices, and the destruction of Jewish life. While the final image of "the cauldron of . . . mercy" invokes hope, it may also be read cynically, the way that poets such as Paul Celan, Jacob Glattstein / Yankev Glatsheyn, Dan Pagis and others accuse, pity, or dismiss the presence of a just and omnipotent God. It calls to mind a legend about human suffering and divine redemption that the Talmud scholar and Auschwitz survivor David Weiss Halivni recrafts as prologue to his 1996

---

65 "Because the Red Osier Dogwood," in Plutizk, *Collected Poems*, 87.

memoir *The Book and the Sword: A Life of Learning in the Shadow of Destruction*.[66] In Halivni's version, the archangel Michael angrily remonstrates God for the murder of children during the Holocaust. God silences Michael by threatening to "return [the world] to null and void." But as the archangel glances back at God, he sees "a huge tear rolling down his face, destined for the legendary cup which collects tears and which, when full, will bring the redemption of the world." Picking up on a legend about messianic redemption, Halivni leads the reader to anticipate that when a sufficient quotient of human and divine pain has been reached—symbolized by the divine tears that collect in the goblet—God will redeem the world. In that scenario, seemingly meaningless suffering becomes meaningful, hastening the onset of the messianic era. But Halivni adds a sardonic twist in his retelling. In his version, as Michael looks on, God's tear bounces off the rim of the goblet, so that most of it spills to the ground, "and the fire of the crematorium continued to burn."

Less ambiguously, the final line of Plutzik's "Prayer in the Seasons of Death" makes clear that the poet, and those praying, live in a diminished world, as yet unredeemed and unrenewed. "Remember us till the new sun greens the earth." The poem imagines such a revivification of Jewish life as possible, but not yet actualized. In portraying the autumnal and winter landscapes, the poem draws upon the flow of those seasons in the Connecticut of Plutzik's childhood and the upstate New York of the final decade and a half of the poet's life. In meshing the ghostly winter of the Jewish past with the contemporary American northeast, and casting the poem as a prayer that invokes the Jewish imperative of memory, the poem links the prayer book and its hope for the spiritual renewal in America with the mission of restoring Jewish life after the devastation.

In a different way, "After Looking Into a Book Belonging to My Great-Grandfather Eli Eliakim Plutzik" also bears the resonances of an engagement with Jewish liturgy. First published in 1959,[67] several years after Plutzik's involvement with the Rabbinical Assembly prayer book project, the poem is not written in prayer form but points to formal prayer service. I will not analyze all the complex elements of the poem here, as it has been amply treated in several incisive essays. In an insightful discussion of the poem, Naomi Sokoloff points to its negotiation of "intergenerational bonds" and "longing for connection with

---

66 David Weiss Halivni, Prologue, in *The Book and the Sword: a Life of Learning in the Shadow of Destruction* (New York: Farrar, Straus and Giroux, 1996), n.p.
67 Hyam Plutzik, *Apples from Shinar* (Middletown, CT: Wesleyan University Press, 1959), 14. Citations of the poem in this essay are from Plutzik, *Collected Poems*, 97.

Eastern European Jewish life,"⁶⁸ and its grappling with ancestral memory and forgetting. For Eric Sundquist, the poem focuses on the poet's "nearly anonymous and unmemorialized"⁶⁹ nineteenth-century ancestors who lie in "speechless graves" while for Cary Nelson those graves signal an "historical and theoretical intervention about diaspora post-Holocaust," noting that the poem "invokes not only the dead of the Shoah who have no living relatives to speak for them but also the vanished European and Russian villages that have no remaining presence."⁷⁰ These essays touch on elements that also underlie Plutzik's engagement with the prayer book project—the saturation of both Jewish memory and Jewish forgetting, the tight bond with unrecollected ancestors, the long arc of Jewish life and Jewish death.

But the poem evokes formal liturgy, as well. In a sense, it is a poem *about* liturgical practice. The book belonging to the poet's grandfather has been identified as a *Tikun Leil Shavuos* (or *Shavuot*),⁷¹ the text of the ritual enacted on the night of the festival of Shavuot. A biblical pilgrimage festival in late spring, Shavuot marks the new harvest; indeed, the Hebrew Bible refers to it as the festival of reaping [*ḥag hakatsir*]⁷² and the day of *bikurim* [first fruits].⁷³ In addition to its agricultural significance, Jewish liturgy calls the festival *zeman matan torateinu* [the time our Torah was given], because the Jewish tradition dates the biblical revelation at Mount Sinai on that day. *Tikun Leil Shavuot* refers to the mystical practice of remaining awake the night of Shavuot, immersed in the study of Torah and its commentaries. The text of the *Tikun* includes the first and last verses of all books of the Bible, several key passages, verses from the Mishna, and readings from mystical texts. The *Tikun* service concludes with the recitation of an expanded version of the Kaddish prayer known as *Kaddish d'rabanan* [rabbi's kaddish], devoted to the memory of the ancient rabbis or sages and their long line of students or disciples. The additional wording of *Kaddish*

---

68 Sokoloff, "Hyam Plutzik and Gabriel Preil: Trajectories of Jewish American Poetry," paper presented at the Twenty-Sixth Annual Jewish American and Holocaust Literature Symposium South Beach, FL, April 25, 2022.
69 Eric J. Sundquist, "Hyam Plutzik's War," *Journal of Jewish Identities* 16, no. 1–2 (January/July 2023): 173, https://doi.org/10.1353/jji.2023.a898144.
70 Nelson, "The Universe Is No Consolation," 15.
71 Jonathan Plutzik, Hyam Plutzik's son, identified the book as a *Tikun Leil Shavuot* at the Twenty-Sixth Annual Jewish American and Holocaust Literature Symposium (April 24–26, 2022), South Beach, FL, in a discussion of Naomi Sokoloff's presentation "Hyam Plutzik, Gabriel Preil, and Trajectories of Jewish American Poetry" (April 25, 2022).
72 Exod. 23:16.
73 Num. 28:26.

d'rabanan bestows blessings on the sages, their students, the students of their students, and anyone who engages in the study of Torah. In the context of the *Tikun*, those reciting the *Kaddish d'rabanan* are, in effect, blessing themselves. In its connection with the *Tikun* ritual, the poem, then, expands the concept of ancestry from bloodline to intellectual and spiritual legacy. In the poem, natural and historical patterns have relegated one's ancestors to anonymity. The elements have long ago eroded the simple wooden markers of their burial places, so that they lie unremarked and unremembered in "blank fields" and "speechless graves."

But liturgy remembers. By naming his great-grandfather in the poem's title, Plutzik retrieves him from obscurity. In invoking Eli Eliakim Plutzik, Plutzik gestures to that other memorial prayer, *Yizkor*, recited in synagogue services on Shavuot. The prayer entreats God to remember the soul of one's departed relatives—and we discern resonances of that prayer in the imperative to "Remember them" and "Remember us" in Plutzik's "Prayer in the Seasons of Death." While congregations recite *Yizkor* communally, each person inserts the name of those that he or she wants remembered, just as Plutzik inserts his great-grandfather's name into the poem's title. Indeed, as I read the poem, the "blank fields" of the opening line that so trouble the poet may be read not only in a geographic sense but in a sociological one. In other words, "field" may refer not only to an open tract of land, but to a missing piece of data that must be filled in, as one fills in a name where a blank space exists in the text of *Yizkor*.

Moreover, while the poem supports reading it in connection with Jewish catastrophe, a mystical tradition associated with the *Tikun* tradition offers a counterpoint to the darkness of death and forgetting. The mystics believed that the heavens opened at midnight on Shavuot, and that if one was awake at that moment, one's prayers reached God directly, and would be fulfilled and bring about redemption. This belief had evolved into folk tales that circulated among Orthodox Ashkenazi Jews, and it is likely that Plutzik had heard some of these as a child. Thus, against the darkness of its imagery, the context of the poem gestures towards redemption that somehow encompasses Plutzik's great-grandfather, and the nameless "no one and no one" of the poem.

Although Plutzik's work on the Rabbinical Assembly in the early to mid-1950s prayer book did not result in a re-energized Jewish American synagogue service, his immersion in formal liturgy nudged the Conservative movement, if only a little. More importantly, it inspired Plutzik to plunge into the fabric of prayer, to compose a set of stunning English renditions of medieval liturgical poems, and to bring his engagement with classical Jewish texts to bear on other poems.

Bibliography

Agus, Jacob. *Guideposts in Modern Judaism*. New York: Bloch Publishing Company, 1954.

———. Letter to Hyam Plutzik. Undated. Hyam Plutzik papers, D.113, Box 16, Rare Books, Special Collections, and Preservation, River Campus Libraries, University of Rochester.

———. *Modern Philosophies of Judaism: A Study of Recent Jewish Philosophies of Religion*. New York: Behrman's Jewish Book House, 1941.

Albo, Yosef. *Sefer ha-'Ikkarim* [Book of Principles]. Accessed October 1, 2024. https://www.daat.ac.il/daat/mahshevt/ikarim/b7-2.htm.

Birnbaum, Mayer. *Pathway to Prayer*. Nanuet, NY: Feldheim Publishers, 2002.

Brown, Michael. "Platform and Prophecy: The Rise and Fall of Rabbi Stuart E. Rosenberg as Foreshadowed in His Early Toronto Sermons on Leadership." *Jewish History* 23, no. 2 (2009) 195–217. https://doi.org/10.1007/s10835-009-9078-y.

Choy, Christine, and Ku-Ling Siegel, dirs. *Hyam Plutzik, American Poet* (2007). Video, 54:41. Accessed October 1, 2024. https://vimeo.com/165907660.

Falk, Marcia. "Author's Preface." In *The Book of Blessings: New Jewish Prayers for Daily Life, the Sabbath, and the New Moon Festival*. San Francisco: Harper San Francisco, 1996.

Fleischer, Ezra. *Shirat ha-kodesh ha-ivrit bi-yeme ha-benayim* [Hebrew Liturgical Poetry in the Middle Ages]. Jerusalem: Keter, 1975; rpt. Jerusalem: Magnes, 2007.

Gordon, Albert I. Letter to Jacob Agus, 5 March 1954. Jacob B. Agus Papers, Library of the Jewish Theological Seminary, New York, NY, ARC.1000.007, Box12.

Halivni, David Weiss. *The Book and the Sword: A Life of Learning in the Shadow of Destruction*. New York: Farrar, Straus and Giroux, 1996.

Katz, Steven T., ed. *The Essential Agus: The Writings of Jacob B. Agus*. New York: New York University Press, 1997.

Langer, Ruth. *To Worship God Properly: Tensions between Liturgical Custom and Halakhah in Judaism*. Cincinnati, OH: Hebrew Union College Press, 1998.

"Minutes of the Prayer Book Committee Breaker's Hotel, 12/28/53." Jacob B. Agus Papers, Library of the Jewish Theological Seminary, New York, NY, ARC.1000.007, Box12.

Moran, Edward. "T. S. Eliot and Hyam Plutzik: 'Hypocrite Lecteur, mon Semblable, mon Frere.'" Hyam Plutzik, Poet. Accessed October 1, 2024. http://www.hyamplutzikpoetry.com/commentarymoran.

Proceedings of the Rabbinical Assembly of America, Fifty-Fourth annual Convention (May 17–20, 1954), v. XVIII

Nelson, Cary. "The Universe is No Consolation: Hyam Plutzik, Jewish Identity, and the Ethics of Post-Holocaust Reading," *Journal of Jewish Identities* 15, no.1 (2022): 5–31. https://doi.org/10.1353/jji.2022.0003.

Plutzik, Hyam. *Apples from Shinar: a book of poems*. Middletown, CT: Wesleyan University Press, 1959.

———. *The Collected Poems*. Brockport, NY: BOA Editions, 1987.

———. Letter to Jacob Agus. 8 November 1953. Jacob B. Agus Papers, The Library of the Jewish Theological Seminary, New York, N.Y. ARC.1000.007, (Box12, Folder 2).

———. "Memorandum to the Prayer-Book Committee," undated. Hyam Plutzik papers, D.113, Box 16, Rare Books, Special Collections, and Preservation, River Campus Libraries, University of Rochester; and Jacob B. Agus Papers, The Library of the Jewish Theological Seminary, New York, N.Y., ARC.1000.007 (Box12).

⸻. "Prayer, from the Hebrew, To Him Who Lights the Earth," undated. Hyam Plutzik papers, D.113, Box 16, Rare Books, Special Collections, and Preservation, River Campus Libraries, University of Rochester.

Reif, Stefan C. *Judaism and Hebrew Prayer: New Perspectives on Jewish Liturgical History*. Cambridge: Cambridge University Press, 1993.

Sher, Steven and Edward Moran. "Hyam Plutzik's Horatio as Post-Holocaust Poem." http://www.hyamplutzikpoetry.com/commentaries.

Sundquist, Eric J. "Blessed Mythmaker: The Poetry of Hyam Plutzik [final]." https://static1.squarespace.com/static/5682cb822399a3aa8df162ec/t/5e3df6c7e14ad269a8b5badf/1581119183903/Blessed+Mythmaker+12-19+final.pdf.

⸻. "Hyam Plutzik's War." *Journal of Jewish Identities* 16, no. 1–2 (January/July 2023), 165–180. DOI: https://doi.org/10.1353/jji.2023.a898144.

Rosen, Tova and Eli Yassif, "The Study of Hebrew Literature of the Middle Ages: Major Trends and Goals," in *The Oxford Handbook of Jewish Studies*. Edited by Martin Goodman, (2004; online edn, Oxford Academic, 2 Sept. 2009), 241–294. https://doi.org/10.1093/oxfordhb/9780199280322.013.0011

Rosenberg, Stuart E. Letter to Jacob Agus. 7 October 1953. Jacob B. Agus Papers, The Library of the Jewish Theological Seminary, New York, N.Y., ARC.1000.007, (Box12, Folder 2).

Seder Tefilot Yisrael: Sabbath and Festival Prayer Book. Edited and translated by Morris Silverman. New York: Rabbinical Assembly and United Synagogue of America, 1946.

Siddur Limot he-hol: Weekday Prayer Book. New York: Rabbinical Assembly of America, 1961.

Sokoloff, Naomi. "Hyam Plutzik and Gabriel Preil: Trajectories of Jewish American Poetry." Paper presented at the Twenty-Sixth Annual Jewish American and Holocaust Literature Symposium, South Beach, FL, April 25, 2022.

CHAPTER 15

Hyam Plutzik's Rod and Creel: Fishing, Jewish Identity, and the Legacy of American Antisemitism

---

Maxim D. Shrayer

Introduction

For the Jewish-American poet Hyam Plutzik (1911–1962), fishing was both a lifelong avocation and a subject of literary exploration. In this essay, the leitmotif of fishing in Plutzik's life and oeuvre serves as a lens through which the poet's

---

Copyright © 2025 by Maxim D. Shrayer.
I would like to thank the volume's editors for the invitation to contribute an essay. I would like to express my appreciation to the estate of Hyam Plutzik for the permission to reprint Plutzik's works, and to the Plutzik family, especially Deborah Plutzik Briggs, Jonathan Plutzik, and Roberta Plutzik Baldwin, for their support and for answering my queries. My profound thanks go to Melissa Mead and Savannah Cid of the Department of Rare Books, Special Collections, and Preservation River Campus Libraries, University of Rochester, for their generous assistance with obtaining materials from the Hyam Plutzik Papers. Edward Moran, a Plutzik expert, generously answered my questions. I rely on his prolegomena to the biography of Hyam Plutzik. See Edward Moran, "The Life and Poetry of Hyam Plutzik," Hyam Plutzik, Poet, accessed September 13, 2023, http://www.hyamplutzikpoetry.com/life-and-poetry. A brief overview of Plutzik's life and poetry is in Edward Moran and Philippe Witte, "A Great Stag, Broad-Antlered: Rediscovering Hyam Plutzik," *Paris Review*, May 8, 2012, https://www.theparisreview.org/blog/2012/05/08/a-great-stag-broad-antlered-rediscovering-hyam-plutzig/. I also benefited from the materials presented in the documentary, Christine Choy and Ku-Ling Siegel, dirs., *Hyam Plutzik: American Poet* (2007), video, 54:40, https://www.youtube.com/watch?v=4zVK4XJYKp4&t=7s.

Jewish questions and Judaic motifs are examined. This essay will also envision the art and craft of fishing as a complex allegory of a Jewish poet's path into the Anglo-American literary mainstream, a career riddled simultaneously with Jewish aesthetic and social anxieties and with Christian religious and racialized prejudices. This essay will argue that it was both Hyam Plutzik's destiny and his choice to live as a lone Jewish fisherman by the rivers of post-World War II American culture.

Of Jewish Fishers and Jewish Anglers

According to Rabbi Emil B. Hirsch, who held a chair of rabbinical literature at the University of Chicago, "the Bible does not mention any particular fish by name," while "the biological knowledge of the Talmud concerning fish was of a very primitive order."[1] Some references to fishing and fishermen are found in the Hebrew Bible, including specific fishing techniques and gear. It was an occupation among some ancient Israelites, and traces of that, such as the "Fish Gate" in Jerusalem (Neh. 3:3),[2] are found in the scriptures. Some allegorical or metaphorical references to fish and fishermen also appear in the Hebrew Bible, specifically in prophetic writings. In Jeremiah 16:15–16, the Lord speaks of gathering the Israelites:

> For I will bring them back to their land, which I gave to their fathers:
> Lom I am sending for many fishermen—
>
>   declares the Lord—
>
> And they shall haul them out;
> And after I will send for many hunters,
> And they shall hunt them
> Out of every mountain and out of every hill
> And out of the clefts of the rocks.[3]

Such fishing tropes later gained prominence in the New Testament, in the episodes depicting the beginning of Jesus's mission and ministry among the Jewish fishermen on the Sea of Galilee (Lake Kinneret). Famously in Mark 1:16–18,

---

1. Emil G. Hirsch, "Fish and Fishing," JewishEncyclopedia.com, accessed August 14, 2023, https://www.jewishencyclopedia.com/articles/6158-fish-and-fishing.
2. *Tanakh: The Holy Scriptures: The New JPS Translation According to the Traditional Hebrew Text* (Philadelphia: The Jewish Publication Society, 5748/1988), 1511.
3. *Tanakh*, 806.

Jesus was walking by the sea of Galilee when he saw Simon and his brother Andrew at work with casting nets in the lake; for they were fishermen. "Jesus said to them: 'Come, follow me, and I will make you fishers of men.' At once they left their nets and followed him."[4]

Figure 1. Raphael, *The Miraculous Draft of Fishes* (1515). The Victoria and Albert Museum. Wikimedia. https://en.wikipedia.org/wiki/The_Miraculous_Draft_of_Fishes_(Witz).

New Testament commentators zoom in on the descriptions of fishing in the Gospel narratives set around Lake Galilee. They rely on the text of the Scriptures and archeological data when they speak of fishing in Jesus's time, sometimes interpreting miracles as historical evidence. Gary M. Burge suggests that "net fishing was the stock-in-trade of the people who lived on the lake, and the Gospels point to Jesus' knowledge of this. Hook-and-line fishing was known but used far less

---

4   *The Revised English Bible with the Apocrypha* (Oxford: Oxford University Press; Cambridge: Cambridge University Press, 1989), 30.

since it yielded fewer fish, but Jesus once told his followers to catch a fish using a single line" (Matt. 17:24–27).[5] In Matthew 17:27, Jesus says to Peter: "go and cast a line in the lake; take the first fish you catch, open its mouth, and you will find a silver coin; take that and pay the tax for us both." Biblical archeologists, notably Mendel Nun, author of *The Sea of Galilee and Its Fishermen in the New Testament* (1989), warn against the danger of reading Gospel narratives, related to Jesus and the fishing communities on Lake Kinneret, as accurate accounts of fishing.[6]

A cursory glance at the history of Jewish civilization reveals that fishing did not constitute a core Jewish occupation or trade, either in biblical times or in the diaspora, even in the areas of Eastern and Central Europe with the largest pre-Shoah traditional Jewish communities. This is remarkable, given the prominence of fish in both Ashkenazi and Sephardic cuisine and the relative ease with which most types of fish could satisfy Jewish dietary laws (kashrut). (A notable exception is the presence of Jewish professional fishermen in the coastal Jewish communities of the Levant and parts of the Black Sea—for example, Thessalonikian Jewish fisherman of the Ottoman and post-Ottoman period[7] and Odessan Jewish fishermen in the nineteenth- and early twentieth-century Russian Empire.) What, then, are the halachic positions on fishing, both as a procurement of food and as a sport and pastime?

In the Hebrew Bible (e.g. Gen. 26), hunting and hunters are more important than fishing and fishermen. The halachic skepticism toward the activity of hunting for animals in the wild, based to a degree on the general prohibitions against cruelty to animals (*tza'ar baalei chayim*) and against wastefulness (*bal tashchit*), extends to—and applies to—fishing, although, perhaps, in a more nuanced fashion.[8] In 2015, Rabbi Yehoshua Pfeffer addressed the subject from

---

5   Gary M. Burge, "Fishers of Fish," *Christian History* 59 (1998), https://christianhistory-institute.org/magazine/article/fishers-of-fish; see also Ray Vander Laan, "They Left Their Nets Behind," *That the World May Know*, accessed September 12, 2023, https://www.thattheworldmayknow.com/they-left-their-nets-behind; James Campbell, "Biblical Fishing 101: Reeling in the First Fishers of Faith," Loyola Press, accessed September 12, 2023, https://www.loyolapress.com/catholic-resources/prayer/arts-and-faith/culinary-arts/biblical-fishing-101-reeling-in-the-first-fishers-of-faith/.

6   Mendel Nun, "Cast Your Net upon the Waters: Fish and Fishermen in Jesus' Time," *Biblical Archeological Review* 19, no. 6 (November-December 1993), https://www.baslibrary.org/biblical-archaeology-review/19/6/11.

7   See Shai Sruogo's illuminating study, "The Mediterranean Culture of Fishing: Continuity and Change in the World of Jewish Fishermen, 1500–1929," *International Journal of Maritime History* 32, no, 2 (2020): 288–304.

8   I am relying on the overview of Jewish views of hunting and fishing by Rabbi Yehoshua Pfeffer , "Hunting and Fishing in Halacha," dinoline.com, November 18, 2015,

a comprehensively historic perspective: "The question of hunting for sport in Halacha was first raised in the seventeenth century, and its main occurrence in responsa literature is in the eighteenth century, when the social status of Jews in some parts of Europe rose and some became landowners. Halachic authorities generally prohibited hunting, for a variety of reasons." Indeed, Yehezkel ben Yehuda Landau (1713–1793) of Prague, author of the responsa *Noda BiYehudah*, states: "How can a Jew actively kill an animal, while motivated by no need other than enjoying himself in hunting?!"[9]

Summing up the responsa on the subject of hunting, Rabbi Pfeffer writes: "Thus, one may kill animals to make a living, but not to be cruel or to kill animals purely for entertainment. Hunting for pleasure is a form of cruelty, and destroys a person's inner qualities and traits." He then asks: "Is fishing similar to hunting? Our intuition tells us that it isn't—hunting is a cruel and bloodthirsty sport, whereas fishing is a quiet and soothing pastime. Might it be forbidden?"

Jewish religious commentators considered whether fishermen inevitably inflict pain on the fish—using hooks or harpoons, for example. Rabbi Pfeffer offers a modern answer to this ancient problem: "Where the fishing trip is required for therapeutic or medical reasons, it is of course permitted—though it remains better to keep the fish for consumption, where this is possible." A traditional Jewish religious sensibility tolerates commercial fishing and fishing for food, but holds negative or skeptical views of fishing for leisure or sport.

As we turn to the lives of Ashkenazi Jews in the former Pale of Settlement in the Russian Empire, where Hyam Plutzik's parents had their deep roots, we note in passing that fishing as a trade or avocation—as opposed to catching fish for use in Jewish cooking (e.g. stuffed carp with added pike and whitefish)—does not leave much of a trace in works by Jewish authors of the nineteenth and early twentieth century.[10]

---

https://dinonline.org/2015/11/18/hunting-and-fishing-in-halachah/. I also benefited from the information posted in 2012–2018 on the discussion board of Mi Yodeya [Who Knows], "Is Catch and Release Fishing Permitted?," mi yodeya, accessed September 12, 2023, https://judaism.stackexchange.com/questions/15616/is-catch-and-release-fishing-permitted and from the summary by Rabbi Aaron Tendler, "Fishing for Sport," JewishAnswers.org, accessed September 12, 2023, http://www.jewishanswers.org/ask-the-rabbi-1040/fishing/.

9   Quoted in Pfeffer, "Hunting and Fishing in Halacha."
10   I benefited from the expertise of colleagues who responded to a discussion of the representation of fishing and fishermen on my Facebook page, https://www.facebook.com/maxim.d.shrayer, on August 29, 2023, and I would like to acknowledge them here: Tony Eprile, Marat Grinberg, Gali-Dana Singer, Thomas Soxberger, Jarrod Tanny, Veronika

In this regard, the Yiddish writer Leon Kobrin (1872–1946), who grew up in Vitebsk and immigrated to America in 1892, is an exception, as one sees in his *Yankl Boyle, from the Life of a Jewish Fisherman in Russia, and Other Stories* (New York, 1898). Another fascinating exception is the Ukraine-born writer Mark Egart (1901–1956), who spent three years in Mandatory Palestine (1923–1926) before returning to the USSR and settling in Moscow. Egart's Russian-language novel *Scorched Land* (first published as a book in 1933–1934 in Moscow) describes the daily lives of halutzim. In one episode, a struggling group of men attempts to revive Jewish fishing on Lake Kinneret. They fail, however, partly because of stiff competition from local Arab fishermen and partly because of the other Jews' residual distrust of the idea of Jewish fishermen.

With some regional exceptions, fishing was not among the common trades and professions of the Jewish population of Eastern Europe.[11] As a leisure activity, it played little part in the lives of traditional East European Jews, regardless of where they lived, be it in cities, *shtetlach* (market towns), or smaller rural communities. The very idea of Jews fishing for recreation did not reach significant levels until the nineteenth century, with the rise of the acculturated Jewish bourgeoisie in Europe and later in the US. In the second half of the twentieth century, fishing became more common as a Jewish pastime in Europe, Great Britain, France, America, and Canada.

Not surprisingly, some of the recent Jewish discussions of fishing focus on sport fishing and, particularly, on the question of catch and release fishing. Is a modicum of pain inflicted on fish by hooks permissible or justifiable? In the blog entry "Jews Don't Fish!?" Rabbi Eric Eisenkramer offers this perspective:

> I practice catch and release. . . . If every fish caught was kept for food, our streams and lakes would soon be empty. . . . And there are plenty of people who find fishing to be a spiritual experience, both Jews and non-Jews. It seems to me that our energy is better spent not worrying about stereotypes, but instead pursuing those activities in life that provide us with fulfillment and meaning, no matter what they are.[12]

Tuckerova. My very cursory consideration of fishing and fisherman in the works of Jewish writers does not extend beyond the 1930s.

11 See, for instance, Judith Kalik's discussion of the occupations of Jews in the Minsk Province of the Russian Empire in her *Movable Inn: The Rural Jewish Population of Minsk Guberniya in 1793–1914* (Berlin: De Gruyter, 1998), 168–169, accessed September 14, 2023, https://www.jstor.org/stable/j.ctvbkk0gx.

12 Rabbi Eric Eisenkramer, "Jews Don't Fish!?!" *The Fly Fishing Rabbi* (blog), December 22, 2008, http://theflyfishingrabbi.blogspot.com/2008/12/jews-dont-fish.html.

Plutzik's Rural Roots in Belarus and Connecticut

Hyam Plutzik was born on 13 July 1911 in Brooklyn to Jewish immigrants, who had journeyed to America in 1908 from the Russian Empire. Formerly of the Minsk province, the village of Lapichi, where Pluzik's parents lived prior to immigration, is located in central Belarus, now administratively part of the Chervyen (formerly Ugumen) district in the Mogilev province. The river Svislach, a tributary of the Berezina, runs through the village of Lapichi, and the area is known for fishing.

The Jewish presence in Lapichi dates to the early nineteenth century. In the records of 1816/1819, fifty-two male and sixty-eight female Jews resided in Lapichi. According to the census of 1897, about a decade prior to the immigration of Plutzik's parents, there were 736 Jews out of Lapichi's total population of 750. In 1926, 709 Jews, or about 85% of the population, were living in Lapichi. Prior to the Shoah, Lapichi was a majority-Jewish Yiddish-speaking small rural community. Soon after the occupation of the area in July 1942, a ghetto was established in there. The Jews of Lapichi and surrounding villages were murdered in three stages in 1941–1942.[13]

Plutzik spent his formative childhood years in rural Connecticut. In 1912 his parents bought a farm in Southbury, a town twenty-one miles northeast of New Haven and thirty-five miles southwest of Hartford. The Plutzik family subsequently moved to the town of Bristol near Hartford. Bullet Hill Brook runs through Southbury. The town is in close proximity of a number of fishing waters, notably Laker Lillinonah and the Pomperaug River. Growing up, Plutzik was likely to fish in local lakes, rivers, and streams, and the principal freshwater fish were largemouth and smallmouth bass, yellow perch, chain pickerel, and varieties of trout. Plutzik may have also fished for saltwater fish in the Long Island Sound. Fishing, with tangible references to the poet's childhood and youth in Connecticut, would later feature in his poetry.

Portrait of a Young Jew as a Stranger at Trinity College

In 1928, Hyam Plutzik entered Trinity College on a merit-based Holland Scholarship. At Trinity, a college with a Episcopalian identity and traditions of religious tolerance, Plutzik majored in English and graduated Phi Beta

---

13   See Vitaly Charny, "Jewish Population for Towns in Minsk Guberniya," JewishGen, accessed September 14, 2024, https://www.jewishgen.org/belarus/lists/vitaly_Town.html; "Lapichi," Yad Vashem, September 14, 2024, https://collections.yadvashem.org/en/untold-stories/community/14621536-Lapichi; Kalik, *Movable Inn*, 64.

Kappa in 1932. According to Edward Moran, during "his senior year at Trinity, Plutzik was associate editor of the college's literary magazine the *Trinity Tablet*, which printed his short story "The Golus" and a cycle of poems titled "Three Paintings." Plutzik went on to Yale University to pursue a master's degree in English, and the first two years of his studies were funded by a special fellowship for Trinity College graduates. His period of study coincided with limited Jewish advancement in the academy and the cultural mainstream during the American 1910s–1930s.

Figure 2. Page from the 1932 *Trinity Tablet* with a picture of Hyam Plutzik. Courtesy of the Department of Rare Books and Special Collections, University of Rochester.

Historians and sociologists have painted a picture of anti-Jewish retrenchment after World War I and of measures aimed at curtailing the number of Jewish students, specifically children of Jewish immigrants from Eastern Europe, at elite private colleges and universities. Already in the 1900s, and especially in the wake of the Bolshevik revolution, Jewish immigrants from the former Russian Empire and other parts of Eastern and Central Europe were regarded as politically suspect, bearers of socialist and anarchist ideas.

To quote from the illuminating research of Jack Dougherty and his colleagues, based on the recently unsealed records:

> At Trinity College... administrative and student leaders expressed explicitly anti-Semitic views from 1915 to at least 1922, and implemented strategies to reduce the number of Jewish students—and to reject all Black applicants—according to Board of Trustees meeting minutes that were long hidden from public view.[14]

As president of Trinity College in 1904–1919, Rev. Flavel S. Luther, mathematician, engineer, and Episcopalian minister, privately expressed opposition to the admission of Jewish students. In 1915, about 10% of Trinity's 250 students were Jewish; they were mainly from the city of Hartford and its environs. Luther advised the board of trustees that the Jewish students' "presence is resented by the other students and has occasioned many protests by the alumni." While emphasizing that Trinity "should do its share in educating these aliens, whatever their race or religion . . . [because] it is only by education that they can ever be assimilated and Americanized," Luther advocated subtle actions aimed at restricting Jewish numbers on campus.[15]

At a 1918 college board meeting, Luther offered a racialized classification of Jewish students based on origins: "a few of the Jews in College who, by reason of exceptional personal qualities, are cordially accepted as good fellows. The other students call them 'White Jews.'" Those were, presumably, scions of acculturated German and Austrian Jews. In the words of Dougherty, Luther "assigned" the children of Jewish immigrants from Eastern Europe "to a lower position in

---

14 See Jack Dogherty and Contributors, "Uncovering Unwritten Rules against Jewish and Black Students at Trinity College," in Jack Dogherty and Contributors, *On the Line: How Schooling, Housing, and Civil Rights Shaped Hartford and Its Suburbs*, May 25, 2024, https://ontheline.trincoll.edu/uncovering-unwritten.html; see the text of the Trinity College Board of Trustees minutes at: https://ontheline.trincoll.edu/images/1915-1922-trinity-excerpts.pdf.

15 Ibid.

the racial hierarchy" and "suggested ways that Trinity might deter their future enrollment, perhaps by mandatory Christian chapel services."[16]

In 1920 Luther was succeeded by Rev. Remsen Brickerhoff Ogilby, who remained president of Trinity until his death in 1943[17] and would play a distinct part in Plutzik's experience at the college and beyond. The Jewish question was high on Ogilby's agenda. To return to Dougherty's account,

> "The number of Jewish students has been a matter of interest to many of us and has concerned two or three," Ogilby told the Board in 1922. . . . He proudly announced that "the percentage of Hebrews in the student body" had declined from 10.5 percent in 1921 to 9 percent in 1922.[18]

One comes across at least two instances of Ogilby's prejudice, both from the years of Plutzik's soul-searching and self-discovery following graduation from Trinity. In 1941 Plutzik won, for the second time, the Cook Prize, an award given to Yale students. His prize-winning long poem Death at the Purple Rim, composed around 1937, was printed as a chapbook; Plutzik sent a copy to Ogilby. As Moran notes, Ogilby's Christmas Eve 1941 letter to the poet oozes prejudice:

> Dear Plutzik,
>
> I have never thought of you as a gardener or a day laborer out of doors. The poem to me smelt too much of the lamp and had very little of the flavor of a New England garden. Most certainly thirty-seven pages is rather long for a real gardener to describe his emotions about the death of a woodchuck.
>
> Please be assured that Trinity College always appreciates the honors received by its graduates. I am glad that you have helped to build up the respect that Yale University should have for its neighboring little cottage.[19]

---

16 Ibid.
17 See J. Bard McNutty, "In Memory of the Rev. Dr. Remsen Brickerhoff Ogilby," *Trinity College Alumni News*, November 1943, https://digitalrepository.trincoll.edu/cgi/viewcontent.cgi?article=1945&context=reporter.
18 Ibid.
19 Quoted in Edward Moran, Afterword to Hyam Plutzik, *Letter from a Young Poet* (Hartford, CT: Witkinson Library at Trinity College, 2015), 90.

Not only does Ogilby write that Plutzik, who grew up in Connecticut, has not figured out how to be a New England poet, the phrase "smells of the lamp" passes a prejudiced value judgement of the poem. In *Brewer's Dictionary of Phrase and Fable* (1870), "to smell of the lamp" means "to bear the marks of great study, but not enough laboured to conceal the marks of labour."[20] Ogilby implies that Plutzik, as a Jew and a stranger, lacks the lightness of idiom and diction *and* the resulting verses are overwrought. Ogilby also deploys the stereotype of Jewish bookishness and Talmudic learning, which, allegedly, stands in the way of the young poet's appreciation (clean and white) of New England pastoral. Ogilby exemplified the genteel, yet widespread antisemitism of the Anglo-Saxon intellectual establishment.

At Trinity College, Plutzik found a mentor in Professor Odell Shepard (1884–1967).[21] A poet, literary scholar, and biographer, Odell taught at Trinity from 1917 to 1946. In 1917 Odell's only poetry collection, *A Lonely Flute*, bearing an epigraph from Part 5 of Coleridge's *The Rime of the Ancient Mariner*, was published in Boston. He is best remembered for *Pedlar's Progress: The Life of Bronson Alcott*, a biography of the prominent transcendentalist and father of Louisa May Alcott, and for *Thy Rod and Thy Reel*, a masterful treatise on fly-fishing, to which I will return below. Unusually for a "WASP" of his time, Shepard was sensitive to the Jewish condition. In the words of Moran, "during the 1930s Shepard was outspoken in his criticism of the growing Nazi menace. In November 1938, he was one of the Christian leaders who spoke at a mass rally in Hartford protesting Kristallnacht."[22]

I would like to draw attention to two significant aspects of Plutzik's apprenticeship with Odell. The first concerns Odell's own poetry. By the time Plutzik had entered Trinity College and was starting to gain his own voice in the early 1930s, Odell had long abandoned his youthful poetry and turned his attention to criticism and biography, the history of fly-fishing, and Connecticut politics. Odell's poems, neoromantic, conversing with Georgian poetry, and in some cases carrying a whiff of Whitman, were already old-fashioned in 1917, the year *A Lonely Flute* came out—and also the year T. S. Eliot's "The Love Song of Alfred J. Prufrock" appeared. Echoes of *A Lonely Flute* survive in Plutzik's own verse.

---

20 Ebenezer Cobham Brewer, *The Dictionary of Phrase & Fable* (Ware: Wordsworth Editions, 1993), 725.
21 Quoted in Moran, Afterword, 89.
22 Ibid., 88.

A LONELY FLUTE

BY

ODELL SHEPARD

BOSTON AND NEW YORK
HOUGHTON MIFFLIN COMPANY
The Riverside Press Cambridge
1917

Figure 3. Title page of Odell Shepard's *A Lonely Flute* (1917).

Consider the opening of the poem "Nightfall" as representative of Odell's poetic vision and technique:

> In a crumbling glory sets
>   The unhastening sun;
> The fishers draw their shining nets;
>   The day is done.
>
> Across the ruddy wine
>   That brims the sea
> Black boats drag shoreward through the brine
>   Dreamily,
>
> And dark against the glow
>   Firing the west,
> By three and two the great gulls go
>   Seaward to rest ...

In the foreword to Plutzik's posthumously published volume, *The Collected Poems* (1987), Anthony Hecht speculates that Shepard's "kindness ... is quietly and covertly honored in that section of Plutzik's most majestic and ambitious undertaking, *Horatio* [1961], and specifically in that section of it titled 'The Shepherd.'" Plutzik could certainly learn the craft of classical versification from Odell's own work, but it is harder to imagine a young Jew whose first language was Yiddish taking inspiration from this antique shop of Anglo-American poetry.

Consider the short, bittersweet, absurdist, and delightfully orchestrated poem "Useful Prepared Speech for the Diffident Author of a Book of Poems Costing Three Dollars and Fifty Cents," which remained in Plutzik's proverbial desk drawer:

> I claim that a poem
> Is merely the proem
> To the author's intending—
> That beginning and ending
> Are the *silence* begun,
> When the talking is done.
> So why should I budge

> If someone should grudge:
> "These poems are costly."
>
> They are golden mostly.[23]

The deliberate use of the archaic term "proem," a preamble or preface to a literary or rhetorical work, evokes the opening poem in Shepard's *A Lonely Flute*. Titled "Proem," it speaks of poetry as a combination of "melodies," "magic," and "low lyric whispers."

More dramatic was the role of Odell as addressee and epistolary confessor during a time of crisis and growth, when, in 1937–1941, Plutzik ached to identify his own poetic idiom and to find a place on the map of American poetry. In May–December 1941, over the course of seven months, he composed a book-length letter to Shepard, beginning it on December 11, 1941, just days before the delayed entrance of the US into World War II. The thirty-year-old poet had finally completed his master's degree and in 1942 he was to enlist in the army. Posthumously published in 2015 as *Letter from a Young Poet* (*Letter from a Young Jew* comes to mind as a saltier alternative), it is simultaneously an autobiography and apologia, as well as an account of Plutzik's Jewish literary and intellectual insecurities and yet realized ambitions.

The bitter aftertaste of Plutzik's treatment by Ogilby and other members of the Anglo-Saxon elite permeates *Letter*'s narrative line. In its first pages, Plutzik reminisces about his last meeting with Odell:

> The last time I saw you I was weeping. It was a day in June in 1933, and Dr. Ogilby had just called me a disgrace to Trinity College. Why? Because some of my work under the Trinity fellowship at Yale was incomplete. So he called me a disgrace, and I went up to your house and asked you whether you really thought I was a disgrace, and you said you didn't, but I, who had been under great nervous strain, wept—rather inobtrusively I hope.[24]

Jewish references—to prejudice, the Shoah, alienation—punctuate the letter, and to respond to those in full must have been a tall order even for a mentor

---

23 Plutzik, *The Collected Poems* (Brockport, NY: BOA Editions, 1987), 241.
24 Plutzik, *Letter from a Young Poet*, 20.

and reader as sympathetic as Odell. "Probably you're not aware to what extent I sympathize with and understand most of the motives, opinions, moods, and attitudes suggested in your letter,"[25] Shepard states in the opening of his letter, dated December 29, 1941. He also takes the unusually bold step of voicing a critical opinion of his college president and colleague: "When President Ogilby called you a 'failure,' he had in mind, of course, a set of standards to which you have never conformed and which you do not at all accept. Neither do I."[26] Tactfully and adroitly, Shepard notes inner formal tensions and imperfections in Plutzik's use of classical prosody in *Death at Purple Rim*.[27]

From a certain Olympian distance, Plutzik's former mentor confirms that his mentee is "at home" in the "Connecticut scene" and will "reach happiness, quiet, peace of mind and heart, not in the city certainly, probably not in any college or university, but in rural New England."[28] Benevolent as it is, Shepard's reply also feels tortured, as if a liberal WASP were to sing "Kol Nidre" at an Orthodox shul; perhaps knowing that, Shepard did not mail his letter. His response speaks volumes about his discomfort at being critical of the young Jew's poem and thus betrays an anxiety of being suspected of prejudice or condescension.

Odell Shepard and the Poetics of Fly-Fishing

Edward Moran proposes that Shepard "inspired Plutzik's own lifelong appreciation of fly-fishing."[29] Shepard still enjoys a following among students of fly-fishing. Both a history and a poetics, *Thy Rod and Thy Creel* came out in 1930, when Plutzik was still at Trinity.[30] Its title is a play on the famous verses from Psalm 23—"Though I walk through a valley of deepest darkness, / I fear no harm, for You are with me, / Your rod and Your staff—they comfort me"[31]—with a

---

25 Odell Shepard, ["Shepard's Response"], in ibid., 81.
26 Ibid., 82.
27 Ibid., 83–84.
28 Ibid., 84.
29 Moran, Afterword, 88.
30 Odell Shepard, *Thy Rod and Thy Creel* (Hartford, CT: Edwin Valentine Mitchell; New York: Dodd, Mean & Company, 1930; rpt: New York: Nick Lyons Books; Winchester Press, 1984), accessed September 19, 2023, https://babel.hathitrust.org/cgi/pt?id=coo.31924051745358&seq=1. I quote the text of the 1984 edition.
31 *Tanakh*, 1132.

deliberate nod to the archaic diction of the King James Bible and, perhaps, a casual pun on the word "creed." Except in the case of fly-fishing, the "rod" is the fishing stick, while "creel" refers to the receptacle, traditionally a wicker basket, where the caught fish are stored.

THY ROD
AND THY CREEL

ODELL SHEPARD

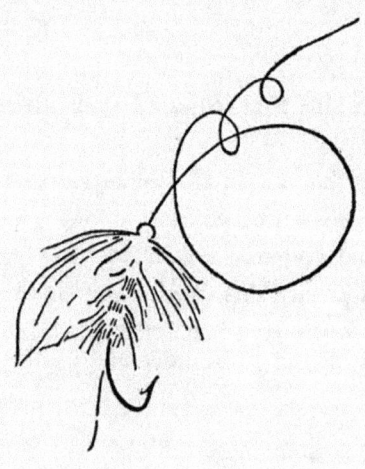

HARTFORD: EDWIN VALENTINE MITCHELL

NEW YORK: DODD, MEAD & COMPANY

1931

Figure 4. Title page of the first edition of Odell Shepard's *Thy Rod and Thy Creel* (1931).

I would like to highlight Shepard's principal points about the pleasures of fly-fishing. While it runs contrary to traditional Jewish views, Shephard's praise of fly-fishing finds echoes in Plutzik's poetic thinking. For Shepard, it has a spiritual or metaphysical quality, and it is in some ways akin to romantic poetry: "The charm of angling, and the strong hold it takes upon many of us, have never been exactly explained. This is not because angling is mysterious in its nature, like poetry, but because its fascination is so inclusive, woven of so many strands. This is a mystery incomprehensible to those who look from outside."[32]

Fly-fishing, Shepard argues, is almost a practice of pantheism; he speaks like a true heir of his beloved transcendentalists: "What can a man desire more when standing knee-deep in a mountain river, rod in hand, with trout on the rise? Here he has earth and air and sky before him, strangely interfused and woven into one element."[33]

Catching trout and other salmonids, Shepard proposes, is ultimately an aesthetic experience: "But beauty is the very stuff and essence of this sport. The trout-fisherman not only has beauty about him and in his hand; he pursues it as his quarry."[34] For Shephard, fly-fishing, as opposed to other kind of fishing—using live bait or spinning lures—is aristocratic and refined. It is not a sport of the masses or for the masses, nor is it a way to procure food: "Something has happened to English trout since that great draft of fishes was taken by one rod on a single night, and something has happened to anglers and angling in consequence. It is now a better sport, fit not only for cooks but for gentlemen."[35]

Finally, Shepard takes on the question of inflicting pain, one that we previously discussed in light of halachic concerns with fishing in general, and catch and release fishing in particular: "How much pain does a trout suffer in the course of a clean capture at the hands of an expert? The answer given me, by men whose knowledge and intelligence I trust, is that he suffers no pain whatever, as we understand pain."[36] Reading *Thy Rod and Thy Creel*—in some ways also a paean to privilege—helps one appreciate how different the young Jewish poet was from his WASP mentor.

---

32   Shepard, *Thy Rod and Thy Creel*, 29; 122.
33   Ibid., 54.
34   Ibid., 114.
35   Ibid., 102.
36   Ibid., 88.

Professor Plutzik and the Postwar Jewscape of American Academic Culture

Cary Nelson characterizes Plutzik's "story [as] fundamentally a Jewish one" and argues that he was "in a deep sense a post-Holocaust poet."[37] The period after the war, in 1940s and 1950s, was when a whole generation of Jewish American poets, born in the 1910s and 1920s, some of them former servicemen like Plutzik, entered the mainstream. When Plutzik was in college and graduate school, few Jewish names were widely known to readers of contemporary Anglo-American poetry. A small cohort of Jewish American poets of Plutzik's age—among them George Oppen (1908–1984), Edwin Rolfe (1909–1954), Muriel Rukeyser (1913–1980; winner of the 1935 Yale Younger Poets Award), and Karl Shapiro (1913–2000)—had succeeded in making themselves visible in the 1930s. Despite his two Yale poetry prizes, Plutzik himself was unknown, although he gained some recognition as a poet on publishing *Aspects of Proteus* in 1949. He reached an audience in the 1940s alongside other important Jewish American voices from his generation and half a generation earlier, such as Delmore Schwartz (1913–1966), David Ignatow (1914–1997), Edwin Honig (1919–2011), Howard Nemerov (1920–1991), and Anthony Hecht (1923–2004), and, in Canada, A. M. Klein (1909–1972).

The decade following the end of World War II was also a time when prestigious private colleges and universities were slowly opening their doors to Jewish faculty in the humanities. Before that, opposition to Jews had not only come from the administration and WASP faculty; members of the student body had also protested access. In 1927, when Stanley Kunitz had completed his master's in English at Harvard and expressed a desire to earn a doctorate, he was told that "Our Anglo-Saxon students would resent being taught English literature by a Jew."[38] In the 1930s, and still in the 1940s, members of the Anglo-Saxon intelligentsia—especially those serving as literary gatekeepers and teaching in English departments—were under the spell of T. S. Eliot and his ideas about culture and tradition. In the Page-Barbour Lectures Eliot delivered at the University of Virginia in 1933, just a short time after the Nazis came to power in Germany, he preached ex cathedra:

---

37   Cary Nelson, "The Universe Is No Consolation: Hyam Plutzik, Jewish Identity, and the Ethics of Post-Holocaust Reading," *Journal of Jewish Identities* 15, no. 1 (January 2022), https://muse.jhu.edu/pub/1/article/840934.
38   Gregory Orr, "Chronology," in *Stanley Kunitz: An Introduction to the Poetry* (New York: Columbia University Press, 1985), xxvii.

The population should be homogeneous; where two or more cultures exist in the same place they are likely to be fiercely self-conscious or both to become adulterate. What is still more important is unity of religious background; and reasons of race and religion combine to make any large number of free-thinking Jews undesirable.[39]

At the University of Rochester, where Plutzik started teaching in 1946, he was apparently the first Jewish professor in the English Department. According to Arnulf Zweig, who studied with Plutzik as an undergraduate in the late 1940s to early 1950s and was later a philosophy professor at the University of Oregon, it was "not hostile [toward Jews] but a WASPy environment."[40] Kenneth S. Rothwell, who had taught with Plutzik at Rochester, also spoke of the discomfort Jewish professors felt: "I have the feeling that he was ... sometimes I thought ... forced to conform to a world that maybe he wasn't any more comfortable than I was."[41]

Speaking of the changing climate of American poetry after World War II, the poet Donald Hall, who got to know (and admire) Plutzik's work as poetry editor of *The Paris Review*, suggested that "It was conventional antisemitism, not in Pound at the time when he was making the broadcasts, but in Eliot, and I think Eliot came to regret it very much. ... A casual racial superiority and sneer."[42] While Hall's own discomfiture with anti-Jewish prejudice is apparent, his words also signal a tendency, to which philosemitic Anglo-American writers and intellectuals of his age are prone, to present literary antisemitism as somehow affected and superficial, rather than deep-seated. That Plutzik himself might have felt differently comes through not only in his prewar reflections (especially in the confessional letter to Shepard), but also in his postwar poetry.

In "The Lowercase Jew" from the eponymous collection of 2003, Rodger Kamenetz places T. S. Eliot before a heavenly court, where he answers to charges of antisemitism. Toward the end of the poem, Bleistein says: "Send him [Eliot—M. D. S] here / to Hyam Plutzik's grandson's bar mitzvah. / For the Jews

---

39 T. S. Eliot, *After Strange Gods: A Primer of Modern Heresy* (London: Faber and Faber, 1934), 20.
40 Quoted in Choy and Siegel, *Hyam Plutzik: American Poet*.
41 Quoted in ibid.
42 Quoted in ibid.

it will seem an afternoon. / For him, a hundred years."[43] In the explanatory note, Kamenetz writes: "Hyam Plutzik wrote a courageous poem, 'For T. S. E. Only,' attacking him for his [antisemitism]."[44]

"For T. S. E. Only," one of Plutzik's most powerful and bitterly polemical poems, appears in *Apples from Shinar* (1959), Plutzik's second full collection. Written in variations of sestets, each of which ends with the words "with our exile," the poem offers a delayed response to Eliot's "Burbank with a Baedeker: Bleistein with a cigar" (1919), which was included in Eliot's *Poems* (1920) and contains verses of unabashed, and hardly casual or playful, antisemitism:

> ... On the Rialto once.
> The rats are underneath the piles.
> The jew is underneath the lot.
> Money in furs ...[45]

(In Eliot's *Poems*, antisemitism is also present in "Gerontion" and "Sweeney among the Nightingales.")[46]

In the words of David P. Goldman,

> No other poet employed so great a talent to elicit as much loathing as Eliot did in the "Bleistein" poems. First published in 1920 and reprinted in all subsequent editions of Eliot's poetry through 1963, "Burbank with a Baedeker: Bleistein with a cigar" depicts a "Chicago Semite Viennese" tourist on the Rialto Bridge in Venice, a nod to Shylock.

---

43 Rodger Kamenetz, *The Lowercase Jew* (Evanston, IL: TriQuarterly Books/Northwestern University Press, 2003), 19.
44 Ibid., 72.
45 T. S. Eliot, *Poems* (New York: Alfred A. Knopf, 1920), Project Gutenberg, accessed September 20, 2022, https://www.gutenberg.org/files/1567/1567-h/1567-h.htm; cf. T. S. Eliot, *Selected Poems* (London: Penguin Books in Association with Faber and Faber, 1952), 32–33.
46 Michiko Kakutani, "Examining T. S. Eliot and Anti-Semitism: How Bad Was It? *New York Times*, April 22, 1989, https://www.nytimes.com/1989/08/22/books/critic-s-notebook-examining-t-s-eliot-and-anti-semitism-how-bad-was-it.html.

Students of Eliot know that he also planted Bleistein in the pages of *The Waste Land* (1922). Goldman reminds us that "the passage was dropped from the initial printings on the advice of Ezra Pound, who thought it too inflammatory, but it appeared posthumously in the annotated edition" edited by the poet's widow.[47]

Here is the evidence of Eliot's poetic degradation of the Jew's corpse—which is also a mockery of Judaism. "Lids" clamor to be read as "Yids":

> Full fathom five your Bleistein lies
> Under the flatfish and the squids.
> Graves' Disease in a dead jew's eyes!
> When the crabs have eat the lids
> Lower than the wharf rats dive
> > Though he suffer a sea-change
> > Still expensive rich and strange.[48]

Plutzik does not only respond to a bout of "T. S. E." bigotry;[49] he also foregrounds an argument about the way a Jew feels on the shores of Gentile culture, a culture which will never be free either of the legacy of Christian Judeophobia or of racialized antisemitism. What is a Jewish poet to do in exile? How is he or she to live in a non-Jewish language? These questions pulsate beneath the surface of many of Plutzik's poems.

---

47 David P. Goldman, "T. S. Eliot and the Jews," *First Things*, March 2021, https://www.firstthings.com/article/2021/03/t-s-eliot-and-the-jews. There is, of course, a rich literature on the subject of Eliot's antisemitism, most notably Anthony Julius's book *T. S. Eliot, Anti-Semitism and Literary Form* (Cambridge: Cambridge University Press, 1995); my purpose here is not to reopen the debate, only to register its existence and impact.
48 T. S. Eliot, *The Waste Land: A Facsimile and Transcript of the Original Drafts Including the Annotations of Ezra Pound*, ed. and introd. Valerie Eliot (London: Faber and Faber, 1974), 120–121, 131.
49 Cary Nelson discusses Plutzik's "To T. S. E. Only" in "The Universe Is No Consolation."

Figure 5. Hyam Plutzik holding a trout, circa early 1950s. Courtesy of the Department of Rare Books and Special Collections, University of Rochester.

In Closing: The Lonely Jewish Poet as Fisherman

A photo from the late 1940s or early 1950s captures an unsmiling Plutzik as he holds up a fish that he has caught—most likely a brown or lake trout. The fish will, presumably, be cooked and eaten. By practicing fly-fishing, yet adhering to the principles of catch and release, Plutzik is both following and not following Shepard's tenets.

A passion since Plutzik's Connecticut childhood, fishing became a favorite leisure during the Rochester years. The area offered many opportunities for freshwater fishing—from Lake Ontario to various local ponds, Genesee River to the nearby Finger Lakes. The freshwater species that are commonly caught in the area include chinook salmon, steelhead, rainbow, brown, and lake trout, walleye, largemouth and smallmouth bass, pike, yellow perch, and carp. Alone, Plutzik would fly-fish for salmonids; with children and family, he enjoyed bait-and-lure fishing. In the words of Roberta Plutzik Baldwin, the oldest of Tanya and Hyam Plutzik's children, "my dad did enjoy fishing a lot." She recalls "waking up at four or five in the morning, very early," and driving with her father to the nearest of the Finger Lakes, Conesus Lake, and fishing from a row boat:

> We would always stop, and we would get bait at some little bait shack, . . . live bait [worms], but he also had a fishing box with various lures. . . . I do know how to put a worm on a hook, and I did learn how to cast. . . . There wasn't much conversation. It was communal in the sense that we were both fishing and we were in a boat.[50]

Figure 6. Hyam Plutzik's fly-fishing reel. Photo by Melissa Mead. Courtesy of the Department of Rare Books and Special Collections, University of Rochester.

Like the two principal trajectories in Plutzik's poetry, the classical and the modernist, which sometimes pulled his poems apart or harmoniously intersected, the intricate and selective art of fly-fishing both conflicted with and complemented the less structured and more democratic diversion of dropping a line and waiting for the fish to discover the bait.

---

50   Roberta Plutzik Baldwin, recorded interview with Maxim D. Shrayer, June 14, 2023.

Fish and fishing references carry distinct semantic tasks and compositional functions in Plutzik's oeuvre. Fishing marks nostalgic associations within scenes of a recollected, idyllic childhood, as is the case in the long prewar poem Death at the Purple Rim:

> ... Such as you and I, whom dignity still holds tightly,
> Can in shoeless and stockingless freedom wade in cool water,
> And think, with a twinge of boyhood, and look in amazement
> At a tiny fish that scampers to shadow and there
> With gills a-tremble munches a mote for his dinner.[51]

While fish betoken an earlier evolutionary form of humanity and act as mythological or ancient creatures, they also communicate the beauty of art and the fragility of artifice. Fish mirror human anxieties, as in *Horatio* (1961), the last book Plutzik published in his lifetime: "the frightened fish maneuver beyond his reach."[52] But people, too, take on ichthyological shapes and forms. In "As the Great Horse Rots on the Hill" from *Apples from Shinar*, the poet admits that as he "observe[s] the ordained explosions on the paper I write / ... [his] hand, too, scintillates, like a strange fish."[53]

A paradoxical poem in Plutzik's retrospective collection *Aspects of Proteus* (1949) conceives of a cycle where evolution develops a fish into a human being, and then imagination, likely that of a fly-fisherman, returns to nature through the dreamy act of creating poetry:

> Absurd Cycle
>
> The wombed thing
> First like a fish
> Will become a man
> And make a wish
>
> For a peck of apples,
> A pint of dream,
> And a leaping fish
> In a stream.[54]

---

51 Plutzik, *Collected Poems*, 70.
52 Ibid., 175. See also other fish references in *Horatio*, in *Collected Poems*, 169, 172, 185.
53 Ibid., 91.
54 Ibid., 34.

In *Apples from Shinar*, in my judgment Hyam Plutzik's most original book, we encounter three poems about fishing and fishermen. Placed, perhaps deliberately, at the beginning, the middle, and end of the collection, each poem represents a facet of Plutzik's passion. I will turn to this triad as I make my closing comments.

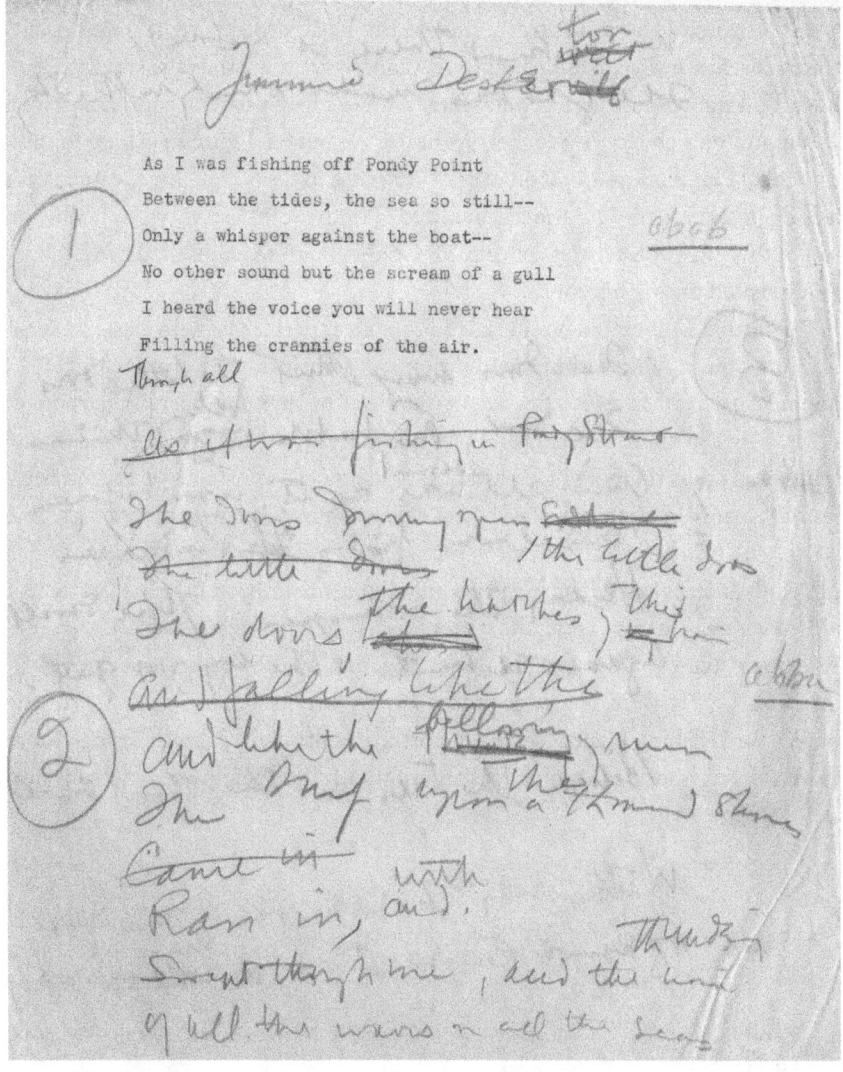

Figure 7. Early draft of Hyam Plutzik's "Jim Desterland." Courtesy of the Department of Rare Books and Special Collections, University of Rochester.

"Jim Desterland," has the Selected Poems by Hyam Plutzik, most in common with Plutzik's prewar poetry, and especially so with the epic Death at Purple Rim. In connection with the title of the poem and the persona it fashions, Norman Friedman suggested that Plutzik "has a way of inventing his own fable-like characters."[55] Moran writes: "As far as I can determine, Jim Desterland was a fictional invention of Hyam Plutzik, though I have never seen any documentation Plutzik provided about this."[56] One could speculate that Jim perhaps anagrammatically echoes Hyam, while Desterland, a non-Jewish-sounding last name with the possible etymological source in the Latin *dexter* ("right"), represents the poet's non-Jewish fishing double. Also noteworthy are the references to "fishing off" "Pondy Point" and "Pondy Pier." Moran sees a possible connection with "a pier in Pondicherry [Puducherry], India ... [but has] found nothing to indicate that [Plutzik] knew of it or adapted it for use in his poem." Jim Desterland is fishing in salt waters, and the fictionalized "Pondy Point" mighty be an allusion to Pont Point, a coastal area in Milford, Connecticut, which Plutzik would have likely visited during his youth.

The formal deliberateness speaks to Plutzik's experiments with classical versification, both staying within the tradition and transforming it from within. This poem consists of five sestets and is composed in rhyming dactylic tetrameter (D4), with the middle caesura and second and fourth truncated feet. The rhyme scheme sustains the poem's exploration of fishing as a portal to hidden mysteries of the universe: stanzas 1 and 4—ababcc; stanzas 2; and stanza 5—abbaab. The circulation of rhyme scheme variants also serves to augment the recurrence of details such as the scream/cry of a gull, but more importantly, the "voice you will never hear" except when the secret "doors" of the universe "sw[i]ng open."[57] Friedman states that Plutzik "is a poet of genuine vision rather than simply of insights. . . . He is, in fact, a cosmic poet."[58] "Jim Desterland," the first of the book's three fishing poems, certainly portrays (saltwater) fishing as much more than sport or hunting for food; it is an experience of a heightened metaphysical self-awareness.

---

55 Norman Freidman, "The Wesleyan Poets: IV: The In-Between Poets," *Chicago Review* 19, no. 3 (1967): 81.
56 Edward Moran to Maxim D. Shrayer, email communication, August 6, 2023.
57 Hyam Plutzik, *Apples from Shinar* (Middleton: Wesleyan University Press, 1959), 12–13.
58 Friedman, "The Wesleyan Poets," 80.

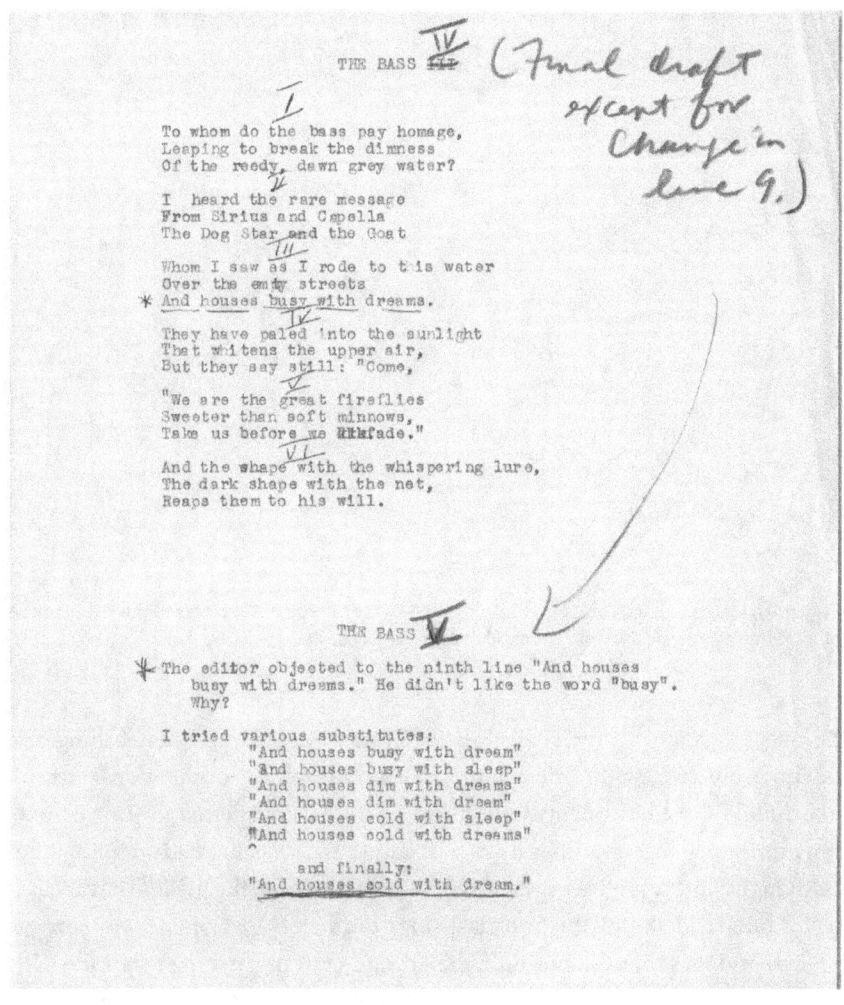

Figure 8. Corrected final draft of Hyam Plutzik's "The Bass." Courtesy of the Department of Rare Books and Special Collections, University of Rochester.

"The Bass," the second fishing poem, also thinks of fishing, this time freshwater, as an enigmatic activity through which people discover hidden connections between themselves and nature (see the text in the Selected Poems by Hyam Plutzik).

The surviving drafts document the care with which Plutzik crafted the poem's six polymetric tercets, their faint rhymes alluding to the terza rima and the Sicilian tercet. The bass leap not only to capture the "great fireflies," itself an act of artistic transference, but also because they are drawn to the people, the ones who will entice them with a "whispering lure" (as opposed to pieces of metal shaped like a fish and replete with triple hooks) and mesh "nets."

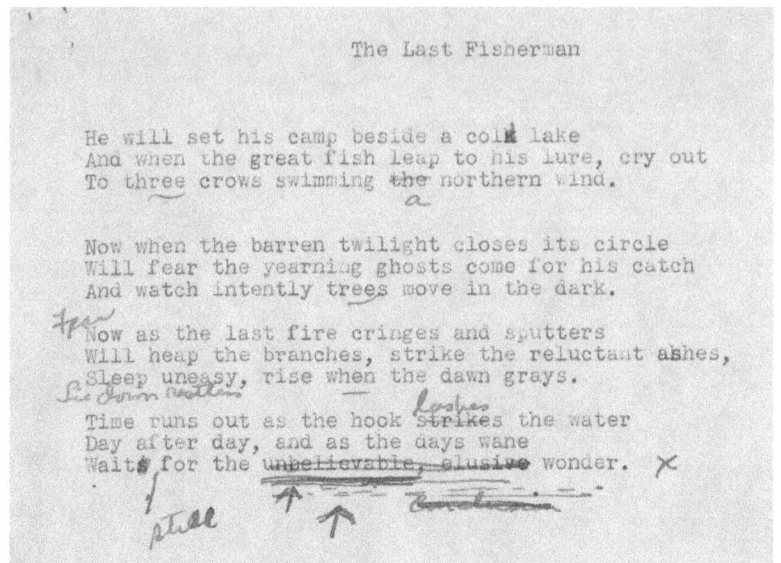

Figure 9. Corrected draft of Hyam Plutzik's "The Last Fisherman." Courtesy of the Department of Rare Books and Special Collections, University of Rochester.

During a reading in the 1950s, Hyam Plutzik said: "I saw that fishing and poetry were two of the most important philosophical occupations. And to conclude, I'll recite a poem about fishing, 'The Last Fisherman.'" This concise poem, which likely describes fly-fishing rather than casting and spinning lures (although Plutzik is a bit vague when he speaks about "the great fish leap[ing] to his lure" and about "the hook lash[ing] the water"), concludes *Apples from Shinar*, and its subject is not only the art and craft of catching fish. Like "The Bass," "The Last Fisherman," also toys with but abandons terza rima, the chosen form of Dante's *Divine Comedy*, and feverishly plays with the form of the Sicilian tercet. Not just fishing, both a sport and a way of procuring food, but assimilation and acculturation are the subject of "The Last Fishermen" (also found in the *Selected Poems* by Hyam Plutzik).

Leaning on the classic formalist dichotomy developed by Russian assimilated Jews, I wish to conclude that Plutzik's best poetry showcases a richly gifted Jewish American poet at the crossroads of archaism and innovation. Plutzik is in conversation with towering English-language poets of high modernism, W. B. Yeats in particular, and with some of the most ingenious and deeply American voices of the 1930s–1950s—Robert Penn Warren leaps to mind. Across languages, Plutzik is also in dialogue with other Jewish poets of his age, whose very existence in post-Shoah culture was a source of internalized guilt—Paul Celan, first and foremost. The poem's "last fisherman" could be also be contextually understood as both the "last poet" and the "last Jew," and the "time run[ing] out" could be interpreted as the finale of Jewish culture in diaspora. There is heaviness and darkness in Plutzik's poems, and their elegance and verbal jouissance only underscores the poet's loneliness.

In "The Last Sermon" section of *The Waste Land*, the Aryan poet-aesthete, whose catalytic impact on modern poetry Plutzik himself resisted, visualizes himself as weeping, but not "by the rivers of Babylon," as the ancient Hebrew singer of exile does in Psalm 137, but somewhere on Lake Geneva in Switzerland. Eliot also sees himself ritualistically fishing in "the dull canal," and a disfigured corpse of a Jew lies there at the bottom:

> By the waters of Leman I sat down and wept . . .
> Sweet Thames, run softly till I end my song,
> Sweet Thames, run softly, for I speak not loud or long.
> But at my back in a cold blast I hear
> The rattle of the bones, and chuckle spread from ear to ear.
> A rat crept softly through the vegetation
> Dragging its slimy belly on the bank
> While I was fishing in the dull canal
> On a winter evening . . .[59]

Apples from Shinar, with its triple crown of fishing poems and its open challenge of antisemitism, appeared in Eliot's lifetime. "Thomas, Thomas, / Come, let us pray together for our exile," Plutzik intones in the penultimate line of "For T. S. E. Only." And he answers his own call with the famous last line of Charles Baudelaire's "To the Reader" in *Flowers of Evil*, integrating it into the final line of his own poem: "You, hypocrite lecteur! mon semblable! mon frère!" Darkly ironic is Plutzik's reminder that Christian poets are readers of Jewish verse, even if they do not want to let Jews into the inner chambers of their culture while condoning the chambers of death.

About three years after the publication of *The Waste Land*, another American abroad, Ernest Hemingway, wrote *The Sun Also Rises* (British title *Fiesta*). When Hemingway's breakthrough novel came out in October 1926, Plutzik was a junior at Bristol High School and the horizon of Anglo-American poetry was

---

[59] T.S. Eliot, *The Waste Land*, Project Gutenberg, accessed September 22, 2022, https://www.gutenberg.org/cache/epub/1321/pg1321-images.html; cf. Eliot, *Selected Poems*, 56.

not dotted with Jewish names. The novel's antagonist, Robert Cohn, a writer and a former boxing champion at Princeton, was based on the Jewish-American author Harold Loeb (1891–1974), with whom Hemingway was friendly in the 1920s in Paris.[60]

Cohn is doubly shunned by the Gentiles—as a Jew and as an artist. In the novel's various registers of malevolence toward him—wrapped inside the overarching authorial voice and spoken by his representative Jake Barnes and other characters—one hears residues of Christian Judeophobia enmeshed with American upper-middle-class unease about associating with "the Hebrews."

The Sun Also Rises culminates with a trout fishing expedition to Burguete, a town in the hills of Navarre, and a disharmonious fiesta in Pamplona. Cohn's intention to fly-fish for trout in the Irati river is evidenced by his asking Jake to "buy him a double-tapered line" for his reel. In the end, Cohn stays behind in Pamplona while Jake Barnes and Bill Compton, his detractors, enjoy a glorious fishing expedition. Does it dawn on Cohn that there is something absurd and incongruous in the image of a Jew fly-fishing with antisemites? I have previously argued that Cohn bows out of the fly-fishing not only because he reacts to the taunts of his Parisian companions, but also because he "Jewishly" rejects the gentlemanly sport and pastime.[61]

Hyam Plutzik, the Jewish American poet, refuses to separate himself from fly-fishing, one of Anglo-American high culture's signifiers. Unlike Cohn, who chooses to drop out of the fishing expedition, Plutzik goes it alone to his premature death.

---

[60] All quotations are from the original edition: Ernest Hemingway, *The Sun Also Rises* (New York: Charles Scribner's Sons, 1926), Project Gutenberg, accessed September 12, 2023, https://gutenberg.ca/ebooks/hemingwaye-sunalsorises/hemingwaye-sunalsorises-00-h.html. On antisemitism and Jewishness in *The Sun Also Rises*, see, for instance, George Monteiro, "Cohn's Descent," *Partisan Review* 64, no. 4 (1997): 620–629; Wolfgang E. H. Rudat, "Anti-Semitism in 'The Sun Also Rises': Traumas, Jealousies, and the Genesis of Cohn," *American Imago* 49, no, 2 (Summer 1992): 263–275; Mary Dearborn, "Ernest Hemingway Was a Great Writer. He Was also an Antisemite: How Do We Grapple with the Remarks the Author Made in His Fiction and in His Correspondence?," *Forward*, July 21, 2022, https://forward.com/culture/451195/ernest-hemingway-was-a-great-writer-he-was-also-an-antisemite/.

[61] I discuss Cohn's fishing expedition in detail in my "Fishing without My Father: Hemingway's Prejudice, Cohn's Fishing Expedition, and the Legacy of Judaism," Arc: Religion, Politics, Et Cetera, November 14, 2024, https://arcmag.org/fishing-without-my-father/.

Bibliography

Primary Sources

Eliot, T. S. *Poems*. New York: Alfred A. Knopf, 1920; Project Gutenberg. Accessed September 20, 2022. https://www.gutenberg.org/files/1567/1567-h/1567-h.htm.
———. *After Strange Gods: A Primer of Modern Heresy*. London: Faber and Faber, 1934.
———. *Selected Poems*. London: Penguin Books in Association with Faber and Faber, 1952.
———. *The Waste Land: A Facsimile and Transcript of the Original Drafts Including the Annotations of Ezra Pound*. Edited and with an introduction by Valerie Eliot. London: Faber and Faber, 1974.
Hemingway, Ernest. *The Sun Also Rises*. New York: Charles Scribner's Sons, 1926; Project Gutenberg. Accessed September 13, 2023. https://gutenberg.ca/ebooks/hemingwaye-sunalsorises/hemingwaye-sunalsorises-00-h.html.
Plutzik, Hyam. *Apples from Shinar*. Middleton: Wesleyan University Press, 1959.
———. *The Collected Poems*. Brockport, NY: BOA Editions, 1987.
———. *Letter from a Young Poet*. Hartford: Witkinson Library at Trinity College, 2015.
The Revised English Bible with the Apocrypha. Oxford: Oxford University Press; Cambridge: Cambridge University Press, 1989.
Shepard, Odell. *A Lonely Flute*. Boston and New York: Houghton Mifflin Company, 1917.; Project Gutenberg. Accessed September 18, 2023. https://www.gutenberg.org/files/34234/34234-h/34234-h.htm.
———. *Thy Fly and Thy Creel*. Hartford: Edwin Valentine Mitchell; New York: Dodd, Mean & Company, 1930. Accessed August 14, 2023. https://babel.hathitrust.org/cgi/pt?id=coo.31924051745358&seq=1. Rpt: New York: Nick Lyons Books; Winchester Press, 1984.
———. ["Shepard's Response"]. In Hyam Plutzik, *Letter from a Young* Poet, 81–84. Hartford: Witkinson Library at Trinity College, 2015.
Tanakh: The Holy Scriptures: The New JPS Translation According to the Traditional Hebrew Text. Philadelphia: The Jewish Publication Society, 5748/1988.

Secondary Sources

Baldwin, Roberta Plutzik. Recorded interview with Maxim D. Shrayer." June 14, 2023.
Ben-Yehoyada, Naor. "The Reluctant Seafarers: Fishing, Self-Acculturation and the Stumbling Zionist Colonisation of the Palestine Coast in the Interbellum Period." *Jewish Culture and History* 13, no. 1 (April 2012): 7–24.
Burge, Gary M. "Fishers of Fish." *Christian History* 59 (1998). Accessed September 12, 2023. https://christianhistoryinstitute.org/magazine/article/fishers-of-fish.
Campbell, James. "Biblical Fishing 101: Reeling in The First Fishers of Faith." Loyola Press. Accessed August 29, 2023. https://www.loyolapress.com/catholic-resources/prayer/arts-and-faith/culinary-arts/biblical-fishing-101-reeling-in-the-first-fishers-of-faith/.
Charny, Vitaly. "Jewish Population for Towns in Minsk Guberniya." JewishGen, August 11, 1998. https://www.jewishgen.org/Belarus/lists/vitaly_Town.html.

Choy, Christine, and Ku-Ling Siegel, dir. *Hyam Plutzik: American Poet*. 2007. Video, 54:40. https://www.youtube.com/watch?v=4zVK4XJYKp4&t=7s.

Dearborn, Mary. "Ernest Hemingway Was a Great Writer. He Was Also an Antisemite: How Do We Grapple with the Remarks the Author Made in His Fiction and in His Correspondence?" *Forward*, July 21, 2022. https://forward.com/culture/451195/ernest-hemingway-was-a-great-writer-he-was-also-an-antisemite/.

Dougherty, Jack, and Contributors. "Uncovering Unwritten Rules Against Jewish and Black Students at Trinity College," In Jack Dougherty and Contributors, *On the Line: How Schooling, Housing, and Civil Rights Shaped Hartford and Its Suburbs*. On The Line, May 25, 2024. https://ontheline.trincoll.edu/uncovering-unwritten.html.

Eisenkramer, Rabbi Eric. "Jews Don't Fish!?" *The Fly Fishing Rabbi* (blog), December 22, 2008. http://theflyfishingrabbi.blogspot.com/2008/12/jews-dont-fish.html.

Friedman, Norman. "The Wesleyan Poets: IV: The In-Between Poets." *Chicago Review* 19, no. 3 (1967): 64–90.

Goldman, David P. "T. S. Eliot and the Jews." *First Things*, March 2021. https://www.firstthings.com/article/2021/03/t-s-eliot-and-the-jews. Rpt: The Claremont Institute for the American Way of Life. Accessed September 20, 2023. https://dc.claremont.org/t-s-eliot-and-the-jews/.

Halpern, Daniel. Foreword to *Letter from a Young Poet*, by Hyam Plutzik, 9–13. Hartford, CT: Watkinson Library at Trinity College, 2015.

Hecht, Anthony. Foreword to *The Collected Poems*, by Hyam Plutzik. xi–xix. Brockport, NY: BOA Editions, 1987.

Hirsch, Emil G. "Fish and Fishing." JewishEncyclopedia.com. Accessed August 14, 2024. https://www.jewishencyclopedia.com/articles/6158-fish-and-fishing

"Is Catch and Release Fishing Permitted?" mi yodeya. Accessed August 14, 2023. https://judaism.stackexchange.com/questions/15616/is-catch-and-release-fishing-permitted.

Julius, Anthony. *T. S. Eliot, Anti-Semitism and Literary Form*. Cambridge: Cambridge University Press, 1995.

Kamenetz, Rodger. *The Lowercase Jew*. Evanston, IL: TriQuarterly Books/Northwestern University Press, 2003.

Kakutani, Michiko. "Examining T. S. Eliot and Anti-Semitism: How Bad Was It?" *New York Times*, April 22, 1989. https://www.nytimes.com/1989/08/22/books/critic-s-notebook-examining-t-s-eliot-and-anti-semitism-how-bad-was-it.html.

McNutty, J. Bard, ed. *In Memory of the Rev. Dr. Remsen Brickerhoff Ogilby*. Trinity College Alumni News, November 1943. https://digitalrepository.trincoll.edu/cgi/viewcontent.cgi?article=1945&context=reporter.

Monteiro, George. "Cohn's Descent." *Partisan Review* 64, no. 4 (1997): 620–629.

Moran, Edward, and Philippe Witte. "A Great Stag, Broad-Antlered: Rediscovering Hyam Plutzik." *Paris Review*, May 8, 2012. https://www.theparisreview.org/blog/2012/05/08/a-great-stag-broad-antlered-rediscovering-hyam-plutzig/.

———. Afterword to *Letter from a Young Poet*, by Hyam Plutzik, 87–95. Hartford: Witkinson Library at Trinity College, 2015.

———. "The Life and Poetry of Hyam Plutzik." Hyam Plutzik, Poet. Accessed September 13, 2023. http://www.hyamplutzikpoetry.com/life-and-poetry.

Nelson, Cary. "The Universe Is No Consolation: Hyam Plutzik, Jewish Identity, and the Ethics of Post-Holocaust Reading." *Journal of Jewish Identities* 15, no. 1 (January 2022): 5–31. https://muse.jhu.edu/pub/1/article/840934.

Nun, Mendel. "Cast Your Net upon the Waters: Fish and Fishermen in Jesus' Time." *Biblical Archeological Review* 19, no. 6 (November–December 1993). https://www.baslibrary.org/biblical-archaeology-review/19/6/11.

Orr, Gregory. *Stanley Kunitz: An Introduction to the Poetry*. New York: Columbia University Press, 1985.

Pfeffer, Rabbi Yehoshua. "Hunting and Fishing in Halacha." *Dinonline.org*, November 18, 2015. https://dinonline.org/2015/11/18/hunting-and-fishing-in-halachah/.

Rudat, Wolfgang E. H. "Anti-Semitism in 'The Sun Also Rises': Traumas, Jealousies, and the Genesis of Cohn." *American Imago* 49, no. 2 (Summer 1992): 263–275.

Shrayer, Maxim D. *Russian Poet/Soviet Jews: The Legacy of Eduard Bagritskii*. Lanham, MD: Rowman & Littlefield, 2000.

———. "Fishing without My Father: Hemingway's Prejudice, Cohn's Fishing Expedition, and the Legacy of Judaism." Arc: Religion, Politics, Et Cetera, November 14, 2024, https://arcmag.org/fishing-without-my-father/.

Sruogo, Shai. The Mediterranean Culture of Fishing: Continuity and Change in the World of Jewish Fishermen, 1500–1929. *International Journal of Maritime History* 32, no. 2 (2020): 288–304.

Tender, Rabbi Aaron. "Fishing for Sport." Jewishanswers.org. Accessed August 14, 2023. http://www.jewishanswers.org/ask-the-rabbi-1040/fishing/.

Vander Laan, Ray. "They Left Their Nets Behind." That the World May Know. Accessed August 14, 2023. https://www.thattheworldmayknow.com/they-left-their-nets-behind.

CHAPTER 16

The Outcasts of Rochester, or, The Fantastic Poetics of Hyam Plutzik

Noah Simon Jampol

Poet Hyam Plutzik was, as tersely stated by his son Alan, "starting to be prominent" at the end of his tragically short life.[1] Plutzik's legacy is, rightfully, his poetic output. He writes poems that are clearly informed by the twentieth-century American tradition, in conversation with its poetic monoliths. Although lacking the notoriety of some of his modernist contemporaries, Plutzik's work similarly wrestles with losses both personal and epochal. His poetic vision accordingly grapples with similar themes and images as contemporaries such as T. S. Eliot, Robert Penn Warren, and even Ezra Pound. As noted by George B. Henson, his work shares a specific DNA with these other modernists: "alienation, war, anxiety in the face of modernity, nature, especially man's relationship to nature."[2] And yet, Plutzik is a poet apart insofar as he is a deeply and explicitly Jewish American modernist. The significance of his Jewishness—and deep concern, within his oeuvre, for the ubiquity of antisemitism—is unambiguous in his best-known poems, particularly the simultaneously ascorbic and conciliatory "For T. S. E Only." But to read Plutzik's body of work—particularly his less obviously (but no less) Jewish works of poetry and prose—above the marine layer of the Holocaust is to misread Hyam Plutzik.

Hyam Plutzik's Jewishness was central to his identity as man and poet, as espoused early in his life: his prose and correspondence, as well as in his poetry.

Copyright © 2025 by Noah Simon Jampol
1   George B. Henson, "Out of His Life He Fashioned a Fistful of Words," in Hyam Plutzik, 32 Poems, ed. George B. Henson (Miami, FL: Suburbano Ediciones, 2021), unpaginated.
2   Ibid.

Eric J. Sundquist, by way of his studied reading of Plutzik's myriad meanings in "An Agadah of Hyam ben Samuel" and the much more explicitly Holocaust-informed "Plan for Work" (a 1960 plan for a poem intended for a Guggenheim Foundation Fellowship), establishes the centrality and potency of the Holocaust within the poet's catalogue and professional trajectory.³ Cary Nelson has thoughtfully catalogued and organized these pieces, making the compelling argument that Jewishness—and a darker sort of Jewishness marked by both the Holocaust and Hiroshima—undergirds Plutzik's work.⁴ Per Nelson's research in the Plutzik Archive at the University of Rochester, the "Plan for Work" was a prospective project grappling with the magnitude of the Holocaust and the limits of representation. Nelson relates:

> to answer that impossible challenge by giving it an uncanny reality, the poem was to open with a scene "in which the six million ghosts appear at midday on Main Street." The poem was also to feature "a section dealing with Anne Frank"; "I expect," [Plutzik] writes in the plan for the poem that she "will become an important figure in the poem. The idea of using her came to me soon after reading her diary some years ago." "I don't know whether I have the ability to do justice to this subject," he advises, "but I shall try."⁵

Here we have an uncertain Plutzik imagining his next work (which would tragically never come to fruition) as a meditation on the challenges of Holocaust representation. The effort to do so deploys the authority of the very real, and nonfictionally bound, Anne Frank, as well as something more fantastic: a virtual haunting by six million ghosts.

Thus, Plutzik, when attempting to reason through a plan for writing the Holocaust turns to the poles of something like nonfiction in Anne Frank and the fantastic of phantasms. Neither is seemingly sufficient for the poet to represent the event, recalcitrant to representation in the spirit of Jean-François Lyotard's metaphor of "an earthquake [that] destroys not only lives, buildings, and objects

---

3   Eric J. Sundquist, "Blessed Mythmaker: The Poetry of Hyam Plutzik," *Hyam Plutzik, Poet*, accessed September 30, 2023), https://drive.google.com/file/d/18y4aXA50KLXS tIN8wD3vcpbFi1qtEEbF/view?usp=sharing from http://www.hyamplutzikpoetry.com/ commentaries.
4   Cary Nelson, "The Universe Is No Consolation: Hyam Plutzik, Jewish Identity, and the Ethics of Post-Holocaust Reading," *Journal of Jewish Identities* 15, no. 1 (2022): 5–31, https://doi.org/10.1353/jji.2022.0003.
5   Ibid., 5–6.

but also the instruments used to measure earthquakes directly and indirectly."[6] Even when considering deploying both realism and elements of the fantastic, Plutzik is tellingly unsure, as if both representational modes are necessary, but insufficient.

If this "Plan" is Plutzik's final and unfinished word on the Holocaust, let us consider one of his first. Eric Sundquist notes: "In a journal entry of June 5, 1944, the eve of D-Day, Plutzik was more succinct, bluntly identifying Hitler as 'the evil one.'"[7] This language—"the evil one"—rightly characterizes Hitler as a different evil from those more banal evils wandering the woods of Connecticut or later stalking the alleys of Rochester. "The evil one" indicates something incommensurate with Enlightenment notions of humanity and establishes both the primacy of the Holocaust in Plutzik's works as well as the discourse he would employ to probe the topic going forward.

Under the pen name Anaximander Powell, Plutzik wrote an explicitly fantastic story: a work of hard science fiction (sf) entitled *The Outcasts of Venus*. He wrote *Outcasts* in 1935–1936, but the short story remained unpublished until after the Holocaust, in 1952. In *Outcasts*, Plutzik once again departs from his aforementioned poetic contemporaries insofar as he writes and publishes within the genre of the fantastic. In the 1936 context of the short story's composition, Plutzik expresses a clear vision: a dichotomous and unwavering view of fascism and good and evil, expressed as classic twentieth-century American pulp sci-fi. And within the 1952 context of publication, we can read a specific trauma that separates him from peers like Eliot and Pound, and finds representation in the fantastic: the reality of post-Holocaust Jewish American identity.

The short story is remarkable both for the presence of Holocaust-inflected imagery (the "Foglands") and its contemporaneous appearance alongside the mass publication of *The Diary of Anne Frank* (1952) and the beginning of the broader dissemination of Holocaust memory and representation within culture in general. Explicit scenes of imprisonment and the gassing of women and children makes it impossible to divorce Plutzik's most fantastic work from what might also be his more Holocaust-inflected texts. Working from *Outcasts of Venus*, we can chart a constellation of poetic works (*The Seventh Avenue Express*, "My Sister," "Cancer and Nova," and "Portrait") in which Plutzik continually turns to the images and tropes of the fantastic to write the personal and collective traumas of antisemitism.

---

6   Jean-François Lyotard, *The Differend: Phrases in Dispute*, trans. George Van Den Abbeele (Manchester: Manchester University Press, 1988), 56.

7   Nelson, "The Universe Is No Consolation," 16.

Sara R. Horowitz argues that the core tension when writing the Holocaust is the "impossibility to express the experience, coupled with a psychological and moral obligation to do so."[8] If a writer is obliged but unable to write, then how might these representations look? Do we attempt to represent or explore the events, lacking a language or mode for representation or inquiry, and return to what Lawrence Langer calls "more traditional forms of expression"?[9] Are these texts characterized by silences, as proposed by Horowitz? Or, as Shoshana Felman and Dori Laub posit, are indirection and metaphor a potential mode of representation for an event whose total effect on its victims may never be fully known?[10]

In her epigraph to *The Norton Book of Science Fiction* (1993), Ursula K. Le Guin quotes—surprisingly—Hannah Arendt: "Storytelling reveals meaning without committing the error of defining it."[11] Horowitz echoes this narratological desire or felt pressure for accuracy, and the challenge (if not outright impossibility) of communicating truth through conventional or "defined" modes of representation, a tension that lies at the heart of many Holocaust narratives. The question remains: Why does Le Guin choose to quote Arendt (known for her 1963 *Eichmann in Jerusalem*), and thereby link science fiction and the Holocaust? What does thinking about Arendt and the Holocaust do for the reader of sci-fi who might just as well have started their journey via an epigraph from any other source capable of speaking to the tension between meaning and reality?

Darko Suvin has pointed to the utility of science fiction as a mode of inquiry, juxtaposing science fiction and myth:

> The myth absolutizes and even personifies apparently constant motifs from sluggish societies. Conversely, [science fiction], which focuses on the variable and future-bearing elements from the empirical environment, is found predominantly in the great whirlpool periods of history, such as the sixteenth-seventeenth and nineteenth–twentieth centuries. Where the myth claims to explain once and for all the essence of phenomena,

---

8   Sara R. Horowitz, *Voicing the Void: Muteness and Memory in Holocaust Fiction* (Albany, NY: State University of New York Press, 1997), 16.
9   Lawrence Langer, *Preempting the Holocaust* (New Haven, CT: Yale University Press, 2001), 2.
10 Shoshana Felman and Dori Laub, *Testimony: Crises of Witnessing in Literature, Psychoanalysis, and History* (New York: Routledge, 1992).
11 Hannah Arendt, qtd. in Ursula K. Le Guin, introduction to *Norton Book of Science Fiction*, ed. Ursula K. Le Guin and Brian Attebery (New York: WW Norton, 1997), 15.

[science fiction] first posits them as problems and then explores where they lead; it sees the mythical static identity as an illusion, usually as fraud, at best only as a temporary realization of potentially limitless contingencies. It does not ask about "The Man" or "The World," but which man?: in what kind of world?: and why such a man in such a kind of world?[12]

Echoing Lawrence Langer's prescription against preempting the Holocaust, Suvin suggests that science fiction is particularly useful for exploring a topic as challenging as the Holocaust without reducing the event to a pedagogical moment that would presume to draw artificial lines of continuity between the world that was and the world that now is—to move beyond myth. The fluid, gray-scale, and problematizing questioning inherent in science fiction as outlined by Suvin points to a definition of the genre as a philosophical and ethical mode of inquiry.

Per Suvin, science fiction is unique because it "is distinguished by the narrative dominance or hegemony of a fictional novum (novelty, innovation) validated by cognitive logic."[13] This "novelty," which is central to the plot and characters of science fiction created by the author, must be (as juxtaposed to myth) a scientific or logical possibility, feasible for the author and reader to cognate within the limits of our universe and its laws—dictates that Plutzik will observe in later works. The goal of deploying this genre, then, is that "all the epistemological, ideological, and narrative implications and correlatives of the novum lead to the conclusion that significant [science fiction] is in fact a specifically roundabout way of commenting on an author's collective context."[14] In turning to the cognitive novelty of sf, Plutzik induces a state of defamiliarization in which rote modes of thinking and writing trauma are exchanged for those less bound, with potential to give voice to silence and provide the writer a new mode with which to, as Dominick LaCapra contends, work through rather than act out their individual and collective trauma.[15]

---

12 Darko Suvin, "Science Fiction as Cognition," in *Speculations on Speculation: Theories of Science Fiction*, ed. James E. Gunn and Matthew Candelaria (Lanham, MD: Scarecrow Press, 2005), 26.
13 Darko Suvin, "On What Is and Is Not an SF Narration; With a List of 101 Victorian Books That Should Be Excluded from SF Bibliographies," *Science Fiction Studies* 14, no. 5 (1978): 44.
14 Darko Suvin, "Science Fiction and the Novum," in *Defined by a Hollow: Essays on Utopia, Science Fiction and Political Epistemology* (Oxford: Peter Lang, 2010), 89.
15 Dominick LaCapra, *Writing History, Writing Trauma* (Baltimore, MD: Johns Hopkins University Press, 2001).

Unpublished until 2023, Plutzik's 1935 dystopian poem *The Seventh Avenue Express* prefigures *The Outcasts of Venus* chronologically, but also insofar as it is a fantastic work, if not outright hard sci-fi. Its central image, the IRT Broadway-Seventh Avenue Line as the surviving infrastructure from an apocalypse establishes a sort of set or storehouse of images for Plutzik for invoking the postapocalyptic. Nelson argues that the images established here as nature overtake the husks of human civilization ("Of rust beneath the new-born, blazing stars) and respond to a fascistic pressure as observed by the young, enterprising reporter Plutzik working the Brooklyn beat.[16] Edward Moran acutely reinforces the centrality of fascism as the substrata of Plutzik's poem, noting that the young poet was well aware of what was happening on the continent and was actively searching for a modality to express his consciousness and concern.[17]

Further, the setting of the poem, the IRT, is subterranean, and Plutzik's description of this setting ("For here in the Earth, here in the home of worms")[18] is alienating, defamiliarizing Earth and rendering a stranger (yet still recognizable) terra, in a gesture towards science fiction. *Seventh Avenue*'s imagery reads like world creation, working a classic trope of the genre as old as the hapless Eloi of H. G. Wells's *The Time Machine* and the laboring masses of Fritz Lang's *Metropolis*: dehumanized human life underground. Hence, this early, dystopic poem presents a fantastic sensibility and praxis for how genre can respond to fascism, suggesting that Plutzik sees poetic value in doing so. *The Seventh Avenue Express* is not outright science fiction; there is no novum. It is also not a piece of post-Holocaust writing. But it is a fantastic and ardently epistemological poem—a poem concerned with the diagnosis of evil, not the ambiguities and shifting definitions therein.

In one early prewar poem, Plutzik leverages elements of the fantastic to characterize a devastating and unnatural loss: the untimely and premature death of his younger sister. "My Sister" (1938) leans on a discourse that includes "monsters" and elements of Eliot's wasteland to explore this deeply personal trauma. Thinking of his sister buried and decomposing, Plutzik begins, imploring the reader: "Imagine the little skeleton lying there— / In the terrible declination of

---

16 Nelson, "The Universe Is No Consolation," 13.
17 Edward Moran, "Honoring the Legacy of Jewish American Poet Hyam Plutzik," *Jewish Book Council*, April 17, 2023, https://www.jewishbookcouncil.org/pb-daily/honoring-the-legacy-of-jewish-american-poet-hyam-plutzik.
18 Hyam Plutzik, *The Seventh Avenue Express* (Rochester, NY: Meliora Press, 2023).

the years— / On the solitary bed, in the crumbling shell of a world."[19] The scale of individual death and his individual pain explodes and is, like an apocalypse, all consuming, the "crumbling shell of a world" recalling "For here in the Earth, here in the home of worms" from *Seventh Avenue* with a posthuman, apocalyptic force and sensibility. But here, the loss of a sister is the loss of a planet, they are equivalent, almost anticipating Derrida's decree that "there is no common measure adequate to persuade me that a personal mourning is less serious than a nuclear war."[20] What follows is the company of monsters and life in the wasteland: "Amid the monsters with lipless teeth who lie there in wait— / The saurian multitudes who rest in that land— / And the men without eyes who forever glare at the sky."[21] Plutzik again deploys the discourse of the fantastic locally, to characterize the extreme and unambiguous horror of human and relational decay. The poem closes by zooming back out, from individual monsters to an entire apocalypse: "And already the fair flesh dispersed, the proud form broken. / The glaciers move from the north and the sun is dying. / And into the chasm of Time alone and tiny . . . / A world of wasteland with the death of just one, with the death of a sister."[22] The collection of images here, mourning the death and decay of a sister are brutal, visceral, and apocalyptic. Such images recall Le Guin's taxonomy of the fantastic—a genre which definitionally interrogates matters of materialistic cause—as the premature death of a sister challenges the speaker's sense of natural order on earth. This is Eliot's wasteland as initiated by the death of a single person—an apocalypse—and, as such, Plutzik presents the reader with fantastic monsters to represent the unambiguously abhorrent.

The Outcasts of Venus, however, remains Plutzik's only outright piece of science fiction and, with respect to its imagery and publication history, also his most Holocaust-inflected. The timing of this publication is particularly striking in light of Ed Moran's observation (in the *Jerusalem Post*'s review of the Israeli debut of the film *Hyam Plutzik—American Poet*) that "Plutzik wrote much of his best work in the mid-'50s as 'consciousness of the Holocaust was beginning to sink in.'"[23] As such: How and in which ways does this "consciousness of the

---

19 Hyam Plutzik, "My Sister," in *32 Poems*, ed. George B. Henson (Miami, FL: Suburbano Ediciones, 2021).
20 Jacques Derrida, "No Apocalypse, Not Now (Full Speed Ahead, Seven Missiles, Seven Missives)," trans. Catherine Porter and Philip Lewis, *Diacritics* 14, no. 2 (1984): 20–31.
21 Plutzik, "My Sister."
22 Ibid.
23 Edward Moran, qtd. in Suzanne Selengut, "Portrait of an Obscure Poet," *Jerusalem Post*, December 11, 2007, https://www.jpost.com/arts-and-culture/entertainment/portrait-of-an-obscure-poet.

Holocaust" appear within this fantastic text written before the war? How do these moves anticipate the poems that would follow?

The Outcasts of Venus, in all of its muscularity, clarity, and force, recalls Richard Blanco's praise for Plutzik's "declarative power" in his foreword to *32 Poems*: "It's not simply the importance of what Plutzik's poems tell me, but that it's told through the voice of an honest and sentient being who is charged with emotional agency, who has something at stake in his poems."[24] This is the voice of a poet who knows "evil" and addresses it with an unwavering voice. There is quite a bit at stake in this pulp and the telling is accordingly vitriolic.

In his 1941 *Letter from a Young Poet*, Plutzik relates to his undergraduate advisor Odell Shephard (Trinity College professor and outspoken critic of the rise of fascistic antisemitism in 1930s Germany) the practical reasons for his literary jaunt into sci-fi—namely: money, albeit not much. Plutzik expresses clear disdain for the paying audience's appetite for the cheap thrills of "low level" (44) writing and the newfound importance of technical specifications (the physics of hard sci-fi that were characteristic of the genre in the mid 30s). Plutzik admits to not having read much contemporary pulp sci-fi, and thus characterizes *Outcasts*—with its brave men in spacesuits and interplanetary conflict—as an "old-fashioned" sort of story out of touch with contemporary tastes (44).

A righteous Earth unified against the Venusian horde is the central tension driving *Outcasts*. The genre-bound sketch of good and evil is clear and unambiguous in their demarcations—as clear as a young Plutzik's castigation of Hitler as "evil." There is no ambiguity—at first sight our protagonist can distinguish them from us (i.e., "That's a Venusian!")[25] These clear delineations of group membership and moral orientation unwaveringly and reassuringly shore up right and wrong, dispelling ambiguities where they would be most uncomfortably felt. These are monsters (*monstrum*) insofar as they indeed warn, portend, and ultimately also remind. They are not, as Jeffrey Jerome Cohen puts it, beasts which occupy "ontological liminality."[26] Rather, they are epistemologically grounded, striking in their direct, distinct, and discrete evil. The illustration by Herman Vestal accompanying the story as published in *Two Complete Adventure Science Books* depicts our heroes penned in—behind them, a monolithic alien structure in the

---

24 Richard Blanco, foreword to Hyam Plutzik, *32 Poems*, ed. George B. Henson (Miami, FL: Suburbano Ediciones, 2021), unpaginated.
25 Hyam Plutzik (as Anaximander Powell), "The Outcasts of Venus," in *Two Complete Science-Adventure Books* 1, no. 5 (January–March 1952), 30.
26 Jeffrey Jerome Cohen, "Monster Culture (Seven Theses)," in *The Monster Theory Reader*, ed. Jeffrey Andrew Weinstock (Minneapolis, MN: University of Minnesota Press, 2020), 6.

background with a swelling mass, arms raised surging towards the protagonists dispelling ambiguities surrounding good and evil. Before them, what appears to be a spaceship is defended by two hostile amphibians: scaled, upright, guns pointing towards the alien humans. The villains explicitly reptilian appearance recalls the "saurian multitudes" from "My Sister," here again, an unwavering and total vision of "evil" linking the personal and the interplanetary. Our heroes are archetypal athletes—near corn-fed in their constitution and continence—and still require space suits and helmets, differentiating them from the mob and the scaled gunmen blocking their egress. The Venusian, devoid of suit and sporting an elongated, reptilian face, completes the epistemologically unambiguous "us vs them" tableau. Seeing the monster head-on, the reader gets the clearest illustration of how different "they" are from "us": in addition to its alien features, the creature is wearing a frock and belt, clearly unfit for space travel yet somehow well at home here in the sick swirling gas of Venus. His gait is unsure, and his expression is befuddled. The reader of *Outcasts* is confronted by this full-page illustration on the right-hand page, directly facing the beginning paragraphs of the narrative. The distinctions between groups, the beautiful and the ugly, could not be more pronounced nor given more primacy.

The illustration promises, and the text delivers, albeit in a more troubling if no less ambiguous manner. When these Venusians appear in groups, Plutzik deploys the discourse of fascism: "From the lighted deck of the ship a company of soldiers came forth, marching four abreast, their black uniforms giving them an air of sorrow." Insignia connote the same: "The iron pentagon on [one officer's] cap showed that he was the commander."[27] The reader's associations at the time of publication with black uniforms and the Nazi iron cross imbues these images and the Venusians themselves with an air of the Reich. These distinctions, as foregrounded by the illustration, refine the scale of difference: "they" are much different from "us," and "their" ugliness is militarized in the key of fascism.

Our Terran heroes from the crash-landed *Firefly* find themselves traversing the fetid Venusian Foglands in search of an exit. These Foglands are a sort of post-Eliot Prufrock-ian wasteland: "No one who has not been in Fogland can imagine the intense darkness of the place.... I had expected to see the glare of the day. Instead I saw nothing but thin streams, a vapor, like fingers brushing the outside of the glass. Otherwise there was no movement in the surrounding murk."[28] These images recall Eliot's description of Prufrock's urban climes: "The yellow fog that rubs its back upon the window— / panes, / The yellow smoke

---

27 Plutzik, *Outcasts*, 89.
28 Ibid., 72.

that rubs its muzzle on the / window-panes / Licked its tongue into the corners of the evening."[29] But with Plutzik (writing science fiction as published and read postwar), we have something more explicitly existential than mere Prufrock; we have not just a city (as explored in *Seventh Avenue*), but an entire planet rendered as menacing and insalubrious. If, in *Seventh Avenue*, we have a more direct connection to Eliot in scale and kind, with his turn toward sf, Plutzik is able to (nearly ironically) transcend the weight of *The Waste Land*.

The earthlings have an existential relationship to the Venusian environment that echoes the existential Jewish experience. "We ourselves, however, felt no hope, and those to whom we spoke must have read our thoughts. We were a small group of aliens in a hostile world."[30] The Foglands—like the wasteland—are "dotted" with "deserted monasteries"; their uneasy and uncertain promises of shelter anticipating those which would shelter the Jews of Europe during the Holocaust.[31]

The imagery of gas, in particular as a mode for torture, emerges eleven pages into the story as it becomes a metonym for the cruelty of these Venusians who quickly turn said gas (initially reserved just for use on senior military leadership Earthlings) on the civilian refugee Terran population of the ship. A "mega-boron gas (commonly known as 'waspfire')" is used in this attack and the results are horrific:

> And so the figures streamed out of the open door, some of them made eyeless now by the gas. We lost count. The deck became littered with dead bodies, our own people, those who had weathered with us the destruction of the *Firefly*. There were women among them, and children. We wanted to turn away and hide ourselves from the carnage, but the picture on the screen held us in its grip. This was the ultimate agony; in comparison with it the wreck of the Firefly and submersion of Section 2 become nothing.[32]

The death by gas of innocent women and children is a horrific and unambiguous evil. That our protagonist and narrator can only bear witness secondhand,

---

29 T. S. Eliot, *The Waste Land: Authoritative Text, Contexts, Criticism*, ed. Michael North (New York, NY: Norton Critical Editions, 2006).
30 Plutzik, *Outcasts*, 72.
31 Ibid., 73.
32 Ibid., 76.

through the screen ("what happened now we saw through the televisor") will echo in the experience of Jewish Americans learning of the similarly ignominious and horrifying fate of their European brothers and sisters from a vexing artificial but very real distance acutely felt in 1952 with the publication, proliferation, and mass market consumption of Anne Frank and her diary.[33]

If, following "My Sister" and *Seventh Avenue*, *The Outcasts of Venus* represents Plutzik's most explicit experiment in the fantastic to speak to the horrific, what of this trend in his later poetic oeuvre? Published in 1959, *Apples from Shinar* is his second collection of poems, written during a time when his "consciousness of the Holocaust" would have been acute.[34] The ethic of these poems stands as firm as young Plutzik declares evil that which he knows to be evil, with the tropes of the fantastic dispatched once more. In this collection, the specific discourse of the fantastic returns in "Cancer and Nova" which recalls and expands the images of the much earlier "My Sister," similarly yoking the cosmic and the corporeal. The scale—local and planetary—considered in the earlier poem are more fully attenuated here, exploding outward, defamiliarizing the readerly process. In this poem, Plutzik reaches for four metaphors, all near befitting the tone of *The Outcasts of Venus*: "The star exploding in the body; / The creeping thing, growing in the brain or the bone; / The hectic cannibal, the obscene mouth."[35] In placing these four images together, Plutzik offers a sort of composite of the fantastic—the monsters of "My Sister" and the *Prufrock*-cum-*Waste Land* of *Seventh Avenue*—on a more cosmic and more terrifying scale. Here the devastation moves beyond the Earth to something simultaneously grander, more intimate—and more terrifying. Although this destruction seems to follow natural laws of materialistic cause and effect (sickness and then death; the birth of a star to its supernova), it is rendered unfamiliar and unnatural—defamiliarized—via fantastic discourse, as if Plutzik is implicating the very cosmic logic of a universe in which stars burn out and cancer kills. The terms here are uncompromising; the destruction described is plainly wrong, evil and awful, with the imagery shoring up this certainty in opposition to the entropy of the body and stars.

In "My Sister," "monsters" characterize the world of decay that follows from the individual loss of a sister. But in 1959's "Portrait," Plutzik applies the discourse of monstrosity to the human condition more broadly. The speaker of the poem entreats: "Notice with what careful nonchalance / He tries to be a

---

33 Ibid., 76.
34 Edward Moran, qtd. in Selengut, "Portrait of an Obscure Poet."
35 Hyam Plutzik, "Cancer and Nova," in *32 Poems*, ed. George B. Henson (Miami, FL: Suburbano Ediciones, 2021), 20.

Jew casually, / To ignore the monster, the mountain— / A few thousand years of history."[36] Herein, Plutzik wields the register of the monstrous with an acute awareness of the Holocaust and identifies a new horror—the horror of the casual relationship between a Jew (including himself) and his Judaism in the wake of the Holocaust. This horror implicates this way of being an American Jew in post-Holocaust America as a monstrous denial of history, shared identity, and shared loss, and treats the magnitude of this denial with befitting severity. There is no ontological question probing the nature of a Jewish identity here. Plutzik is unambiguously and wholly a Jew and argues for the existence of an ethical component to a Jew's self-awareness. The monster here can thus be read twice over—first, as a castigation of the behavior of aspirational, casual, (sometimes) ethnicity-denying, "passing" Jews; and secondly, as the "monster" that comes to also characterize the unbearable historical weight of being a Jew, the scale of which is "the mountain." As expressed in Plutzik's construction, to confront one's Jewishness is to confront something logos-defying and deeply recalcitrant yet unceasingly demanding of exploration and expression in a post-Holocaust universe.

Plutzik's examination herein of this willful denial of the weight of history under the incalculable weight of post-Holocaust Jewishness—via the mathematics of the monstrous, and fantastic fractions—offer the poet a singular lexical fuel and opportunity for the expression of unflinching moral absolutism within the post-Holocaust literary tradition. This is Hyam Plutzik amongst the modernists, transcending that would-be coterie as he plumbs the internal viscera and stares unflinchingly upward at a dark and blinding sky, creating from this language of indirection a lexicon for attempting to represent the reprehensible be it local or epochal.

Bibliography

Arendt, Hannah. Quoted in Ursula K. Le Guin, Introduction to *The Norton Book of Science Fiction: North American Science Fiction, 1960–1990*, edited by Ursula K. Le Guin and Brian Attebery. New York, NY: W.W. Norton & Company 1993.

Cohen, Jeffrey Jerome. "Monster Culture (Seven Theses)." In *Monster Theory: Reading Culture*, edited by Jeffrey Jerome Cohen. Minneapolis, MN: University of Minnesota Press, 1996. http://www.jstor.org/stable/10.5749/j.ctttsq4d.

Derrida, Jacques, Catherine Porter, and Philip Lewis. "No Apocalypse, Not Now (Full Speed Ahead, Seven Missiles, Seven Missives)." *Diacritics* 14, no. 2 (1984): 20–31. https://doi.org/10.2307/464756.

---

36 Hyam Plutzik, "Portrait," in *Apples from Shinar* (Middletown, CT.: Wesleyan University Press, 1959), 31.

Eliot, T. S. *The Waste Land and Other Poems*. New York: Knopf Doubleday Publishing Group, 2021.
Felman, Shoshana, and Dori Laub. *Testimony: Crises of Witnessing in Literature, Psychoanalysis, and History*. New York, NY: Routledge, 1992.
Frank, Anne. *The Diary of a Young Girl: The Definitive Edition*. Edited by Mirjam Pressler. New York: Anchor Books, 2022.
Friedländer, Saul. *Probing the Limits of Representation: Nazism and the "Final Solution."* Cambridge, MA: Harvard University Press. 1992.
Henson, George B. "Out of His Life He Fashioned a Fistful of Words." In *32 Poems*, edited by George B. Henson, Miami, FL: Suburbano Ediciones, 2021.
Horowitz, Sara R. *Voicing the Void: Muteness and Memory in Holocaust Fiction*. Albany, NY: State University of New York Press, 1997.
James, Edward. *Science Fiction in the Twentieth Century*. New York, NY: Oxford University Press, 1994.
LaCapra, Dominick. *Writing History, Writing Trauma*. Baltimore, MD: Johns Hopkins University Press, 2001.
Lang, Fritz, dir. *Metropolis*. United States: Paramount Pictures, 1927.
Langer, Lawrence. *Preempting the Holocaust*. New Haven, CT: Yale University Press, 2001.
Le Guin, Ursula K. Introduction to *Norton Book of Science Fiction*, edited by Ursula K. Le Guin and Brian Attebery, 15. New York: W. W Norton, 1997.
Lyotard, Jean-François. *The Differend: Phrases in Dispute*. Translated by George Van Den Abbeele. Manchester: Manchester University Press, 1988.
Moran, Edward. "Honoring the Legacy of Jewish American Poet Hyam Plutzik." *Jewish Book Council*, April 17, 2023. https://www.jewishbookcouncil.org/pb-daily/honoring-the-legacy-of-jewish-american-poet-hyam-plutzik.
———. Quoted in "Portrait of an obscure poet," by Suzanne Selengut. *Jerusalem Post*, December 11, 2007. https://www.jpost.com/arts-and-culture/entertainment/portrait-of-an-obscure-poet.
Nelson, Cary. "The Universe Is No Consolation: Hyam Plutzik, Jewish Identity, and the Ethics of Post-Holocaust Reading." *Journal of Jewish Identities*, 15, no. 1 (2022): 5–31. https://doi.org/10.1353/jji.2022.0003.
Sundquist, Eric J. "Blessed Mythmaker: The Poetry of Hyam Plutzik." *Hyam Plutzik, Poet*. Accessed September 30, 2023. https://drive.google.com/file/d/18y4aXA50KLXStIN8wD3vcpbFi1qtEEbF/view?usp=sharing from http://www.hyamplutzikpoetry.com/commentaries.
Plutzik, Hyam (as Anaximander Powell). "The Outcasts of Venus." *Two Complete Science-Adventure Books* 1, no. 5 (January–March 1952), 66–112.
———. *Apples from Shinar: A Book of Poems*. Middletown: Wesleyan University Press, 2012.
———. *Hyam Plutzik: The Collected Poems*. Rochester, NY: BOA Editions, 1987.
———. *Letter from a Young Poet*. Trinity College and the Estate of Hyam Plutzik: Hartford CT, 2015.
———. *The Seventh Avenue Express*. Rochester, NY: Meliora Press, 2023.
———. *32 Poems*. Edited by George B. Henson. Miami, FL: Suburbano Ediciones, 2021.
Rousset, David. *L'univers concentrationnaire*. Paris: Hachette Littérature, 1998.
Suvin, Darko. "On What Is and Is Not an SF Narration; With a List of 101 Victorian Books That Should Be Excluded from SF Bibliographies." *Science Fiction Studies* 14, no. 5 (1978): 44.
———. "Science Fiction and the Novum." In *Defined by a Hollow: Essays on Utopia, Science Fiction and Political Epistemology*, 89. Oxford: Peter Lang, 2010.
———. "Science Fiction as Cognition." In *Speculations on Speculation: Theories of Science Fiction*, edited by James E. Gunn and Matthew Candelaria, 26. Lanham, MD: Scarecrow Press, 2005
Wells, H. G. *The Time Machine*. London: Penguin Books, 2005.

CHAPTER 17

This Is My Letter to the World: On Hyam Plutzik's Big Epistle

Jenny Browne

Dear Hyam Plutzik,

"To hold a letter addressed to you and see your own name in another's hand is to feel an unsettling kind of pleasure. Even before you've opened the envelope, your identity has been refracted through someone else's. The invitation is both estranging and thrilling: *Could you become the person whose name you read there?*"

The italics above are mine, as I returned to this passage in Kamran Javadiazadeh's essay "Can Rilke Change Your Life?" and to this question in particular, several times when reading through your ambitious epistle *Letters From a Young Poet*. It also feels important to bring up Rilke anytime one talks about poets and letters, which I intend to do here.

Your own "letter," which clocks in at eighty-five pages, was officially intended for Odell Shepard, your undergraduate professor at Trinity College, but as someone who's been teaching poetry to undergraduates for many years now, I feel personally invited to listen in.

"This letter I feel is becoming a bit inchoate," you begin, "but I suppose that is inevitable when one has seven years worth of thought on the edge of one's mind and wants to put it down all at once."

And some pages later, "The trouble is that in a mystical work of this sort one sometimes loses track of just what one wants to say; the feeling of unreality which one is trying to put down on paper eludes one's grasp [Someday] when I have an unworried month to myself (if I ever do) and rearrange my thoughts and can follow the elusive threat through the labyrinth, I shall try to rewrite it, if I can."

Copyright © 2025 by Jenny Browne

Soon enough, passages like this had me feeling that if Yeats was correct in suggesting, "out of the quarrel with others we make rhetoric; out of the quarrel with ourselves we make poetry," which I believe he was, one might extend his argument to argue that letters to others are also letters to ourselves.

Yours certainly is.

All to say, I've been meaning to write.

More specifically, I've been meaning to write *back*. To you. Eventually, I decided to shape these remarks into the something like the shape of a letter—and by now, *letters*—knowing full well they wouldn't be received, or answered, at least not in the traditional sense.

Mostly, I'm hopeful this response might somehow stand in for the one I wish you could have, and perhaps even *should* have, received, back when you might have really used it.

To state it more plainly, as you did, "My reasons for writing you? They are complex."

Warm Regards,
Jenny Browne

Miami Florida
September, 2015

Dear Hyam Plutzik,

I was sitting in the lobby of The Betsy Hotel in Miami, Florida when I first came across your book. I'd yet to learn about your family's connection to the most excellent dogs, and cheese popovers, I'd also encountered in said lobby. To be honest, I didn't know who you were either and was mostly intrigued by your reversal of Rilke's positionality, but I'd also been thinking a good bit about epistles, or letter poems, and even more about epistolary work in general. So by *epistolary* here I really just mean any kind of writing that uses the formal properties of a letter to both create and complicate meaning, a gesture of direct address, for starters, as well as the agreed-upon fiction we're now engaging in, namely that these are actual letters to you.

And isn't there a certain thrill is reading other people's mail?

And if this is indeed a real letter, might it also contain something as domestic, as cute dogs and popovers, perhaps even a weather report? (My god what a scorcher this summer has been!) as well as more searching queries: *Why does* this poem seem to have been written? What has happened that insists this encounter be recorded? How is it better than silence?

I often begin my own poetry classes with questions like these. And in the silence that follows, a mix of slow nods and furrowed brows signal back equal parts ambition and insecurity. I like teaching epistles to young poets in part because they come with a built-in antecedent scenario, namely the notion that a real or imagined me sitting here right now needs to tell a real or imagined you something important. It helps to have a place to start, and a listener in mind. The letter form also creates additional dramatic tension through the implied premise I can't tell you this important thing directly, for whatever reason.

I've also been known to suggest (okay, rant) in class about how all poems are ultimately about time, and how the epistle expands narrative possibilities by evoking this present tense compositional event that points both backwards and forwards as we imagine the reception of the letter, the reading, the re-reading etc. etc. In her book *Epistolarity: Approaches to Form*, Jane Gurkin Altman uses the term *temporal polyvalence* to suggest that any statement in an epistle forges bonds with innumerable moments, past, present, and future.

It took you seven years to write your letter. Is it a letter? A coming-of-age memoir? Perhaps a novella? Seven years! I mean if what I've heard on NPR is correct, you were made of entirely new cells by the time you finished. I'm not certain about this detail, or of the logic behind many of my more cavalier declarations in poetry class. Still, lines like "In all this was involved the question of Time and its nature, and the mystery of our existence in it" suggest your true subject was indeed time itself.

I can recognize so many of my own students in your urgent, searching words. I also recognize something of myself.

Truly, Jenny B.

San Antonio, Texas
May 2013 / May 2023

Dear Hyam P.,

Today I found myself thinking back a decade or so to a particular spring afternoon here at Trinity University in San Antonio and suddenly I realized that I really needed to tell you a story.

It's a Thursday afternoon and office hours are long over when I hear a sharp knock on my door. I open it. There stands a young man. He is red-faced and seems to be gasping for air. Let's call him Vlad, which *was* his name. (And yes, that's a nod to Robert Creeley. Of course, you don't know him but he also wrote loads of letters, and letter poems. One to Larry Eigner begins "Your letter at hand, and much obliged. I'll try to go into some of this, while there's time.")

Are you still with me? Here in the deepening illusion that this is an actual letter? If so, let's take things a step farther and imagine you are standing there when I open the door.

Do I invite you inside?

Vlad is premed, if I remember right. Not a great poet, but he follows directions with diligence and enthusiasm. He has also shared, through the content of his poems, a deep interest in power lifting. For a moment I wonder if this was why he looks so sweaty? Or maybe he's just run up the three flights of stairs?

"Can I help you?" I say, half-wishing I had some Gatorade to offer. I have a sense that he, like most second semester seniors is, well, *completely freaking* about his future.

"No no no, I just, I mean maybe, I don't know. I just wanted to talk to you about something real quick is all."

Quick. I like the sound of that. "Come on in," I say.

"Well, the things is, see . . ." He sits down across the desk from me and takes another slow jagged breath. I wait. I'm not a particularly patient person by nature and I do have a few important things to do before heading home. I hope he doesn't waste my time. Speaking of wasted time, is the black hole of my inbox really an important thing? Oh Hyam, rest happy to have missed this "innovation."

"Well, you see," Vlad tries yet again, clearing his throat and coughing into his elbow. Oh god, is he going to get me sick too? "I mean it's just that some days I get to the end of the day and I think to myself, *Well, I just lost a day.*" I nod, understanding the topography of this feeling more than he likely imagines. "But then," he says, wiping his forehead with the back of his hand, "on other days it's like I get to the end of the day, and I think to myself, I just *gained* a day. And well, *I just really want to know how I can get more of those kind of days?!*"

I don't reply. Heck, I don't even blink.

I was truly saddened to learn that the recipient of your letter, your own professor, had not, in your lifetime, replied. I'm a little irritated too, as this kind of council was/is a part of our job/s.

But at the same time, when thinking about you, I think of Vlad, and the terrific audacious faith of him in believing, that I (or anyone) actually has the answer.

All the best, JB

Dear Hyam,

"This is my letter to the world. / That never wrote to me." So begins one of Emily Dickinson's not-so-private conversations with isolation, and with mortality.

Or consider these opening stanzas of Bishop's "Letter to N. Y. (for Louise Crane)":

> In your next letter I wish you'd say
> where you are going and what you are doing;
> how are the plays, and after the plays
> what other pleasures you're pursuing.
>
> taking cabs in the middle of the night,
> driving as if to save your soul
> where the road goes round and round the park
> and the meter glares like a moral owl,
>
> and the trees look so queer and green
> standing alone in big black caves
> and suddenly you're in a different place
> where everything seems to happen in waves...

I love how Bishop's graceful rhyming quatrains announce the poem as both a real letter, and not. Something is wrong with trees, but more importantly something is wrong with the distance between us. Faced with this, the speaker of the poem orders and bends time, imagining in the present tense what her friend might be seeing without her, and in doing so creates a felt sense of longing, a desire to be closer, together, even *one*.

The relationship between mentor and mentee is often tricky, part project, part worship, part merging.

"... the trouble with me," you wrote to Shepard, "was that I was impatient with details and wanted to reach the stars at one swoop and without any intermediate stages of approach." And some pages later, "Six months have passed since I wrote the preceding page of this letter. The insubstantiality of this beast called time that eats us all! But some mileposts have been reached and passed in this period, and now that I have a chance again to go back to this letter, I really must finish it quickly. You are a busy man I know, and it is only because I have become an optimist in these last years that I think you have accompanied me thus far."

"Judge tenderly of me," Dickinson concludes.

Maybe the *you* here is Higginson, the line an effort to preclude his certain editorial corrections, but the you is also *us*, her future audience, reading this line today, together, as one, so it were, so long after she is gone.

You too did your share of fantastical futuring:

> "As to my plans I shall (disregarding for the moment the implications of the war) get myself a job somewhere in the Midwest and teach the literature that I love, no doubt in time wed some comely wench, as yet unmet and entirely unaware (poor girl) of the absent-minded and ashes on the rug scattering husband who awaits her; get myself a house on the edge of a river somewhere; write certain things that intelligent men and women will not be displeased with (God willing). I hope sometime to have time enough to stop and look at things without feeling that I am loafing and ought to be doing something else ... A somewhat domestic scenario is it not? Still, it is certain that my life will never stagnate. The things most people take for granted I do not take for granted. The world of sense, on whose existence my neighbors seem to rely implicitly I know is thin as a dragon-fly's wing. Who is this creature of flesh and bone that, on a world whose position in the universe and the gradation of things no Copernicus will every completely explain, walks amongst things of dimension, color and texture and booms forth sound like a veritable frog in the marsh?"

What exactly was Odell Shepard supposed to say in reply to this?

Technically, he did write back, although I understand he never posted the letter. I don't know if he ever was the person you made him into on these pages, but I can see clearly how you were writing your way toward the person you imagined you could become.

Sincerely, Jenny

Freetown, Sierra Leone
September, 1991

Dear Hyam,

The first poem I ever wrote was also a letter. I was nineteen and had left the Midwest to spend a year in West Africa. Like most nineteen-year-olds, I stepped off the plane puffed with all sorts of notions about how I would change the world. Mostly I wrote loads of bad poems about sunsets and red clay roads and sent them across the ocean with a rather eighteenth-century understanding of audience, knowing it would take weeks, even months, for them to arrive, and that they would surely be read aloud to my aunts and uncles and cousins at Thanksgiving.

I probably should have taken the advice in an even earlier epistle, that of Horace, whose *Letters to Piso* serve to council on the art of poetry and includes the suggestion that that we should read widely, strive for precision, find best criticism and most importantly put our poems away for nine years before sending them to anyone.

In his poem "The Dishonest Mailman," Robert Creeley writes:

> They are taking all my letters, and they put them into a fire.
> I see the flames, etc.
> But do not care, etc.
> They burn everything I have, or what little
> I have. I don't care, etc.
> The poem supreme, addressed to
> emptiness—this is the courage
> necessary. This is something
> quite different.

I love the tonality of teenage defiance in all those etc. etc. etcs. At the same time, the last four lines (and especially, *The poem supreme* . . .) feel decidedly Rilkean. And despite the place *Letters to A Young Poet* holds on many a college sophomore's bookshelf, I'm starting to wonder about some of the advice it contains.

That famous "living the questions" bit still holds up, but Rilke's letters read differently from this distance. That Javadiazadeh *New Yorker* piece I mentioned in an earlier letter is in part a review of a new translation that includes Kappus's original letters along with Rilke's replies, several of which detail the young poet's suicidal ideation. Knowing this, Rilke's question about whether Kappas "would die if he were not allowed to write" feels chilling. As is the dictum, "What we need after all, is only: solitude, a vast inner solitude." I think you needed more than that. I think we all do.

Warmly, Jenny B.

May 2023
Belfast, Northern Ireland

Dear Hyam,

When I was your age is a potentially dismissive way to begin a letter, but of course I mean when I was the age you are on the pages of *Letter from a Young Poet*, as I too was in my early twenties when I really committed myself to this thing (idea? myth?) called "being a poet."

Mostly I flailed around for years listening for strange and musical language, stumbling upon inspiration, applying for jobs both bad and good, losing friends and finding love. I also spent (too) many hours in a (too-bright) Barnes and Noble up off I-10, nursing a drip coffee and reading poetry journals I couldn't yet afford. On one of those visits, I came across a letter/essay that seemed written especially for me. And maybe for you too. I've read it dozens of times over the years. I guess you could say it has emerged as my favorite example of the "letters to and from young poets" genre. Is it a genre? I think so, or I think it should be.

I'm actually sitting in a pub in Northern Ireland right now, and through the miracle machine of time and space compression and expansion that is the internet I can track down a pdf of that 1997 issue of *American Poetry Review* which contains Irish poet Eavan Boland's "Letter to a Young Woman Poet."

"I wish I knew you," she begins, "I could stand for a moment in that corridor of craft and doubt where you will spend so much of your time."

Remember that *temporal polyvalence* business I also mentioned earlier? Hold my beer, as I will now attempt to travel both forward and backwards inside this sentence, doing my best to suggest how a woman in her early fifties in Ireland writing to the imagined young woman poet I was just becoming in San Antonio becomes the woman in my early fifties that I am now, writing to you, long gone from this bodily realm, but still.

What can we possibly have to say to one other?

Perhaps only that across oceans, religions and genders, Boland's arguments about history and who gets to define who or what a poet really is made room for both your youthful intensity and the heart of a mature poetic vision. She was never my teacher in the physical realm, but she is one now and forever. I wish she could have been yours too, writing back:

> When I read poems in the library I felt as though a human face was turned towards me, alive with feeling, speaking urgently to me about love and time. But when I came across the idea of the poet I felt as if someone had displaced that speaker with a small, cold sculpture: a face from which the tears and intensity were gone, on which only the pride and self-consciousness of the Poet remained. I had no words for this. And yet I began to wonder if the makers of the poem and the makers of the idea of the poet could be one and the same.

In the elegant afterward to *Apples from Shinar*, a collection of your own poetry, David Scott Kasten suggests "Another poet would find the importance of poetry in its intimations of immortality. For Plutzik the importance is not that it's the place where the temporal reveals the eternal but where the eternal gives way to the temporal."

Kasten also details the limitations of trying to define you as a war poet, a Jewish poet, and even a modernist. Like you, Boland pushes back at Eliot, specifically his notion that, "We can only say that it appears likely that poets in our civilization, as it exists at present, must be difficult. Our civilization comprehends great variety and complexity, and this variety and complexity, playing upon a refined sensibility, must produce various and complex results. The poet must become more and more comprehensive, more allusive, more indirect..."

In writing her way toward the conviction that a middle-aged woman's life in the Dublin suburbs washing the dishes as the sun goes down was also the life of the capital P poet, she concludes:

> the fact was and is, that the words, decisions, insistences of poets and canon-makers—but more canon-makers than poets—had

determined the status of my machines, my medicine bottles, my child's hand reaching up into mine. They had determined the relation between the ordinary object and the achieved poem. . . . It was harder than I thought proper to record the life I lived in the poems I wrote.

It will be harder than you think, I might have told Vlad, meaning both poetry and life, but you can do it.

I might have given him your poem "The Importance of Poetry or the Coming Forth from Eternity into Time," (Also, dude, what a capital T title!) which begins: "Beyond the image of the willow / there is a willow no man knows . . ."

There is a willow beyond this one, sure, but there is also this willow, right here, let me show you.

"And the willow-image do grace to a bird / And the ghost on the roadway gives them word/ Not for forever only a day."

What can we truly ask of our histories, our teachers, our words, and what days we have left?

Dear Hyam, thanks for living the questions.

Dear Hyam, thanks for writing.

Your fan,
Jenny

Bibliography

Altman, Janet Gurkin. *Epistolarity: Approaches to a Form.* Columbus, OH: Ohio State University Press, 1982.

Bishop, Elizabeth. "Letter to N. Y." In *The Complete Poems, 1927–1979.* New York: Farrar, Straus and Giroux.

Boland, Eavan. "Letter to a Young Woman Pot." *American Poetry Review* 26, no. 3 (May 1997): 23–36.

Javadiazadeh, Kamran. "Can Rilke Change Your Life?" *New Yorker*, May 2021. https://www.newyorker.com/books/under-review/can-rilke-change-your-life.

Pipenbring, Dan, "Robert Creeley's The Dishonest Mailman." *Paris Review*, May 2014. https://www.theparisreview.org/blog/2014/05/21/robert-creeley-the-dishonest-mailmen/.

Plutzik, Hyam. *Apples from Shinar*. Middletown, CT: Wesleyan University Press, 2011.

———. *Letter from a Young Poet*. Limited special ed. Hartford, CT: Watkinson Library of Trinity College, 2015.

Vendler, Helen. *Dickinson: Selected Poems and Commentaries*. Cambridge, MA: Harvard University Press, 2010, 237–38.

SELECTED POEMS

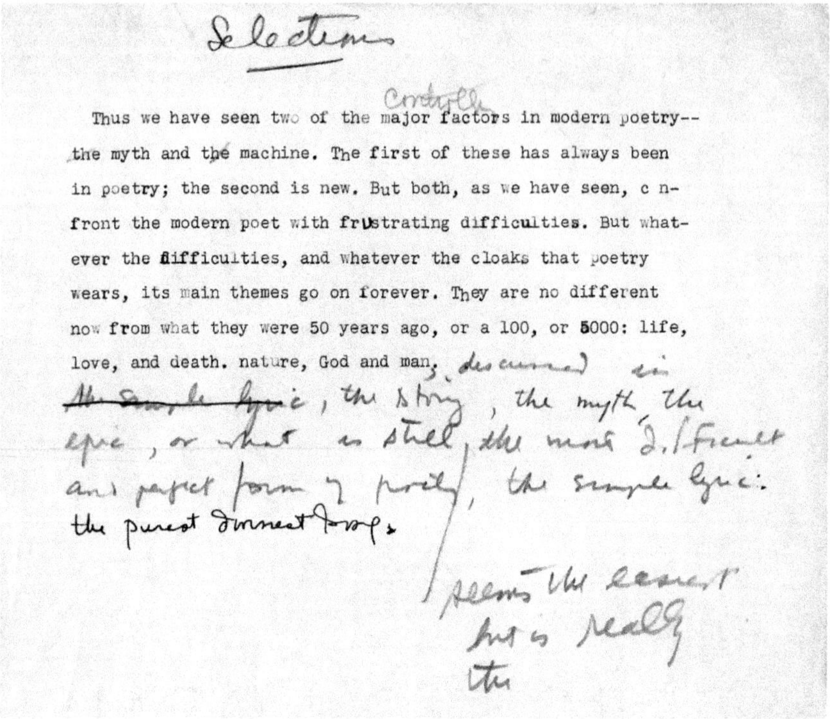

Selections

Thus we have seen two of the major factors in modern poetry—
the myth and the machine. The first of these has always been
in poetry; the second is new. But both, as we have seen, confront the modern poet with frustrating difficulties. But whatever the difficulties, and whatever the cloaks that poetry
wears, its main themes go on forever. They are no different
now from what they were 50 years ago, or a 100, or 5000: life,
love, and death. nature, God and man.

[handwritten marginalia, partially illegible: "Cordially" / "described in the simple lyric, the story, the myth, the epic, or what is still, the most difficult and perfect form of poetry, the simple lyric: the purest innermost form." / "seems the easiest but is really the —"]

Unpublished literary material from the Hyam Plutzik Archives at the University of Rochester, used with permission.

Selected Poems

Abner Bellow	340
Absurd Cycle	341
After Looking into a Book Belonging to My Great-Grandfather, Eli Eliakim Plutzik	341
A Letter to Someone at Mt. Palomar	342
An Agadah of Hyam Ben Samuel	345
And in the 51st Year of That Century, While My Brother Cried in the Trench, While My Enemy Glared from the Cave	345
An Electromagnetic Phenomenon	346
An Equation	347
As the Great Horse Rots on the Hill	348
Because the Red Osier Dogwood	349
Beware, Saunterer, of This Desperado, a Mr. Bones, a Bad Actor	350
Bomber Base	351
Cancer and Nova	352
Commentary	353
Connecticut Autumn	354
Dante in Our Time	355
Divisibility	356
The Dream about Our Master, William Shakespeare	357
El Anon Al Kol	358
Elaboration on a Phrase of Rabelais	359
Elegy	359
Entropy	360
Exhortation to the Artists	360
For T. S. E. Only	361
God and My Father	363
He Inspects His Armory	364
Hiroshima	365
I Have Read in the Book of the Butcher Boy	365
I Imagined a Painter Painting Such a World	366
If Causality Is Impossible, Genesis Is Recurrent	366
Jim Desterland	367

Jonathan and the Snow	368
Kaddish	368
L'Cho Dodi	369
Magen Avot	371
My Sister	372
Next Time I Shall Not Burn the Beehive	373
Of Objects Considered as Fortresses in Baleful Space	374
On Hearing That My Poems Were Being Studied in a Distant Place	375
On the Last Survivor of Our War, 1861–1865	376
On the Photograph of a Man I Never Saw	377
Patterns of Earth	377
Portrait	378
Requiem for Edward Carrigh	379
Sprig of Lilac	380
Strange Diners at the Café Parnassus	381
The Airman Who Flew over Shakespeare's England	383
The Bass	384
The Begetting of Cain	385
The Belated Birds Having Taken Their Leave	385
The Camorra	386
The Chinaman and the Florentine	386
The Devil with the Minus Sign in His Right Hand	387
The Geese	387
The House of Gorya	388
The Importance of Poetry, or the Coming Forth from Eternity into Time	390
The King of Ai	391
The Last Fisherman	392
The Marriage	392
The Milkman	393
The Miracle	394
The Mythos of the Man from Enoch	395
The Mythos of Samuel Huntsman	396
The Old War	397
The Priest Ekranath	398
The Premonition	400
The Zero That Is All	400
Those Who Write after Freud	401
To Abraham Lincoln, That He Walk by Day	402
To Pablo Picasso, on his *Guernica*	404

To My Daughter	404
To the Predynastic Egyptian Who Rests within the Entrance of the Metropolitan Museum	405
To Those Who Look Out of the Window	405
Two Hearts and an Arrow	406
Trio for Two Voices and a Woodwind	407
Useful Prepared Speech for the Diffident Author of a Book of Poems Costing Three Dollars and Fifty Cents	409
Winter, Never Mind Where	409

Long Poems

Death at The Purple Rim (excerpts)	410
Horatio (Prologue, The Ostler)	412
The Book of Metamorphoses	418
The Seventh Avenue Express	422

Abner Bellow

What wanders under the meadow—
An inverse horrible shadow?

As our feet pace ground
And our heads are high in air
There are upside-down people
Pacing below us there.
They are no longer than a steeple.
They never make a sound.

One follows me where I go.
Sole to sole are our feet.
We are two mad acrobats
Where earth and air meet.
I have tried to escape tiptoe,
But his tread is quick as a cat's.

What wanders under the meadow?
I tire fast in this balance
On the tightrope of the world,
The pursuit in the silence
And the hours fear-filled
In the sad dance with the shadow:

The long lank shadow
Pacing under the meadow.

Absurd Cycle

The wombed thing
First like a fish
Will become a man
And make a wish

For a peck of apples,
A pint of dream,
And a leaping fish
In a stream.

After Looking into a Book Belonging to My Great-Grandfather, Eli Eliakim Plutzik

I am troubled by the blank fields, the speechless graves.
Since the names were carved upon wood, there is no word
For the thousand years that shaped this scribbling fist
And the eyes staring at strange places and times
Beyond the veldt dragging to Poland.
Lovers of words make simple peace with death,
At last demanding, to close the door to the cold,
Only *Here lies someone.*
Here lie no one and no one, your fathers and mothers.

A Letter to Someone at Mt. Palomar

Though you reach forth past that hot pinwheel of Messier
And gobble, like a monstrous turkey with red eyes,
The farthest kernel of fire in our half-heaven,
Beyond Ophiuchus, you will never come to the end
Of this metaphor our world. Confusing mirrors
Are cocked at strategic angles along the walls
And ceiling of this immense translucent chamber
Where the suns follow their ceremonious paths
And we the littler ritual of breath: where no door
Or window exists except (in its odd corner)
The panel through which the occasional dubious shape—
The serpent, the saint, or the ghost—enters quietly,
To sour our theories and give us our dose of madness.

Consider then, to use some archaic counters,
This odor of death and the rose, as we walk the world
Sniffing the scenery. A machine would be more explicit;
A formula have less of passion and nonsense;
Only a poem would give us this strange odor
Of death and the rose together; a fragment only,
This sudden awareness cast between nothing and nothing.
A metaphor, this damned evasive face
That peeps wherever we look, a masked henchman,
A god, a demon, a stick or a stone. Enough
To spy on the desk our fragmentary symbol
Which we may observe, as archeologists
Worry a scrap of parchment, extrapolating
The shape of the whole work, and thence the heart
Of the artist himself: here that old unhappy romantic,
With a consciousness full of more shadow than light,
Obsessed by the moral sense that we call form,
And you logic or law. And what remains
Is, as it were, some epic simile
Full of outrageous sounds, furies and posturings.
Since we cannot break this frame, so let us turn
To the world we have, within. If the sum of things

Is an apparition shaped in a mirror darkly,
Each fraction must be of this same deceptive stuff—
Or say that every atom of a symbol
Is of itself symbolic. Wise men would be
More numerous than ninnies; brooks run uphill;
And one and one be four, if parts outreached
A whole in level of reality,
Like a hat on a ghost. No, in this vast chamber
The suns follow their ceremonious paths;
And we our ritual of breath; and all between,
Their individual, formal dance. See here
Where action is accidental, most at random,
In a crowded street the automatic movement,
The hypnotized walk and talk, as if the world
Were bowing and scraping, acting a part by rote,
Like Hakagawa among his Titians, or Nanki-poo
And his stilted friends as the play opens. They rise,
Don clothes and wash their faces, work thus and thus,
Laugh at a fly, kiss in the evening, sleep,
Die as the script demands, in an etiquette
Of strictest but hidden command, though the will is free
As a butterfly in a gaudy flower-patch.
And ever standing for something beyond themselves,
They laugh and cry, say mother, pace their game
To the formalism of their inanimate comrades,
The house, the falling apple, the cigarette,
The clock, indeed the telescope on the hill—
All in vast conspiracy, except
The dubious shape that squirms through the crack in the wall . . .

So you will not pass the bounds of the world-symbol,
Nor come to the new Indies, and smell the spice
Of the secret mountain, and hear the tribes singing.
The crooked mirrors hanging upon that sky
Will give you yourself only, as a protean gargoyle,
Skinny or fat or horsefaced. But the hungering spirit
Will wash away the joke: the quest itself
Stand as out quintessential pattern and doom,

With its old brother constants death and pain.
Let the silent dome turn and the glass glitter.
And the nighttime sky be brilliant and clear. O study
Your subtle emulsions and your photographic plates,
The spectral and radiant records, dwarf and giant
(With other children reading a story). Peer forth
At the faint, livid spirals, wonderful
In the black cosmos. I would be with you there.

An Agadah of Hyam Ben Samuel

It is the function of a match to be scraped against roughness,
To flare to fire, and to become ashes.

Once there was a match in the days when matches could speak
That complained: "Why should I be hurt?
The surface of the match box is unnecessarily rough.
I question the justice of the universe.
Why cannot I and my friends
Live in our match box in comfort and amity?
Is fire necessary?

At which a gigantic voice cried out in the workshop:
"Both the beauty and utility of a match
Are in their burning."

And in the 51st Year of That Century, While My Brother Cried in the Trench, While My Enemy Glared from the Cave

This star is only an augury of the morning,
Gift-bearer of another day.

A wind has brought the musk of thirty fields,
Each like a coin of silver under that sky.

Precious, the sound of breathing of wife and children
In a house on a field lit by the morning star.

An Electromagnetic Phenomenon

What the trees know that grow in graveyards
Isn't pleasant. With your fingers curled in their eyes
What can you say, even with your little leaves,
Even in sunlight? No, I shall go elsewhere
To a field here where only grass has died,
Pure green from drinking a radiance from space.

You there, whose nerves are a net flung upward,
Veins of mind, feeling with vague fingers
To catch birds and starlight, butterflies and the sun!

The birds are flying in and out of the living fingers.
The starlight touches the blood with cold tremor.
The sun and the butterflies tangle in the threads of mind.
A current of music is set up by the flying birds,
The starbeams, the butterflies, the sun, as they shuttle through
       the bent fingers and threads.

Finer than cobwebs in the dew
The threads pierced the eyes, ears and flesh of the listener:
Look, there is a cobweb in my head!
I heard something.
What I heard I shall not tell you, having already told you.

An Equation

For instance: $y - xa + mx^2(a^2+1) = 0$

Coil upon coil, the grave serpent holds
Its implacable strict pose, under a light
Like marble. The artist's damnation, the rat of time,
Cannot gnaw this form, nor event touch it with age.
Before it was, it existed, creating the mind
Which created it, out of itself. It will dissolve
Into itself, though in another language.
Its changes are not in change, not its times in time.

And the coiled serpent quivering under a light
Crueler than marble, unwinds slowly, altering
Deliberate the great convolutions, a dancer,
A mime on the brilliant stage. The sudden movement,
Swifter than creases of lightning, renews a statue:
There by its skin a snake rears beaten in copper.

It will not acknowledge the incense on your altars,
Nor hear at night in your room the weeping . . .

As the Great Horse Rots on the Hill

As the great horse rots on the hill
    till the stars wink through his ribs;
As the genera of horses become silent,
    the thunder of the hooves receding in the silence;
As the tree shrivels in the wind of time,
    as the wind Time dried the locust tree—
Thus you prepare the future for me and my loved ones.

I have been in many towns and seen innumerable houses,
    also rocks, trees, people, stars and insects.
Thieves, like ants, are making off with them,
    taking them to your old ant-hill.
Thus you prepare the future for me and my loved ones.

What spider made the machine of many threads?

The threads run
    from time's instants to all the atoms of the universe.
In each instant a wheel turns in your head, threads go taut,
    and one of a quintillion atoms is transmuted.
Thus you prepare the future for me and my loved ones.

I observe the ordained explosions on the paper as I write,
The pinpoints of flame in the wood on the table, and on the wall
(Like a battlefield at night, or a field where fireflies flicker).
My hand, too, scintillates like a strange fish;
Fires punctuate the strange faces on the road;
A pox, a fever, burns in the tissues of the hills.
Thus you prepare the future for me and my loved ones.

As the great horse is transmuted on the hill
Till the stars wink through his skull;
As the stars become husk and radiance;
As the locust tree is changed by the wind Time;
As the wind Time too will lapse, will blow from another quarter—
Thus you prepare the future for me and my loved ones.

Because the Red Osier Dogwood

Because the red osier dogwood
Is the winter lightning,
The retention of the prime fire
In the naked and forlorn season
When snow is winner
(For he flames quietly above the shivering mouse
In the moldy tunnel,
The eggs of the grasshopper awaiting metamorphosis
Into the lands of hay and the times of the daisy,
The snake contorted in the gravel,
His brain suspended in thought
Over an abyss that summer will fill with murmuring
And frogs make laughable: the cricket-haunted time)—
I, seeing in the still red branches
The stubborn, unflinching fire of that time,
Will not believe the horror at the door, the snow-white worm
Gnawing at the edges of the mind,
The hissing tree when the sleet falls.
For because the red osier dogwood
Is the winter sentinel,
I am certain of the return of the moth
(Who was not destroyed when an August flame licked him),
And the cabbage butterfly, and all the families
Whom the sun fathers, in the cauldron of his mercy.

Beware, Saunterer, of This Desperado, a Mr. Bones, a Bad Actor

Saunterer on this autumn track
That edges the garden, brown with brown,
Along by the hickory tree remember
To avoid the place where the dead rat lies.

Else how will you breathe untainted the sweet
Rot of the indolent cucumber,
Apple-smell, stubble-reek, pumpkin-vinegar?

Someone is taking all the parts
In this season's performance—ha! leaping the footlights
Where your beating blood is most gay with his masking,
Marks your time too with his ticking bomb.

Bomber Base

The machines are quiet before the day's struggle.
Geometric lines subtend the air at random.
In the half-dark, propeller, wind and fin
Loom out of space. A searchlight lifts a far
Pillar of white and a flare falls slowly,
In isolation, so calm, so secretly.

There are many messages coursing the earth
In this wartime night: of command, terror, despair;
In guttural syllables, in soft; by lights in the sky.
And none so beautiful as the white flare sinking
On a distant field, in East Anglia the ancient.

And space is full of the mutter of engines passing
Over the clouds, like a great organ playing.

Now the thatched farmhouse sleeps in the dark
Among wakeful men, moving swift to their task.
The runways stretch silent; somewhere in the blackness
The guards stand, unseen, longing for home,
And a woman's arms, a warm bed in a house.
Upon the fields the stone weapons of dead men
Lie awaiting the outcome, which they will survive.
And the bomb-trucks move down the deserted perimeter
Where the cold North Sea wind stifles all.

Listen: the King's airmen are at large tonight.
But this is no story. Already the enemy
Touches them with his instruments. His guns poise.
Already fragments of metal puff out in the sky.
The bombs shatter the factory and many are blasted.
The broken machine crashes into the hill.
The young men die in manifold agonies.

Cancer and Nova

The star exploding in the body;
The creeping thing, growing in the brain or the bone;
The hectic cannibal, the obscene mouth.

The mouths along the meridian sought him,
Soft as moths, many a moon and sun,
Until one
In a pale fleeting dream caught him.

Waking, he did not know himself undone,
Nor walking, smiling, reading that the news was good,
The star exploding in his blood.

Commentary

> *Once, when I entered the Holy of Holies to burn the incense, I saw the Lord of all Hosts sitting on a high and exalted throne, and He said to me: Ishmael, my son, bless me."*
>
> —The Talmud

I
He is lonely then within the pale of the palace—
The Enthroned Will, whose fingers must ever shore
The pitiful islands against the destroyer of all.

To guard the breath of the violet for its time,
And Helen's face, and the gay moment the sun
Touches the street in the town where children play.

To shale and reshape forever the crumbling substance
Yet see the ruin so quickly, the figurines
Wasting in air, the brush-strokes graying in ash.

If only once out of the flow, the river,
To make the lasting, the perfect—O to create
What will endure for the creator's time.

II
Lonely, lonely in the pale of the palace.
Once there were others, rivals, Ammon or Zeus.
Brother or foe, to bring the blood to the face,
Or who fashioned himself a mate out of the ground,
For eternity, his paltry thousand years.
But to shape and reshape forever the dust, the dust.

III
And the desperate tricks, the man or the nation beloved.
The disguises: dream or fire or a cloak by the gate
Of an unknown city, beyond the candlelight's friendship,

Where the guard cries out who goes, and sees no thing
But the darkening sand and a desert bird wheeling
With the cry that a gull makes on an empty coast.

O he is lonely in the pale of the palace—
The Enthroned Will, whose fingers must ever shore
The pitiful islands against the destroyer of all.

Connecticut Autumn

I have seen the pageantry of the leaves falling—
Their sere, brown frames descending brokenly,
Like old men lying down to rest.
I have heard the whisperings of the winds calling—
The young winds—playing with the old men—
Playing with them, as the sun flows west.

And I have seen the pomp of this earth naked—
The brown fields standing cold and resolute,
Like strong men waiting for the end.
Then have come the sudden gusts of winds awaked:
The broken pageantry, the leaves upflailed, the trees
Tremor-stricken, the giant branches rent.

And a shiver runs over the remnants of the brown grass—
And there is cessation . . .
The processional recurs.

I have seen the pageantry.
I have seen the haggard leaves falling.
One by one falling.

Dante in Our Time

Across the barrier through a gate unguarded
Came Alighieri, restless still for knowledge,
To the hell of the living, Count Ugolino's pasture.
Unguided, along the twisting roads of the world,
The dark cloak passed, and the burning eyes
Read out the book of our shame, till weary at last
He returned by the devious route to the bed of torment
Which for presumption was his for eternity;
And to the gray philosopher beside him,
The Athenian, questioning, of frank face, he said:

*I went like Ulysses once more into the morning.
And those who still at this fagot-end of days
Walk on the earth in the purlieus of the sun
I saw them, burning in their fire.*

          *Yes,
They are still after so many years attempting
To define themselves; they still grasp after shadows.
They are still uncertain, for their knowledge brought to them
What you without knowledge knew: that the Thing itself
In its essence is nothingness. Therefore they have built
Upon ciphers their huge structures not more real
Than the angels we spun out upon a pin
Before the acrid earth taught us the truth.*

*I saw also a boy and girl walking
Side by side, into the immense dusk
Till they disappeared. And the smoke rose
Old as a campfire over city and city.*

*Again on a bridge I met her, Beatrice.
I turned, but she passed. That day was a deer bleeding.
And again within me there came the madness to write
The infinite yearning, the babbling hell in my spirit.
O Merciful! It is not joy I ask for,
Nor desire for joy, for I have killed that monster:
But to sup on the quiet of pain on these plains of Acheron.*

Divisibility

The limitary nature of a wall
Is partial only, to keep out dogs and insects,
Contain the furniture, exclude the rain.

But space flies through it like a mad commuter.
Rooms are thus always strange, as if you entered
Another by error in the same hotel,

And saw incredulous no known landmarks,
The bed moved, new luggage on the floor,
And a window staring at you from the wrong corner.

And desire goes through a wall as wild geese
Pass and cry over reedy waters. Memory
Knows no walls. They are elementary limits.

Only a fool would cut the sea with a knife,
Or say to wind: Exceed this line at your peril.

The Dream About Our Master, William Shakespeare

This midnight dream whispered to me:
Be swift as a runner, take the lane
Into the green mystery
Beyond the farm and haystack at Stone.
You leave tomorrow, not to return.

Hands that were fastened in a vise,
A useless body, rooted feet,
While time like a bell thundered the loss,
Witnessed the closing of the gate.
Thus sleeping and waking both betrayed.

I had one glimpse: In a close of shadow
There rose the form of a manor-house,
And in a corner a curtained window.
All was lost in a well of trees,
Yet I knew for certain this was the place.

If the hound of air, the ropes of shade,
And the gate between that is no gate,
Had not so held me and delayed
These cowardly limbs of bone and blood,
I would have met him as he lived!

El Anon Al Kol

God who is commander of all creation,
Blest by the praying lips of his multitudes,
Fills all space with his greatness and goodness,
Surrounding himself with knowledge and wisdom.

High above the spirits of heaven,
Honored like a hero on a splendid chariot,
He marshals his powers before his throne,
Purity, Justice, Grace and Mercy.

Good are the lights our God has made,
Sun, moon, the wandering planets,
Of whom it is said: They know their mission
To rule the worlds with the strength of their shining.

With fulness of light, with outpouring of splendor,
With bright beauty over the universe,
They celebrate their rising and setting
According to the awesome will of their maker.

To him they render glory and honor,
Acknowledge in glad song his kinship,
At whose command the sun flamed forth,
Whose skillful devising shaped the moon.

The hosts of the sky, the fixed and wandering stars,
    cry his praises:

Seraphim!
Orphanim!
Hayot Ha-Kodesh!

The spirits, instruments of God, named after fire—
The spirits named for a whirling wheel—
The spirits called the Creatures of Heaven—
All chant his grandeur and might.

Elaboration on a Phrase of Rabelais

To return to a city where you lusted once
Is to come to a place older than Damascus,
With huger shapes of myth than Gilgamesh
Or Ishtar who went down naked to the water.

Though a man hail and tell you he remembers
When the first house was axe-shaped in the forest,
It is old beyond the nether ruin at Knossos,
Or Chinon the oldest city in the world.

Elegy

He walked quietly among the loud ones,
In the first world and the eternities following,
Till the pale flame of the spirit sank
And flickered out in the last wilderness.
There on a plain vast and shadowy
Come at last those who have run their course,
Where the minions of God regard them coolly and see
As in a fog the starved fires sinking.
It is pitiful how long the test goes on.
Some swagger and shout but he walked quietly.
Some were lonely, but there was a kindred spirit
That passed with him through the metamorphoses
And failed beside him after the race was done.
Together they spurned the immense coils of Being.
The poised darkness, the blows of the answerless Ocean.

Entropy

I have seen the wound that matter makes in space,
The hole in the blank sheet of white paper.
On a day the name of no dead demon could hold
I saw the tension of Being in all things,
Bearing them up against the tightening spring
Of infinite number and the fires of nebular torment
Till the last day, when they lie crushed like a moth
In a child's hand, or a thing under the sea.

Exhortation to the Artists

> *Rabbi Elazer once became sick. Rabbi Jochanan came to visit him ... Rabbi Elazer was weeping. "Why do you weep?" asked Rabbi Jochanan. "I weep," said Rabbi Elazer to him, "for the beauty which will decay in the earth." "For that indeed," Rabbi Jochanan said, "you ought to weep," and both wept.*
> —The Talmud

Two weeping for beauty perished, husband
And wife, lover and mistress, friend and friend,
    Shall mark the world's end.

As I was spinning a fable for this page,
There came ghosts weeping, two and two,
    In pity, dolor, or in rage.

Against the pillars of the heartless temple
Throw, whom knowledge blinded, your brute skill
    Though it is yourself you kill.

He crushes the sparrow fallen among the rocks;
The hunter is trapped with his quarry; the man and the fox—
    Even the little mouse on the hill.

For T. S. E. Only

You called me a name on such and such a day—
Do you remember?—you were speaking of Bleistein our brother,
The barbarian with the black cigar, and the pockets
Ringing with cash, and the eyes seeking Jerusalem,
Knowing they have been tricked. Come, brother Thomas,
We three must weep together for our exile.

I see the hunted look, the protestation,
The desperate seeking, the reticence and the brashness
Of the giver of laws to the worshippers of calves.
At times you speak as if the words were walls,
But your walls fell with mine to the torch of a Titus.
Come, let us weep together for our exile.

We two, no doubt, could accommodate ourselves:
We've both read Dante and we both dislike Chicago,
And both, you see, can be brutal—but you must bow down
To our brother Bleistein here, with the unaesthetic
Cigar and the somber look. Come, do so quickly,
For we must weep together for our exile.

O you may enwomb yourself in words or the Word
(The Word is a good refuge for people too proud
To swallow the milk of the mild Jesus' teaching),
Or a garden in Hampshire with a magic bird, or an old
Quotation from the Reverend Andrewes, yet someone or
        something
(Let us pause to weep together for our exile)

Will stick a needle in your balloon, Thomas.
Is it the shape that you saw upon the stair?
The four knights clanking toward the altar? the hidden
Card in the deck? the sinister man from Nippon?
The hordes on the eastern horizon? Come, brother Burbank,
And let us weep together for our exile.

In the time of sweet sighing you wept bitterly.
And now in the time of weeping you cannot weep.
Will you wait for the peace of the sailor with pearly bones?
Where is the refuge you thought you would find on the island
Where each man lives in his castle? O brother Thomas,
Come let us weep together for our exile.

You drew us first by your scorn, first by your wit;
Later for your own eloquent suffering.
We loved you first for the wicked things you wrote
Of those you acknowledged infinitely gentle.
Wit is the sin that you must expiate.
Bow down to them, and let us weep for our exile.

I see your words wrung out in pain, but never
The true compassion for creatures with you, that Dante
Knew in his nine hells. O eagle! master!
The eagle's ways of pride and scorn will not save
Though the voice cries loud in humility. Thomas, Thomas,
Come, let us pray together for our exile.

You, hypocrite lecteur! mon semblable! mon frère!

God and My Father

I look down
With the eye you call Aldebaran, the angry one
Of a bull of my dear land of Bashan,
And the mild eye Arcturus, lord of eyes.
The width of my forehead is your ninety parsecs;
My right arm grips the throat of your Dragon.

On the spheres lit by the light of my eyes,
Made indeed by the word of this light, for long
I have heard creatures crying, and seen things
Better lost in the darkness toward Andromeda
Where another strength takes over, perhaps a better,
Which I feel feeling my outstretched fingers sometimes.

These three years,
Yours not mine, not as formerly
Can I lose myself elsewhere.
I might ignore the weeping
As a customary noise which one forgets.
It is a silence that will not let me be

Coming out of a hole in the earth,
Where he lies
With the open psalm book over the ruined heart.

I cannot turn from the page.
Through the six feet of earth, or the whole earth
As the sphere turns, as the spheres turn,
Though my forehead is your ninety parsecs
The eyes burn and focus on those words
(Charging that I be with him now)
Which will not burn away, yet burn like words on a wall—
Or a waste field, out of a tree.

And my right arm is near the Pole Star;
My left, on the ambiguous frontiers.

He Inspects His Armory

Phoebus, the car
And the galloping horses
Are dead, dead,
And in their stead
Inanimate forces
And a minor star.

Cynthia too,
Whom Edmund and John
So quaintly adored,
Ignored, ignored,
Wrinkled and wan,
A hag in the blue.

And Zephyrus eke,
Vulcan or Thor,
Are all together
Weather, weather,
And nothing more.
Useless as Greek.

Remains the least
Of the living for art—
Loneliest, latest,
The greatest, greatest,
The occult heart
Of the talking beast.

Hiroshima

The man who gave the signal sleeps well—
    So he says.

But the man who pulled the toggle sleeps badly—
    So we read.

And we behind the man who gave the signal—
    How do we sleep?

And they below the man who pulled the toggle?
    Well?

I Have Read in the Book of the Butcher Boy
(In time of war)

I have read in the book of the butcher boy, William of Avon,
Of the deathless thyme; I have read of the wild thyme growing.
Be patient, gypsy, and we shall seek for that place.
We shall set our house there on that fragrant hill,
Deathless too, over the thyme-sweet stream,
With a road as brown and clean as an autumn leaf
Passing beside it for friendly feet to tread.
No mouse will lurk there, or fourteen-legged bug
Trespass its corners as in a lesser house.
No pug-nosed dog will snarl from its lawns, but a gentle,
Sad-eyed and shaggy-eared being as wise as Buddha
Will sit magisterial on the porch to guard us
From villain and bore. Never will hoarse old rooster
Raise up his odious cry at dawn to wake us:
A small red bird on a limb by our window will be
The bell of morning for us through the long years.
And we shall look down at the brown road to see
The butcher boy pass there idling upon his wheel
As butcher boys do, whistling a lilt to life;
The postman will pass there and other wise men also.
Sons will come to us there through the long years.
We shall grow old but mist and road and stream,
In that coign of things, shall give us youth eternal,
By the fragrant thyme of the happy butcher boy's singing.

I Imagined a Painter Painting Such a World

Like successive layers of leaf that dwindle the sunlight
Are the overlapping cumulative shadows
Projected by things, which huddle in them darkly
Within the greater shadow: suffering.

Breaching the shores of matter a swell of shadows
Destroys all sanctions of formal separateness;
And objects, transposed of vesture, take doubtful values
Like hulks vaguely discerned under the tides.

What inner or outer flames may shine are random
In the one, shadowed sea where all things melt,
While through all, the superior dark, the subjective night
Encloses and bathes the universe.

If Causality Is Impossible, Genesis Is Recurrent

The abrupt appearance of a yellow flower
Out of the perfect nothing, is miraculous.
The sum of Being, being discontinuous,
Must presuppose a God-out-of-the-box
Who makes a primal garden of each garden.
There is no change, but only re-creation
One step ahead. As in the cinema
Upon the screen, all motion is illusory.
So if your mind were keener and could clinch
More than its flitting beachhead in the Permanent,
You'd see a twinkling world flashing and dying
Projected out of a tireless, winking Eye
Opening and closing in immensity—
Creating, with Its look, beside all else
Always Adamic passion and innocence,
The bloodred apple or the yellow flower.

Jim Desterland

As I was fishing off Pondy Point
Between the tides, the sea so still—
Only a whisper against the boat—
No other sound but the scream of a gull,
I heard the voice you will never hear
Filling the crannies of the air.

The doors swung open, the little doors,
The door, the hatch within the brain,
And like the bellowing of ruin
The surf upon the thousand shores
Swept through me, and the thunder-noise
Of all the waves of all the seas.

The doors swung shut, the little doors,
The door, the hatch within the ear,
And I was fishing off Pondy Pier,
And all was at it was before,
With only the whisper of the swell
Against the boat, and the cry of a gull.

I draw a sight from tree to tree
Crossing this other from knoll to rock,
To mark the place. Into the sea
My line falls with an empty hook,
Yet fools the world. So day and night
I crouch upon the thwarts and wait.

There is a roaring in the skies
The great globes make, and there is the sound
Of all the atoms whirling round
That one can hear if one is wise—
Wiser than most—if one has heard
The doors, the little doors, swing wide.

Jonathan and the Snow

Snowflakes were falling as I rode homeward.
Snowflakes! Snowflakes! and I no longer young.

Out of a place in the dark that moved with me
They struck the glass, died, were brushed off.
And I, no longer young, drove faster, faster.

At the door they came at my face like little bees
And I, "Snowflakes, you knew me on Good Hill.
And now..." Jonathan laughed in the doorway. And they,

"It is simple. We love those who laugh at us.
Go sit by the... damned fire and write your poems."

Kaddish

Render greatness and holiness to the mighty name of God,
    throughout the world which he has created according to his will.

May his kingdom flower in your time and in the time of the whole
    house of Israel, quickly, soon. And to this let us say Amen.

May his mighty name be blest for eternity.

Cry laudation and honor to that holy name which is above all the
    praises and adorings of our world, and all its consolations.
    And to this let us say Amen.

May our prayers be answered, may the supplications of all Israel
    find favor with our Father in heaven. And to this let us say
    Amen.

May his heavenly peace touch us, may long and good life be given
    to us and all Israel.
May he who establishes peace on the heights bring peace and
    comforting also to us and to all Israel. And to this let us
    say Amen.

L'Cho Dodi

Quickly, friend, the bride is come.
Princess Sabbath is her name.

Recall the Sabbath, keep it holy.
God, in one command, said duly.
He is one. His name is one;
His the praise and His the glory.

To greet the Sabbath let us haste.
Through her blessings we are blessed—
She who was by God's intent
First in goal, though fashioned last.

Holy nation, royal town,
Rise above your ancient ruin.
Leave the valley of your grieving
For the mercy God has shown.

Shake the bitter dust away.
Dress as for a holiday.
By the hand of Jesse's son,
Save me, God—so must you pray.

Hurry then! O hurry then!
Rise in brightness: light has come.
God's high glory blesses you.
Quickly, quickly, sing His song.

Leave confusion, no more shame.
Why the downcast face, the moan?
You will yet be comforted
The holy city built again.

He who spoiled you will be spoiled,
And who consumed you be consumed.
God delights in you, my people,
As a bridegroom in his bride.

Rightward, leftward you will win
If to God your soul you turn
Through the power of David's house.
Let us laugh and sing this tune.

Come in peace, Crown of the Lord—
Come gaily, come happily—
To the people of His word.
Come O Bride! Come O Bride!

Magen Avot

He whose word in times past was a shield to our fathers,
      and whose command will at last give us immortality—
There is none like him!
Because le loves them, he brings now the holy tranquility
      of the Sabbath to his people.
Let us therefore serve him fittingly, with fear and awe,
      and let us bless him.
The God whom we praise, the Lord of peace, make this
      Sabbath holy.
To us, a people already rich in the delights of the
      spirit, he gave this sacred seventh day,
To celebrate and recall the creation of the world.

My Sister

Now the swift rot of the flesh is over.
Now only the slow rot of the bones in the Northern damp.
Even the bones of that tiny foot that brought her down.

Imagine a land where there is no rain as we know rain.
Not the quick dashing of water to the expectant face,
But the weary ooze of spent drops in the earth.

Imagine the little skeleton lying there—
In the terrible declination of the years—
On the solitary bed, in the crumbling shell of a world.

Amid the monsters with lipless teeth who lie there in wait—
The saurian multitudes who rest in that land—
And the men without eyes who forever glare at the sky.

And the ominous strangers ever entering.
Why are they angry? They keep their arms to themselves.
Comfort themselves in the cold. Whisper no word.

And the black dog has come, but he does not play.
And no one moves but the man who walks in the sky—
A strange man who comes to cut the grass.

Seventeen years...

And already the fair flesh dispersed, the proud form broken.
Memory! Where are the ligaments to bind—the glowing cords—
As in this hand once touched, this hand that writes?

Seventeen years have passed and the way grows steeper.
The glaciers move from the north and the sun is dying.
And into the chasm of Time alone and tiny...

The Man of War sits in the gleaming chair.
Struts through the halls. The Dispenser of Vengeance laughs,
Crying victory! victory! victory! victory!

Victory.

Next Time I Shall Not Burn the Beehive

Next time I shall not burn the beehive
Where in hexagonal cells the city's future,
Divided already into golden bodies,
Prepared for entrance into a cosmos
Of calyxes and summery airs—

Nor, before, let loose under the eaves
The skillful, poisonous vapor smelling of naphtha.

At the first spurt of the gas, despite the netting,
Two frightened members of the commonwealth
Launched themselves past my ears.
I jumped from the ladder, waited, soon returned
To give them the long-enduring stroke of grace.

Later, having ripped the hive away
And thrown it to the ground some distance off,
When I poured the gasoline upon it I saw
Things with closed wings straining to get out.

Of Objects Considered as Fortresses in a Baleful Space

I and the other intruders,
The oak and stone my brothers,
Stare at one another
Upon the plain of nothing.

As if to ask what wonder
By willing or by blunder
Could lead to this encounter
Upon the plain of nothing.

(As if to ask what meeting
Could overmatch the wonder
Of opaque hostile Being
Emergent out of nothing.)

The nothing is a glitter
Wicked, a frosty water,
Upon which no words scatter,
Not hallo, sob or laughter.

Upon their petty islands
The something and the something,
Knowing or blank, in silence
Await the will of nothing.

One, one, and one,
Mysteries of the moon,
And the always never-guests,
None, none.

On Hearing That My Poems Were Being Studied in a Distant Place

What are they mumbling about me there?
"Here," they say, "he suffered; here was glad."
Are words clothes or the putting off of clothes?

The scene is as follows: my book is open
On thirty desks; the teacher expounds my life.
Outside the window, the Pacific roars like a lion,

Beside which my small words rise and fall.
"In this alliteration a tower crashed,"
Are words clothes or the putting off of clothes?"

"Here, in the fisherman casting on the water,
He saw the end of the dreamer.
"And in that image, death, naked."

Out of my life I fashioned a fistful of words/
When I opened my hand, they flew away."

On the Last Survivor of Our War, 1861–1865

I must write quickly; time does not wait for art.
Now he is dying and the wave is wholly spent
On a shore thirty thousand days from the storm's heart.

The dead that Mathew Brady saw by the wall
Call too loud now to be denied.
The generals, the loser and the winner.
The audience at Ford's Theatre is calling.
Infantry and artillery,
The foragers, the skirmishers, the irregulars.
General Hood's trumpets are signalling bivouac for the night.
The magnificent beards are calling, the moustaches, the
       strange hats.
(The guns in the town squares are uttering salvoes of silence.)
Mr. Lincoln and Mr. Davis have called and left their
       addresses.

Farewell, drummer boy—
(My God, how the storm of the generations passes,
How each wave is lost at last in the sand.)

On the Photograph of a Man I Never Saw

My grandfather's beard
Was blacker than God's
Just after the tablets
Were broken in half.

My grandfather's eyes
Were sterner than Moses'
Just after the worship
Of the calf.

O ghost! O ghost!
You foresaw the days
Of the fallen Law
In the strange place.

Where ten together
Lament David,
Is the glance softened?
Bowed the face?

Patterns of Earth

Now the new grass is vivid with dandelions,
As last night the ancient sky was constellated.

And the Scorpion, the Dog, Perseus, and Hercules
Are less than the gold children of my field.

Whom I will name quickly, for their time is flying:
The Butcher, the Baker and the Candlestickmaker.

They will be gone in a fortnight, fluff upon the wind,
And the bullies of the sky will resume their mastery.

Portrait

Notice with what careful nonchalance
He tries to be a Jew casually,
To ignore the monster, the mountain—
A few thousand years of history.

Of course he personally remembers nothing,
And the world has forgotten the older objections—
The new ones not being socially acceptable:
Hangdogs, hiding in the privies and alleys of the mind.

It is agreed
That he of all men has gained the right to his soul
(Though like the others he no longer believes in one).
He lives in his own house under his oak.
He stands by his car, shod in decently-grained leather.
He is smiling. His hair is peacefully in place.
His suit is carefully pressed; his cravat harmonious.

Whose father, it is whispered, stubbornly cried old clothes
       and bric-a-brac,
He of all men might yet be master of self, all self-possession,
Were it not (how gauche and incredible!) for the one
       ill-fitting garment—
The historical oversight in the antique wardrobe—
The shirt, the borrowed shirt
The Greek shirt.

Notice how even when he is at ease he is somehow anxious,
Like a horse who whiffs smoke somewhere nearby faintly.
Notice with what nonchalance,
The magazine in his hand and the casual cigarette to his lips,
He wears a shirt by Nessus.

Requiem for Edward Carrigh

The sudden translation to the bottom of the hill,
To be with the dull stones and the sterile earth
After the bitter climbing of forty-four years.

You who postponed the quiet amenities,
The lazy conversation after lunch,
The cigarette in mid-afternoon, the daydream
When a certain wind came to your window
Out of that young, beautiful sea, the Atlantic.

Night. Nighttime in the earth.
The body settles patiently into eternity.
Time moves, yes, but like glacial ice.
The tireless eyes stare out of the sky, answering nothing,
And the silence is august and terrible.

While we were lost in our petty commerce
Of coming and going (that day a barking dog annoyed us,
A buzzing insect, a lagging clock)
You suddenly left your house, your city and your country,
Traveling in the night, few knowing,
To fight with a dark archangel in a desert.

Already there is no one to call to.
The body of Edward is not Edward,
Nor the ashes of Gregory Gregory.
Alexander is no longer Alexander in the earth.

Nothing can be done but something can be said at least.

Sprig of Lilac

Their heads grown weary under the weight of Time—
These few hours on the hither side of silence—
The lilac sprigs bend on the bough to perish.

Though each for its own sake is beautiful,
In each is the greater, the remembered beauty,
Each is exemplar of its ancestors.

Within the flower of the present, uneasy in the wind,
Are the forms of those of the years behind the door.
Their faint aroma touches the edge of the mind.

And the living and the past give to one another.
There is no door between them. They pass freely
Out of themselves; becoming one another.

I see the lilac sprigs bending and withering.
Each year like Adonis they pass through the dumb-show of death,
Waxing and waning on the tree in the brain of a man.

Strange Diners at the Cafe Parnassus

The saddest thing I saw
Was not the war-brought sorrow
But at lonely tables,
Teeth at elbow,
With lips drawn back
Like Ugolino,
The mythmakers
Eating their own marrow.

"Sailor, reaper—
As once they did—
For a hundred years
Have brought no food.
Nor does manna fall now
From the orchards of God
For the mouths of the blest—
Or the damned.

"The brain starves.
The wit sickens.
And the visionary energy
Is darkened.
We have become
Sponges, blackguards;
And Love, our father,
A public cuckold.

"The fever out of hunger
Has brought the private illusion,
The hallucination,
And the convulsion,
The sly aside
And the crude explosion,
The needle, the gun,
And the leap into the ocean—

"While Goat giggles
And Cousin Ostrich:
'Do as others do
When you're in Carthage.
Don't dwindle: Adapt
To the prevalent pottage—
Wheels, nuts
And this shiny clockwork.'"

The Airman Who Flew Over Shakespeare's England

A nation of hayricks spotting the green solace
    Of grass,
And thrones of thatch ruling a yellow kingdom
    Of barley.

In the green lands, the white nation of sheep.
    And the woodlands,
Red, the delicate tribes of roebuck, doe
    And fawn.

A senate of steeples guarding the slaty and gabled
    Shires,
While aloof the elder houses hold a secret
    Sceptre.

To the north, a wall touching two stone-grey reaches
    Of water;
A circle of stones; then to the south, a chalk-white
    Stallion.

To the north, the wireless towers upon the cliff.
    Southward
The powerhouse, and monstrous constellations
    Of cities.

To the north, the pilgrims along the holy roads
    To Walsingham,
And southward, the road to Shottery, shining
    With daisies.

Over the castle of Warwick frightened birds
    Are fleeing,
And on the bridge, faces upturned to a roaring
    Falcon.

The Bass

To whom do the bass pay homage,
Leaping to break the dimness
Of the reedy, dawn-gray water?

I heard the rare message
From Sirius and Capella,
The Dog-Star and the Goat,

Whom I saw as I rode to this water
Over the empty streets
And the houses cold with dream.

They have paled into the sunlight
That whitens the upper air,
But they say still, "Come,

"We are the great fireflies,
Sweeter than soft minnows.
Take us before we fade."

And the shape with the whispering lure,
The dark shape with the net,
Draws them to that shore.

The Begetting of Cain

Longing at twilight the lovesick Adam saw
The belly of Eve upon the golden straw
Of Paradise, under the limb of the Tree.
He thought that none was near, but there were three
Who were upon the mortal grass that dusk,
Under the wispy cloud, breathing the musk
Of the young world. Creature of pointed ear,
Of the cleft-hoof and the tight-mouthed sneer,
The other passes, wound round within his thought.
And Adam in his mounting passion caught
The white shoulders of that woman there . . .
All were engulfed—these two, the birds of the air,
The burrowers of the earth, by the quenchless mind
Roaming insatiate on the lowland, blind
In its lonely hunger, lusting to make all things
One with itself. Brief as the flutter of wings
Was his mastery, though ranging through world and void
To the dusk-star shining. But all, all were destroyed:
The two on the odorous earth in the garden there;
The beasts, the birds in the nest, the fireflies in the air.

The Belated Birds Having Taken Their Leave

The belated birds having taken their leave, suppose
This instant or two of barely falling flakes,
Each of a certain splendor, the time of our stars.

While the marrowbones shake, consider
What shift of weather precipitated those,
And the walkers upon the grass where that snow sinks:

The glee on the upturned faces. Imagine
Arms raised on a hill to catch at Vega.
"That one I call Antares, and—"
                            "Why do you cry?"

"This snowflake died before I could give it a name."

The Camorra

They meet me at midday in implausible places;
They strike at me with their daggers and when I cry out
I am told there are no invisible highwaymen.

I say that even at noon in the public streets
Where crowds are chattering, fingers brush my throat
And a whisper reveals the conspirators are here.

O they plotted this before Adam was born,
To track us like hounds till we falter at last and fall
Though we laugh behind doors and wear clever disguises.

For they were not all thrown in the burning gulf.
There are those who remained behind and at convocations
Fawn at the Lord and mumble the words of Hosannas.

The Chinaman and the Florentine

This man for forty years studied a leaf;
This man, the scattered leaves of the universe.

This man lies in the earth at Ch'ang-hsi;
This, in a crypt at the crossroads in Ravenna.

The Devil with the Minus Sign in His Right Hand

As the unexpected world to an angel who slept
Through the seven crucial days is the sudden poem:

"See the abyss and the golden chain pendent,
And the yellow midges there circling the ether.

"Within those rings the radiant jewel alone—
Red, red, and the green richness within.

"But what black things wings from the lower quadrant?
See where he nears, breaking that timeless bliss!"

The Geese

A miscellaneous screaming that comes from nowhere
Raises the eyes at last to the moonward-flying
Squadron of wild-geese arcing the spatial cold.

Beyond the hunter's gun or the will's range
They press southward, toward the secret marshes
Where the appointed gunmen mark the crossing

Of flight and moment. There is no force stronger
(In the sweep of monomaniac passion, time)
Than the will toward destiny, which is death.

Value the intermediate splendor of birds.

The House of Gorya

In the house of Gorya, in risen Jericho,
Six dark men sat in heathen Hadrian's hour.
The servant who brought them the black loaf of bread
And the wine as meagre as Rabbi Hanania's face
Startled their talk of the slavish Empire
That stretched from Judea out to the great ocean.
Down in the streets the hungry dogs whined.
There were thin children crying in all the realms
Of Caesar the fat-faced god, while rich men sold
Themselves and their goods, and whored for pleasantry.
Couriers posted the roads with little fish
To tingle the stomach and make the wine taste sweeter.
In unknown myriads, slaves labored and died.
Wherever there was an idol of stone or thought
Gaily the worshippers came to bow and yield.
And the ruined temple greyed on the holy hill.
In Jericho, in a room bare and dark,
Where the lame Isaac brought them bread and wine:
"There is but one—" As Rabbi Hanania poised,
Bending so that his black beard was thrust
Like an omen over them, they heard a voice speak forth:
"There is but one in this generation of man
Bearing such worth that the spirit of God touches him.
But this age is unworthy of him." All turned as one
To where Hillel sat, as quiet as a boy
That listens to the memories of old men.

Like a chariot of the Roman conqueror,
The years have thundered across the vision of ages
Releasing the bronze and iron shapes from their prison.
Their rust thins through the sky. The horses become
Shadows, pressing silent hooves to the ground,
To the road sunken beneath the imperial grass.
In the long two millennia between
That dot of time and us, his name who sat
In the six, in Gorya's house that day, beats thin

In the veins of history as a sleeper's pulse.
O he is fortunate thus to remain in the shadow,
Where only the Talmudist dreaming thinks of him
That he was not thrown to the nations to be torn
Like a deer by dogs; to be sullied and shouted over.

There will arise, in the repletion of time,
In every age the chosen one, its saint,
Whom the later days will corrupt when the great minds,
The sharp imaginations that discovered him,
Perish, and the little spirits play with history.
In the epoch of great crimes and sanctimony;
The hour of the learned bigot, the well-groomed barbarian;
Of immense knowledge and the conscience dead;
The murderer who loves humanity; and the king
With a newer title, lording it in his halls;
The willing slaves, multifarious in their abasement;
The hungry children, the rich, worthy whoremasters—
In the time of unworthiness he will be hidden.

I seek that house in all the streets of the world
And the twilit room with the great fire burning.
I shall climb the stair at last and open the door.
There will be six men sitting there.
There will be talking among them, as among brothers.
Fragrant from the shadows the smoke of tobacco will rise.
And old or young, one will be recognizable
For his dignity, his knowledge and his suffering.
He will not know for what he has been chosen.
Perhaps his face will be Africa or Asia.
Perhaps in the sudden moment of recognition,
When all the faces turn as one upon him,
It will not be toward the master or the guest,
But to the lame servant waiting mute in the corner.

The Importance of Poetry, Or the Coming Forth from Eternity into Time

Beyond the image of the willow
There is a willow no man knows
Or watches with corruptible eyes.

Deep in a field where no man goes
Nor bird flies
The willow fronts an empty road.

The bird hovers in other skies:
World where only these wings exist.

And elsewhere, alone, upon an abyss,
The man is marching down a road.

As the rays of the sun are drawn together
By a curved glass and rekindled to fire
So, to the poppies life and death,
So does desire
Draw them and bend them and bind them so,
So the noise of the wings can at last be heard
And the willow-image do grace to a bird
And the host on the roadway give them word
Not for forever, only a day.

The King of Ai

They hanged the King of Ai at eventide
On a high tree at the gates of the gutted city,

And the smoke rose out of the ruck of the city
Where the fierce captains shouted at eventide.

Now on the tree the rope was heavy at eventide
Where the gods lay broken under the ash of the city.

He turned once more toward the ravished city
And the head swung slow toward the eventide.

Ah, the smell of blossoms at eventide
From the almond trees beyond the gates of the city:

But the tightened rope on the tree at the gates of the city
And the swaying shape in the air at eventide.

God, God, for the evil done at eventide
For the bloody knife and the torch on the doomed city,

And the girls who screamed on the sand by the gates of the city,
With the strange seed within them at eventide—

O God be merciful at eventide:
Remember him you condemned by the flaming city,

Where he lies under his cairn at the gates of the city,
And the vultures circle the sky at eventide.

The Last Fisherman

He will set his camp beside a cold lake
And when the great fish leap to his lure, shout high
To three crows battling a northern wind.

Now when the barren twilight closes its circle
Will fear the yearning ghosts come for his catch
And watch intently trees move in the dark.

Fear as the last fire cringes and sputters,
Heap the branches, strike the reluctant ashes,
Lie down restless, rise when the dawn grays.

Time runs out as the hook lashes the water
Day after day, and as the days wane
Wait still for the wonder.

The Marriage

On a certain night they dreamt of the silent nations,
The ghosts of the unborn.

Unclasped and separate, like effigies on a tomb,
They lay
Under the canopy of galactic eyes.

They rose and entered a dark ship.
They saw the snow falling on the plains and the mountains
And the ice clasping all in its arms.

The Milkman

The milkman walks with mysterious movements,
Translating will to energy—
To the crunch of his feet on crystalline water—
While the bad angels mutter.

A white ghost in an opaque body
Passing slowly over the snow,
And a telltale fume on the frozen air
To spite the princes of terror.

One night they will knock on the milkman's door,
Their boots crunch hard on the front-porch floor.
One-two, open the door.

You are the thief of the secret flame,
The forbidden bread, the terrible Name.
Return what is left; go back where you came.

One-two, the slam of a door.
A woman crying: Who is there?
And voices mumbling beyond the stair.

Is there a fume in the frozen sky
To spell that someone has been by,
Under the sun and over the snow?

The Miracle

Under the cliff of Betterton
A soldier bathing in the sun
In the mild waters of Betterton.

Into the waters of Betterton
When dusk was near he went alone
At the firing of the sunset gun.

A gull is crying across the bay
On that day and another day.
The soldier heard and hears that cry

To the running moment: *Stay! stay!*
Over the valley of Ajalon! ...
O and the one who cried was I.

War is done and that time is done,
But nothing changes at Betterton.
Much is lost but a strange thing won.

The Mythos of the Man from Enoch

Faintly against the stars,
From the northmost march to the Crab,
I see the undulant outlines
Of the vast, ameboid Spirit.

Foggy grains of fire
Light the tortuous paths
Within the hungry hands,
Brain, body and feet.

Time is already victim
And at only the farthest milestone
Is there space pure as water
Upon a delectable mountain.

I cannot reach those ranges.
Hours become a lifetime
As I linger at each crossroads
Waiting the blow on the cheek.

God is brutish life!
God is the living ether!
Within these strange entrails
We must build our beautiful houses.

The Mythos of Samuel Huntsman

If I should round the corner quickly—
Or suddenly turn my head—
I know I'd catch them preparing the scene,
Painting a tree or hanging the moon,
Arranging houses and streets exactly
In the desperate game which is God's.

For I have seen through their plausible lies—
That of a uniform world,
And cities existing beyond these hills,
Or on rain-wet pampas ferocious bulls,
A logic of morrow and yesterdays
Or real seeds under this field.

The surface is thin as a gilding of oil
Upon an enormous lake
Deep as infinity, void as a gas,
On which they plant the lying rose
To delude the sniffing child or the fool.
But me they cannot expect

To wink forever, never to turn
And look at their empty stage
Of space starless and planetless
Where they swarm to cover some nakedness,
A ravaged fruit tree perhaps, some sin
That calls to me to judge.

One question has to be wrestled down
Before I smash this façade:
Are they worlds, these other men, Thomas or Roger,
Like me, with their plague of conjurers
Or but lesser dolls in the scene of one
Who will deal alone with God?

The Old War

No one cared for the iron sparrow
That fell from the sky that quiet day
With no bird's voice, a mad beast's bellow.

Sparrow, your wing was a broken scar
As you blundered into the mother-barley.
Sparrow, how many men did you bear?

"Ten good men, pilot and gunner—
Trapped in the whirlpool, held by no hands,
Twisting from the truth with curse and prayer.

"Ten good men I bore I my belly—
Not as the mother-barley bears.
Ten good men I returned to her there."

> *Thunder rolling over the barley!*
> *Fire swarming high and higher!*

Home again to the barley-mother—
Ten good sons, pilot and gunner,
Radioman and bombardier.

The Priest Ekranath

                        I who am sanctified—
Having lain with the holy harlots at Askelon
On the roof of the great temple under her visage
Who graces with splendor the night in the god-filled sky:
Mother, rich-wombed mistress, whose thighs are forever
Rising and falling like the tides in the roadstead of Gath,
To strike with fear the arid and impotent damned
And assure the fruit of field and man and animal
With Adonis and her chosen, fortunate priests—
Must tell you of these barbarians from the mountains,
From the anarchic hills come to destroy us,
Recent siftings out of the east and south.

They call her the White One or the White Lady
But do not worship her nor any mother-goddess,

I have seen them on the high days in Askelon
When the harlots dance naked through the gala streets
For the joy of Adonis and the blessed thirst of the loins
Turn away angry, cursing these holy bodies,
Crying, "Let them be stoned and their evil wombs ripped up."
They hate delight. They have but a lone god
And he is their enemy. I met a certain one:
Sly as a jackal yet arrogant as a lion,
Rough-bearded, out of the desert, desperate
With his private phantoms, his eyes like an animal's
(Fearful, and darting here and there, yet ready
To spring and rend), his hair and garments filthy
With the rot of caves, his skin flayed red by scorpions.
Though his nights are writhings of fire, he will not clasp
The salvation of sweet flesh, but for sustenance
Communes with this impossible imageless demon,
Stuff of a barren race, who has tainted him
With a sickness I cannot fathom, an evil spirit
Like the guilt which dogs a murderer. So always
He looks behind him, before, and within himself,

And the voice he hears becomes this maniacal thundering
On our sunlit streets and before our gleaming temples,

What I saw in the eyes of this vagrant (one of a tribe
Cultureless, without iron, art, or altar)
Was the whole world made somber, and man lonely
In a proud empty heaven like a hell,
Estranged from the field and the beast and his own body
And kin to the mothering earth only in death.
I cannot break this knot, but I know he thought—
And I thought too in the wizardry of that moment—
Our sun washed cities despicable and meaningless,
Our splendid artistic productions abominable,
Our majestic pantheon foul as a kennel,
The harbor jostling with keen ships and mariners
From the farthest ocean, trivial as a sigh.
And joy unimportant too. The dignity of sorrow
Was the only blessing under the cloud of his god.

I say these are faces of stone no years can weather.
They scheme to take your ease. Listen, you nations:
They will lure you from your spontaneous ecstasies
And positive possessions, and with themselves,
Carry you forth on arduous pilgrimages
Whose only triumph can be a bitter knowledge
Out of the suffering they make our worth,
They see the desert in the growing leaf:
That is their sickness. The sky will be darker then;
The White Lady of splendid thighs and bosom
Without a seedsman or a harvester,
A pallid virgin; and the lands beneath
Dark with this god and people, I who am wise
Through the sacred harlots' embraces know the syllables
(Ah, they are powerful and barbarous!)
Of the secret incantation that gives them strength.
Hear how they thunder! Listen: *Issachar
Levi simon reuben judah dan
Zebulun asher naphtali menassah ephraim.*

The Premonition

Trying to imagine a poem of the future
I saw a nameless jewel lying
Lurid on a table of black velvet.

Light linked there like eyes half-lidded,
Raying the dark with signals,
Lunar, mineral, maddening

As that white night-flower herself,
And with her delusive chastity.

Then one said: "I am the poet of the damned.
My eyes are seared with the darkness that you willed me.
This jewel is my heart, which I no longer need."

The Zero That Is All

If these lesser things are subsumed within the Good—
These corrupt shapes: desk, mirror or tree—
The falsely transliterated, strangely planed
Creatures of eyesight and the sentient bones
(Themselves in the web of the spider), then all times
Are poses of the one actor, Time: he
Who is ape of eternity, and the acorn neglected among leaves
Encircles, now in this very heartbeat, a forest
Of oaks that have no horizon; and the still white egg
On the tablecloth in the hush of morning is turbulent
With the cackle of a universe of chickens;
And still it is hot noon on the sea Tethys
Where the protoplasmic slime begets Aphrodite
Whose belly is history till the moon falls
And the last spore flames like Andromeda.

Those Who Write After Freud

Though clarity
Is a form of sincerity,

And confusion
Of evasion,

With what dexterity
They run to obscurity,

Set up a maze
As a hiding place,

Become by choice
A mysterious voice,

Against the yell
Of the Hound of Hell!

But he is nearer
Than throat or ear.

He laughs within:
The original sin

That the learned Jew
Discovered anew

In the fabulous gulf
Of the self.

To Abraham Lincoln, That He Walk by Day

On the rich, florid hillsides of Alabama,
The Negro hovels lean, affronting the sun.
Bringer of the dogwood blossoms and the wild rose.
Father Abraham—they need you, Father Abraham!
There are still those in the hundred and sixtieth year
Of this majestic republic for whose sweet sake
Your men fell in the Wilderness and at Murfreesboro,
And you yourself to the mad assassin's bullet,
Who when they enter the house of the kind master
Must come to the back door, skulking like dogs.
O Father Abraham, let me spin you this brief story,
Since you loved stories and children and were always patient.
Do you remember pompous Stanton and Seward,
How they fumed and grunted at the chill cabinet meetings
When you dared to pause—with the Rebels so close you could feel
Old Stonewall's breath, or his teeth. on the back of your ear—
To tell the tale of some simple farmer or blacksmith?
Let me tell you then of a charwoman, Mr. President—
And one whose ancestors sat in the sun so much
She was born black; now with a trouble on her,
That her little son, though warned most solemnly
Would walk through the front door when he came to us.

For he would forget: it seems that he did not know
The importance of this in his training to be a man.
He won't forget for long, Father Abraham!
He will see soon that he must bend and cringe:
Be a jester and sing doleful songs;
We will expect him to smile, and steal a little
(Though not too much, for we make an example of those);
Accept old clothes and be deeply thankful for them;
Be shiftless, childlike, irresponsible;
Be condescended to, without pride, a good nigger;
And perhaps die young, ridden with consumption.

O Father Abraham, our sleep is quiet in this republic.
Not usually do we fret about hunger and epidemic.
But daily this enormous wrong multiplies:
That men are denied the gracious and simple thing
Which your country storekeeper, your lawyer of Springfield,
Bear with them always, the dignity of man.
Devious is the slavery, ugly. smug and hooded:

The occasional terror but the constant threat of terror.
Have you heard of the fashionable women speak of their servants?
Behind them stood a man with a rope. whip and gun.
Whom they would not acknowledge at the front, or the back door
    either.
O Father Abraham, you know how wrongs grow fat
On victim and doer, swallowing them both:
One is destroyed, the other corrupted and tainted.
The weary ages of injustice and brutality
Do not fade out like a flying spark in the smithy.
They burn deep and smolder till the full time
When all, guilty and innocent, are consumed.
For each man who is strung up, shot or castrated,
Do you not think we shall have to pay a debt?
For the daily callous rebuff, infinitely repeated
(At the Gulf, the Lakes, the eastern and western oceans)
To millions of men and women and their children,
Must not there be a time of remorse and agony?
For the man who said, "Some hemp must be stretched soon,"
And the man who retorted lamely, acting the coward,
Are we not already rotten? Is not the fruit falling already?
For the President, Senators, Judges and Congressmen,
And the citizens, and the clergymen asleep in hosannas to God,
Who forget, and do not see, and accept amiably,
While the stink of the evil is on highway, house and shop,
Will not this republic grieve in later days:
For whose sweet sake your men died in the Wilderness
And you took the road to the mad assassin's bullet?

To Pablo Picasso, on His *Guernica*

That black bull of yours, Pablo,
Proves that in Spain, Pablo,
God and the Devil are often hard to tell apart.
That is the Spanish problem, Pablo.

To My Daughter

Seventy-seven betrayers will stand by the road,
And those who love you will be few but stronger.

Seventy-seven betrayers, skillful and various,
But I do not fear them: they are unimportant.

You must learn soon, soon, that despite Judas
The great betrayals are impersonal

(Though many would be Judas, having the will
And the capacity, but few the courage).

You must learn soon, soon, that even love
Can be no shield against the abstract demons:

Tome, cold and fire, and the law of pain,
The law of things falling, and the law of forgetting.

The messengers, of faces and names known
Or of forms familiar, are innocent.

To the Predynastic Egyptian Who Rests Within the Entrance of the Metropolitan Museum

Lying with head hidden and a ragged arm
Covering the sockets of your eyes, you fend yourself
Against the world, the hell by the flooded river:
Look upon us! we are not those who hurt you,
But give you this tomb in a mausoleum of granite
Which even the King would have longed for, drawing the sweat
From your living flesh and your children's. The place of evil
Where you met the jackals and were thrown into the pit
Is not here, where the civilized people pass and whisper
On the long clean streets.
Your score is paid and the demons long since mollified.
O do not think there is darkness in our days.
Look upon us. We are not guilty, guilty.

To Those Who Look Out of the Window

To those who look out of the window at night
This passing moment, within the bounds of our city:
We are not many, standing in the dark by the window,
With the cool and starlit air brushing the face
And our eyes hungry for the light-givers,
The luminous ones, brightening the reaches of the sky.
Of them our neighbors, the thousands and thousands,
Under all the rooftrees in the obscure streets and alleys,
Let us not be reminiscent or piteous,
If, in the coils of the serpent sleep long since,
All unresisting they have become earthen.
—But feel the brush of the wind on the face, the bath
Of the light, the torment of beauty deep in the throat;
And strive, in secret, this brotherhood so small,
To climb the stairway out of the dust a moment
Before the lying down to sleep and the surrender.

Two Hearts and an Arrow

Deserted railroad sidings on Sunday
Adumbrate the rust of our future,
When the antiquarian will comment,
"No, they were not wholly detestable.

"Though the barbarians burned the libraries,
And the rocks are still radiant from their warring,
See, I have found in their more casual inscriptions
Hints of tenderness or only moderate hate."

Trio for Two Voices and a Woodwind

You for whom the waters of no spring are sweet:
Consider, in their respective empires, vegetal and animal,
Men and trees, bearer of the sceptre.

Laughing, our leafy Caesar might shrug,
"A pusillanimous cousin!" (as we would refer
To a ring-tailed monkey or an indiscreet baboon)—
Or, "an oversized, ambulatory mandrake,"
Or better, "a carrot, defective, cloven."

Man, however, must sooner or later lecture:
"A tree is a river system,
Continental, a lovely schema against a background
Of sky brightness and earth green and brownness:
Tiny dark runnels, myriad yet distinct, starting up there
      in the light,
Becoming rivulets, always traveling inward as if drawn
      by hunger,
Becoming brooks, creeks, tributary rivers,
And the one great river flowing into a planet.
The tree is the antecedent symbolism.
A man must always be part of the tree of the living;
A tree, of no man, of itself only.
What, tell me, feeds on pure air and energy?
And what, as in the beginning, on the bitter fruit of a tree?"

Excellently done, Professor.—
And you whose tears drip poison into the well:
No longer will you be restless when the belief they offer you—
As, under the very noses of the archangels,
The oldest story has secretly winked it—
Has a tree as its god or prophet.
The animals with nimble forefeet, hitherto the only voluble
      observers,

Have long been biased.
There are no bears, swans or heroes among the constellations—
Only, throughout all space, branches budded with fire,
From which, in an ether where never a wind shivers,
Sift and sink the burning flower-flakes of time
(Breathgiver, incendiary, refiner of the sorrowful metal
That rises, walks and sings like a man;
Whitener, when the flakes are ashes,
Of philosophical skulls in a valley.)

Useful Prepared Speech for the Diffident Author of a Book of Poems Costing Three Dollars and Fifty Cents

I claim that a pome
Is merely the poem
To the author's intending—
That beginning and ending
Are the *silence* begun
When the talking is done.
So why should I budge
If someone should grudge:
"These poems are costly."

They're golden mostly.

Winter, Never Mind Where

The illusion is one of flatness: the sky
Has no depth, is a sheet of tin
Upon which the blackened branches and twigs
Are corroded, burnt in
By a strong acid:

Hang there, outside the squares of pane—
Work of a gruff but extraordinary artist,
Who has done good things in pastels too,
In summer scenes, leaf-stuff
And the placid

Nuances of snow.
Since, as we know,
Genius is superior to praise or blame.
He will not mind if I suggest:
"Fewer cold subjects please (they do not please!).
Really, your leafy stuff, Sir, is best."

Death at *The Purple Rim* (excerpts)

This beast I killed lived under a stone wall,
And every day he came to sun himself
On the warm rocks, in the pleasant afternoon.
I worked in the garden, and the earth was rich,
Clinging to hoe and heel, as gold, alas,
Clung not to hand. And pausing, I looked
At the motionless elm and the hawk winging afar
In the sunlit air, and the butterfly's trembling wing
This was a little valley all to myself
In Connecticut's northern hills . . .
. . . .

                                           But you—
I see you entering life in a jaunty youth:
No Ben who chewed an undignified loaf on High Street
And tugged at his suitcase and heard a merciless wench
Laugh with white teeth from a doorway—a personage rather
The world bowed deeply to greet: whose resplendent doorman
Ushered you in with deference, called for a page
To relieve you of bag and bundle, and to the room clerk
Whispered that this was no passing fool—indeed
Was a noble and affluent scion of Venezuela,
Incognito, Don Antonio Pez y Mañana y Mosca,
Arrived to savor the sights: was a friend of the owner's;
Was to loll at the owner's expense in a spacious room
That faced the ocean, and have his drinks on the house.
And as you moved forward, the bellboys cleared you a path
With worshiping, callow eyes; and people whispered;
And a girl who sat there alone with long legs crossed,
And naked arms, and tresses of laughing yellow
Gave you that ancient look that only the young
Can thoroughly understand—nor was she aloof
When encountered later at leisure. So dreamt you away
The tedious early years, the wind in your face,
Blushlessly sipping the famed and the blushful claret,
The cool and strength-giving Collins, the sweet Manhattan;
Throwing a coin on the spinning wheel nor caring

Of win or loss; drawing on paper vain squares
And aimless configurations, nor thinking of time
Wasted or looming; fondling the yellow locks,
Nor thinking of old and lantern-jawed letters suggesting
Celestial disapprobation.
. . . .
Return then to your garden, your sweet labor.
But why are your shoulders heavy, what curse is upon you?
What holds you back? The garden smiles in the sunlight.
From its mound of sod the arms of the tiny beetle
Beckon you gaily on. What menace looms there?
Angels are figments and burning swords are but fables.
Why do you turn? O whither? Tell me! Tell me!
Why are your shoulders heavy? What ill lies upon you?

Horatio   *(excerpts)*

Prologue

It is fifty years since the Prince Hamlet died,
In the fateful duel, touched by the poisoned rapier,
With Claudius the King and the wretched woman:
Since I, finding no sleep that night in my chamber,
Went out on the platform where the guard stood—
Bernardo, my friend—staring down at the city.

"What ghosts could come tonight if they so wished!"
He said. "O good Horatio, nothing is answered us.
Look at the town so silent there below.
How well they sleep there, so unlike the unhappy
In the high tower that the thunderbolts of Christ
Can strike so easily. You are watching here;
And the new king lies upon his bed
With eyes open; and the new ghosts, trembling,
Pass from room to room of the strange house
Wondering at the dark corner, like children."

"Do you think," I asked, "that the Prince Hamlet trembles
When he opens a door there? I see him moving
With head erect, curious, sniffing the air
Like an eager hound, till he reach the last portal—
Where, it is true, he will pause, to let his mind
Thrust to the truth and grapple with it before
His hand rips back the curtain and he sees—"

"Himself!" Bernardo whispered, "dead at the arras,
Pierced with his own sword."

                 "What do you mean?"

"He died," Bernardo said, "willing that end,
Because the dungeon of life hemmed in his spirit:
A voyager, no coward cringing from life.
At last, after a sum of meaningless days,
He took up the gage, and now, the new ghost,
He finds that the first question answered is—self."

"Perhaps," I said, "that is the only secret
We will know on the glad day, my friend Bernardo,
When the hooded priest closes our eyes. And we—
You and I in a minute will comprehend
The whole of this incredible labyrinth
Of our mortal years and souls. But he was a king—
No, not of some narrow warren of lust and murder—
But as he, Hamlet, sensed it, of infinite space.
If self is the answer, we know then what our prince
Will be engaged in for eternity—"

A clock struck.

    "And you, Horatio,"
Bernardo broke the thought, "what will you do?"

"Fulfill a dead man's final wish—and then—"

The rumble of armored footsteps on the flags
Left unsaid what would not have been said.

The Ostler

To the sound of the strange hooves on the midnight cobbles,
By the inn at Weser, Richard the ostler came running.
The lantern, held high, made caverns of his eyes
And his gaping mouth.

    "Ha, have you heard the news?"

"Attend to my horse," I said. "What news, my friends?"

"From the court. Marry, but she was a bitch.
No, no, a ditch, in which merry Hamlet dabbled
When the mood caught him! I hear that he was lecherous
As my neighbor's seventy goats—but he's dead now,
And the King and Queen also."

    "Of what do you speak?"

"You come from the north, yet have not heard the news?
The witless Hamlet who murdered his father last year
Has poisoned the good King Claudius and the Queen
With some hellebore he poured in their ears as they slept—
That he got from a ghost he waylaid on a stair—
But the staunch nephew of Norway, Fortinbras,
Tipped up this fiend with a happy thrust of his rapier
And rules now as our King, for which God be blessed."

The lantern shook in his hand.

        "But consider," I said,
"I come from the court. I am Horatio

Who—"

"A pleasant lie! I know you. You're a scholar
Going to study Pluto and Harris Tuttle
At Wittenberg, I'll wager, with the other drunkards.
Horatio passed through our town this very week
(Though I did not see him)—a smooth and ample man,
The very mark of a courtier. Why, his sash
Was yellower than gold. He was the one
Who unmasked the wicked prince. He says that this Hamlet
Had him a bouncing doxy called Olivia
With whom he would play his game of double or nothing—
You know what I mean—we have a few such here
For your use, my master, and free of the pox I'll warrant—
If you have but a penny. Wait till I stable your horse
And I'll lead you to her. But tell me now, is it true
(If you came from the court, I mean) that when roaring mad
He would stick a straw in his nose and croak like a chicken
Wagging his head like this, or piss in the moat
From the upper windows, singing of Gog and Magog
(Two devils he played at dice with)? I have heard
He wore a pot for a hat and sometimes orated
To a fish or a dead man's bones or the empty air.
But tell me more of this madness."

                    I turned away
And took a few steps into the dark of the courtyard
And saw some stars, and retracing my footsteps went
Into the stable where the quiet-breathing horses
Buttressed the dark with a greater gloom—the lantern
Was dim in the corner.

            "You will learn soon," I began,

"All this you tell me is lies—" and paused, remembering
The friendly, beloved voice telling Horatio—
None other—to guard the hurt honor and name.
"Believe me," I cried, "I am Horatio,
Friend of the dear Prince Hamlet—"

                        "How dear, when he murdered
His own father?"

        I explained it patiently:
"That crime his uncle, later King Claudius,
Committed by pouring poison in his ear
As he slept—"

        "But that's how the cunning Hamlet killed
The King and Queen—by poison—"

                    "He did not kill them—"

(I was still civil, for truth was my sole mistress.)
"He stabbed the King—"

                ("Ha!")

                "—as the murderer
Of his father."

        "Simpler and simpler," he said. "And the Queen?"

"She died of poison—"

                "Poured in her ear by her son?"

"No! drunk by her and brewed by the King himself!"

I shook my head.

   He closed in briskly:
"To kill his wife?"

    "No, to poison Hamlet
If the tainted rapier did not work."

     "What rapier?"

"The one," I said, mouthing it through my teeth,
"That young Laertes wielded in the duel
With Hamlet."

    "What duel, and who was this Laertes?"

"Son of Polonius the Councillor!"

"I've got you there! His name was Rosencrantz."

"Rosencrantz—" I remarked, breathing heavily,
"Rosencrantz was a student friend of Hamlet's."

His eyes gleamed like a devil's as he whipped back:
"Ah, you are wrong, but that was Guildenstern!—
And tell me, how if Laertes wielded the rapier
Did Hamlet stab the King with it?"

     "In fighting
They changed their weapons—"

      "Was this Laertes mad
As the Lord Hamlet was? And tell me, pray,
Why should the King, as you say, will ill of Hamlet
To murder him?"

    "Because the Prince discovered
That Claudius had killed the old King Hamlet . . ."

Once more I paused, weighing again a retreat
From this unworthy foe and battlefield.
But a vow made at the sanctified hour of death
Is a stubborn metal—and I said quietly:
"Listen to me, I am Horatio,
Friend of the most gentle, honest prince
The world has seen, young Hamlet. Once at midnight
He met the ghost who called for him—"

                        "The ghost
He snatched the poison from upon the stairs?"

"The ghost of his father, who told him how this Claudius
Had poisoned him to get his throne and queen.
He asked revenge—"

                        "Then Hamlet killed the King?"

"No, not then, uncertain if this ghost
Were real or not and if he spoke the truth
(And baited by a subtler qualm or two).
But when the King grew pale during the play
And mumbled his repentance in his prayers,
He was assured that this was brother Cain—

"For this he judged him guilty? My face is pale
From listening to you here. Am I a murderer?

And I say my prayers too. Soon you'll declare
The whore Olivia who sang foul songs
In the whole castle's ears was never ploughed,
And Hamlet not a madman but philosopher—
Like your Pluto and Harry Tuttle.... And hold a moment!
Did not your Hamlet kill kind old Polonius?"

"By accident. He thought he was a rat."

"Get out, or I might think you one tonight.
And sleep alone. You'll have no wench from me."

The Book of Metamorphoses

If, long since, our shepherd's tale had become
A crazy piper's tune, what shall I say
Of the words that issued now from that old mouth?
A dark dimension suffuses the time and place,
And much besides that puzzles the questioner.

Voices were urging: "The riddles! Give us the riddles!"

And he, bold, down his long and rheumy nose:

Who is the wielder of Fang's sword in the sea?

Who is the spying fox in the fox's den?

Who is the unknown wolf, the beaked voyager,
The limping weasel, the beast on padded feet?

Who is this who comes as a wanderer
To the shepherd's fire or far to Rome City?

Who is the tree felled by the woodchopper?

Who is the victim—wolf and lamb and deer?

Who is the digger, digging over the world?

Who is the gnasher of teeth on the sea shore?

Who is this who flees from the house of God?

To each of these riddling questions the hoarse answer
From the rest of the crew was "Ambleth!" "Ambleth!"
                                        Then:
"Sing of the changes, old one!"
                        And the teller,

Tremulous, lord of a strange echo:
"I sing of the changes of Ambleth as the sun dies,
As the moon grows old, as the fever of high summer
Crisps the grass, as the sparrows flying southward
Are touched by the odor of time like a beaked bird
Overtaking them, and they fall like blasted leaves."

The Virgilian sigh sank in the rude throat.
A pause, and the bell of a boy's voice asking:
"Will you not let me help you, father?"

                                                        "Aye!"

The old man first, the younger chiming in antiphon:

"Now he moves carefully in the seas' depths
With the Sword of Fang tightly gripped in his hand
While the frightened fish maneuver beyond his reach."

        "Now Ambleth the fox comes to the foxes' den,
        Knocks at the door sobbing, asks for entrance.
        'I was chased by the hunters' dogs yesterday,
        Escaped, have lost my way. Let me come in.'
        Resting deep in the burrow, he looks around
        Through half-closed eyes, or cautiously sniffs the air,
        Or rising, circles room, and carelessly peers"
        Into the black and the branching tunnels beyond.

"Now at the edge of a restless wolf pack in Thule
Wolf Ambleth mingles with the company.
'You haven't seen me before? Through the indulgence
Of your noble king, I joined you yesterday
Before he struck at the herd of antelope
One licks his chops still over that feast.
Nothing could be more sweet, except perhaps—'
And he watches closely the expression of the other—
'Some *humble* meat fit for a delicate *fang*.'"

"Now a beaked voyager he hunts the mountains
Of Germany. to find a remote cousin,
A miser, he says, who rarely stirs from his eyrie,
As if he guarded some precious, new-killed game."

"Now to the wood a limping weasel comes
Seeking a home, being too weak to dig.
'Is there some den, tell me, in this neighborhood
Left empty, where I may rest till my paw heals?'"

"Now he looks at night with gleaming eyes
And wanders with padding feet, beyond the fires
Of Europe and Asia, and the deserts of Africa,
And the barbarous cries in the nameless forests of
    Vinland."

"Who comes now in the guise of a wanderer,
At the time of dusk, to the shepherds' campfire?"

"Now a northerner enters Rome City
To visit the catacombs where the martyrs are buried
And inspect the niches behind the mounded skulls."

"Now for a little while in a little field
The dogs and crickets that live in the nerves of the grass
Whisper and ask, ask and whisper, sending
A delicate message, like a slow ripple in water,
Beyond their border: 'When? Where? Tell us.'"

"But the wolf pack turns on the wolf in the hills of Scythia.
Beaks suddenly rip at the beak on the cliff.
The long-necked thieves murder the long-necked spy
As he sits at ease after dinner, smacking his lips.

"Now three foxes follow Ambleth the fox
Like hounds, though silent, over hill and brake.
His tongue lolls as the chase narrows. He doubles
And crosses water. When skirting the edge of a farmyard
He pants alarm to his ancient enemies

Whom he can outwit, he knows, as often before,
If they will but loosen the foul grip on his shadow.
Ah, on a sorrowful hilltop he turns at bay
To the red mouths circling and closing in."

    "Now the lamb steals softly out of the fold
    To lure the wolf, while the leaves of the beech rustle.
    The rabbit is taking a promenade in the wood,
    Whistling a tune, while the oak listens and waits.
    A deer goes down to the water and drinks too long
    While the fir tree nods. And a wicked woodcutter
    Comes and fells the fir. But a snake lunges
    Out of a bush, biting deep in his heel.
    A hawk fastens the head of the snake to the ground.

"Digging, digging. He digs a mine, a well,
The foundation of a house, a city of houses,
And graves, graves, the earth probed with a pick.
War makes many and the black plague more.
He poisons the water and invites the kings to battle.
Now a city is burnt, the foundation lies open.
The sea lays open the secrets of the cliff—"

    "He gnashes his teeth on the shore—

                                   The foam rises
In the mouth of Fox Ambleth as he jumps to his feet
To murder his neighbor's cub. The limping weasel
Forsakes his supper to stalk and crush the butterfly
That idles over his camp. And the wolf halloos:
'Fellows, I know where a forester's child lies sleeping!'
Now smoke is vomited out of the mouth of the mountains.
The earth rumbles and shakes and the river suddenly
Rises to flood, and a loosened star hisses
Down from the sky . . ."

The Seventh Avenue Express

Argument

*In a finite, involuted world, the world of the
here and now, are imprisoned men confronted by glimmerings
of the not-here and bearing in their eyes the knowledge
of the not-now. It is a tunneled world they live in, and
both sound and thought, matter and aspiration, are driven
back upon themselves; they cannot escape and are frustrated.
Here men stand with their hands, upraised—not
in adoration of the gods but to protect themselves from
the material forces which would undo them. In their very
resistance they are degraded. But in their resistance,
too, they are noble, for there are others sitting and
standing beside them that are already too brutalized to
resist; time and the forces of nature move by them without
meaning: stolidly they sit in the earth, symbols of
the destroyed and the destroying. On the streets they
are not seen, in the sunlight; only here, in the accursed
earth do they congregate—evil memories and fore
bodings that would be forgotten by the others, the real,
who though harried by hunger and the obduracy of their
surroundings, still are staunch, still hold up their
hands in defiance.*

  *What do we do, we men.? We read the stories of
ourselves, but our thoughts are on something outside
ourselves, something to be possessed and which will
give us forgetfulness. Fer always our comrade death
Is implicit, hinting his betrayal. Ever to each he
turns some facet of his darkness. One will die, and
tonight. Another, in woman's compassion and in beauty,
Knowing death as an ultimate hatefulness, will meanwhile
spun it by struggling against the lesser. Another
is the self-killer, whose hand the involuted
world has driven back into his skull. Another is a
woman mourning– after her child's death and thus her
own; of this there is no philosophy. Another already
lies in the grave, but is in our company. Another is*

the watcher, knowing death with the knowledge of all.
His mind too is driven back into its caverns by the
walls of the repellant universe; and he sees that
this which confounds us is as breath in the nostrils,
not a severed ill but parcel of this lost road of
time on which we move, this tunnel we follow astray.
And distantly, he sees, the world and the moment go
by us, and the sun sinks into a west unfathomed.
This is the world-city he speaks of, and the road of
the universe.

I
In a world finite but Euclidean,
Over parallel lines that never meet-
Twin bands of steel, luminous under the lamps-
The Seventh Avenue Express runs swift
And rhythmless, its windows throwing pale
And fretful cubes of light on tunnel walls.
This world is finite, curved into itself.
Like snakes the humps of sound lash out, retreat
From wall and stanchion, thud on flesh—the clash
Of wheels on rails, the throb of motors like
A heart, the agonizing gasp of brakes,
And axles' shriek, and voices' murmuring.
For here in the Earth, here in the home of worms,
Voices are prisoned, speak with urgency
From mouths that sag in weariness.

*

Their hands uplifted (fingers clenched on straps),
Not in salute to dictator or king,
Uneasily and million figures sway.
And this is the sign by which we shall be known:
The clenched hand raised aloft and not in prayer
Or execration of God; but only to hold
The body as the machine throws it aside.
Until this city is the haunt of wolves,
The skyline rounded like the sunken teeth

Of an old man, the buildings tumuli
Of rust beneath the newborn; blazing stars,
No hour of the day or night will pass
Without these clenched hands raised beneath the earth
And not in prayer or execration of God.

*

The sun is waning in an unseen West
The hour is seven; the red and green lights pass.
The tunnel's roof sinks down until the sky
Becomes a morning legend: Jew and Slav,
Saxon and Roman hold their place; they move
Their jawbones with deliberation, cheeks
Tightened and loosened over resin drained
From the trees of jungles; eyes restless, seeking
An unfound focus; bodies compressed, unloved
Yet touching each other, yielding yet unyielding.

II
Among them are those things that mimic men . . .
The lost are here. The eyes are quicksands that take
And do not give; bury without a trace;
Accept without protest; destroy without
Remorse, implacably, the beautiful,
The foul, the generous, the pitiful,
The strong, the shaking masonry, the clash
And howl of whirling iron, and the lights,
Purple and red and spectral, the shuddering
And clamor of voices, the scoriae of thoughts.
(How like brute mouths these faces swallow the world!
Drink without thirsting! Ingest without hungering!)

*

The immediacy of Time is not for them;
That is for us who grasp the day and night.
For them there are no years, no hateful powers
To stand against, or, in the pulsing heart,
Raise pity. Yet in the caverns of the brain
The gaunt beasts paw the rack and kill and feed

Unsated upon the carcass of the world
That festers there, within each gaping skull--
For· what they see they kill. That is their doom . . .
And here in the earth, this strange cosmopolis,
They sit with body bent, dejected; eyes
Filming the light but neither thought nor passion;
And fingers inert and jaw seeking the chest.

*

They spurn the ostracism of the dust.
Bestial and arrogant, they resurrect
Nations that death has outlawed, Mayan, men
Of Mu, the savage-mouthed, the oval-faced,
The pendant-eared. Impossibilities
And ghosts are palpable before us; dreams
Confront us; monsters from stele and monolith
Stand in our midst, posturing, with rigid limbs.

III
On the streets of the city, the lines of an intricate crystal,
Symmetric, yet bearing asymmetry's faltering imprint--
The stigma of hands, of wavering flesh the creator–
On a stony, repellant expanse, the face of a crystal,
The flesh-wrought faces of men are moving, rejected.
On a crystal's glittering surface restless they wander:
The Negro and Slav, the Mongol and Saxon together,
The Jew with his hunted eyes and the Magyar hunter,
The Negro and Slav, the Mongol and Saxon, hunting.
Never the naked earth, but the stone below them.
Around them the pitiless stone they have raised for their dwelling.
They sought a refuge from nakedness; found them a prison.
And they cannot escape. From their houses the infinite windows,
Range upon range, the eyes confound them with blindness.
And the doors delude them, lead nowhere, lead inward and inward.
Wherever they tum, the stone interposes, betrays them.
Upon them its wound and within· them its mark of estrangement--
Wherever they turn, the stone interposes, betrays them.

*

Cn the streets of the city, the lines of an intricate crystal,
Geometric, farflung, and gleaming in darkness; by nighttime
A flaming tiara set on the forehead of rivers;
Many faceted, glowing with strange and ominous power;-
(Have you seen the bridges alight in the yielding darkness?)
By day a lair of shadow, dull and metallic.
There lave I walked and seen by sun and by lamplight
The faces of men. I have seen the faces of hunters.
Ql a crystal's glittering surface restless they wander:
The Negro and Slav, the Mongol and Saxon together,
The Jew with his hunted eyes and the Magyar hunter,
The Negro and Slav, the Mongol and Saxon, hunting,

Never the naked earth, but the stone below them.
Below them the treacherous stone they have mastered, their
    master.
What roots can they sink in this ground? What sustenance
    gather?
This is their homeland; they move distraught and impatient.
The mouth turns downward; the eyes speak the language of
    hunger.
What roots can they sink in this ground? What sustenance
    gather?
But where are the strangers who sit in the tunneled darkness?
The mimics of men? Of earth forever the outlawed?
I have not seen them above on the streets of the city.
Do they only exist as parts of their tunneled darkness?
Much have I wandered by sun and lamplight, nor ever
Have seen these masks of the dead, these putty faces,
These shapes degraded, these insolent, craven figures.
Do they only exist as parts of their tunneled darkness?
The passive shadows completing a page of twilight?
Fragments of this the hell, the nightland we pass through?
Or are they men like ourselves, the men of the city,
The distrait, the impatient, the fevered with infinite longing,
Who enter beside them, who sit in the tunneled darkness
With mouth turned downward and eyes aglitter with hunger?
(O see how their fingers wove forever unquiet:
The day they grasp, and the night: the skirts of a phantom.)

IV
They read the annals of their fellowmen
In cities, in the air, under the sea.
The annals of their fellowmen they read:
How someone killed his wife, and someone raped
His grandmother, and one begot quintuplets.
They see the picture of a chorus girl–
And in their eyes the look that Moses hand,
Seeing the rich and hoped-for earth afar–
To be or to possess: their hungering.
They read the words their prophets speak to them.
The good! the great! the beautiful! the true!
Whose memory shall outlast by far this age!
Men of the flaming word! the flaming sword!
King Arthur Brisbane, aye, and Walter Winchell!
They who have tapped the thin, elusive wire
That leads directly to the mind of God!
King Arthur Brisbane, aye, and Walter Winchell!

*

In the far era of the setting sun,
When this our city is the haunt of wolves—
The skyline rounded like a young girl's breasts—
And campfires bum along the Battery;
And frogs croak out their loving song where once
The suave, tophatted gentlemen made love;
And Al Smith and the tower that he built
Are food for speculation—vermiform
And archaeological—their memory shall remain:
King Arthur Brisbane, aye, and Walter Winchell.

*

And were I the Lord Jehovah or one of these—
Say, were I God omnipotent or Walter
Winchell his prophet, foreknowing things unknown,
Unrealized, within the womb the seed
Of manchild, action, stroke of statesmanship,
Then would I know that this man dies tonight—
The man with the green tie and flabby face—
He does not know that he shall die tonight.

He scratches the stubble on his chin, and lifts
His eyes, and sees with half-awakened lust
A red gash of lips, a curve of breasts,
A girl, a naked triangle of throat.
He does not know that he shall die tonight.
He shall descend at Forty-second Street,
Turn to the left, climb weary stairs until
His lungs are breathless as an unprimed pump;
See lights flare forth and neon bulbs brand deep
His retinas, and feel his knuckles brush
The skirts of someone he shall never know;
Smell sweat, perfume, and carbon gas, and sense
The cold wind blowing down the avenues,
And hear the honk of home like vagrant geese—
(He does not know that he shall die tonight)—
Turn left, and walk through tumult till an arm
Seizes his shoulder and a hand grips his;
And milky eyes look down on him and say
He must remember Thursday night to come
When they shall drink and banquet and discuss
The villainy of those who govern them . . .
Will he be there? He smiles complacently.
Of course he will be there. Of course. Of course.
(He does not know that he shall die tonight).
He walks, and on the edges of the sky
Sees moving words of fire threaten him
With baldness, boredom, evils great and small.
He stands upon the curb impatiently.
He has no time. No time. No time, he thinks.
In doom he walks among his fellowmen,
Enters a portal and a final door.
His heart grows clamorous; he sees in pain
The segment of a tower like a knife
Beyond a curtained window in the night.

V
Slim as the fuselage of the far-off plane
That pits its beauty against the yellow cloud,
In the luster of afternoon, in the fair sun,
In the cool vapors of the shining sky,
Her body rests; but here, in the earth, but here
In the home of dreams: and her arms like the wings far-off
She reads the book of Kant, and sees a world
Of noumena, phenomena, and forms;
And lifts her eyes and sees a world of pain.
And questions: are they congruent these worlds?
And shuts the book and in the world of pain
She walks, and sees the hunger in men's eyes;
And knows there are no patterns of the mind,
No metaphysics to limn hunger's face . . .
She yields her to the tyranny of years.
She knows she will grow old, that she will die
In some yet unborn day, as others died
(As she has read about or heard) in days
With them a myth. That is an inference
That cannot be eluded, though the mind
Be quick--be quick as little Mignon's feet . . .
Of little Mignon's dancing feet she thinks,
And thinks of death, that it should come to her.
That it should come to her, passes belief . . .
Perhaps, if she will die, she is a dream.
She is a dream perhaps, surely a dream
Within the dream the world makes in her eyes.
For there between her and the world of pain-
Between her and the piteous land she saw--
A sudden veil has fallen, and like snow
The fields of peace and silence compass her.
And she with them is comrade, she, a dream . . .
How grave the dark eyes' wonder and the smile!
How grave, with dark eyes wondering, she turns
And feels the solid arm beneath her coat
To reassure herself she is no dream.
She is no dream; she will grow old and die . . .
She yields her to the tyranny of time;

Foresees her doom and ours and gives consent.
Gravely she bows her head—but shall she yield
To tyrants who themselves with us are slaves?
The mascara and the boresome look, the yawn,
The stilted glance, the mask, cannot delete
The mark the whip has made on every face.
She sees with anger where the whip has lain.

She is impatient at the urgent wrongs.
She knows her sons will fight them days to come—
As she herself this day and other days—
As she herself this day, and other days.
(The dark eyes' wonder and the dark eyes' woe!)

She walks through open doors; under tall trees.
She sees a planet on the verge of heaven.
She smooths her forehead where a wayward curl
Disturbs the order of the universe.
She sees a spire and a distant glow . . .
That day she saw a boy with roving eyes.
The bridges alight she saw in the spectral dusk.
At noon she saw a child under the El.
That hung fantastic across a dusty street,
A drowsy daddy-longlegs in the sun . . .
She leaves the universe outside, and shuts
The door. Over a desk she bends her head.
Her fingers move with nervous pace; she draws
The picture of a child under the El.
And weaves herself a web of dream, and then
Within the web she is herself enmeshed.

VI

One stands by the ocean of madness. Perceptibly
The water eats the shore. And hands claw up
To reach him. Arms stretch forth. Green faces swell
Out of the mist, a mob crying the kill.

He nears the outposts of madness, and he sees
Strange sentries beckon him. He hears them call
In a soft language that he vaguely knows.
Is this the foe he feared? He has been tricked,
He thinks. These are his friends that call to him . . .
The shells scream in the sky, The Very lights
Delineate a darkened land. The din
Of the lost battle whips his memory.
Has he betrayed himself? He holds his skull
Within two hands, and turns, and stumbles back.
Again the tunneled world. He hears the clash
Of wheels on rails, the throb of motors like
A heart, the agonizing gasp of brakes,
And axles' shriek and voices' murmuring.
This world is finite, curved into itself,
Outside there is no faring—and within
A spiral winds into the heart of Naught.
His clenched fist beats his forehead and drops down
Limply. once more the rout of hope. Well,
Today and tomorrow he shall compromise
With these the indignities, the goading wrongs,
The griefs. But next day she shall climb the stair
Slowly, and shut the door slowly, and put
A bullet in his brain.

VII
Ishtar was naked once, but she was a goddess.
She can strip off her clothes and still be clothed.
Though she be clothed she is naked, naked.
She is no goddess. She is Eve the woman . . .
She remembers the rude hands to her breasts, remembers.
Remembers the field. Remembers the cry. Remembers
The pain, remembers. She remembers the darkened room.
She remembers a child in the darkened room, remembers.
And over mascaraed, tired eyes she draws
A small gloved hand—a small gloved hand she draws.

VIII

In a Jamaica churchyard near the El,
That shakes the bodies of the quick and dead—
Daylong the rushing trains frighten the earth—
On crumbling brownstone written saw I this:

>Here
>Of N
>Peter
>Januar
>So sev
>O cruel

O cruel the enigma that wrestles with the brain,
Not angel in darkness but devil day and night.
This is not whim: the inscrutability
To questioning that the earth confronts us with.
There is a crevice where the climber thinks
The peak will bare to him truth manifest.
On the talus of a cliff he will lie quenched.

Of Peter, oh, what can be said? what written?
What, in obliquity of speech, expressed
To fit within the table of right and wrong?
Even the words are lost that bounded him . . .
In the cosmopolis, the city, all are unknown;
All are anonymous, both, living and dead;
Living and dead, both are anonymous:

And pass with turned-up cloak that hides the face
Through dark and the rapacious wind of Time.

IX

He sits in a corner lest the world surround him,
And sees with pity men outflanked by fate---
Hunters at bay--and thinks that he has heard
They are the victims of their masters' sins—
They are the victims of their masters' sins.

                          *

He thinks he knows them but he knows them not.
He does not know himself, nor does he know
Her he embraced, or who has heard his voice
Over the table and the pungent smoke.
He calls a name and knows not whom he calls.
He seeks himself by strange and devious ways:
By night on windy platforms, and by day
On streets where he the seeker and himself
Are lost. An opened door is mystery.
A cloud surrounds him as he mounts the stair.
He sits within four walls, watching a clock.
He fears the ticking clock; would see himself
A brain and heart unburdened by viscera.
He sits within four walls and holds his skull
In his two hands; and thinks how from each skull
A world is haloed forth, to clash, and pass
Each other world in silence in the dark.
He watches mystified before a glass
The image of the shell he occupies.
He sits within four walls and watches a clock.

He seeks the meaning of the growing grass,
The withering leaf, the soft arms he knew.

(And here in the earth, here in this tunneled world,
This strange cosmopolis, munchers of meat
Sit stolidly, at rest, their fangs at rest.)
He seeks the meaning of the luminous plain
He saw in a dream as the island where men live.
(And Protoanthropos stalks through the swaying cars.
His head just forward and his knees are bent.
A bestial leer looks through his half-closed eyes.
His long hands hang beside him and he hawks
The tragic annals of his fellowmen—
Murder and death, murder and perfidy.)
He searches the faces for the clue to life,
As severed into selves such as himself,
That he might know what being bears his name.

(And sees the dormant eyes, expressionless
As the clicking shutter of a camera.
With unconcern are raised the naked masks,
The wrinkled tarpaulins of flesh stretched out
On skulls; the grimaces, stony, yellow there,
Blunt as the chisel of hunger that carved them out;
The nets of blood shrunken like dying streams;
Faces that flee the light—the lost, the lost.
The phototropic faces of the damned.)
He sees how men are confounded by the past—
The intricate ear, the simian jowl, the nostrils—
Their forebears that ever mock them through their eyes.
(The lost are here. The eyes are blotters that write
Unwittingly imperfect images,
Caricatures, impudent blasphemies
Of the precise geometry of light
And line in a coherent universe.
Impress without expression; without hate
Mar and degrade; volition, write deceit;
Or malice, blur the naked knifelike lines
That plot a world from chaos; breach the dikes
Guarding an island of reason against the sea.
What the exact world brings to them they take,
Invert, disperse, distort, corrupt, betray.
How like brute mouths these faces follow the world!
Drink without thirsting! Ingest without hungering!)

He seeks the meaning of the growing grass,
The withering leaf, the soft arms he knew.

X
It was April once and at the city's end.
And thin as a glowing filament of wire
Shortly after sundown rose the moon—
A crescent poised above the bones of trees
Awaiting resurrection in that Spring.
And in the west the planet Venus rose
Near the horizon, so in that darkening sky

We formed a triangle in empty space—
There was a pattern poised above the earth...
And underneath, the others held their course,
Bewildered, errant as a drunkard's step:
The man with the green tie and flabby face!
Peter!
The man with the spats!
The woman in gray!
The boy with the roving eyes!
Ishtar! Ishtar!
The girl with the naked triangle of throat.

*

In what configuration do they move?
Under what cloud, O under what reproach?
What is their course? What path does Peter take,
He who is dead and he who dies tonight?
Have those two lines converged at last for one?

As blood moves in the veins, so do they move.
There is a world outside, but that is death.
Their world is finite, curved into itself.
Their world is finite, they indefinite...
As blood flows in the veins, so do they flow,
In the same channels forever, day in and out.
We walk a path that has been walked before
And think we forge a new road into Time.
Outside there is no faring for us; and
Within there is no path—no path but this
The spiral, winding to the heart of Naught.
Can we transliterate into our speech,
Our tongue of darkness, the language of the sun?
Our eyes probe upward, outward, inward—probe,
Asking the how of how, the why of why,
The what of what—until the burdened mind
Reels like a dizzy rat upon a turntable,
The silly subject for experiment.

XI
We wander in an alleyway of Time,
And faintly in the distance hear the drum
Of traffic on the highway—on the road
Untaken by our sires. In the streets,
Gaunt houses front us, chill our blood; the cries
Of hunger harrow us. And prostitutes
Beckon to sordid entrances. And eyes
As furtive as a thief's hands covet us,
Upon the Earth, the ancient slaughterhouse.

All things are unfulfilled here, passions lurk.
Thoughts are velleities and words are thoughts.
The forest crouches underneath the streets,
Biding its time here, even on Broadway.
This is the past we pass through, not the present.
Into the past we wander, the present is elsewhere.

Contributors

Victoria Aarons holds the position of O. R. and Eva Mitchell Distinguished Professor of Literature in the English Department at Trinity University in San Antonio, where she teaches courses on American Jewish and Holocaust literatures. She is the author or editor of thirteen books, including, most recently *The New Jewish American Literary Studies* (2019); *Holocaust Graphic Narratives: Generation, Trauma, and Memory* (2020); *The Palgrave Handbook of Holocaust Literature and Culture* (2020); and *Memory Spaces: Visualizing Identity in Jewish Women's Graphic Narratives* (2023), which received the 2024 Jordan Schnitzer Award in Jews and the Arts. She serves as judge for the Edward Lewis Wallant Award and is on the editorial board of *Philip Roth Studies, Studies in American Jewish Literature, Partial Answers,* and *Women in Judaism*. Aarons is series editor for Lexington Studies in Jewish Literature.

Kristin Boudreau is a scholar of US literature and culture, engineering education, and critical university studies. She teaches poetry for the Clemente Course in the Humanities and is professor of English at Worcester Polytechnic Institute, where she helped to implement a new tenure track for teaching faculty.

Jenny Browne is professor of English and creative writing at Trinity University. Her most recent collection is *Fellow Travelers: New and Selected Poems*, from TCU Press. A former James Michener Fellow at the University of Texas, she has received the Cecil Hemley Memorial Award from the Poetry Society of America, a National Endowment for the Arts Fellowship in Poetry and two Literature Fellowships from the Texas Writers League. Her poems and essays have appeared widely, most recently in *American Poetry Review, Bennington Review, Copper Nickel, Oxford American,* the *Nation,* and the *New York Times*. She served concurrent terms as the 2016–2018 City of San Antonio Poet Laureate, and the 2017–2018 State of Texas Poet Laureate. In 2020 she was the Distinguished Fulbright Scholar in Creative Writing at Seamus Heaney Centre at Queens University, Belfast, Northern Ireland.

Edward Brunner is professor emeritus at Southern Illinois University, Carbondale. His published books include studies of Hart Crane with an emphasis on *The Bridge*, W. S. Merwin's career from 1945 to 1988, and Cold War poetry (apart from the "fifties poem"). Individual essays in various journals and book chapters examine the poetics of the hoax, the extended sequence in American poetry from 1990 to the present as public art, and newspaper comic strips from 1930 to 1955 aimed at an adult readership.

Hilene Flanzbaum is the editor and contributor to three essay collections: *The Americanization of the Holocaust*; *The Holocaust across Borders*; and *Jewish Women in Popular Culture*. She was also the managing editor of *Jewish American Literature: A Norton Anthology*. Her literary criticism, creative nonfiction, and poetry have appeared in *Ploughshares*, the *Massachusetts Review*, *Tikkun*, *O!*, the *Yale Journal of Criticism*, and many others.

Sandor Goodhart is professor emeritus of English and Jewish studies at Purdue University in the Department of English. He directed the religious studies program (2018–2020), the classical studies program (2007–2011), the philosophy and literature program (2005) and the Jewish studies program (1997–2002). He is the author of seven books on literature, philosophy, and Jewish studies, among them *Of Levinas and Shakespeare: "To See Another Thus"* (2018; co-edited with Moshe Gold), *Möbian Nights: Reading Literature and Darkness* (2017), *The Prophetic Law: Essays in Judaism, Girardianism, Literary Studies, and the Ethical* (2014), *Sacrifice, Scripture, and Substitution: Readings in Ancient Judaism and Christianity* (2011; co-edited with Ann Astell), and *Sacrificing Commentary: Reading the End of Literature* (1996). He served as guest editor for a special issue of *Shofar* 26, no. 4 (Summer 2008) on Emmanuel Levinas, as co-editor (with Monica Osborne) of a special issue of *Modern Fiction Studies* 54, no. 1 (Spring 2008) on Emmanuel Levinas, and as editor of a special issue of *Religion, An International Journal* 37, no. 1 (March 2007) on René Girard. In 2012 and 2013, he co-hosted (with Benoît Chantre) an international conference on Emmanuel Levinas and René Girard ("Du sacré au saint") at the Bibliothèque Nationale de France and the École Normale Supérieure. He is a founding board member of the North American Levinas Society (currently in its seventeenth year), the former president of the Colloquium on Violence and Religion (2004–2007), and the author of over one hundred essays.

Sara R. Horowitz is professor of comparative literature and Humanities and former director of the Israel and Golda Koschitzky Centre for Jewish Studies at York University in Toronto. She is the author of *Voicing the Void: Muteness and Memory in Holocaust Fiction*, which received the Choice Award for Outstanding

Academic Book, and served as the senior founding editor of the Azrieli Series of Holocaust Memoirs—Canada (series 1 and 2). She is the editor or co-editor of *Shadows in the City of Light: Paris in Post-War French Jewish Writing* (2021); *Hans Günther Adler: Life, Literature, Legacy* (2016) which received the Canadian Jewish Literary Award; *Lessons and Legacies of the Holocaust Volume X: Back to the Sources* (2012), *Encounter with Appelfeld* (2003) and other books. In addition, she is founding co-editor of the journal *KEREM: A Journal of Creative Explorations in Judaism*.

Noah Simon Jampol is the writing program coordinator and assistant professor of English language and literature at Bronx Community College, The City University of New York. His work on morality, the Holocaust, and the fantastic has been published in *Literary Matters, Slayage, Robert Penn Warren Studies, Shawangunk Review, Developmental Studies,* and *Cognition*. His most recent work is the co-authored book, *Not of the Living Dead: The Non-Zombie Films of George A. Romero* (2023).

Rodger Kamenetz is professor emeritus of English and religious studies at LSU and founder and first director of its Jewish studies minor. He is the author of fifteen books of poetry and prose, among them *The Lowercase Jew* and *The Missing Jew: Poems 1976–2023*. He lives and works in New Orleans.

Phyllis Lassner is professor emerita at Northwestern University. Her publications include studies of Holocaust literature, film and art, and of women writers of the 1930s, World War II, and after. In addition to many articles, her books include *British Women Writers of World War II, Colonial Strangers: Women Writing the End of the British Empire,* and *Anglo-Jewish Women Writing the Holocaust*. Her most recent book is *Espionage and Exile: Fascism and Anti-Fascism in British Spy Fiction and Film*. She co-edited the volumes *Antisemitism and Philosemitism in the Twentieth and Twenty-First Centuries,* and *The Palgrave Handbook of Holocaust Literature and Culture*. She also co-edited the new edition of Gisella Perl's memoir *I Was a Doctor in Auschwitz*. She was awarded the International Diamond Jubilee Fellowship at Southampton University, UK and serves on the education and exhibition committees of the Illinois Holocaust Museum and Education Center.

Holli Levitsky is founder and director of the Jewish studies program and professor of English and Jewish studies at Loyola Marymount University in Los Angeles. She held the 2001–2002 Fulbright Distinguished Chair in American

Literature in Poland, fellowships at the Center for Advanced Holocaust Studies at the United States Holocaust Memorial Museum and the Schusterman Institute for Israel Studies, was Florida International University exile studies scholar in residence, and co-directs the annual Jewish American and Holocaust Literature Symposium. She works primarily in the areas of Jewish American literature, Holocaust studies, and exile studies, and has published articles, book chapters, and essays in these areas. Most recently, she is editor or co-editor of *Communist Poland: A Jewish Woman's Experience* (2022); *New Directions in Jewish American and Holocaust Literature: Reading and Teaching* (2018); *The Literature of Exile and Displacement: American Identity in a Time of Crisis* (2016); and *Summer Haven: The Catskills, the Holocaust and the Literary Imagination* (2015).

Cary Nelson is Jubilee Professor of Liberal Arts and Sciences emeritus at the University of Illinois at Urbana-Champaign. His thirty-six authored or edited books include a number devoted to modern poetry, including *Revolutionary Memory: Recovering the Poetry of the American Left*, a book that includes a long essay about Jewish-American poet Edwin Rolfe, whose collected poems Nelson coedited. He has repeatedly written about Holocaust-era poetry, including antisemitic poetry commissioned by the Nazis. He is completing a book about German antisemitic poetry and a book about reactions to the October 7, 2023, Hamas massacre in Israel.

Monica Osborne is a former professor of literature, film, philosophy, and trauma studies. Her scholarly work deals primarily with representations of trauma in art, film, and literature. Osborne is a regular contributor at both *Newsweek* and the *Jewish Journal of Los Angeles*, where she is editor at large. She has also written for the *New Republic*, the *Chronicle of Higher Education*, the *Los Angeles Review of Books, Forward, Areo*, and other magazines, academic journals, and edited collections. Her book *The Midrashic Impulse and the Contemporary Literary Response to Trauma* examines theoretical modes of writing in literature about the Holocaust and other genocides. She is co-director of the Jewish American and Holocaust Literature Symposium with Dr. Holli Levitsky.

Jacqueline Osherow is the author of nine collections of poetry, most recently *Divine Ratios* (2023). She's received grants from the John Simon Guggenheim Foundation, the National Endowment for the Arts, the Ingram Merrill Foundation, and the Witter Bynner Prize from the American Academy and Institute of Arts and Letters, as well as a number of prizes from the Poetry

Society of America. Her poems have appeared in many magazines, journals, and anthologies. She is distinguished professor of English at the University of Utah.

Timothy Parrish is a writer and critic who teaches at the University of California, Davis. He's the editor of *The Cambridge Companion to Philip Roth*. His Pushcart Prize-nominated story "Philip Roth's Final Hours" appeared in *Raritan*. His novella *The Critic* appeared in *Ploughshares*. His most recent critical book concerns the democratic vision of Ralph Ellison. His fiction and critical work have appeared in *American Literary History, Modern Fiction Studies, Contemporary Literature, Vestal Review, Sonic Boom*, the *Raw Art Review*, and *Equinox*, among other places.

Stella Setka is professor of English at West Los Angeles College, where she teaches courses on multiethnic American literature and film and directs the honors program. She is the author of *Empathy and the Phantasmic in Ethnic American Trauma Narratives*, and she has published essays on ethnic American literature and women's writing in various edited collections and academic journals, including *Modern Fiction Studies, MELUS*, and *Mosaic*. She is currently at work on a second book project that examines the use of midrash in contemporary Jewish American literature.

Maxim D. Shrayer, bilingual author, scholar, and translator, is a professor at Boston College. His books include *Immigrant Baggage* (2023), *Waiting for America* (2012), *Leaving Russia* (2017), *Of Politics and Pandemics* (2020), and *Kinship* (2024). Shrayer's works have been translated into thirteen languages.

Naomi Sokoloff is a professor in the Department of Middle Eastern Languages and Cultures at the University of Washington (Seattle), where she teaches Hebrew and modern Jewish literature. She holds the Samuel and Althea Stroum Chair in Jewish Studies and she is the author of *Imagining the Child in Modern Jewish Fiction* (1992). Her most recent books include *Since 1948: Israeli Literature in the Making*, co-edited with Nancy E. Berg (2020), and *What We Talk about When We Talk about Hebrew (And What It Means to Americans)* (2018), which was also co-edited with Nancy E. Berg and which won a 2019 National Jewish Book Award. She has published widely on Israeli and American literature, commenting on work by Diane Ackerman, S. Y. Agnon, Yehuda Amichai, Aharon Appelfeld, Louis Begley, Ch. N. Bialik, Alona Frankel, David Grossman, Primo Levi, Etgar Keret, Jerzy Kosinski, Primo Levi, Savyon Liebrecht, Rutu Modan,

Yehoshua November, Cynthia Ozick, Hava Pinhas-Cohen, Henry Roth, Philip Roth, Avraham Shlosnky, and Myra Sklarew, among others.

Eric J. Sundquist is the Andrew W. Mellon Professor of Humanities Emeritus at Johns Hopkins University. His books include *To Wake the Nations: Race in the Making of American Literature* and *Strangers in the Land: Blacks, Jews, and Post-Holocaust America*.

Betsy Winakur Tontiplaphol is professor of English at Trinity University, where she teaches courses in nineteenth-century British literature, poetic form, and other topics. In addition to numerous essays, she is the author of two scholarly monographs: *Poetics of Luxury in the Nineteenth Century: Keats, Tennyson, and Hopkins* (2011) and *The Pointe of the Pen: Nineteenth-Century Poetry and the Balletic Imagination* (2021). She is also the co-editor of *The Literary Taylor Swift: Songwriting and Intertextuality* (2024).

Index

Aaron (biblical), 50
Aarons, Victoria, 1, 51, 122–23
Abraham (biblical), 19, 53
absences, 48, 68, 95, 114, 159, 162–63, 239–40. *See also* Holocaust
Adam and Eve, 22–23, 102. *See also* Garden of Eden
Adonis and *Adon*, 18, 43
Adorno, Theodor, 37, 48, 237; "Cultural Criticism and Society," 36
African Americans, 53
"After Looking into a Book Belonging to My Great-Grandfather, Eli Eliakim Plutzik," 25–26, 48, 230; compared to Preil's "Chapters of Time, His and Mine," 9, 74–76, 79–84; family/cultural heritage and, 75, 80–81, 84, 86–87, 275; Holocaust and, 248–49; impersonality and, 81, 196; Jewish liturgy and, 82, 84, 274–76; memory and, 275; in non-conversational language and about the unspeakable, 82; retrieving Plutzik's great-grandfather from obscurity, 276; simplicity of, 81–83; text of poem, 79
Aggadah vs. Halacha, 16, 30, 177, 238
Agus, Jacob, 254–63, 266–71; background similarities with Plutzik, 258–59; Conservative movement and, 260, 270; failure of prayer, book revision project and, 271, 271n61; family background and education of, 259, 259n21; *Guideposts in Modern Judaism*, 260; Holocaust's legacy and, 261; *Modern Philosophies of Judaism*, 259; Plutzik's liturgical translations and, 261–62, 268–70
Ai, conquest of (biblical), 27–28
Ajalon battles. *See* Joshua (biblical)
Albacín (Jewish quarter of Grenada), 55
Albo, Joseph, 268–69
Alexander the Great, 133
Allen, Woody: *The Front* (film), 98
Altman, Jane Gurkin: *Epistolarity: Approaches to Form*, 327
Amalek and Amalekites (biblical), 23, 27–28
American Studies, transnational turn in, 84
Améry, Jean, 37n11
Anath/Anat (Canaanite goddess), 43
Anglo-Saxon intelligentsia and antisemitism, 196, 196n11, 286, 289, 292, 296, 308
antisemitism: Britain's first blood libel against the Jews (1144), 149–50; Claudel and, 156; demonization of those who demonize the Jews, 65; disavowing humanity of Jews, 240; Eliot and, 3, 12, 13, 20, 49, 75, 172, 174–75, 201–5, 209–12, 230–31, 296–98, 299n47; elite private colleges and universities and Anglo-American literary mainstream excluding Jews, 13–14, 196, 196n11, 286–89, 292, 296; Europe of late nineteenth century and, 48; Hemingway and, 308; Israel's founding provoking, 43; Jewish writers trying to minimize their identity in face of, 157–58;

Ogilby and, 288–89; Plutzik and, 13, 20, 37, 38, 73, 158, 194, 231, 236, 241, 307, 312, 314; pogroms and forced exile inflicted by those believing God on their side, 42, 149–50; Pound and, 297; WWII and, 22. *See also* Holocaust; Nazis and Nazism
apple motifs, 19, 55
Apples from Shinar (Plutzik): critical reception of, 44, 235–36; fishing as theme of poems, 303; Greek mythology and, 19; Holocaust pervasive throughout, 39, 47, 307, 322; Judas and, 193–94; Kastan's foreword in special edition, 55, 333; Keats and, 222; last poem in first edition of ("The Last Fisherman"), 115, 230, 306; linked to leftists of 1930s, 55; Lurie's review of, 158n6; Platonic invisible world and, 199; preface of, 54, 225–26; published (1959), 35; Shinar as location of Eden and, 19, 55; title of, 225–26; written after founding of Israel, 42
Apter, Emily, 137–38
Arendt, Hannah, 315; *Eichmann in Jerusalem*, 59, 315; *The Origins of Totalitarianism* and banality of evil, 59
Aristotle, 133
ars poetica, 17, 241
Ashkenazi Jews, 9, 75, 85, 276, 282–83. *See also* Eastern European Jewish life
Aspects of Proteus: first retrospective collection published by Plutzik (1949), 2, 35, 302; history of evil in, 240n26; Holocaust as subject, 39; impersonality and, 205; lark in "On the Airfield at Shipdham" akin to Proteus, 150; "My Sister" as earliest poem in, 47, 65; poems from rejected *House of Gorya and Other Poems* in, 8, 29; Proteus as shape-shifter and, 19; reaching 1940s audience receptive to Jewish American poets, 296; "The Three" eliminated from, 179
assimilation, 13, 20, 48, 230, 287, 306
Auden, W. H.: Eliot and, 3; "In Memory of Sigmund Freud," 6; "Musée des Beaux Arts," 25, 195; Plutzik and, 2, 3, 5; "Refugee Blues," 5–6; Rich and, 5; "September 1, 1939," 6
Austin, J. L.: *How to Do Things with Words*, 104

Baldwin, Roberta Plutzik (daughter), 301
Bar Kokhba Revolt, 16, 31
Barrie, J. M., 147
bat kol (echo of prophecy), 30, 30n23
Baudelaire, Charles: "To the Reader" in *Flowers of Evil*, 205, 212, 232, 307
Bavli, Hillel, 74
Belleforest's *Histoires Tragiques*, 127
Benet, Steven Vincent, 168
betrayal, 11–12, 192–206
Betterton, Maryland, 26, 26n21, 146, 146n21
birds: in "The Airman Who Flew over Shakespeare's England," 149; in "The Begetting of Cain," 58; in "An Electromagnetic Phenomenon," 58; in "The Geese," 21, 48–49, 91, 104, 219; in *Horatio*, 136–37, 136n24; in "The Importance of Poetry," 9, 94–95, 98–101, 102, 104, 105, 108; in "The Old War," 25, 41, 151; in "On the Airfield at Shipdham," 150–51; in Shakespearean song and sonnet, 150
Birnbaum, Mayer: *Pathway to Prayer*, 269
Bishop, Elizabeth, 14; "Letter to N. Y. (for Louise Crane)," 329
Blake, William, 209

Blanchot, Maurice: *L'écriture du désastre* (*The Writing of the Disaster*), 89, 90, 104–5, 106, 155
Blanco, Richard, 319; foreword to 32 *Poems* (Plutzik's poems in Spanish and English), 319
"Blessed art Thou" and *barukh*, 268–69
Bloch, Chana, 73
blood libel against the Jews, 149–50, 150n33
Bloom, Harold, 158n6
Boland, Eavan, 333–34; "Letter to a Young Woman Poet," 332–33
Boudreau, Kristin, 11, 192
Boyer, Paul, 119
Brady, Matthew, 53
Brett, Lily, 59
Brooks, Cleanth, 197
Browne, Jennifer, 10, 14, 325–34
Brunner, Edward, 7, 10, 45, 46, 60–61, 117, 152; *Cold War Poetry*, 52, 65
Burge, Gary M., 281

Cain (biblical), 23–24, 247
Camorra references, 22, 41, 244–45
Campbell, Joseph: *The Hero with a Thousand Faces*, 19
Celan, Paul, 14, 37, 59, 245n43, 273, 306–7; "Todesfuge," 65
Chaucer, Geoffrey: *The Canterbury Tales*, 204
Chess, Richard, 73
Christianity: of Eliot, 211, 231–32; fishing tropes in New Testament, 280–82, 281; *Horatio* and, 129; Judeophobia of, 299, 308; knowledge of, as requirement for professorship, 196–97n11; Plutzik's respect in address to Eliot, 201n26; separating from Judaism, 174; Shepard as Christian leader speaking out against Nazis, 289; "The Three" including along with Greek and Judaic traditions, 179, 180. *See also* scriptural citations
Civil War, 53
classical civilization and history in Plutzik's work, 19, 38, 170, 179–81. *See also specific mythological figures and specific classical authors*
Claudel, Paul, 156
Cohen, Jeffrey Jerome, 319
Cold War, 10, 18, 24, 125n13; *Horatio* and, 117, 122, 124–25; unsettled post-WWII peace and, 152
Cole, Peter, 73
Coleridge, Samuel Taylor, 224, 227, 228, 289
comic book industry, 124n11
concentration camps, 10, 45, 48, 61, 68, 157. *See also* Holocaust
Conservative Judaism, 252–54, 253n2, 256, 260, 261, 270, 276
consumerism, 48
covenant with Jewish people, 32
Cowper, William, 147
Creation parables, 16, 20, 22–23, 24, 27, 178
Creeley, Robert, 328; "The Dishonest Mailman," 331
cynicism, 64, 273

dandelions, 141, 218–21
Daniel (biblical), 27n22
Dante Alighieri, 174, 204–5; in "The Chinaman and the Florentine," 217; *Divine Comedy*, 306; *The Inferno*, 128, 175, 194; Plutzik comparing Eliot to, 233, 234
David (biblical), 42, 43
Day-Lewis's translation of *Aeneid*, 265
death as theme, 83, 156, 162–64, 219–20, 272. *See also* concentration camps; Holocaust

death camps. *See* concentration camps; Holocaust
decay and decomposition, 21, 90, 93, 163, 194–95, 200, 226, 317–18
Delbo, Charlotte, 37
Derrida, Jacques, 37, 60, 318
Des Pres, Terrence: *The Survivor*, 89, 93
Diaspora, 29, 31, 48–49, 72, 175, 178, 243, 256, 282, 302, 307
Dickey, William, 123–24, 126
Dickinson, Emily, 2, 5, 11, 14, 169, 329, 330
Dilke, Charles, 223
dogwood, imagery of, 7, 227, 229, 273
Donne, John, 199
door imagery, 119, 199, 230, 232, 234
Dostoevsky, Fyodor: *The Possessed* (aka *Demons* or *The Devils*), 22n13
double consciousness, 3, 3n4
Dougherty, Jack, 287–88
dreams: "end of the dreamer" in "The Last Fisherman," 115; in *Horatio*, 122–23, 133; Ozick writing of pre-Holocaust time, 165; in "Prayer in the Seasons of Death," 272; primordial images in, 210; sequel writing and, 122
DuBois, W. E. B., 3n4
Dunbar, Paul Laurence, 3–4; "We Wear the Mask," 4

Eastern European Jewish life, 74–75, 82, 86, 275, 284, 287. *See also* Ashkenazi Jews
Efros, Israel, 74
Egart, Mark: *Scorched Land*, 284
Egyptian mythology, 21
Eichmann, Adolf, 5, 53, 59n32, 158
Eisenkramer, Eric, 284
Ekronites, 42n19
Elata-Alster, Gerda, 239

Elazer and Jochanan dialogue from Talmud, 246–47, 364
Eliakim, 80, 80n25. *See also* "After Looking into a Book Belonging to My Great-Grandfather, Eli Eliakim Plutzik"
Eliezer (rabbi), 23
Elijah (biblical), 27n22
Eliot, T. S.: antisemitism of, 3, 12, 13, 20, 49, 75, 172, 174–75, 201–5, 209–12, 230–31, 296–98, 299n47; Auden and, 3; Baudelaire and, 212, 232, 307; Boland and, 333; Broadway plays in verse by, 125; cleverness of, 203; conversion to Anglicanism, 232; Dante and, 233, 234; as exile like Plutzik, 49, 173, 201, 212; impersonality and, 11, 196, 198, 202, 205; influence of, 2, 4, 6, 11–12, 168–70, 171–72, 196–97; Kamenetz on, 211–12, 297–98; Keats and, 223, 233–34; on Metaphysical poets, 3, 203; modernism of, 204; Plutzik's engagement with, 11, 179, 183, 197–98, 201–2, 312, 314, 320–21; Plutzik's poem ("Critique") and, 171; Plutzik's poem to ("For T. S. E. Only"), 11–13, 20, 49–50, 171–73, 175–76, 201–5, 212–13, 223, 230–34, 298, 307, 312, 365–66; Stevens on, 202
Eliot, T. S., works by: *After Strange Gods*, 209; "Burbank with a Baedeker: Bleistein with a Cigar," 49, 172, 175, 200–201, 203, 209, 211–12, 231n19, 298; *The Complete Poems and Plays*, 211; *Four Quartets*, 20; "Gerontion," 210–11, 298; "The Love Song of J. Alfred Prufrock," 12, 208–9, 289, 320–21; "The Metaphysical Poets," 3; *Poems* (1920), 49, 175, 203, 298;

Poems: 1909–1925, 197, 207; "Sweeney Among the Nightingales," 209, 298; "Tradition and the Individual Talent" (essay), 2–3, 196, 197, 199, 233; "The Waste Land," 2, 4, 4n6, 128, 172, 197, 200, 202, 209–10, 232, 299, 307, 317, 318, 321
ellipses in works of historical trauma, 241, 241n30
Emerson, Ralph Waldo, 199
empathy, 13, 36, 53, 203, 224, 230–33, 246–48
Empson, William, 121n7
English history and cultural heritage, Plutzik's poems engaging with, 10–11, 147, 149–50, 152. *See also* Horatio
En Jacob: Agada of the Babylonian Talmud, 16, 238, 246
Enoch (son of Cain), 24
entropy, 90
equations, 9, 90
eternity, 59, 62, 182
ethical considerations, 13, 119, 239–50, 261; of Jewish memory and forgetting, 252; Levinas on, 241–42, 245, 245n43; midrashic awareness and, 239–40, 245; in post-Holocaust reading, 61; weight of, 246, 323; of WWII, 145–46, 151–53
Europe: antisemitism of late nineteenth century, 48; Jewish writers turning away from, 4. *See also* Eastern European Jewish life
evil, 6, 22, 24; banality of, 59; bearing witness to, 54; beauty and, 56; in history and in the present, 57, 58–59; unlimited human capacity for, 8, 57, 59–61, 66. *See also* Holocaust
exile of Jews. *See* Diaspora
existentialism, 21, 107, 231, 321

Falk, Marcia, 73, 269
fascism, 11, 31, 38, 46–47, 54, 157, 314, 317, 320. *See also* Nazis and Nazism; totalitarianism
fate, 41, 49, 150
Feast of Unleavened Bread, 25
Felman, Shoshana, 315
fertility ritual of Hebrew tradition, 25
Fiedler, Leslie, 128
fish and fishing, 13–14, 279–84; "Absurd Cycle" and, 302; "As the Great Horse Rots on the Hill" and, 302; "The Bass" and, 305, *305*, 306; Eliot's "The Waste Land" and, 307; fly-fishing as Plutzik's leisure activity, 300–308, *300–301*; fly-fishing as Shepard's lifelong pursuit, 293–95; Halacha on, 282–83; Hemingway's "The Sun Also Rises" and, 308; Horatio and, 302; "Jim Desterland" and, *303*, 304; "The Last Fisherman," 306–7, *306*
Fishbane, Michael, 16
Fishman, Charles Adés, 240
Flanzbaum, Hilene, 1
Ford Foundation Fellowship application describing plan to write Holocaust poem. *See* Holocaust, *for* unwritten (but proposed) poem by Plutzik on
foreboding, sense of, 157, 159, 164. *See also* Holocaust, *for* Plutzik's poetic evocation of
Franco, Francisco, 54
Frank, Anne, 35, 36, 313; *The Diary of Anne Frank*, 314
Frazer, James: *The Golden Bough*, 25, 25n19
Freedman, Jonathan: *The Temple of Culture*, 196–97
Freud, Sigmund: *The Interpretation of Dreams*, 122

Friedman, Norman, 126, 126n17, 304
Frost, Robert, 74, 168
Fry, Christopher, 125
Fussell, Paul, 143

Garber, Marjorie, 122
Garden of Eden, 19, 22–23, 55, 58–59, 102
Gardner, Brian, 145
Gath (biblical), 42
genocide, 16, 22, 50–51, 261. *See also* Holocaust
ghosts: as both being and not being, 95, 112; in "Exhortation to the Artists," 247–48; in "The Importance of Poetry," 101, 102, 108; in Plutzik's proposed Holocaust poem, 35–36, 67–68, 73, 247; in "Prayer in the Seasons of Death," 272–73; in Shakespeare's *Hamlet*, 114, 120–21, 121n6, 124, 136–37; of unborn because parents among Holocaust dead, 63; of war comrades who do not return, 145
Ginsberg, Allen, 73n11, 170; "Howl," 4–5
Gitelman, Lisa, 117
Glatstein, Yankev, 74, 273
global order, remaking of, 32
God in Plutzik's work, 20–21, 27–28
golden calf, worship of (biblical), 50
Goldman, David P., 298–99
Goliath (biblical), 42
Goodhart, Sandor, 1, 7, 9, 89, 161, 165
Gordinsky, Natasha, 75–76
Graham Jorie, 59
Grand, Sue: *The Reproduction of Evil*, 162
grave markers and tombstones, 48, 79–81, 276
Graves, Robert, 11, 127–28, 129, 147, 169; *The White Goddess*, 127, 129
Greek classical references. *See* classical civilization and history in Plutzik's work

Grierson, Herbert J. C., 197
grieving. *See* mourning
Grossman, Allen, 73
Grosz, George: *Cain, or Hitler in Hell* (painting), 23–24
Gubar, Susan, 36
Guggenheim Fellowship application describing plan to write Holocaust poem. *See* Holocaust, *for* unwritten (but proposed) poem by Plutzik on
Guggenheim Foundation fellowship application (1960), 8, 17, 35
guilt: from nuclear weapons use, 46; survivor guilt, 61, 114
Gunn, Thom, 168

HaAm, Ahad, 183
Hadar, David: *Affiliated Identities in Jewish American Literature*, 86
Hadas, Gershon, 271
Hadrian (Roman emperor), 29–31
Halacha: vs. Aggadah, 16, 30, 177, 238; on fishing and hunting, 282–83
Halivni, David Weiss: *The Book and the Sword: A Life of Learning in the Shadow of Destruction*, 273–74
Halkin, Simon, 74
Hall, Donald, 297; Plutzik's letter to (November 24, 1968), 55, 66–67
Hanania, Rabbi Joshua ben, 30–31, 32
Hardy, Thomas, 114, 147
Harlow, Jules, 252
HD, 74
Hebrew: "After Looking into a Book Belonging to My Great-Grandfather, Eli Eliakim Plutzik" and, 82; earlier American Hebraists and elevated language, 74; Jewish literature broadened to include American Hebraism, 84–85; Preil writing in, 71, 73, 77, 79, 82–83

Hecht, Anthony, 296; "The Book of Yolek," 2–3; introduction to Plutzik's *Collected Poems* by, 2–3, 5, 64, 168–69, 291; "More Light! More Light!," 59; on mutability of truth in Plutzik's *Horatio*, 50; selecting Plutzik's poems for *The Collected Poems*, 179
Heidegger, Martin, 107, 124, 181
Hemingway, Ernest: *The Sun Also Rises*, 307–8
Henry VIII (English king), 150, 150n34
Henson, George B., 312
Heracles (Hercules), 20n8
Heschel, Abraham, 170, 179, 181
Heyen, William, 59
Hillel the Elder, 30, 32, 72
Hinman, Robert: "A Memorial to Hyam Plutzik," 166
Hiroshima, 10, 24, 39, 59–61, 68, 122, 313
Hirsch, Ed, 210
Hirsch, Emil B., 280
historical subject matter, 6, 16, 18, 142–43. *See also* classical civilization and history; English history and cultural heritage; Jewish history and topics
Hitler, Adolf, 22, 27, 46, 50, 54, 56, 157, 314, 319
Holocaust, 4–5; accountability for, 244–45; "After Looking into a Book Belonging to My Great-Grandfather, Eli Eliakim Plutzik" and, 248–49; "An Agadah of Hyam ben Samuel" and, 8, 15–17; "An Aggadah" and, 177; Allied plan not intended to save Jews, 152n45; avoidance of topic by writers, 8, 13; awareness of poets of, 4–5, 10, 60; "The Begetting of Cain" and, 59; "Bomber Base" and, 41; as break with God and history, 177, 178, 273; claustrophobia in poetry about, 45; as defining event of twentieth century, 66, 75; "Elegy" and, 153; eternal evil's legacy, 59; "Exhortation to the Artists" and, 247–48; Fishman's anthology of American Holocaust poetry, 240; "For T. S. E. Only" and, 175–76; as God's judgment upon Diaspora, 29; *Horatio* and, 10, 113, 122, 123, 237, 260; human capacity for evil and, 59–61; "If Causality is Impossible, Genesis is Recurrent" and, 105–9; *Letter from a Young Poet* and, 22, 242–43; linkage to arc of Jewish history, 11, 161, 165, 177–79, 243, 261, 275; "Next Time I Shall Not Burn the Beehive" and, 18; "The Outcasts of Venus" and, 14, 314, 318–22; Plutzik's anger over, 152, 248; Plutzik's obsession with, 113–14, 240, 260; Plutzik's poetic evocation of, 39, 75, 156, 159, 160–62, 164–65; "Portrait" and, 47–48, 93, 112, 322–23; Preil compared to Plutzik in regard to, 75; range of poems about, 37, 148n29; Remembrance Day concert (2007), 10; science fiction and, 314–19, 321–24; term coming into use, 175; testimony of survivors, 8; time and, 93, 106–9; "Two Hearts and an Arrow" and, 44–46; unwritten (but proposed) poem by Plutzik on, 4, 8, 10, 17, 24, 31–32, 34–36, 66, 68, 73, 90n1, 113, 131, 160, 165, 236–38, 247–48, 313–14; Yad Vashem's role to document victims, 81. *See also* concentration camps
Homer: *Iliad*, 120n4; *Iliad* translation by Richard Lattimore, 265; *The Odyssey*, 19
Homeric *Hymn to Demeter*, 25
Honig, Edwin, 296

Hopkins, Gerard Manley, 68
Horace: *Letters to Piso*, 331
Horatio (Plutzik), 10, 117–38; Ambleth character representing Hamlet, 127, 129, 216; ancient Greek and Roman thought in, 170; "The Book of Metamorphoses" (Part Two), 129, 422–25; Carlus dialogue, 50–51, 125–26; Cold War and, 117, 122, 124–25; confessional verse in Horatio's voice, 131–32; continuity of parts, 135; critical reception of, 236; cynicism and humor of, 64; determining subject of, 112–13; Dickey's review of, 123–24, 126; failed telling of Hamlet's story and, 94, 215–16; fish and, 302; goal to live life in the fallen's stead and not to forget them, 131; grief as prelude to Cold War and, 122; "The Harrowing of the House of Eyes" (Part Two), 129; Holocaust and, 10, 113, 122, 123, 237, 260; Honorio character representing Horatio, 216; manuscript, 187; misconceptions of *Hamlet* and, 50; mockery of mob mentality in, 130; as multilayered poems, 137; outsiders and exclusion in, 130–31; Part Three as workbook for unwritten Holocaust poem, 137; publication (1961), 35; as Pulitzer Prize finalist, 117, 236; role of Horatio in *Hamlet*, 117–18; "Salon on the Rue Galantiere," 54; as sequel to *Hamlet*, 24, 112, 117, 128–29, 168; "The Shepherd" (Part Two), 115, 126, 127, 291; surreal imagery in, 134; text excerpts, 416–21; time in coda of, 135–36; as underground myth, 126–31; as verse drama, 123–26; war overtaking nature in, 150; wounding as repeated event in, 124

Horowitz, Sara R., 13, 252, 315
Hughes, Ted, 8, 18, 168
humor, 17, 38, 38n16, 45, 64, 86n31, 130, 164, 169, 204, 223
Hyam Plutzik Fellowship, 7, 10
hypocrisy, 232

Ignatow, David, 296
impersonality, 11, 192–206, 233
"The Importance of Poetry" (The Importance of Poetry or the Coming Forth from Eternity into Time) (Plutzik), 9, 94–109, 334; allusion to creation in Genesis, 99–100, 102, 104, 109; awareness of the posthumous in, 107–8; compared to *Horatio*, 112–13; compared to "Of Objects Considered as Fortresses in a Baleful Space," 109–11; compared to "Portrait," 111–12; cosmological dimensions and, 102, 114; divided into two parts, 9; equations created in, 9, 90; the eternal and, 96, 108–9; "front," meaning of, 98; Holocaust and, 106–9; "hover," meaning of, 98–100, 109; Kantian realms and, 96–97, 104; language that denotes vs. language that describes, 100; last line of, 107; metricality of language in, 102–3, 109; performativity of, 9, 103–4; poetry as way of asking questions, 106; poetry as witness to tradition, 109; relationship of two parts, 101–4, 108; rhyming, 102; situations described in first part, 101; text of poem, 94–95, 101, 394; time as subject matter, 106–9; title's hidden meaning, 95–96, 108–9
"the infinite within the finite" (Levinas), 96
irony, 3, 63, 74, 82, 163
Israel, 16, 28, 42, 43, 77, 179

Ixion (mythological), 156, 159, 164, 179–82

James, Henry, 114, 125, 125n13, 132n23; *The Ambassadors*, 132; *Aspern Papers*, 200
Jampol, Noah Simon, 14, 312
Jarrell, Randall, 59n32
Javadiazadeh, Kamran: "Can Rilke Change Your Life?," 325, 331
Jeffers, Robinson, 168
Jericho, 27–28
Jewish American and Holocaust Literature Symposium, 7
Jewish American identity: American identity prized in, 4, 241; crafting artistic identity, 86; criticism of overemphasis on Ashkenazi Jews, 85; duality of, 1–2, 18–19, 84, 86n31; fluidity of Jewish culture and, 75; modern Jewish American poets, 5, 13, 14, 72, 73, 236, 244, 296, 306–7; multilinguality and, 71–72, 75, 84; Plutzik and, 37, 42, 55, 158, 306, 312; post-Holocaust, 314; Preil and, 71
Jewish history and topics: abrogation of Christianity and, 174; aggadah's role, 177; comparing Plutzik's and Preil's poetry in regard to, 72; cycle of suffering and renewal, 19, 26, 75; extrapolation to universals, 32; fishing as occupation, 280, 282; Heschel and, 170, 181; Jewish theology compared to Greek ontology, 181; in Plutzik's poetry, 3, 18, 38, 72, 90n1, 168–70, 259; in Preil's poetry, 86n31; tragedies of, 8, 32, 46. *See also* antisemitism; Eastern European Jewish life; Holocaust; *specific biblical characters, locations, and events*
Jewish identity and Jewishness: "casually Jewish," 13, 47, 93, 111, 158, 230; compared to Yankee's identity, 4, 241; Hecht and, 3; Nelson on, 137, 242, 296; Plutzik and, 8, 11, 12–13, 17, 18, 20, 38–68, 72, 157, 158, 168–84, 213, 221, 230–31, 235, 238, 253, 259, 263, 312. *See also* Jewish American identity
Jewish literature: broadened to include American Hebraism, 84–85; crafting artistic identity of Jewish American poets, 86; definition and characterization of, 85. *See also* modern Jewish poets
Jewish War (68–70 CE), 16, 30
Jews: American Jews' responsibility for Jewish continuity, 261, 274; exclusion from elite private colleges and academic jobs, 13–14, 196, 196n11, 286–89, 292, 296; Faustian bargain of Nazism and, 56; as others, 43; as people of the book and of conscience, 56, 243; solidarity among, 231. *See also* antisemitism; Conservative Judaism; Holocaust; Jewish American identity; Jewish history and topics; Jewish identity and Jewishness
Johnson, Samuel, 113
Jonah (biblical), 27n22
Joshua (biblical), 27–29, 72, 146–47
Journal of Jewish Identities' special issue: "Post-Holocaust Culture and Jewish Identity" (2023), 7
Joyce, James, 14, 128
Judas (biblical), 61, 193–94, 205
Justice, Donald, 169

Kabbalah, 20, 96
Kaddish prayer, 21, 26, 41; *Kaddish d'rabanan* (rabbi's kaddish), 275–76
Kamenetz, Rodger, 12, 208; "The Lowercase Jew," 211–12, 297–98; *The Lowercase Jew*, 213

Kant, Immanuel, 96–97, 104, 107
Karp, Abraham, 253n2
Kastan, David Scott, 55, 62, 168, 222, 233–34, 333
Katzenelson, Yitzhak: "Song of the Murdered Jewish People," 17
Keats, John, 12–13, 222–34; on Coleridge, 224, 228; "Egotist" letter to John Hamilton Reynolds (February 1818), 224; Eliot and, 223, 233–34; "negative capability" letter to his brothers (December 1817), 223–25, 228, 232, 233; Plutzik's Keatsian qualities, 225–30, 233–34; on poet as "most unpoetical of anything in existence," 225, 230, 233; "poetical character" letter to Richard Woodhouse (October 1818), 224–25; on Wordsworth, 224; works by: "Beauty and Truth," 225; "Ode on a Grecian Urn," 147; "To Autumn," 226, 227n16
Klein, A. M., 296
Klepfisz, Irena, 73
Kobrin, Leon: *Yankl Boyle, from the Life of a Jewish Fisherman in Russia, and Other Stories*, 284
Korean War, 60
Kreymborg, Alfred, 235–36
Kristallnacht, 47, 161, 163, 243, 289
Kunitz, Stanley, 296
Kyd's *Spanish Tragedy*, 120n4, 127

LaCapra, Dominick, 316
Landau, Yehezkel ben Yehuda, 283
Lang, Fritz: *Metropolis* (film), 317
Langer, Lawrence, 316
Lanzmann, Claude, 59n32
Lassner, Phyllis, 10–11, 140
Lattimore's translation of *Iliad*, 265
Laub, Dori, 315

Leavis, F. R., 197
Lee, Laurie, 145
Le Guin, Ursula K., 315, 318
Letter from a Young Poet (Plutzik's letter to Shepard, 1941), 14, 194; on antisemitism, 20, 297; Browne's reply to, 14, 325–34; Camorra reference in, 22, 41, 244–45; composition of, 292; on evil's rise, 54, 57; identity issues and, 199, 292; on Jews as people of the book and of conscience, 56; midrashic awareness and, 241–44; Nazi book burnings and, 45, 243; on science fiction writing, 319; Shepard's unmailed reply to, 293, 330; title allusion to Rilke's *Letters to a Young Poet*, 37
Levi, Primo, 37
Levinas, Emmanuel, 96, 107, 159–60, 241–42, 245–46n43; "Poetry and the Impossible," 156–57; *Totality and Infinity*, 242
Levine, Philip, 73n11
Levitsky, Holli, 1
Lewis, Alun: "All Day It Has Rained," 148
Lincoln, Abraham, 53
Lisitzky, Ephraim E., 74
Llewelyn, John, 247
Loeb, Harold, 308
Logan, William, 146n20
Longenbach, James, 201
Lorca, Federico García, 54, 55
Lowell, Amy, 74
Lowell, Robert, 5; *Life Studies*, 5, 131; "Memories of West Street and Lepke," 5; "The Quaker Graveyard in Nantucket," 5
Lurie, Margot, 38, 44, 73, 158n6, 235
Luther, Flavel S., 287–88
Lyon, Phillipa, 143
Lyotard, Jean-François, 313–14

MacGreevey, Thomas, 197
MacLeish, Archibald, 125, 168
Mann, Thomas, 128
Mantegna, Andrea: *St. Sebastian* (painting), 200
matches trope, 8, 16–17, 102–3, 176–78
mathematics as subject matter, 18, 22n12, 86n31
Matthiessen, F. O., 121n7, 132n23, 197
McCarthyism, 52, 98, 125n14, 152
memory, 1, 13; in "After Looking into a Book Belonging to My Great-Grandfather, Eli Eliakim Plutzik," 275; assimilation and, 48; of Britain from serving in war there, 149; of Holocaust, 10, 53, 68, 108, 273; in *Horatio*, 123–24, 126, 133–34, 137; Jewish imperative of, 53, 87, 274; *Letter from a Young Poet* and, 241; traumatic events and, 237–40
Messiah: legend of messianic redemption, 274; remaining hidden, 32, 32n26
Midrash Eleh Ezkerah ("Ten Martyrs" prayer), 31
midrashic awareness, 2, 7, 8, 13, 31–32, 237–50; "The Camorra" and, 245; ethical engagement and, 239–40; "Exhortation to the Artists" and, 246, 247–48; explanation of midrash's origins and role, 238–39; in Holocaust context, 68, 239, 249–50; *Letter from a Young Poet* and, 241–44; Levinas and, 241–42; poetry and, 240; truth and clarity and, 244
Miller, David, 37, 60, 68, 148n29
Mintz, Alan, 74, 77
Mintz, Stephen, 30
minyan of ten men parallel to ten-man crew on bomber, 26, 41
Miron, Dan, 85

mitzvah of *bikur cholim* (visiting the sick), 246
modern Jewish poets: as American modernists, 72, 171–72; as heirs to rabbinical tradition, 16, 238; Jewish American poets, 5, 13, 14, 72, 73, 236, 244, 296, 306–7. *See also specific poets by name*
Moran, Edward: on blood libel in England, 150n33; on "Elegy," 153; on "For T. S. E. Only," 201, 201n26; on *Horatio*, 142, 237, 260; on "Jim Desterland," 304; on Plutzik at Trinity College, 286; on Plutzik's best work, 318; on Plutzik's consultancy with Conservative movement, 253n2; on Plutzik's response to Holocaust, 152n45, 318–19; on Plutzik's unwritten poem on Holocaust, 35, 90n1, 160; on "The Seventh Avenue Express," 317; on Shepard, 289, 293
Moses (biblical), 27, 27n22, 30, 30n23, 50, 72
Mount Sinai, 26, 51, 275
mourning, 26, 31, 32, 48, 61, 151, 176, 246, 318; *Yizkor*, 276. *See also* Kaddish prayer
Mussolini, Benito, 46, 54
mysticism, 30, 256, 275–76. *See also* Kabbalah
mythological subject matter, 18, 20, 62, 123, 126–31, 142, 155, 179–81; science fiction and, 315–16

Nazis and Nazism, 5, 18, 22, 23–24, 56–57, 320; antisemitism as template of, 240; Arendt on evil of, 59; beautiful German landscape and, 56, 151–52; book burnings by, 45; Faustian bargain of, 56; German and Western culture failing to control, 56;

Heidegger compromised by, 124n12; *Kristallnacht* (1938), 47, 161, 163, 243, 289; Nuremberg Laws (1935), 47; opening of first concentration camp (1933), 157; as pagans, 43. *See also* Holocaust
Nebuchadnezzar, 19
negative capability: Keats on, 12, 223–25, 228, 232, 233; Plutzik and, 226, 230
Nelson, Cary, 7–10, 34; on *Aspects of Proteus*'s coverage of history of evil, 240n26; on Jewish identity, 137, 242, 296; on *Letter from a Young Poet*, 241; on "The Old War," 151; on Plutzik as "not a poet of consolation," 193; on Plutzik's response to Holocaust, 75, 152, 152n45, 157, 236–38, 249, 260–61, 275, 313; on Plutzik's unwritten poem on Holocaust, 90n1; on "Portrait," 242; *Revolutionary Memory*, 52; on "The Seventh Avenue Express," 317
Nemerov, Howard, 8, 18, 296; "D Day Plus 20 Years," 144
Nemo, Philippe, 159–60
Nessus, 20, 20n8, 48, 112
New Criticism, 127–28
New Testament, 174. *See also* scriptural citations
Norris, Margo, 145
November, Yehoshua, 73
nuclear/atomic weapons, 44, 45, 119. *See also* Hiroshima
Nun, Mendel, 282

Ogilby, Remsen Brickerhoff, 288–89, 292–93
Old Testament (Tanakh), 174, 179. *See also* scriptural citations
Oostdijk, Diederik, 144–45
Operation Barbarossa, 56
Oppen, George, 296

Ormsby, Eric, 158n6, 168
Orwell, George, 134
Osborne, Monica, 10, 11, 155, 237, 239–40
Osherow, Jacqueline, 7, 12, 215
osier dogwood, imagery of, 7, 227, 229, 273
Ovid: *Metamorphoses*, 20n8
Ozick, Cynthia, 73; "Rosa," 165

Pagis, Dan, 59, 273; "Written in Pencil in the Sealed Railway Car," 36
Pale of Settlement, 168, 243, 283
Parrish, Timothy, 11, 168
Pegasus, 62
performativity of Plutzik's poetry, 9, 103–4
Pfeffer, Yehoshua, 282–83
Philistines (biblical), 42, 42n19, 43
philosophy as subject matter, 6, 86n31, 96–97, 118, 160, 170
Piercy, Marge, 73
Piette, Adam, 144
Pinsky, Robert: "Poem about People," 194
piyyut translations, 256–57, 262, 266
Plath, Sylvia, 8, 18; "Cut," 5; "Daddy," 5, 59; "Lady Lazarus," 59
Plato, 199
Plutzik, Alan (son), 312
Plutzik, Eli Eliakim (grandfather). *See* "After Looking into a Book Belonging to My Great-Grandfather, Eli Eliakim Plutzik"
Plutzik, Hyam: anthology of works by, 6; birth (1911), 18, 37, 71, 158, 258, 285; brevity of career of, 2, 73, 222, 312; change in writing style after war service, 198; characteristics of poems chosen, 6; Connecticut and, 18, 38, 86, 160, 285, 304; critical reception of, 235–36; death (1962), 35, 73;

early poems of, 155–67, 179; economic pressures of, 258; Eliot's *Poems: 1909–1925* personal copy of, *207*; exulting in poetic powers, 217–19; family background and education of, 1–2, 8, 18, 22, 37–38, 158, 169, 238, 258–59, 259n21, 285; family/cultural heritage as subject of, 26, 79, 86; favorite topics of, 6, 86n31; fishing avocation of, 279–80, 285, 300–308, *300–301*; gravestone and inscription, *191*, 221; Holocaust as subject of unwritten poem, 4, 8, 10, 17, 24, 31–32, 34–36, 66, 68, 73, 90n1, 113, 131, 160, 165, 236–38, 247–48, 313–14; languages spoken in early childhood, 1, 9, 38, 71, 158, 169; literary canonization of, 2–7, 222; as neglected poet, 38, 73, 87, 158–59, 158n6, 168, 235, 296, 312; photographs of, *185, 189–90, 300*; as Pulitzer Prize finalist, 8, 18, 71, 117, 158; as secular Jew, 221, 238, 255; Trinity College for undergraduate education, 285–93, *286*; on University of Rochester faculty, 7, 18, 38, *185*, 196, 297, 300; Yale Poetry Awards won by, 18, 155, 168, 288, 296; Yale University for master's degree in English, 18, 38, 159, 286, 292. *See also* Plutzik, Hyam, works by; wartime letters to his wife, Tanya; wartime poems

Plutzik, Hyam, works by: "Abner Bellow," 6, 21n11; "Absurd Cycle," 302; "An Agadah of Hyam ben Samuel," 7–8, 15–17, 72–73, 176–77, 220–21, 313; "An Aggadah," 177; "The Airman Who Flew over Shakespeare's England," 11, 24–25, 39, 148–49, 151, 178; "And in the 51st Year of That Century, While My Brother Cried in the Trench, While My Enemy Glared from the Cave," 60–61; "As the Great Horse Rots on the Hill," 61–62, 194–95, 228, 302; "Autobiography," 197–98; "The Bass," 305, *305*, 306; "Because the Red Osier Dogwood," 7, 227, 229, 273; "The Begetting of Cain," 22–23, 58–59, 72n3; "The Belated Birds Having Taken Their Leave," 220, 389; "Beware, Saunterer, of this Desperado, a Mr. Bones, a Bad Actor," 226–27; "Bomber Base," 24, 39, 40, 142, 143, 145, 148, 182, 183, *186*, 215; "The Book of Metamorphoses" (Part Two of *Horatio*), 129, 422–25; "The Camorra," 41, 244–45; "Cancer and Nova," 92–93, 220, 314, 322; "The Chinaman and the Florentine," 217, 390; *Collected Poems*, 2, 35, 38, 44, 54, 168, 179, 238, 291; "Commentary," 16, 21; "Creativity and Poetry" (essay), 134, 170, 171; "Critique," 171; "Dante in Our Time," 21n11, 359; "Death at the Purple Rim," 11, 64, 156, 160, 165–66, 288, 293, 302, 304; "The Devil with the Minus Sign in His Right Hand," 22, 391; "Divisibility," 6, 216–17; "The Dream about our Master, William Shakespeare," 227–28, 229; "Elaboration on a Phrase of Rabelais," 24; "El Anon Al Kol," 19, 181, 273n64; "An Electromagnetic Phenomenon," 170; "Elegy," 62, 153, 195; "Entropy," 58, 240, "An Equation," 20–21, 22n12, 58, 90–91; "Exhortation to the Artists," 16, 246–48; "For T. S. E. Only," 11–13, 20, 49–50, 171–73, 175–76, 201–5, 212–13, 223, 230–34, 298, 307, 312; "The Geese," 21, 48–49, 91, 104,

219; "George Hobbs," 38n16; "God and My Father," "The Golus" (short story), 286; "The Harrowing of the House of Eyes" (Part Two of *Horatio*), 129; "He Inspects His Armory," 20; "Hiroshima," 24, 46; "The House of Gorya," 8, 29, 31–32, 34–35, 68, 72–73; *House of Gorya and Other Poems*, 8, 29; "Identity," 6; "If Causality is Impossible, Genesis is Recurrent," 6, 91, 105–9, 199, 228; "I Have Read in the Book of the Butcher Boy (In Time of War)," 143; "I Imagined a Painter Painting Such a World," 62, 92, "In Memory of Sigmund Freud," 6; "Jim Desterland," 118–19, 199, 229–30, 232, 303, 304; "Kaddish," 48, 181, 273n64; "The King of Ai," 27–28, 72n3, 178; "The Lark at Heaven's Gate" (Chapter 5, *Horatio*), 150; "The Last Fisherman," 89, 115, 230, 306–7, 306; "L'Cho Dodi" (or *Lekhah Dodi*, "Come My Beloved"), 18, 181, 273n64; "A Letter to Someone at Mt. Palomar," 20; "Magen Avot," 181, 273n64, "The Marriage," 63; "The Milkman," 21, 64–65; "The Miracle," 26–28, 72, 146–47; "My Sister," 11, 21n11, 47, 65–66, 156, 159, 162–66, 314, 317–18, 320, 322; "The Mythos of Samuel Huntsman," 63, 199, 228–29; "The Mythos of the Man from Enoch," 24; "Next Time I Shall Not Burn the Beehive," 18, 123n10; novel about dictatorship (unpublished), 46; "Of Eternity Considered a Closed System," 176; "Of Objects Considered as Fortresses in a Baleful Space," 21, 94, 109–11; "The Old War," 25–26, 39, 41, 63, 151, 195; "On Hearing That My Poems Were Being Studied in a Distant Place," 7, 112, 115–16; "On the Airfield at Shipdham," 11, 39, 150–51; "On the Last Survivor of Our War, 1861–1865," 53; "On the Photograph of a Man I Never Saw," 32, 51–52, 72, 72n3; *The Outcasts of Venus* (science fiction novel), 14, 152, 314, 317–22; "Patterns of Earth," 218–19; "The Poetic Process," 192, 205; "Poetry and Myth" (lecture), 18; "The Poetry of Myth," 25n19; "Portrait," 13, 20, 32, 47–48, 55, 72, 93, 94, 104, 106, 111–12, 157–58, 181–83, 230–31, 242, 314, 322–23; "Prayer in the Seasons of Death," 272–74, 276; "The Premonition," 63, 228; "The Priest Ekranath," 42–44, 42n19, 128; "The Protean Universe" (lecture), 19, 21, 25n19; "Requiem for Edward Carrigh," 64; "The Seventh Avenue Express," 46–47, 64, 156, 314, 317–18, 321, 322; "The Shepherd" (Part Two of *Horatio*), 115, 126, 127; "Sprig of Lilac," 19, "Strange Diners at the Café Parnassus," 128; "Those Who Write after Freud," 21n11, 171; "The Three," 11, 155–56, 157, 159, 163–64, 166, 179–81, 182, 183; "Three Paintings," 286; "Time and the Poem," 176–78; "To Abraham Lincoln, That He Walk By Day," 53, 170, 178; "To My Daughter," 7, 11, 189, 192–93; "To Pablo Picasso, on His *Guernica*," 54; "To the Predynastic Egyptian Who Rests within the Entrance of the Metropolitan Museum," 6, 57, 178; "To Those Who Look Out of the Window," 218; "Two Hearts and an Arrow," 45–46; "Two Voices and a Woodwind," 63; "Useful Prepared Speech for the

Diffident Author of a Book of Poems Costing Three Dollars and Fifty Cents," 176, 291–92; "Winter, Never Mind Where," 63; "The Zero That Is All," 20–21, 21n11, 22n12, 91–92. See also "After Looking into a Book Belonging to My Great-Grandfather, Eli Eliakim Plutzik"; Apples from Shinar; Aspects of Proteus; Horatio; "The Importance of Poetry"; translations of liturgical works by Plutzik
Plutzik, Jonathan (son), 214
Plutzik, Mollie (sister), 162. See also Plutzik, Hyam, works by: "My Sister"
Plutzik, Roberta Ann (daughter), 189
Plutzik, Samuel (father), 15, 162n16, 169, 176, 178, 190, 221, 238
Plutzik, Tanya Roth (wife), 10, 38, 75n14, 189, 213–14, 235n1. See also wartime letters to his wife, Tanya
Plutzik, Zach Hyam (grandson), 214
poetry: balancing between idealization and reality, 12, 78, 215; as beginning of thinking, 11, 159–62; challenge of the impossible in, 217; contemporary poetry evaluated by Plutzik, 170–71; as gift, 177; Keats's definition of, 229–30; major themes as eternal, 170; midrashic thinking and, 240; Plutzik considering as something both won and lost forever, 176, 178; relevance to modern world, 169; understanding made possible by, 157; as way of asking questions, 106; as witness to tradition, 109
postapocalyptic tropes, 38, 46, 47, 155, 317
post-Holocaust poetry, 59–60; "An Agadah of Hyam ben Samuel" as, 15–17; of Apples from Shinar, 42; consolation not offered by, 50, 62, 152, 193; ethical burden of reading, 61; "House of Gorya" and, 31; Jewish identity of Plutzik and, 38–68; Miller on, 68; mourning without end, 61; Plutzik as post-Holocaust poet, 11, 13, 68, 157, 236–38, 296
Pound, Ezra, 3, 74, 128, 210, 297, 299, 312, 314
Powell, Anaximander (Plutzik's pen name), 14, 314
prayer and liturgy: Plutzik interweaving into his poems, 13, 252, 272–76. See also translations of liturgical works by Plutzik
Prayer Book Committee of the Rabbinical Assembly. See Rabbinical Assembly of America Prayer Book Committee
Preil, Gabriel, 71–87; "Chapters of Time, His and Mine," 9, 75–78, 82–83; compared to earlier American Hebraists, 74; compared to Plutzik, 9, 74–76, 79–84; family/cultural heritage as subject of, 75, 77, 80, 84, 86–87, 86n32; Hebrew romanticism rejected by, 74, 86n31; influences on, 74, 86nn31–32; languages spoken and written in, 71, 73–74; modern English verse and, 74; as neglected poet, 74, 87; nostalgia and lamenting lost world, 75–76, 78; straightforward approach in speaking to reader, 83; writing in Hebrew, 71, 73, 77–79, 82–83
prosopopoeia, 36, 42
Proteus, 2, 19, 150
psychological issues as subject matter, 123
Pulitzer Prize, Plutzik as finalist for, 8, 18, 71, 117, 158
puns, 96, 109

Rabbinical Assembly of America Prayer Book Committee, 13, 252–55, 253n1, 254n5, 257, 261; Agus's interim report to, 270; memorandum from Plutzik to, 262–63, 266, 267. *See also* Agus, Jacob

Rabelais, François, 24

Raphael: *The Miraculous Draft of Fishes* (painting), *281*

Regelson, Abraham, 74

Reilly, Catherine, 143–44

Reznikoff, Charles, 72; *Holocaust*, 37

Rich, Adrienne, 5, 73

Richards, I. A., 197

Rilke, Rainer Maria, 14, 326, 331; *Letters to A Young Poet*, 37, 37n11, 331–32

Rochester Poetry Society, 55

Rolfe, Edwin, 52, 296

Roman classical references. *See* classical civilization and history in Plutzik's work

Romanticism: English poets and, 90, 222; Keats and, 222–23; Plutzik and, 106, 151, 198, 199, 222–23; Preil's rejection of Hebrew romanticism, 74, 86n31

Rosenberg, Stuart E., 255

Rosenzweig, Franz: *The Star of Redemption*, 95–96

Ross, Alan: "Naval Base," 145, 146

Rothenberg, Jerome, 73

Rothwell, Kenneth S., 297

Rowland, Antony, 37

Rudolf, Anthony, 72

Rukeyser, Muriel, 5, 73n11, 296

Sabbath, 179, 181–83

Salmon, Rachel, 239

Samael, 23, 23n15

Samson's destruction of Philistine temple (biblical), 248

Sanders, Julie, 117n1

Satan/Devil, 22–23, 133, 243

Saxo Grammaticus, 113, 127

Scholem, Gershom, 21, 32n26

Schwab, Gabriele, 162

Schwartz, Delmore, 2, 296

Schwartz, Howard, 72

science as subject matter, 6, 21, 22, 58, 86n31, 90, 170, 179, 182

science fiction, 14, 47, 152, 314–18. *See also* Plutzik, Hyam, works by: *The Outcasts of Venus*

scriptural citations: Genesis, 23, 96, 179; Genesis 1, 92, 102, 163; Genesis 1:1, 99, 100; Genesis 1:1–2, 161; Genesis 11, 19; Genesis 11:1–2, 226n14; Genesis 11:4, 226; Genesis 11:7–9, 226; Genesis 12, 19; Genesis 26, 282; Exodus 14:14, 27; Exodus 17:8–14, 27; Exodus 17:8–15, 27; Exodus 17:16, 27; Leviticus 23, 25; Deuteronomy 25:17–19, 27; Numbers 7:89, 30n23; Joshua 6:21, 27; Joshua 8:26–9, 28; Joshua 8:35, 28; Joshua 10:11–14, 27; 1 Samuel 5, 42n19; 1 Chronicles 17:17, 77n16; Nehemiah 3:3, 280; Job 26:7, 21; Psalm 1, 208; Psalm 23, 293–94; Psalm 42:5, 31; Psalm 137, 307; Jeremiah 16:15–16, 280; Jeremiah 18, 194–95; Lamentations, 17, 31; Daniel 1:2, 19; apocrypha: Enoch, 22n13, 23n15; Matthew 17:24–27, 282; Matthew 17:27, 282; Mark 1:16–18, 280–81; John 13:28, 205; Revelation, 23; Revelation 19:20, 42

Sefer Ha-Aggadah (Bialik & Ravnitsky, eds.), 16

sequel writing, 122. *See also Horatio*

Setka, Stella, 13, 235

Sexton, Anne, 8, 18

Shakespeare, William, 2, 112–13, 147, 168, 223–24, 232; *Antony and*

Cleopatra, 200; *Cymbeline*, 150; *Hamlet*, 54, 94, 95, 112, 114, 115, 117–22, 124, 127, 136, 137, 168; *King Lear*, 223; *The Merchant of Venice*, 200, 201; *Othello*, 200; Plutzik's poem on ("The Dream about our Master, William Shakespeare"), 227–28; Plutzik's visit to Stratford-upon-Avon home of, 142, 143; *Richard II*, 112–13; Sonnet 29, 150; *The Tempest*, 209
Shapiro, Karl, 296
Shavuot (Feast of Weeks), 25–26, 79, 275–76
Shepard, Odell, 325, 330; fly-fishing and, 293–95; *A Lonely Flute* (poetry collection), 289, 290, 292; as mentor to Plutzik, 289; "Nightfall," 291; Plutzik's letter to (*See Letter from a Young Poet*); "Proem," 292; *Thy Rod and Thy Reel*, 289, 293–95, 294
Sher, Steven, 153, 160, 237, 253n2, 260
Shinar, 19, 55, 226, 232
Sholem Aleichem, 17, 73
Shrayer, Maxim D., 13–14, 279
silence, 4–5, 13, 36, 80, 111, 176, 195–96, 242, 249
Silkiner, Benjamin Nahum, 74
Silverman, Morris, 252, 266–67
Sisyphus (mythological), 159, 165, 180–81
Sklarew, Myra, 73
Slberschlag, Eisig, 74
snowflakes, 220–21
social and political issues as subject matter, 118, 123, 134, 137–38, 170
Sokoloff, Naomi, 7, 9, 71, 274–75
Solis-Cohen, Solomon da Silva, 253
Spanish Civil War (1936–39), 54–55
Spears, Monroe, 125
stars and constellations, 20, 218–20, 317, 322

Stein, Gertrude, 114
Stevens, Wallace, 2, 11, 74, 168–70, 202
Sundquist, Eric J., 7–8, 10; on "After Looking into a Book Belonging to My Great-Grandfather, Eli Eliakim Plutzik," 275; on "An Agadah of Hyam ben Samuel," 313; on "The Airman Who Flew over Shakespeare's England," 149; "Blessed Mythmaker," 38; on "The Old War," 41; on Plutzik's early poetry's allusions to Jews and Jewish traditions, 72, 96; on Plutzik's journal entry (June 5, 1944), 314; on Plutzik's response to Holocaust, 152n45, 260–61; on Plutzik's Talmudic references, 238, 246; on Plutzik's unwritten poem on Holocaust, 90n1; summarizing poetic range of Plutzik, 145n16; Szenes's influence on Plutzik, 177; on "Time and the Poem," 178
sun standing still (biblical event), 27, 27n22, 147
survival of the remnant (Jewish people), 28, 248
Sutzkever, Abraham, 59
Suvin, Darko, 315–16
synecdoche, 36
Syrkin, Marie: *The Story of Jewish Resistance*, 17
Szenes, Hannah, 178; "Blessed Is the Match," 17, 177–78

Talmud, 16, 23n15, 31, 78, 168, 238, 246, 269, 280
Tanakh (Old Testament), 174, 179. *See also* scriptural citations
Tantalus (mythological), 155, 163–64, 180, 181
Thoreau, Henry David: *Walden*, 241
Tikkun Leil Shavuot, 26, 79, 275–76

time as theme, 90–93, 95, 106–9, 114, 116, 182, 307, 327; aging and, 194–95; history as acts within time, 183; in *Horatio*, 93, 106–9; sanctification of time, 181. *See also* eternity
Titus (biblical), 173–74
Tontiplaphol, Betsy, 12, 222
totalitarianism, 18, 22, 24
Tower of Babel (biblical), 19, 226
transcendentalism, 295
translations of liturgical works by Plutzik, 13, 73, 252–78; Agus preferring more literal translations, 268–71; closing blessing (*Pesukei dezimra*) of morning prayer service, compared to Silverman's translation, 266–67; "El Anon Al Kol," 19, 181, 273n64, 362; importance of revitalization of postwar Jewish spirituality, 266; "Kaddish," 48, 181, 273n64; later prayer books ignoring Plutzik's translations, 271; "L'Cho Dodi" (or *Lekhah Dodi*, "Come My Beloved"), 18, 181, 273n64, 373–74; "Magen Avot," 181, 273n64, 375; memorandum from Plutzik to Prayer Book Committee of the Rabbinical Assembly, 262–63, 266, 267; modernizing language of prayer, 263–72; *piyyut* genre, 256–57, 262, 266–68; Plutzik's work unpublished until several included in *Collected Poems*, 272; policy set by Rabbinical Assembly Prayer Book Committee, 257; ripple of formal liturgy into Plutzik's poems, 252, 272–76; *Seder Tefilot Yisrael: Sabbath and Festival Prayer Book* selections, 263
trauma as theme, 14, 94, 108, 114, 118, 159–60, 162–66, 240. *See also* Holocaust
tribes of Israel (biblical), 44, 44n21

Trinity College, 285–93, *286*
truth, 50–52, 132, 244, 315
Tu Fu in "The Chinaman and the Florentine," 217

understanding made possible by poetry, 157
University of Rochester, 7, 18, 26n20, 38, *185*, 196, 297; Plutzik Poetry Series, 159
the unspeakable, writing about, 82, 113, 119
Untermeyer, Louis, 236

Van Den Bogaerde, D.: "Steel Cathedrals," 148
Van Doren, Mark, 198n15
verse drama, 123–26
Vestal, Herman: illustration for *The Outcasts of Venus*, 319–20
Virgil, 205; *Aeneid* translation by C. Day-Lewis, 265

Wagenblass, John, 64
Waits, Tom, 89
Wannsee Conference, 56
Warren, Robert Penn, 306, 312
wartime letters to his wife, Tanya, 10–11, 140–53; (July 1, 1942), 26n21, 146n21; (May 18, 1944), 141; (May 29, 1944), 39–40, 147; (June 5, 1944), 144, 153, *188*; (June 7, 1944), 152; (June 8, 1944), 142; (June 16, 1944), 146; (July 2, 1944), 149; (July 25, 1944), 140; (August 14, 1944), 152; (August 28, 1944), 147; (January 22, 1945), 145; (April 18, 1945), 142; (May 14, 1945), 55–56, 151–52
wartime poems, 10, 22–26, 39, 140–54; Norfolk memories of Plutzik becoming, 141–42; Plutzik's connection

with British wartime poets, 147;
WWI legacy, 143–44
Wells, H. G.: *The Time Machine*, 317
West, Benjamin: *Death on the Pale Horse* (painting), 223
Wheatley, Phillis, 3
Wheelwright, Philip, 128
White, Thomas, 59
Whitman, Walt, 18, 74, 75, 170, 199, 241, 289
Wilbur, Richard, 8, 18, 126n17
Williams, William Carlos, 4, 4n6
Williamson, George, 197
Wilson, Edmund, 197
Wordsworth, William, 90, 161, 224
World War I, poetic legacies of, 143–44
World War II: Auden's poetry and, 6; D-Day invasion preparation, 10, 22, 140, 142–43, 147–48, 148n26, 152, 182; ethical challenges of, 145–46, 151–53; God's role in victory, 27; heroism and, 63; Jews as slaves under Hitler, 22; Pearl Harbor bombing, 244; Pegasus ridden by Bellerophon as British insignia, 62; Plutzik lamenting losses of, 153, 183; Plutzik serving in, 22n14, 26, 39–40, 41, 53, 55–56, 118, 120, 146, 183, 261; Plutzik stationed at Shipdham Air Base (Norwich, Britain), 10, 22, 25, 40, 140–43, 195; postwar judgment on, 24–25; refugees to America from, 152. *See also* Holocaust; wartime letters to his wife, Tanya; wartime poems

Yad Vashem, 81
Yale Poetry Award, Plutzik winning, 18, 155, 168, 288, 296
Yale University, Plutzik's master's degree in English from, 18, 38, 159, 286, 292
Yeats, William Butler, 306; "Leda and the Swan," 23
Yerushalmi, Yosef, 179
Yiddish: Eliot and, 212–13; Plutzik and, 1, 9, 38, 71, 73; Preil writing in, 71
Yizkor, 276

Zangwill, Israel, 252
Zelda [Schneerson Mishkovsky], 81
Zisquit, Linda, 73
Žižek, Slavoj, 37
Zukovksy, Louis, 5
Zweig, Arnulf, 297

Editors

Victoria Aarons is Distinguished Professor of Literature at Trinity University where she teaches courses on American Jewish and Holocaust literatures. She has published fourteen books, including *Holocaust Graphic Narratives: Generation, Trauma, and Memory* and *Memory Spaces: Visualizing Identity in Jewish Women's Graphic Narratives*, recipient of a 2024 Jordan Schnitzer Book Award.

Holli Levitsky, Professor of English at Loyola Marymount University, has authored and edited *Communist Poland: A Jewish Woman's Experience; New Directions in Jewish American and Holocaust Literature: Reading and Teaching; The Literature of Exile and Displacement,* and *Summer Haven: The Catskills, the Holocaust, and the Literary Imagination*, among other writings.

Hilene Flanzbaum taught American, Jewish-American, and Holocaust literature for over thirty years. She has edited three collections, *The Americanization of the Holocaust, The Norton Anthology of Jewish-American Literature,* and *The Holocaust Across Borders*.

www.ingramcontent.com/pod-product-compliance
Lightning Source LLC
Chambersburg PA
CBHW052041220426
43663CB00012B/2392